# Dafydd and Goliath

# Dafydd and Goliath

Dafydd Gittins

CPW

Columbia Publishing Wales Limited.

First Published in the UK in 2000 by:
COLUMBIA PUBLISHING WALES LIMITED.
Glen More,
6, Cwrt y Camden,
BRECON LD3 7RR,
Powys. Tel/Fax 01874 625270.
Wales. UK.



A CIP catalogue record for this book is available from the British Library and The National Library of Wales.

ISBN 0-9538945-0-9



Cover Design and Typesetting by AuthorsAdvisoryService.Com

Printed in Wales by: Creative Print and Design Wales,
Ebbw Vale NP23 5SD.

# Acknowledgements

Petronella Wyatt, Daily Telegraph.
Brendon Williams, Western Mail.
David Meacham, Brecon and Radnor Express.
Jackie Hadley, Western Telegraph.
Joel Bennathan, Tooks Court.
The Staff of Douglas Jones Mercer.
Mark Lynas, One World.
Dafydd Wigley MP.
Elfyd Llwyd MP.
BBC Wales.
Comsat UK Ltd.
Gavin D Smith. [Whisky a book of words]

## Special Thanks to

Gareth Barrett.
Jane Gittins.
John Williams (Col. Patch)
John Rogers.
Steve Spalding.
Paula Rogers.
Tony James.
Nick Ainger MP.
The Welsh Books Council.

Christine Chambers.
Roger Jones (new still operator)
University of Surrey (Process Engineering Department)
Sheryl Law (Hilton - Tenby)
Peter & Pam Saxon
Glenda, Kim, Karen, Alan, Rose, Gofer (Welsh Whisky)

## My. Family

Gillian Gittins and Gareth Lee Gittins.
Marjorie Georgia Gittins and Ronald Gittins.
Michael Gittins and Peter Gittins.
Auntie Rose and Uncle Ted.
Len Skinner. Kay and Paul Williams.

Many individuals have helped and encouraged me to write this book and I am indebted to them. I apologise if I have failed to mention anyone.

The author wishes to thank and acknowledge the invaluable assistance of The authorsadvisoryservice.com

# Contents


| | | |
|---|---|---|
| | *Introduction* | *ix* |
| 1. | *Chequers the Raid* | *1* |
| 2. | *My Early Years* | *15* |
| 3. | *Rock and Roll Comes to Town* | *23* |
| 4. | *A Time of Change* | *29* |
| 5. | *The Break* | *41* |
| 6. | *Hamburg Calling* | *55* |
| 7. | *Homeward Bound* | *73* |
| 8. | *Welsh Whisky: The Early Days* | *83* |
| 9. | *Birth of an Enterprise* | *89* |
| 10. | *The Rocky Road Ahead* | *101* |
| 11. | *The Prince of Wales* | *107* |
| 12. | *Upward and Onward* | *117* |
| 13. | *The Recession* | *125* |
| 14. | *Export! Export!* | *135* |
| 15. | *The Take Over* | *155* |

16. *The Sea Empress Legacy* 163

17. *The Snowball Effect* 171

18. *The Nightmare Begins* 179

19. *The Civil Conspiracy* 191

20. *Where do we go From Here* 199

21. *The Struggle for Survival* 207

22. *Fairwell to Brecon* 219

23. *The Scales of Justice* 229

24. *Justice Most Foul* 241

25. *The Twist and Turns* 255

*The Aftermath* 267

*Epilogue* 269

*Chronology of Events* 273

*Short Story* 285

# INTRODUCTION

This autobiography tells the true story of Dafydd Gittins who rediscovered Welsh Whisky and exported it around the world He then ended up in prison after a two year court battle costing £2,000,000 for the heinous crime of 'Knowingly Know'.

An intriguing mystery evolves around a handful of drugs sold to police in an under cover police operation at a nightclub he owned in the sleepy West Wales seaside resort of Tenby, a rural area recently ravaged by the infamous Sea Empress disaster.

Despite the fact he was not at the club on the fateful night and there had been no other such drug related incidents, he was sentenced to 12 months imprisonment having been found guilty of vicarious liability, purely on the evidence of under cover police officers which was later proved false. The results are appalling, it cost the State millions, and the cost to him much, much more.

Having been a former Chairman of the CBI in mid-Wales, a founder director of the Training and Enterprise Council, fought two parliamentary elections for a fledgling Plaid Cymru paving the way to devolution, and considered a captain of industry. He had no previous convictions, how could this have happened? Why did it happen?

By bringing a point of basic law to the forefront of the English Legal system and representing himself in the Royal Courts he exposed a great injustice, or was it a sinister conspiracy?

This is a story built around a dream that may still come

to fruition, if it fails it certainly will not be for the want of trying. A continuous fight for recognition against immense opposition from the establishment, bureaucracy and the multinational Scotch Whisky Companies. All entwined with Wales' struggle for international identity, regained nationhood and the scandals that surrounded the Sea Empress dubbed 'The Unnatural Disaster."

He has said, "We all strive for something, some more than others but we all have a dream and some have a mission. Whether or not this ever works out in the end is just another of life's mysteries. None of us are sure what it is that's out there when we start. We all know what we have in store at the end. It's that middle bit which is tricky. The unknown! My life is no different, but my tricky bit certainly warrants a book or two. They say life is a bitch, I don't know if that's true. Let's just say life can be a tunnel of love with the ghost train thrown in for good measure and that's for sure. It is certainly how I describe my life, as the contents of this book will reveal!"

In some small way his life reflects some of what has happened in the latter half of this century. His achievements have been many but when the tide turned, good fortune fell from his grasp. All the positive things achieved in his life meant nothing. He had to look for inner strengths that had always seemed to come to his rescue in the past. Would they once again prevail?

Everyone hopes, and tries to rely on others, sometimes it works but in reality when your back is against the wall and the chips are down, it is you and you alone who will win or lose. In his case this is only partly true. He was fortunate to have friends and family who stood by him in the fight to clear his name, regain his dignity and perhaps, one-day, his fortune.

Wales is a small emerging nation with a history far greater than its geographical size. Until very recently its international standing could be described as non-existent, yet beneath it all, Wales and its people had surprising influence and involvement throughout the world, least not in North America. This story reflects the battle of one Welshman who re-discovered an ancient Welsh art long forgotten. Although regarded as a truly Celtic craft it belonged commercially to Scotland and the multi-national Companies who now own this celebrated industry. Whisky is the 'King' of spirits the 'water of life' it has more mystique, mythology and Celtic intrigue, than any other drink known to mankind. It was fought over in days of 'Olde' and nothing has changed. As the big multi-national conglomerates jealously guard what they think is theirs and theirs alone!

When Welsh Whisky awoke after a slumber of some 70 years and a history going back to the 4th century. He tried to reclaim its rightful place at the table of the new millennium; it was met with disbelief and bureaucracy but had surprising popular success. Its rebirth received a quite incredible world wide media attention that dwarfed its commercial success. Many sang its praise, from President Jimmy Carter to Prime Minister John Major Welsh Whisky was a hit!

This story also reflects a momentous time of change, the last fifty years of a millennium. From confusion and hope after the Second World War to fleeing from revolution in Iran to the peace and tranquillity of mid-Wales. From the Fifties through the Sixties and life in 'Swinging London', 'free love' and the incredible music of the era. This decade was one of the most exciting times of any century. New freedoms, wealth and prosperity, he feels privileged to have experienced this time as a young struggling musician from the country to the

'Big Smoke'. Sex ,drugs and Rock and Roll are all part of the tale.

The story behind Welsh Whisky is sometimes humorous, and sometimes fraught with anguish. It includes true stories of international 'skulduggery' and reflects well the title of the book it self.

The noble fight that David had with Goliath back in time is still very apt today. With a new age opening its pages on chapter one, let us hope that his revelations help others to fight injustice and gives heart to those who fight on against all the odds.

The moral of this tale is never give up, no matter how hard things get. With a little bit of humour, a glass of good cheer and the undying knowledge that you are right, you can win through in the end.

Through the dark days in prison Dafydd knew that what had happened to him was wrong. It was an abuse of power by the Authorities and wrecked many lives. It brought British Justice to yet another very low ebb. This story illustrates a prime example of the panic and paranoia that drugs have brought to our everyday life. Drugs are an evil we need to combat but at what cost? Will our new dawn sound the rebirth of a modern day 'Spanish Inquisition' or will we solve this dire problem through common sense and reason? Read this story and judge for yourself, maybe someone has the answer and balance we need.

Let us keep 'big brother' where he belongs, at our service not increasingly as our jailer. It is evident that the United Kingdom desperately needs a written constitution, a 'Bill of Rights' to stop the ever growing number of miscarriages of justice that have become so common place today; tomorrow it could be you! But it is just conceivable that this book will help to prevent that?

Dafydd has tried to be as accurate as possible with the sequence of events and recollections of what people said at the time If he has mis-quoted anyone he appologizes. This is a true-life story that reads like an adventure novel, but then life is just that! Any criticism levied at the British Legal System is meant to be constructive, an effort to help reform for the common good.

"Maybe justice is like football, we invented the game, but we don't play it very well at present!" - Dafydd Gittins, Readers Digest May 2000.

# 1

# Chequers The Raid

"Gareth".
I called to my son to get ready. It's Friday afternoon, the 5th of September 1997. We're in Brecon getting ready to go to Saundersfoot for the weekend. The usual rush of picking him up from school and packing the car with all his paraphernalia, including guitar and amplifier. Never goes with out them. He's13, big for his age and quite an accomplished musician already.

At last we finally get into the car and start off at 5pm, complete with our dog Pebbles, a little black and white Jack Russell cross. It's a bright autumn afternoon, and with blue skies all the way, it should be a great weekend.

We made a quick stop at Carmarthen for a bite to eat, some ribs and chips, and sat out side the 'takeaway' in Lammas Street to eat our spicy ribs and enjoy the sunny afternoon; I had no idea of what was to happen to me later that night.

On the last leg of our journey, we pulled in to Saundersfoot, a small fishing village a few miles outside the coastal resort of Tenby on the beautiful Atlantic coast of West Wales. I had to drop Gareth off at his mother's, my soon to become ex-wife. She's living with her boy friend off and on and this weekend she's staying with him.

I waved Gareth goodbye saying ; "See you tomorrow, we'll take the boat out if the weather's fine. Call me in the morning I'll be at the cottage".

The cottage is the small bolthole, I bought back in 1991. A quaint little three bedroom home close to the harbour which I enjoy using most weekends. It had become even more useful since acquiring a Night Club just outside Tenby called Chequers, about two years ago in 1995. Being Friday, and on my own, I planned to call over to the Club, see how things were going, and maybe have a night revelling with the crowd. Something I did two or three times a month.

I had hired a manager, Gareth Barrett, to run the Club. He was one of my best friends and took care of the day to day running of the place. I had had a partner, Richard Jones, but he had dropped out a year after we took the place on. Richard had worked for me for over ten years in my Welsh Whisky business in Brecon. [Something I'll explain later on as the story unfolds.] He was in his thirties with dark cropped hair, quite stocky but a good-looking cheeky chap with the nickname, 'Gopher'.

Prior to selling Welsh Whisky Richard had asked me to back him in order to buy the leasehold of the Club. He did not want to work for the new company in Brecon and he convinced me that he could make a success of the Club. I in a moment of madness backed him financially and thought my role would be little more than advisory. However, although taking on this commitment had been his wish and was in fact to be his enterprise, I had now been left 'holding the baby'.

He had decided to return to Brecon, and ironically ended up working for the new company. So here I am with a nightclub on my hands. Not something I really wanted but I had little choice after signing my name to the lease and committing myself to many thousands of pounds.

Thankfully I had Barrett to step in and help out. He was a fairly street wise guy in his late forties, a Billy Connolly look a like with a mane of long dark curly hair. He was a native of nearby Carmarthen but had spent many years living in Tenby. He had a very dry Welsh humour, something you needed in the night club business. Barrett was my right hand man and someone I could rely on.

The club had turned out to be a bit of a nightmare and one hell of a struggle. Petty bureaucracy was driving me to distraction. I had walked into an ongoing feud between the previous owners of the Club and the Local Authorities. My erstwhile partner had been aware of this, but I was blissfully ignorant to the extent of the hostility. Something that would cost me dearly!

For some time I'd been thinking of selling the place even though business was good. It was just one headache after another. From noise abatement to blocked drains. Pot holes in the car park, to the ever-virulent Licensing Officer with the very apt nickname of 'Chimp', otherwise known as Police Constable Tony Davies. A rather odd character in his early fifties with a large head, a perpetual grin, and 'Brillcreamed' black hair. He had been Licensing Officer for over twelve years, which in its self was unusual. He did his job with relish. He was a little man with a lot of power, especially if you were at the wrong end of his grace and favour regime.

PC Davies and I had crossed swords a few years before I had entered the night-club business, but I had been unaware of it at the time and had still not put 'two and two' together! Chequers, was a medium sized club, which we called a 'country club'. It was in fact a bit of a mis-match of a pub that served a near by caravan park, 'Bogey's bar', and a 500 seater nightclub that operated mainly at weekends. The Club had seen better days needing more and more renovations. I had been pouring money into it, trying to refurbish and decorate as an on-going process. The Club was about 4 miles outside Tenby in the West Wales County of Pembrokeshire. A sea side town suffering greatly from the economic effects of the infamous Sea Empress disaster of February 1996.

Although the area is one of outstanding beauty, it is an unemployment black spot, and one got the impression that the Local Authorities wished to keep it that way. The police certainly gave that impression by the way they regulated with a very heavy hand. Considering it was supposed to be a tourist area, pubs and clubs were under the continuous and zealous imposition of petty rules and regulations. Certainly I had never experienced anything like it in other parts of Wales. Normally the Police are very supportive and helpful to business, certainly that was the way I had found them to be elsewhere. Tenby seemed to be different.

Chequers had been raided several times over the past few months on various obscure pretexts. The last one consisted of fifteen police officers and about the same number of County Council officers. They raided at half past midnight to cause maximum disruption. The end result being a caution for having a sign on the front door the lettering of which was not regulation height, and dirty toilets. Considering the time of night and the fact I had 500 people in the Club, this was not a great surprise to me. However, this pettiness was a typical example of the ongoing war of attrition against the Club and myself.

After finally dropping my son off, I continued down the road to the Cottage. Watered and fed the dog then took a nice long bath, opened a bottle of wine and started to get ready for the evening. In fact I was feeling pretty good. I rang Barrett at the Club and told him I'd be over later on. He was in fine spirits and said

"It should be a good night."

He had a top DJ booked called 'Angel'. How wrong could he be?

It was the final 'Up for It' night of the season and should be very busy. 'Up for it' was a trading name for a local DJ Danny Slade who had teamed up with a hairdresser called Andy Price. Andy had a number of salons in the Pembrokeshire area and Danny had some slots on National Radio Wales.

Both Danny and Andy were in their late twenties. Andy always wore black and had a smart punk appearance, a lady's man with a hint of rugged good looks. Very much the wheeler-dealers type.

Danny was the eternal surfer but a little over weight, wore round spectacles and liked to wear Bermuda shorts. He was always the jovial type and laughed a lot. A nice 'wouldn't hurt a fly' sort of guy. They were both successful at what they did and made an odd but good team. The 'Up for it' team organised and marketed Friday evenings at the Club. The arrangement had worked well and we had seen some top DJ's, such as Judge Jules, Scott Bond and Dominik Lee Williams, to name but a few.

I arrived at about 8.40pm and went straight through

to 'Bogey's, the side bar which we tended to use before and after closing time of the main part of Chequers. There were already a few people milling about and things were just starting to open up. Not all the staff had arrived yet and there was a lot to do before we opened up fully, no real panics in fact a fairly easy atmosphere.

Things didn't normally start to get busy until 10-10.30pm, so there was plenty of time. Barrett was upstairs in his flat, sorting change and trying to iron his trousers at the same time, I was chatting to a very pretty girl I knew called Penny who did the backdrops for the various DJ's.

I was totally unaware what was happening at the front of the Club. The first hint I had was when 'Chimp' appeared through a door behind the bar at Bogey's which joined the main club.

My first thoughts on seeing him was, "what the hell does that bastard want now?"

He called me over with his usual smirk.

"Have you got a minute Daf?" he said with a knowing grin.

I followed him through the door, past the cellar and into the main Club. I was to be confronted with an army of police officers pouring in like some sort of SAS siege.

My mind was numb trying to make sense of what was happening around me. Everything seemed to be in slow motion as I walked further into the Club and onto the dance floor.

I was introduced to an Inspector who asked me to stand over by the stairway at the centre of the Club, which led to the balcony. All the while police officers scurried about as if they were looking for something but couldn't find it. Then another officer who I was later to know as Detective

Constable John Davies started to talk to me. A well built man in his mid-thirties. He looked more like a farmer than a policeman and wore some kind of yellow 'flak jacket'.

"Are you Dafydd Noel Gittins proprietor of this Club" he said in a toneless voice and with a face like thunder.

"Yes I am" I replied in shock. "What the hell is going on?".

"I have a warrant for your arrest under the Misuse of Drugs Act!"

With that he thrust a piece of paper in my face then just as quickly stuffed it back in his pocket.

"Place your hands out in front of you"

"why?" is all I could utter before my hands were cuffed!

At the corner of my eye I could see Barrett being followed by 'Chimp' and two other officers. He was already hand cuffed. Barrett had the same look of disbelief as I must have had.

I was led to an alcove at the back of the club and told to sit and wait. Barrett was told the same and was seated about 3 metres away from me.

The next to be arrested and cuffed was Christian Torkington; he was a tall thin young lad of 21 with a mop of long curly hair who worked for Andy Price. Christian handled the door money on the 'Up for it' nights. Why they had arrested him I had no idea. The whole night seemed to be a bad dream, some sort of sick joke gone very wrong.

By now the 30 or so customers who had arrived at the club early, had been herded onto the dance floor in the centre of the club, along with some of the staff. The police ordered them to put their hands on top of their heads, as if playing out some role in a Hollywood style Chicago gangster movie. The whole situation was becoming a farce. The police had obviously not found what they were looking for and were franticly searching around. By now they had a sniffer dog with them a large German Shepherd they called 'Spliff'.

'Chimp' had disappeared back to Barrett's flat at the top of the building. The police were now taking people one by one to the toilets to strip-search. Myself, Barrett and Christian sat staring at the spectacle that unfolded before our eyes. I kept turning to Barrett saying. "What the hell is going on?"

He just shrugged his shoulders and shook his head repeatedly. Occasionally punctuating his gestures with "fuck knows?" and "that bastard Chimp has finally gone off his head, this is taking the bloody piss!"

The police set up a table by the stairway leading to the balcony. A women police officer and three men had spread out a floor plan of the club  and were studying it and pointing at areas of the building.

As I mentioned before Chequers was not a vast place but big enough. The main club area consisted of approximately 1,600 square metres. There was a small foyer where people entered and paid their admission fee. This led into the main club through swing doors. The dance area had a polished wooden floor. To the left was a large semicircular bar and several alcoves bordered the whole area. It was a fairly typical nightclub lay out with a wooden, banistered stairway, that separated in a curve to the right and left, leading to an upstairs gallery surrounded by more wooden banisters, which over looked the dance floor. Brightly coloured artistically printed 'Back drops' hung from the banisters, proclaiming 'Up for it'.

There was another small bar and a dozen round tables

and chairs on the balcony. There was also a small dance floor at the far end of the balcony bar where couples went to 'smooch' the night away! The Club was normally dimly lit by numerous spot lights and of course the myriad of coloured lights, strobes and laser disco lights that gave it that 'night-club' atmosphere on the dance floor, but left the alcoves more intimate and comfortable.

However, when the police entered the way they did the staff had switched on the halogen lights that we used at the end of the night to call 'time to go home'. These lights lit the whole place up rather starkly, exposing the renovation work that still needed to be done, and giving the place a cold dreary look that the dim lighting had hidden

The police were starting to settle down a bit; the frantic panic was subsiding. Customers were allowed to sit down on stools placed on the dance floor. Then one by one were permitted to leave after being strip-searched. One and half-hours had passed laboriously by. There were just two young girls left sat nonchalantly chatting to each other while waiting to be searched.

One of the bar staff had been arrested. Dione Wales a lovely girl in her late twenties with flowing blonde hair. Apparently she had been found with a small amount of 'wacky backy' (Cannabis leaf) in her handbag. She looked at me with tears in her eyes as if it was all her fault. We were then told by one of the officers who brought us some cigarettes that a 'bouncer' Chris Boyle had also been arrested. He was found with steroids in the glove compartment of his car. The officer raised his bushy eyebrows to the ceiling and sighed

"I rather be collecting tolls on Cleddau bloody Bridge than this shit!"

It was now 11pm, two hours had passed and it was finally my

turn to be strip-searched in the gent's toilets. I walked slowly over with two officers. Once in the toilets I was asked "drop your pants" by one of the officers. Not an easy task when handcuffed. The officer looks apologetic and started to undo my belt and lowered my pants in a half-hearted manner. Took a look, then gave me a quick frisk and all was done, nothing found. I was led back out into the club and then through the front doors to a waiting police car.

I knew one of the officers in the car as 'Auto' a burly ginger headed lad in his late twenties. I used to drink with him occasionally in The Royal Oak pub in Saundersfoot.
He shook his head saying
"Sorry about this Daf. Nothing to do with me".

As I bent down to get into the squad car I could see a small crowd from the Caravan Park had gathered by the entrance to the car park. Barrett used to refer to them as the 'out to lunch bunch'. They looked amazed by it all as I sped away into the night headed for the police cells at Haverfordwest.

The 25-mile trip took less than 20 minutes. We cruised through the country lanes and byways, lights flashing blue and white, splintering the darkness of the night. My mind was racing trying to make sense of it all. The officers said very little. They just wanted to get me to the police station and off their hands. There was an air of embarrassment but I kept asking 'Auto', " What's this all about, why didn't any one warn me if there was a problem at the club?"
No answers were given, the car continued winding its way to Haverfordwest. Maybe I would find some answers there?
On arrival at the police station I asked to have the cuffs removed they were beginning to hurt.

"As soon as I get you inside Daf, as soon as I get you inside"

Auto repeated. I got out of the car and went through a doorway into the duty sergeants' reception office. Good as his word 'Auto' removed the cuffs. It felt good and I rubbed my wrists to get the blood flowing and ease the pain.

The reception area was small, brightly lit, and in need of a lick of paint. A police sergeant stood behind a counter and began writing down my name, address, and date of birth. The usual formalities, the paper work! He did it with that look of longing for retirement, his hair was getting greyer and he was still working night shifts.

I started to say " I want to see a lawyer."

"All in good time" said a young plain-clothes detective with his feet up on the table behind the duty desk.

"Don't worry it's a nothing charge it's not you they're after!" He continued as he kept flicking a pen with his thumbnail.

"Nothing charge? Doesn't look like that from here", I replied in a tone of despair.

"What is the bloody charge away?" I continued.

"You haven't been charged yet sir, we are holding you under suspicion of Section 4(1), the Misuse of Drugs Act 1971 while CID carry out further investigations" retorted the sergeant still filling in the endless forms.

"Where are the other guys?" I enquired.

" Pembroke Dock Sir" The sergeant then brought me a telephone "You can phone your own solicitor if you wish or you can make use of a duty solicitor. Your choice sir"

"I'll take a duty solicitor for now, I just need some advice. Can I phone my wife please?"

"Help your self-sir. Is there anyone else you would like to phone?"

"I'd like to ring the Home Secretary if I knew his fucking number, this has got to be political. I wouldn't know what a drug looked liked if it jumped up and bit me?"

"Very droll sir"

I rang my wife Gill; she answered the phone after the first ring.

"Is that you?"

"Yes" I replied with the tired bewilderment of all the night's events and a disbelief of the situation I found myself in.

"What's going on? Colwyn Howells the head doorman has been up to see me and said you had been arrested! I've rung everywhere. No one would tell me where you where" Gill sounded concerned but relieved that she'd found me.

"I'm in Haverfordwest Police Station, they raided the Club just before 9pm but I've only been here a few minutes"

"But it's nearly mid-night Dafydd!"

"I know but they kept us at the Club for two hours while they searched the place. The others are down at Pembroke Dock I'm here on my own". She paused for a while and said 'I'll be over straight away"

The sergeant was still filling in his forms and I informed him that my wife Gill was on her way. He looked up from his paperwork and smiled saying, "I don't think that's allowed-but I'll see what I can do. In the mean time a Mr. Paul Cowper of Lowless and Lowless Solicitors will be over shortly to see you. However I'm going to have to lock you up while we wait, things will start to get busy very soon now. It always does this time of night on the weekends but I'll do what I can. I've also sent out for something to eat and a coffee, you hungry?" I made no reply, I just gave a blank look.

He continued "DC John Davies will also want to see you sometime, possibly tonight but certainly first thing

tomorrow. I'll try and make things as comfortable as possible"
"OK!" I resigned myself and followed the sergeant to the adjacent cell and stood inside as he closed the door on me. This would be my 'pit' for the night.
Gill arrived at 12.30 a.m. the same time as the duty solicitor so she had to wait. Paul Cowper was a thin man with sunken cheeks. In his mid-forty's he looked like he had had a long day. He was as equally puzzled as I was but could not offer much help and just said.

"We'll have to wait until the morning. I've got to go back down to Pembroke Dock now to see the others and the arresting officer DC Davies, I'll know then what it is they have or haven't got and when they intend to release you. In the mean time say nothing."

I was too dazed to protest and just wanted to see Gill. Apparently it was against the rules but the sergeant was allowing it. Gill's face was white. She is a very beautiful woman in her early forties with immaculate blonde hair and looks more akin to a twenty-year-old. Although we had lived our separate lives for a few years we still had a very strong bond between us. We chatted in my cell for about fifteen minutes before a dowdy, stern faced women police officer came in and said it was time to go.
I gave her a gentle kiss and we parted saying

"See you in the morning love, I'll sort things out in the morning" How wrong could I be?

I looked around my filthy, drab and dimly lit cell. I hadn't really noticed it before. In fact nothing had sunk in. There was a jangle of keys and my cell door opened; the duty Sergeant brought me a plastic cup of coffee and a burger. I looked up at him but said nothing as he placed the food and drink on a small ledge next the 'bed', a stone slab with a thin, well-worn mattress and a green string blanket. He left in silence as I looked at the steam rising from the coffee and began to realise for the first time that this was for real. How on earth had this happened? Why had it happened, and just what was it they were looking for at the Club? Thoughts started to spin and buzz in my head.

This was going to be a very long and lonely night. I reached for the coffee took a small sip and started to reflect on my life. With hand on head and bowed over the cup of steaming liquid my mind embarked on a journey back in time!

# 2

# My Early Years

'I was born in Abadan. With a name like Dafydd one could be forgiven for thinking that this was somewhere in the Rhondda. It is in fact several thousands of miles from that famous valley and sits on the border between Iran [Then Persia] and Iraq. It is the oil rich port of the Shatt al Arab in the Persian Gulf. I am the third and youngest son born to Marjorie and Ronald Gittins. My brother Michael was the eldest, born in 1944 and Peter the middle boy was born in 1946.

I was born in 1949, the 19th of December to be precise. In the dying days of the British Empire and a bloody conflict was raging over the ownership of the vast oil fields of southern Iran. The political leader Mohammed Mossadeq led a relentless battle against the entrenched British and the Anglo-Iranian Oil Company, for whom my father Ron worked as a chemist. My dad had left his native Brymbo near Wrexham, North Wales in 1921 to pioneer the newly discovered wealth that lay beneath the swampy mash lands of the delta and the arid deserts beyond.

I remember very little of my life there, my birth was

registered with the British Consulate at Khorramshahr as David Noel Gittins. David is the English spelling of the Welsh name Dafydd. We fled Abadan at the height of the riots in 1951, first flying to Switzerland then onto London before finally arriving in Brecon. We had to leave everything behind, although at a later date one of Dad's Persian friends managed to crate a lot of the valuable carpets and antiques that he had collected over the years and ship them secretly to Wales.

One of the reasons we stopped off in Switzerland was so that Dad could access his Swiss bank account and draw some much needed cash. There were strict currency controls in the U.K. at this time so Mum stuffed bundles of white paper five pound notes in my carry cot mattress and they hoped for the best. I guess that, with all the confusion at the time, we managed to slip through British Customs at London Airport untroubled.

Brecon was my mother Margorie's adopted home, being born just across the border in Hereford. Her parents George and Lily Hargest ran a beautiful old Tudor pub called the Blue Boar in a part of Brecon called the Watton. They had moved there in the early Twenties after running several other pubs in the Welsh Marches towns of Hereford and Ludlow.
Mum and Dad took the lease on a Hotel called the Towers in a nearby village called Talgarth. It was a long way from the ravages of war, riot, and the unsettled world of the Middle East.

This was Mid-Wales, amidst the lush green hills of the Brecon Beacons and the babbling rivers of the Usk the Honddu and the meandering Wye. One would be hard pressed to find two places that were so different.

The Towers Hotel was a tall gothic stone built building

that overlooked the village square. There was a huddle of shops, two banks and the village hall that doubled as a cinema at weekends. The main source of employment in this relevantly prosperous area was farming and two large hospitals. One, the Mid-Wales, was a psychiatric and recuperation sanatorium, and the other, Bronllys ,was a TB and convalescent unit which treated miners from the South Wales Valleys suffering the effects of coal dust inhalation.

My brothers went to the local school but I was too young and spent my days crawling up and down the large wooden staircase to the up stairs bedrooms. (Something of a novelty after the large bungalow of Abadan). Food rationing was still in force after World War II but was not something enforceable in Mid-Wales. The local farmers would sell my Dad the odd side of bacon and baskets of golden brown free-range eggs for the huge breakfasts that Mum cooked at the Hotel.

Tourism was not really an industry in those days and the main guests at the hotel would be visiting specialists working at the nearby hospitals, or travelling salesmen. However, on one occasion we had the famous mountaineer and explorer Sir Edmund Hillary and his team as guests for a few weeks. They were in training for their forthcoming assault on Mount Everest in the Himalayas. The hills of the Brecon Beacons and Black Mountains, which over look the Wye Valley, offered good practice for the foothills of Nepal. The entry in the hotel guest register was a prize. Mum and Dad proudly showed off the page where Sir Edmund had signed in.

My Dad was a very jovial fellow with thickset shoulders and balding head and deep brown eyes. He enjoyed a glass of Robert's of Aberystwyth brewed beer and a chat with the farmers in the 'snug' bar. He smoked untipped Senior

Service cigarettes, quietly puffing away as he served behind the bar. Those were the heady days before the plethora of rules and regulations that plague our lives today.

We only stayed at the Towers for about 18 months before moving to another small hotel in Brecon. In 1953 we moved to the Angel Hotel in a part of Brecon called the Struet. It was another Brewery owned hotel. This time the Brewery was Simmons of Newport.

The Angel was a smaller building than the Towers but had a huge garden and car park. Running above the car park was the railway viaduct. A monstrous multi arched stone bridge, which crossed the River Honddu at the bottom of our garden. My Dad kept 30 or 40 chickens in a large wire fenced enclosure, these supplied the fresh eggs for Mum's famous breakfasts.

Tuesdays and Fridays were market days in the town. A 'hustle, bustle' time, and our car park was used by many local farmers who set up 'shop' under the arches of the viaduct. One old chap I remember as farmer Russell from Merthyr Tydfil, sold hundreds of wild rabbits. A local delicacy that had found great popularity during the times of food rationing.

A very busy time was market day, Mum and Dad worked hard pulling pints of beer, glasses of whisky and local cider for the thirsty farmers and market traders who came from far and near to sell their produce.

Mum preferred it here, as we were closer to the rest of her family. She was a very good looking woman, with blonde Marilyn Monroe style hair and a similar figure, although the life style of the pub was starting to put the pounds on a bit, but it suited her. She was a fun loving person who enjoyed socialising. She had travelled the world with Dad and was something of a celebrity in the town because of it. Most people had only travelled overseas during the War. Foreign travel was a rarity in those days.

Mum's family was centred on the Blue Boar Inn. She had two sisters that I called Aunt Rose and Aunt May. Aunt Rose lived at the pub with her husband Bernard, an ex-solider. They ran the pub for Granny after the death of my Grand Father George. May lived in Redditch in the West Midlands of England but visited quite regularly. Then there was Uncle Teddy who was a Squadron Leader in the Royal Air Force and Stationed at RAF Cranwell where he taught electrical engineering. He had been a Battle of Britain pilot, winning many decorations, and the family always looked forward to when he came home in his open top MG sports car.

Dad's family were always something of a mystery to me, all I ever really knew was that he had a brother who kept a pub called the White Rabbit in Luton just north of London. He had a son Dennis Hamilton Gittins who was quite a famous actor in the Fifties. He was married to the actress Diana Dors. Although I can't remember ever meeting any of Dad's side of the family, they certainly cropped up in conversation from time to time.

I started my education in the autumn of 1955 at Mount Street Infants school, only a hundred metres up a small hill from our pub. A 'prefab' building put up shortly after the War and attached to the main stone built primary school of the same name. It was a happy childhood in a friendly Welsh Border town, with friends and family always around. Those days are a little hazy, and it seems that the sun always shone in the summer and the snows always came in the winter. I can remember the first time my brothers and I witnessed our first snow at Talgarth. It was a sight to behold and I've liked snow ever since. A source of wonder, a cleansing frosty feel that heralded the coming of Christmas and Santa Claus.

In 1956 we were to move yet again. This time just a mile down the road when mum and dad bought the freehold of The Camden Arms Hotel. Obviously this is what they wanted, a pub not leased from a Brewery. A 'free house'.

The Camden was just across the road from the Blue Boar in the Watton. A long tree lined road that led to the Town Centre, from the great stone edifice of the Army Barracks at the other end. In those days Brecon was still a Garrison Town, the home of the South Wales Boarders Regiment, made famous by the film Zulu. This was to be a permanent move. Our new 'pub' is a Georgian built, end of terrace, Welsh stone building, joined at the rear to several rambling cottages and sheds of various ages. One of these had housed the old Phillips Brewery that closed during the War.

It was much smaller than the Towers, roughly the same size as the Angel, but without the very large garden and car park. Dad had also bought the house next door, number 20. The original idea was to extend the pub, incorporating number twenty, but this never happened. In stead it became a three-bedroom annex to the hotel side of the pub's seven bedrooms and later let to the Army as a 'married quarter'.

Life in Brecon was good. My brothers kept pigeons and I had two ferrets and Timmy the polecat, along with Muggles a funny old sausage dog and numerous cats with names like Soey, Jumbo and Tiger. I became a fully-fledged member of the Gas Works gang and the Fantastic Four. Spending many a summer's day running down Gas Lane to the Island Fields where I learnt to swim in the River Usk. Here we sailed down the rapids on an old tyre, jumped off 'big rock' swam to the 'point' and swung on a big rope tied to an over hanging tree just at the bend of the river.

With my pals, Jocko, Emlyn, Wayne and Chris, we lit campfires and tickled fish to cook with baked beans on an old piece of corrugated tin. Those were the days, before television, when parents did not need to worry where their children were. A far more innocent time when kids actually had a childhood, unlike today. In fact, during school holidays, we only went home to sleep and get more baked beans, bread and a bottle of orange squash for our daily feasts by the river. Occasionally we would get some penny sweets and a bottle of Tizer.

Sundays was a day for the family. We had to go to Sunday school in the morning and lunch was at 2pm sharp, when we all sat in the lounge around a huge oak table that groaned with the weight of the food laid upon it. A ten pound piece of best Welsh beef was not unusual. Chicken on the other hand was considered a luxury but there were always plenty of garden fresh vegetables, tureens overflowing with piping hot buttered spuds and every one's favourite, Yorkshire pudding and onion gravy.

The Watton Methodist Chapel was just a few yards from the Camden, which was handy for the thirsty congregation who went to Sunday morning service. The pubs in those days were officially closed on a Sunday but our little back bar was always full before and after chapel, when the gents drank pints of foaming mild beer, the ladies sipped sherry and the vicar drank port wine. All would say what a wonderful sermon he had given, and it would inevitably be the fire and brimstone variety, warning his flock of the evils of the demon drink. But the odd glass of port wine was medicinal and Gods work was thirsty toil after all. Such was the philosophy of the day and why not, the War was long past and Rock and Roll was just around the corner.

# 3

# Rock And Roll Comes To Town

Rock and Roll hit Brecon on a Saturday night in the late Fifties. The Coliseum, one of the two local cinemas, showed the film Rock Around the Clock with Bill Hailey and the Comets. I must have been eight or nine years old at the time and sat in absolute wonder at the spectacle that unfolded before my eyes. People actually got up and started dancing in the aisles. The film was already a few years old but it was new to Brecon.

Shortly afterwards my brother Mike took up guitar lessons and my brother Pete begged Mum for a set of drums. I started to sing in front of the mirror using an old hairbrush as a microphone. It wasn't long before Mike and Pete formed a band called the Amazons with two of Mike's friends.

In 1961 I took my 'eleven plus' exam and came 102nd out of 110 assuring me a place at the Brecon Secondary Modern School. This was something of a disappointment to my parents, as my eldest brother Mike went to Brecon's Christ College one of Wales' premier private schools, but at least I followed in the footsteps of my other brother Peter, who also attended the Secondary Modern. In fact I followed in Peter's shadows for many years to come, he had become something of an athlete, later to be voted Wales' best all round male athlete by TWW (Television Wales & the West).

I could never say that I liked school. I found it difficult and boring, and longed for the last 'bell' of the day when I could run off and play with my mates. On one such day in the early summer of 1962 as I was running home, I spotted a strange ariel on our main chimneystack Dad had bought a television! As I rushed in through the back door and into the lounge, quickly followed by Jocko and Emlyn, there was Dad, feet up, cigarette in one hand, glass of beer in the other, watching the tennis at Wimbledon. We sat and watched in awe, the only other person who had a 'telly' in our neighbourhood was Mrs Pallardy. Once a week our gang would pool our pocket money to buy her a bottle of Mackeston Stout so that we could sit in her front parlour and watch 'Quatermass'. It was the scariest show on telly and we loved it, but her telly was tiny with just a 12-inch screen and a very dark picture.

Now we had our very own telly with a huge 21-inch screen. Needless to say I became very popular with all the other kids in the street. It wasn't long before T.V. ariels started springing up all over town, this was the Sixties, and as the man said "you've never had it so good."

Now on Saturday afternoons, instead of going to the old Palace cinema in the Watton and paying our 7 pennies to sit in the 'bug run' to watch the afternoon film, we all went to Jocko's house to watch the 'Lone Ranger and Tonto'. It wasn't long before the old Palace closed down and was redeveloped into a car show -room and garage

The happy world of my family came suddenly to an end in 1963 when my Dad was rushed into hospital and died. The years of toil in the oil fields of Persia had taken their toll. He had long suffered from the recurring effects of Malaria that finally led to complications and thrombosis.

I will remember forever my mother's face when I ran into the hospital. She stood crying in the corridor. I had returned home from school one windy afternoon to be met by my brother Mike who gave me the sad news. I said nothing and just rushed out and ran up the big hill to the War Memorial Hospital. Mum was totally devastated. Her eyes said it all.

The funeral is a total blur to me. All I can remember was that Dad had obviously been well liked and it was a big affair. Half the town turned out to pay their last respects. For weeks afterwards people came to offer Mum their sympathies and a veil of sadness descended on the family. It was time for me to grow up; perhaps faster than I would have done had my father lived longer

Dad had provided well for the family, money worries didn't seem an issue. Dad had also been a prominent Freemason and I think they helped Mum a lot after his death.

Mum decided she needed a holiday. Mike and Pete didn't want to go but I did. We went to the travel agents, which also doubled as a fishing tackle shop and general newsagents. It was perched on the end of the Usk Bridge that separated Brecon town from the small suburb of Llanfaes. We collected a handful of holiday brochures and spent the next few days deciding where to go. The options in those days were not as great as today and she left the final choice to me; Majorca!

We flew from Rhoose Airport near Cardiff in an old DC4 Argonaut on a wet blustery September afternoon. The flight would take over 5 hours with a re-fuelling stop in Barcelona. We hit a lighting storm over the Pyrenees Mountains, the planes four prop engines spluttered and droned noisily through the stormy night. Lighting flashed left and right as I peered out of the porthole window. I was 13 years old and this was just like a story from one of the comic books I used to read with gusto. We finally touched down at Palma Airport in the dead of night. The storm was far behind us, and all you could hear when the cabin doors opened was the chorus of crickets in the still warm night air of this Spanish Isle.

Our journey to Puerto de Soller took several hours. By the time we got to the Costa Brava Hotel we were both shattered and totally exhausted from the long trip. I woke up that first morning, not quite sure where I was. I looked around our twin bedded room and at the light peeping through the drawn curtains. Leaping out of bed and peering through the window, the sight that greeted my eyes was amazing. The bright blue waters of the Mediterranean Sea sparkled at the clear blue sky. I drew the curtains aside a little further and opened the windowed door that led to a small balcony over looking Puerto de Soller's horse shoe shaped bay. I was careful not to wake Mum; I wanted to breathe in this magnificent sight. It was only 8.30am and the day was already starting to warm up. A faint smell of coffee and hot bread wafted from below making me feel hungry. I had only drunk coffee once or twice and that was the old 'Camp' coffee and chicory mix, I was soon to be in for a treat!

I was the first person from my school ever to have visited Majorca, probably one of the first from Brecon. This was paradise and I hoped that my father was in such a beautiful place. I just had to wake Mum to see this magnificent sight.

We spent two fantastic weeks here, a time I will always remember and place I would surely return to one day.

Tourism had only just began to happen in Majorca in the early Sixty's, but already hotels were shooting up on every available sea front site. Puerto de Soller however, was still relatively unspoilt, and popular with the rich and famous. The actress Peggy Mount was staying in the hotel just up the road from us and one day the small fishing village was absolutely buzzing when John Wayne's yacht sailed into harbour. It dwarfed the Spanish Navel vessel moored next to it.

Late one morning the hotel owner knocked on our door, she was English and married to a Spaniard, a large but glamorous lady with big ornate glasses. "Marjorie!" she exclaimed in a very excited voice.

"Come quick, you'll never guess who's just popped in for a drink?" She was right we had no idea. Mum hurried down stairs to the bar and I followed.

There, sat at the bar talking to the lady's husband, was John Wayne, the 'Duke'. I was stunned; Mum was over the moon and was soon introduced to the great man himself. She then turned around and said

"And this is my youngest son David"

I just froze, this was John Wayne the Cowboy I had seen on the silver screen of the Palace cinema back home. A huge hand stretched out towards me and we shook hands.

"Well, how are you young man, enjoying your vacation?"

I looked back in disbelief, nodding and replying

"Yes thanks".

With that my mum, the hotel owners, and several other people closed in to talk to the great man. I melted into the back ground and watched and listened as everyone tried to talk at the same time.

He seemed very relaxed and laughed and chatted away for the next half-hour or so before a taxi came to take him back to his yacht. He was very much like his screen character. He even walked like he did in all those westerns as he disappeared through the front door of the hotel and into his waiting car. The boys back in Brecon were not going to believe this. Only then did I think of my camera up stairs in the bedroom!

We teamed up with a family from Cardiff who had two teenage daughters. This was my first real attraction to girls. They were several years older than me, but it didn't stop me dreaming and certainly gave me the incentive to learn to dance.

The cost of living in Majorca was a fraction of that in Wales. A fine dinner with wine cost no more than a bag of fish and chips from our local 'chippy' back home. Even at an early age I would try anything. I had my very first taste of Lobster, Paella and Suckling Pig and I drank wine with every meal. I even tried the local Brandy at 4 old pennies a glass but preferred the wine.

All good things come to an end but the flight back home was smooth and in daylight. I waved Majorca farewell from my window seat and watched it grow smaller as our plane headed back to Wales.

# 4

# A Time Of Change

The thought of going back to school was not something that I relished but I had to make an effort. Life without Dad was strange, but we all had to pitch in to help Mum. She now had to run the pub on her own but Mike left Christ College and did his final exams at the Brecon Boys Grammar School. This meant he could help Mum in the pub. Peter decided to join the Navy and would leave home soon.

As my brother's band was winding down, so I had started my own and we borrowed their equipment. The early rock and roll bands and later Cliff Richard and the Shadows had influenced them. We, on the other hand, were now listening to The Beatles, Rolling Stones, The Animals and The Small Faces. We converted the old brew house at the back of the Camden into our rehearsal studio, and also practised at the Army Cadet hut where I was a member. Major Goodwin used to let us use the old wooden Nissan hut provided that we cleaned it up.

It was on a Summer Camp in Southport just outside Liverpool that I first heard the Beatles and the Mersey Sound.

I was a full corporal in the Royal Artillery attached to the South Wales Borderers Regiment Army Cadet unit. I loved every minute in the Cadets, playing Rugby for the County side and representing Wales Command in Discus and Shot Putt at the U.K. tournament at Taunton in Somerset, winning a gold and silver medal. Although I never reached the same standards as Pete, I was very pleased with myself.

We played our first 'Gig' in 1965 at a small village hall just out side Brecon. It was also to be my first real sexual experience. To date, apart from the odd grope behind the 'bike-sheds', and a few snogging parties with some of the girls who lived in the Watton, I was still very much a virgin. What happened after our performance changed that. A very pretty teenage 'County-set' girl with a posh accent came up to me and asked if I'd like to go out side with her for a chat. Years before these 'County' sorts would not have been seen dead at a Village Hall dance, but things were changing fast.

As soon as we got around the back of the hall she pounced on me, she'd obviously done this before so I let her carry on. As she went to work on my 'John Thomas' I thought to myself " the sixth form girls at school won't even talk to me let alone this!"

Before 'Daddy' picked her up, she asked if we would like to play for a Young Conservative pyjama party, which we did. It turned out to be a feast of young nubile Felicity's and Cynthia's cavorting about the large County Seat of a local noble. We were like kids in a sweet factory. Life in the band certainly had its rewards!

I was the lead singer of our band 'The In-Sect' with Tweedy on Bass, Rob Whittaker on Lead guitar, Guy on Rhythm and Gus on Drums. We started playing various

Church halls in and around Brecon, transport was our biggest problem, but some how we seemed to manage, someone or other would ferry us about. In 1966 we decided to change our name to 'The Mists of Time' I'm not sure why, but we did. Soon we were playing two or three nights a week. We played the Honey Cavern in Bronllys, considered at the time a major venue in Mid-Wales. Bands such as The Rolling Stones, Swinging Blue Jeans, Them and The Honeycomb's were just a few who performed there on the way up the ladder to stardom.

We started writing and performing our own songs, but the band was plagued with arguments. This was usually over girls or not being committed enough. Sid our drummer was a lot older than us and had a job, which meant he had other considerations. Guy left the band to live in Swansea and was replaced by Roger Leakey who played bass so Tweedy swapped over to Rhythm.

A turning point came when we played at the guildhall, Brecon, for the Christmas school 'mob' dance. This was one of the high lights of the year if you were a teenager in Brecon during the Sixties. We supported an up and coming band called 'Next of Kin' from Ebbw Vale. But that night we stole the show when the zip on my hipster bell-bottom trousers broke and out popped my 'John Thomas' (I wasn't wearing any underpants). The girls went wild, I thought it was my singing and it was a good five minutes or so before I realised what had happened.

That night I met a girl called Ruth Evans. She was five years older than me but thought my 'singing' was 'fantastic'. She was very attractive with shortish brown 'Mary Quant' style hair that curled around her face. She was a fiery, passionate woman who worked in the local chemist shop. I'd seen her around the town but she had never given me a second look, until now. We were to embark on my first serious and very intense love affair.

Ruth thought I was far too good for the band and should seek my fortune in London. Which to every ones surprise, including my own, I did. My mother was devastated and the guys in the band were not very happy either. I had to hand in my cherished Army Cadet uniform, (by now I'd risen to the rank of colour sergeant). I felt apprehensive, and unsure of what lay ahead.

They say love is blind and I guess that's true but in hind sight it was my best move. I was totally useless in school and job prospects at home were very limited, especially if you had no educational qualifications. I had saved up a hundred pounds or so from my earnings in the band and Mum said to phone home if I needed more. We boarded the London bound train one July morning, and a few hours later arrived at Paddington Station. Ruth had been to London before and knew of a small bed and breakfast in Ladbroke Road.

We stayed there for a few days making love ten times a day, she was insatiable and so was I. We just couldn't get enough of each other. London was alive; this was the era of 'swinging London and Flower Power'. However, our money wouldn't last forever and the record companies were not exactly queuing up to offer me a multi million pound contract. I'm not quite sure how we did it but we managed to get into a Civil Service hostel in Hampstead's Belsize Park Gardens. It was £3 a week all in and a great part of town.

The hostel was split into two female and one male blocks, converted from large Victorian terraced houses. I shared a large room with two other guys, one a tall ginger headed Irish guy from Shannon, and the other a short dark hared English guy from Maidstone in Kent, both of whom were Civil Servants. Ruth had her own room in the women's block, which proved to be handy for my newly acquired sex drive.

Ruth found a job with the Brook Street Employment Services as a temporary secretary, while I went from one audition to the next. I guess I was perfectly happy with her bringing in the money but one Monday morning I decided to get a job just to hedge my bets. So, it was off to Camden Town Youth Employment Centre where I entered the world of opportunity.

After only minutes of walking into this large red brick building I was offered all sorts of jobs. London was booming and there were far more jobs than there were people. I really fancied travel so they gave me a card to go immediately to Russell Square for an interview with Frames Tours. This I did 'immediately!' The interview consisted of, "how soon could I start?" I replied "how much?" "Nine pounds!" came the quick reply "ten!" said I.

"Nine pounds ten shillings and I'll throw in £2 a week in luncheon vouchers. Here's the address, report to the manager I'll ring him to expect you, what's your name again?" Back home I would have thought £4 per week good money in those days, to argue the 'toss' would be unthinkable but this was London in the Sixties.

So, I found myself on the 'Tube' headed for Golders Green, then a bus to Temple Fortune. I couldn't believe they wanted me to start today, but I had nothing else to do, EMI had not replied to my last request for an audition so why not go for it! The small but very busy travel agent was opposite the John Lewis Supermarket and National Provincial Bank. This was a very wealthy, predominately Jewish part of North London.

I opened the glass door, walked up to the counter, and there was the most gorgeous women I'd ever seen. She was in her late twenties with long raven black hair and ruby red lips. I introduced myself and she exclaimed oh! You're Welsh. Now, I had not realised I had an accent until I came to London. My point of view being that they had the accent not me. So, before I could enquire as to how she knew, she came from behind the counter so I could see her mini skirted legs that disappeared up to heaven, who was I to argue? Who cared?

Her name was Leigh and was the assistant manager, the manager was away sick but would be back tomorrow.

"Let me introduce you to the other members of staff, this is Jean"

I would be the forth member of staff but they were on the look out for more. It appeared that the turnover of staff was quite high but for the life of me couldn't think why. Before long it was closing time, I'd done nothing more than talk to Leigh and Jean in between them seeing an endless stream of customers.

As soon as I got back to the hostel I told Ruth the good news that I'd found a Job. She was not exactly thrilled, saying that I should concentrate on getting into a new band. I ended up celebrating my first job with my roommates at the Great George Pub in Hampstead, complaining about the price of beer in London at half a crown a pint!

My job at Frames Tours-Temple Fortune proved enlightening. As I've said I was not much good at school but no one asked, my saving grace being my 'gift of the gab' and Leigh's helping hand.

The manager turned out to be a very dry humoured chap who lived with his ageing mother in Hemel Hempstead. He was a Harry Corbett (young Steptoe) look alike but with thick horn-rimmed glasses. He was totally besotted by Leigh, but she had a boy friend, a very rich one twenty years her elder; and he was Welsh! They lived together in a 'posh' apartment near-by. The job at Frames was her little bit of independence.

The other girl Jean was in her early thirties, Irish and totally proud of her magnificent breasts, which she kept feeling? I found this a bit distracting but never complained when she rubbed up against me from time to time behind the counter and pinched my bum. Both Leigh and Jean took great delight in teasing this athletic young Welsh boy with a 'very nice arse'.

My relationship with Ruth was becoming very strained. The only time we could make love was if I sneaked into the girl's block and up to her room. There was a dragon of a matron who lived there and could smell men at a hundred yards. Every time was like an SAS sortie, knowing that if I got caught they would throw me out. As yet I could not afford a Penthouse on Park Lane so I had a lot to lose, but, the thought of Ruth's warm firm body waiting for me over ruled the fears and I became quite expert at clandestine manoeuvres. My Army Cadet training served me well.

My first real psychedelic experience, a taste of real flower power, was in December 1967. Ruth and I were invited to a party at a large apartment overlooking Primrose Hill. She was 'Temping' for an Indian Businessman called Previn in the West End. He invited her, and we were not sure if I was included in the invite, but we were still 'going out' together, so I tucked a four-pint can of Watney's Red Barrel under my arm and off we went.

Now; at all the parties I'd been to before, including those in London, a four-pint can was a prerequisite. Alas, not here. Previn had a better stocked bar than the Hilton, my large can provided much amusement with the assembled 'in-crowd', and a little bit of embarrassment to Ruth who had told me not to bring it. Most people wore Kaftans, beads, and flowers in their hair. I on the other hand wore my newly acquired (from Carnaby Street) red Beatles style army jacket, blue bell-bottoms and Cuban healed boots. Pretty suave I thought!

One thing I had not succumbed to was the drug scene, and thankfully I never did. Booze was enough for me although I was still under age it was by far the lesser of two evils. I could handle booze; being brought up in a pub it was never a big deal to me.

Apart from the copious amounts of liquor available there was also Wacky Backy (marijuana) and pills which were, presumably, LSD. It was hard to tell who was 'pissed' or who was 'high'.

Previn was paying Ruth a lot of attention, and as she was deliberately ignoring me, I began to wander around the various rooms of the apartment. In the dimly lit rooms strobe and projector lights beamed vivid liquid patterns of light on the walls and ceilings to the sounds of Pink Floyd, Eric Burton and Procul Harem, occasionally punctuated by Ravi Shankis sitar music. I could just see, through the haze and coloured lights, couples making love on large oriental 'bean bags'.

As I entered one of the huge mirrored bedrooms two young hippie girls came up to me

"Just love your jacket man, you want some 'weed''.

"No thanks Luv there's enough in the atmosphere to

turn a gelded ferret on"

"Wow-a gilded ferret"

"No, not a gilded. Never mind!"

With that they led me to a large bed to experience 'free love'. I just went with the flow, it seemed the most natural thing in the world to do, and do it I most definitely did. Since going out with Ruth I didn't dare so much as look at another woman (certainly when she was around.) She had more than a drop of fiery Celtic blood flowing through her pretty veins. The following morning I awoke in a daze the girls were already up walking around the apartment completely naked with not a care in the world. Why not? They had incredible bodies, truly beautiful.

Previn walked in wearing a flowing silk dressing gown and holding two massive glasses of Bucks Fizz.

"How was it dear boy"

"Bloody great" I replied rubbing the sleep from my eyes.

"Where's Ruth"

"Went 'miles ago' dear boy" Previn said in his educated Indian tones.

This was the first time I'd really seen Previn properly; he was in his early forties, short but had very distinguished good looks.

"The girls tell me you have a wonderful gilded ferret" He continued with a knowing smile.

"Ah? Oh yeah, well I guess you could call it that! Heard it called worst."

"You are so amusing dear boy-no wonder Ruth finds you so interesting-she tells me you're a singer in a Rock Band"

"I'm not sure she's so amused with me now-boyo!"

Previn handed be a large glass of Bucks Fizz that had more

fizz than bucks but it did the trick. I could certainly get used to the good life.

"Why don't you join me for lunch and a few drinks- you can tell me all about your band"

"Well thanks Previn but I quit the band back in Wales, been looking around London for a break and besides my Bank Balance couldn't stand the strain"

"I wouldn't hear of it dear boy, my treat, besides the girls are hungry, always are, especially after your gilded ferret".

The gilded ferret became something of a 'buzz word' that raised a roar of laughter every time it was mentioned. But what the hell I thought, I'd rather make people laugh than cry, which is probably what I'd done to Ruth.

Previn turned out to be a really nice guy, as usual I'd got it all wrong, Ruth had been trying to get Previn to introduce me to some of his friends in the record business. Over lunch at his favourite Indian restaurant in Swiss Cottage he told me he had an import/export business but two friends of his ran a record company that did cover versions. Ruth had been plaguing him to introduce me. That made me fell really great! God knows what I was going to say to her when I got back to the hostel.

After a sumptuous curry lunch, Previn offered me a lift home. Belsize was not that far so I declined saying I needed the walk besides I had to think of something to say to Ruth. Previn gave me his home number and we shook hands, I gave the girls a genteel kiss good bye, they giggled saying "look after that ferret of yours!"

It was late Sunday afternoon. Despite being early December it was not cold and a weak sun still brightened the sky. It took me fifteen minutes or so to walk back to the hostel. Ruth was sitting in the large bay window of the hostel peering down the road, soon as she saw me she came out to meet me. There was no escape!

She had a frown that would pierce steel, before I could say anything she slapped me across the face and said, "See you after work tomorrow-don't be late" and went back inside.

I felt relieved at least she was talking to me!

# 5

# The Break

I met Ruth in the Common Room of the Hostel at 6pm 'as ordered'. She told me to take the following day off work.

"I've arranged for you to make a demo disc tomorrow at 11am. The studio is in Turnham Green. I'll see you in my room at 10pm tonight; don't be late". With that she left and I went up the pub with my mates.

Needless to say I did my SAS manoeuvre and got into her room just after 11pm. After a little bit of retribution we made love but were even more intense than usual.

The following day we took the 'Tube' to Turnham Green. It was a small recording studios near the Station. Ruth introduced me to the Guy who ran it and she gave him my sheet music and we got straight into it. I was to record two songs that I had written some months ago in Wales. 'Body and Soul' and 'This Town is too big for me'. After an hour of rehearsal with two of the studio session musicians we started to record. By 4pm we had finished and every body except me was happy with the result. Ruth seemed thrilled and so did the studio boss, but I felt I could have done better. I needed more rehearsal time and I needed a band. I never really thought of myself as a solo singer.

We sent copies of the Demo Disc to various record companies without luck. Ruth began to get more and more distant and eventually moved out of the hostel and into her own flat in Hampstead Village. I had never really talked to Leigh about my aspirations of being a pop singer, but one Friday afternoon at work the subject arose. She seemed fascinated and suggested we went for a drink after work to talk about it.

There was no pub in Temple Fortune so we had to take a taxi to the 'Spaniards Inn' Hampstead. Here I poured my heart out to this most beautiful of work colleagues any one could possibly have. There was magnetism between us but she was faithful to her boy friend. He was a millionaire and I was a young lad just starting out what else could she do. We held hands and I swear a charge of electricity flowed through my veins. I had never looked at anyone the way I looked at Leigh that night; we gazed into one another's eyes as I revealed my life history to her. She told me to follow my dreams, only I could be the master of my destiny. No one else could ever lead me to the stars, I must do what ever was needed myself, and it would be a very long road indeed.

We parted that evening with a very long lingering kiss that made my head spin, she left by taxi and I walked up the hill to Hampstead Village. Strolling through that misty December evening, my head still reeling, I came across another pub, the 'Jack Straws Castle'.

"What the hell I'll have another pint then head for the hostel." I thought to myself, with a little sigh.

The pub was heaving, Hampstead's 'hooray-henry's' were out in force. I ordered a pint of larger and sat in a corner looking a bit sorry for myself.

"Well how the devil are you old boy" I looked up it was Previn!

"Bloody hell you get about-how are you-good to see you, I was miles away, busy day, bloody awful day. Sorry Previn I'm in a world of my own at the moment" I said in one breath.

"Calm down dear boy-I hope its nothing to do with my little party?"

"No way Previn; No its all about my lack of success Ruth had such high hopes and I'm afraid I've let her down"

"Let me introduce you to a friend of mine, I'm sure she can help you out dear boy"

Previn introduced me to a party of people loudly drinking Champagne in an anti-room of the pub.

"This is Vicki" Said Previn pointing to a lady in her late twenty's with long strangely hair and thick rimmed glasses, she had a sort of trendy 'hippie' look.

Vicki turned out to be Vicki Whickham the presenter of Ready Steady Go. The forerunner to Top of the Pops 'the' pop TV programme in the country.

I sat down next to Vicki and we began to chat, I don't think she was into men but who gave a damn! The main thing was she seemed interested in my singing. She asked me to audition for a new record label. I gave her my telephone number at work thinking it was the Champagne talking and I'd never hear from her again. Monday morning, as I was rushing around the small office at Frames' Tours Leigh called me to the telephone, it was Vicki Whickham. "Could I come to see her tomorrow?"

The following evening I walked into a small top floor studio just off Oxford Street. There were about ten other people waiting to be auditioned and I took my place in the queue. Eventually it was my turn to go through into the auditioning room where Vicki and two musicians sat. She greeted me with a little hug and I handed over my sheet music to the pianist.

The audition went well, I sang the same two songs, I had written back in Wales and recorded at the demo session. 'Body and Soul' and 'This town's too big for me'. Vicki seemed very pleased and asked if I could come to her offices the following Friday. She was currently the A & R director of Toast Records a subsidiary of Major Minor Records. Their other artists included Deep Purple and David McWilliams who had huge hits at the time.

I was over the moon to say the least and rushed back to Hampstead to tell Ruth what had happened. She knew nothing about this latest audition. With all the dead-ends I'd been down so far, I felt it best not to tell her. Besides, things were not going too well between us. She didn't seem very pleased to see me, but eventually let me into her flat when I told her I had some great news! I recounted the story of bumping into Previn and being introduced to Vicki Whickham, who used to present Ready Steady Go. How she had asked me to audition and now wanted to sign me to Toast Records.

Ruth sat open-mouthed on the settee, wearing her red dressing gown, her face beginning to brighten as I revealed my good news.

"Why didn't you tell me?" she said with a wicked smile.

"Well I thought it might be just another let down. I've not exactly had much luck lately. This came totally out of the blue, it could have been just another disappointment"

As I spoke she stood up undoing her dressing gown

and letting it drop to the floor revealing her beautiful naked body. Walking over to me she fell to her knees saying in a hushed voice. " You're such a naughty boy-you know you should tell Ruthy everything"

With that she undid my zipper and blew my mind away. She had never given me a blowjob before, Ruth very much ruled our relationship and demanded that I pleased her and got really moody if I didn't, tonight would be different!

The following morning I arrived at work exhausted and an hour late. The manager grunted something at me and gave me a pile of filing to get on with. As I struggled with my task Leigh whispered

"Tell me all about it after work tonight-my boy friend is away for a few days."

I spent the next two days in a dream world. Ruth became insatiable and kept going on about what to do with all the money I was going to earn, and Leigh's skirts were getting even shorter (was that possible?).

When Friday came I rang work to say I was sick with flu and wouldn't be in. The manager made a grunting noise and said, "See you Monday".

I arrived at the offices of Toast Records at 11am. They were just around the corner from Carnaby Street, that bastion of Sixties fashion. Vicki came out to reception and while we greeted she introduced me to a stunning black girl, Rosetta Hightowers, a soul singer from the United States who had just signed for Toast. I then went in to see 'the boss' Mr. Solermann, a large man wearing horn rim glasses. He had typical Jewish features and a broad welcoming smile.

"Vicki's told me all about you. You write songs as well I hear. That's wonderful" he beamed.

"I have a publishing contract for you as well. How

many songs have you written."

"Four or five I guess" I replied a little in awe of it all.

"Your going to have to get busy. What name are you going under-Vicki you thought of a name yet" Mr. Solermann was talking faster as he pulled a big fat cigar from his desk draw.

"How old are you my boy?"

"I'll be seventeen next week, and I'd like to go under the name of David Noel if that's OK with you"

"Great-sounds great, what you think Vicki?"

"Yeah! Its good" she answered "kind of folksy-I like it".

Solermann turned back to me

"Eighteen yah, your parents are going to have to sign their approval, are you in the Union. Vicki is he in the Union?"

I interceded.

"Yes I am. I joined the Rhondda branch of the musicians union last year"

"The Rhondda branch no less, great we got a regular Tom Jones here!" Solermann then proceeded to hand me a pile of documents.

"Here my boy, take these home with you for your parents to see. Get em back as soon as you can. Take him for lunch Vicki"

With that we went off to a trendy restaurant near Soho accompanied by Rosetta and a lady from their P.R. department.

In transpired that Rosetta could not obtain a permit to work in the U.K., and the record company was trying to get her married off to a British national. For one minute I thought it might have been me. Thankfully this was not part of the deal. Although the thought of the honeymoon certainly had its appeal, she was gorgeous, and a really nice person. However, the thought of trying to explain something like that to Ruth would have been an experience I was glad I didn't have to even contemplate!

Christmas was approaching and I was looking forward to going home for the first time since leaving in July. I rang Mum on a regular basis but was missing her, and feeling home sick. I had posted the recording contract to Mum for her to look at and sign. She was ever so proud and got the local newspaper to print a story.

I left work on the afternoon of the day before Christmas Eve and went straight to Paddington Station to catch the 'Pullman' express to south Wales, Ruth met me on the platform. One of the perks of working for a travel agent was reduced prices, and sometimes, free travel. The old blue Pullman was the height of luxury train-travel at the time. It would put modern British rail travel to shame. Each seat was reserved and full 'silver service' meals were served at each table. I had changed into my sky blue silk caftan that I bought the previous Sunday at Petty Coat Lane Market. I thought I really looked the part of the up and coming pop singer.

Ruth and I dined all the way to Newport and consumed several lagers and a bottle of 'Mateus Rose' wine. Our plan was to get a connecting train to Abergavenny, then a bus onwards as the line to Brecon had been axed a few years earlier in the 'Beeching cuts'. Instead we opted for a taxi to take us the 40-mile trip home dropping Ruth off at Llangynidr on the way. The taxi cost £5, with a £1 tip [a lot of money then] the taxi driver seemed happy with the deal and we chatted merrily all the way home.

It was great to finally arrive at the Camden Arms; it was just before midnight, on a starry still cold night. It was good to breath the clean mountain air of home and to see the stars twinkling in a velvet black sky; something of a rarity in the Smokey grey skies of London. Mum had waited up and was so pleased to see me. We sat in the empty front bar, she pulled herself a large Scotch and Soda and a pint of lager for me, which I drank thirstily before retiring to my old bedroom.

The story in the local Brecon & Radnor Express had certainly raised my popularity in the town, and with my shoulder length hair and silk caftan I also looked the part as I walked through Brecon the following day. It was good to be home.

My brother Mike was working for the General Post Office Telecommunications (GPO), after serving an electrical apprenticeship at a local store, Bulwark Radio. He also helped Mum in the Pub. My brother Pete arrived home from the Navy, he was serving in the Fleet Air Arm in Plymouth. Mum arranged for someone to look after the pub for an hour or two and joined us three boys for a 'drink around town'. She was so proud of her three boys, but still insisted on calling me her 'baby'.

We stood in the 'cocktail lounge' then known as 'Dolly's bar' after the charismatic barmaid Dolly Mayo, at the Wellington hotel in the Town Square. We laughed and sang, (one does in Wales!) as we revealed our various tales and caught up on the local gossip before returning to the Camden. The Christmas holidays passed quickly and it was soon time for me to return to London. What would be in store for me in the New Year of '68?

My mind was now firmly on making a hit record, but I could not give up my 'day job' just yet. Working at Frames Tours was not so bad and had its pluses. Besides cheap travel we were often invited to numerous tourist board parties. We were also a theatre-booking agency and I had the opportunity of obtaining free tickets to the many West-End theatres.

This became quite a passion for me; I especially liked the Brian Rix farces and the new musicals like 'Hair' and 'Fiddler on the roof'. On one occasion I had an invitation to the Soviet Embassy for a party hosted by the department of culture and tourism. The manager didn't like going to these 'do's' and would give the invites to Leigh, who in turn gave them to me.

The Embassy 'bash' was really lavish, with buckets of fresh caviar; Russian Champagne, canapé's of every sort and of course Vodka. In fact every flavour of Vodka one could imagine, along with Cossack dancing, choirs and folk dancing. All this at the height of the cold war was of course to impress, at any cost. Tourism to the Soviet Union was practically non-existent, but what the hell, a party was a party.

I thought that was wonderful until I went to the Spanish Embassy, they were courting a thriving and fast growing tourist industry. It was still in the days of President Franco but the Spanish flair for food, colour and fiesta was very much alive. Unlike the Soviets' they didn't have to pretend to be having a good time! Usually after such parties, which tended to end before 10p.m. We would move on to a club such as the Marquee to hear bands like Jimi Hendrix, The Yard Birds and Eric Burdon.

It was early February by the time the record company started to work on me. We started with a photo shoot on Hampstead Heath and several sessions at Toast's offices, hearing various song submissions and ideas. I had still not come up with a song that anyone thought good enough as an 'A side'. Then one day Vicki rang me to say she had found a song that was just right for my first single. I listened to the demo tape sent in by the songwriter but didn't like it at all. It was a folk-blues number in totally the wrong key and style for me. So memorable was this song that I can't even remember the title of it to this day.

Having no manager I was a lone voice of opposition in the decision to record this song. Even Ruth told me to follow the advice of the record company 'they knew best!' to be honest I went with the flow on that very premise. The first recording schedule had to be cancelled because of a raging toothache that started two days before. It turned out to be an abscess, which probably came out in sympathy with me for having to record this unmemorable song!

Despite my protests that I needed some serious rehearsal sessions to get my voice around this song, the record company insisted that I get into the studio immediately. Unfortunately, I did.

The day is etched upon my brain [apart from the name of the bloody song]. The recording took place at Chapel's Studio, Bond Street, one of London's best. The recording studio was on the second floor, above Chapel's Music publishing Co, and was very impressive. It was nothing like the small 4 track studio in Turnham Green, this was very much Hi-Tech, state of the art 32 track and totally professional. Unlike me.

I arrived at 10am although I was not due to record until the afternoon. I thought that if I could get a feel of what was going on I could be more relaxed. Rosetta was recording in the morning; she'd obviously met mister right? And she made it look so easy.

Following me were three teenage blond girls from the North of England, who I guess had the same idea as me about getting into the atmosphere of the studio. They were very pretty, all with the same straight honey blond hair, angelic faces, micro skirts, small tight bodies and large breasts. (Who needs a voice?)

For the first time I was very nervous and not my happy go lucky, cock sure self. There was a studio full of professional session musicians, violins the lot. Never having sung in a remote booth with earphones on did not help. I guess some people take to it like a duck to water but not me.

Because of union regulations at the time, I mumbled through both tracks along with the orchestra the best I could. My own song 'This town's too big for me' was OK. But the 'A' side was proving very difficult I sang out of tune most of the way through it. Vicki then told me to go for a break and come back in 20 minutes, this I did. Then I spent the next two hours trying to get the 'A' side right without the session musicians present. I can only say I failed. The key changes were beyond my vocal capabilities.

I left the studio a very disappointed man and headed for the nearest pub where I found the three girls from 'Up North' and some of the session musicians drooling over them. I had hoped they would not notice me coming in, I wanted to sit in the corner with a pint and wallow in self-pity.

"Hi!" Said the slightly tallest of the three. "You're the singer from the Studio?"

With that the three girls came over, my heart sank.

"You got a great voice" She carried on in a very broad Liverpool accent.

"Thanks, but I think I really cocked it up" I replied sipping my cold flat lager.

"No we thought you were great!" The girls all said in harmony. They giggled and then two wiggled back on their high heels to rejoin the session musicians.
The taller one continued in a quiet tone. "Your lucky mate we had to shag our way here, you got talent, get your self-a manager. Tell the bastards you want a better song. If you want to see me later on here's the number"
With that she scribbled down the phone number of her hotel and stuffed it in my hand, gave me a kiss on the lips and wiggled back to her pals. I gulped down my flat lager and left. A few yards down the road a hand felt my shoulder.

"Hey! Hang on son lets have a beer in the next one" I looked around and it was one of the session musicians, I think he was the lead guitarist.

"Ah! Shit man I just want to wallow somewhere on my own" I said trying not to be impolite but wanted to be alone.
" I know-just a quick one then I'm going back with the girls"
We went into the next pub, at least the lager wasn't flat and I'd resigned myself to a friendly chat.

"Look kid! Vicki was way out of order whisking you into a studio like Chapels without rehearsing. She's on a time frame with Solermann, looking for a big hit. Don't take it to heart, get yourself a manager or you'll be eaten alive." We chatted a while then he left saying "if you want some fun the girls are up for it!"
As much as I wanted to, I declined and took the tube back to Belsize Park. For the next few days I avoided Ruth and pretended with Leigh at work that everything was fine. It was about two weeks before I heard anything from Toast Records. They sent me a copy of the recording I'd made, along with a letter asking me to call in to see Vicki, which I did a few days later.

We both agreed that my performance was not really up to standard and she gave me an introduction to Deep Purple's manager.

"Go along and see him, I'm sure he can help. Perhaps you've got some new material that he could work on with you" Vicki said hopefully.

Before going to see him I decided to take a day off work and record some songs on an old tape recorder I had. Setting every thing up in my bedroom at the hostel I began to record three numbers without any backing. Singing away into the microphone I noticed that the tap was dripping in the wash basin in the corner of my room. Still holding the microphone I went to switch in off.

The next thing I remember is waking up on the other side of the room with the head of the tap still in my hand, shaking like a leaf, my hair standing on end as if I'd been given an afro perm. If the screw holding the head to the tap had not given away I would have died that day. I'm sure some people would have turned to religion there and then, joining some sect of monks to praise the Lord. I certainly prayed in thanks to the Lord and my guardian angel, then went straight to the pub and downed several pints of Strongbow cider, I've liked the beverage ever since. I was obviously destined for something but was it singing?

My meeting with the Deep Purple manager went well and he set me a task that if successful would have prolonged my recording career. Could I get hold of the master tape from Toast? If I could he would work with me. However, the answer to that was no. Try as I may the record company would not let me have it. Then I discovered that someone else had released the song and that was the end of that.

A group called Vernons' Brass Foundry released it that

spring, it never made the chart, which was some comfort to me, but I'm sure Vernon was gutted.
I did however record some cover versions of chart hits for Regent records and went under the grand name of 'various artists' and that was virtually the end of my 'pop' career.

Things at work plodded on until the manager left and later Leigh decided to work for Lunn Poly Travel. Leigh's departure made me determined to broaden my horizons and look for a new beginning.

# 6

# Hamburg Calling

Things at Frames ToursTemple Fortune became chaotic after the departure of Leigh and the manager. They sent a large black lady from head office to take charge. She was the spitting image of the TV chef Rusty Lee and had the same sense of humour.

Jean was still there, but she also soon departed. She left a goodbye note and wrote herself an airline ticket to Dublin. We were joined by a young cockney boy who spent most of the day dreaming; of what I'm not sure. Then Marilyn joined us. A thin girl with large breasts. She came from Hendon and was the same age as me but very much the 'little girl' with big doe like eyes. I liked her a lot.

By this time Ruth and I had more or less finished and I found a new sexual awakening. It had been increasingly apparent that the wealthy matrons of Temple Fortune and Golders Green found me attractive. There was a steady stream of these well-preserved, well-dressed, bored ladies, frequenting the travel agency. You could not call them housewives; they had maids for the mundane duties. One husband actually paid me to take his wife to a posh dinner dance at the Hilton Hotel Park Lane, on the pretext he had other commitments that weekend in Brighton, 'wink-wink!' and I'm sure his secretary was part of the itinerary.

Mrs. M. had booked several cruises and a trip to Israel through me over the past six months or so. She was in her late thirties, with shoulder length, raven black hair. She wore lots of make up and dressed immaculately I had already been to 'lunch' at her place on two occasions, but apart from a lingering kiss or two and a feel of her ample breasts I had not gone any further. The night at the Hilton would be very different. Her husband had booked a suite for the night and I had to hire a Tuxedo (dinner suit). I'd never worn one before, normally my trusty black suit and a 'dickie bow tie', would suffice. I was not unaccustomed to high living or swanky 'do's', but I must admit this little soiree was in the big league. The whole place smelt of wealth and the women were dripping in diamonds, including Mrs M.

She kept introducing me to her friends "as her travel agent" I went with the flow and thoroughly enjoyed the attention of her female friends, although some of the men were a little suspect! Nearing the end of the evening she invited me to her sumptuous suite for a nightcap before I returned to my hostel. A large bottle of champagne was cooling in an ice bucket.

"Open it for me darling while I just freshen up" she said, before disappearing into the bathroom.
I found a 'hi-fi' in the room, along with several LP's including Sergeants Peppers Lonely Hearts Club Band. I put on 'Lucy in the Sky with Diamonds', my favourite track, then popped the cork.

She emerged from the bathroom dressed in black

stockings and suspenders, uplift bra and high-heeled shoes. (You can't beat perfection). The only freshening up she'd done was to apply a new coat of bright red lipstick to her pouting lips and comb down her raven black hair. It was time to play with the big girls! Mrs. M. taught me things I had only dreamed of, here was I, Dai boy, making love to a beautiful Jewess in a suite at the Hilton-Park Lane, life's' not all bad!

Airlines and travel had been a great source of wonder for me. So, deciding that I needed a change, I wrote to all the major airlines enquiring about a job. The first to reply was Lufthansa German Airlines. They enclosed an application form and a request for references.

I rang Mum and told her that I couldn't see any future in pop singing and had an opportunity of working for an Airline. As usual she supported me and arranged for some very impressive character references. My old Colonel from the Army Cadets, and the Chairwoman of Brecon magistrates, both gave me flowing references. She also decided to come to London for a few days to see me.

As for the reference from my employer, who better to write it than myself. Our new manager spent most days off sick, so that left me, at sweet eightteen the senior member of staff! Mum was very much a larger than life character and I arranged the red carpet treatment for her. I booked her into a good hotel in Hampstead, arranged theatre tickets and dinner at the Savoy Hotel 'GrillRoom'.

As I've said before, working for Frames did have its perks. Having by this time virtual carte blanche for what I did in the office, I was able to get some very substantial discounts. In fact when booking the Savoy restaurant I told them I was the new hotel-booking manager for the whole group of companies and was taking my Mum for a celebration dinner.

As Frames were a major player in the tourism game the Savoy did me proud. Two bottles of Champagne on the house and the Maitre d' mooning around as if I were Royalty. No bad for a country boy I thought!

However, even with the discounts I was skint for weeks afterwards. Still it was all worth while, and good to see Mum enjoy herself. She had been used to the good life so I had to show that her 'baby' was doing OK in the 'big city'.

Having sent off my application and references to Lufthansa I received, almost by return post, a request to come for an interview. When the day came, I dressed in my one formal suit and made my way to Heathrow Airport. Here I was confronted by two men, one a big German, the other a small thin Englishman. I took an instant dislike to the thin Englishman, Mr. Arthur Thorn-Davis, and he to me. On the other hand Herr Lehman, the boss or Station Manager and I got on very well. Having studied Lufthansa's time table and publicity leaflets, which were mailed to all the major travel agents, such as Frames, I was pretty au fait with what they were doing as a Company. Herr Lehman at least seemed impressed.

Thorn-Davis just kept on about my school examination certificates, which of course, I did not have. I told him I'd given them to the personnel office at Frames and they had not returned them. He didn't believe me, but Lehman just asked when I could start.

"When do you want me to start?" was my answer.
His answer was that I should report to Heathrow Airport in seven days time. I was to fly to Hamburg for a six months training course. The pay was double what I received at Frames and on top of that I would receive free living accommodation and a daily allowance or 'Tagers Geldt'. The job? Flight dis-

patch. I didn't have a clue what that was, but hey, I'd learn!

I had not seen Ruth for a few weeks, and co-incidentally, she had moved in with a German girl called Brigitte. When I called to see her she was very cold. After telling her that I was going to Hamburg for six months, I asked if I could stay with her for a few days. I had to book out of the hostel and would need a place to stay. Reluctantly, she agreed, then introduced me to Brigitte.

She was tall and attractive but not a pretty girl, with short black hair and a broad German accent. It turned out she was from Hamburg and chatted away with me to the great annoyance of Ruth. I gave notice at Frames. That resulted immediately in the head office personnel manager ringing me. He practically begged me to stay. He obviously knew I was very popular with the customers, especially the big spending Jewish matrons who constantly invited me to lunch or, if their husbands were away, for dinner. Suffice it to say I ate well during my time at Temple Fortune.

Despite an offer of more money I was determined to go to Germany and make a fresh start. On my last night in London I stayed at Ruth's flat. There was only one bedroom but two beds. I slept in one and Ruth and Brigitte slept in the other. It was a long bitter night for me that I longed to get over. As morning broke I got up, dressed, grabbed my bags and made for the tube station, trying not to wake them. As I neared the station I heard a voice calling my name, it was Ruth, still dressed in her red dressing gown and running down the road. She flung her arms around me.

"I do love you Dave, you must know that, its' just we've changed. Please write to me" With that we kissed and said goodbye.

On arrival at Heathrow I met Herr Lehman who introduced me to five other guys and two girls who were also going on the course at Hamburg. We boarded the Boeing 737 on a bright early summer's morning, chatting and laughing, wondering what lay ahead. A few hours later we arrived at Hamburg's Fleusbutles Airport and then went onto the airline's college.

I shared a spacious twin room with a guy from Hounslow named Bruce. He called me, Taff, which was I think, the first time anyone had called me that. It didn't bother me, coming from Brecon my Welsh accent was very soft. Bruce however, had a very broad London accent and talked 'twenty to the dozen'. The Germans found him hard to under stand.

At the college were students from all over the world. It wasn't a big establishment, probably about 60 or 80 on various training courses, approximately 20 to a class. On the first evening we had a chance to meet every one over a few beers at the local bar next door. I became a great friend with an American guy from New York, Joachime Legner. Joe was a typical New Yorker with a heavy accent, a slight lisp, and an incredible sense of humour.

We had all been given 200 German Marks advance. To put that into perspective a large bottle of good German beer was just one mark. Our first night was a great success as parties go but the hangovers in the morning were not conducive to studying. Never the less, class started at 8am sharp and we were all present and correct. Lectures were from Monday to Thursday, 8am to 5.30pm, with a one-hour lunch break and a couple of short coffee breaks. On Fridays between 8.30 and 10.30am we would sit an examination of what we had learnt that week. The rest of the day was spent learning about the Company and its structure, finishing at 4pm with the result of that morning's test.

The weekend was basically free but we were obliged to revise and prepare for the following weeks study. Our lecturer started by explaining the course, I listened attentively as I really wanted to know what this new job entailed. As the lecture wore on I realised that my academic qualifications were well below what was required. Still, I had never let that bother me before so I sat and listened, wrote notes, and pretended that it was well within my capability.

The parameters of the course, which initially ran for six weeks, entailed sitting an exam at the end of each week. I had to get a 75% pass mark in at least 4 exams to qualify at the end of the course. I was the youngest student in the entire college, and with many having university degrees I was also the least qualified, this was going to be very interesting. I gave it my best shot but the results of my first exam found me out. Getting just 25% was a big shock to my lecturer who immediately sent me to see the college psychiatrist. I had not been the only one to fail but the other two achieved around 60%.

He gave me the full treatment. Lying on a couch, I was confronted with a bespectacled Martin Bormann look-alike, complete with stereotype German accent.

"Vhat do you think is wrong Herr Gittins, are you sick for your home in Engoland!"

"I'm from Wales" I said looking at the ceiling as he made notes on his pad.

"Ya! I have read your Dylan Thomas at University. Verr goot  Under Ze Vood nien!"

That was more than I had ever done. Welsh Literature and history were hardly taught at school in the Sixties, it was almost as if they didn't exist. I had heard of Dylan Thomas, but only from Joe Legner who had read his poetry.

"Yeah a great poet I like him a lot" I said, hoping he

would not ask which of his poems I liked best.

"Now tell me vhat you think is wrong Herr Gittins, your exam result was very confusing. Is English your mother tongue?"

I guessed he was referring to my atrocious spelling! I explained to him that my academic achievements were not on a par with the other students. I'd learnt my job at Frames 'parrot fashion', but I did reasonably well there, and I was willing to learn if given the chance. I just needed more tuition than the others.

He looked perplexed, I was to learn that the Germans didn't like making decisions. He set about asking me a series of question such as,

"What comes into your mind when I say the word blue!" Which I relied "Black" and so on.

After he had completed his analyses he asked me to come back in an hour. That hour seemed an age. If they decided I was a hopeless case it would be back to London first thing in the morning, with no job and no where to live. I would probably have to re-pay the 200 marks; most of which I'd lost playing cards with Joe. It was a dark prospect; going back into the office to face the 'doctor' my lecturer and the College Principal. Fortunately they gave me the benefit of the doubt, along with a stern warning that if I didn't improve dramatically I would be shipped out.

After the meeting my lecturer offered to give me an hour's tutoring each day after class for the next two weeks, I readily accepted. That week it was head down. While the others enjoyed the delights of Hamburg I stayed in and studied for the first time in my life. My lecturer was brilliant. I was obviously something of a challenge for him. He told me that although my first exam results were dreadful the aptitude test showed promise.

Joe also stayed behind and helped me with my studies, bringing me the odd beer or two to ease the stress. I think he felt a bit guilty about fleecing me at poker. In fact he taught me a valuable lesson and I've never been much of a gambler since, certainly not betting on cards or the roll of the dice. Other forms of life's gambles were still very much in my blood.

Friday morning came around again and the two-hour test that lay ahead was my last chance. This test was more to do with mathematics and problem solving. Weight and balance of an aircraft, fuel calculations, alternate airports in case of bad weather etc. Unlike the previous test, which was more academically focused on written English. A few minutes before 4pm the results of our test arrived, my heart was in my mouth. The lecturer starting reading out the results to the class in alphabetical order, I was almost half way down the list. The first two had failed as they had in the previous test getting around 60%. When it came to me I was numb. "Mr. Gittins 79%" I was riveted to my chair, I couldn't believe it, I knew I had done much better but this was great!

The highest mark was Joe's 91%, but a total of four had failed to hit the pass mark. Feelings were a little mixed. I was sad for those who'd failed, but also relieved, and 'chuffed' that I'd actually passed. I wasn't out of the woods yet but it was Friday night and I could collect another 100 marks from the cashier's office. Joe, Homer and I headed for the 'Reeperbanh', Hamburg's infamous red light district and entertainment centre for wine, woman and song. Unlike London's sleazy Soho the Reerbahn was fun-city, even the girls liked to party here.

At the end of our six-week course just 14, including the

seven from Heathrow, out of the original 20 remained and I was one of them, surprisingly ending up 3rd in the class. I'd never studied so hard in my life. For Joe it was easy, and he cruised through the whole thing. For me it was blood sweat and tears, and I owed a lot to him and the lecturer.

It had been intended that our crew returned to Heathrow Airport at the end of our studies. Instead we ended up working at Hamburg Airport for twenty weeks before finally returning to London. A new crew of students came in from London for the same course. This time the class were all from London, and Marilyn the young girl who'd worked with me at Frames Tours, was among them, I couldn't believe it!

We said our goodbyes to the rest of the students on our course as they flew back to their various airports. I was sorry to see Joe go back to JFK New York, but felt sure I'd see him again one day. Our crew moved out to an apartment block at Fulsbuttle near the Airport and commenced our work experience after a week of home leave. They even gave me a free ticket, flying Hamburg-Frankfurt-Dublin-Cardiff and back. On my return I spent many evenings back at the college, getting to know my future colleagues and of course, showing off my smart new airline uniform.

I spent some time with Marilyn catching up on the news from Temple Fortune. She got fed up when I left and applied to Lufthansa for a job. I knew she fancied me, and I her, but apart from a kiss and a cuddle it had never gone further. No more long-term relationships for me I wanted to play the field. We all got on together very well and made friendships that lasted for many years after. Hamburg was a fun city and living there opened my eyes to a whole new way of life. The U.K. seems almost repressive compared to Germany. The cost of living was lower but the standard was much higher.

Pubs didn't close at 10.30pm as they did in London in those days. In fact some pubs didn't close at all and most were open until 2am. The food was excellent and cheap. The Germans loved to party and although they were hard to get to know at first, I soon found myself being invited to endless parties.

Their attitude to sex was completely different to the U.K. Even the new liberal attitude that had swept through Britain in the swinging Sixties was tame in comparison. Prostitution was open and legal with very little, if any, stigma attached. There were no great hang-ups about nudity, and it seemed almost obligatory for married people to have affairs. The romantic intrigue at the Airport could have been made into one of the hottest 'TV soap's' of all time.

Nightlife in Germany was fantastic. Compared to Wales at that time it was light years ahead. Even London had nothing like the nightlife of Hamburg apart from the 'Rock Scene'. But to some extent even that had been imported. The Beatles had found success at Hamburg's Star club (where I made a pilgrimage), and many British and American bands played concerts in the City.It was extremely difficult to imagine what Germany had been like during the War, little more than twenty years previous. Certainly they would never talk about it, it rarely cropped up in any conversation, even in jest. It was amazing how well they had done rebuilding their economy. Certainly they had invested in training, in Britain it was practically non-existent. We still maintained the old vestiges of class and the aristocracy; suppressed during the 1960's they still remained a reality. But not in modern Germany.

Hamburg had become my University; I learnt so much during my six months stay. I left a much wiser and a better educated person. My only regret is that I hadn't learnt very much German, oddly enough it was not a requisite of the job.

English being the language of the airline industry and most Germans spoke it fluently. But I had picked up a fair smattering. It was with mixed feelings that I returned to London. I had nowhere to stay and ended up sleeping on the floor at Bruce's' home in Hounslow, where he lived with his parents. However, I soon moved into a house near Heathrow with two girls and two guys who had been on the second course at Hamburg.

Mike Sessions was slightly built but like me enjoyed the good life. He came from the Home Counties. Ralf was totally the opposite, a bit of a 'Billy Bunter' with round spectacles he looked and acted much older than his age. Sue and Jenny were both nineteen, a bit neurotic but full of fun we all got on remarkably well. I remained at Lufthansa for seven years or so and travelled the world. I took mum back to Majorca and my Brother Mike on a fabulous round the World trip, starting in New York and staying a few days with Joe and his girlfriend before going on to the Far East.

One of the great perks of working for a major airline like Lufthansa was the free or highly discounted travel, of which I took full, advantage. We also enjoyed generous holiday leave of up to six weeks a year. The most memorable trip was with three of the guys from work, Mike Sessions, Tony Foskitt and Mike Overton. We set off on a four-week tour of Australia and the South Pacific in 1969, flying Pan Am nonstop to San Francisco where we stayed for a few days eating seafood on Fisherman's Wharf, taking in the sights and riding the tram up the steep road to Nob Hill, then down like a roller coaster to the Bay. For me going to San Francisco was another pilgrimage to the music scene of the era. Flower Power had faded from London but it was still alive and well here, fuelled by the unpopular but escalating Vietnam war.

We even went to an anti-war concert in Golden Gate Park and heard Scot Mackenzie sing 'If you're going to San Francisco'.

Our next stop was Honolulu and Waikiki beach. We stayed in a huge pink hotel over looking the ocean. From our balcony you could see the most incredible sun sets in the world. You could also observe the Waikiki hookers ply their trade on the street below. Large American businessmen on vacation and dressed in garish flowered shirts and Bermuda shorts, would waddled up to them and haggle over the price as their wives shopped in the Malls near by. The Hawaiian Islands are truly beautiful but thoroughly spoilt by commercialism. Our next destination was the exotic islands of Fiji where commercial tourism had not yet taken a major foothold.

Being airline staff on free tickets we were known as P.A.D.'s (passengers available for disembarkation). The Pan Am flight to Nandi (Fiji) had only three seats left and I drew the short straw to take the next available. This turned out to be an American Airlines B707 cobmi-freighter with six tonne of cargo and just a hand full of passengers. In fact the cabin staff out numbered the passengers.

Despite a fairly bumpy flight through Pacific storms over the International date line, I spent most of the time drinking Californian Champagne and chatting with the cabin staff. One of the girls was based in Sydney and we arranged to meet up when I eventually got there.

When I arrived at Nandi Airport I had hoped to be met by the lads. Instead I was greeted by a very attractive Fijian lady with large brown 'come to bed' eyes.

"Are you Mr. MacGittins-Sir!" she said in a low enquiring voice. "Well you got most of it right, it's Gittins, Dave

Gittins"

"Will you come with me please Sir. I have a limousine waiting to take you to your hotel" Bloody hell I thought to my self, either its incredibly cheap in Fiji or the boys have won some money playing cards on the flight down. There was no sign of the lads so I presumed they were at the hotel. I followed her out to the parked limo at the front of the small terminal building. Getting in, I was greeted by another Polynesian beauty, wearing a sarong slit all the way to heaven exposing the most incredible legs.

"Would you like a glass of wine or a nice cold beer Mr. MacGittins?" She purred pointing to a pull down mini bar. Putting my eyes back in their sockets I blurted out

"I'd love a cold beer"

With that the limousine pulled away into the warm Fijian night air and headed to whom knows where. Who cared? I spent the next 40 minutes or so drinking ice cold beer and getting very friendly with the natives, or at least, one particular native. I was a little disappointed when we eventually arrived at the hotel; I could have stayed in that limo for the rest of the holiday.

When I entered the hotel the royal reception continued. I was convinced the boys had arranged an elaborate wind up and just went with the flow. My room turned out to be a fabulous bungalow suite, complete with Jacuzzi, over looking a spacious pool in palm tree lined exotic gardens. My hostess began to unpack my suit case and suggested that she would keep me company for the night "if you like-sir!" My mind was now racing, this place must cost a fortune and I haven't even been asked for my credit card or passport, and where the hell were the boys? Then I thought, 'what the heck', if the worst comes to the worst I could afford one night, anyway its not really my fault if this is all a mistake. With that there was a knock on the door, come in I shouted thinking here they are!

"I'm afraid there's been a terrible mistake-sir!" said a well-dressed gentleman as he opened my door.

"Could you please come to reception so we can sort this out?"

"I knew it, this is a joke isn't it?" I chuckled as I followed the gentleman back to the reception area.

At reception, instead of seeing my erstwhile buddies, I began to hear a very loud, slightly irate American chap He was wearing an enormous ten-gallon hat and cowboy boots. He was somewhat 'pissed off' that he had not been met at the airport as arranged and "did they know who he was" etc.

I though I'd better intervene before the guy has a 'thrombi'. I explained what had happened to all and sundry, there was a pregnant pause before the very large irate American chap saw the funny side of the situation and burst out laughing.

"Well the least I can do is buy you a cold beer before I try and find my friends" I said apologetically.

"The hell you will partner-this is on the house!" He glared straight at the manager who nodded profusely and guided us to the cocktail lounge.

He sat on a barstool as if he was saddling up a horse and called to the bar tender

"Two Heinekens and two shots of JD".

"My name's Dan, Dan MacGittins, from the great state of Texas." With that we shook hands and slugged back the Jack Daniel's, banging the emptied glasses on the bar.

"Pleased to meet you Dan. I'm Dave, Dave Gittins from Welsh Wales"

We sat and talked for a while and I told him about the girl

from the limo who was still in 'his' room. He told me he was an 'oil baron' and had bought a stake in the chain that owned this fabulous hotel, and with that the boys appeared.

"Where the heck have you been?" They said in unison.

"I could say the same about you buggers. Anyway come and meet Dan from Texas and I'll tell you all about it." Needless to say we were not staying at this luxury hotel with hot and cold running hostesses. It turned out that the guys had rented an old car that broke down on the way to the airport. We were booked into a run down old shack a few miles away at LaTouka harbour. The following morning I awoke to the whirr of a ceiling fan and the tropical wildlife chorus of the South Seas islands.

Our plan for today was to take a boat from LaTouka harbour to a small island called Tai. There we would spend 10 days. The boys had made a deal the day before, 7 dollars US a day, fully inclusive of accommodation, food and drink! We set sail in a rickety old boat crewed by a hand full of large fit jovial Fijian men wearing rugby shirts. The boat Chugged out on a sapphire blue sea. The journey would take two hours and several crates of cold lager beer.Tai Island was a paradise, gentle swaying palm trees, white sands and straw huts. We jumped from the boat into the shallow surf, the cool water felt good from the heat of the sun that burned down from a crystal clear blue sky as we paddled ashore.

Our home for the next ten days was a large straw hut over looking the beach. It had four bamboo beds with mosquito nets, and little else. Meals were served buffet-barbecue style on the beach. The bar was a make shift bamboo hut that served beer and Tiki, a lethal fiery hooch made by the 100 or so villagers who lived on the Island. That evening we made our way to the little beach bar for an evening of local culture.

It was out of 'season' and we were the only tourists there! The guys from the boat were at the bar drinking beer with Tiki chasers. There were a number of other islanders there including several females. Now, in Polynesia (especially in the sticks where we now were) big is beautiful, and the local beauties were 'big' as were their men folk. However, sat in the corner of this bar in the middle of the vast Pacific Ocean was a group of 'ugly' girls.

To us westerners these 'ugly' girls were absolutely gorgeous, slim but well blessed. They had long black flowing hair and as they smiled their brilliant white teeth shone out from perfect olive brown faces. The guys from the boat thought we were mad when we made a beeline for them and began chatting to these 'wall flowers'.

After a few beers, a laugh and joke we paired off with our little 'wall flowers'. We were now in the age of free love, but the Polynesians invented it long ago, before missionaries interfered at the turn of the century. Thankfully I don't think they made it as far out as Tai Island. I walked along the beach leaving behind the lights of the bamboo bar, and the gentle but erratic hum of the electric generator, and then looked up into the clear night sky. There before me was an unprecedented celestial sight. A billion stars shone and twinkled punctuated by an occasional streak of light from a burning meteor.

My new-found 'girl friend', untied her sarong and walked naked into the white tinged surf. She knelt in the water, her perfect young body silhouetted in the starlight. She scooped up two hands full of seawater and threw it skyward. All the colours of the rainbow twinkled as the water splashed back into the sea. The surf was full of tiny phosphorus fish that became luminous at night. You didn't need drugs to trip out here, the whole place was a trip all on its own. Complete with psychedelic fish! Off came my jeans and T-shirt and into the surf I went. I had died and gone to heaven! Our time on Tai Island went much to quickly, we spent our days swimming, fishing with the men from the village in outrigger canoes, playing 'beach' rugby with coconut husks, helping to unload the daily supply boat and drinking beer with Tiki chasers. And making love!

Meal times were a great occasion. Baked fish and coconut for breakfast, curried goat or prawns for lunch and BBQ suckling pig or rock lobster for dinner along with mountains of fresh fruit. All washed down with copious amounts of Fijian or New Zealand beer. We made many friends on the Island. One of the village boys even took me back to his family hut to show me his prize possession. A framed photo of a great rugby hero, Barry John. Before we left I gave him one of my Welsh youth athletics vests, with the embroidered three feathers of Wales. 'Just like Barry John!' Fiji was a beautiful place with warm friendly people and I hope to return one day. Wonder if its still the same? One thing for certain, I lost my heart to Fiji!

Our next stop would be Sydney before meeting up with my friend from American Airlines. We then headed up to Koolangatta and Queensland's Gold Coast, exploring Australia's wondrous Great Barrier Reef for the remainder of our holiday.

# 7

# Homeward Bound

Over the next few years I worked in many different departments of the airline. Going from flight dispatch to booking co-ordination and then customer services. I ended up running the lost and found department, searching for lost baggage-world wide. From the Indian Government delegation's missing luggage, to a plane full of drunken seamen from Bremerhavan whose bags were loaded on the wrong aircraft, it was all in the line of duty.

It was quite a stressful job but I was left very much to my own devices. The shift pattern suited me fine; work four twelve-hour shifts, two late ending with two early, then four days off. During this time I started returning home to Brecon on a regular basis. With the building of the Severn Bridge and the new M4 motorway it was a much quicker journey. In 1972 I joined Plaid Cymru's London Branch and started playing rugby again, although I couldn't get into London Welsh. Instead I played for London Transport at Osterley Park. Here I met the Irish population of London, becoming very friendly with a number of Irish guys. Some worked for Lufthansa others with London Transport. They were so very proud and nationalistic. I guess this started to rub off on me, my thoughts began to focus on my homeland. Wales.

At this time I was living in a large flat in Earls Court which I sub-let to numerous Australian and South African pack-packers.

The arrangement worked well, although half the time I didn't know who was staying there, the rent was always paid and I met some very interesting people.

We used to frequent a 'den of iniquity' called the Zambizee Club just off Earls Court Road. It opened from 2pm to 2am, whether it was legal or not, who knew? But the pubs closed at 2.30 in the afternoon and reopened 6pm to 10.30pm, so the Zambizee club at five shillings annual membership was good value and had a more civilised attitude to opening hours. Occasionally I would go out with my Irish friends to pubs and clubs in Hammersmith and Kilburn. We would listen to Irish show bands and down pints of Guinness; it was like being in Dublin. On many occasions at the Hammersmith Palace, a huge dance hall built in the fifty's, the band would make a collection for the IRA from the stage! I couldn't believe it! The Irish were so defiant I could not help but admire them. The English thought they were thick and stupid but it was obvious to me the Irish were having the laugh.

We frequented pubs like the Dublin Castle in Kilburn and the Father Murphy in Sudbury where the Irish republican movement thrived. Being Welsh as opposed to being English I was accepted in this circle and invited to many a Sunday lunch by my new Irish buddies. All this started making me homesick for the first time. London was exciting, diverse, and perverse but above all it could be very lonely. The whole scene began to have no rhyme or reason any more. The Sixties and its enlightenment had faded. A new age was forging ahead reflected by the on coming of 'anorak' rock, as in John Travolta and Mott the Hupple!

My involvement with Plaid Cymru became more intense, although I strongly believed that Wales did not have to follow the violent path that Ireland had gone down to achieve home rule. By 1973 my visits back to Brecon became almost weekly, picking up the pieces I'd left behind in so much that I had left home so young and now spent more time with Mum. However, my flamboyance was as strong as ever and Brecon now had a nightclub. At this nightclub, called Nythfa, I met my lovely future wife Gill.

For a town as small as Brecon, Nythfa was quite sophisticated and compared favourably with many clubs in London. Gill used to go there most weekends with her friends Paula and Judy. I felt really 'cool' in my white safari suit that shone out in the ultra violet disco lighting. She thought so too, and we soon began dating. The atmosphere in the club was certainly conducive to romance; it was the place to be in Brecon.

Gillian Skinner was nineteen, very shy, but stunningly attractive with long brown hair that fell to her waist. She attended teachers training college at Wrexham with her friend Paula, who was also a budding cabaret singer and Gill's complete opposite, not shy at all! Ours was not a whirlwind affair it sort of just happened over many months. We became an 'item', together whenever I was in Brecon. Although Gill was shy in public she had a ferocious temper and was wildly jealous, similar in many ways to Ruth. This didn't bode well with my 'roving eye', so it was just as well that I lived in London most of the week. Our relationship would never have lasted in those early days before she mellowed a little. Ours was to become a really true love, a love rarely found.

My involvement with Plaid Cymru continued to grow and I became seriously inquisitive about Welsh History. I even wrote a book about the great Welsh patriot Prince Owain Glyn Dwr, Entitled, 'The Son has risen.'

Whenever I finished an early shift at Heathrow I would travel into town to the British Museum's reading room to study. I absolutely loved that temple of knowledge, spending many a long hour there sifting through forgotten volumes of ancient books.

It was at the British Museum in Russell Square that I discovered the works of the Mabanogion, The Red Book of Hergest, the Black Book of Carmarthen, the Laws of Hywel Dda and the Statues of Wales. A total discovery to me, the only Welsh history I had learnt at school revolved around Edward I and the conquest of Wales.

About this time I became very friendly with a Scots guy called 'Scotty-White' who'd transferred from Dusseldorf. He was short and overweight with wire rimmed glasses, but had a tremendous gift of the gab. The way Scotty could 'pull the birds' was incredible, you'd think he was John Travolta. It just goes to show; sometimes looks are not everything and he certainly couldn't dance! Scotty had many friends in Dusseldorf having worked there for several years. I had never been there, so we decided to fly over one weekend to a party.

It was a huge industrial city but the 'Ald Stat' (old town) was full of character. We went to Scotty's old 'local', 'Diggers Bar' to play dice and drink Dusseldorfer Union Pils, from large German stein glasses. It was here I met Anna the epitome of German womanhood, twenty-three years old, standing six feet tall with long natural blonde hair a forty-inch bust and legs that mere mortal men can only dream about (or is that dribble about).

She stood at the end of the bar drinking beer with some of Scotty's mates. At first I thought she was a 'hooker', dressed as she was, in skin tight leather hot pants and a boob tube straining to hold in her large firm breasts.

As it turned out, she also worked for Lufthansa as a secretary in the cargo office. Scotty knew her and introduced me. She immediately transfixed me with her deep blue eyes and in a haughty accent asked me.

"Spreaken zie Deutsche?"

"Ein bisen" was my babbled reply to which she turned to Scotty (who was fluent) and laughed saying (in German which, I understood).

"How come he works for Lufthansa and can't speak German properly?"

"Because he's Welsh, got a big cock, and he's on missionary work. You want another beer Anna?"

With that Scotty got another round and Anna became very interested in what ever I had to say. I spent the next two days at Anna's flat. What transpired between Anna and me could not be described as love; it was sheer carnal lust; the most intense sexual experience of my life. There are few true nymphomaniacs in this world; sex to Anna was a religious experience and I felt privileged to have worshipped at her Altar.

Returning to Diggers bar Sunday afternoon feeling drained but elated, I thanked Scotty from the bottom of my heart for the introduction to Anna. Had she been around during World War II we would never have won. She was capable of taking on the entire Allied Army all by herself. They would have been too 'knackered' to have even contemplated an assault on Berlin, where incidentally she was born.

Two weeks later I received a phone call at my office in Heathrow.

"Anna here!"

She had been transferred for six weeks to the cargo base at Heathrow Airport, on relief! 'My God' could I take it? Could London take it? Was this the invasion that Winston Churchill had feared? Then I thought 'Gill!' How the hell was I going to sort this one out? We weren't engaged or anything but she was the nearest I'd got to a regular 'girlfriend' at the time.

Anna looked different in her Airline uniform but nevertheless she was still awesome to say the least. She was sharing a flat in Knightsbridge, not far from my apartment in Earls Court, which pleased Anna greatly. I even ended up taking Anna to Brecon for a weekend; Gill was back in College at Wrexham. Our relationship hadn't really got off the ground yet it would many months before that started to 'gel.' Taking her to Nythfa was an experience all on its own. Grown men drooled at the sight before their eyes. She wore a skin-tight short black dress and thigh length black PVC boots with 4 inch heels. By the time Anna had returned to Dusseldorf I was a physical wreck. I never heard from her again. Apparently she married a very wealthy businessman in Berlin some years later. I'm sure the East Berliners tore down the wall brick by brick with their bare hands when they found out that Anna was back in Town!

Slowly but surely, my relationship with Gill began to flourish and in 1974 we talked about getting engaged. That same year I had been selected as the official Plaid Cymru parliamentary candidate.

In May of that year a general election was called and I

took three weeks unpaid leave to fight it. Being elected as a Nationalist in the Brecon and Radnor constituency was an outside shot to say the least. Plaid had only won one seat in Westminster back in 1966 when Gwynfor Evans won an historic by-election in Carmarthen. He later lost it in the 1970 general election. After an intense battle I lost to Labour. They won the seat from the Tory's. I polled 2,099 votes, a substantial increase on the previous Plaid showing in 1970 of less than a thousand. Plaid Cymru was making inroads and Welsh politics were changing at last. After the election I decided to leave Lufthansa, receiving a small redundancy package I returned home. I suppose I had some ambition of going into full time politics but in reality I'd had enough of life in London.

I helped Mum to run the pub. My brother Mike was engaged to his soon to be wife Jane who lived near by, but he had no interest in the licensed trade. My other brother Peter was still in the Royal Navy fleet air arm and had married the year before to Loraine. Gill joined me in running the pub and it became inevitable that we would get married sooner or later. At this stage we were inseparable and very much in love.

Around this time I got involved with a business partner, Maldwyn Morgan, who was also chairman of the local Plaid Cymru branch, and we began to market Welsh Mead from the pub. Mal was a larger than life character in his late thirties. He had been involved in various enterprises, mainly agricultural, so how we ended up selling Mead, I'm still not sure. We formed a Company called Powys Promotions Ltd (Hyrwyddwyr Powys Cyf (in Welsh)), after selling over a thousand cases of our Mead; 'Cambria Welsh Celtic Mead', mainly from the back of an old Bedford Van in and around North Wales.

Another General Election was called for October 1974; the new Labour Governments slim majority in the May election, which ousted Edward Heath's Government, had failed to hold on to power. I was made Plaid Cymru's spokesman on water resources, an important role for a 24 year-old, considering the heated debate that surrounded water issues at the time. It was only a few years previously that the Free Wales Army (FWA) had bombed several reservoirs supplying the English Midlands. As 'shadow minister of water resources' I would play a significant role in this election.
I would appear on Television news not only in Wales but in the English Midlands as well. I also addressed the Party conference in Aberystwyth. This time I polled 2,930 a figure still not exceeded by Plaid in Brecon & Radnor to this day. Labour won conformably and Harold Wilson was returned to office.

My main claim to fame over this period was the 'help a toad cross the road campaign'. The Western Mail reporter Roger Dobbson rang me one day and asked if I would champion such a scheme. British toads were in decline and thousands were being squashed by cars as they migrated between rivers and ponds. This was before our more enlighten views on wild life conservation so I got considerable stick from my constituency committee. Nevertheless I carried on with this crusade; the story made front-page news and spread worldwide. For many years others continued the campaign, and it resulted in the road signs we now see of a red triangle and a picture of a toad. The decline of our frogs and toads was halted and I like to think I played a small part in helping at least one of God's little creatures along the way.

This was not a complete end to my political life but now I had to concentrate on making a living. Mal had decided to buy a big pub in Merthyr Tydfil, the old Railway and

Locomotive. This enterprise was not successful, the pub was busy enough but it was wild, like the town it self. This large industrial 'valley's' town was beset with problems following the demise of the heavy coal and steel industries of Wales. Unemployment was rampant, but the people's slavish support of the Labour party was never rewarded,
even though the party itself was born in Merthyr Tydfil when James Keir Hardie became the first Member of Parliament for the newly formed Labour Party in 1900.

He was a Scotsman from the coal belt of Lanarkshire and was first elected to Parliament as a socialist representing West-Ham south in 1892. In fact he represented both seats until 1905 then just Merthyr until 1915. Finally losing his seat reportedly because of his strong pacifist beliefs and his opposition to the Boar War. Merthyr had a proud industrial history fuelling the British Empire with coal, and steel for ships and armaments. Sadly the area never saw the fruits of its toil and typified the title of the famous book by Alexander Cordell. 'The Rape of the fair country'.

The pub was frequented by such local celebrities has 'Malcolm the Axe' and his faithful dog Rufus, 'The Bo-Bo boys' and 'Mad Kelly' to name but a few. I was involved in the running of the pub with Mal, but I was not happy. Merthyr was a relatively violent place, Saturday night 'punch-ups' were common and the pub got 'trashed' several times. I pulled out after less than a year and Mal left shortly after. At the same time we continued with our Mead business and during a delivery to Ruthin Castle at some time late in 1974 I came across a bottle of 'Welsh Whisky'.

On seeing this bottle of very rare amber gold I just knew there had to be a market for its revival and my quest began!

# 8

# Welsh Whisky - The Early Days

Ruthin Castle was a magnificent 14th Century seat of the Earls of Denbighshire. It had been converted into a large hotel that hosted medieval banqueting nights. Hence their thirst for Mead the honey brew of Knights of Old. Behind the bar in a fine glass cabinet stood a single bottle of 'Royal Welsh Whisky' produced at Bala in 1895. Like most people I had never heard of Welsh Whisky. My mind started to see a new enterprise unfold. In the immortal words of 'Del Boy', this time next year we'll be millionaires!

On my return to Brecon I told Mal of my discovery. He in turn rang an old friend who was now running a pub not far from Bala, the White Lion at Cerrigydrudion. He was none other than Ronnie Williams the other half of the famous Welsh comedians Ronnie and Ryan. Not only had Ronnie heard of Welsh Whisky but had a lot of memorabilia from the old Bala Distillery at his pub. Mal and I set off for Cerrigydrudion to see Ronnie and gather some historical background to the mysterious Whisky.

Indeed; Ronnie had a lot of information, including old

advertising posters, photographs and leaflets produced by the distillery's owners, The Welsh Whisky Company at the turn of the century. The Whisky had won a gold medal of excellence at the great Chicago Exhibition of 1901. It had been a very large enterprise with an issued share capital in 1890 of £100,000 pounds. The Bala distillery closed in 1906; suffering from the onset of prohibition in the United States, its main market, and the feverish advance of the temperance movement sweeping post Victorian Wales, led by the 'seemingly pious' David Lloyd George.

Ironically the building ended its life as a concentration camp for Irish dissidents during the First World War. Then, we are led to believe, puritanical villagers levelled it to the ground.

Further research showed that Whisky making was very much a Celtic tradition originating on Bardsey Island just off the North West Coast of Wales in the 4th Century, and spreading to Ireland with St. Patrick, who took Christianity, (and whiskey), from Wales to the shores of the Emerald Isle. The alchemy of distillation was probably introduced to the British Isles by missionary monks visiting on merchant ships from the eastern Mediterranean; Bardsey being an early Celtic Abbey. "The Isle of Twenty Thousand Saints". It was ruled at the later end of the 4th Century by Rhaullt Hir a warrior monk, 'fired by the spirits of the still'.

The Whisky had Royal patronage from Queen Victoria and the Prince of Wales. So large was the enterprise it had its own rail link connecting it to the industrial heartland of Great Britain and the seaport of Liverpool.

We later discovered that there had been a scattering of smaller farm distilleries dotted around Wales but little was known of these; except for a number of small distilleries established in Pembrokeshire during the reign of Henry VIII (1491-1547).

The word 'Chwisgi' was first attested in 1784, by which time a small native whisky industry had been established in Wales.

The burden of excise duties was first introduced in 1643 to finance the army. This unpopular tax was also introduced to Scotland in 1644, but then lapsed, only to be reimposed in 1693. The imposition of Excise Duty forced most producers 'underground'. Illicit distillation was certainly not restricted to Ireland and Scotland; with out doubt it was also practised in parts of Wales and England,

the argument of the day being that 'If a southern English farmer can make cider from his own apples without paying duty on it, why should a farmer in Scotland, or for that matter in Wales, not distil whisky from barley grown in the same manner?'

In 1781 the government banned private distillation and authorised the excise man to seize whisky, whisky making equipment and later even horses and carts used in the transportation of illicit spirit. A premium of one shilling and sixpence, a princely sum in those days, was offered to anyone handing in an illicit still to the authorities. This measure backfired as many shrewd smugglers gave up old worn out pieces of equipment and bought new ones with the reward money!

The government had to reduce duty in 1784 through the Wash Act. They also simplified regulations regarding the legal production of whisky in order to reduce smuggling and illicit production, but this measure was short lived and duty trebled in 1793 to help pay for the war with France.

One man from Dale in Pembrokeshire emigrated to

the United States and founded the Evan Williams Distillery at Bardstown, County Kentucky in 1783. It still flourishes today as a major brand of American Whisky. He was the first man to distil whisky in the Louisville area.

Kentucky developed as a 'whisky state' from the time Thomas Jefferson, another Welsh-American, then Governor of Virginia (1779-81) and later the 3rd president of the United States (1801-9), granted settlers sixty acres of land in the County of Kentucky on which they could grow corn. Turning excess corn into whiskey became a form of 'currency' that improved with age and was much sought after.

A hazier story is that of Jack Daniel. The name Daniel certainly has origins in Cardiganshire and several Daniel's immigrated to New York in the early part of the 19th Century. Jack was born in New York in 1846 to a very large family and left home at the tender age of seven? He went to work for a Methodist preacher and distiller by the name of Dan Call. He eventually settled in Lynchburg Tennessee and established the Jack Daniel's distillery; the first 'registered distillery' in America. In 1866 the Federal Government introduced a whiskey tax, although whiskey making in Tennessee dates back to at least the late eighteenth century.

When considering Jack's non-conformist background, it is quite conceivable that he was second generation Welsh. Ironically Lynchburg is still a 'dry' county to this day which may prove a further link to its religious Welsh founding fathers. It does show a sense of Welsh humour in that they allowed the manufacture of the 'demons-brew', but only for sale outside of the County.

Our first attempt at recreating a Welsh Whisky had all the elements attributed to a 'Heath Robinson' method of production.

A few weeks before Christmas in 1974 from large dark cellars under Mal's house in Alexandra Road, Brecon, we decanted raw whisky from two oak casks, one malt and one grain, imported from Glasgow for our experimental blend 'Swn y Don' (sound of the wave). Together with Mal's children, we filtered the spirit through muslin and measured an appropriate amount of Brecon tap water to reach the required strength, adding a little burned sugar to enhance the colour. Finally we carefully poured the newly blended whisky into amber bottles, capping them with plastic stoppers bought from Morgan's the local chemist. We had antique gummed labels designed and printed by Y Lolfa in Aberystwyth, all in Welsh, we lovingly licked and smoothed them on to the bottles. The birth of Chwisgi Cymreig had arrived! This method of production carried on for about nine months before Mal's wife Ann got fed up with us traipsing in and out of her house carrying crates and bottles.

In September 1975 I finally married Gill and we decided to buy the Camden Arms from Mum. The wedding was a grand affair in an old forgotten church in the foothills of the Brecon Beacons. A beautiful 15th Century stone edifies, hidden away behind the ancient oak trees of Cantref. Gill looked positively stunning in a classic white gown she had made herself. It was a perfect day for two people who loved each other very deeply.

Originally I'd wanted an old Celtic style wedding, a 'Priodas Cyswllt', presided over by Druids, and held under a Hawthorn tree. Gill's Dad Len however, was not keen on the idea. Mal was best man and also helped to run the bar, (stocked from the Camden; catering provided by two pals who were cooks at the local Army Barracks), at the reception in the nearby Talybont Village Hall. Many of my old buddies from Lufthansa came, including Scotty, who was now living in Tarre Hute Indiana.

Paula, Judy, Kay and Cathy, another of Gill's best friends, were bridesmaids, all dressed in pink gown's that Gill had spent weeks making. With over two hundred guests, as with most Welsh Weddings, much ale would flow; the festivities lasted until the early hours.

The following day after sobering up at Brecon's Bishops Meadow Motel, we headed out in an old car I'd borrowed from one of the reception cooks. Kevin was a sergeant in the Welsh Guards and one of our regulars at the Camden. We honeymooned in the little City of St. David's on the west coast of Pembrokeshire, all paid for from the profits of the reception bar. We had never been so happy, and thought our love and friendship would last forever!

# 9

# Birth Of An Enterprise

The following year Mal decided to go back to his agricultural business and I carried on the Whisky enterprise from the Camden Arms, changing the product name to Swn y Mor (sound of the sea).

Gill and I applied for a rural business grant from the newly formed Development Board for Rural Wales. We wanted to renovate the old brew house at the back of the pub into a bottling and blending house for the whisky.

We formed Brecon Brewery Limited and, after considerable bureaucratic wrangling with the Development Board, obtained a soft loan of £25,000. This paid off the bank-bridging loan I had used to pay Mum for the pub and left me with enough money to renovate the brew house.

I employed Dai 'Rum' and his mate Griff to carry out the renovations, which they did to perfection. Fortified by many gallons of beer, rum and of course whisky, they built the new brew house in just three months, even laying a Terrazzo tiled floor. Dai was a bald headed long-distance truck driver with a lecherous laugh and girlfriend in every major city, he could turn his hand to most things. Griff was a wafer thin chain smoking 'brickie' with a wife three times his size that 'pestered' him at night. He would often turn up for work at six in the morning.

During this time a new by-pass was being built around Brecon and many of the workmen who came from near and far drank at the Camden. They also provided most of the material to build the brew house and 'tar-mac' the yard and car park. They even built me a new beer garden. With the influx of workers building the new by-pass, Gill's cooking and the kudos of the Whisky brew house, the Camden became very busy.

Mum lived just across the road in Conway Street and visited the pub every day, still very much 'Auntie Marge' and still as large as life. Mum loved her whisky and soda, so my new enterprise met with her wholehearted approval. Shortly after moving into the Camden, Gill's sister Kay moved in with us. Gill's mum Belle had died the year before and their father Len, a tall good looking man in his fifties was devastated by his wife's sudden death from an undetected brain tumour and couldn't cope with a teenage daughter. Kay was about fourteen at the time, a pretty girl with natural blonde hair and all the mood swings of a growing teenager but I got on with her well. She became almost like a daughter to me.

We invested in some new bottling and blending equipment but our production methods were still relatively primitive. However, our output was growing by the day though my blend was still very much in its experimental stages. The regulars at the Camden became my enthusiastic and willing 'guinea pigs,' enabling me to gain immediate feed back on my 'blend from the likes of Charlie James a character of folklore, hard working farm labour, to council roadman and gardener extraordinaire. He had a fiery nature, a heart of gold and a singing voice to match Carreras. Or the rotund meat worker Gwynn M.M. who got drunk on rum during the liberation of Europe and single handily stormed an entrenched German machine gun post, blowing it up with hand grenades and winning the Military Medal in the process.

He recounted the tale many a time as he sat in the back bar with his brother Danny, Jack the Roller and Tom the Lock, all drinking pints of Westons Cider.

"There I was boys, two bottles of 'Nelsons blood' (Rum) the night before, liberated from a bloody big house (Châteaux) ,thumping headache and this bloody German machine gun, bang, bang bloody bang all night long. So I thought, right you buggers Gwynn Sarnau's got your ticket and over I went running like a banshee on heat. Grenade in each hand pulled the pins with my teeth, I had teeth then, and lobbed them one after the other. Blew the Nazi bastards back to Berlin I did, bang bloody bang. Well the Major comes up to me see,"

"Gwynn you mad bastard I've never seen the likes of that in my life, you're a bloody hero, I was just about to call the retreat."

"After that the King himself gave me the MM. Himself mind you"

'Duw duw" exclaimed his tireless audience every time he retold his great tale of war!

The pub was full of characters from labourers to gentry. There was John (English) Pugh who became one of my best friends. A local squire who farmed Watton Villa, he was born just across the border in Ross on Wye, and insisted he was English. A great chap and a huge loss to us all. When he died in 1985, Brecon Rugby Club, of which he was a feverent supporter, renamed their ground after him, Parc de Pugh. John would sit at the bar and argue 'black was blue' with his friends Dai 'Dwr' Evans, head press officer for Welsh Water who had their headquarters near by. And Colonel Gil Roach the commandant of Brecon Barracks. The discussion would inevitably revolve around the fortunes of the Welsh Rugby Team.

Gil was a Lieutenant Colonel in the Gurkha Rifles, a towering man from Pembrokeshire who always drank 'Guinness wine'.

"If you'd be so kind sir and what ever my reprobationous friends would care to partake of " would be his call.

Dai Dwr with his large gin and tonic, Pugh his whisky shandy (whisky and lemonade with copious amounts of ice) and Gil; they would sip and debate the afternoon away.

We employed two full time young attractive bar maids Jackie and Cheryl, and one part time very smart ex-landlady Joan Davis, plus Stan 'the Man' as 'potman' and general factotum. Everyone gave a hand with bottling even, Joan in her high heels and designer frocks. Stan was a taller version of 'Popeye' who always wore an old brown hat and puffed away at his trusty Brier pipe. His catch phrase was "Me do!" which was about all Stan could say due to a bad speech impediment, but he was as strong as an Ox and a willing worker. Although, you had to be very precise when telling Stan what to do. On one occasion I asked him to load a trailer with builders rubble, leaving him to get on with the job I returned to the bar. An hour or so passed by and thought I'd better check on old Stan, to my horror he had almost buried the trailer. I hadn't told him how much I wanted loaded.

On another occasion, John Pugh asked him to dig a posthole at the entrance to his farm. When John came up to the pub I enquired after Stan, when John told me the job he was doing my mind flashed back to the trailer. We both jumped into John's pick-up truck (PEU 1) and headed down to the farm. Low and behold all we could see was the smoke from Stan's pipe and scoops of earth flying up out of the crater that Stan was beavering away in. Had we left him there all day he'd have ended up in Australia!

The big occasions at the Camden were the five nations rugby championships. Wales were coming to the end of their 'golden' years having seen the end of the likes of Barry John, Gareth Edwards, JJ and John Dawes. Nevertheless Wales was still a force to be reckoned with and the pub would be packed on match days.

Because of the nonsensical licensing laws that still prevailed in the mid-Seventies we had to watch the match behind closed doors. Pub's closed at 3pm and reopened at 6pm, kick off was usually 2.30pm or 3pm. The 'boys' and ever increasingly the 'girls' too would gather at 1.30pm and the 'lock-in would commence at 2.30pm. We would set up a large screen TV in the bar and Gill would provide free curry, rice and chips.

Match days were more for our younger customers, the 'wool boys' like Spike and Charlie Edmunds who worked for Gill's dad at the Wool factory. The atmosphere compared to any pub near the 'hallowed' turf of the Arms Park. These were great occasions, especially if Wales won, and went on until 'stop-tap' later that night and sometimes into the early hours of the following morning. Quite often the following Sunday morning a busload returning to North Wales from the match at Cardiff would call in for a 'pit stop' and the festivities would recommence. I had built up a number of friendships supplying our whisky to pubs in North Wales. Not least

Aneurin Jones of the Dolbadan Hotel, Llanberris. He was a great fan of Swn y Mor and one of our best customers in North Wales.

During the years 1976 to 1979 the sales of Swn y Mor grew slowly but surely, we were supplying specialist stores which included Harrods of London and Howells of Cardiff. Apart from the standard bottles, we started bottling it in old style earthenware jugs that became much sort after tourist souvenirs. This expanded our sales to the coastal resorts of Tenby, Aberystwyth, Barmouth, Rhyl and Llandudno.

The product was also starting to attract some media attention. Journalists from around the world started picking up the occasional stories put out in the Western Mail. I began to give interviews on the telephone to national radio stations fascinated by the forgotten history of Welsh Whisky. One sunny afternoon in 1981 while I was sweeping out the yard in front of the 'brew house', a smartly dressed bespectacled American gentleman approached me.

"Hi, your wife Gill said I'd find you out here, my name is Peter, Peter Bordeaux President of Sazerac Wines and Spirits, New Orleans."

We went into the back bar and he began to tell me how the concept of Welsh Whisky excited him. He saw huge potential in the American market, as his company was one of the biggest independent producers and distributors of liquor in the US. I explained that my production capacity was minuscule, producing just a hundred cases a month, duty paid. At this stage our production was too small for a bonded facility that would allow us to export. I stored duty free stocks of raw whisky in a bonded warehouse in Cardiff, drawing down casks on a need to use basis because I had to pay duty up front.

I had what was called a compounders licence from HM Customs to carry out my operations in the 'brew house'. Unlike small producers in France or Spain UK regulations were not conducive to small-scale production. We would have to make a big leap and set up a full blown bonded warehouse operation before I could even think of going into the export market. He explained that the first thing we needed to do was to get the whisky recognised by the US authorities. There was no category for Welsh Whisky it needed to be created. If this were successful his company would back an expansion programme for Brecon Brewery.

Unwittingly this was to lead on to my first battle royale with the Scotch Whisky Association, and they in turn would incite Customs and the Ministry of Agriculture Fisheries and Food (MAFF) to become involved.

Peter Bordeaux invited Gill and I to make a trip to New Orleans to discuss matters further and see his set up there. In September 1981 we boarded a plane at Heathrow bound for Florida for a short holiday before flying on to New Orleans. John Pugh took charge of the pub while we enjoyed a much-needed break on Long Boat Island off the coast of Sarasota. On our first day we headed off in our hire car to the 'Point' and discovered 'Fast Eddies'. 'Warm beer and lousy food' read the sign out front; so in we went. We dined on delicious lobster salad washed down with Californian Chardonnay and looked out over the sun-drenched Gulf of Mexico. A week later we flew onto New Orleans.

Mr. Bordeaux and several Vice Presidents of the Company greeted us at the airport, whisking us away in a big black limousine straight to their offices on the outskirts of the city. They showed us a huge production facility churning out thousands of bottles of liquor a hour. A far cry from our little brew house in Brecon. The board of directors at Sazerac seemed delighted with the prospect of importing Welsh Whisky to the States, they had already made application to the Bureau of Firearms, Tobacco and Alcohol (BFTA) for an import licence for Swn y Mor. Over the next few days Peter showed us the sights of New Orleans, a fascinating city that still had a strong French influence.

The cuisine of this Southern City was outstanding. From 'Mud-bugs' (Crawfish) eaten by the bucket full, washed down with cool beer, to the finest French-Creole lobster Jambalaya, prime Châteaux-Briane of beef or a hot spicy Gumbo, accompanied by exciting 'New World' wines of great distinction.

When Gill and I managed to get away on our own we visited the noisy Jazz Bars of Bourbon Street and small dark blues clubs off the side streets where we listened to Negro artists 'cry the blues' to the hypnotic rhythm of the 'bayou guitar'. A magic sound I still love today. On our last night we dined in style at the famous 'Captains Table', a real taste of Southern Grandeur, an old plantation style building reminiscent of the Clark Gable film 'Gone with the Wind.' We started with a Louisiana salad bowl followed by a medley of Cajun seafood. We consumed a whole magnum of Champagne and finished with a good Cognac, coffee, and a 'humungous' cigar. Before we left for Wales, Peter presented me with a Certificate making me 'An Honorary Citizen' signed by the Mayor of New Orleans dated the 21st September 1981. The hospitality we received knew no bounds.

Returning to Wales my task was clear, to get Welsh Whisky officially recognised. We had shipped to New Orleans six cases of Swn y Mor as samples to be tested by the Federal Authorities. These test proved favourable but when the

B.F.A.T contacted the British Embassy in Washington the response was simply 'never heard of it'. The Embassy contacted HM Customs in London who in turn contacted me. A very senior customs officer, a Mr. Crowther, rang me, enquiring in a very condescending voice, about my product and a communiqué he'd received from Washington. I informed him that I was blending duty paid products, holding a compounders licence issued from their Merthyr Tydfil office, and the description 'Welsh' was not held in contention by the home authority responsible; namely Powys County Council.

A few days later an officer from Cardiff visited me to obtain more details about what I wanted to do. I explained that I wanted to move my operation to larger premises on the newly established Ffrwdgrech Industrial Estate and produce under bond so that I could export. This would be the first time that I was made aware of the Scotch Whisky Associations interest in my endeavours. The SWA were concerned that I had applied to the US authorities for recognition. They were also concerned that I was calling the whisky 'Welsh'.

I told the officer I was 'touched' by the SWA's concern but determined to expand the business. He smiled and said he'd like to help but I might have a fight on my hands as they were putting pressure on both the Ministry of Agriculture and the Customs head quarters at Kings Beam House London. Somehow the story got into the Western mail and from there to the London 'Daily Telegraph'. The story suggested that Customs were being 'intransigent' and obstructive in not allowing me to export my Welsh Whisky. The next time the senior officer from Kings Beam House contacted me he was very irate. I explained that the story had not come from me, it must have been the Americans! The Customs official answer was that my operation was far too small to warrant a bond, I countered this by informing them that there were no 'operational' bonds left in Wales only warehousing bonds. There was a need for such a bond, regardless how small my business was at present and that I would pursue my application.

They invited me to a meeting at Kings Beam House in London to discuss the matter. I duly attended to be confronted by a permanent under secretary from MAFF, two MAFF officials, two Senior Surveyors of Customs and Excise and two other men with distinct public school accents who did not reveal who they were representing. Perhaps this confrontation was meant to intimidate me but it did the opposite. Entering this historical temple of money collectors should have filled me with apprehension but all I expected was to see a couple of customs officer to discuss my business expansion plans not, what I was to be confronted with.

On entering an oak-panelled boardroom on the top floor of this huge building, I met with my 'interrogators'. I was surprised by the size of the reception committee but didn't show it, merely sitting down at the end of a long table looking back at the grey suited gentlemen. Crowther introduced me to those assembled and proceeded to 'chair' the meeting. There was cordiality but little humour. That gave me a 'gut' feeling, so before he got started I did.

"Well thank you gentlemen for inviting me along. I must say I didn't expect such a welcome nor am I prepared for the 'third degree' you are undoubtedly about to give me. I've come along today merely to discuss the matter of granting a bond to my Company in order that I may export my products without the imposition of UK duty as my competitors North of the Boarder are allowed to do. My other reason in coming to London today is to have lunch with my friend Dafydd

Wigley at the House of Commons to discuss the exact same thing! Had I known the nature or hidden agenda of this meeting I would have brought Mr. Wigley along to observe and advise."

With that they looked at each other in disbelief. Bidding them good day, I left.

I hadn't arranged to see Dafydd Wigley that day but as he was a good friend and was now the sitting Member of Parliament for Caernarfon and the president of Plaid Cymru needless to say I'd soon be on the phone to him. He wrote directly to the minister responsible for Customs and Excise, and the Minister of Agriculture, pointing out that there was flexibility in the regulations should local needs so require. Customs relented and said that, providing I could secure suitable premises, a bond would be granted. My next problem was to persuade the Development Board to lease a unit on the Ffrwdgrech industrial estate to me and then to sell the Pub to finance it. In the mean time the US authorities accepted the registration of Swn y Mor Welsh Whisky. Sazerac wrote me saying they would place a confirmed order of 1,000 cases to be delivered to New Orleans as soon as possible.

My application for an industrial unit was initially met with scepticism but on reading press coverage of my U.S. success they changed their attitude. By the end of 1982 Gill and I bought a new house, 'Glen More', just off Camden Road in Brecon, sold the Camden Arms, and secured a lease on two 1,500 square foot industrial units from the Development Board for Rural Wales. We had also doubled the sales of Swn y Mor on the home market. We bought a second hand automatic bottling line and various other pieces of equipment. Customs granted our 'bond' shortly after moving in to the new building, so we were now ready to go. Sazerac placed an order for 1,000 cases of Swn y Mor worth £20,000 to get us started, but it would take us some months to fill such an order, which at the time represented a years production.

# 10

# The Rocky Road Ahead

Brecon now had its first bonded warehouse at 14-15 Ffrwdgrech Ind Est, two newly built units which we knocked into one. A new page in the long and struggling history of Welsh Whisky had turned.

The sale of the pub had given us much-needed working capital but I now had much greater overheads without the positive cash flow that the pub had provided in the past. The bond saved me from warehousing costs in Cardiff and paying duty on losses that occurred in production, evaporation, spillage etc. Everything now depended on sales and getting paid. We'd hardly been in the new premises a few weeks when I had a letter from Trading Standard's saying that a new Food and Drink labelling law had come in and I was to make a submission of my Welsh Whisky labels for approval under the new 1983 Act.

As we strove to for fill the American order we continued to expand our efforts at home. We decided to develop a new product based on the growing popularity of cream liqueurs such as Baileys Irish Cream. Setting about creating a recipe for the product, I got in touch with a Creamery in near by Llangadog, between us we developed a blend of fresh cream, honey and whisky. I struck on the name Merlin but decided to spell it Merlyn and tried to register it as such. A large wine and spirit distributor in London, who had registered Merlin many years before, contacted us and explained their prior registration. After some correspondence with the company one of their directors visited us at Brecon, he was a real gentleman from the 'old school' and the company he worked for was a household name. We sat and drank a few glasses of Swn y Mor before he presented me with a waver note to the trademark Merlin saying,

"We haven't used this mark for years and as I'm retiring next month you may as well have it but make sure you renew it in your own Company name"

I was 'gob-smacked' this was a very generous gesture that meant I did not have to destroy all the Merlyn labels I'd already prematurely printed.

We finally completed our 'huge' order for Sazerac which entailed bringing in several of my old 'Camden-gang', including good old John Pugh, to help out. It had been a mammoth task, one we had not really been ready for, and we experienced many production problems along the way. Nevertheless we were now ready to ship.

The Launch of Merlyn in the spring of 1983 was low key but again attracted substantial media coverage. The media attention prompted the Milk Marketing Board to contact me with regard to a joint promotion. Merlyn needed the equivalent of six pints of milk to produce so it was a good promotion for added value milk usage.

I was of course interested, but could they provide the money required? Surprisingly they did, this resulted in

Merlyn becoming a successful product in our portfolio. In the meantime the buyer from Harrods rang me to say they would like to do a promotion of Welsh products and as we had been supplying them with Swn y Mor for a few years could I help? He gave me an order of six cases of Swn y Mor and 'we'll try a couple of cases of Merlyn.' I said no problem, "I'll deliver them myself and see you to discuss the promotion at the same time".

Delivering the order myself in an old blue ford van was to prove a good idea. Telling the guy at the goods entrance that not only was I delivering the goods but also had to see the food and beverage director, he allowed me to park in the Harrods delivery bay. Arriving at the Wines and Spirits department I could see the Director talking and joking with a bald headed American looking chap who looked vaguely familiar. I stood patiently clutching my bag of samples, (the new Merlyn and a new packaging idea for Swn y Mor, old fashioned stoneware 'crock' jugs), plus a loaf of Bara Brith, a Welsh currant bread loaf for the directors secretary who had asked me to bring her some. She was east European and had spent a holiday in North Wales, loved Bara Brith, but couldn't get it in London.

I had met the Director before an elegant man in his late fifty's and when I caught his eye he immediately said

"Ah Mr. Gittins the Welsh Whisky Gentleman!"

With that the American gentleman turned around, it was Telly Savalas, (Kojak) the actor. Who exclaimed

"Welsh Scotch,I like this guy already" with that we shook hands and I said.

"Not only do I have whisky today but my new Merlyn Whisky Cream Liqueur, and Barra Brith for your secretary", and I handed a brown paper package to the Director.

After explaining to Mr. Savalas what Barra Brith was, the three of us went through to the tasting room. A little party started to ensue as I poured samples of Merlyn and Swn y Mor, the Director's secretary joined us, she was over the moon with the Bara Brith and cut slices for us to enjoy with our whisky. By this time we were on first name terms and 'Telly', puffing on a giant cigar took a look at his watch and said he had to get to London Weekend studio's, so I volunteered to give him a lift. The Director thanked me for the samples and said he would place an order for the whisky crocks and mail it to me. Telly said

"Put a couple of cases on for me and ship it."

Walking down to the bowels of Harrods and through the back door to the loading bay I pointed to our mode of transport, an old blue escort van that had seen better days. The guys in the loading bay looked in disbelief but quickly asked 'Telly' for his autograph and with shaking heads and smiles one remarked

"Well I've seen it all now Kojak in a van!" then shouted over to me "you can park here any time you like Mr. Whisky!"

Off we went to Upper Ground the LWT studio's over looking the south bank of the river Thames. Pulling up out side 15 minutes later 'Telly' said

"Heh! Park up come in I owe you a drink."

He spoke to the doormen who said they'd keep an eye on the van and in I went. 'Telly' went off to his interview and someone took me upstairs to the roof top bar. I was introduced to a fellow Welshman, Tom James, the props and sets manager who I later became great friends with. We all had a laugh about my meeting with 'Kojack', who later joined us with one of LWT top brass for a drink, having refused to go to the VIP suite.

We spent a pleasant half-hour or so and he actually said "who loves ya' baby" when I introduced him to Tom James.

Driving back to Brecon that evening I giggled to myself. Who the hell will believe this one? It was to become a dinner conversation of mine for many years to come. Further more I had gained new customers to prove it; the LWT bar not to mention 'Kojak!' Some weeks after my trip to London, I received a letter from Trading Standards informing me that they had no objections to my Swn y Mor Welsh Whisky labels. The Scotch Whisky Association had failed again!

However, my troubles were not over, the consignment shipped to New Orleans had thrown a 'haze' (a sediment of insoluble compounds). I couldn't understand it. The product in Brecon was OK. I was to learn later that the change in temperatures during the long journey to New Orleans had caused precipitation within the whisky. In the old days they got around this phenomenon by bottling in green or amber glass so you couldn't see it. The modern way was to chill or freeze filter the whisky but this tended to strip much of the flavour. I hadn't carried out enough research and development in the filtration method I was using.

Having employed some herbal compounds in the filter medium I was purely trying to recreate an old recipe. I'd not really found out what various different types of herbs could do to filter out the insoluble matter. Facing this problem lead me to carry out further research into filtration and the usage of herbs. The problem would plague me for years.

# 11

# The Prince Of Wales

On the 21st December 1983 my son Gareth was born. My greatest achievement after eight years of marriage, we finally had our own family. I would recommend to any father that he attend the birth. It was the most incredible experience. One I will always cherish. Gill's sister Kay had left home to work in Exeter after splitting up with her boy friend, just when we needed a babysitter! The business survived the hazing problems of the Swn y Mor shipment to New Orleans, and we added a new product to our portfolio. Tafski Imperial Welsh Vodka. The media loved the name with banner headlines like 'World Launch of Tafski!' It didn't rival Smirnoff but it did add to our growth. My plan was to launch one new product every year. In 1984 this would be Glan Usk Welsh Dry Gin, then in 1985, Prince of Wales Malt Welsh Whisky.

The growth of Malt Whisky had been dramatic during the eighty's and Prince of Wales was an instant hit. We used malt from Speyside, vatting and filtering through my improved herbal system. Impressive packaging was the key. With such an 'up-market' product this proved expensive, especially when we also decided to bottle it in a Rugby Ball shaped porcelain container holding half a litre. I used the three feathers symbol on the label and attempted to register the name. At first this was rejected by the Trade Mark Agency, I then managed to register it as Owain Glyn Dwr, Prince of Wales, after the last Welsh Prince of Wales.

All went well until Westminster Trading Standards office wrote to me complaining about the name and the use of the three feathers. Someone from the Royal household had purchased a bottle at Harrods then enquired with the Local Authority about the legality of the name and the use of the feathers. A battle royal ensued that created much needed exposure for the product. Prince Charles' office wrote to me demanding that I desist from using the name and remove the feathers. People wrote from near and far in support of my product, informing me that Prince Charles had not issued a single warrant to a Welsh manufacturer. Several professors of heraldry wrote saying I was entitled to show 'fielty' to the Prince of Wales by ancient right going back to the 12th century. Plaid Cymru intervened saying the label supported the 'real' Prince of Wales Owain Glyn Dwr. And so the argument continued. In the end we came to a compromise if I removed the feathers the Palace would not complain about the name. The headline was; 'Dafydd has his feathers plucked.'

As a result of this furore a Japanese importer came to see me and we started to ship to Japan. We even registered the actual name 'Prince of Wales' in Japan. Despite the incredible bureaucracy that confronted exporters to Japan in the eighty's, Welsh Whisky was received with open arms. The authorities even placed it in a favourable tax category. This of course infuriated my 'friends' in the SWA who then, after conceding their lost cause over the 'Welshness' issue, proceeded to challenge whether or not it was in fact whisky because of the herbal filtration. This issue too was 'Scotched' after a series of tests carried out on my products in Wales and Japan.

To promote Welsh Whisky and in particular Prince of Wales we under took our first overseas trade exhibition at Foodex-Tokyo.

Together with a friend of mine Richard Harpur, (who'd offered to give me a helping hand), I travelled out with the help of a Department of Trade grant. We would be the only exhibitors from Wales and one of just a handful from the United Kingdom. Our newly appointed agent met us at the airport after a horrendous flight with Aeroflot via Moscow, and took us to the Palace Hotel. Tokyo was a marvellous vibrant city bustling in Japan's economic boom. The only drawbacks were the prices. Things were three times the cost as in Wales. Thankfully the DTI grant and the great generosity of our Japanese agent softened the blow.

Now. I had often heard about the Japanese like of a drink or two but I was to find out first hand! No sooner had we checked in to the hotel and had a quick freshen up, we were on our way to a welcoming luncheon party. Here we would meet the other executives of Sure Liquors, our agent Mr. Takahashi's family business.

We received a regal reception at a traditional Japanese restaurant in an area of Tokyo called Akaska. The hospitality was formal but surprisingly warm and friendly with much hand shaking, bowing and business card exchanges. The drinks began to flow. The meal consisting of a large array of tasty morsels such as Sushi, Tempura, rice, and sauces both hot and spicy. After lunch we had a brief tour of the Sure Liquors offices before going back to the hotel for a few hours. At 7pm prompt we were picked up for a dinner engagement at a very swish Geisha house. This was a great honour, our hosts for the evening would be the Bar and Restaurant Guild of Tokyo and both Harpur and myself were expected to make speeches.

We in the West have heard about Geisha houses but very few of us have had the privilege to ever be invited to one. It was nothing like our minds eye image of an up-market 'knocking-shop'. Indeed it was the complete opposite, a bastion of refined Japanese culture. The Geisha girls were immaculate in their traditional costumes. Like little dolls with bright red lips and white faces, scurrying around taking off the men's shoes and jackets, placing slippers on our feet, and silk robes which they wrapped around us before we were ushered into a private dining room accompanied by haunting string music.

The decor was delicate and tastefully sparse but not empty. The ambience formal, there was a ritual of protocol closely observed by the Japanese that we tried to emulate as best we could. The most senior executives and their guests entered the room first then by descending order of seniority or importance the others. The Geisha girls lined the room, bowing as we entered. The chairman of the guild chanted something in Japanese and the girls replied in unison. There was a large low level table that we all sat around crossed legged on cushioned stools. Warm Sake was brought and poured by the girls who kneeled down beside each gentleman. At a toast, 'Kampai', all the men raised their small porcelain cups in the air repeating the chant, then in one swallow downed the smooth but deceptively strong Sake rice wine. This happened several times before our charming Geisha Girls served the first part of what was to be a veritable banquet.

Neither Harpur or I spoke a word of Japanese, and as

our agent Mr. Takahashi was seated at the top of the table with the chairman, the proceeding were a little hard to follow. Thankfully my Geisha spoke a little English and when she didn't understand she just giggled and poured me another drink. When the main course arrived, 'Saibu Saibu.' (A myriad of meats, fish and vegetables cooked on the table using a pyramid charcoal cooker). The chairman made an announcement then in walked a girl carrying a bottle of Prince of Wales Welsh Malt Whisky on a silver platter, followed by several others bearing the same amber liquid. Not knowing what to do I stood up and bowed then everyone clapped followed by much laughter, the party had begun!

We were twelve gentlemen, so twelve bottles were placed on the table, one apiece. Large 'highball' glasses, buckets of ice and jugs of water were placed before us. The girls set about preparing our 'Mizuwari' a ceremony all by itself. Whisky diluted 1 to 6 with ice and water. As we eat 'Saibu Saibu' the 'highballs glasses' were never empty. As the evening wore on I found myself chatting away to the guys opposite, they in Japanese and me in English, Harpur doing the same. I guess when the whisky takes hold any language becomes universal. The toast had now changed from 'Kampai' to 'Iechyd Da'. Our hosts found this incredibly amusing laughing and clapping every time. My Geisha Girl had given up translating and was giggling so much I thought she was about to wet herself.

It was now time for speeches. The chairman got to his feet helped by his geisha and began to recite his prepared speech. Takahashi had come over to me in order to translate. He talked about "our friends and colleagues from Wales and how he so enjoys the Welsh Whisky. He could not believe that Gittins San and Harpur San had never been to Japan before because we seemed so much at home and that he must visit Wales soon''

It was now my turn, standing up with glass in hand I thanked my hosts then continued to prattle on, forgetting to pause so that Takahashi could translate. It didn't seem to matter, every time I mentioned Wales, whisky or the Prince of Wales I received a cheer. Finally I bowed to all seated, gestured to Harpur to stand up and we raised our glasses to the chairman and proudly proclaimed Iechyd Da Japan!

This brought the house down and I'm sure my Geisha Girl had a religious experience, her face was the epitome of utter amazement. Meanwhile Takahashi stood, still pondering whether there was any point in translating what I'd said during my ten-minute speech. After all every one was in 'stitches' including the chairman and the 'heard it all before' Geisha Girls. We had certainly broken the ice, the chairman invited us for a drink at his club afterwards. Heaven knows we had drunk more than enough already but it would be impolite to refuse. So off we went to the 'Ginza' to party on.

After we were 'poured' into our hotel at 4am we were informed that Mr. Takahashi would pick us up at 8am prompt and take us to the exhibition centre. Thanks to the valiant efforts of a chambermaid we rose, showered, dressed and were waiting in the hotel lobby fortified by a pot of strong black coffee, when Mr. Takahashi arrived. Having declined a traditional Japanese breakfast of sticky rice and raw egg.

Mr. Takahashi seemed surprised to see us? He remarked. ''You samurai. So much whisky, so much party yet you look fine!''

We had obviously passed our test of stamina!

Spending the rest of the morning overseeing the setting up of our exhibition stand our heads slowly cleared, refreshed by a swift beer in the exhibition centre's canteen.

Having told Mr. Takahashi that Harpur and I had a mutual friend who lived in Osaka and we'd made arrangements to meet up with her at our hotel later that afternoon, he drove us back. Anna Roberts was teaching English at Osaka University and spoke fluent Japanese. This would prove a god send as very few people spoke English and we had no Japanese. Getting back to the hotel proved another god send, as we managed to get a few hours rest before receiving a phone call from reception telling us that Anna had arrived.

It was marvellous to see Anna, a familiar face from back home; she too was delighted to meet up with us. We retired to the top floor where the DTI had set up a 'club' room and complimentary bar for the British exhibitors. The free bar was most welcome as a bottle of beer in the hotel cost £7. The bar also proved to be a practical idea as we could invite potential customers for a quiet drink and sample of our 'wares.' All the British exhibitors, of which there were 12 food and drink companies in all contributed to the bar, including Welsh Whisky.

Anna stayed with us for a few days in our executive suite and even helped out on the exhibition stand. She not only spoke Japanese but also she came from Brecon and knew a fair bit of the background of my Company. This greatly impressed Takahashi and also many visitors to our stand 90% of whom were Japanese and spoke little or no English. The British Ambassador, an impressive chap, became fascinated by Welsh Whisky and I think Anna. She was a petite pretty girl with deep brown eyes, in her mid twenties exuding energy and confidence. He invited us for drinks at the embassy the following evening.

The British embassy was a massive complex over looking the gardens of the Imperial Palace. The acreage alone must have been worth millions of pounds. The drinks party turned out to be a very stuffy affair but it was interesting to see around this ornate 'palace' built during a time of empire and grandeur.

Our trip to Japan had been a resounding success. Takahashi had taken many orders for Prince of Wales and Swn y Mor. We had become great friends and met many warm and friendly people. It was hard to believe that less than a generation ago we had fought a long bloody war with these people. How things change through the course of time. Before we left I decided to return some of the hospitality which had included chartering a bus complete with bar and hostess to take Harpur and I to see Hakone National Park and Mount Fuji.

With the recommendation of the Chairman of the Bar and Restaurant Guild, I booked a good restaurant and invited six leading lights of the drinks trade and a senior vice president of a major Japanese bank we had met to dinner. Takahashi was unable to come but the bank vice president spoke fairly good English so he could help with any translations. Takahashi pointed out that I should have a business card printed in Japanese. Anna had left so I explained to the concierge at the hotel that I wanted

Dafydd Gittins, Prince of Wales Welsh Whisky, C/O the Palace Hotel, to be printed on the back of my regular business card. Card exchanges in Japan was a ritual, no card no person it seemed to me.

On entering the Restaurant I presented my card to the Maitre d' who immediately turned it over to the Japanese printing. His face lit up. Saying 'Ah so' he led us to the bar for an aperitif before dinner. The waiters seated us at the centre table of a beautiful dining room with much ceremony. The décor was a mix of Western and oriental; very grand. We dined on superb Kobe beef washed down by Château Neuf de Pape and several 'Mizuwari'. At the end I was expecting a hefty bill that would probably melt my American Express Gold Card. My guests were impressed by the impeccable service and attention we received at this gracious establishment. Calling over the Maitre 'd for my bill he whispered in my ear in broken English "No bill sir we very honoured"

My immediate thought was that they would send the bill to my hotel. The hotel concierge had made the final arrangement for me so they would add this to my hotel account. Maybe that's how they did things here. I was positive none of my guests would have paid, that would have been impolite as this time they were my guests. Leaving the restaurant, again with much ceremony, I eventually bided my guests farewell and took a cab back to my hotel. It had been a great success my guests seemed ecstatic over the whole evening, the bank vice president commenting that he must use this restaurant himself for entertaining. When I got back to the Palace Hotel I went straight to the club bar to tell Harpur and the other guys about the evening.

Harpur had been entertaining a young Japanese girl he'd met at Food-Ex. She spoke good English having spent some time at Oxford.

His first words to me were.

"And how much did that little lot cost you?"

To which I replied

"I don't know?"

"Too pissed to read the bill were you"

"No not at all I think their sending it to the hotel, it's got to be a grand, but the head waiter just said no bill we very honoured?" Harpur couldn't believe this. So I continued.

'It all started when I presented my card. After that this

Maitre d' – headwaiter to you – started bowing and scraping as if I were Royalty or something. I mean the meal and the service was out of this world!"

"Give us a look at your card?"

I gave him one of my cards pointing out that I had it printed in Japanese on the back by the hotel concierge. Harpur looked at it then handed it to the Japanese girl, who immediately burst out laughing! She stood up took a bow and said

"Ah so your Royal Highness very honoured to meet you!"

"What?" I exclaimed in puzzlement.

"Well according to this Gittins San you are Dafydd Gittins His Royal Highness the Prince of Wales care of the Palace."

"You've got to joking I don't look anything like the Prince of Wales-I'm twice this size and I've got a beard"

With that she laughingly replied

"Sorry Gittins San, but all Westerners look alike!"

Harpur retorted

"It could only happen to you-you 'Jammy' sod, I'll get the beers in"

I never did get that bill and as we flew back to London I could picture in my minds eye the restaurant sticking up a plaque 'by appointment to HRH Prince of Wales'.

# 12

# Upward And Onward

In 1986 I sought expansion capital for our Company and met with an acquaintance of mine from Cardiff. David Richards was the finance director of a large wine shippers and bonded warehousing company, Luc Lacerre Et Fils Limited, who had recently merged with a fast expanding Public Company H. Young Plc. Over lunch at the Armless Dragon in Cardiff we struck a deal and he introduced me to John Wydham Lewis and John Wilson, directors of H. Young Plc.

John Wilson was the boss. A straight talking Yorkshireman, he swore a lot but was a very shrewd businessman. Lewis was a large jovial Cardiffian who liked his wine. David Richards was a true gentleman; a public school educated chartered accountant originally from Mountain Ash but who had lived in Cardiff for many years. Our Company, Brecon Brewery now became part of the H. Young Group of Companies but would trade independently. To begin with this worked extremely well giving our Company access to new markets and much needed expansion capital. I was also appointed to the Board of H. Young Operations Limited a group holding subsidiary.

During the early part of 1986 the ex-President of the United States paid a visit to Wales to pursue one of his favourite past times, fly fishing. He was visiting the famous Welsh fishing expert 'Moc' Morgan and we received a visit from his entourage after President Carter received a bottle of our Prince of Wales Whisky. He had commented how much he had enjoyed its mellow flavour. Among the entourage was a senior journalist from the Wall Street Journal. Like most journalists I know he liked a 'drop' of whisky and he certainly appreciated the smoothness of Welsh Whisky and decided to do an in-depth report on the emergence of our little known industry.

When the article came out I was flabbergasted and impressed by the fact it appeared not only on the front page but continued on several inside pages. SWA had also put in their 'ten penny' worth but it came over as sour grapes. Had I have taken out the column space in advertising in would have cost $100,000 dollars. The result was even better, receiving a deluge of letters from the States enquiring about our products and where could they buy them? An importer from San Francisco rang me asking if we were represented in the States. Our previous deal with Sazarac now being defunct the answer was of course no.

We had been shipping to Canada for some years but in rather small quantities of a few hundred cases a year. The Canadian market was a State monopoly, difficult to penetrate, and very much influenced by the larger US market. So it was important to get back into the larger American market. The San Francisco importer decided to come over to Wales immediately to discuss a distribution deal. The outcome being that we concluded a new distribution contract with Cannon Wines

Inc of San Francisco. Having already received US Federal approval for Welsh Whisky the bureaucratic procedure was far simpler this time around. We set about a major sales campaign in the States, up grading the packaging of Prince of Wales, producing publicity material and I went over on promotional tours. G.Q. Magazine did a feature about Welsh Whisky and myself, as did several US in-flight magazines all the time adding invaluable publicity.

Malt Whisky had become very much an 'in' drink in the US with many trendy bars offering a wide selection. Our big advantage was being the only one from Wales. However, we were unable to mount a major advertising campaign, the cost of which was way beyond our means. Instead we settled for the niche market and looked for slow but steady growth.

The SWA continued its war of attrition no matter how much it continued to backfire on them. A typical example of this being reflected in an article by the lovely Petronella Wyatt of the Daily Telegraph when commenting about their on going gripe. She quotes Mr. Hugh Morrison the then general director of the SWA.

*" But back to the whisky. The Scotch Whisky Association, Mr. Morrison told me, is engaged in a dispute with the Ministry of Agriculture. The cause: a man in Wales who is producing something called 'Welsh Whisky'. There is, of course no such thing. Mr. Dafydd Gittins from Brecon, however, is selling two brands of this, entitled Prince of Wales and Swn y Mor.*

*I discovered, after some research, that Mr. Gittins is contravening the EC Drinks and Spirits Regulations Act. This is because he does not possess a distillery. Whisky must be distilled and matured for three years in Wales before it can be called Welsh Whisky. Instead, Mr. Gittins is buying Scotch Whisky which, is often 'aromatised' using Welsh herbs.*

*"That is not whisky at all" said Mr. Morrison. "And with herbs, it is not whisky at all."*
*Mr. Gittins, nonetheless, is exporting his beverage as far afield as Japan, where, I imagine, they are blissfully unfamiliar with EC regulations. "It's ridiculous," Mr Morrison told me. "But our talks with the Ministry of Agriculture are what you might call constructive."*
*I wish him luck. Mr. Morrison is intelligent, hard-working and surprisingly abstemious-he possesses all the virtues, in fact, which drive a man to drink."*

I think Ms Wyatt summed it up very well. Having lost their 'Welsh' argument back in 1983 they were now wholly focused on the 'herbal' element. Countering their argument by pointing out various 'grey area' practises of theirs such as added Sherry or Port to finish off whiskies would from time to time enrage them. The odd thing about all this is that I was very friendly with several of their members who were only too pleased to do business with me.
I generally travelled up to Scotland two or three times a year to buy 'fillings' which is new immature whisky for laying down, and older, generally malt, whiskies for blending or vatting.

Visiting my old friend John Macdonald at Tomatin Distillers in Inverness always turned into quite an occasion. He was a real character who had little time, for in his words, "the poncy public school accountants who have taken over the industry."

John was a Highlander and had worked in the whisky industry for thirty years 'man and boy'. He drank single malt Tomatin, watered down with Burn water. Whenever I visited there would be no Tea or Coffee; instead John would produce a Decanter of 'amber gold' and a large jug of peat coloured water straight from the burn. This would be followed by a trip to the nearest pub for a lunch of steak and eggs. The Japanese had bought Tomatin, Scotland's largest Malt distillery but John had been left very much in charge.

Another character I dealt with was John 'Jack' Milroy who owned a whisky and fine wine emporium in Soho. Originally from Scotland he and his brother Maurice had moved south to London in the late sixty's. The two brothers were highly regarded in the industry, Maurice writing numerous books and articles on Scotch whisky. Jack was a big bearded cuddly man who loved the good life. I looked forward to my visits to see him. Within five minutes of being in his office he would invite me to lunch with some celebrity or the food and beverage manager of one of London's top hotels.

On one occasion he asked if I'd like to come with him as a guest to Cliveden Hall in Berkshire the once home of the Astor family. It had also featured in the Profumo affair and the film Scandal about his relationship with Christine Keeler back in the early sixties.

The only way to describe Cliveden is luxuriously grand, not only once the Astor residence but previously that of several Dukes and a Prince of Wales. Jack was dining with a group of Japanese industrialists who wanted to purchase the contents of a fine wine cellar and a number of rare Malt whiskies. We drove to Cliveden in Jack's burgundy coloured Bentley, rolling up the mile long drive way in style. The Japanese came by helicopter and had booked a whole wing over looking the spacious swimming pool and immaculate gardens. We joined our hosts in the grand wood panelled lobby that was almost covered with fine art and lit with huge crystal chandlers.

We shook hands and exchanged cards with eight

smartly dressed Japanese gentlemen, all of who were in their early thirties apart from one grey haired chap in his late fifties. While we went through the ritual of introduction, I noticed Lord King the chairman of British Airways walk in, and from the corner of my eye could see Lord Snowdon chatting away with a group of matrons festooned with diamond and pearl jewellery. Sitting down to glasses of Champagne and canapés, the manager came over to greet Jack who he knew well. I commented on how wonderful Cliveden Hall was. Jack had introduced me and added 'this is Mr. Welsh Whisky'. With that the manager offered to give me the grand tour which I eagerly accepted, leaving Jack to discuss the more confidential financial details of his deal with the Japanese.

To describe this beautiful building as a hotel would not do justice to its grace and charm. It was more akin to opening up a Royal Palace as a play 'den' for the rich and famous. The landscaped grounds extended down to the river Thames, they looked glorious on this sunny summer evening as majestic weeping willows swayed gently in the warm breeze.

I rejoined my hosts in the malt whisky bar where we were to dine. This was a cosy cellar bar stocked with hundreds of different malt whiskies, supplied by Jack's company. Our bar snack was to consist of Oysters to start followed by Lobster cooked anyway you wanted, washed down with bottle after bottle of Dom. Perrigeon Champagne. Then the serious drinking commenced as we selected various malt whiskies to 'round' off the meal. I suggested drinking these in brandy balloons in order to appreciate the delicate aromas of the individual whiskies, especially Prince of Wales. By the end of the evening Jack had sold the Japanese the contents of a wine cellar he had purchased from a French aristocrat fallen on hard times. He also sold them a mixed container (1,000 cases) of various malt whiskies including Prince of Wales. The deal totalled over a million pounds.

It was just after mid night when I realised there was no way I was going to get back to Brecon that night. I hadn't planned staying the night. Cliveden was full despite its £400 a night price tag, Jack invited me to stay at his home in near by Maidenhead but being some what worse for wear I didn't think Jack's wife would appreciate me rolling in unannounced and staying the night. Instead I ended up sharing a taxi to the Holiday Inn at Heathrow with a lady whose romantic evening with her 'gentleman' had gone awry. We sat together in the back of the cab, her thanking me profusely for sharing the ride, and then through my 'merry haze' I thought I recognised her.

"I've met you somewhere before" I exclaimed "Hampstead! You were one of Previn's girls!"

"Well blow me down I thought I recognised you too. The gilded ferret. The Welsh boy, weren't you a pop singer? What a small world!" Her eyes lit up as her mind raced back all those years to Hampstead and the swinging Sixties.

I persuaded her to join me for nightcap at the Hotel. When we got to the lobby bar I could see her more clearly, she was still a very attractive woman now in her late thirties with shoulder length Auburn hair, well spoken and expensively dressed. She oozed wealth and breeding. I couldn't remember her name but her face and mannerisms had stuck in my memory all those years. Ordering myself a pint of cider and her a gin and tonic she grabbed my arm and said.

"To hell with it I'll have a pint of cider as well."

We chatted about old times and the many changes in our lives. She had married a wealthy something in the city chap and divorced. With no kids she got bored, then started working for a high-class escort agency in Mayfair that paid really well. Her date for the evening had got seriously drunk, had a pang of conscience, paid her off and told her to get lost.

"All part of the game darling! Let me get the next round" She said then waved to the barman to fetch us a fresh round of drinks.

It must have been three in the morning before we went to bed. She stood up saying

"Well come on sweetie its all bought and paid for you might as well enjoy!"

This presented me with a dilemma. Although Gill and I had what was now commonly regarded as an 'open' marriage, apart from outrageous flirting I'd not actually done the 'dirty deed' during our marriage. On the other hand?

My dilemma became philosophical as no sooner had we entered the bedroom she striped to her suspenders and black stockings and unclipped her bra to reveal the most magnificent pair of double D's. With hands on hips she swayed back and forth saying.

"What'd you think sweetie had em' done in Harley Street bloody good job what?"

Arriving back in Brecon that afternoon I was totally knackered and still in a daze from an incredible night. She even paid the hotel bill

"My treat sweetie, here's my number give me a call next time your in town and…(In a whispered tone) well what I said last night about being a tart, it was a load of tosh, fell out with the old man last night. The boring old bastard probably still snoring is head off back at Cliveden. Still lovely seeing you again, must do it again sweetie. Simply must fly!"

Blowing a kiss she disappeared into a taxi!

# 13

# The Recession

In 1989 we parted company with H. Young Holdings and became independent once again. In was a fairly amicable separation and I was still on friendly terms with the Chairman John Wilson. We wanted to expand into a new building and develop a full-blown distillation unit. The Group had other plans so the division was inevitable and suited all concerned.

One of my first ports of call was the Bank of Wales; I'd dealt with them in the past and knew several of the directors there. Putting forward a new revised business plan the Bank agreed to help. My next hurdle was the Development Board for Rural Wales.

Despite the fact I knew many of the DBRW's leading lights I had never found them particularly helpful. My impression was that their main brief was to support and encourage 'inward investment.' Their support for indigenous companies seemed lukewarm. Nevertheless they had a brand new 10,000 square foot unit on a new industrial development park, lying idle, less than a mile away from our unit on the old Ffrwdrech Industrial Estate.

It would take me nearly two years to finally get the lease on this new building. It had stayed empty as the British economy started to slide into recession, and property prices collapsed for the first time since the Great Depression of the early thirty's.

At the end of 1990 my mother Marjorie died after several months of illness. Her passing was almost like the end of an era. Known as Auntie Marge to many, a true character dearly missed in a world that was slowly becoming devoid of such personalities.

In September 1991 we moved to our new building which we intended to turn into Wales' first commercial distillery since 1906. I had formed a new Company the year before to spear head the expansion; The Welsh Whisky Company Limited was born. The down side of all this expansion was my marriage. As we had drifted together in the mid-seventies, Gill and I now drifted further apart. It's not easy working and living together. Gill began to feel trapped and started staying out late at night. She had dyed her hair blonde and it suited her. As they say, blondes have more fun!

In the early summer of 1991 I bought the cottage in Saundersfoot. I guess it was an escape from the ever-increasing arguments at home. My son Gareth was seven so the cottage by the seaside was a great new adventure. I'm sure he wasn't oblivious to what was happening between his mum and I, but he probably thought it was normal. Perhaps it was, certainly we were not the only parents to be splitting up.

He had attended a Welsh language school, Ysgol y Bannau in Brecon, since he was four and had already started to play the guitar and drums. He had begun with classical guitar lessons at school and seemed to take to it like a natural born musician. Ironically his idols were Sixty's bands like

Status Quo and Pink Floyd, instead of the Punk and Rap groups of the time.

Moving house is said to be a traumatic experience, moving factories is even worse In the autumn of '91 we moved to the new factory unit on Parc Menter. After several months installing and converting plant and machinery we finally limped back into production. It was shortly after this that I met two doctors from the University of Surrey.

Dr. Ron Schultz and Dr. Dave Farraday were introduced to me in the George Hotel one rainy afternoon in Brecon. By an old friend and soon to become a non-executive director of Welsh Whisky John (Patch) Williams.

Patch was a tall slim retired Lieutenant Colonel of the Parachute Regiment originally from Tywn North Wales but now firmly settled in Brecon. The 'Para's' have a long association with Brecon and Ron Schultz had also been an officer in the Para's, although he was Australian by birth.

Ron and Dave both specialised in process engineering, which encompasses distillation, and were based at Surrey University in Guildford. Dave was a fairly typical looking boffin, In his early thirties, he was well on his way to becoming a senior lecturer, as Ron, in his early fifties, already was.
He was very laid back with a large nose and short black hair, his broad Australian accent still present, despite living in England for some twenty years.

As we supped several pints at the corner of the bar we began to formulate a partnership, and the basic idea of an innovated distillation unit. Explaining that I wanted a far more efficient method of distillation for whisky production, Ron and Dave scribbled away on scraps of paper procured from the busy bar maid, while patch puffed endlessly away on one cigarette after the other.

Ron gazed at his empty pint glass then at the pile of papers on the bar, in his broad 'Aussie' brogue he declared.

"Well men, I think we just might be able to do it!" Dave nodded in agreement and removed his oversized spectacles to wipe away the haze from Patch's smoke.

"Chaps, I think this calls for another round" retorts Colonel Patch as he waves over to our ever helpful bar maid.

This was the beginning of an eventful relationship that would last for nearly a decade:

The next few years were tough, we had decided to build a visitor centre around the experimental still that Surrey University was building for us. In fact this 'tourist' facility would prove my best idea yet, it would ease cash flow in a falling home market.

We opened the centre to much 'pomp and ceremony' in May 1993. The Secretary of State for Wales at the time, David Hunt, doing the honours. The DBRW had somewhat highjacked the affair but, needing their support I didn't really mind. For the first time they realised that Welsh Whisky was an excellent source of much needed 'good' publicity at a time when there was little for British Industry gripped, as it was, in what seemed like a never ending recession.

At the time I was chairman of the Confederation of British Industry for Mid-Wales, having been elected the year before. A position I enjoyed, finding it both interesting and conducive to good business in general.

The visitor centre proved a success from day one; it attracted a lot of free publicity being the only one of its kind south of Edinburgh. This was just as well as advertising was expensive. We were soon welcoming busloads of visitors from all over the world. The town was to benefit from the spin off from the tourists who came especially to see the 'distillery and visitor centre.' At its height in the summer of 1995 we saw over 50,000 visitors.

Our theme was more Disney than the Scottish roll-model, it was billed as a 'journey through time' 'the Welsh Whisky experience.' It consisted of a large shop displaying for sale the now enlarged array of products that we produced on site. Swn y Mor deluxe blended Welsh Whisky. Prince of Wales 10 year old malt, Prince of Wales Special Reserve, Merlyn Welsh Cream Liqueur, Tafski Imperial Welsh Vodka, Glan Usk Welsh Dry Gin and our latest addition Dewi Sant Welsh Mead Wine. Plus a selection of Welsh Crafts and food products which contained Welsh Whisky, like Jams, preserves, fudges, Bara Brith etc produced by other local firms.

The shop led on through a double door into an audio/visual theatre. This was designed like an old monastery and included a robotic monk. The visitors sat on old Chapel Pew's and watched a 7-minute video tracing the history of Welsh Whisky through the ages from the 4th century. The robotic monk called 'Dafydd' narrated through the video film, his mouth moving in sync with the film.

After the film people walked through a series of exhibits depicting the various times in history. A monastic apothecary 4th century, a farm still from Henry the Eight's 15th century, a smugglers cove 17th century, the story of Evans Williams, Jack Daniel and early American distillers, the Old Bala distillery of 1890 then a glass panel looking out to our new copper experimental still. Then a small exhibit about the Brecon Beacons and the importance of water to the production of whisky. Before going through a mock up of a bonded warehouse full of oak casks and back into the shop for a tasting. The tour was fun and educational. People from around the world would visit and sign our ever-burgeoning visitor's book.

With a difficult home market struggling through the recession, we looked more and more to our export markets. Patch had joined our board to help with this sector, he also came up with a novel idea to help Airborne Forces Charities raise money and at the same time increase our sales of malt whisky.

We struck a deal with General Glyn Gilbert to produce a commemorative 'Airborne Forces Whisky' to mark the 50th year of the historic but fateful Arnhem Landings in 1944. We launched at Arnhem in 1993 the year before the bi-centenary, with the help of our Dutch importer Van Wees B.V.

Mr. Van Wees senior met us at Skipol airport and took us all for lunch. He was a tall thick set Dutchman in his sixties, white hair, distinguished looking and very conservative.

I had managed to persuade Gill to come along with Patch and his wife Jo. Although she was never keen on coming on these trips, I thought it too important for her to miss. It would be an experience.

Van Wees took us to a very 'in' restaurant the Canard Savage, not far from Skipol and on the way to our Hotel the 'Kleinzwitserland' in Heelsum. After being seated by a charming waitress and ordering an apéritif Patch, a face like stone demanded to see the manager.

No one said a word I looked at Van Wees and shrugged my shoulders not knowing what Patch's problem was. The waitress scurried out to get the manager he quickly arrived to see what this problem was. As he neared our table his face lit up

"Patch you old bastard!"

Patch stood up and they hugged each other. Jo began laughing. Obviously she had known but didn't let on. Van

Wees looked puzzled by it all until Patch introduced us.

We had no idea that Van Wees was going to invite us to lunch, or which restaurant .It turned out that the manager whose name was Rudi was an old friend of Patch from his days at the Army Staff College.

Rudi used to manage the Kleinzwitserland Hotel where Patch stayed on many occasions when lecturing on defence studies to the Dutch Army. He had lost touch with Rudi but knew he had bought a swish restaurant and bar near Skipol and took a guess. Our lunch turned into something of a reunion party and the food was superb. Van Wees ended up with a new customer for his range of fine wines and spirits. It was a pleasant start to our weekend.

The following day we attended an emotional ceremony at the small, secluded cemetery in Arnhem. There were about two thousand veterans, family, friends and towns people. A lone bugler played the last post, followed by a piper playing a sad and haunting highland battle hymn quietly ending before the sweet sound of a Welsh Choir lilted through the breezy sunny morning. The gentle song Myfanwy echoed to the silence of those who prayed for fallen comrades.

We stood riveted by the whole spectacle. Tears welled in the eye and goose bumps bristled. I felt both proud and sad. War will be the epitaph of mankind. It brings out the worst and the best and leaves that eternal question why?

After the ceremony we retired to the 'Harkenstien' hotel now a museum to the Airborne Landings.

The Para's had set up a field kitchen in the museum grounds that produced the most wonderful canapés and sweet meats. A second ceremony took place here for Polish veterans of the Landings. Until now they had been unable to attend the annual event at Arnhem, but now democracy had returned to

Poland after nearly 50 years of Communist rule, it was at last possible. The Polish veterans would be receiving their long over due medals from the Dutch Government in gratitude of their undoubted bravery all those years ago.

We provided whisky for the toasts and for the old boys who preferred something a little more warming than white wine. Later that afternoon we went to the 'drop zone', where units of the 10th Parachute Regiment re-enacted the 'drop' of '44. The crowd had now swollen to 20-30,000 people who lined the vast Common to watch the troops fall from the sky their chutes swishing through the wind as they glided earthward. A memorable day. One that I felt privileged to have shared. Even Gill felt moved by it all.

We returned to our hotel in time for a swim and sauna before dinner. It was little wonder that this hotel was so well renowned. Built like a huge Swiss chalet set in a pine forest it had every amenity, including an indoor swimming pool, sauna, Jacuzzi' and beauty parlour.

Looking forward to a soak in the Jacuzzi I hurried down to the ground floor after changing into my swimming trunks. As I opened the door to the Jacuzzi out walked a young lady completely naked. She said something to me in Dutch and pointed to a door just behind me that had 'karten" printed on it. I quickly open this door for her which led out into the garden and the early evening sunlight.

She stood in all her glory arms out stretched steam evaporating into the cool evening air. Still holding the door open and gazing at this wonderful sight Patch's wife Jo came up behind me. Looking around at her I said clearing my throat. "Jo, this would never happen in Brecon!" Then limped off into the Jacuzzi room before rigor mortis set into my nether regions.

We had booked dinner in the hotel's Michelin starred restaurant the 'DeKromme Dissel' a separate chalet set in the spacious hotel grounds.

The dinning room had beautiful oak beams, split-level, with a gigantic grand piano and a roaring log fire. The antique mahogany tables were laden with expensive silverware and candelabra. It was possibly the most romantic restaurant in which I have ever dined.

After a glass or two of Champagne we were handed large menu cards written in French but with no prices. Jo spoke French and I had eaten in enough French restaurants to understand a menu can only describe the meal at stupendous. Rounded off with Grande Balloon glass of Airborne Forces Welsh Malt Whisky! Sipped to the serenade of the grand piano, played by none other than the head chef.

It had been a wonderful weekend in Holland and we were to raise many thousands of pounds for Airborne Charities.

However nothing could rekindle what it was that Gill and I had felt for one another. Our marriage was a over, and had been for several years. I knew I still loved her and in her own sometimes-unemotional way she still loved me. Had she found someone else? Who, I didn't want to know, I just blocked it out and got on with my life.

# 14

# Export! Export!

After our trip to the Netherlands I decided to concentrate our sales efforts to exporting. Thailand was fast becoming a tiger economy in the booming Pacific Rim.

Our first trip to Bangkok was sponsored by the Chambers of Commerce Export Research Scheme. Patch and I spent two weeks in this hustle bustle, polluted but fascinating Capital City. Our mission? To secure import licences, and a good importer. Easier said than done!

We stayed at a small friendly business hotel called the Tantawan situated close to the banking centre and the infamous Pat Pong entertainment area. In was run by a strikingly good-looking Swiss lady called Claudia. A friend of Patch's, Mike Jones, had recommended it to us.

Mike was a retired major in the SAS working for the Thai military as a security advisor. He was to prove invaluable in getting us introduced to the Bangkok business community and the all-important military. We became members of the British Club, which was only a ten-minute walk from the hotel. It was an Oasis in this crowded, motor gridlocked city.

The King of Thailand had given it to the British Community at the turn of the Century. It occupied several acres of prime land in the heart of the banking centre and must be worth a fortune. It was a large old colonial style building fronted by lawns, a swimming pool and tennis court.

When you passed through the gates to be saluted by uniformed Thai guards. It was as if you had stepped into an English Country manor estate. The noise and pollution of the city diminishing as you walked up the driveway to the club-house.

Mike introduced us to members of the club and we ended up joining the Saint David's Society of Bangkok [I still have the embroidered polo shirt they gave me] Everyone was jolly and seemed extremely pleased to see us. Mike had already told them of our visit to Thailand and they put on a bit of a 'do' for us with drinks and finger snacks.

We met dozens of interesting people; they worked either for the diplomatic corps, large financial institutions or large industries like Rolls Royce, ICI and BP. Some had lived here for many years others a few months on secondment. Not all the members were from the UK. There were several Irish, Australians, Canadians and even a Swede.

The Welsh were well represented. In fact a lady from Cardiff, Liz Shepherd who worked at the British Embassy, was in charge of the social calendar of the club and they had a thriving Rugby side. Brecon RFC had been there on tour the year before, on route to Hong Kong.

We were also introduced to several interested importers; one of which was the Leonowens Company. A Firm of traders founded by a relative of Anna Owens. She had been governess to the Royal Court of King Chulalongkorn (1853-

1910) made famous by the film the King and I. Born in Wales, she came to Siam as it was known then, in the late 19th century to teach English.

Because it was so difficult to travel around the city, Mike suggested the best way to meet the right people was to throw a party. With the help of our new found friends we were able to book the Foreign Correspondence Club on the top floor of the impressive Dusit Thani Hotel.

Mike had a Thai secretary, Ranuka, who translated for us and worked hard sending out invitations. The British Embassy had been kind enough to ship a dozen cases of Prince of Wales 10 year old Malt through diplomatic channels so we had samples for people to taste.

Everyone rallied around leaving Patch and myself very little to do. Even the Steward of the British Club, Dave Bell pitched in. Consequently our 'little' party was the buzz around Bangkok's business community. We even over-heard a conversation in our adopted 'local' The Crown Royale, a pub in Pat Pong frequented by many top businessmen and run by an ex Air America veteran of the Vietnam War, Izy.

On the day of the party Patch and I made our way to the Foreign Correspondence Club to be greeted by Ranuka and Mike. A large display of our whisky made a centrepiece to the cocktail bar. Posters adorned the walls, and ladies in traditional Thai costume stood ready with information leaflets about Welsh Whisky. An impressive buffet had been set and I had also ordered a free bar for our guests in addition to the Prince of Wales whisky that we would provide. The party was scheduled from 6pm to 8pm.

As we nervously awaited the arrival of our first guests, Patch and I fortified ourselves with a few beers.(Inevitable when free booze is on offer). The Press were the first to arrive which was a good sign, but would tie me up for a while giving interviews and left Patch and Mike to do the honours of greeting the growing numbers of guests. In all just over a hundred people showed up. We had expected half that number but luckily the Club was well prepared for the extra numbers.

The big coup was that a number of top military brass showed up, including a senior general. This also impressed the delegation from the British Embassy who were amazed at our guest list, considering Welsh Whisky was a relatively small company and totally unheard of in Bangkok until a week or so ago.

Even the managing director of Johnny Walker Scotch (Far East) turned up; 'tongue in cheek' we'd sent him an invite. Their Company dominated the market in the Far East and was the biggest selling imported whisky in Thailand. The Thai General saw the funny side of this and began to exude many compliments about the superior quality of Prince of Wales over 'Johnny Black'. He wanted to order some for the officer's mess. I explained that we were still awaiting an import licence and label approval. He spoke good English and had attended the British Army Staff College where Patch had been a lecturer although they hadn't met before.

With that charismatic Thai smile that epitomises its people the General assured me that such details would not be a problem. Looking over at the Director from Johnny Walker, he said "anyone who can invite the enemy to his camp with such charm and hospitality deserves a break, leave it to me Gittins Khun!"

The 'Prince of Wales' had won again. After our guests finally departed at around 9.30pm, my mind finally came around to the 'little' matter of the bill. A free bar for 3 ½ hours, fabulous canapés and six hostesses, I thought my Gold Card would go into 'melt down'.

The Club Stewart presented me with an invoice on a silver platter. I took a quick look and couldn't believe it 12,000 bhat a little over £300 pounds sterling the lot! Most people had drunk Prince of Wales but even so I could never get over how inexpensive Thailand was. Retiring to the Crown Royal to celebrate our successful launch we took in some of Bangkok's exotic nightlife. A subject that could fill several volumes all of its own? This town made Amsterdam and Hamburg look tame.

We would return to Thailand several times . But back in Wales I had new challenges to meet. Gofer (Richard Jones) who had worked for me now for nearly ten years as sales director was struggling with the home market. The visitor centre was doing well and we had a gem working for us here Karen Mellors, she was a natural with the tourists a little 'scatty' but they loved her. All in all I had a good team but the recession continued to cause cash follow problems. The big supermarket chains were slow in paying and a number of our smaller customers were closing down. We decided to factor our sales ledger, an expensive option but one that offered more flexibility than the Bank. It also afforded us debt protection in the export market but unfortunately not for the home market. In the early nineties the UK economy was something of a mess. Interest rates soared to an all time high and company failures continued to grow.

Normally one would build a solid home market before exporting but the situation was not conducive. Duty rates were totally out of step with our partners in the European Union, nearly three times higher than the EU average.

People were travelling to the Continent to buy their spirits in ever increasing numbers. They were no longer restricted to duty free allowances. Provided they bought 'down town' they could bring as much as they liked back to the UK providing it was for own consumption. Often prices were cheaper down town than in the duty free stores.

Our next push was France. We had made some in roads in Holland and Germany but France was the 'plum'. The statistics showed that France was now the third largest market in the world for whisky with the US and Japan first and second respectively. A large slice of those sales was the re-export back to the UK either legit or otherwise? I would visit Paris, Nantes, Nice, Calais, La Havre and St. Malo in pursuit of sales. Success was limited but nonetheless we had a foothold and things would grow slowly but surely.

In the spring of 1994 we went back to Thailand to take part in the South East Asia Hospitality Exhibition, and to follow up our trip of the previous autumn. We had found an agent in Bangkok who would undertake the importation and distribution of our products. Our plan was to support the agent at the exhibition then take a well-earned holiday in Thailand.

A number of my pals from Saundersfoot also decided to fly out and meet up with Patch and myself. This would turn out to be one of the best holidays I'd had in many years. We flew out at different times on different airlines but all met up and stayed at the Tantawan.

Our 'motley crew' consisted of Colonel Patch and me, 'Fast Eddy' (Eddy Price) who kept a shop in Saundersfoot. A larger than life chap weighing in at 22 stone (308 lbs.). 'The Major'. (Richard Lawrence) A renowned character around the village an 'Arthur Daley' type of likeable rouge he had just inherited some money and had never been abroad before. Finally Tony Jones a small 'dapper' chap who owned a night-club and a dozen pubs in Pembrokeshire. All of them in their early forties.

The exhibition was held at the newly built Queen Sirikit Centre. It was a showcase to the now highly sophisticated hotel and tourism industry of South East Asia. This new centre made places like Earls Court and Olympia look positively 'tacky,' the facilities were superb.

Our newly appointed agents JKL Industries had done us proud, with a large well-positioned stand 'manned' by five beautiful Thai girls neatly dressed in yellow mini shirts and tailored jackets that bore a badge proclaiming 'ask me about Welsh Whisky?'

The guys behind JKL were English with a lady Thai partner. Like most business in the Far East they were traders in all sorts of commodities, booze being just one.

The Welsh Whisky stand received much attention, something of a spin off from our previous trip, which received some good press and media coverage. I even ended up doing a video for the exhibitions promoters.

The whole show was fascinating with ice carving demonstrations where I watched huge blocks of ice being transformed into works of art. Swan's, elephants, temples and leaping fish. Bar tenders emulating the film Cocktail, mixing exotic drinks throwing them in the air with a twirl. Chefs' were creating the most sumptuous banquets representing food from all over the world, an incredible event.

Food in Thailand is taken very seriously and one could describe the country as the France of Asia. It is also an art form the presentation even in the humblest of establishments is impressive.

We all took turns on the stand including the guys from Saundersfoot. The end result was orders from Thailand, Mainland China, Singapore and Malaysia.The exhibition lasted four days, it had been hard but rewarding work, but now it was time to play. Coincidentally on the last night the British Club held their annual dinner dance at the luxurious Oriental Hotel. We were all invited to attend this grand affair and as all the guys had brought their tuxedos off we went.

It was easy to see why the Oriental keeps being voted one of the top hotels in the world; it just oozes luxury with an emphasis on service

There were about 300 people at dinner and the food was a traditional Thai banquet. Beef and Pork Sate`, Pork wrapped in noodles, Fried Spice Fish, See-Krong Moo Ob. [five spice pork], Khao Clook Gapi [Shrimp paste fried rice] and so on. All washed down with Shingha beer and long whisky and ice hi-balls.

At the end of the evening we were treated to a lift back to the hotel in a 'pink' Rolls Royce. We then all decided to go down to Pat Pong. You can imagine five merry Welshmen dressed in their best Tuxedo's walking down Bangkok's notorious red light district. The girls thought it was Christmas!

We ended up in a dubious night-club called the 'Pink Pussy' (I think!) where nubile young ladies did incredible things with Ping-Pong balls. I've never taken the humble table tennis ball for granted since.

The Major fell madly in love, he had several times already that week but apparently this was the real thing. The Colonel was far more concerned about the temperature of his beer; Fast Eddy had made a life long friend of the buxom 'Mama San', Tony had sloped off somewhere; And two totally naked young ladies confronted me with the question where was 'Walesland'? And could I possibly take them there? (Who was I to refuse!)

The following morning the guys wanted to go to Pattaya a large coastal resort set up during the Vietnam War for American Forces R and R leave.

Colonel Patch had to shoot off with Mike Jones to a military base for a few days and I needed to tie up a few loose ends with our agents. So Eddy, Tony and the Major went as advance guard with instructions to telephone me at the Tantawan to let me know where to find them.

A few days later I took a bus to Pattaya, something of a perilous journey, the bus taking the boys there earlier had overturned (luckily without injury) so I was a little apprehensive, thankfully my trip was uneventful but driving standards are somewhat haphazard and not for the faint hearted.

I was to head for a hotel called the 'Flipper Lodge' which I eventually found. No sooner had I deposited my bags in my bedroom came a knock on my door. A 'bell boy' stood at my door saying that the major had sent him, and I was to go with him. Sitting on the pillion seat of a Yamaha 50 I was duly whisked to 'Sabai Sabai Land', a top massage parlour of some repute. On entering this 'temple' to the goddess Aphrodite and red flock wallpaper I was greeted by the 'Mamma San' who led me up the stairway into a large lounge bar over looking a huge glass 'gage' where some fifty or so beautiful Thai girls sat dressed in their best frocks.

"You friend of Major" said Mamma San in broken English and a smile as wide as the Severn Bridge.

"I believe you could be correct" was my reply. A little puzzled but nonetheless impressed. She continued.

"You have nice cold beer-on the house-then you pick two girls-beautiful girls no!"

Being somewhat 'bus lagged' the thought of a relaxing massage had a great appeal. Thai massage both traditional and the more intimate body massage knew no equal. in the deal here I was to get both.

After finishing my very welcome cold beer I told 'Mamma San' it was impossible to choose they were all too beautiful. So she did the honours and selected what could only be described as two extremely stunning young ladies in their early twenties with long flowing jet-black hair and perfect olive skin.

What happened to me over the next hour or so should most definitely be on the National Health Service. Words fail me but suffice it to say 'it would never happen in Brecon' mores the pity! After my welcome to Pattaya the 'bell boy' who had waited patiently outside whisked me away in a cloud of tail pipe smoke to meet up with the 'boys'. They were 'encamped' in a local hostelry with the cheapest beer, the eternal karaoke and the best 'Thai Curry in Town.'

The following morning I woke up,thankfully,in the Flipper Lodge Hotel. Breakfast was served late by the roof top swimming pool and bar. We all seemed to arrive about the same time sporting various degrees of hangover from the night before. It was amazing what a cup of coffee, scrambled eggs, toast and 'tamarind' juice followed by a gentle swim can do.

The Major and I decided to go for a walk along the beach to clear the head even more. As we strolled along the empty beach of North Pattaya we came across a couple of beach lounge chairs under some shady palm trees. No sooner had we sprawled out on these than two young girls in their late teens appeared.

"You want beer?" They said smiling with bright white teeth, glowing faces and eyes that sparkled like the sea itself. I looked at the Major and he at me. In harmony we replied

"Yes please!"

We spent about three or four hours on the beach drinking ice cold Kloster beer from their 'cold box' while they manicured, pedicure and massaged us with coconut oil.

They even rustled up a stir-fry lunch of prawns and vegetables cooked on a small charcoal fire as the Major and I chatted away putting the world to rights looking out on to the Bay of Siam.

The world seemed pretty good, After paying our 'beach tab' of 500 baht (about £12.50) we strolled back to the hotel in the glorious sunshine and gentle breeze of North Pattaya Beach. It had been along time since I had been able to 'switch off' and relax, forgetting about work and my lost marriage. It was much the same for the Major who by the way was not a military man like Patch. He got his 'nick name' from his days playing for Tenby United Rugby Club-'the galloping major' because of the way he ran-but that's another story!

The Major had just gone through a tough divorce so the attention of a little female company was more than welcome. It's hard for guys in their middle years especially in the UK. I know the 'Women's-Lib' brigade frowns at the thought of such antics but believe me we couldn't have cared less. These girls made us feel great, we did them no harm and they in turn earned a living.

The following day the consensus of opinion was that all of us liked our food. Given that Thailand is a gourmet's paradise it was time for some serious 'lunch'. Off we went to

South Pattaya and a restaurant highly recommended by the manager of our hotel. By this time Patch had re-joined us from his military jaunt 'up jungle.'

Two Jeeps arrived to take us to an eatery built on stilts, a pier going out to sea. Here you selected your food raw like a supermarket before going into the dining area. The choice was immense ranging from fresh Siam Delta Crawfish, Tiger prawns, and fish of all shapes and sizes to beef steaks. Plus an array of every vegetable and fruit known to mankind.

The deal was to select what you wanted place it in a basket and take it over to your table, including booze, a cross between a restaurant and a supermarket. The food would be cooked at the table anyway you wanted and the drinks served as and when you required making sure they were nice and chilled at all times.

We sat overlooking the rolling waves of the Bay of Siam cooled by sweeping breezes that relieved the heat of the tropical sun. A veritable feast of gigantic Crawfish, Rock Lobster and a medley of fried fish, noodles and stir fry vegetables placed before us with great ceremony, all washed down with bottle after bottle of ice cold beer.

Life felt good chatting away with my mates, laughing and joking about old times the future and our escapades. Needing a pee I made my way to the toilet hidden behind a flimsy bamboo wall at the far end of the restaurant. Feeling relaxed and content as I emptied the beer from my bladder, I suddenly felt the presence of someone behind me. Then a pair of hands on the back of my neck and a warm clammy sensation. In quick response I swung around sending my would-be assailant flying through the frail bamboo wall into the restaurant, sprawling in a hail of dust and shattered bamboo.

Silence fell up on the previous chatter of the diners.

The boys looked-on in disbelief as I walked through the remains of the wall.

"The bugger tried to put his hands round my neck in the bogs"
I explained pointing to the heap on the floor as a small once brown face now the colour of chalk dust raised his head to say.

"Velly sorry sir"
He then lifted his hand to the air waving a small white towel as if to surrender.

"Cool towel for neck-keep refresh?"
I looked around at all the starring eyes putting my hand to my forehead.

"Well you might have said something first I'm very protective when my old 'toggers' out"
With that Fast Eddy burst out laughing, then the whole restaurant. I helped the little man to his feet still apologising for his indiscretion. The other waiters helped too, and the manager started bowing and apologising, in unison with his waiters.

Two American sailors came over to me with tears of laughter in their eyes.

"Well buddy I've seen it all, thought we had a good old slug out to join, you guys have a beer with us-looks like your having a rare old time"

Our 'lunch' lasted until 7pm before we decided it was time to move on. Before leaving we settled our 'tab' and shook the hands of each of the waiters, but my 'towel boy' was nowhere to be seen. I never did get used to the custom of someone putting a cold towel on the back of my neck and massaging my shoulders while I was taking a pee.

Three of us returned to Wales after a much earned rest and

memorable holiday full of adventures, laugher and romantic encounters. The Major had decided he liked the place so much he'd stay until the money ran out. That was to last six months before he got deported for not paying a hotel bill (or so he said?) Fast Eddy bought a bar in Hua Hin and married the daughter of a police captain who he later brought back to Wales, but it didn't last.

I visited Eddy the following year to see his bar 'Fast Eddy's' right in front of the plush Melia Hotel. Eddy's new family flocked around me like bees to the honey pot. Being separated thus 'single' I was fair game. Some people think Thailand is all about bar girls. Believe me its not, for every bargirl there's ten ordinary ladies looking for romance. Westerners are very much in demand.

At a barbecue on Cha Am Beach a very wealthy lady propositioned me. After making 'doe-eyes' at me all afternoon she asked me to follow her over to her brand new Range Rover. Opening up the boot she pointed to bails of 1,000 baht notes. She spoke very little English so I had to call over Eddy's wife 'Do Do' to translate. The up shot was, she had three million (£75,000) baht all bailed up ready for banking, the weekends take from her bars. If I married her there was more where that came from?

At the beginning of 1995 business was good especially our export sales. I turned my attention to Cyprus, a growing market for us, having shipped out regular consignments for the past four years. Our agents there were ship chandelier's, big business in the Cypriot port of Limassol. So I decided to pay them a visit to see if we could expand trade.

My son Gareth was now 12 and I decided to take him along making a little holiday of the trip. The Cypriots as most Mediterranean peoples, love children so this was no problem.

Gareth was excited about going on holiday with his dad and I got to spend some time with him.

We stayed at the Mediterranean Beach Hotel in Limassol a beautiful four star establishment with its own beach and three large swimming pools. Our agents knew the owners and they gave us a lovely suite overlooking the pools and the azure blue sea of Akrotiri Bay.

Michael our agent, was a large gent in his fifties who wore dark glasses, and looked like a larger version of Aristotle Onassis the Greek shipping magnet. He picked us up at the hotel the day after we had arrived and took Gareth and I for dinner.

We entered an old Greek taverna called 'Famagusta'; the owners like Michael had been displaced from the north of the Island during the Turkish invasion in 1974.

Sat at an enormous table in the centre of the Taverna was a group of six burly gentlemen. They were ships captains from the near by docks and did much business with Michael's Chandlery. Introducing Gareth and I with great gusto like long lost brothers the introduction then extended to the owner of the taverna and his entire family. The captains all had gifts for Gareth, watches, transistor radio and two-toy remote controlled speed boats. I thought he might be a little over awed by it all but took it in his stride showing great appreciation, particularly for the little boats.

Gareth sat with Michael and two captains from Athens while I sat with the others. After several glasses of Ouzo the banquet got underway, a Greek Mase` both fish and meat. There were so many dishes and they just kept coming it was like feeding the 'forty thousand' I don't think I've ever seen so much food on one table. There was wine and beer in abundance and lemonade for Gareth although he did sip a glass or two of white wine.

The great joy about mixing business with pleasure is you get to do and see things which, as a regular tourist you wouldn't. The idea of making a 'bee-line' to the industrial dock area of Limassol in search of a great meal would not be high on the agenda of your regular tourist. But in fact this was the best Greek Restaurant and food I have ever experienced.

We arrived back at the hotel around 1am Gareth was a little sleepy but had done really well. His politeness and appetite had impressed our hosts, Gareth liked his food and enjoyed trying different cuisine.

The following day we spent at ease around the pool soaking up the glorious sunshine. The hotel was not full being out of season. Most of the guests came from Russia, huge people dripping in gordy gold rings and bracelets, and that was just by the poolside sunbathing!

When the pool cleared as the sun went down that evening Gareth and I decided to play with his remote controlled speedboats. They were not sophisticated but your regular 'made in Taiwan' plastic toys. They raced across the large pool then by turning the control would speed back across. We played racing for ages closely observed by two giant men who we had seen that morning sun bathing with their families. These guys had Mafia stamped all over them, their mannerisms, gold bracelets and loud clothes, and just the way they looked.

Eventually they walked over to us puffing large cigars and holding pint bottles of Keo beer. In a deep accented voice, the larger one (if that was possible) called out to me.

"My friend! You English?"

"No we're Welsh!"

This confused him but he was smiling and with a grunt they both sat down beside us.

"You?...."

"I'm Dafydd and this is my son Gareth"

"Ah! I George and this Surgay"

"pleased to meet you" I replied shaking their hands.

"You have much fun with boats no?"

"Yeah, Gareth's boat mad"

"Could Surgay and I have a play too?"

Now these were guys whose job descriptions probably included extortion, international arms smuggling and god knows what but obviously paid very well were totally fascinated by two toy boats. I guess the kid remains in all of us.

I passed my control to George and he began to race with Gareth. His face was a picture like a ten year old getting his first bicycle at Christmas. Surgay was looking a little sheepish so Gareth handed him his control unit.

These two huge guys sat at the side of the pool dressed in Bermuda shorts and Hawaiian shirts, heavy gold jewellery puffing foot long cigars; playing race with toy boats.

They were so excited chattering away in Russian as the boats sped across the pool and back again. George's boat got back first and he was ecstatic waving his arms in the air as if he'd won the Olympics.

"Bravo! Bravo!" cried Surgay (obviously George was the boss?)

"Da! Da!" retorted George. Then turned to me and said.

"Where you buy boat-much fun Da!"

"It was a gift from a business friend to Gareth"

"I give you five hundred dollars-each boat?"

"Look I'd love to but they were gifts, you don't sell gifts-tell you what I'll do Gareth and I are going for diner there's a great taverna across the road. You play with the boats"

"And family?" he interrupted.

"Yah sure and the family. Anyway tomorrow I need to go down town I'll ask my friend where he bought the boats buy you some then you pay me back-deal"

"Da! Da! I bring boat to your room I know where you live"
(Pointing his cigar to my balcony)-there!" putting his hand in his pocket he gave me a crumpled up bank note"

"No! Hey man there's no need"

"Da! Da! You and.... err...Gareth-dinner on me-so much fun!"
I put the note in my pocket with out looking and Gareth and I left for dinner.

"What was all that about dad?" Gareth enquired "What about my boats?"

"Don't worry he'll bring them back in the morning. Anyway its good to share and its time to eat!"
At the Taverna I retrieved the scrumbled up note from my pocket. It turned out to be two notes each fifty Cypriot pounds worth 140 pounds sterling.

"You can have anything on the menu Gaz - George is paying!" Raising my glass to invite a toast our glasses clinked it was now time to order.

We got back to our room around 11.30pm I went straight to the balcony – lo and behold George and Surgay were still at it now accompanied by all their family and friends. Much merriment was ensuing and the betting was furious. I later found out they had sent out for no less than three sets of replacement batteries to keep going-such were the stakes!

Sure enough George returned the boats the following morning. True to my word I found out where I could buy some replacements that turned out to be a little toy store in the old part of town. They had three sets left I bought the lot for £30 sterling. George was over the moon and it turned out to be the cheapest holiday I have ever had?

# 15

# The Take Over

Our trip to Cyprus had been a success both for Gareth and the business. The ship's captains had placed orders with Michael for many thousands of pounds for Welsh Whisky. However, the home market continued to slide until one week no less than three large customers went bust owing us a lot of money. Ominously the largest loss was an Edinburgh based wholesaler.

Things went from bad to worse very quickly. Cash flow became tight. Had the defaulting customers been from overseas we would have been covered by export insurance. Not only did we lose the cost of the goods but also the vast duty paid to Customs.

Thankfully I was with the Bank of Wales, the high street Banks were panicking like mad. They were foreclosing on businesses left right and centre, in my opinion they undoubtedly fuelled the recession. Our Bank certainly wasn't in the mood to extend credit limits, but at least didn't pull the plug at the drop of a hat like the big boys. So we had time to go the WDA (Welsh Development Agency) hopefully they might have a solution?

I was quite friendly with the Deputy Chairman Dr. Roy Bichan, telling him of our plight he suggested having a word with the Chairman David Roe-Beddow. He had contacts in the Far East who wanted to invest in Wales. Within a week or so he had put us in touch with a Taiwanese Company called the Nice Group. The introduction would led to Patch and I flying out to Taiwan to see them.

Negotiations got under way with the object of gaining both investment through share purchase and sales through an exclusive distribution deal. The Nice Group was a large food manufacturer and distributor through out the Far East. They were hard negotiators but wanted a foot hold in the ever-growing international whisky market.

Talks went well, with a great deal of much welcome input from the WDA and David Roe-Beddow himself. The Bank held back any pre-emptive action it may have been planning, giving me time to manoeuvre.

Arriving back from Taiwan we thought we had brokered a deal whereby the Nice Group took a 35% stake in Welsh Whisky and an exclusive distribution contract to sell our products through out the Far East. The Taiwanese came to Wales to sign the deal together with their London Lawyers, Allen and Avery. After showing them around our premises and visitor centre, things changed.

During their visit we gave them a presentation of our new experimental still which was now fully operational. We had produced several batches of whisky, proving not only did it work but was highly efficient. Nice Groups Chairman took great interest in the technology behind the still. The following day we all met up at the WDA's offices in Cardiff to put the final touches to the deal.

The mood had changed. The negotiating became intense, new parameters were put forward. The 35% stake was now not enough and they wanted three directors on our board, and we had offered only one.  After several hours we were going nowhere. Adjourning the meeting they left for London, requesting a telephone conference from the offices of their London lawyers the following morning.

Gill and I met with our lawyer Felix Macintosh of Hugh James, Jones and Jenkins a large firm of solicitors in Cardiff. The three of us sat glumly around a conference phone listening to the ever-increasing demands of the Taiwanese. It soon emerged they wanted total control but would offer very little. When they made their final condition that I guarantee the trademark 'Prince of Wales' be registered in Mainland China under their Company name! Gill looked at me and I looked at Felix then said:

"Thank you for your time but if we don't revert back to the original deal agreed in Taiwan we might as well stop now."

That was the end of that, Gill and I left with mixed feelings of disappointment and a determination to fight to keep the Company going.

A few days later I had a phone call from a chap called Derrick Wilshee, someone I'd met some years ago when he worked for Ansells Brewery. He had moved on to The Coca-Cola Company as a bottling and commissioning engineer. Recently he'd been involved with a company based in Essex who exported cars to Thailand. They wanted to diversify and he had heard through the 'grape vine' that I was looking for investment.

Derrick, a large jovial midlander in his mid-thirties, and his colleagues from 'MDT International Plc' paid me a visit to discuss possibilities. They were typical East Londoners, 'suited and booted' with heavy cockney accents. Paul was a good looking tall dark hared guy in his late twenties, his partner Roger a short man with a limp, horn rim spectacle and dyed black hair. Both seemed genuine enough proposing a contract bottling deal.

Paul had some good idea's for new Vodka and was keen to get started. We talked about the Nice Group deal that had fallen through and they indicated that they might wish to invest.

Around this time Richard Jones (Gofer), my sales director, came to me with another totally unrelated proposition. A friend of his in Tenby owned a nightclub called Chequers. He had lost his drinks licence and was looking for someone to take over the club.

Gofer wanted to take the club on. He had worked for me for ten years. He needed a change and apparently the club was a 'gold mine' it would be a good opportunity to run his 'own' business. He could also promote our products there too and continue working for Welsh Whisky on a part time basis. On the face of it seemed OK and with falling sales on the home front maybe this could be a worthwhile diversification.

I met with his friend Robert Davies and his sister Hettie who had been in partnership at Chequers. I knew little or nothing about the club although I owned a cottage in near by Saundersfoot. It did have a reputation of being a busy club and more 'main stream' than the other clubs in the area. They were offering a relatively low rent and staged lease premium that gave us a six-year lease providing we moved quickly and re-applied for a new liquor licence.

Gofer engaged a local firm of solicitors in Tenby to apply for a new licence. After some correspondence the solicitors informed us that it would be highly unlikely that we would ever get the place re-licensed. There was strong police objection particularly from the Licensing Officer Tony Davies. We tried to contact Tony Davies who eventually sent us a letter refusing to discuss the matter with us. Not accepting this I contacted a senior officer at Tenby Police Station, who agreed to a meeting.

Sitting in a small office on the top floor of Tenby police station in April '95, Gofer and I chatted away cordially with an Inspector. Then in walked PC Tony Davies. I recognised him at once from an encounter a few years previously at Brecon Jazz Festival. He had been seconded to advise on licensing issues during the festival, but instead went round laying down the law with a heavy hand upsetting all and sundry. To the extent where, as Chairman of the CBI in mid-Wales, I was asked by many business people in the town to write a letter of complaint. In fact I had witnessed his arrogant style of policing first hand and wrote to the chief constable complaining of such.

Nothing of this issue was mentioned at the meeting that, by now was monopolised by PC Davies who deliberated in great detail about how bad the previous licensees had been. He and Gofer seemed to be getting on quite well especially when Gofer explained that he was going out with a WPC in Brecon and they were to be engaged. At this juncture I said,

"Well, I'll leave you to discuss this with Gofer, he's going to be running the club if we get the licence, I'll see you later." And with that I left and met up with Gofer an hour later in a nearby Pub.

A month later we were granted the licence when it was suggested that if I became a co-licensee, there would be no police objection. Gofer opened the Club at the end of May and

I continued my negotiations at Welsh Whisky with MDT International.

The home market continued to be a major problem and the recession had spread to the Far East. The Thai economy was nearing collapse; Japan too looked very shaky I had no option but to broker a deal with MDT.

In August '95 we signed a distribution contract whereby they would guarantee a certain level of sales, leaving us to concentrate on production and the profitable visitor centre. Furthermore they invested a capital sum for an equity stake. This eased pressure from our bankers to reduce borrowings.

It looked as if I had solved our problems. At the beginning we worked fairly well together, although Gill had grave reservations. Our Club Chequers was being run as a partnership completely separate from Welsh Whisky and was doing well.

The Honeymoon with MDT was to be short lived. Within a few months sales dropped even further and they defaulted on minimum quotas. Their own 'core' markets, the sale of Volvo cars to Thailand and Taiwan, had nose-dived along with their cash flow.

What ensued for the next six months was a classic boardroom clash. Although Gill and I still held the majority shareholding MDT held the purse strings. They had also won the backing of the DBRW (Development Board for Rural Wales) to the extent that a development grant, which was due to be paid to Welsh Whisky, went straight to MDT.

This happen during my last export sales trip to Canada, one of my most successful, getting extended listings for Prince of Wales, Swn y Mor and Merlyn in British Columbia, Alberta, Manitoba and Ontario Liquor Boards. (Canada operates a State Alcohol monopoly.)

Another incident occurred during by visit to Canada, which would haunt me for years to come. On the 15th February 1996 the Sea Empress ran aground near Milford Haven, Pembrokeshire.

Staying at the grand Vancouver Hotel, in Vancouver City I over heard the news broadcast on the local TV station. The plight of that fated giant oil tanker was followed intensively by the world media. Every time I switched on the TV during the ten days I was there, the events of the disaster were headline news. Over 72,000 tonnes of crude were spewed onto the magnificent coastline of the Pembrokeshire National Park.

At the time no one knew how badly this event would effect the tourist-dominated economy of West Wales. No one foresaw the scandals that would surround the whole pollution affair, nor the monumental struggle for compensation that would ensue for many years to come.

By the spring of 1996 Gill and I had agreed to sell out. We would still hold a stake in the Company and be retained on a generous consultation contract for two years, plus a six-figure lump sum paid over three years.

Quite frankly I was worn out by all the financial juggling and was looking forward to doing something else after 21 years of Welsh Whisky-perhaps I would write a book? My thoughts were obviously mixed but philosophically I thought it was time for someone else to have a go. How wrong could I be?

Gill stayed on and worked a few days a week to assist a smooth change over. I on the other hand, hardly ever went near the plant after signing the contract of sale in July 1996. There was continual conflict between myself and the new directors from MDT. They had completely opposite views to me and wanted to take the Company into the main stream market. I on the other hand thought it should retain its unique and very Welsh identity, growing within a niche market that had little or no direct competition.

No sooner had I left Welsh Whisky than Gofer decided he'd had enough of running the Club and left to join Yates Brothers, the wine lodge and wholesaling group. Having backed him financially over the Club business I had to take over and protect the investment. Having foolishly signed a personal guarantee during all the pressure and distraction the previous year, I moved, on a more permanent basis, to my 'holiday' cottage in Saundersfoot. I maintained my links with Brecon, but I set about running the Club. I had run pubs in the past and of course been involved in the liquor industry for many years but running this nightclub would prove my eventual down fall!

# 16

# The Sea Empress Legacy

Taking over Chequers in the summer of '96 was a fairly uneventful affair. Gill and I had in fact been running the administrative side of the business since first taking it on the year before and had visited on a regular basis. There were two main problems to deal with, both inter linked. One the effects of the Sea Empress disaster, and the other an application Gofer had made, encouraged by the land lord, to extend the hours of the club to 4am in line with other night clubs in the larger cities of Swansea and Cardiff in the hope this would off set the down turn in business due to the falling numbers of tourists to the area caused by the oil spill. One might have thought that our application to extend hours might fall on sympathetic ears considering the damage caused to business in the area by the oil pollution affair. However, local government policy was to play down the whole sordid mess.

The first oil spill meeting I attended was organised by the Tenby and District Licensed Victuallers Association (LVA). We were told that the insurers of the tanker owner, together with the International Oil Pollution Compensation Fund

(IOPCF) had deposited one hundred million US dollars to meet immediate compensation claims.

Everyone was advised to fill in notice of claim forms and to monitor very carefully any down turn in business. The impression given by those who addressed the meeting and more so subsequently from other concerned organisations was that the IOPCF would deal with the claim swiftly and efficiently. The reality was to be very different!

From the very start when that huge ship ran aground on the rocks at St. Anne's Head Milford Haven, for reasons still unknown, a conspiracy of 'cover up' unfolded. On that blustery morning of Thursday the 15th February 1996, Texaco had informed the Port Authority that a berth was available and the ship should be allowed to dock. A pilot was despatched alongside the supertanker, one hour and 20 minutes before one of the lowest tides of the year the ship steamed towards the port. Suddenly, without warning the tanker grounded at the entrance to the Haven and began to leak oil. For the next seven days tugs and rescue workers battled to dislodge the stricken vessel. In vain they tried to contain the rapidly spreading slick of toxic crude. Violent gales lashed, tides ebbed and flowed but the ship stayed fast at the entrance to the Haven. It had been thought she was stuck fast to the rocks but this was not the case. At each high tide between the 15th and 18th February she could have been brought safely into port, or taken out to sea, saving any further damage.

What happened was a disaster of indecision; the ship took further damage as she rested on the jagged rocks at each low tide. In a famous radio exchange between the harbourmaster and the pilot who reported that the ship's engines were working and she could be brought into port. The harbourmasters reply was,

"I'd say bring her in, but I've got a roomful of people telling me not to"

No one has ever found out who these people were. Speculation has been rife but the question remains unanswered

By Sunday evening, as the weather worsened, the Sea Empress had been held fast for three days at St. Anne's Head. Only 2,000 tonnes of crude had been lost at this stage. By the following Thursday, after seven full days of blundering, she limped into port under her own power. By this time more than 72,000 tonnes of toxic crude had been lost. The spill was to damage 175 miles of fragile coastline, 35 sites of Special Scientific Interest, 20 National Trust properties, a marine nature reserve, thousands of business's and untold wildlife.

When I'd returned from Canada at the end of February I took a trip to my cottage. The smell was the first thing that hit you as you neared the coast, like a fuel station. Clean up operations were well in hand, thousands of people worked night and day to rescue sea birds, clean beaches, rocks and coves. Attempts were made to recover some of the oil, in total just 3,000 tonnes were recovered, of the later officially admitted 73,450 tonnes lost. The Local Authority tried playing things down to counter the daily media coverage that continually showed the truth of the matter, depicted in a TV scene of Tenby Harbour awash with crude oil, washing in and out on the tide. The Wales Tourist Board coughed up some extra money to market the area but where was compensation money? Shouldn't some of that been made available for this?

The Milford Haven Port Authority was fined four million-pounds by the environment agency. This money would come straight out of the local economy, the port being a major employer in an employment black spot. Yet the compensation money from the IOPCF would be very slow in coming. The Pembrokeshire County Council would be one beneficiary but only for the work they had carried out. Some hoteliers, fishermen and a handful of others received some form of compensation, but the payments could not be described as generous, and probably little more than the interest that the fund would have accrued. Certainly nothing like the funds extracted by the US government from the Exxon Corporation over the smaller Valdez spill.

An inquiry was called for by the Shipping Minister Lord Goschen, who was described by biologist Tim Deere-Jones as; "A complete Pratt" and dubbed him,

"Groschen who doesn't have a notion about the ocean, even hardened oil industry professionals were laughing at him."

The Minister had even spurned an offer of help from a Norwegian vessel. He stamped on any attempts to have the area declared an EC disaster area because it would have been bad for the Government's reputation. It would also have forced the Government to recognise the extent of the disaster and their failings to provide proper tug facilities in the Western Approaches. The tug that was supposed to have covered the Pembrokeshire coastal area was off the Portuguese coast on legitimate business. However, there was a Chinese tug in the area, one of the most powerful in the world. Apparently none of its crewmembers spoke English so a desperate call was made to a local Chinese restaurateur to translate!

The enquiry by the Marine Accident Investigation Branch of the Department of Transport involved civil servants investigating their own colleagues. The local MP, Nick Ainger (Labour), commented

"It's wrong to ask a civil servant working in the same department to actually investigate the political actions of a minister. Because of this, the report is likely to be little more than a 'whitewash."

Our club was just 400 metres from the coast, a small inlet called 'Franks cove.' Caravan parks surround the whole area and campsites normally busy with tourists from Easter onwards were conspicuously empty in spring and summer of 1996.

Our application for extended hours met with unbelievable hostility. P.C. Davies immediately leapt in with an objection. The licensing officer for the County Council initiated a petition of objection; something I learnt several years later from the now ex-manager of our rival club the Night Owl. I had originally thought it had been initiated by the residents of the nearby Village of Penally. From the day we made our application for extended hours in an effort to off set the effects on business caused by the oil spill, we came under siege from the local authorities.

The first hearing was to be a farce. I represented myself before the assembled members of the licensing sub-committee of the Council, made up of some ten or twelve persons, all seated on an elevated podium.

Also present were PC Davies, two other police officers one of which was a Chief Inspector, two fire officers, three environmental health officers, several other officials including the Council's own licensing officer, members from the Penally Community Council, two 'concerned elderly residents' and of course members of the local press. The large Council chamber was almost full for this 'impartial' and specially convened hearing. A huge bundle of papers was placed before me, papers that should have been made available weeks before. A volume the size of War and Peace, deposited on my table as I sat alone in this hostile chamber gazing around at eyes that refused contact with mine.

As the proceeding got underway, with little acknowledgement of my presence, I got to my feet and interrupted.

"Mr. Chairman may I be permitted to comment?"

The sub-committee's Chairman a tall thin man in his seventies peered at me from behind his bifocals.

"What appears to be the problem Mr. Gittins" he grunted in reply.

"Well Sir, this weighty document placed before me"

"What about it Mr. Gittins?"

"Well Sir, this is the first time I have ever seen it. Surely I should have been privy to its contents prior to the hearing?"

As the Chairman looked over to the Council's Licensing Officer a silence fell on the Chamber.

"Is this correct Mrs Rees?"

She was flustered; Mrs Rees, was a greying woman who looked older than her years, her husband was a police constable, deputy to the erstwhile PC Davies, and sat at the back of the chamber listening intently.

"No Sir, it was definitely sent out to Mr.Gittins"

"And when was that Mrs Rees?" The Chairman retorted in a now weary voice.

She fumbles through her papers looking even more flustered, and then came upon what ever it was she was looking for as if she didn't already know the answer!

"Um...Yesterday Sir"

The Chairman wiped his brow, knowing full well that this charade has all been a waste of time. I rose to my feet again clutching the weighty tome of papers. For the first time the Chairman looked me in the eye, at least for a second.

"Yes Mr. Gittins?"

"If Mrs Rees posted this yesterday then it will I'm sure be delivered to the Club sometime later today.... It's 10.30am now and we receive our post in Penally between 11am and Noon...presuming she posted it first class! Hardly satisfactory considering this is September and my application was made in June. I therefore request an adjournment."

After some discussion among the members of the committee he reluctantly agreed to an adjournment and I immediately walked out, leaving PC Davies and his assembled cronies to squabble amongst themselves as to whose fault this waste of time and money was. The document did arrive at the Club but the following day, and set a pattern of what would ensue for the next three to four years.

It would be several weeks before I presented my case to the licensing sub-committee. The weighty volume of documents prepared by the council took a lot of reading and a lot of believing. Between the time of these two hearings a loss adjuster from the IOPCF paid us a visit. He went through the motions with a smirk on his face but it would be almost a year before I would hear from him again. P.C. Davies ran up a vast list of complaints, including a lot of 'hearsay' incidents that had happened 'on route' to the Club. These were mainly during the time the land lords Robert Davies and Hettie Jones ran the club and, of course, mostly unknown to any one, including the management. The Environmental Health people complained about excessive noise. Bearing in mind the club is half a mile from the nearest residential house, and that the elderly residents complaining lived two miles away and spoke of the Club being a 'bad place where youngsters went to drink and make trouble.' This was not something I viewed as a serious matter

I made an impassioned plea that the Club had been there since the Sixties and that the extended hours requested were to combat failing business due the oil spill. Further to this even the Association of Assistant Chief Constables had recommended that extended hours helped control public nuisance, people leaving premises on a more staged basis, instead of all piling out at the same time.

It all fell on deaf ears, PC Davies wanted our hours cut from 2am to 1am. The Sub-Committee agreed; this left me with 21 days to appeal to the local Magistrates. Although I knew this would be a waste of time and we would eventually end up appealing to the Crown Court.

# 17

# The Snowball Effect

Gofer was still the co-licensee so we both attended the Magistrates Court in February '97, this time we had a solicitor. He found a technically that would allow the Magistrates to throw out the Council's decision. They refused to do this siding with the Council and the Police. We informed them we would appeal to a higher court, this allowed us to stay open until 2am until it was heard. In the mean time the council slapped a Noise Abatement Notice on us, but with a compromise that they would monitor noise levels and to inform us if the new insulation work we had carried out was effective.

From here on the authorities declared open war on the Club. Squad cars would sit in our car park all night, a road block was set up one Friday night in March '97, and cars going in and out of Tenby were stopped and searched. Council and Police Officers would inspect the club at midnight. Disrupting our disco nights, they would count plasters in our first aid kit to see if we had the correct amount, inspect outside lighting, our video equipment, toilets, signs, anything.

About this time we entered into an agreement with

'UpforIt' promotions, Danny Slade and Andrew Price, to run high profile events at the club, and I took on Gareth Barrett to manage it. The 'Upforit' nights proved extremely popular, the Club grew busier or as they say in the business 'the Club was banging', but unknown to us the Police had started operation 'Snowball' We knew nothing about these undercover operations until much later!

PC Davies, who had now earned the nickname 'Chimp', continued his visits and we became aware of increased police activity in the area. We received no warnings, cautions or directions from anyone during this period, and we certainly didn't expect the unprecedented actions they were secretly planning.

The business was moving back into profit. It was being featured in music magazines like 'Mix Mag', 'Time Out' etc., and top DJ's played 'Chequers' for the first time. Clubbers came from near and far, teenage holidaymakers were impressed by the wicked sounds, the rainbow of laser lights and the swirling smoke. The sounds and atmosphere equalled anything on offer in the big cities. Mid-week we experimented with live bands, cheap drinks and even line dancing.

In between the petty harassment from the authorities, I quite enjoyed the whole scene, although I did tend to spend most of my time in the more sedate 'Bogey's bar. Despite everything it was a happy club employing a lot of people and providing enjoyment and entertainment to even more.

At the end of a busy night some of the staff, my self and Barrett would enjoy a relaxing drink together with the inevitable 'groupie', one perk of owning a nightclub was the endless supply of women, young and not so young. It never ceased to amaze me what these girls wore to a club, as little as possible seemed the order of the day. The most outrageous were the young single 'mums' who had finally found a baby sitter for the night or their parents had the kids for the weekend. They were out for fun, with a capital 'F'! Men were mere 'babes in arms' when it came to raunchy and uninhibited sex. To these girls the Club was a fantasy, an escape from the life they led at home.

Barrett and I became good friends with many of these girls, they would confide in us, seek advice and reveal their woes and frustrations of life on the dole struggling to bring up a young child. Pembrokeshire has its fair share of divergence between rich and poor, especially in towns like Milford Haven and Pembroke Dock. Hard to believe in such a picturesque county. Some had found themselves pregnant after a quick shag behind the bike sheds at school, or a drunken affair with a casual boy friend. With others it was a meaningful relationship that ended abruptly. All this could be forgotten if only for a few hours as they stepped into the flashing lights of Chequers and a fantasia world of sound, colour and who knows, maybe romance?

Occasionally the owners of a local Indian restaurant would join us bringing along a huge take-away curry, as would one or two Tenby pub owners. These little social gatherings in Bogey's bar went on until dawn, serenaded by one of the best jukeboxes in Wales, pumping out the new sound of 'Cool Cymru' such as the Manic Street Preaches and Stereophonics!

One evening in late May, Barrett over heard Police Officers talking in a Tenby pub, this was our first indication that the police were stepping up their activities. It was something about a drug operation conducted at Chequers! He rang me the following morning informing me he'd requested a meeting with the Police but no one wanted to talk to him. He persevered and a month later two officers called to the Club to discuss it with him, he later rang me at my home in Brecon. Apparently there had been an undercover operation at the club at the beginning of May and certain drugs had been purchased. They told him to tighten up his act but offered no assistance and little or no advice. This surprised me as several weeks earlier I had written to PC Davies requesting the setting up of a training scheme for staff, teaching them what to look out for as far as drugs were concerned. I had been a founder director of the Training and Enterprise Council in Powys during my term as Chairman of the Mid-Wales CBI. I offered my services to help set up such a scheme and to arrange funding. I received no reply.

We were both shocked by the revelations of the two officers who had spoken to Barrett. Neither of us suspected drugs dealing at the Club, we were not naive but had never seen it going on. We had briefed the door staff on many occasions to be on the look out. We even employed a firm of security guards recommended by PC Davies on one of his regular visits. This firm had been approved by the council and had completed the compulsory training courses to qualify as registered doormen. The head doorman, Colwyn Howells had continuously told us "there is no drug problem at Chequers".

Considering the police presence around the Club any drug dealer would be foolish to say the least even to attempt it. It was far more likely that clubers would buy and consume their 'E's' or smoke their 'pot' before coming to the Club. Everybody knows that the drug culture is wide spread, its not restricted to nightclubs.

On July 12th 1997 the Police and Council mounted yet another raid just after Mid-Night. 30-40 Officers and

Officials including Mrs Rees and her husband PC Rees poured into the Club. I was informed they had monitored noise levels that exceeded those set by the Noise Abatement Notice. A sign in the lobby was not of the correct size lettering, and the toilets were dirty. They seemed totally unconcerned when I pointed out that the council had agreed to monitor sound levels months ago and to inform me of any adjustments needed. They completely disrupted the evening and I was forced to close at 1.15am. The whole affair was beginning to wear me down.

Unfortunately Barrett had not been there that night; his mother had been taken ill but he too was getting fed up with all this harassment. We decided to run the Club until the end of the summer season then sell up. Barrett was firmly of the same opinion as me; we had walked in to a minefield. We were embroiled in a civil conspiracy to close the Club at any cost. Not only this but we faced a continued barrage from the owner of the nearby caravan park. He had a long-standing dispute with Robert Davies, which made matters even worse. This was something Gofer had played down when he left me holding the baby. A letter arrived at the end of July informing me that our appeal for extended hours was to be heard at Swansea Crown Court at the end of August, some five months after the Magistrates refusal.

Deciding I needed a holiday I took my son Gareth to Paris for a week of culture, relaxation and Disneyland. The City was packed but thanks to British Airways and my 'Airmiles' account they found us an apartment hotel near the rue de Republique. His holiness the Pope was in town to give mass; pilgrims from all over the world had descended on the French Capital to rejoice. The glamorous Princess Diana and her illustrious lover Dodi Al'Fayed were here, Paris was obviously the place to be and even the weather was positively glorious.

Our hotel was full of priests from Chicago and Boston who were having a 'ball'. The hotel had a large open courtyard with tables and chairs around a fountain where you could picnic alfresco. We often shared a bottle of chilled Rose` wine with the reverend fathers before Gareth and I ventured out to find one of Paris' many excellent little restaurants. We made the most of this rest by visiting everything from the Picaso museum to Disneyland. We found a great jazz club near Notre Dam and watched the most amazing 'Hip-Op' dancing I'd ever seen, but it was soon time to return home and my continuing battle with Pembrokeshire County Council and PC 'Chimp'.

Returning on Sunday night to Brecon we learnt of the terrible car crash that had killed Princess Diana and Dodi Al'Fayed. We had travelled through the same tunnel under the River Seine that very afternoon. Two beautiful people cut down in their prime seeking only happiness. I guess we will never know what really happened but I for one remain to be convinced that this had been an accident.

While I had been away the police had charged Barrett with perverting the cause of justice! A girl we knew from Saundersfoot had been charged with possession of amphetamine and had been banned from all licensed premises as part of her bail conditions. Barrett, blissfully unaware of this, rang her and asked if she could wash a pile of bar towels for him. He had a big night in the club later and couldn't get to the laundromat, she had obliged. The same day the landlords had decided to call in the bailiffs over a rent dispute, Barrett eventually sorted this out with the help of Gill. Needless to say he had his hands full that day.

The following day police offices arrived to question him

about the Girl; they had information she had visited the Club. Barrett explained but couldn't be absolutely certain about the time she left the Club after dropping off the washed bar towels. He said 6 to 6.30pm, apparently she had left at 7.05pm and she was under a curfew of 7pm as well as the licensed premises ban. As incredible as it seems they actually charged him, this ridiculous charge was later to be dropped when Barrett refused to take a caution instead of going to Court. The Crown Court hearing we were to attend that week over the extended hours turned into a nightmare. My solicitor had left the firm unexpectedly and the barrister was not fully briefed. However, he informed me the council and police were out for blood, having spoken to their barrister. They were going to call up wards of thirty witnesses, the trial could go on for weeks and the cost would be astronomical. Even if we won the authority would appeal costing even more. My solicitor should have informed me of this eventuality. Although our barrister was perfectly willing to carry on, could I stand the costs, win or loose?

I talked it over with Gofer who had been summoned to attend as joint licensee. He told me that in a conversation with PC Davies in the waiting room he had been told that Barrett had previously been done for possession of Cannabis and they were going to bring this up. This of course was a lie, but at the time I did not know and it frightened the life out of me. I didn't know what to believe anymore. "Bloody hell what next?" Ran through my mine over and over again.

Capitulation was my only option and I withdrew the appeal, which meant the hours of the Club would now be decreased to 1am! They had got what they wanted surely things couldn't get any worse? After leaving Court I rang Barrett to tell him the news, he was 'gutted' and swore blind he had never been charged with possession of cannabis. I told Barrett to prepare for next Friday as normal it's the end of the summer season 'Upforit' have a major DJ booked so we're committed. I'll be down as early as I can then Saturday we'll all discuss the future of the Club.

# 18

# The Nightmare Begins

I awoke as the light of day flickered through the small dusty cell window. The plastic cup that once held coffee was still in my grasp.

"Where was I? Surely last night was all a dream!" Were the thoughts that slowly pierced my hazy mind. There was a jangle of keys as my cell door opened and in walked a policewoman carrying a steaming cup of coffee.

"Good morning Mr.Gittins, did we sleep well?" I hardly noticed what she looked like as she handed me another plastic cup. I looked at my watch, it was 7.30am.

"PC Davies and DC Davies will be along to interview you later-would you like some breakfast?" She continued in a monotonous voice.

"No thanks, when is my solicitor coming and can I ring my wife?" I replied in one breath.

"I'll ask the duty sergeant, sure you don't want some breakfast?" I shook my head and sipped the tasteless coffee as she turned and walked out, locking the cell door behind her.

It was 3pm before officers Davies and Davies turned up

to interview me. One reason we have 'nick' names in Wales is to identify people. While I was waiting for them to turn up, the duty Sergeant let me watch Princess Diana's funeral on T.V. I said a little prayer for her and Dodi and pondered my own fate.

My solicitor, Paul Cowper, turned up a few minutes before the officers and we had a brief chat in the corridor before going into the interview room. PC Chimp and DC Davies interviewed me for two hours. Apparently they had found a 'haul' of drugs discarded on the floor of the Club. They presented me with this 'haul'. It consisted of six or seven small empty clear plastic bags. Similar to those you buy dart flights or lighter flints in. Holding one of these bags to the light DC Davies said.

"See! Traces of white powder!"

I strained my eyes to see these offending specs of powder that looked like particles of dust.

"And here we have a 'E" he said, holding out an exhibit bag containing a small white tablet cut in half.

"And here we have Cannabis leaf found on one of your bar staff!"

Pointing to another exhibit bag that held a pouch of Golden Virginia rolling tobacco.

'This!" PC Chimp interrupted and DC Davies held up in yet another exhibit bag.

"Is a piece of Cannabis resin found in Mr. Barrett's flat."

The piece of resin was a small brown ball half the size of a marble.

"Of course they will have to be analysed, but its obvious what they are." Said DC Davies as he stowed away the exhibits.

"I'll have to take your word for it, I wouldn't know what a drug looked like if it jumped up and bit me. All I can say is I'm shocked and flabbergasted, I can't believe you found them at Chequers, I can't believe you found those on the floor. No way."

My reply seemed to up set them and they insisted that they were serious and that this was a serious matter. DC Davies then proceeded to ask a lot of questions about Andrew Price and the 'Up for it' promotions before PC Chimp chirped in saying.

" I told you not to take on that Club, it attracts drug dealers like bees to a honey pot!"

They also talked about an undercover operation carried out at the beginning of May, when officers bought several 'E' tablets and amphetamines at Chequers. The interview concluded just after 5pm, leaving me more confused than before. Surely all this could not be over the litter they had shown me in the interview, there had to be more to this!

The Chimp quickly disappeared leaving me to talk to DC Davies who informed me they would release me after they had interviewed Barrett and Torkington. With that I was returned to my 'cage.' For the rest of the day I remained in my cell, pacing up and down. Gill had been allowed to see me briefly and had dropped off a couple of packs of cigarettes that I smoked continuously. Although I'd been told what they were holding me for I had not been formally charged. The duty sergeant periodically let me out of the cell for a chat and a cup of coffee, he told me they had until 11pm to charge me or he would release me. In any event he couldn't see why they would want to detain me any further, I'd given a statement that should be enough.

I looked at my watch for the hundredth time. The

deadline was just minutes away, and in rushed a breathless Chimp and DC Davies to charge me formally with "Knowingly Allow" and they wanted me detained until Monday morning to be brought before Haverfordwest Magistrates Court. That second night would be even worse than the first. At midnight two drunken Irish Gypsies were brought in shouting and bawling. They were locked up in two separate cells adjacent to mine and kept up a barrage of abusive language all night. They had refused to give their names and address' so all night long an officer would come back and forth to shout.

"Paddy you ready to tell me your name?"

To which the two Irishmen replied in harmony.

"Fuck off you pig!"

Sunday morning, much to my relief I was to be moved to Pembroke Dock to join Barrett and Torkington. The two officers' that came to transport me prepared the handcuff's for the journey. The duty sergeant said it wouldn't be necessary.

"OK Sarge' if you say so"

With that I walked out into the fresh air and the awaiting squad car.

The Pembroke Dock detention block was like the Hilton Hotel compared to the squalor of Haverfordwest police station. It was a purpose built centre with proper facilities and an exercise yard.

It was good to see Barrett and Torkington again, perhaps they could explain what the hell was going on. After a much-needed shower I was able to sit down with them to discuss the harrowing events of the past few days. Again this was not strictly allowed but the duty sergeant was an experienced and fair-minded officer who thought the whole situation was 'bizarre'; a word I would hear many times. Barrett explained.

"Well they interviewed us in the morning then they went up to see you. Chimp and DC Davies returned late afternoon and began pacing up and down the stairs waiting for a phone call. They were obviously waiting for a very senior officer to give the go ahead. They got nothing from me, because there isn't anything. They just kept on about Andrew Price and could I give them some dirt. I told them to bog off, I hardly know the guy, but they obviously think he's into something big!"

I interrupted.

"Well they told me when they left they were off to interview you two. Chimp asked about Andrew Price and were we in partnership with him. I found this strange. I also can't understand why Chimp is so involved if this is supposed to be a 'drug' investigation."

Barrett, with his usual banter blurted out.

"You've got to be joking; Chimp probably set the whole thing up. What did Gofer tell you at Swansea Crown last week, I'd been done for possession; well Chimp obviously got the date wrong! Anyway, they got this phone call about 9.30-10pm and started jumping up and down as if Swansea had won the FA Cup. Who ever it was had given them the thumbs-up. They got 'fluffy' (DC Lewis) to charge us while they raced up to Haverfordwest to do you before the 'witching hour.' They're holding us here on the pretext that if we get out we're going to warn off Andy Price and Danny Slade. Which is the biggest load of bollocks I've ever heard, they know full well where they are and the bloody world probably knows where we are!"

With that DC Davies walked in and got a bit irate that we had been allowed to talk to each other. He went over to the Duty Sergeant.

"What the hell's this?"
The Sergeant replied in no uncertain terms.

"I get crack-heads, shit-heads, piss-heads and for once I've some gentlemen in here; so fuck off and do what ever it is you're here to do."

DC Davies then proceeded to fingerprint, photograph and all the other recording of details required by law. As he did this with me he kept asking about 'Price'.

"Why don't you 'shop' him, you know he's a drug dealer, its only a matter of time before we get him, why don't you save your self, you know your going down!"
To which I just shook my head.

"You've got it totally wrong. Andy's a regular guy, he's a local businessman, and anyway, apart from the Up for It night's I hardly know him."

Monday morning arrived. We were all carted off to Haverfordwest Court this time in handcuffs. We were bundled into holding cells in the bowels of the courthouse together with a handful of other prisoners. The two Irishmen, who still hadn't given their names and three 'crackheads' who were actually smoking dope in the cell. The Irishmen went first and were bound over to keep the peace after giving their names and the whereabouts of their caravan.

Next went the 'crackheads', two returned to the cells after telling the prosecution barrister she was. 'An ugly old bastard who should be locked up with a dildo to put a smile on her face' or words to that effect. So they said. Their young mate had been given a conditional discharge, much to his disappointment, he was looking forward to joining his friends in Swansea 'Poke'!

Now it was our turn. We walked up the steep steps to the Courtroom under guard and stood in line in the dock. I guess we all looked a little dishevelled after three days in custody with little sleep or edible food. Nevertheless we thought justice would prevail.

The small Courtroom was full, Gill was there looking as radiant as ever. How the hell we had ever drifted apart I would never know. I knew I loved her, always had and always would. She would prove, as ever, to be my best friend in life, what a fool I'd been! Torkington's family and a number of onlookers and press were there, together with various police officers including Chimp and DC Davies. The CPS barrister Magie Hughes, a look alike of the wicked witch of the North in the Wizard of Oz, got to her feet and spat forth the prosecution allegations.

"These men are charged with allowing Chequers nightclub to be used as a drug-dealing den. They are worse than the dealers themselves. We all know the vast sums of money involved in such dealings and the misery and corruption it causes. These are serious charges that have justifiably been brought following a raid on the Club last Friday night when a number of drugs were found including class 'A' drugs."

Barrett and I looked around to see who she was talking about. Torkington just looked up at the ceiling in disbelief. Barrett and myself shared the same solicitor, Paul Cowper, who was looking more dishevelled than we were. He must have been on duty all weekend. He got up and started to babble on about my good character and why neither of us should be detained any further.

Torkington's solicitor then rose to ask why the Court was even contemplating detaining any of us. To this Magie Hughes said.

"There are two other suspects at large, Price and Slade if we release these defendants they might warn them off."

Torkington's solicitor objected saying the police knew perfectly well where both Price and Slade were. He called Torkington's father to the witness stand who gave evidence that the police had actually been talking to Slade only the day before. He was on his way back from Belfast where he had been Disc Jockeying. Price on the other hand was in New York at a hairdresser's convention but the police knew his travel arrangements.

All this fell on deaf ears, the Magistrates would have none of it. They automatically took the CPS's side with out question. The only concession they made was for Torkington because he was a juvenile and gave him conditional bail. Barrett and me were sent down for seven days on remand while the police continued their investigations.

Out of the corner of my eye I could see the smirk on Chimps face as we were escorted back to the holding cells. Getting over the initial shock of being sent to prison for something I did not do and had no precedent for such scant evidence and a first offence. This was bad enough but it was the thought of the vindictive people who had orchestrated this whole charade that would motivate me to seek eventual justice, but I knew even then that I would not find this in Pembrokeshire.

Barrett and I would share a cell for the next seven days in Swansea 'Poke' a condemned Victorian monolith of penal servitude. If it hadn't been for his philosophical sense of humour I would not have survived this indignity as well as I did. It was bad enough being handcuffed and marched out to the awaiting Reliance 'sweatbox' truck, sealed in a metal cubicle for the two hour journey to Swansea picking up prisoners from other Courts on the way. We drove through the huge wooden gates of that dank prison then watched as they shut tight behind the prison truck and the outside world. I felt a complete outcaste the lowest point of my life had been reached! After being released from the confines of the 'sweat box' we were filed up a stark metal staircase to the reception hall. The 'crackheads' thought it was home from home they were almost glad to be back.

We were fed and then one by one our names were called out for processing. The reception officer looked at my charge sheet; a little puzzled he enquired.

"What you in for Gittins?"

"Knowingly allowing premises to be used for drugs, I own a nightclub" I answered in the same puzzlement.

"You got to be joking, you don't get remanded for that!"

"Well, that's what I thought"

The officer shook his head.

"You must have some form then?"

"No nothing at all, it's a bloody nightmare!"

"You and curly together?" The officer pointed to Barrett.

"Yes, Barrett, he's the Club manager"

"Over here Mr. Barrett. Look, you and Mr. Gittins take a seat and we'll sort you out after the rabble. Sorry about the grub, I'll see if I can get you some sandwiches" He then turned to his colleague and showed my charge sheet.

"Here look at this Dai, every fucker's going to be locked up before long!"

After this we were treated well. Barrett was given the number BF4798 and me BF4799. But most of the time the officers or 'screws' as they were known inside, called us Mister. This gave us a lot of respect among the other inmates. The worst part of the next seven days was being locked up for 23 hours a day. Sometimes one of the officers would open our door and let us out for a chat and a cup of tea. They were very sympathetic and curious about the charge. On our first full day while walking around the prison yard for 20 minutes exercise, Barrett and I were offered every drug known to man.

I mentioned this to one of the officers during our regular chats. His reply summed up the situation.

"I know it's rife and well reported, we do our best. If we can't stop it, you as a club owner got no bloody chance. There's more drugs in here than Boots the chemists"

Those seven days past slowly; though Barrett had settled in well. Our cell was the best stocked in the prison and we became very popular. He managed to get good coffee, cigarettes, sweets, and salt etc. We had daily newspapers sent in and a pile of mail from well wishes and friends.

Gill instructed a new firm of solicitors from Swansea; Douglas Jones Mercer. My new 'brief' Del Cudd would be representing me at the next Court hearing at Haverfordwest and Barrett opted for Paul Cowper of Lowless and Lowless Tenby, in the hope that this time round he would be bright eyed and bushy tailed. On Monday 15th September 1997, a bright sunny morning we headed back to Haverfordwest in the 'sweatbox'. As we approached the Cleddau Bridge the truck broke down at the tollbooth.

The 'crackheads' thought it was hilarious, they had been joined by their young friend who had been so 'miffed' about being discharged the previous Monday he went straight outside and started smashing cars in the high street. He joined his friends on the Tuesday. They were now on their way, like us for a second hearing. If we ever got there. We finally arrived at the Court in time for the lunchtime recess, this meant waiting in the holding cells again.

After a brief meeting with my new solicitor we met up with Andy Price and Danny Slade. They had voluntarily surrendered to the Tenby police as soon as they arrived back in Wales. It transpired that Danny had spoken to the police by telephone on the Sunday before we were 'sent down'. Andy had been in touch through his office and the police even knew what flight he was on. The police's pretext was just the first of many lies to follow.

Thankfully we were first on after the lunch break. This time the mood of the Court was more relaxed. Maggie Hughes was nowhere to be seen nor could I see the Chimp. Christian Torkington joined us in the 'dock' and all five of us stood as the Magistrates entered the court. This time five defending solicitors stood up in turn to deliver a barrage of reasons why no one should be detained any further. My solicitor reiterated that on reading from the 'scant' evidence available there was no charge to answer and I should be released immediately.

The Magistrates agreed with release but the charges and the investigation would continue. We were all bailed with various conditions; one of mine was not to reopen the Club in any circumstances. I was also ordered not to talk to the other accused including Barrett; until they were informed we'd shared a cell for the past seven days.

It felt great being able to walk out of that courthouse into the fresh air, we met up with Gill, and she took Barrett and I for a very much-needed pint or two at a nearby pub. Barrett had been ordered to live at his mothers' house in Carmarthen and I had to return to Brecon. We both had to report to a local police station weekly. The battle was about to begin!

# 19

# The Civil Conspiracy!

A few days after my release I received a revocation of licence notice from the Police. It had been issued while I was on remand. They cited the drug allegations and breaches of the Public Entertainment's Licence the latter of which I had not even been charged with yet! I always thought one was innocent until proved guilty but this was obviously not so in Pembrokeshire. The notice read as follows.

*That Richard Jones, joint licensee, lives and works in Brecon has not visited the premises in over twelve months, has no control over the day to day management of the premises, and therefore is not a fit and proper person.*

*Dafydd Gittings is not a fit and proper person as he* ***has*** *knowingly allowed and suffered the premises to be used for the sale supply and use of Classes A, B, and C controlled Drugs. He has also totally ignored all safety measures imposed as a condition on his Public Entertainment Licence thereby risking the lives and safety of his customers.*

*Signed INSP E.DAVIES 10/9/97.*

They couldn't even spell my name right, but the emphases

had to be on the word 'has' (I hadn't even been tried). I wasn't to receive the list of accusations regarding the P.E.L breaches for another few weeks, they would be based on a 'multi-agency visit' on the 12th July '97.

A few days after I received the Revocation Notice, I received yet another surprise. A High Court Writ from the Scotch Whisky Association, or to be more precise, from two of their members Matthew Gloag & Sons (Famous Grouse) and Chivas Brothers (Chivas Regal). Although the Writ included MDT and Welsh Distillers; they had changed the Company name from The Welsh Whisky Co Ltd, the crucial part was that they named me personally. They were accusing me, after almost 25 years of whisky blending and production, of breaching European Regulations (EEC) No. 1579/89. I guess the best time to kick someone is when there're down.

My next court appearance in connection with the drug charge was to be the 21st October 1997. It was quickly adjourned because the CPS, Crown Prosecution Service, had not typed up any of the statements and could not present any firm evidence. My bail conditions were relaxed and the passport I had surrendered would be returned.

On the 30th October Tenby Magistrates declined jurisdiction and a procedural debate would occur on the 4th December without the defendants being present. A day later I had to attend Tenby Magistrates yet again to defend the revocation licence order. What transpired could only be described as an affront to democracy, natural justice and common sense. Ignoring the fact that I had not been tried, let alone convicted of any offence. The Magistrates accepted hearsay evidence as presented by PC. Tony Davies (Chimp) and revoked our liquor licence. Gofer had a solicitor who attempted to get the Magistrates to administer fair play and I defended myself on the ethos that the whole affair was 'sub judice'. They would have none of it and revoked the licence.

One would have thought that considering I was unable to open the club or suffer it to be opened as part of my bail conditions. A fair-minded bench would have deferred judgement until the due process of law had taken place. Then made a decision based on facts. It did not end there. The County Council repeated the same thing on the 9th December when they revoked the Public Entertainment's Licence. It was little more than a 'Kangaroo Court.'

Gofer defended the action; I was too pre-occupied with the on going drug case but had requested an adjournment on the same grounds as I did to the Magistrates. Furthermore I had been excluded from talking to Gofer because he was now a prosecution witness. Neither I, Gofer nor anyone else understood this turn of events other than a further attempt by the local authorities to suppress the due course of justice. While all this was going on I received a phone call from Gill. She was still working a few days a week at Welsh Distillers. She was very concerned about large shipments of spirits, in and out of the warehouse, that had not been produced there.

MDT had already defaulted on the first major payment to us for the sale of our shares. We had been pushing them for payment but had been 'fobbed off' with excuses. With my mind on other things I had not really pressed the matter.

I suggested that Gill get in touch with Customs, as we had always had a good working relationship with. Senior Officers at Customs asked Gill to effectively work undercover. They were working on an operation called 'Trap.' The information that Gill was able to supply them proved to be the vital piece of a large jigsaw puzzle they had been working on for several months.

I paid a visit to the warehouse to find it filled to the ceiling with thousands of cases of French Brandy, Rum, Vodka and Scotch. But very little Welsh Whisky.

Customs contacted me and I concurred with Gill's misgivings. They asked me to keep an eye on things after I told them I was seriously considering putting in a liquidator. I had already spoken to a friend of mine in Cardiff, Paul Harding who was a partner with a major insolvency practitioner. My initial concern was the defaulted payments from MDT, but now I had been asked to assist Customs and Excise unravel a major smuggling ring. This meant delaying any action on my, or Gill's part in calling in the receiver.

Meanwhile MDT was trying to fight off the SWA in the High Court. The Writ that had been issued in September was supposedly aimed at them and not me, or so I was told. In fairness they did consult me over the matter but little more. I was adamant that we should fight it all the way, I had already been given a ruling back in 1983 and Trading Standards had had advice in 1995 that what I had been doing all those years was perfectly within the regulations. As with all the advice I gave to MDT they ignored it and went for a 'strike-out'. Bearing in mind the power and influence the SWA could yield a strikeout was a long shot which of course failed. However the biggest mistake the SWA made was to name me on the writ, personally. This allowed me to take the issue further.

Pressure from the Pembrokeshire authorities continued and Gofer and I were back in court for P.E.L breaches and Noise Abatement offences going back to 12th July '97. Considering they had already refused our Public Entertainment's Licence, these proceedings were, in my option, little more than malicious but I guess they already knew what the out come would be.

On the 31st January 1998 at Tenby Court we faced an array of charges. Breach of noise regulations, was a notice put upon us the year before to keep within noise regulation NR35. (The sound of a quiet library according to a HSE book I had read), 22 metres from the club entrance. Our solicitor Peter Douglas-Jones of Douglas Jones Mercer, explained that the Council had promised to monitor the Club and advise as to the effectiveness of sound insulation improvements made at the Council's behest. That way adjustment could have been made to the sound system at the Club in order to comply with the notice.

The Council admitted this but told the Magistrates they had been unable to do so because of bad weather conditions. E.g. If it rains or the wind blows the sound these elements make is greater than the sound level they had set, NR35 could only be monitored on a still dry night like the 12th July '97. Lack of staff was another excuse. For this heinous crime our Company was fined £8,000 with £400 costs! As a first offence, under normal circumstances we would have expected a fine of £100.

As for the breaches of the P.E.L. 6 out of 8 charges were dropped these were the so-called safety charges. Such as a doorman with out a torch, or a doorman wearing his identity badges in the wrong place etc. What remained was a charge of dirty toilets; 1am in morning after 500 happy clubbers had availed themselves of the facilities, and a statutory sign with lettering the wrong size. It should have had 25mm lettering and the Council official measured it at 15.5mm. Had fair play and reason been the order of the day we would have expected a warning, instead we were each fined £1,000 per breach plus costs. The total for the day amounted to £12,000 plus £800 costs.

Our solicitor closed his book in disgust turned and walked out after looking straight at me saying.

"We appeal even if I do it for nothing, this is an absolute disgrace."

My reply was simple.

"Well Peter you now know what we're up against!"

A local resident replying through the letters column of the Tenby Observer following media coverage of the case summed it up in a letter entitled 'Is this Justice!'

He pointed out that the Council themselves had been accused of dirty toilets at Fishguard Town Hall, where there was a weekly food market. 'Mould growing up the walls and no water in the cracked wash hand basins. One of the theatres owned by the Council had operated with out an entertainment's licence at all.'

Another article that appeared sometime later in a small column reported another nightclub in the Tenby area that was prosecuted for over crowding. They had almost twice the number of people in the club as permitted a very serious safety offence. They were fined £500! A Tenby restaurateur was arrested after police found him in possession of £600 worth of Cocaine. Fine £600 and still in business! Conversely a man was fined £40 with a conditional discharge for possessing fifty pence worth of cannabis!

As my own drug case wound endless on I was faced with problems at Welsh Distillers. The amount of illicit booze going through the warehouse was alarming. Customs told me to hold fire with my liquidation order. I was also concerned that large amounts of cash could be diverted from the

Company. The longer this was allowed to go on the worse it would get.

Gill had discovered other irregularities concerning an escalating amount of duty, accounted for, but not paid over to Customs. She persuaded the directors of MDT, who were firmly in control, to make a full disclosure to Customs, which they eventually did. The sum being in the region of £250,000. Customs made a deal with them to pay it at £20,000 a month. They were far more interested in the goods being exported and needed more time to trace these goods.

Gill was working with Customs on a regular basis, phoning them when deliveries left the warehouse, and giving them details of the consignment and where it should be going. Thanks to Gill's vigilance Customs uncovered a ring operating between South Wales and London. The sums involved were enormous, estimated at £17,000,000.

Following a meeting in late March 1998 with Paul Harding the insolvency practitioner I decided April 6th would be the cut off date. Customs were happy as they had enough evidence and told me there would be no come back on Gill. 'She had been invaluable to them.'

At 9am Monday morning April 6th 1998, myself and Paul Harding presented the controlling directors of Welsh Distillers with an insolvency notice for defaulting on payments to Gill and myself of £150,000, among other issues.

# 20

# Where Do We Go From Here

The hardest part of taking the liquidation action was telling the staff they had lost their jobs. In the main MDT had got rid of most of the old staff who'd worked for Gill and I but there were still a few left. The move was inevitable if it hadn't come from me it would have come from elsewhere. The Company was in serious debt and there were many anomalies concerning large cash transactions that should have been paid into Welsh Distillers. The one ray of hope for the staff was that I was prepared to mount a rescue attempt for the Company.

The Liquidator immediately put me in charge of the building and the Company's residual affairs, this had the full approval of Customs. No sooner had this been done than the DBRW turned up. I had beaten them to it by an hour. Being the freeholder of the building they were going to change all the locks and evict everyone for non-payment of rent. Reluctantly they had to allow me time to assess the Company's affairs and to leave me in charge of the building. As it turned out MDT had not paid the rent for almost a year, when Gill and I ran the Company had we been but a month overdue the DBRW would have been banging on my door with bailiff's.

After everyone had left I had a good look around. It was a weird feeling to be back, this had been my 'baby' what had they done? The large stock warehouse was literary full with thousands of cases of spirits. Millions of pounds worth from God knows where. Even the production area was stacked to the ceiling with pallet loads of Brandy, Rum, Vodka and Scotch.

The bottling plant, now silent, had been busy bottling Vodka day and night for transhipment to the Continent but it was now more likely to be stashed away in an east London shed or a Birmingham warehouse. My large shinny copper still had not been 'fired-up' since I left almost two years ago. The Visitor Centre looked run down and ignored. They had totally destroyed what took over twenty years to build. Was it my fault? Did I walk away too soon or too easily? Many thoughts went through my head as I looked around what was once a thriving business employing over thirty people, now silent. Would I ever get it back?

For many weeks we sifted through mountains of paperwork. Gill assisting Customs to piece together various paper trails leading to the destinations of goods, and I with the Liquidator trying to unravel the accountancy system and find where certain payments had gone.

Customs finally took away the vast majority of spirits; a total of sixteen articulated lorry loads with a value of over two million pounds. Before doing this they arranged T.V. and media coverage after asking my permission. I found that a little bit strange but it seemed they didn't want to jeopardise my rescue bid for the Company and would only film the contraband goods not Welsh Whisky products. The big boss of Customs, Mel Scudimore, came to do the T.V. interview as this was the largest haul of contraband goods ever seized in Wales. After thanking Gill and I profusely for all the help and assistance Customs left us to get on with trying to put the Company back together again.

We made legal history on a day back in March, when, after a lengthy debate at the Tenby courthouse the Magistrates tried to block our right for an 'old style' committal procedure, whereby a stipendiary magistrate hears the facts and decides whether or not to proceed. That day will never be repeated as cases now go straight to Crown Court.

It had started on the 26th May and lasted until the 1st of June 1998 at the Shire Hall Haverfordwest. The stipendiary came from Cardiff a Mr. Watkins and by this time a sixth defendant had joined us, although no one could understand why his case had been joined to ours. It had been alleged that a chap by the name of Brett Goodridge had been seen handing over a twenty-pound note in the toilets of Chequers on the 4th July 1997 by a group of drunken military police. They had admitted in their statements that they had been the worse for drink on the night in question. He was also charged with supplying cannabis in the town Pembroke Dock.

The Shire Hall was another old Victoria building that also housed the Crown Court. It was oak panelled, dark and festooned with heraldic coats of arms. Things started well. The police gave evidence, which the Clerk of the Court had to record on tape in an abbreviated version. This was the same man from the Tenby Court who had orchestrated the magistrates there, but the Stipendiary magistrate was having none of it. The stipendiary had to keep correcting him saying. 'He didn't say that he said……etc'

'Chimp' was there lurking about at the back of the Court, he was apparently off duty and wasn't going to give verbal evidence but had submitted the list of incidents produced at the revocation hearing. This was in support of the first three charges, that drug dealing at Chequers had been going on over a long period. The prosecution called a number of witnesses. The four undercover police who said they purchased a number of drugs at the Club on the 2nd May '97. These being four ecstasy tablets and two wraps of amphetamine, they also said they had been offered 'blow'; cannabis resin.

All four officers commented that the vast majority of people at the Club were drinking bottled water, indicative of drug taking. They also said that the water had been turned off in the toilets inferring that we were aware of drug taking and profiting from vast sales of bottled water. None of the officers said that I was present when this was happening. They suggested it was so blatant and open that the Club's management must have known.

With regard to the raid of the 5th September '97 one of the lead officers, Sergeant Morris, stated that when he entered the Club that night everyone was drinking bottled water. The connection with Bret Goodridge was even more obscure he being accused of selling drugs in the gent's toilets on the night of the 4th July '97, an off duty military policeman had seen him taking a twenty pound note from another man!

They also called three doormen and one of our resident DJ's to give evidence against us. Two of the doormen and the DJ stated quite clearly that they had never seen drugs being dealt on any night. However the other doorman, Colwyn Howells who was also the Head Doorman and the prosecutions chief witness, inferred that although he too had never seen drugs being dealt at the Club as such, he had seen Barrett take drugs. Howell's written statements varied considerably from the evidence he gave in the witness box. He was very nervous and confused, obviously under pressure. Considering it was his job to detect and prevent drug taking or dealing at the Club, it was strange that he had not been accused with the rest of us.

The charges against Price, Slade and Torkington of being members of the management of Chequers were tenuous at best. They merely ran the 'Up For It' promotions on a Friday night, organising the music and marketing the event. Whereas Howell's firm, Howells Security, was permanently contracted to the Club and very much part of the management structure of Chequers.

After the third day of the hearing the Stipendiary threw-out the three charges relating to any long-term drug abuse at the Club. He was bullish about his decision, not even retiring to contemplate. The list of incidents compiled by PC 'Chimp' was in the main based on hearsay and conjecture, i.e. 'a male person arrested on route to Chequers found in possession of Cannabis' and so on.

The Stipendiary gave me the impression that he was of a mind to throw the whole thing out of Court there and then! I felt sure that had the hearing continued through to Friday he would have done just that. Instead he had another case to hear on the Friday and two of the defending Barristers had other engagements so the hearing was adjourned until the following Monday.

As we sat down to continue another day of the hearing on Monday morning I could sense a change of attitude by the Stipendiary. He looked agitated, eager to move things along much quicker; the police gave evidence about Bret Goodridge and the incident supposedly witnessed by a military policeman. Colwyn Howells was recalled to give evidence about the events that took place on the 4th July '97. How two of the MP's approached him saying they suspected Goodridge of supplying drugs in the gent's toilets. He had searched Goodridge and found nothing but decided to eject him from the Club. This he said was countermand by Andrew Price, saying throw the 'pigs out, pigs are pigs'. Howells said he had to escort the MP's into Bogey's Bar for their own safety. A charge Price strongly denied.

This was enough for the Stipendiary, unlike the proceeding Thursday he decided to retire to consider his decision. This was bizarre, we hadn't even been charged for any transgression pertaining to the incident of the 4th July '97, not even Goodridge, his charges related to an alleged supply of cannabis on the 27th August at Pembroke Dock.

Returning after about twenty minutes the Stipendiary had decided that Price, Torkington and Slade were part of the Club management. Their attitude towards the police, military or otherwise gave concern, therefore, there was a 'Prima Facie' case to answer and the remaining charges should be attested at Crown Court. The defence barristers were dumbfounded by his 'U'-turn.

I had asked my barrister to have a word with the stipendiary about costs. My purse was seriously lacking after nine months of legal wrangling. I had no solicitor at court and my barrister was very junior. He was a bit hesitant to do, protesting it was the job of a solicitor, but I insisted. While the others filed out my barrister and I approached the Bench to ask for Legal Aid. Surprisingly not only did he grant this but also costs to date.

It would be another eight months before we got to Crown Court and over seven months before we would receive 'prime disclosure' of the prosecution case against us. Through out this time correspondence would pass back and forth clocking up huge legal costs on both sides. All the while the stress and stigma of criminal charges hung over our heads.

# 21

# The Struggle For Survival

In June 1998 Gill and I divorced more out of necessity than anything else. Being embroiled in one legal battle after another coupled with the loss of my income from Welsh Distillers and Chequers Night Club I could see no point in dragging Gill down with me. In fairness to her she had stuck by me all the way and despite our estranged state I very much doubt if we would ever have formally divorced had the Chequers affair ended at the 'old style' committal stage. Following the frustrations of the committal process at Haverfordwest, where we had chipped away at the charges and at lest secured Legal Aid and costs, I would begin my quest to revive Welsh Whisky.

Two old friends of mine, Tony James and Alun Evans, joined my crusade. Alun owned a large pub in Hirwaun near Aberdare and had previously been a customer of mine when he owned and ran Gwalia Wholesale, a drink wholesalers that went bust during the recession, later acquired by Carlsberg Tetley.

Tony was in the coal industry having developed several large open cast-mining schemes in South Wales. Alun and

I had been helping him put together a business plan to develop a new site in the Neath Valley. This unfortunately never got off the ground but we had built up a good working relationship together. Tony was a 'Merthyr' gentleman, who spoke his mind and had a heart of gold. In his fifties but not in the best of health, he had over the years built up a fortune from coal. He now joined me in the Welsh Whisky venture.

Alun, a portly bearded chap in his late forties who I'd known for over twenty years, had been associated with the licensed trade all his life. After his bankruptcy he had managed to hold on to his family pub the Glancynon Inn and Carlsberg kept him on as a sales representative. He was very well connected and sympathetic to my plight.

Before I left Welsh Whisky in '96 I had been working on a European Research Scheme with the University of Surrey relating to the experimental still. My objective was to revive this scheme and use it as a catalyst to the rescue bid. My greatest hurdle was securing a new lease, or to purchase out right, the building in Brecon from the DBRW(Development Board for Rural Wales). This would prove easier said than done.

The Liquidator had kept the assets in tact, in fact Welsh Whisky could have restarted at the push of a button. This would have been the best prospect for all concerned, even the many creditors.

The DBRW were concerned about reprisals from the Scotch Whisky Association, but I explained that they had only won a technical victory when Welsh Distillers went 'bust'. Had they not defaulted on costs then the whole thing would have been resolved at a hearing over the preliminary issue. Had there been a breach of European labelling regulations or not? In any event it would not effect any new company formed to revive the production of Welsh Whisky at Brecon. It was reluctantly agreed by the DBRW that we could bid for the freehold of the building, and they informed us that there were several other interested parties.

Alun introduced me to someone interested in helping us revive the Company. He was Brian Morgan a well-known economist with the Cardiff School of Business. A trendy-looking man in his late forties well versed in business start-ups and rising finance. In a further effort to strengthen the board of our now newly formed company, Dragon Corporation, Dr. Roy Bichan the former vice-chairman of the WDA and Graham Dale a property developer from North Wales joined us. The European Commission allowed me to restart the research programme with Surrey University and bid for funding. If successful it would prove invaluable in raising bank funding and investment in the new company.

In July '98 the Liquidator decided to sell off the assets of Welsh Distillers because the DBRW had still not made up their mind about selling us the building. We would now have to bid along side anyone else if we wanted to stay in the game. We took a major gamble in successfully bidding for these assets but felt sure the DBRW would see this as a firm commitment on our part. The bank certainly did and backed us with an offer to provide a mortgage if we would purchase the building from the Development Board.

In that same month I had to attend to the appeal against the fines imposed by Tenby Magistrates for P.E.L. breaches and Noise Abatement Notice infringements. This was heard at Swansea Crown Court and was another capitulation. Gofer and I met with our barrister for this episode a few days before. He was another junior but had a little sparkle about him. However, his advice was depressing. After reading through his notes and speaking to the barrister for Pembrokeshire County Council he advised us to drop our appeal and 'fall upon the mercy of the court.' We had a case but the Council was going to fight it all the way, calling many witnesses, expert and otherwise.

According to our barrister, the Judge appointed to our case was apparently something of an ogre and very pro-establishment. We therefore took his advice and withdrew our appeal but would appear before the Court to argue mitigating circumstances, in what is known as a 'Newton' hearing. Having withdrawn our appeal the council sent just one official to assist their barrister. Otherwise the courtroom would have been awash with council officials and who ever else they could have seconded to give damming evidence against us. Their barrister started by complaining about the very short notice we had given when withdrawing our appeal. But he didn't labour the issue. The Judge seemed unimpressed as were the two advising magistrates seated either side of him, neither of which was from Pembrokeshire.

I passed a note to my barrister telling him I wanted to take the stand. He looked back at me shaking his head, but I insisted and he relented. After he had given a very good deliberation about the change in circumstances that had forced our decision to withdraw the appeal, to save costs and 'everyone's' time, I was called to the witness box. This was very much a gamble. Thinking that if I could appeal to this man's sense of fair play then perhaps we stood a chance, after all we had been fined over £12,000 for very minor infringements. The noise abatement offences were little more than trumped up but you needed serious money to fight these very technical accusations.

After taking the oath I nervously told my tale to the

Judge and Magistrates.

"Your honour's I've been kicked into a ditch and I'm trying desperately to climb out of it. In fact I've so many mountains to climb I'm not quite sure which one to attempt first. I've lost everything and to be fined the amount of money that I've been fined is totally unfair. If I have to pay this extraordinary fine then somehow I will, but for the life of me, at this moment in time, I don't know how I can!"

The Judge interrupted me here and looking me square in the eyes enquired

"You're a well-known businessman Mr. Gittins, surely..."

"The answer to that Sir is, was! This case, coupled with other 'mountains' before me means I'm unemployed, but I am trying to restart my original business. I was divorced last month and admittedly I protected my family by not contesting it but I'm sure you would do the same thing in my shoes."

I looked over to my barrister who was shaking his head in disbelief. Then I looked back at the Judge and Magistrates who where muttering to each other before adjourning for lunch.

Gofer and I went to a nearby pub, the Wig and Pen, for a much-needed drink before returning to the court. My barrister was not confident saying.

"Well worth a try, but I can't see how the Judge is going to react because we had to withdraw the appeal."

The Judge reacted all right and to everyone's astonishment stated.

"Withdrawing the appeal has presented me with something of a problem but I've listened to what Mr. Gittins had to say. Therefore I'm reinstating the appeal."

With that the prosecution barrister stood up to protest

but stood down as the Judge lowered his spectacles and continued.

"The noise abatement charges, which are quasi-criminal, I see no public interest in pursuing. These are therefore discharged. The P.E.L. fines against Mr. Gittins will be reduced to £1,500 and Mr. Jones £1,000. Mr. Jones to pay off at £20 per month and Mr. Gittins within six months of receiving a formal demand. If he can't do it after that period he will come back to the Court and I'll consider a further reduction." It would be eighteen months before I received that demand!

It was now back to my rescue operation fuelled by trying to win back not only my old job, but also many of the loyal staff I'd employed in the past. I felt a deep sense of responsibility for the first time in my life, I was unemployed and beginning to know what it felt like.

Our bid for the Brecon building was in, my partners had invested cash and I was further in debt. At the end of August I was summoned to Brussels to present our case for funding. This I thought would be the final hurdle.

I flew out from Cardiff to meet up with Dr. David Faraday and Martin Fosbrook from the University of Surrey. We would make a formal presentation to DGXII, the scientific research arm of the European Commission. We made our submission to a senior science officer of the Commission. A small 'fuzzy' headed man totally devoid of humour. I'd visited the Commission several times before when I was with the CBI arguing Wales' corner for Objective One Status but I'd never come across anyone as intense.

We had to convince this 'boffin' that our Experimental Still, not only worked, but if it's technology was extended throughout the industry it would reduce energy consumption considerably. After three hours we achieved this seemingly impossible task. Our written submissions had been extensive but I guess they wanted to see our personal commitment. Although interrupted by the MDT take over we had all spent many years putting this project together, we had now secured hundreds of thousands of pounds in funding against all the odds. I faxed the good news to my partners and I went for a well-earned drink in a small bistro in down town Brussels. Being physically and mentally drained I decided to make a little holiday of the trip and took a train up to Amsterdam.

It was August Bank Holiday weekend back home but in Amsterdam it was festival time. The City was packed for an international music festival. I couldn't get near the tourist offices to book a hotel and thoughts of abandoning my little holiday flashed through my mind until I remembered a previous visit I'd made many years ago.

In 1993 I'd visited the Amsterdam Chamber of Commerce as part of our Arnhem memorial campaign. I made a bee-line for their offices and explained my plight. They couldn't help me out with a hotel in the centre but a conference had been cancelled in a five star hotel on the outskirts of town. Explaining my reduced financial position the very helpful lady there said,

"No problem I'll see what I can arrange."

I couldn't believe my luck, she booked me into the Okura, a five star Japanese owned hotel about three miles from the centre of town. I had an executive suite for three nights for a total of one hundred pound sterling. Lying in my Jacuzzi, glass of wine in one had and a fine Dutch Cigar in the other, I really thought things were about to change for the better. That evening I made my way up to the rooftop bar and restaurant for a quiet few beers before heading into the City to see the festival. The bar was almost empty, just one other guy drinking large whiskies, a youngish well-dressed Arabic looking chap. I ordered a beer and said Hi and he acknowledged by inviting me to join him at the bar. We started chatting, he told me his name was Anwar and that he was on a business trip from the Middle East. It turned out he was a junior Finance Minister for one of the Gulf States.

It's always amazed me how fellow travellers tend to enjoy one another's company. Being from completely different cultures and backgrounds makes little difference provided the conversation is interesting and the atmosphere is convivial. I recounted my trials and tribulations and my success in Brussels that would hopefully lead to resumption of my past fortunes. With that Anwar turned his head towards the doorway leading into the bar.

"My friend, I'm sure things will change only for the better!"

I looked around to see what he was looking at and there walking in were two very attractive young ladies. He got up to welcome them, kissing them on each cheek and shaking hands like long lost friends.

"Come meet my new friend 'Daveed' "

The girls were in their early, twenties both blonde and had east European accents. I wasn't sure if they were professionals or not, if they were I suspected they were expensive and out of my league. Anwar ordered a bottle of Champagne, what else? And we sat at a table by the large windows that overlooked the suburbs of Amsterdam. Feeling a little awkward because of my financial state I thought I should make my excuses and leave them to it. Anwar sensed this and said

"Excuse please I need a quick word with my friend."

This was even more embarrassing and we went over to the far side of the bar for a whispered chat. I explained.

"Anwar I can't afford this, as I said before things have changed for me, I've enough for a good weekend around town having a laugh and a few beers but..."

"It is not a problem my friend, its not what you think. I met these girls at the Investment Bank and invited them for dinner. I hate dining alone. It's my treat, I understand what you told me, its no problem, you do the same for me one day, come, enjoy."

I could not refuse such genuine hospitality, but felt bad that I'd jumped to the wrong conclusion. The girls were from Moscow and worked for a major Russian bank in Amsterdam where Anwar was doing some investment business.

My few quiet beers turned into a very memorable night! We finished the Champagne then made our way down to the lobby into a Taxi and off into the city centre. He had reserved a table at an exclusive Lebanese restaurant. The two young ladies were really charming, Anwar had certainly clicked with one and they ended up holding hands and staring deeply into each other's eyes for the rest of the evening.

We went onto a nightclub and then the casino, where surprisingly, I won fifteen hundred guilders (£500). Exhausted, we returned to the roof top bar at the Okura, it must have been 3am. After a quick nightcap Anwar and his lady would bid us good night and disappear, leaving me with the other girl named Inga.

We had danced, dined and talked pleasantries all evening but I expected no more than a peck on the cheek from this very beautiful young Russian lady before she said her farewell. Instead she stood up, all six feet of her, grabbed my hand and said;

"We go your room now it late-no!"

As soon as we got into my suite she went straight to

the bathroom and with a little squeal she exclaimed

"Jacuzzi-I love Jacuzzi" and immediately striped naked. I stood in the doorway gazing at the incredible sight of a beautiful young lady, in all her glory bending over turning the taps to fill the tub. I thought to myself 'my luck must be changing, at last!'

We awoke at 10am to a knock on the door; room service. With that the door opened and a maid entered wheeling a trolley. Rubbing my eyes I turned to Inga.

"You order room service?" she shook her head. The maid revealed the mystery,

"Compliments of..." before she finished Inga and I replied "Anwar!"

The maid withdrew and Inga jumped out of bed to lift the silver domes on the trolley to discover a veritable feast of scrambled eggs, two pots of Caviar, Melba toast and instead of coffee a large bottle of chilled Champagne. She was like a kid opening her Christmas presents and so was I. Inga left at mid day and Anwar had checked out to fly home, but left me a note, 'hoping I'd enjoyed the evening' and his business card.

Switching on my mobile phone to ring home I notice there were several messages. Before I could retrieve them it rang. Gill was on the line.

"Sorry to interrupt your little break in Amsterdam but we've had a letter from the DBRW this morning, they've sold the building to someone else and 'the bastards' want us to move all the plant and machinery out within seven days!"

My run of luck had been short lived, there was nothing I could do to change the situation over a holiday weekend but it did give me time to contemplate the issues.

The new company, Dragon Corporation, now had a million-pound research project with funding from the

European Commission and partners in Finland, Belgium, Italy, Ireland and England. We had the best part of three-quarters of a million pounds worth of plant, machinery and stock and no base for any of it! As they say the rug had been taken from under our feet. What I needed now was a bloody magic carpet!

It was obvious to me that the deciding factor not to sell the building at Brecon to Dragon was due to the drug allegations against me - there could be no other logical reason.

# 22

# Fairwell Brecon

I spent the remainder of the weekend with Inga, flew back to Cardiff early Tuesday morning, and reached Brecon in the afternoon. I immediately rang the Development Board. They informed me they had agreed to sell the building to an Italian company, rejecting our offer because they were concerned about the SWA litigation and our ability to rescue the core business. The only concession they gave me was an extension of time until the end of the month. I had been in possession of the building since the beginning of April, it was now the beginning of September, all the effort and hope completely wasted. It was a heartbreaking experience having to dismantle the Still, bottling line, blending vats and most of all, the unique Visitor Centre. As we torn down the structure I knew how it felt like to be raped!

Alun Evans had organised storage in a warehouse near Aberdare; the plan now was to bid for Alun's old wholesale depot in Penderyn, a small village in the Brecon Beacons. Carlsberg had closed it down a few years before and it was up for auction. Building a brand new distillery at Penderyn would be a bold and expensive project but we were fully committed. The HSBC Bank backed us all the way, and Rhondda Canon Taf County Council welcomed us with open arms. The headlines in Brecon's local paper, the Brecon and Radnor Express read; the obituary, 'Welsh Whisky Bids farewell to Brecon.' After twenty-five years the production of whisky in Brecon would be confined to the history books, as would the DBRW, it was merged into the WDA shortly after. The closure of Welsh Whisky would be their epitaph. To add insult to injury the Italian Company would move out in less than eighteen months!

In November '98 I was awarded full Legal Aid to challenge the SWA. This was just as well because my funds had been completely exhausted. My role with Dragon Corporation was merely advisory, I was effectively unemployed and still facing criminal charges over my past ownership of Chequers nightclub.

The Club was still closed as part of my unprecedented bail conditions; I couldn't even allow or suffer it to be opened. The future looked bleak.

Dragon managed to buy the Gwalia Depot and plans were in hand to build a brand new distillery. I was now living back in Saundersfoot and had finally been given a date for the full trial to be held at Swansea Crown Court 26th January 1999. We would receive final disclosure of evidence on the 11th January, sixteen months after the event.

Gill and her friend Paula drove drive me to Court each day. On the first day Gill's car broke down and I arrived at Court with seconds to spare. All six of us stood solemnly in the dock in Swansea's Guildhall, which doubled as a Crown Court when the new Court building across the road was full. After swearing in the jury the trial started with Brett

Goodridge, although I could never understand why he had been included in our trial. The Crown Prosecution Service was represented by an old chap with a game leg. Tom Granville-Jones, started by offering no evidence against Goodridge. The poor lad told me he had spent four months on remand. He was a young man in his early twenties and like the rest of us had had these charges hanging over him for nearly eighteen months.

The Judge, Mr. Michael Burr, instructed the jury to find him not guilty. After we all shook his hand he immediately left the dock, felt relieved but angry. The Jury retired while the Judge spoke to our barristers on how long they expected the case to last. He appeared quite relaxed and came out with a surprising remark when addressing Andrew Price's barrister Miss Elfed Evans. I hadn't heard the question but the Judge remarked.

"Yes I know if young club goers consume lots of water its indicative to drug taking-that's the crux!"

The Jury was recalled and we all in turn were asked our names and how we pleaded to the charges against us. We all replied in turn with a firm. "Not guilty."

The prosecution led the case; the point they had to prove was that we had a case to answer. All the witnesses called except two would be police officers as they had been unable to find any independent witnesses to testify against us. They had obtained one hostile statement against Barrett from a part time cleaner who had worked at the club for a short time. The statement had been taken under suspicious circumstances and she refused to attend Court pleading mental stress. Apart from that they would rely on the head doorman Colwyn Howells. My co-licensee Richard Jones would also be called as a prosecution witness but he said very little.

Howell's evidence was confused to say the least and he was called back several times because it differed not only from his written statements but also what he'd said at the 'old style' committal. He was clear when asked if I was the type of person to condone drugs.

"Most definitely not. Had I thought that I would not have worked there!"

But he inferred that he had seen Barrett rolling something saying, 'I'm in for a good night to night!', and that he had seen him with a white tablet in his hand. Barrett's brief challenged this by asking Howell's if the 'white tablet' could have been a mint! He said he wasn't sure.

The first police witness was a detective sergeant who had entered the club on the night of the 5th September '97 raid. He said that when he looked around the Club shortly before 9pm everyone was drinking bottled water. He could see no alcohol at all on the tables or on the bar.

A WPC gave evidence regarding the 5th September '97, saying she entered the club at 9pm and at 9.02pm had found a split ecstasy tablet under a table on the balcony where three persons were sitting. When questioned by the defence she admitted that she had not questioned these people, she actually knew one of them and her instructions had been not to question them! A succession of police officers came and went giving mundane statements of little relevance. The drugs found on the raid of the 5th were shown to the Jury, and a forensic scientist gave evidence as to what they were. The street value of the broken 'E' tablet, the small ball of resin, the contents of a tobacco pouch and the small clear plastic bags that held traces of amphetamine was less than twenty pounds!

The trial would last two weeks Andrew Price's barrister took the lead on behalf of the defence with my barrister Huw Rees saying very little. The highlight of the prosecution case came from the military policemen that attended the Club off duty on the night of the 4th July '97. They had flown the three MP's from Cyprus to give evidence, something I found totally bizaar as this evidence concerned, in the main, one of the charges against Goodridge and his case had been dismissed at the very start.

The MP's admitted they were the worse for drink on the night, but stated they could smell cannabis but they never actually saw anything being dealt, only the twenty-pound note being given over in the toilets to Goodridge. The CPS got away with it by saying they wanted to illustrate the level of control that Andrew Price had over the Club when he allegedly ordered their removal from the premises. However the MP's couldn't remember this ever happening, just that they felt unsafe and were moved to another bar.

The next would be the undercover officers from the night of the 2nd May '97. The lead officer, when asked to produce the 'haul' of drugs they had purchased that night had to explain that these drugs had been 'lost' or destroyed along with his note book. They did have a forensic report but not the drugs themselves. Now I thought, the whole charade will end here.

The defence called for a recess to challenge the Judge, but he would have none of it and resumed to hear the evidence of all four undercover officers. Their evidence focused on the bottled water consumption at the Club and that the water in the toilets had been turned off or just a trickle. The prosecution said this had been a sharp practise by the management to profit from the 'vast' sales of bottled water so we must have known drugs were being dealt.

My barrister asked the arresting officer DC John Davies if he had made an audit of the Club's computer, this would obviously prove the scale of bottled water sales. His reply was no, despite the fact that the police had seized the computer and held it for a year. It seemed to me totally unbelievable that the police had not carried out an in-depth audit, this evidence would either corroborate or not what the undercover officers were saying. The Judge made no observation over this crucial piece of evidence!

Considering the relevance of this information as the only means of knowledge that I would have of alleged drug abuse, any Judge wishing to uncover the truth would have challenged the officers statement and why the CPS had not demanded such an audit.

The undercover officers confirmed that I was not present in the Club that night, but drug dealing by a young black man known as Teito Payne was open and blatant. He was dealing close to the bar and the bar staff must have been aware, doormen were also walking around the Club they must also have been aware. And most people were drinking bottled water.

Justice Burr seemed totally oblivious to the fact that no bar staff had been called to give evidence and their written statements and those of the door-staff contradicted this evidence. I sent note after note to my barrister to challenge this but he said he wanted to keep his 'powder dry.' Price's barrister did, but her brief was to merely prove that her client was not part of the management and so even if drugs were dealt he had no responsibility. The water issue cropped up time and again; the Police had made an elaborate smoke screen around this. We had evidence to show that our bottle water sales were moderate and in any event the consumption of mineral water was now a part of modern society. Young people especially are far more abstemious when driving, and young girls prefer it to 'fattening' beer.

The police brought in evidence previously rejected at the 'old style' committal hearing alleging long-term drug abuse at the club. The Jury was sent out on a number of occasions when this inadmissible evidence was heard, they were in and out like 'yo-yo's.'

By Thursday of the second week the prosecution had concluded their case. The Jury was again asked to leave while all five-defence barristers made legal arguments to the Judge that there was no case to answer, quoting various precedents in law.

The Judge adjourned for the day to give his judgement the following morning. On the Friday morning we reconvened to hear his verdict. My barrister was convinced that the prosecution had no case.

Justice Burr split the case in three parts. Firstly the issue of who was part of the management of the Club. It was clear that Barrett and myself were, me being the co-licensee and he being the manager in charge. Although why he never challenged the fact that Gofer was also the other licensee and hadn't even been charged will forever remain a mystery, the issues here being strict or vicarious liability. He conceded there was no clear evidence at all to say that Price, Torkington and Slade were part of the management so they would be dismissed from the proceedings.

The second part being the charges relating to the 5th September '97. He stated "had all the drugs found at the Club been found on one single person it would have amounted to little more than simple possession." He dismissed all charges concerned with the raid and any 'hear say' evidence of any prolonged drug abuse at the premises.

There was however Barrett's single charge of possessing cannabis in his flat and this would remain a separate issue.

The third part concerning the undercover operation on the 2nd May needed further debate. He contested that knowledge could be reasonably argued over the level of sales in bottled water. The charges concerning that night and that night in isolation should be answered. He wanted to continue the trial with Barrett and myself on this single issue. Both my barrister and Barrett's barrister Stephen Rees (no relation to my barrister Huw Rees; now you know why I have used 'nicknames' a lot) protested saying that the Jury were by now totally confused. The Judge reluctantly agreed and ordered a re-trial after calling back the Jury to find Price, Torkington and Slade not guilty of all charges and Barrett and myself not guilty of any charges relating to the 5th September '97.

We left Court with mixed feelings and reassurances from my barrister and the solicitor's clerk David Williams, who had attended the trial in the absence of my solicitor Del Cudd. They felt sure that now Price had been acquitted the CPS would not proceed. We all met at the Wig and Pen pub for a drink and a discussion with the other guys and their barristers and hear the consensus of option. Everyone felt the CPS has very little evidence but felt uneasy about the Judge who was relatively inexperienced. He had been a civil lawyer and his understanding of the criminal code concerning torts and strict liability was suspect.

The one piece of advice that turned out to be profound was not to under estimate the CPS barrister who was very experienced and highly respected. He may appear to be an old dodder but in reality he most certainly wasn't.

For the next three months both my lawyers and

Barrett's would badger the CPS to drop the case. During this time I had signed off the dole and started self-employment as a business consultant. My main projects being the European Research Project and the setting up of the new distillery at Penderyn. Successfully negotiating an advance of funds from the EC of 250,000 euro's I organised a project launch to be held at the new council offices near Pontypridd. This would be a first for Wales with partners flying in from several European Countries. All this time I was under the considerable stress of being hauled back into Court to answer the trumped-up, but potentially devastating drug charge. All my friends, family and colleagues remained convinced the case would be thrown out.

# 23

# The Scales Of Justice

On the 26th April 1999 the re-trial commenced at Swansea's Crown Court. Barrett and I stood alone to answer three counts of to knowingly allow or suffer the sale of drugs at our premises. Barrett faced a further charge of possession of cannabis resin allegedly found in his flat but it had been agreed this would be heard separately and would not form part of this trial. My barrister arrived with his arm in a sling having fallen from his horse over the weekend and appeared to be in some pain. David Williams again attended in the absence of my solicitor. The case would last a week and focus on the events of the 2nd May '97. The presiding Judge His Honour Michael Burr.

After swearing in the Jury, a mixed bunch of elderly and middle-aged men and women, apart from one young chap sporting an earring. We commenced the 'nth round of this long and expensive drama; my 29th appearance in court.

The CPS would lead with police evidence. PC 'Fluffy' Lewis, no longer with the drug squad but moved back to uniform, gave an impassioned speech from the box, he had received 'zero co-operation' from Chequers.'

A number of other officers gave mundane statements, then we came to DC John Davies the arresting officer. I sent a note to my barrister to ask DC Davies again if he had carried out an audit of the Clubs' computer. This time he said "yes" he had, but couldn't retrieve anything of relevance; only till receipts of money taken on the night. He could not differentiate between alcohol sales and water sales only monetary values. I sent another note to my barrister.

'The computer does not produce till receipts-it's a stock master and at the first trial he said he hadn't conducted an audit.'

He repeated the question and the officer repeated his answer I can only surmise his reasons for merely repeating the question, as opposed to challenging the fact that not only had the officer changed his story but where was this audit? Was he waiting for the Judge to raise the question or even the CPS to make comment?

None of this happened I felt uneasy and any confidence I had in my barrister was certainly dwindling. Why wasn't he being more assertive?

The main thrust of evidence would be from the undercover officers; one by one the three WPC's and the detective constable 'waxed lyrical' about the vast consumption of bottled water. How the water had been switched off in the toilets and how no one had been searched by the door staff on entry. They produced photographs of the drug dealer Teito Payne taken on the night, posing with the undercover WPC's? Ironically he was holding a bottle of Budweiser!

One WPC's said it was all so blatant she had seen clearly the dealing going on. Barrett's barrister challenged this saying, from where you were standing some 10 to 15 feet away in a dark busy nightclub with strobe disco lighting and smoke swirling she could plainly see what was going on? She was emphatic, it was as clear as daylight! Blatant! I turned to see one of the jurors' writing down this remark.

It was then ascertained that in total the officers had witnesses or took part in some ten or twelve transactions over a four-hour period. That there were some 500 people in the Club and the 'bouncers' were continuously patrolling inside the Club.

Next came Colwyn Howells, he was a little more coherent this time around and in answer to prosecution questions described the music at the Club as 'head banging rubbish' 'Rave music'. He reiterated his experiences of Barrett with the white tablet and some substances in a silver foil wrapper. But he also reiterated that neither he as head doorman, nor any of his staff had seen anything untoward that evening. He further stated that I never interfered with his security work and never suspected me of ever being involved or condoning drugs. He then turned to the Judge and said.

"Look can I say something here. If you ask me you have the wrong people in the dock!"

Granville-Jones stopped him short.

"No speeches Mr. Howells just answer the questions."

The prosecution then moved on to the issue of the water being turned off. Howells admitted his other occupation was that of a plumber and that there had been one occasion when someone complained about the water in the toilets, but he was vague. He then inferred that Barrett might have tampered with the stopcock but had never witnessed such an act.

Gofer my co-licensee took the stand for the prosecution but again said little or nothing other than when questioned by my barrister. He agreed that he found it strange that he too was not in the dock and as to the question of water said water sales at the Club were not excessive, maybe 3 or 4% of turn over. The statements that Barrett and I had made while in police custody were read out in court. An odd practise where by the arresting officer reads out his words and the prosecution barrister reads out the defendants words. Now, all words have inflections and you can guess which ones they would use. Granville-Jones would have made a passable Shakespearean actor had he ever failed his 'Bar' exams. During this farcical episode Granville-Jones started to read out the passage concerning Barrett's Cannabis charge, the one the CPS had agreed not to mention. The Jury gave out a gasp! This had never been mentioned I could imagine their thoughts. There was I anti-drug employing a manager accused of taking them himself.

The Jury was sent out as our two barristers protested at this blatant breach of confidence. The accusation against Barrett of processing a minuscule amount of cannabis would be tried separately if at all. Granville-Jones apologised profusely; with a little grin on his face.

The defence barrister's lodged their protest saying this would be ground for appeal if the matter arose but the Judge dismissed it and recalled the Jury. As the prosecution case drew to a close and the jury was sent out yet again our two barristers Huw Rees and Stephen Rees made a call to the Judge of no case to answer. Again quoting various precedents such as R. vs. Galbraith (1981) and Sweet and Parsley (1970).

It fell on deaf ears, he would have none of it. There was no evidence to say I was present that night. No evidence that Barrett or I had actually observed any wrongdoing, no previous convictions, and no evidence that the Club had any history of serious drug problems. In fact there had never been any arrests at the Club at all until we were held at the raid of the 5th and there was no evidence that we had been asked to do anything by the police that we refused to do.

Despite all logic the Judge would not stop the case, he wanted the Jury to decide. He was convinced the sales of bottled water as reported by the under cover officers was true. Yet he never bothered to consider the facts. The police had the opportunity to corroborate the oral evidence conclusively by analysing the Club's computer. They now confirmed they had made an audit yet never produced one. They said they had till receipts yet never produced any. They also said they purchased drugs but never produced any.

The trial continued, first Barrett giving evidence then me. The CPS's barrister Granville-Jones came into his own. He crossed swords with Barrett almost immediately he entered the witness box.

"Mr. Barrett you said you are totally anti-drugs yet Mr. Howells says he saw you rolling a piece of silver foil in your hand one night exclaiming!

'I'm in for a good night tonight' what did that mean?"
Barrett looked him in the eye saying.

"Well you tell me."
Granville-Jones hunched his back and replied.

"Well didn't you mean you had some substance which you were about to take!"

"No-no way."

"Then what was in this silver foil?"
Barrett hands in the air.

"It might have been a condom!"

"Come, come Mr. Barrett a condom in a silver wrapper?"
Barrett; as quick as a whippet.

"Well how you'd buy yours then Mr. Jones?"
The Judge intervened.

"I don't think there is any need of such banter Mr. Barrett."
And so the cross-examination continued.

He remarked on PC 'Fluffy' Lewis' comment of zero co-operation from the management at Chequers. Barrett countered this by informing Mr. Granville-Jones it had been him who called the police in the first place to find out what was going on. 'Fluffy' had ignored his calls on several occasions and at the end of the day the advice he begrudgingly gave was fully adhered to, what more co-operation could he give? Granville-Jones continued by asking Barrett who was in charge of the Club on the night of the 2nd May '97. Barrett's reply was simple, he was. He was the Club manager and that he had been delegated as the person in charge as part of the P.E.L regulations. It was now my turn I didn't have to give evidence but twenty months of 'pent' up frustration had to be vented.

Granville-Jones asked me why I'd never co-operated with the police, and wasn't it true that PC Tony Davies had warned me not to take the Club on in the first place because; 'It attracted drug dealers like bees to a honey pot'.

My answer to that was that I had co-operated with the police, it was Tony Davies who had recommended Howell's Security. I had also written to him about organising a training course. Being a former director of Powys Training Council I was aware that training in our industry was poor. He never replied! We issued anti drug leaflets and posters after Mr. Barrett's meeting with the two drugs squad officers in June '97. Howell's security were not only recommended by the police but licensed and trained by Pembrokeshire County

Council as a requirement of the Public Entertainment's Licence. They had 'carte blanche' when it came to security and drug detection at the Club. Patrons to the Club were searched on a random basis but door-staff are limited in what they can do when searching people. The Judge interrupted saying. "Surely it doesn't stop there."
I replied.

"Well, what else could we do?"

The Judge continued

"You could have mounted your own under cover operation!"

"We have neither the training nor the resources to do that. If the police had wanted us to, then why didn't they ask. In fact they had carried out another undercover operation at the Club but found nothing. I had asked Mr. Howells on numerous occasions about drugs at the Club and he always told me there was no problem."
Granville-Jones came in with.

"O! And you believed him; he wanted to make a speech from the witness box."

"Well he is your witness!"

He then changed the subject into a long dialogue about the 'Up for It' nights and how they had been run as 'Rave' nights with 'head-banging' music organised by Danny Slade and Andrew Price. Did I not tell the police when applying for the licence I would not run 'Rave' nights but would be more up market? But of course when that didn't work I turned to these 'Rave' nights and everyone knows the type of persons they attract!

I explained that they were not 'Rave' nights. Danny Slade was a well respected Radio Wales DJ and the DJ's we had on those nights were top people, playing a variety of modern dance music.

He then moved on asking if we had video cameras at the Club. He was flicking through the incident report produced by Tony Davies that had been dismissed as hearsay at the 'old style committal'. I thought my barrister might have objected but he didn't. I informed Granville-Jones that we did have video cameras' at the Club, both out side and a couple of dummy ones inside. Inside we relied on the door staff to observe. Pointing to the document he carried on.

"Well according to this they weren't working on several occasions."

I replied it was nonsense, and if he was referring to PC Tony Davies report he should also note we had reduced so called incidents at the Club by 33% over the corresponding 28 month period when the previous owners ran the Club. The Judge stopped the line of questioning there.

Granville-Jones then went on to the episode of the military policemen on the 4th July '97. Again I thought my Brief would challenge him or even the Judge. I thought the case was about the 2nd May in isolation?

"Didn't you allow a drug dealer to re-enter your Club?"

I was dumbfounded and informed him that if he was referring to Bret Goodridge he was not a drug dealer, he had never been convicted of any such offence. Anyway I was not present that night, Mr. Barrett and Mr. Howells dealt with it, I only found out about the incident the following day. He continued by saying that didn't they want to eject the MP's in favour of a drug dealer! Before I could reply properly the Judge adjourned for lunch. During the lunch hour I asked why my barrister hadn't intervened, I thought we were dealing with the 2nd of May in isolation. He just said I was doing fine.

As soon as we resumed Granville-Jones looking straight at me said

" When Barrett and Howells informed you about the drug dealer incident of the 4th July, did they tell you what happened to him and the MP's?"

I explained that they had but it had already been taken care of there was little I could do, I wasn't there that particular night.

"So you couldn't have cared less?"

"Mr. Jones, of course I cared but Barrett and Howells had dealt with it."

He sat down saying

"I see-no further questions."

My barrister asked me a few questions about my back ground, that I had never been involved in any form of drug abuse, that I was a well know and prominent businessman, a former chairman of the CBI in mid-Wales with many other business commitments other than the Club. He also asked me to state that when I was at the Club I spent most of my time in Bogey's Bar, although I did walk around the nightclub area periodically but relied heavily on my staff.

The last witness would be my ex-wife Gill. She had been running the accounts of the Club and analysed the invoices and receipts. She had prepared a series of graphs based on monthly bar sales showing the various percentages indicating the sales of beers, spirits and water etc. Bottled beer was by far the biggest selling product with water sales accounting for 3 or 4%. If we sold our entire monthly stock on the 2nd May it would not have equated to anything like the accusations of the undercover police, that the vast majority of customers were drinking bottled water at the Club.

This was the first time we had been able to present any evidence to support our claim that the undercover officers were not telling the truth.

It would be the biggest anti-climax of the trial. The Judge made some remark about how he liked graphs and the prosecution made a few grunts. My barrister enquired whether this evidence was to be contested and Granville-Jones shook his head. There was no debate. Yet this issue had been the pivot of the prosecutions case.

Next, the defence made their plea of no case to answer. The prosecution rejected this by saying of course we knew of the drug dealing but had decided to turn a blind eye to the obvious. Presentations took up the rest of the day. Granville-Jones fell asleep at one stage to be woken by the Judge. It was an effective distraction during the summing up process. The Jury seemed totally bored by it all.

The following morning Judge Burr summed up giving a lot of credence to the evidence of the undercover officers. He did balance it slightly by pointing out the graph's that Mrs Gittins had produced, but with little weight behind his observation of what they actually revealed. He pointed out the charges; one count each of allowing Class A Ecstasy, Class B Amphetamine and Class C Cannabis to be purchased at the Club on the night of the 2nd May 1997.

He briefed the Jury on what knowledge meant in this case. They must decide if we had done enough to prevent drug abuse or did we 'turn a blind eye.'

It was difficult to know what the Jury was thinking; they looked a little confused. We would have to wait three and half long hours for their verdict, and we were not allowed to leave the court building. When the Jury finally decided they were ready we were ushered into the dock and stood facing the Jury as they delivered their verdict. Barrett was convinced they would ether throw it out or find him guilty but felt there was no way I could be found guilty.

They gave their verdict on Barrett first. Count 1 not guilty! Count 2 not guilty! Count 3 they were unsure but after a very short intermission they came back with a not guilty!

As they turned to give their verdict on me my stomach began to churn.

Count 1 guilty!   Count 2 guilty   Count 3 not guilty!

There was a look of complete and utter disbelief on the faces of the people assembled in the court. Gill was crying and I was numb. Barrett was shaking his head repeating.

"No way, no way."

The Jury quickly filed out. I shook Barrett's hand in congratulations and contemplated by own fate.

The Judge declined to sentence me, saying he wanted to consider it in more detail. I was allowed bail to appear before him in three weeks time. Leaving the dock I tried to speak to my barrister but he had left the Court. I spoke to the solicitor's clerk David Williams who could say little other that he was totally shocked. He had been a Police Inspector and couldn't believe how the hell the Judge had allowed the case to go the distance and what the Jury had been thinking was beyond comprehension. They had found the person in charge of the Club and present, not guilty and the person who was absent guilty? But what was I guilty of? The perpetrators of the crime had not been arrested in the Club but several weeks later. The offending handful of drugs could not be produced and the one piece of solid evidence that could prove my innocence had been ignored!

I shed several tears before walking out into the street and over to the Wig and Pen for a stiff drink! My future was now looking extremely bleak!

# 24

# Injustice Most Foul

A few days after the shock of being found guilty of 'knowingly allow' I met with my barrister to discuss the next stage. He was full of apology and said he would mount an appeal directly after sentencing. My confidence in him was at very low ebb but I had little choice but to hope he could at least make the Judge see some common sense. He informed me I could very well be looking at a custodial sentence but the CPS seemed willing to accept a fine or community service. In any case we would lodge an appeal as we had more than enough grounds.

Meanwhile I still had to organise the European Research Project and got working on this to take my mind of the conviction. My friends and colleagues could not believe it. Everyone was convinced I would not be sent to goal and letters of support arrived daily. After arranging the 'kick off' meeting for the Research Project to take place on the 20 and 21st May 1999, I received a call from my solicitors clerk David Williams. The sentencing would take place on the 21st May. I told him I'd be unveiling the European Project that same day. Was there anyway of postponing it? He replied that he very much doubted it but would try. He rang back a few hours later, miraculously, the court had agreed to delay sentencing until Monday the 24th, reiterating that he had never known them to do that before. Normally the date would be 'cast in stone' unless it suited them. Surely this was a good sign!

The launch of the Research Project was a tremendous success that attracted a lot of media coverage. I was interviewed for television news and the national and international press covered the story. I addressed a packed auditorium of scientists, university professors, financiers, industrialists and government officials. The Court case seemed a million miles away. My business colleagues were impressed and Gill felt proud of my achievement against the odds. Even I couldn't believe I'd managed to keep everything on track, how I'd not suffered a nervous breakdown I'll never know. I kept saying to myself, I've done nothing wrong! Monday the 24th May arrived; Gill and Paula drove me to Court accompanied by my friend Colonel Patch.

My solicitors had prepared an impressive portfolio of testimonials and references endorsing my good character, and many public and charitable works. A letter explaining the great importance of the research project I was engaged in with the European Commission and a glowing report from the probation service as to why I should not receive a custodial sentence. A letter from my doctor explaining I suffered blood pressure and stress problems from this prolonged affair also endorsed my plea for compassion.

Patch went before the Judge to give me a character reference explaining my good works for Airborne Forces Charities. Furthermore he was senior Guard Force inspector for the Ministry of Defence. One of the Camps he inspected was the Penally Army Camp close to Chequers nightclub and there had always been a good relationship between the Camp and the Club. The Judge became flustered and stopped Patch in mid sentence saying

" Well we had different evidence from three MP's so we shouldn't go into that."

He started moving papers from side to side and was obviously taken aback by what had been laid before him. He retired to consider my punishment, returning after ten minutes or so to read out his decision.

After giving a flowing account of my impeccable character and the way in which I had behaved throughout my entire period of bail he sentenced me to twelve months imprisonment! Everyone waited with baited breath for him to continue with 'to be suspended.' But it never came, just the words "take him down." I was looking straight at him but he never raised his head, he could not look at me. He stood up, turned and disappeared. The Court Usher had to find a Dock Officer to take me to the cells. Throughout both the trials and the committal proceedings there had never been the need for a Dock Officer.

I looked over to Gill and felt her anger. The charade had finally ended in farce. British Justice would be called into disrepute yet again. Even Granville-Jones looked astonished and the Court Usher blushed with embarrassment. He asked me to wait a few minutes while they found someone to take me to the cells, saying,

"Look I'll make sure your family can see you down stairs in the cells. I'm really sorry about all this, its bloody ridiculous!"

Walking down the steps from the courtroom to the bowels of the building and holding cells is a very lonely walk.

Every step a step into the unknown a dangerous world apart from friends and loved ones. My head spun all my achievements all the good things I'd done accounted for nothing. When I reached the bottom of the stairs an officer met me and asked if I'd like a cup of tea. There were some forms to fill in then I could see my friends.

After the paperwork my barrister and solicitor came to see me, saying they'll file an appeal immediately. Then Gill, Paula, Gareth Barrett and Patch came in. Barrett called the officer and gave him £40 in cash and sixty cigarettes saying I'd left it behind up stairs. The officer gave me the cigarettes and put the cash in my wallet which would then be taken to the prison and put into a canteen account.

I spent twenty minutes or so with Gill and the others before I had to leave to be placed in a cell. After a few minutes in the cell a very distraught young lad from Cardigan who'd been sentenced to eighteen months for fighting joined me. We would share a cell in Swansea Prison for the next two weeks.

Returning to that Jail as a convicted prisoner was the worst experience of my life. If I had done something wrong it would have been much easier to accept. Being the victim of a miscarriage of justice is everyone's nightmare I never thought it would happen to me but lying on a cold metal bunk bed the reality began to dawn.

That first night was dreadful. Through the bars of my cell window I could see Swansea Bay. A chilling wind blew across the white-topped waves in the early evening light as ships steamed across the horizon to who knows where? A poem I wrote at the time best describes how I felt.

*Day and night I wrote.*
*In Swansea Bay and prison poke.*
*Through bars of sea and winds so cold,*
*That night I grew so old.*
*In Swansea Bay and prison poke.*

*Jangle Keys and echo sound.*
*No good night from screw in black.*
*Doors that slam-they go bang! Bang!*
*In Swansea Bay and prison poke.*

*Stone of rock, soot of black,*
*Colours of my day, colours of my night.*
*They keep me in or keep me out.*
*With spinning thought, it's lonely now.*
*In Swansea Bay and prison poke.*

On my second day I had an unexpected 'legal' visit thinking it to be my solicitor with some good news. Instead of my solicitor it turned out to be a bailiff who served me a writ from my bank Lloyds-TSB for the immediate repayment of my overdraft! The following day my barrister turned up to report that the trial Judge had refused to hear an appeal application. He would now lodge the appeal with the Royal Courts of Justice in London. When I'd been on remand 18 months previously the prison officers treated me well and couldn't believe the charges against me. Thankfully they were to treat me with the same respect and showed even greater disbelief over my conviction. Both my cellmate Robert Brown and I had requested to be moved to an open prison. Before that could happen we had to be categorised and our state of mind had to be assessed.

Brown was extremely distraught, he had a young family, his wife having given birth to a son only a week before he was convicted. He had fits of crying and talked continuously, I was concerned that he might do something irrational. I kept telling him to hold back his emotions when the officers talked to him otherwise he would spend his entire sentence in Swansea. There was no way he would be transferred to an open prison if he were emotionally unstable. Taking him under my wing probably helped me more than him. It took my mind off my own despair.

We were both desperate to be transferred. Swansea was full to bursting point and the officers were concerned about the numbers of first time offenders being sent down by the courts. Forty percent of new admissions were now first timers. The authorities were now operating a politically motivated stance of zero tolerance. All very well but it creates enormous problems. Not only can the prisons not cope; but also the future burden on society will be high.

A prison sentence is devastating to most people; their future employment prospects become grim. There are those who deserve prison and should not be allowed back into society, but jailing people for relatively small and first time misdemeanours erodes the significance of a jail sentence. After a spell inside it is often the case that the original jail sentence becomes self-perpetuating when those released find it impossible to find gainful employment. They then turn to crime encouraged by their new 'friends'. It is inevitable after any length of time incarcerated that you will meet people you would not have met out side. It does not happen in all cases but in many. Too many!

Luckily, after two weeks that felt like two years I was transferred to Prescoed Open Prison. After spending an average of 22 hours a day locked up Prescoed was literary a breath of fresh air.

After driving through the leafy lanes of Monmouthshire we arrived at what looked like a 1950's army camp. After processing we were shown around our new home. Instead of a cold dank cell I had a little bedroom to myself. As humble as it was it seemed like a palace compared to the accommodation at Swansea. My cellmate remained in Swansea Prison for a further two months. One chap who came with us in the 'sweat-box', relieved at finally getting away from 'bang up', was turned away because he was disabled, despite posters in the reception unit declaring the Prison Service's non-discrimination policy; he returned two months later after lodging several protests. Prescoed would remain my home for the next three months. Again the prison officers were to treat me very well. One of the senior officers was from Brecon and I knew his family well. I did not receive any special favours but he was a link with home.

Being a working prison one had a choice between jobs and education. The open prison system was a far more civilised approach to penal servitude. It is not suitable for every prisoner because you could just walk out if you were of a mind to. It revolved around trust and privilege, if you transgressed punishment meant back to 'bang up' never to return.

At first I opted for full time education in the computer centre which I found invaluable and I gained an RSA diploma in computer literacy. After a few weeks I got the Librarians job and switched the computer course to the evening, but as the computer centre was at the back of the library I managed to combine both. Running the library was not only the prime job in any prison but would prove a crucial move in my fight to clear my name. I began by reading legal textbooks and then managed to obtain an up to date copy of 'Archbold' the bible of our legal system.

My fight against the Scotch Whisky Association had not gone away either. On the 11th June 1999, whilst incarcerated and against all the odds I won a mile stone rearguard action. My 'civil' legal team headed by Hugh Hitchcock solicitor, and barrister Robert Onslow, managed to over turn the High Court Injunction won through default by the SWA the previous year. I would have no such luck with my criminal team Huw Rees lost the first stage with the application to the 'Single Judge' despite what I thought was a good 'perfected grounds' of appeal submission. But I thought he was missing the pivotal point, it was at this stage, I felt I had to continue the fight alone.

Among the inmates there were several solicitors convicted of various acts of misappropriation of client's accounts. Nevertheless they had a wealth of knowledge and they would assist me with an addendum, which I would prepare for the 'full court' application for leave to appeal.

When the first stage had been lost several well-meaning officers told me that I now risked having my sentence doubled if I continued with my appeal. But I knew I was right and had no option but to fight on, somewhere, somehow I would get justice.

Gill had mounted a petition on the outside obtaining hundreds of signatures, and posters appeared throughout South Pembrokeshire and Brecon. 'Free Dafydd'. She, on my behalf, wrote to Dyfed Powys Police asking for a copy of the audit that DC John Davies said he had made of the Clubs' computer but never produced in Court. We received no reply. I asked my solicitor Del Cudd to write demanding a reply but nothing happened. It appeared to me that it was inconceivable that the police would seize the computer yet fail to obtain its data. This to me was the central issue that my barrister had failed to pursue.

While I waited for my appeal to be heard it was time to get on with doing my sentence. Another turn of fate would be that the person Gill had assisted Customs to convict for Wales' biggest smuggling operation, Mickey Oliver, a likeable cockney rogue in his early fifties, arrived from Cardiff Prison to spend the rest of his six and half year sentence at Prescoed. One of his co-conspirators was still awaiting trial after being extradited from Spain. Gill was on stand by as a key witness in his trial scheduled for September. Here was I languishing at her Majesty's pleasure with the man my ex-wife had helped put away and it was not his first time by any means. He was what you may call an 'old lag' having spent time at such salubrious institutions as the Scrubs and Pentonville.

Although I was a bit apprehensive when he approached me, (there are few secrets in side), he had been told who I was. Nevertheless, and surprisingly there was no animosity. He had resigned himself knowing that what he had been convicted of he actually had done. There was no bitterness; in fact we got on quite well together. Mickey was a popular guy with a great sense of humour. On many an evening he would retell his many escapades over endless cups of tea and biscuits on the lawns outside our 'wing' a bungalow style building housing twenty or so inmates in single bedrooms.

The summer of '99 was long and warm, my days were spent working in the library, and evenings walking around the extensive grounds or sharing a 'brew' and a laugh with the other guys.

Cards was a popular past time but not for me, I had never played cards since losing my first months salary while working for Lufthansa in Hamburg and apart from the odd flutter, gambling was not really a vice of mine. But I would sit with Mickey and his 'Gang' and talk while they played a game called 'Kalukkie', sometimes all night. I called them the 'Kalukkie' Kings and wrote them a poem as a keepsake.

*'The cards unfold the tables set.*
*The Kalukkie Kings begin to play.*

*The deal is dealt.*
*Win or Lose, the Kings will choose.*

*Oly's in and Tuggers not.*
*Massy heaves and Jimmy grieves.*
*The night is long the music strong,*
*Smoke begins to slow.*

*As doggie's mount they begin to count.*
*Hand by hand the Kings reveal.*
*Cards are kind and cards are not.*
*For one must win and one must not!*

*Night draws in cells doors call.*
*Time to fold, pack grows cold.*
*Day by day, hand by hand,*
*Freedom calls, the pack goes back.*

*The Jokers sing the final song.*
*The Kalukkies sail that homeward track?'*

Boredom is the main problem in jail, in Swansea it was excruciating but at Prescoed there were things to occupy your mind. I had learnt to master the computer, something I'd always wanted to do but never found the time. Writing had also become a major pass time for me. Short stories and poetry became a passion. Prescoed was a small prison with just eighty or so inmates, twenty of whom were young offenders. An experiment to stop bullying when the jail was entirely made up of Y.O.'s. In the main it was a good idea the only bullying that I ever saw at the prison was amongst the youngsters and was usually stopped by the older guys.

As for homosexuality I never saw any, even at Swansea. If it went on it was very discreet.

There was a lot of humour inside, a major safety valve but not all the humour came from the prisoners the officer's could hold there own. One of them, who I came to know as Sandy, missed his vocation and should have been on the stage. He had several duties one being the legal aid officer and one the 'AIDS' awareness advisor. His seminars were hilarious but he got the message over.

On the whole the staff were dedicated, if you were willing so were they. The object was to try and get you back into society; not an easy task. The majority of offenders I met were either 'white collar,' petty criminals or 'long termers' at the end of their sentences. The inmates of HMP Prescoed were made up of struck off solicitors, 'iffy' stockbrokers, 'book fiddling' businessmen, fraudsters and tobacco and alcohol smugglers. Their lives wrecked, families broken and fortunes lost.

We also had a prisoner of Principal. Eric Man from Pembroke, who suffered with arthritics but found cannabis relieved his suffering. He was serving twelve months for growing the offending weed in his garden and led a campaign for its legalisation which had a fair amount of public support. The Young Offenders on the other hand were inevitably there for possession of cannabis, joy riding or theft.

At the end of the day they all had to face an uncertain future. Most were guilty of their crimes and were paying a heavy price. Others were arguably not, but the complexity of an appeal and the appalling legal advice they had received made the prospect of due process a remote possibility. As I see it, the open prison system is better structured to give offenders some hope and possibility of getting back to work as there is a fairly sophisticated structure of work related and educational support in place. This is not the case in closed prisons and the repercussions of over crowding and hopelessness endemic to those institutions, is probably, the biggest cause of the ever rising crime rate we see in the UK today.

All in all my days at Prescoed were bearable. I felt comforted in my unshakeable belief that I had committed no crime and no matter how long it took or how much effort I needed to expend I would win in the end. By August I was getting home leave every other Sunday Gill would pick me up at 9.30am and get me back to the Prison by 5pm.

It was a welcome respite but nerve raking getting back on time. A minute late and you were on a serious charge. But it was worth it for some home cooking. Prison food wasn't all bad. Sometimes at Prescoed it was reasonably good with such gourmet delights as fish fingers and curry sauce! Swansea on the other hand was uneatable slop, and I simply refused to eat porridge! A great comfort during my time in jail were letters, I received hundreds, either direct to the prison or Gill would bring those sent to my house when she visited.

Dafydd Wigley MP, Plaid Cymru's president, wrote to me several times pledging his support and arranged for Elfyn Llwyd MP, Plaid's legal affairs spokesman to advise on the addendum appeal papers I had drawn up with the help of my fellow in-mates.

Christine Chambers an old friend from Brecon sent me regular supplies of stamps, which enabled me to reply to the letters I received thus giving me a lifeline. All these things helped me cope with this dark chapter in a once colourful and productive life.

Towards the end of my time I was allowed to attend some meetings in Cardiff. I needed to sort out business affairs with my partners. Brian Morgan had visited me several times but surprisingly Alun Evans did not. I knew Tony James was unwell and couldn't, but Alun's decision not to visit was a mystery.

We held a meeting in Brian's offices at Cardiff University to discuss the European Project and the building of the new distillery at Penderyn, all of which had been seriously delayed by my untimely imprisonment. I realised that what had happened to me had caused my colleagues great embarrassment, but I prayed they would stand by me.

The meeting did not go very well, Brian was OK but Alun was distant. I agreed to work on some documents and address various technical questions arising from the distillation project. Other than that there was no firm offer to take me back as an advisor, in all fairness they wanted to see how I got on with my appeal and I had to accept that. But in reality they had dumped me.

On the way back to Prescoed after the meeting, Gill received a call from Customs and Excise on her mobile phone. The long awaited trial against Mickey Oliver's co-defendant had been listed at Newport Crown Court the following week. They were most anxious for her to give evidence on behalf of the Crown, which she readily agreed to do. Ironically when I got back to prison Mickey already knew all the details. I wasn't going to mention it for obvious reasons.

His co-defendant was pleading not guilty but Mickey was worried he would change his plea and make a deal with Customs. On the 2nd September 1999 my solicitors finally received a letter from Dyfed Powys Police denying that they had ever taken the computer from the Club. Ten days later I was released on the new electronic tagging scheme and had to reside at my Cottage in Saundersfoot.

This latest twist would prove crucial. We had clear evidence they had taken the computer and even held in for a year. I couldn't fathom out why they now decided to deny it! There was nothing logical about such a statement. But then, nothing had been logical about this case from the very beginning!

# 25

# The Twists And Turns!

A few days before my release I rang Gill to make the final arrangements. She was a bit distraught and informed me she had received a phone call from Customs saying they no longer required her to give evidence at the second Newport Trial. Mickey Oliver's co-defendant had changed his plea to guilty so none of the witness' were now required. However, she had also received a recorded delivery letter saying she was being prosecuted herself over alleged irregularities at Welsh Distillers! I told her that was impossible. Customs had informed me on several occasions during the time I was in charge of the distillery, on behalf of them and the liquidator, that she was immune from prosecution. That was certainly my understanding.

The directors of MDT had been charged more than a year previously of various alleged breaches of the Customs and Excise Management Act. There had also been allegations that they were involved in the diversion of goods from the bonded warehouse at Brecon. Gill had put her self at considerable risk helping Customs piece together the whole intriguing network of bogus companies and elaborate paper chases. Through her, not inconsiderable efforts, they had been able to recover some seventeen million pounds worth of goods that would otherwise have found there way onto the UK market. These facts had been revealed at Mickey Oliver's trial. There had to be some mistake! I honestly thought the world had gone mad! But it would be a long time before this saga unfolded. Although there were no allegations against me, I would not let Gill face this alone. It was yet another mountain to climb but I had to fight my battle first.

On Monday the 13th September 1999 I left HMP Prescoed. My first port of call was the Wellington Hotel, Brecon. Peter and Pam Saxon, two good and loyal friends, laid on a Champagne breakfast for Gill, Gareth and myself. Next I had to drive to Saundersfoot and ring the Probation Service to tell them I was at my residence and waiting for the 'tagging' company. No sooner had I put the phone down than friends from the Village started knocking on my door to welcome me home. By the time the 'tagging' people arrived a full-scale party was ensuing.

Electronic tagging had been introduced at the beginning of that year after various trials in England. It was proving to be successful and extremely cost effective for the Government. The real cost of keeping someone in prison is around £1,000 a week whereas 'tagging' costs a little more than £50 per week. Had it not been introduced I would have spent a further two months inside. Tagging is not an option to all prisoners, only those deemed, after careful checks, of not being a threat to the public. It consists of a watch type of transmitter attached to your leg. In the house there is a monitor connected to the telephone line. A curfew is set; mine was 10pm until 8am. (Normally it's 7pm to 7am). If you leave the confines of the house during that time a signal is sent down the phone line to a central monitoring centre. If that happens you are in breach of your release conditions and face arrest and immediate return to a closed prison for the rest of your sentence. Statistically less than 5% break the 'tagging' curfew and I suspect that fair proportions of these are technical. On a number of occasions the special tagging phone would ring at night to say they were not getting a signal at such and such a time. It turned out that the bathroom was a 'blackspot.' They had to come out to reset the transmitter range. As welcome as tagging was, I remained a convicted prisoner striving for vindication but I now had the freedom to pursue my appeal with vigour. The first thing I would do was to get the original manufacturer of 'the' computer to analyse its data in detail.

Comstat UK Limited retrieved the vital evidence for the offending night the 2nd May 1997 and confirmed Gill's reconciliation of the overall annualised consumption being less than 4% of sales. Although the retrieved data showed that on the night of the 2/3rd May some 207 bottles of water were sold, they only accounted for less than 1 in 5 of all drinks sold and less than 12% of total cash sales. This hardly reflected the evidence given at the trial when the Police Officers had reported that "the vast majority of people were drinking bottled water!"

The Officers themselves admitted to consuming bottled water all evening to 'blend in' and could have accounted for 15 to 20% of these sales alone. Which might explain their frequent trips to the toilets. Yes! Water sales had been higher than normal that one night but hardly cause for concern. The Company analysed other Friday nights at random and showed sales of less than 10%, less than 5%, and some nights none at all, including the night of the 5th September '97 when the police raided in force and arrested me. That night a senior officer gave evidence in Court saying, "he saw no alcohol being consumed only bottle water."

Having been given a telephone number at the Royal Courts, and because I was unrepresented, the name of a case-worker was passed onto me. When I rang her, Ms. Claire Kerr informed me that my leave of appeal hearing was scheduled for the beginning of November.

We spoke for a long time, she had obviously done her homework not only did she know much of the case background but complimented my preparation of appeal papers and the addendum document. I had also made an application to attend Court; this seemed a problem because technically I was still incarcerated. Under the rules I was not entitled to attend the 'Leave' application hearing. However, she said she'd see what could be done. Ringing me back the following day she confirmed, uniquely, that the Registrar of the Court had allowed my attendance and would allow me a short address to the Court. After making all the arrangement to travel to London while under home curfew, which meant informing my probation officer David Norcross, asking permission from the Governor of HMP Prescoed, and arranging with the 'tagging' company to suspend my curfew, the date was changed to the 26th November. The change of date was disappointing but something I had learned to expect during the past two years.

When the time came, although feeling apprehensive at standing before the Royal Courts to argue my case, I also felt confident. My pal Peter Saxon accompanied me as moral support and sat waiting for the three Judges to arrive. Being told to attend Court at 10.30am at 11am the Judges arrived, apologised, and informed me my case would be heard at 2pm. Neither the CPS nor the police were going to attend!

Pete and I had a late breakfast in the George Inn, a pub directly opposite the Royal Courts. Finally my case started promptly in court 6 at 2pm before Lord Justice Evans, Justice Alliott and Mrs Justice Ebsworth.

Coincidentally a short distance away in an adjoining courtroom Mohammed Al'Fayed and the former MP Neil Hamilton were locked in litigation and the whole place was swarming with media and press.

Sitting in the wooden stalls looking around the ornate oak panelled room, lined with countless volumes of law books, then to the high podium where my Judges would peer down upon me the Royal Coat of Arms embellished in the wall behind them, I knew that if I failed here it would be the end, life as I knew it would never be the same again.

The Judges read out a synopsis of the case, charges and sentence given. They then referred to my 'addendum' to the grounds for appeal, referring to the 'new' computer evidence and my challenge to the whole ethos of the conviction. After this they called me to the front of the Court to answer some questions. Lord Evans asked me was the computer evidence available to the trial Judge?

My answer; "not in its current form merely monthly averages"

I then went on to say my barrister had advised I had no case to answer and concentrated on this fact alone. We knew the police had taken the computer and there must have been a reason for this but no one, the CPS or the Judge, had demanded an independent analysis of the data.

They asked me if I had any further observations to which I continued.

"The police took the computer for a purpose. They accessed its data banks found the truth and suppressed it. There can be no conceivable belief that they did not make a full audit of that computer. They held it for a year, now they say they never took it, yet in the first trial they admitted they took it but made no audit. In the second trial they admit they did carry out an audit but could find only till receipts from a system that does not produce such receipts and we never even saw those receipts!"

I then quoted a phrase in Latin 'A actus Non Facit Reum Nisi Mens Sit Rea' and repeated my allegation that the police had taken the computer for a reason then suppressed that evidence.

With a brief smile Justice Alliott said.

"Yes, yes we get your point and there's no need for jargon, you've been most helpful."

They adjourned for a while to consider. On return Lord Evans gave the task of reading out their judgement to Justice Allilott.

I had won! Leave to appeal had been granted and my legal aid reinstated. Although I still had to win the full appeal I had succeeded where my legal advisors had failed. I was no longer a convicted criminal and would not have to serve the rest of my twelve month sentence on probation. Before leaving the Court I gave a press statement to Strand News Agencies whose reporter had followed the case with great interest.

Boarding a South Wales bound train at Paddington we celebrated in the buffet car, bumping into Dafydd Williams, Plaid Cymru's General Secretary, on his way back to Cardiff. He bought me a well-earned can of Strongbow!

Stopping over in Brecon for a few days I then returned to Saundersfoot and opened my mail. Low and behold there was a summons from Pembrokeshire Magistrates Court to attend court for non-payment of a fine imposed by them in February 1998.

Apparently papers from the appeal at Swansea's Crown Court in July '98 had only just arrived at Haverfordwest pertaining to the P.E.L. breaches at Chequers back in the summer of '97. I was to appear before Tenby Magistrates on Friday December 10th to be 'means tested'. The Clerk of the Court would be the same chap as at the 'old style' committal hearing. However, this time round he was very conciliatory. Explaining to the Magistrates that I wasn't here for non-payment of the fine as such, because it had taken some 16 months for the papers to arrive back from the appeal court in Swansea and no payment demand had ever been sent out.

He suggested to the bench that in view of my circumstances they write the fine and costs off. The Crown Court had substantially reduced it from the original fine anyway. The chairman asked me about my Royal Court Appeal and I explained my success in being granted leave. The bench retired to consider their decision returning within a few minutes. They decided to cut the fine in half to £750 to be paid at £20 per month, in the light that if I win my Appeal against the drugs charges I must stand to get considerable' compensation from the State. To monitor my 'process' I had to re-attend at the end of January. They just couldn't let go. But they did wish me luck!

Winning at Appeal is no easy task. I had legal aid for a barrister only, and under the rules should use the same one as at the original trial. I refused this point blank, it was then put to me that the Court would choose one, again I refused it was then agreed I could choose my own. Through a recommendation I chose a Mr. Joel Bennathan of Tooks Court London. The protocol of having to deal through a solicitor had been waived so I was able to communicate directly with him. After speaking to Joel on the phone we arranged to meet at his London Chambers to plan the full Appeal. The hearing had been scheduled for Friday the 18th February 2000. I met my new barrister for the first time just a week before.

Joel was an amiable chap in his late thirties from the Home Counties; his wife coincidentally was from Llangors near Brecon. We got on very well together, an important point for me, and sat down for a two hour work session to plan the appeal, drawing up the basis for a skeleton argument focused on the 'addendum' that I had put before the previous court.

The Court had directed we concentrate on the water issue but left the door open for us to pursue other avenues of edict. Joel thought the whole affair to be bizaar, finding it difficult to imagine that the case ever got to court in the first place.

Looking at the facts, we were concerned with a single incident, no hard evidence of any prolonged misuse at the premises, the small amount of drugs involved and that the person legally in charge on the night, and present, was acquitted. No previous convictions what so ever and the only inference of knowledge was the evidence given by the undercover officers that the vast majority of customers at the Club were drinking bottled water! The irrefutable computer evidence seriously damaged this single and very tenuous piece of evidence.

He contended that the observations by the undercover

officers on the night were gross exaggerations, both of water consumption and the sale of drugs. Joel also contended that the whole ethos of the conviction was unsafe, with or with out the computer evidence. It would be hard to get the Court to overturn a jury's verdict, but he thought this case was more than strong enough. The Appeal was heard at 11am on Friday the 18th February, before Lord Justice Kennedy, who replaced Lord Rose at the last minute, Mr. Justice Morison and Sir Charles MCCullough at court 6, Royal Courts of Justice in the Strand, London.

I took my son Gareth along, it was important to me that he see his father cleared after all this time. He had suffered as much as anyone seeing his dad jailed and our small family torn apart. Hopefully I would be vindicated but nothing is certain and winning an appeal is no easy task.

This time the CPS would be represented, but not by their trial barrister Mr. Granville-Jones. A replacement, Mr. J. Davies attended. The Police did not show-up. DC John Davies sent his apologies. He was away on holiday in Portugal.

The prosecution came up with a counter to the Computer evidence saying that it only covered the period up to midnight and that further water consumption could have taken place between midnight and 2am the following day before the Club closed.

The CPS had brought this up the day before the hearing, luckily Joel had the forethought to contact the Computer firm directly to verify the exact period the print out covered, which was until 3am.

When this failed the CPS contended that customers were drinking bottled water until the officers left the Club. Joel pointed out the officers didn't leave until 1.30am so was the CPS inferring that 1,058 alcoholic drinks were served and consumed in the last half-hour? He withdrew his comment!

From there on in the prosecution conceded every issue raised, then Joel put forward a second leave of appeal concerning the whole ethos of the conviction. The Appeal Judges immediately accepted this submission.

*"The acquitted co-defendant, Barrett, was the bar manager. In respect of virtually all aspects of the Prosecution's case, it is submitted that the case against him was stronger, in that: -*

*Barrett was actually in the bar on May 2nd the Appellant was not.*
*The sales at the bar of water or anything else, would have been happening in front of, and through, Barrett.*
*The low water pressure/water turned off was due to Barrett, if anyone?*
*Barrett was aware of police activities about this time.*
*Barrett was suggested to have actual contact with drugs.*

*It is accepted that the Honourable Court will only exceptionally interfere with a jury's verdict on this general basis. It is submitted, however, that the principle in R-v-Cooper 1QB267 is still good law.*
*It is further submitted that the combination of paucity of the evidence, the Appellant's age and character and acquittal of Mr Barrett ought to persuade the Honourable Court that this conviction is unsafe.*

The Court adjourned for a short while for the Judges to make their decision. Joel looked confident and began introducing me to two lady barristers who had come to observe. Telling them I was the person who presented his own 'leave' to the Appeal Court. They looked impressed and commented on what an unusual and interesting case this was.

After just five minutes the Judges returned Lord Kennedy asked Mr. Justice Morison to deliver the verdict. We had won! On both issues!

It was clear to the Appeal Court that I had done nothing wrong, it was also clear that Mr. Barrett had done nothing wrong. Yet, the security staff who had been hired after a recommendation from the police and would, if anyone, should have seen what was going on, were not even accused of knowledge or condoning any drug abuse. The question I now asked myself was, did it ever happen in the first place? If the undercover officers exaggerated the water issue what else was untrue?

Joel then addressed the Court again, informing them that his costs had been met by Legal Aid, but I had represented myself at the crucial Leave Application and had assisted him greatly in putting the final Appeal together, because he had entered the fray at the last minute, so to speak. Could the Court consider meeting my out of pocket expenses for the various trips to London? Again with a smile they agreed.

"As long as it didn't include first class rail travel!" Quipped Lord Kennedy.

As we left the Court in jubilation I shook many hands and hugged my son. When we got out side the courtroom I shook Joel by the hand and thanked him profusely; he had done me proud. Before we left he said.

"Well Dafydd, you are now once more of impeccable character. I can't give you back the time you spent in jail but I'm sure you'll tackle that and other issues later on. I'm sorry the system let you down in the first place but you've gained a lot of admiration!"

Gareth and I left the Royal Courts for a celebratory drink or two in the George, joined by some supporters from Tenby and Saundersfoot who had travelled to see the outcome. After making a number of phone calls to tell Gill, Barrett and numerous friends the good news I was asked to go around to the BBC studio's at nearby Bush House by BBC's Melanie Dole to make a live broadcasted interview. The Newspaper headlines heralded ''Whisky man off the Rocks!'' (Brecon & Radnor Express) ''Freed entrepreneur plans to sue'' (Western Mail) ''Licensee wins spirited fight.'' (Western Telegraph) ''Former Whisky King Wins Appeal!'' (BBC Wales Today).

UK legal journals would report the case and the outcome would form legal precedent. Right had vanquished wrong Dafydd felled Goliath but at what cost, would I ever regain what I had lost and why did it ever happen?

# The Aftermath

At the time of going to press I am battling, along with Barrett, Price, Slade and Torkington, for compensation. The Home office is investigating the whole sordid issue but the results are not expected for some time. A claim has been lodged with the Club's Insurance Company and claims issued against Dyfed Powys Police. These total several million pounds and will also take many months to conclude.

Following my watershed victory at the Royal Courts two Cambridgeshire charity workers were released pending an appeal. They had been given sentences totalling nine years for the noxious offence of to knowingly allow drug taking at a hostel they ran for the homeless. Like me they had huge public support. Had my case failed then carers, licensees and others in charge of establishments throughout the United Kingdom would have remained at serious risk of prosecution and conviction of vicarious liability despite a lack of actual knowledge, or the fact they had taken steps to prevent drug taking on their premises.

However, it must be emphasised that we should all

remain vigilant and report anything suspicious to the police immediately. We all have a duty to fight the evil of drugs.

I am no longer a part of either the new Welsh Whisky distillery or the European Commission funded research project, both of which were started by me and would have been my future career but for the damage caused by the actions of the police, and the personal attacks during that time by the Scotch Whisky Association. However, instead of crying into my whisky I've formed a new business in the publishing and entertainment's industry funded by the proceeds of this book. I live in hope of one day making Welsh Whisky again, after all, it formed a large part of my life and provided pride, enjoyment and employment to many.

My son Gareth has recently joined a rock band called Ricochet and their first recording should be out at the end of 2000. I feel sure he will enjoy much success in the music business. As they say watch this space!
I've moved back to Brecon and made a start on my second book, an historical novel to be called The Son Has Risen, and a musical film script with Danny Slade called 'Sound Bites.' A TV documentary drama is planned based on 'Dafydd and Goliath' and who knows, it may even be made into a block-busting film!

My ex-wife Gill and I remain the best of friends. She has moved to Saundersfoot and runs her own small accountancy firm. However she remains embroiled in a battle with HM Customs over duty irregularities at Welsh Distillers/MDT despite all the assistance she gave Customs at the time in bring to book the 'Oliver Gang'. I hope all goes well for her and natural justice and common sense will finally prevail. As for me I'm starting out all over again 'young' free and single and looking forward to my next 50 years, who knows what will happen this time round!

# Epilogue

After the euphoria of victory would come the long hard struggle for compensation for the co-defendants and myself. Some would rightly say that recompense should be automatic but alas it's not.

When the 'Sword of Damocles' pointed at my head, I faced a roller coaster to ruin loss of liberty and years of uncertainty. When I was wrongly convicted I paid an immediate and heavy price. Conversely when it was proved that I bore no guilt the scales of justice should tilt in my direction compensating for the wrongs done, for I too am a victim, and what happened to me could happen to you. It has happened to many others with devastating consequences. People have languished for many years in prison before justice finally prevailed.

The Police in the main do a good and valuable job and often complain about lack of resources. Hopefully my case will help them focus their finite means and question why or how such a case, costing thousands of man hours and millions of pounds, was ever brought, and the motives of the officers

who instigated this travesty from the beginning.
The Crown Prosecution Service should be far more subjective and independent, the Courts more consistent and unbiased. Our legal profession at all levels seems little more than a lottery and the whole system is overloaded and in serious need of reform. Easy words-hard task!

If citizens of whatever country can not rely on their judicial system then they are let down and unprotected by their elected representatives in Government.

*"Justice is like a game of football, we invented the game but don't play it very well at present!"*
Dafydd Gittins the year 2000.

# Chronology Of Events

**R. V. Dafydd N. Gittins.**

2nd May 1997: Undercover operation at Chequers nightclub. Purchase of various drugs to the value appx £77. 5 Ecstasy tablets and two wraps of Amphetamine.

27th May 1997: Three persons arrested in Carmarthen in connection with this supply. Tito Payne, Andrew Blakey and Sharon Potter.

5th Sept 1997: Tito Payne pleads guilty to 5 counts of supplying drugs at Chequers on the 2nd May 1997.

5th Sept 1997: Gittins, Barrett and Torkington arrested at Chequers nightclub in connection with events occurring on the 2nd May. Police find one 'E' tablet where three people were sitting. They are neither arrested nor questioned. A number of empty 'wraps' found after an extensive search and a small piece of cannabis in the managers' flat. Manager was not present during the search of his private quarters. Allegedly PC Tony Davies spent some twenty minutes in Barretts' flat alone. Computer and other items seized by police as evidence.

7th Sept 1997: All three Charged with 9 offences of being involved in the management of premises and knowingly permitting the supply of controlled drugs. Barrett is also charged with 1 offence of possession of cannabis.

8th Sept 1997: Appeared at Haverfordwest Magistrates Court. Bail application made, bail refused remanded in custody because two other suspects still at large.

8th Sept 1997: Slade arrested after surrendering at Tenby Police Station. (He had been working in Northern Ireland)

10th Sept 1997: Price arrested after surrendering at Tenby Police Station. (He had been away in New York at a hairdressing convention) Police issue revocation of licence notice.

15th Sept 1997: Appeared in Haverfordwest, bail application made, bail granted with conditions, case adjourned until 21st Oct 1997. A Brett Goodridge, is joined to our case making it 6 defendants.

3rd Oct 1997: Tito Payne sentenced to 2 years imprisonment. He had previous convictions dating back to 1995. Andrew Blake 4 months and Sharon Potter community service.

21st Oct 1997: No typed statements received from police, matter adjourned to 30th Oct 1997. CPS accepts that this sit-

uation is unacceptable.
30th Oct 1997: Jurisdiction declined by Tenby Magistrates, matter to proceed to committal adjourned until 4th Dec 1997 for review. Advocates only to appear.

31st Oct 1997: Club license revoked 'Dafydd Gittins is not a fit and proper person as he **has** knowingly allowed and suffered the premises to be use for the sale, supply and use of classes A, B, and C controlled drugs.' Despite the fact he had not even been tried in any court, magistrates refused to accept this fact. Hearsay evidence compiled by PC Tony Davies accepted by Tenby Magistrates Court. **Alleged act of sub-judice?**

4th Dec 1997: application for adjournment made by prosecution. CPS indicates that they would serve the statements by end of next week. Adjourned until 15th Jan 1998.

9th Dec 1997. Pembrokeshire County Council refuses to renew P.E.L. licence, because of noise and safety allegations, none of which proven or tried in a court of law. **Alleged act of sub-judice?**

17th Dec 1997. Appeal to Crown Court over revocation withdrawn due to lack of funds.

15th Jan 1998: supplied with committal papers at Court, case adjourned.

31st Jan 1998. Magistrates fine Company, United Clubs (Wales) Ltd. £8,000+costs over two breaches of noise abatement notices. Gittins and Jones £2,000+costs each over two breaches of P.E.L. regulations. (Dirty toilets and a sign with incorrect sized lettering). Immediate appeal to Crown Court Legal Aid awarded at later date.

26th & 28th Feb 1998: representations made in relation to whether the committal should be old or new style. Case adjourned for special Court before Tenby Magistrates. Adjourned until 12th March 1998 to fix date for the hearing. Defendants not required at hearing.

12th Mar 1998: adjourned for 1 week to enable defendants to canvass availability of Council. Adjourned until 19th March 1998.

19th Mar 1998: date fixed for committal before the Magistrate 26th May 1998 at Haverfordwest Shire Hall.

26th May 1998. Old style committal in relation to 3 counts of permitting the supply of control drugs over a prolonged period. Found no case to answer the 3 counts were thrown out. Police incident report complied by P.C. Tony Davies rejected as hearsay, no substance.

1st June 1998. The old style committal for six counts of permitting the supply of control drugs and one count of possession. These charges were committed to the Crown Court for PDH set on 29th June 1998 and related to two dates the 2nd May and the 5th September 1997.

28th Jun 1998: informed by listing officer that PDH should now take place on 30th June 1998.

30th June 1998: PDH Swansea Crown Court made. Disclosure to be made within 14 days.

24th July 1998: Appeal at Swansea Crown Court HH. G. O. Edwards presiding against PEL and Noise accepted. Company fine reduced from £8,000 to zero; Gittins' fine reduced to £1,500 later to £750 then zero and Jones £1,000 over minor P.E.L. breaches.

7th Sept 1998: Mention requested in order to put pressure on the CPS to comply with their directions.

13th Oct 1998: Defence solicitors have still not received primary disclosure from CPS or a date for mention.

11th Jan 1999: Final disclosure received.

25th Jan 1999: Case at Swansea GuildHall starts. HH Mr Justice M. Burr. Bret Goodridge acquitted by direction of the Judge at start of hearing after spending four months on remand.

Case revolves around the water issue. Police maintain that on the night of arrest 5th Sept 1997 DS J.J. Morris states no one at premises drinking alcohol only water. (We have written statements to this effect). Under cover officers all state the same for the 2nd May 1997. DC. Davies says no audit of computer had been made but he had 'till receipts!!!' showing monetary value of takings from a computer that does not produce such receipts.

5th Feb 1999: Slade, Torkington and Price acquitted as not

being concerned with the management of the club. 3 counts concerning the 5th Sept 1997 against Barrett and Gittins dismissed. The remaining 3 counts concerning the under cover supply on the 2nd May 1997 remain as does Barretts possession of cannabis count. New trial ordered. Judge saying that the vast sales of water that the police said were being consumed at the Club should have alerted management to abuse.

Feb-Mar 1999: Several requests to CPS from defence solicitors of Gittins and Barrett to halt proceedings there being no case to answer!

26th April 1999: Case against Gittins and Barrett starts at Swansea Crown Court. Again under cover officers state the water issue, which is accepted by the Judge Mr. Burr when he refused an application of no case. DC Davies on this occasion states that he had carried out an audit of the club's computer but nothing could be found apart from till receipts! These receipts were never produced nor the audit! Judge accepted this and the fact that the prosecution's case relied only on the water issue. Water consumption was the only evidence of knowledge in this case but neither the Judge nor CPS had called for an investigation into the computer's data banks to corroborate the police evidence.

30th April 199: Gittins found guilty on two counts of knowingly permit supply, even though he was absent from the actual club that night. Barrett was acquitted of the exact same charge even though he was present and legally in charge of the Club in accordance with the P.E.L. regulations.

24th May 1999: Gittins sentenced to 12 months imprisonment even though he was in the words of the Judge 'of impeccable character.'

27th May 1999: Application for appeal made to trial judge refused.

June 1999: Several letters to DC Davies Dyfed Powys Police asking him to reveal details of the till receipts and computer data retrieved.

15th July 1999: Appeal refused by single judge, again over the water evidence given at trial by police.

2nd August 1999: Gittins renews his appeal after dismissing his trial barrister and requests the Royal Courts to represent himself.

2nd Sept 1999: Finally received reply from DC Davies. He states that no computer was ever seized from Club!!!

13th Sept 1999: Gittins released from prison on electronic tagging.

23rd Sept 1999: Gittins files his addendum to perfected grounds of appeal; citing clear evidence that the police seized the computer and that data retrieved from this computer showed that police evidence was untrue. Only a minority of customers were consuming water on the night of the 2nd May 1997. In fact water consumption was not excessive on any night. The computer further revealed that on the 5th Sept 1997 no water at all was purchased at the club in direct contradiction to police evidence. (However, because counts relating to any alleged drug misuse on the 5th Sept 1997 had been dismissed by HH Judge Burr at the first Swansea hearing this would not form part of the appeal.)

26th Nov 1999: Gittins represents himself at the full court of appeal. The court accepts his computer evidence, which had been corroborated by the computer manufacturer Comsat UK Ltd. He states in court 'that the police had seized the computer for a reason, had accessed it and found the truth, which they suppressed'.

Lord Evans allowed his leave of appeal on the 'water issue' only but left the door open for other issues to be raised and reinstated Legal Aid.

18th Feb 2000. The Lord Kennedy quashed his conviction on the water issue and a new leave was submitted on the day over the whole ethos of the case being unsafe, this too was accepted by the Court. Gittins was vindicated as having done nothing wrong.

1st June 2000. Civil Legal Aid awarded to pursue action against Dyfed Powys Police, after an Access to Justice, a new government body, committee hearing.

20th June 2000. Home Office mount investigation. Compensation under the Criminal Justice Act 1988 section 133 is sort.

Compensation claims being complied amounting to millions of pounds

**Observations of the events.**

Despite no actual evidence that Mr. Gittins would have known that drug abuse had occurred at the Club on the night in question. The police fabricated at its worst or exaggerated at best the amount of bottled water being consumed at the Club. They did this knowing that the Court would deduce that if this fact had been true then the management of the Club would have knowledge of drug abuse associated with excessive water consumption, a fact widely publicised in the media.

By fudging the evidence that the police had seized the Club's computer system and held it for some 12 months they succeeded in suppressing conclusive evidence which, would have revealed the true facts in this case.

It is unbelievable that the police went to the trouble of seizing the computer and holding it for a long time yet did nothing with it.

They stated that they had retrieved till receipts but the system at the club did not produce any. What the system produced was a stock master, showing a complete break down of sales and products sold.

Their actions were allegedly deliberate and malicious with the sole object of jailing an innocent man and justifying their elaborate and extraordinary actions to close down the Club and cause maximum distress and damage to that person.

The Appeal Court ruled that the appellant had done nothing

wrong and previous courts had ruled that a chronology of alleged incidents that had supposedly occurred either at the Club or on route to the Club were merely 'hear say'.

The trial Judge had erred when he refused the first leave to appeal, the acquittal of Barrett being totally inconsistent. Further he jailed Mr. Gittins against medical advice causing further distress, but he had obviously been influence by the misleading police evidence and Mr. Gittins' staunch refusal to plead guilty.

The CPS withheld full disclosure for 16 months; even then it appears that full disclosure never took place, certainly with regard to the computer and the mysterious till receipts.

Had the CPS and/or the police, conducted this case properly and been open and truthful, this grave miscarriage of justice would never have occurred.

Being clear that Mr. Gittins has been a victim of alleged malice by a Crown agency; namely Dyfed Powys Police it is only right that he sues for compensation and restitution. Mr. Gittins was wrongly prosecuted and convicted and paid a very heavy price of liberty, livelihood and wealth.

# FREE DAFYDD

## AN HONEST AND INNOCENT MAN

## A TRAVESTY OF JUSTICE

GAOLED FOR KNOWINGLY ALLOWING DRUGS TO BE SOLD ON THE PREMISES

A CHARGE VEHEMENTLY DENIED

***A LIVING NIGHTMARE THAT CAN HAPPEN TO ANY LICENSEE***

*We believe that Dafydd is an innocent man and has been made a scapegoat*

## NOT GUILTY

*TO LICENSEES: If you think that Dafydd is an innocent man, please put an X in the box and display in your window*

*TO ANYONE ELSE: If you believe that Dafydd is innocent, please sign the petiton in his support available at the bar*

Dafydd Gittins: Co-Licensee of Chequers Nightclub, Crackwell, Penally, Nr Tenby.

# The Strange Case Of The Nightclub Owner Who Knowingly Knew, Or Not
# By
# Dafydd Gittins

This is a tale of a hapless licensee found guilty of knowingly knows, contemplating his fate with the dish of the day. A regal feast of Fish Fingers and Curry Sauce.
This robust delicacy is served on a regular basis in the most salubrious and exclusive dining hall at one of Her Majesty's least known prisons. A small institute of penal servitude, hidden away among the beautiful, rolling green hills of Southeast Wales.

"This humble, yet complex dish." He thinks to himself in quiet contemplation. "Represents the whole judicial system of the entire United Kingdom."

The odd combination of crass modern British cuisine and mysterious exotic spice of old empire embroils a perplexity of culture, indecision and humour. Of course this Epicurean delight should only be served with good old British chips, bringing back that sense of order and discipline to what could otherwise be viewed as an indulgence of luxury. The diners have, after all, infringed Her Majesty's laws. Sobriety and respect must prevail at all times.

How could such a dish be compared to the awesome colossus of the British legal system? Well, like the dish, it is befuddled and inconsistent. Laws are made by a series of Parliamentary Committees like chefs with a menu or recipe. Concoct something, pass it for debate by the Houses of Commons and Lords (both of which boast excellent restaurants) then eventually hand it down to the Learned Judges to make a sauce, I mean sense, of. No law or dish is ever simple; when committees take charge that would never do. It needs to be interpreted, cogitated and regurgitated many times by people, not forgetting the army of lawyers who generate a vast industry from such delights. One must argue precedent, meanings and merits. What did these chaps in Parliament really mean by it all? Who knows?

The Judge in his role as Maitre'd, has to decide if the law has been transgressed or not. If he can make neither head nor tail of it he, or she, passes it down to the Jury to decide and they remain clearly baffled by the task ahead. If the Judge couldn't fathom it out then the poor sod standing in the dock must be guilty. Or is that innocent? A vexing dilemma to be sure ponders the foreman of the Jury.

You see fish fingers, like the law, should be straightforward enough. Add the curry sauce and what have we got? A mad chef perhaps? Do these people in Parliament really know the secret of the universe? It needs further examination to reveal the mystic meaning of this statement of absurdity or legislative genius. Let us examine this hideous crime of 'knowingly know.' Before we do, let's reflect upon considered opinion of this lofty aspect of English Law.

Professor Card extols ''neither Parliament nor the Courts appear so far to have considered fully the answer to the question. A Cardinal Principle of Criminal Law is embodied in the maxim 'Actus non facit reum misi mean sitrea.' (An act does not make a person legally guilty unless the mind is legally blameworthy.)

How does the celebrated Professor Williams view it?

''Neither the Judges, Parliament nor Government care a straw that they are making a Piggery of the Criminal Law.''

Well our esteemed fellows are agreed. But is the Learned Judge intrepid enough to concur?

What we have before us is cryptically clear. No evidence of guilt but a covering of curry sauce. Does this mean he must have known? What about the chips? Surely some one who eats chips can't be all bad? A stout fellow no doubt. But the police said he must have known and a great saga will unfold. The Barrister for the Crown Prosecution Service is a confirmed vegetarian and has only fallen asleep twice throughout the whole trial but woke up for lunch and tea. Surely this must be grave?

The Judge studies the menu. The CPS has laid the table, no knife and fork but I think we see a spoon.

"I know." Says the Judge at the end of the prosecution's case.

"I can't make rhyme or reason of this dish, I mean case."

"The law is absolutely helpfully unclear, of this I'm sure. But is this fish or foul? Did he knowingly know or knowingly not? I know I'll listen to the offering from the defence. This dish needs spice and besides the Jury look hungry I'll throw them a bone."

The defence is adamant, absolutely almost certain that this is no charge at all. Knowingly knows can not be proved. The only evidence comes from the undercover police and they concocted the whole thing in the first place. They must have read the recipe book upside down. It's their job to lie, I mean lay the table we know but this time they have laid it the wrong way round so we can't blame them or can we?

"Anyway enough of the defence" The Judge remarks to himself.

"The defendant added his own curry sauce when he, with impudence pleaded not guilty. Therefore, he must know something we do not. He says he never 'knowingly knew.' He wasn't at the nightclub at the time and fish fingers are definitely not allowed in his hostelry. His staff agree to boot! A good point thinks the learned Judge but what matter that. He is charged with 'knowingly know' and every one knows that nightclubs are thoroughly naughty places (the ones I know certainly are)."

The Learned Judge cogitates what is laid before him. He must have known that fish fingers and curry sauce were blatantly served to the under cover police officers, who popped in his club that fearful night in question. But did I not hear his waiters, I mean bouncers and the manager agree in tandem that the serving of fish fingers and curry sauce is not tolerated at the Club? How could the accused have known? Not even they saw it. Nor anyone else, as the facts are told.

Only the dutiful officers of the law caught three diners devouring the dish in the dark recesses of his Club were privy to the 'e'vil deed. Four officers no less, disguised as anorexic foodies. They saw it! Plain as night, clear as black print on a crows backside. So come, come observed the Learned Judge, "you must have known!"

Such dishes are on offer in clubs and pubs up and down the land. Some of the finest establishments in the Realm go far beyond the pitiful helping at your Gaff, Guv.

"So tell us did you knowingly know, even if you never saw, heard or thought…."

"He wasn't there M'lud" coughs the Barrister for the defence.

"Who said?" Rebuffed the Judge.

"The police M'lud" whispers the cowering barrister.

"Clever bugger, I've got your number my lad" The Judge mumbles under his wig so hot.

The Judge begins to roll.

"What steps did you take to enforce the prohibition of such unlawful enactment's." He bellows from on high. "It is common nonsense which everyone knows, others have tried and failed to eradicate such wrongdoing. You should have followed the prime directive; you should have followed the written procedure. It is no defence that no such enlightenment's exists just because no one has the answer to your predicament, will not wash with us and that for sure!

But the Jury must decide, the die is cast to know or not to know that is the question-I think?"

A weighty hush descends upon the Court. "Has the Jury reached its verdict?"

"Yes M'Lud we have" the foreman replies and the hushed Court awaits with baited breath.

"We all agree guilty it be! In any case we're all fed up it goes on too long. Even if he did 'knowingly know' or not! How the hell do we know what he knows; it's all a load of fish fingers and curry sauce anyway. The CPS and police are most flamboyant chefs, so we have made a parody to fit this silly crime. Guilty and let some one else debate its hidden meaning, we're off for tea!"

The Judge is full of glee. "'Tis not I who made this jolly foe pa. The man is good and true but that is no defence, so down you go my boy. We'll gorge on this for years to come while you dine at Her Majesties pleasure at the Prescoed Café. The strange case of Fish Fingers, Curry Sauce and Knowingly Knows, will go down in history. So bring on the Caviar and blancmange, that's real crap for that I'm certain sure!"

*Written by Dafydd Gittins at HMP Prescoed shortly after the second trial at Swansea Crown Court in 1999, a humorous and satirical rendering of the proceedings. Originally written as an entry to the Andrew Groves Short Story Prize, Prison Reform Trust July 1999.*

*Quote 1. Prof. Richard Card. Professor of Law De Montfort University Leicester. 13th Edition Criminal Law 1995.*
*Quote 2. Prof. Glanville Llewllyn Williams. Professor of Law. Cambridge University and Aberystwyth University of Wales. 'A Textbook Criminal Law 1984.'*

English as a Lingua F

CW01641890

English as a Lingua Franca (ELF) is a term used to describe the use of English as a common language for communication between speakers whose first language is not English. Providing a unique and original perspective on this subject, Istvan Kecskes explains the language behavior of ELF speakers, through the lens of Gricean pragmatics. This study successfully brings together the main viewpoints of the Gricean paradigm into ELF research, to discuss and better understand the nature of ELF interactions, as well as explaining how Gricean pragmatics can benefit from investigating and analyzing ELF. Each chapter presents intriguing ideas that put existing knowledge into a new perspective, such as interactional competence, intention, implicatures, the semantics–pragmatics interface, and modality. New terms and viewpoints such as language use mode, deliberate creativity, temporary extension of the system, emergent common ground, and modality continuum are introduced into the ELF debate.

ISTVAN KECSKES is Distinguished Professor of the State University of New York. He is the President of the American Pragmatics Association and the CASLAR (Chinese as a Second Language Research) Association. He is author of *Foreign Language and Mother Tongue* (2000, with Tunde Papp), *Situation-Bound Utterances in L1 and L2* (2003), and *Intercultural Pragmatics* (2013). He is the founding editor of the journal *Intercultural Pragmatics*.

# English as a Lingua Franca

*The Pragmatic Perspective*

Istvan Kecskes

*State University of New York, Albany*

CAMBRIDGE
UNIVERSITY PRESS

**CAMBRIDGE**
**UNIVERSITY PRESS**

University Printing House, Cambridge CB2 8BS, United Kingdom

One Liberty Plaza, 20th Floor, New York, NY 10006, USA

477 Williamstown Road, Port Melbourne, VIC 3207, Australia

314-321, 3rd Floor, Plot 3, Splendor Forum, Jasola District Centre, New Delhi - 110025, India

103 Penang Road, #05-06/07, Visioncrest Commercial, Singapore 238467

Cambridge University Press is part of the University of Cambridge.

It furthers the University's mission by disseminating knowledge in the pursuit of education, learning and research at the highest international levels of excellence.

www.cambridge.org
Information on this title: www.cambridge.org/9781107503373
DOI: 10.1017/9781316217832



First published 2019
First paperback edition 2022

*A catalogue record for this publication is available from the British Library*

*Library of Congress Cataloging in Publication data*
Names: Kecskes, Istvan, author.
Title: English as a lingua franca : the pragmatic perspective / István Kecskés, State University of New York, Albany.
Description: Cambridge ; New York, NY: Cambridge University Press, 2019. | Includes bibliographical references and index.
Identifiers: LCCN 2019020260 | ISBN 9781107103801 (alk. paper)
Subjects: LCSH: English language – Variation – Foreign countries. | English language – Globalization. | Lingua francas.
Classification: LCC PE2751 .K43 2019 | DDC 427–dc23
LC record available at https://lccn.loc.gov/2019020260

ISBN 978-1-107-10380-1 Hardback
ISBN 978-1-107-50337-3 Paperback

# Contents

*List of Figures* — *page* vi
*List of Tables* — vii
*Acknowledgments* — viii

Introduction — 1
1 The Nature of English as a Lingua Franca — 15
2 Linguistic Creativity in ELF — 45
3 Interactional Competence — 69
4 Sociocultural Background Knowledge — 91
5 Speaker's Intention — 113
6 The Semantics–Pragmatics Interface — 137
7 Implicatures — 159
8 Modality — 184
9 Dialogic Sequences and Odd Structures — 206
Epilogue — 232

*References* — 236
*Index* — 258

# Figures


| | | |
|---|---|---|
| 1.1 | Recent linguistic theory of language | *page* 22 |
| 1.2 | Kecskes' definition of language | 23 |
| 1.3 | The result of the interplay of the English code system with the Chinese sociocultural background: Chinese variety of English | 24 |
| 1.4 | English as a Lingua Franca; native English; outer circle English | 25 |
| 5.1 | The perceptual salience triggered by the brand name | 125 |
| 8.1 | The continuum representing epistemic modality on the one side of the continuum, and deontic modality on the other side | 191 |
| 8.2 | Merging semantic criteria | 198 |

# Tables


| | | |
|---|---|---|
| 2.1 | Type-1 and Type-2 creativity | *page* 58 |
| 8.1 | Modal categories | 188 |
| 8.2 | Modal devices | 193 |
| 9.1 | Criteria for odd structures | 214 |
| 9.2 | Possible hearer- and speaker-strategies in reaction to OSs | 216 |
| 9.3 | Selected MCs and lack-of-clarity markers in VOICE | 218 |
| 9.4 | Speaker strategies in our dataset | 222 |

# Acknowledgments

This book has grown out of a classroom experience. In the spring of 2016 I taught a graduate class on English as a Lingua Franca. During some heated debates with my students about the available literature in ELF, I realized that what we were really missing in the discussions was a perspective that reflects the Gricean way of thinking. My students were the first with whom I discussed my views about ELF, and who helped me shape the contour of this book. After that course I started to develop presentations on different aspects of ELF, such as formulaic language use, deliberate creativity, sociocultural background knowledge, and the semantics–pragmatics interface. I made these presentations in many universities all over the world where I received invaluable feedback from researchers and graduate students. I would particularly highlight the support I received at the National Research Tomsk State University, Russia; Sorbonne University, Paris, France; Donders Institute for Brain, Cognition and Behavior, Nijmegen, The Netherlands; Complutense University of Madrid, Spain; University of Messina, Italy; University of Queensland, Brisbane, Australia; Guangdong University of Foreign Studies, Guangzhou, China; University of Belgrade, Serbia, just to mention a few. I really appreciated the feedback that I received from scholars such as Rachel Giora, Alessandro Capone, Michael Haugh, Jesus Romero-Trillo, Tatiana Larina, Markus Bieswanger, Olga Obdalova, Robert Sanders, He Gang, José Sánchez Fajardo, and others. I would also like to thank two of my doctoral students, Hahn Dinh, Limei Zhang and Sepideh Yasrebi for their help with the manuscript and references.

But again, my most sincere gratitude goes to my wife, Dr. Tunde Papp, whose intellectual support cannot be compared to anybody else's. Writing a book occasionally makes one's life difficult. You often need someone to discuss some issues with. Tunde was always there for me with her thoughtful suggestions and careful reasoning that always put me back on the right track. You can judge yourself how right that track was.

# Introduction

## I.1 Why Have I Written This Book?

I have already written a book on *Intercultural Pragmatics* (Kecskes 2014). Did I not address issues on lingua franca there? Yes, I did. Then what on earth am I doing here? Well, I have been wanting to bring some pragmatic perspective into the heated debate on English as a Lingua Franca (ELF hereafter). It is not so much that there is no pragmatics in that discussion – there is! – but that it is not exactly what we, pragmaticians, call pragmatics (I shall return to this issue later). So what this book is about is most aptly characterized by the subtitle: "The Pragmatic Perspective" on English as a Lingua Franca. I do not write this book specifically for second language acquisition (SLA) scholars, applied linguists, ELF experts, or language teachers and not even only for pragmaticians. I have written it for all scholars who are interested in a very timely and intriguing question: Is lingua franca communication changing the way we think about language? Should we rethink, revisit, and/or revise what our standard knowledge and way of thinking is about language use in general? So please do not expect me to review the huge, rapidly burgeoning literature on ELF (although I do that where I find it necessary). My goal is not to give a synthesis of what we already have, rather to raise and discuss unanswered and partly answered questions, and approach existing knowledge from a new perspective. The focus is on issues concerning pragmatics, such as interactional competence, intention, the semantics–pragmatics interface, context, implicature, and modality. I intend to revisit these issues from an ELF perspective: what new knowledge (if any) can ELF add to the debate about the issues above, and what can ELF researchers learn from pragmaticians so as to better understand what goes on in ELF communication? So this is basically a two-way street in that I will regularly relate L1 pragmatics findings and thoughts to ELF and vice versa. I sincerely believe that the two fields can learn a lot from each other.

In my book on *Intercultural Pragmatics* (2014), I emphasized that I did not wish to ignore or replace the Gricean paradigm. On the contrary, my aim was to broaden the scope of Gricean pragmatics in order to explain not only what happens in L1 communication but also in interactions that include nonnative speakers. My problem with the current research on English as a Lingua Franca turns on the sentiment shared by many, namely what Jenkins calls "language with no native speakers." Well, if there are no native speakers there is no natural language.[1] What we have then is only a code-system without a heart and soul. Just think about computer programming "languages" such as Java, COBOL, Prolog, C++, Python, or others where there is a one-to-one relationship between code/sign and meaning. Take Esperanto, for instance, which failed to become a lingua franca because it lacks the real "human touch." It has no native speakers who could shape the language according to their needs, so that the language would reflect their ways of thinking. Esperanto lacks the unique relationship and interplay between the code system and users which should be a bidirectional dynamic process expected to result in the transformation of both sides as it occurs in natural languages. The question for us to answer is how English as a Lingua Franca differs from Esperanto and English as a Native Language (ENL) use. First of all, in ENL, the code system (English grammar) and its conventionalized use are the result of natural language development with its own sociocultural background, unlike in Esperanto where the code system has been artificially developed. The English language has native speakers whose language use and development of the code system are rooted in a dynamically changing sociocultural background. But in ELF those native speakers of English do not participate in the language game. This makes the whole thing tricky and unique. ELF interlocutors make use of a code system that has been developed according to the needs of a speech community other than theirs. So they just "borrow" that code system for their own communicative purposes, and use it and shape it according to their needs in temporary sociocultural situations where English is used as a medium of communication.

Therefore, I will consider ELF a language use mode in which all participants have an L1 other than English. My definition of ELF goes like this: *ELF is a way to put a variety, or several varieties of English to use in interactions between speakers whose L1 is other than English.* Here arises the basic problem for ELF research, namely the fact that what the "players" have in common is that they are native speakers of a language other than English.[2] The question remains: *how would these interlocutors use the English code system with a mind dominated by and wired to another code system with a different sociocultural background?* Let me explain this issue by means of an analogy with another medium, namely, painting: The way I think about language can be compared to the way in which Amedeo Modigliani understood the function of

[1] I am fully aware of the debate about the term "native speaker." Later I will return to explain what is meant by this term in this book.

[2] Based on Wittgenstein's "language game" metaphor, I will often refer to interlocutors as "players" or "gamers."

human eyes. Eyes are the mirror of the soul just as language is the mirror of human mind. The eyes in Modigliani's portraits are different from any others.[3] Sometimes the eyes look like almonds, sometimes they seem to be empty holes. Very rarely do they resemble real human eyes. At first glance, they do not express anything, but when you look into them you see – or feel – the model's soul. It would be hard to find another artist able to express so much with such unrealistic, single-colored eyes that occasionally even appear to be blind. Some of Modigliani's portraits, however, have fully painted eyes, like the later portraits of his wife, Jeanne Hebuterne. In the earlier years of their relationship, Modigliani once said to her, "When I know your soul, I will paint your eyes." Sometimes it happens that Modigliani paints two different eyes, like those in the portrait of Max Jacob, which is considered one of Modigliani's masterpieces. What he wanted to show with those eyes is that with one eye Max is looking at the outside world, while with the other he is looking within himself. On another occasion, when Leopold Survage saw his portrait painted by Modigliani, he asked his friend, "Why have you only given me one eye?" Modigliani's answer: "Because you only view the world with one eye, with the other you look within yourself."

How does this all relate to language and ELF? Soul operates mind and mind operates language. To quote Tertullian (A treatise on the soul): "We, however, affirm that the mind coalesces with the soul – not indeed as being distinct from it in substance, but as being its natural function and agent."[4] So the mind is a natural agent of the soul, and as such operates language. Through language the mind facilitates the inner reflection of the outside world. In the case of ELF the "eye" is unique because it mirrors the complexity of a mind that has to work with the blend of two (or more) reflections of the outside world: one that is attached to L1 and the other being developed through L2 or Lx. The two are intertwined. Both of them require the maintenance of some kind of a norm system. So the question is: whose norms do/should the ELF speakers follow? Since they communicate in L2, the answer should be that ELF speakers are expected to follow both the grammatical and communicative norms of L2 (English). The issue, however, is not that simple: If their mind works with the blend of two reflections of the world, then they appear to need to make special efforts to follow the norms of L2 and overcome the dominant effect of L1. And here arises yet another problem. ELF occurs in temporary speech dyads or communities. There is evidence (e.g., House 2003; Kecskes 2007, 2013, 2015; Canagarajah 2014) that when people spend even a short time together they inherently, instinctively attempt to create their own norms

[3] Information in this part of the text was collected on the Internet.
[4] *Sacred Writings of Tertullian*, vol. 1. p. 224. Jazzybee Verlag: Altenmuster: Germany. 1922.

no matter how temporary the time together will be.[5] In order for the norms to be organized into a relatively definable system, they need to be developing for a significant amount of time. This is not the case in lingua franca where the dyads and speech communities are usually temporary. It is difficult or even impossible for ELF speakers to create long-lasting norms of their own although they attempt to do so no matter how temporary the dyads or speech communities are. That is why it is a mistake to compare lingua franca to "interlanguage" (Selinker 1972) as some scholar do. ELF is not a "developing system" of a nonnative speaker. As I have said, it is a language use mode, a "variable way" of using English (Seidlhofer 2011: 77) and not a variety of English. Consequently it is not right to try to squeeze ELF into the Kachruian three categories: "inner, outer and expending circle." Also, I do not agree with Mauranen (2003) that Kachru's model is outdated. I think ELF simply does not fit into that model because it is neither norm-providing as American English or British English is, nor norm-developing in a way as Nigerian English, Iranian English, Chinese English, etc. are. ELF is a language use mode, and as such it is more fluid and flexible with its temporarily developed and temporarily existing "intercultures" and norms than any variety of English. So, it does not make much sense to compare it to the Kachruian varieties that usually have a describable structure with their norms and rules.

## I.2 Why Is This Book Needed?

ELF as an independent research field has been growing very quickly. There is an increasing amount of empirical work focusing on ELF interactions: see, for instance, Jenkins, Cogo, and Dewey (2011), for an overview, and the latest books by Archibald, Cogo, and Jenkins, (2011), Bowles and Cogo, (2015), and Vettorel (2015); and databases such as the Vienna-Oxford International Corpus of English (VOICE), the Asian Corpus of English (ACE), and the Helsinki ELFA Corpus, which all focus on aspects of language in lingua franca interactions. Furthermore, there was a special issue in the journal *Intercultural Pragmatics* (2009), edited by House, with the title of "The pragmatics of English a Lingua Franca." *Journal of Pragmatics* (2011, 43/4) also published a special issue dedicated to the pragmatics of English as a lingua franca edited by Björkman. Several excellent books have been published on English as a Lingua Franca (such as Jenkins 2007; Seidlhofer 2011; Mauranen 2012; Björkman 2013; Deterding 2013; MacKenzie 2013; Baker 2017) just to mention a few. Björkman's (2013), Holmes and Dervin's (2016), Deterding's (2013), and

[5] Of course, the more time they spend together the stronger those norms are going to be.

Baker's (2017) works are parts of the series in the Developments in English as a Lingua Franca (DELF). There have been some significant developments of ELF in specific settings such as business English as a lingua franca, academic English as a lingua franca, or ELF for Asian or European people (e.g., Du-Babcock 2009; Kankaanranta & Planken 2010; Mauranen 2012; Ehrenreich 2016; Liu & Liu 2017). Books like Björkman's *English as an Academic Lingua Franca* (2013), and Kirkpatrick's *English as a Lingua Franca in ASEAN* (2011), highlight these developments. The field also has a (relatively) new journal (*Journal of English Lingua Franca*). As mentioned, these developments demonstrate a rapidly increasing interest in the field.

One of the reasons why I think this book still can add something to the existing and ever-burgeoning scholarship is its unique perspective that is based on the Gricean paradigm. ELF research has been carried out mainly from the perspective of applied linguistics and second language acquisition even when the focus has been on ELF pragmatics with an interest in strategies interlocutors use in communicative processes (e.g., House 2009a: Seidlhofer 2009a; Bjorkman 2010, 2013; Mauranen 2012; Murray 2012). Less attention has been paid to the theoretical issues of pragmatics underlying ELF language use including utterance formation (not speech acts), intention, explicature, implicature, semantics–pragmatics interface, role of context, salience, relevance, and linguistic behavior in general. No current pragmatic theories have been applied to explain lingua franca use (at least to my knowledge). Consequently, there seems to be a need for a book that discusses the language use and behavior of lingua franca speakers from the perspective of current pragmatic theories with an attempt to answer the following questions: Can current pragmatic theories explain lingua franca communication in which basic concepts such as common ground, cooperation, intention, implicature, presupposition, salience, relevance, and politeness. gain a new meaning? Do we need a new pragmatics theory for lingua franca interaction, or what we have to do is just adjust and/or modify the existing approaches according to the requirements of this type of communication? And, of course, the main question: With no native speakers participating in the language game how much will players stick to the original rules of the game?

That said, I think this book can be useful for both theoretical pragmatics on the one hand, and applied linguistics and SLA on the other. It would help both sides understand that neither the monolithic (rigid, formal, structure-based) nor the heterolytic (fluid, hybrid, intersubjective, community practices-based) approach is good enough to reveal the real nature of language, especially language use. Both sides should loosen up and let some fresh air into their disciplines acknowledging the equal importance of form, structure, cognition, and the individual factors on the one hand and the hybrid, fluid, socially determined factors on the other. In other words, the former cannot exist without the latter. They form a symbiosis that requires scholars on both sides to analyze language use as a reflection of the dual nature of human beings: we are both individuals and social beings at the same time. This fact is reflected in our communicative behavior. Recent neurological experiments on mirror neurons can be interpreted as confirming human beings' dual nature, as well as the interaction of their abilities (Rizzolatti & Craighero 2004; Arbib et al. 2005).

## I.3 How Can the Book Be Useful for Theoretical Pragmatics?

### *I.3.1 Monolingual Bias in Current Pragmatic Theories*

According to UNESCO data, the number of multilinguals exceeds the number of monolinguals in the world. But if multilingualism is considered 'normal,' shouldn't this affect the ways linguists build their models of language and pragmaticians develop their models of meaning and language behavior? I argue that given the rapid growth in the world of the number of people who speak more than one language and the increasing importance of intercultural interactions in communicative encounters, the main linguistic and pragmatic models must also be evaluated on their capacity to explain multilingual competence, multilingual language use and its traces appropriately. However, this is not exactly what is happening. As I discussed elsewhere (Kecskes 2014), in the dominant monolingual approaches that govern mainstream pragmatics today anything that is "societal" (Mey 2001) and/or whatever pragmatic phenomenon has not reached "grammaticalized" status (as Levinson calls it; 1983: 9) on principle is excluded from consideration in many versions of pragmatics. This is how Jacob Mey (2013: 488) described the current situation:

> It has been the custom for partisans of linguistics to fire away from their hideouts and shoot down pragmatics (of the 'wrong' kind) as being 'continental' (Levinson 1983:2), as "not stringent enough" (as one colleague of mine once told her students), or simply as being outside the realm of scientific description (as many linguists and semanticists seem to believe, witness the fact that they, intentionally or unconsciously, omit any mention of the 'other' kind of pragmatics in their writings.

The assumption then of standard pragmatics about the nature of communication is that it depends on there being commonalities and conventions between speakers and hearers. These commonalities, conventions, common beliefs, shared knowledge, and the like all create a core common ground, a kind of collective salience on which intention and cooperation-based pragmatics is built (see Kecskes 2014). However, when this core common ground appears to be missing or limited – as is the case in lingua franca communication –

interlocutors cannot take them for granted, rather they need to negotiate and co-construct them, at least temporarily. So there seems to be a shift in emphasis from the communal to the individual. It is not that the individual becomes more important than the societal. Rather, since common ground is limited, it should be created in the interactional context in which interlocutors function as core common ground creators rather than just common ground seekers and activators as is mostly the case in L1 communication. The nature of intersubjectivity therefore seems to be being changed. That is to say, *there is more reliance on language created ad hoc by individuals in the course of interaction than on prefabricated language and preexisting frames.* So the role of individual with his/her individual background, prior experience, language use habits, and creativity in general increases. Deliberate creativity (see Kecskes 2017) rules instead of exiting norms and formulaic, prefabricated language. In the case of interlocutors who use a common language and whose L1s differ, the lack of full control over language skills (L2) and lack of full knowledge of conventions, beliefs, and norms of the target language (L2) used as the medium of communication may lead *to a more conscious approach to what is said, and how it is said.* This is where mainstream pragmatics and lingua franca pragmatics significantly differ. The more conscious approach in ELF shifts the emphasis from societal to individual, results in co-construction of common ground (rather than relying on exiting core common ground of the target language speakers), and brings closer "what is said" to "what is communicated" than in L1. To a large extent, interlocutors have to rely on semantic analyzability rather than on figurative and prefabricated, formulaic language. So the semantics–pragmatics interface issue has to be revisited. All of this should certainly affect the way we evaluate speaker intention and production, hearer comprehension and implicatures in lingua franca interactions. There is more conscious and careful recipient design involved in these interactions than in L1 communication in which interlocutors do not have to deal with language skill issues and may rely on more spontaneous speech and less monitoring. This kind of recipient design may change the way we think about what is said, and what is beyond what is literally said.

Theoretical pragmaticians worry if they let some "fresh air" in, that will surely ruin the logical structure of language, jeopardize truth conditions, and break how presuppositions work: in one word, that change will put everything into the air and ruin systematicity, which is so important for each human language system. Not a bit of it. This book tries to demonstrate that ELF, although it is just a language use mode, does not mean anarchy in language use, and it does not entirely lack systematicity. If, however, we want to describe ELF, we need to make some changes to our way of thinking about how language works.

### *1.3.2 The Pragmatic Analysis of English Lingua Franca Gives a New Twist to the Main Tenet of Current Pragmatic Theories: The Semantics–Pragmatics Interface*

According to the traditional view, it is up to semantics to tell us what somebody literally says when s/he uses an utterance of a given type, and it is up to pragmatics to explain the information one conveys, and the actions one performs, in or by saying something. King and Stanley (2005: 117) formulated the basis for the semantics–pragmatics divide as follows: "pragmatic content is what the speaker communicates over and above the semantic content of the sentence."

However, the issue is not that simple and the border-line debate (see for summary, Korta and Perry 2015) is a never-ending one.

Analysis of lingua franca utterances and discourse can give a new twist to the debate. The process of inferencing for lingua franca hearers in intercultural interaction usually differs from that of L1 hearers. Native speakers do inferencing usually top-down, while lingua franca speakers mostly rely on bottom-up processing. For lingua franca speakers the semantic content is very often the conveyed content (cf. House 2002, Kecskes 2007). There is evidence that semantic analyzability has some kind of priority in lingua franca interactions. Some studies concluded that interlocutors were reluctant to use language that they know, or perceive to be figurative or semantically less transparent (e.g. Philip 2005; Cieślicka 2006; Kecskes 2015). So for nonnative speakers (especially those with lower language proficiency) participating in lingua franca interactions, pragmatics gets very close to semantics, particularly if we look at this issue from the traditional mainstream pragmatics view, where there is little pragmatic enrichment and/or saturation.[6] In L1 communication, however, "what is said" rarely coincides with "what is communicated." This is why Gricean pragmatics gives such importance to implicatures: "Speakers implicate, hearers infer" as Horn (2004: 6) said. However, in lingua franca interaction what the speaker says frequently coincides with what s/he actually means. The meaning, that is to say, of the utterance is usually limited to its literal sense. In L1 communication, on which current pragmatic theories are built, there may be much more of a gap between what is said and what is meant than in lingua franca communication. In the case of the latter, it is of utmost importance that the speaker should mean close to what s/he says, otherwise the hearer may have difficulty figuring out the speaker's intention because of limited core common ground, nonexisting frames, restricted familiarity with shared knowledge and few mutual norms. Figurative and formulaic language use does not help the communication process as much as it does in L1, for the latter requires

[6] I will return to explain "saturation" and "pragmatics enrichment" (Recanati 2004, 2012) in the next chapter.

background knowledge rooted in the culture the target language represents. This is precisely why we need to address the following crucial questions: Whose common ground do the interlocutors rely on in lingua franca interaction? Does speaker implicature always go beyond semantics, or sometimes speaker implicates what is literally said?

Does ELF use mean that there is less pragmatics and more semantics for lingua franca speakers? No, not quite so. (As we will see later, the issue is more complicated than that.) Lingua franca interaction may disabuse us of the prevalent current view in some pragmatic theories that posit a divide between pragmatics and semantics. Analysis of ELF use demonstrates the validity in theoretical pragmatics of those propositions that emphasize the function of pragmatics in ways beyond the mere filling of the gap between semantics and conveyed content. Bach (2007: 5) argued that it is misleading to speak of the border, or the "interface" between semantics and pragmatics. This mistakenly suggests that pragmatics somehow takes over where semantics leaves off. It's one thing for a sentence to have the content that it has and another thing for a speech act of uttering the sentence to have the content it has. Even when the content of the speech act coincides with that of the sentence, that is still to be understood as a pragmatic act, something for the speaker to intend and the hearer to figure out. So Humpty Dumpty's maxim (Lewis Carol 1871, *Through the Looking-Glass*) is truer than ever before: "When I use a word, it means just what I choose it to mean – neither more nor less." When a lingua franca speaker produces an utterance, it usually signifies more or less what its compositional meaning is. I will return to this issue in some of the upcoming chapters.

## I.4 How Can the Book Be Useful for Applied Linguistics and SLA?

### *I.4.1 Calling Attention to the Fact That Dismantling the Concept of "Language" Will Not Help*

Since Firth and Wagner (1997) questioned some key dichotomies dominating second language acquisition research in their article, there has been quite a strong tendency in SLA and applied linguistics research to dismantle the concept of language (as it is traditionally understood) based on the Haugenian approach, according to which "the concept of language as a rigid, monolithic structure is false, even if it has proved to be a useful fiction in the development of linguistics. It is the kind of simplification that is necessary at a certain stage of a science, but which can now be replaced by more sophisticated models" (Haugen, 1972: 325). We can respond to this Haugenian approach with a quote from Leibniz (1976 [1679]): "*si nihil per se concipitur, nihil omnino concipietur,*" meaning if "nothing is understood by itself, nothing at all will ever be understood." Why is this important? It is true that what we call "language" is a scientific abstraction, and what we actually have is the instantiation of this abstraction in different dialects and varieties. This does not mean, however, that we do not have to have a "core," a basic abstraction to which we relate the "concrete" occurrences/substantiations of language. English as a Lingua Franca is not a language, it is not a normative phenomenon, it is a temporary "community of practice" – a "language use mode" (Kecskes 2007) – that may develop into a variety if, and only if, it is used for a longer period of time in a relatively definable speech community. There is hope for that in the European Union. This basically explains why ELF research appears to be most intensive and extensive in Europe.

### *I.4.2 Grammar versus Pragmatics*

It seems to me that one of the main dangers in ELF research is the emphasis of pragmatics over grammar: "Is one more primary in communication than the other," House (2003: 46) asks, "and are they in fact separable? Would pragmatic strategies enable one to communicate successfully irrespective of the level of grammatical proficiency?" One can argue that the general view is that ELF facilitates harmonious communication mainly through pragmatics rather than grammar. Canagarajah (2007) claimed that ELF speakers cannot depend on "preconstituted forms of meaning." What happens is that they activate complex pragmatic strategies that help them negotiate their variable form. However, we have to be careful with this statement because everything depends on what we understand by "preconstituted forms." If what Canagarajah means by "preconstituted forms" is formulaic, prefabricated language then he is right. But grammar is also preconstituted. And so is semantics. If we think otherwise, that will dismantle language. Grammar and semantics represent preconstituted knowledge which serves as a basis for semantic analyzability and general language use. ELF speakers seem to prefer semantically transparent language. This was claimed in Section I.3.1, and will be shown later in this book.

As I have said, analysis of ELF use demonstrates that pragmatics doesn't just fill in the gap between semantics and conveyed content, and that it operates even when there is no gap. Pragmatics is there when the utterance is formulated and/or interpreted, just like grammar. Pragmatics and grammar work together (see Ariel 2008), they are inseparable, they support one another. Higher grammatical skills help learners to overcome some pragmatic problems in language production (classroom learners); likewise, higher pragmatic skills help to get meaning through even if grammar is poor. This is especially true for ELF.

### I.4.3 *Lingua Franca Interaction Is a "Success-and-Failure" Process Rather than a Collision of Cultures*

This book adopts a view according to which intercultural interaction is a "success-and-failure" process rather than a collision of cultures, which was the dominant view for a significant period of time and still occasionally is. For instance, the editorial of a 2006 edition of the *Journal of Intercultural Communication Research* claimed that "during intercultural communication, the message sent is usually not the message received" and that "intercultural communication necessarily involves a clash of communicator style" (Neuliep 2006: 1). This is not surprising given that intercultural communication as a field of inquiry was basically constituted as an analysis of misunderstandings (e.g., Gumperz 1982; Gudykunst & Kim, 1992; ten Thije 2003; Zhu 2015). What is unfortunate, however, is that when misunderstanding occurs in intercultural interactions, people usually start to search for cultural differences for a cause without considering other factors. That view was summed up by Gass and Varonis (1985: 340) in the following way:

> NSs [native speakers] and NNSs [nonnative speakers] are multiply handicapped in conversations with one another. Often they may not share a world view or cultural assumptions, one or both of which may lead to misunderstanding. In addition, they may not share common background . . . that would permit them to converse with shared beliefs about what Gumperz and Tannen (1979) call the "semantic content" of the conversation. Furthermore, they may have difficulty with speaking and interpreting an interlocutor's discourse as a result of a linguistic deficit.

I think that the view summarized (but not shared) by Gass and Varonis is lopsided because its focus is on failure only, and there is no mention of success. ELF speakers almost always succeed and get their message through, just as NSs do in L1 communication. Seidlhofer (2004: 218) observed that "misunderstandings are not frequent in ELF interactions," and she went on to add that "when they do occur, they tend to be resolved either by topic change, or, less often, by overt negotiation using communication strategies such as rephrasing and repetition."

Furthermore, the focus of attention in the field of intercultural communication shifted beyond misunderstanding at the beginning of the 2000s (see Clyne, 1994; Koole & ten Thije 2001; ten Thije 2003). Several studies have attempted to answer the question of how people with different cultural and linguistic backgrounds act and react in intercultural discourse, how common ground or intercultural understanding is established, and what new discourse structures result from intercultural communication. In a study of cross-cultural, cross-linguistic communication, Kidwell (2000) proposed to use a "success approach" that has as its aim explicating the resources that enable participants to accomplish their communicative tasks. Koole and ten Thije (2001) argued that rather than working deductively from cultural differences to communication, an inductive analysis of interaction should be applied to discover whether actors orient to group differences at all, and if so, in what terms these groups and their boundaries are defined. I think that the way in which empirical answers can be found for patterns and problems in lingua franca interaction is a detailed and nuanced analysis of concrete communicative events. This has been going on in the field of ELF since its inception. It is a very positive tendency that the overwhelming majority of claims about ELF, whether they are acceptable or debatable, have been made on the basis of detailed analysis of concrete language data, interactions, and language production. But I need to mention here one of the main problems (at least in my opinion) that is connected to the use of English as a Lingua Franca. We can call that the "everything goes" approach. I concur with MacKenzie's criticisim that "Most ELF researchers will have you believe that when communication takes place in English as a lingua franca, ideally in the absence of those pesky NESs, collaboration is total, misunderstanding are vanishingly rare, and harmony prevails" (MacKenzie 2014:140). It seems to me that some researchers go too far when talking about "no-errors" in lingua franca interactions. Cogo and Dewey (2012) claimed that "deciding what constitutes an error is . . . not a particularly ELF-compatible way of thinking about language." Pitzl, Breiteneder, and Klimpfinger (2008) called errors by ELF users "creative innovations." I think it is a serious mistake to call the way and means by which ELF interlocutors try to overcome their difficulties and lack of knowledge of the target language "creativity." If we do consider those ways and means "creativity," then we do not quite understand the essence of human creativity in general. Human creativity is always in some sense a response to a regulating order. Creativity and variation are impossible without reference to "existing patterns." Csikszentmihalyi (1999: 314 –315) argued that "'new' is meaningful only in reference to the 'old'. . . . Without rules there cannot be exceptions, and without tradition there cannot be novelty." This is true for any kind of human creativity including linguistic creativity, pragmatic creativity, or whatever creativity we are talking about. In ELF communication we use a language called English that has a structure, its standards and norms of "putting together" (grammar), and recommended standards and norms of usage (social behavior) that we should, at least to some extent, keep in mind as a guide lest communication in ELF become chaotic and uneven. What we can mainly detect in lingua franca interactions is not necessarily just creativity. Rather I would call that *ingenuity* of the speaker-hearer. This refers to the ability of the interlocutor to overcome difficulties that mainly derive from proficiency issues, lack of knowledge of sociocultural background of the target language, limited common ground, unfamiliarity with communicative frames in the target language, and other issues. This ingenuity may include accommodation, resourcefulness, pliancy, and forethoughtfulness that all come in handy when trying to overcome communication problems.

## I.5 Theoretical Guide

As discussed in Section I.1, the goal of this book is not to work out a theoretical frame for ELF, rather to offer several alternatives that could be used to explain what takes place in ELF interactions. Still, because of the nature of these interactions in which the individual is blended with the social, the main line of thinking in this book has been shaped by the socio-cognitive approach (SCA) proposed by Kecskes (2008; 2010; 2013; 2014) and Kecskes and Zhang (2009). I would like to emphasize that SCA is not only a theoretical frame but also a guide that determines my approach to the questions at hand. SCA emphasizes that there is a dialectical relationship between a priori intention (based on individual prior experience) and emergent intention (based on actual social situational experience), and egocentrism (individual) and cooperation (social) in any human interaction. In this approach, interlocutors are considered social beings searching for meaning with individual minds embedded in a sociocultural collectivity. SCA argues that Grice was right when he tied cooperation to the speaker-hearer's rationality. However, egocentrism must be added to speaker-hearer's rationality. We human beings are just as egocentric (as individuals) as cooperative (as social beings). *Egocentrism* in the SCA is not used in a negative sense, but rather it refers to attention-bias that is the result of prior experience of individuals that affects their way of thinking and actions including communication (e.g., Giora 2003; Barr & Keysar 2005; Colston & Katz 2005). Therefore it means that interlocutors activate and bring up the most salient information to the needed attentional level in the construction (by the speaker) and comprehension (by the hearer) of the communication. There is nothing negative about egocentrism if the term is used in this sense.

It is also important to highlight that communication is a dynamic process in which individuals are not only constrained by societal conditions but they also shape those conditions at the same time. In the process of interaction, human beings show their two sides. They cooperate by generating and formulating intention that is relevant to the given actual situational context and their recipient(s). At the same time their egocentrism means that they activate the most salient information to their attention in the construction (in the role of speaker) and comprehension (in the role of hearer) of utterances. The interplay of these factors shapes their communicative behavior.

Based on the SCA, I argue that the nature of lingua franca interactions differs from that of L1 interactions. But this difference is not about lingua franca communicators having more misunderstandings and problems than L1 communicators. *It is about their different and/or modified routes to success.* Interlocutors in lingua franca interactions have to be inventive and ingenious when commonalities and/or conventions are missing or limited. This ingenuity has a profound effect on how intersubjectivity works in lingua franca interactions. Intersubjectivity captures the way a person understands and relates to another, and by which we share experiences with one another. The goal of intersubjective acts in communication is to eliminate the difference between two or more subjective perceptions and/or definitions of reality. How interlocutors do that in lingua franca interaction is worth exploring and discussing. This is what I am trying to do in this book.

# 1 The Nature of English as a Lingua Franca

## 1.1 Brief history

Contact languages used among people who do not share a first language have been around for many centuries. In different periods of time, for instance, Greek, Latin, Arabic, Portuguese, and several other languages have performed this function (see Ostler 2005). Several scholars (e.g., Graddol 1997; Phillipson 1998) agree that English has been serving as a lingua franca as a result of colonization from the late sixteenth century. However, nobody mentions another very important reason – at least in my opinion – why English has become the lingua franca of the world. I think it is mainly because the English language unites the two major branches of the Indo-European language family – Germanic (both North and West Germanic) and Neo-Latin – which has created a unique structure and vocabulary that cannot be compared to any other language in terms of diversity of origins. Let me quote here James D. Nicoll (1990: 22), who wrote the following epigram on the English language: "The problem with defending the purity of the English language is that English is about as pure as a cribhouse whore. We don't just borrow words; on occasion, English has pursued other languages down alleyways to beat them unconscious and riffle their pockets for new vocabulary."[1]

Of course Nicoll exaggerates quite a bit but there is some truth in what he says. English as a Germanic language has a grammar and core vocabulary inherited from Proto-Germanic. According to estimates, the core vocabulary deriving from Germanic languages is about 26–29 percent, while the Greek-Latin word stock is 64–66 percent (see entries in Wikipedia, and Corson 1995). This has a profound effect both on language acquisition and language use, which is rarely taken into account by language teachers and researchers. Words of Germanic origin constitute the bulk of the vocabulary in everyday conversation (see Jackson 2013). These words tend to be short, consisting of one or two

[1] A follow-up to the original post acknowledged that the spelling of 'riffle' was a misspelling of 'rifle.'

syllables (e.g., take, cut, put, go). There are special word-formation processes in English that attempt to increase the number of words that look like and behave as Anglo-Saxon words:

CONVERSION: the change of a word from one word class to another. (e.g., There have been *ups and downs* in their life).
ABBREVIATION: vet (veterinarian), ad (advertisement), lab (laboratory)
BLENDING: *blog:* blend of web and log; *smog*: blend of smoke and fog

Vocabulary is an important issue for ELF because people whose L1 belongs to the Germanic branch or the Neo-Latin branch use English quite differently from those whose L1 is outside these two groups of languages, like Chinese, Korean, Russian, Turkish, etc. Words of Anglo-Saxon origin are identified with everyday conversational and informal language, while words of Greek-Latin origin are said to represent written and formal language, more sophisticated style, and the language of science. Anecdotally – there is no proof for this, at least to my knowledge – Anglo-Saxon words are said to be used 62 percent of the time in everyday conversations in English. The problem for ELF speakers is that most figurativeness, metaphorism, and formulaicity in English are expressed by Anglo-Saxon words, which, mainly because of their simple syllabic structures, are completely unmotivated for speakers whose L1 does not belong to the Germanic or Neo-Latin language groups. And now let's go back to ELF history.

The field of ELF as an independent research paradigm did not exist until the start of the new millennium, although there were some publications available even earlier that discussed the phenomenon (e.g., Firth 1996; Jenkins 1996; Firth & Wagner 1997; House 1999). An important event in shaping the field was Jenkins's book (2000) on ELF pronunciation in which she identified some formal and functional features of pronunciation, and argued on the basis of these features that native English pronunciation is not optimal in ELF communication contexts. Later, Jenkins was joined by Seidlhofer (2001: 133) who argued that while ELF was "the most extensive contemporary use of English worldwide," little description of this linguistic reality was currently available. She called for conceiving of speakers of lingua franca English as "language users in their own right" (ibid.). The paper established a basis for an empirical research agenda for ELF. This was followed by the compilation of the first ELF corpus, the Vienna-Oxford International Corpus of English (VOICE) at the University of Vienna, under her directorship. Two years later came the launch of a second major ELF corpus: the corpus of English as a Lingua Franca in Academic Settings (ELFA) in Finland under the leadership of Mauranen (2003). Also, the third major ELF corpus and the Asian Corpus of English (ACE) was begun in Hong Kong, with Kirkpatrick (2010) and his team.

In the last two decades, the field has been burgeoning and drawing the attention of various scholars from many disciplines such as applied linguistics, second language acquisition, discourse analysis, and English language teaching, but not necessarily pragmaticians. Most of the studies that were written about ELF pragmatics have had an SLA, interlanguage pragmatics, and discourse perspective (e.g., House 2009a, 2014; Björkman 2011; Murray 2012; MacKenzie 2014).

## 1.2 What Is ELF?

Before discussing definitions of ELF, let me start with a quote from Mollin (2006: 1): "English as a Lingua Franca seems to be the Yeti of English varieties: everyone has heard of it, but no one has ever seen it." Yes, I believe that this is very true. The more scholars try to 'grab' it, the more it escapes. It is because ELF does not have 'substance' the way we think about a variety, a dialect, or a language. In short, it comes and goes. Nonnative speakers come together (sometimes even repeatedly), use English as a Lingua Franca between themselves, and then they go different ways, and nothing remains from what they have created temporarily while they used English as a Lingua Franca. This is how the real nature of the phenomenon that we call ELF can be described briefly. So it is almost hopeless to look for patterns, norms, conventions, and common ground in this language-use mode, at least in the way we traditionally understand these terms. So there was some truth to what Seidlhofer (2011: 77) argued when she said that ELF is not a variety of English but a variable way of using English. Widdowson (2012: 21) was also right when he claimed that looking for some kind of 'construct' is the biggest challenge for ELF research: "Descriptions of ELF already give some indication of the nature of this construct, and identifying its essential features is, I think, one of the major challenges of ELF research in the future." What is problematic though is that in spite of all that was said above, most of the definitions of ELF – no matter whether they include or exclude English as a Native Language – contain reference to a 'language' or 'language system' (as we shall discuss in the following paragraph). My point is: If ELF were a language or a language system, it would be possible for us to describe it on the basis of its standards, norms, and rules. But this is not the case. And please do not consider me a 'normativist' because of what I have just said. It is just that when we talk about language as such we usually mean a system whose structure and usage are describable, as we will see.

Another important issue for the field of ELF is the debate about the inclusion of English as a Native Language (ENL). Here are some definitions of ELF that reflect either inclusion or exclusion. Firth (1996) argued that ELF is a "contact language" between persons who share neither a common native tongue nor a common (national) culture and for whom English is the chosen foreign language of communication' (Firth 1996: 240; emphasis in original). According to Mauranen, ELF is "a vehicular language spoken by people who do not share a native language" (Mauranen 2003: 513). These two definitions clearly exclude English as a Native Language. On the VOICE website, the following definition of ELF is given: "an additionally acquired language system which serves as a common means of communication for speakers of different first languages." In my opinion this definition also excludes ENL. However, with some unique twist, Jenkins, Cogo, and Dewey (2011) argued that this definition, in fact, includes ENL because "ELF is not the same as English as a Native Language (ENL hereafter), and must therefore be 'additionally acquired' by NSEs too [albeit that their starting point renders the task easier] (Jenkins et al. 2011: 283). Isn't this a bit strange? Do they really argue that native speakers of English are expected to acquire ELF to communicate with other ELF users??!! So, am I missing something here? Jenkins et al. (2011) further explained their approach. They argued that according to Firth's perspective, native speakers of English are indeed excluded from ELF communication because they cannot be considered as 'foreign language' speakers of English. They also added that ELF and English as a Foreign Language (EFL hereafter) are two entirely different phenomena. Yes, I absolutely agree with them on this. However, not for the reasons that Jenkins (2006) and Jenkins et al. (2011) gave in their publications, but simply because *when EFL learners with different L1s speak with one another they use English as a Lingua Franca*. ELF is constituted by EFL or ESL learners/users who enter into this language use mode (ELF) when they talk to each other. Here is Jenkins et al.'s first argument when explaining the differences between English as a Foreign Language and English as a Lingua Franca:

> ELF is part of the GLOBAL ENGLISHES paradigm, according to which most speakers of English are non-native speakers (henceforth NNSEs), and all English varieties, native or non-native, are accepted in their own right rather than evaluated against a NSE benchmark. By contrast, EFL is part of the MODERN (FOREIGN) LANGUAGES paradigm, according to which most interaction involving non-native speakers is with native speakers of the language, and non-native speakers' goal is to approximate the native variety as closely as possible. (Jenkins et al. 2011: 284)

What I believe is this: First of all, they can argue that ELF is part of the Global Englishes paradigm only if they consider ELF a language or a variety of the English language. This is against what Seidlhofer, Mauranen, Firth, House, and several other scholars say because they do not consider ELF either a language or a language variety in spite of the fact that they often refer to ELF as a "language," as we have discussed. Second of all, it is not quite correct to consider EFL as a paradigm in which most interaction involving nonnative speakers is with native speakers of the English language. In fact, in most cases, EFL learners would appreciate the chance to speak to native speakers. Further, in our globalized world English is used more often between nonnative speakers representing different L1s and varieties of English than either between native speakers or between native speakers and nonnative speakers (see Graddol 2006).

Moreover, Gramkow Anderson (1993) characterized ELF in the following way: "There is no consistency in form that goes beyond the participant level, i.e., each combination of interactants seems to negotiate and govern their own variety of lingua franca use in terms of proficiency level, use of code-mixing, degree of pidginization, etc." (Gramkow Anderson 1993: 103). Referring to this definition, House (2003) emphasized that in it we have the most important ingredients of a lingua franca, such as negotiability, variety in terms of speaker proficiency, and openness to the integration of forms from other languages. She argued that all this reminds one of "interlanguage" (House 2003: 557), and continued with a quote from Selinker describing interlanguage: "the observable output resulting from a speaker's attempt to produce a foreign norm, i.e., both his errors and non-errors. It is assumed that such behavior is highly structured . . . and it must be dealt with as a system, not as an isolated collection of errors" (Selinker 1972: 55). I cannot agree with House on this issue. In fact, ELF has nothing to do with interlanguage that refers to the inner language development of an individual L2 language learner. Interlanguage is an evolving system: the more developed this system becomes, the more it is describable and definable. *ELF is not about the diachronic process of language development. It is about the synchronic use of several varieties of English by the speakers whose L1 is other than English.*

At this point we need to summarize what is common in ELF speech communities. First, in ELF temporary speech communities all participants use a common language that is not their L1. When they use the common language they usually rely on the variety of English (e.g., Chinese English, German English, Hungarian English, Korean English) that they learned/acquired in an English as Foreign Language or English as a Second Language environment. Second, they do not necessarily follow the original rules of the game of ENL and are very flexible in their language use, making negotiation of meaning their priority. In doing so, ELF speakers pay special attention to their partners' varieties. In this way they produce a temporary variety of English that disappears when the temporary speech community dissolves. Leyland's analysis (2011) of ELF conversations suggests that ELF users, despite not adhering to standardized rules, achieve mutual intelligibility through negotiating their own variety of ELF depending on each others' "proficiency level, use of code-mixing, degree of pidginization, etc." (see Gramkow Anderson, 1993: 108) as well as various discourse strategies. Leyland argued that the form of ELF interactions is entirely variable and cannot be standardized. Thus, I think ELF can be best understood *if we think about norm-development as a part of human rationality*. What does this mean? People inherently try to categorize, standardize, and normativize different phenomena in the world in order to better understand, describe, and discuss them with other human beings. I believe that I need to quote Leibniz (1976 [1679]) again to explain this endeavor of human beings: "*si nihil per se concipitur, nihil omnino concipietur*" ("if nothing is understood by itself, nothing at all will ever be understood"). Norm-development in language in general is part of this human endeavor. Based on two of my studies (Kecskes 2007, 2015), I argued that lingua franca speakers start to develop their own norms even when they spend only a short time together. The more time ELF speakers spend together, the more norms and standards of language and contact they will develop. This is so because spending time together creates a speech community. *ELF interaction creates temporary speech communities.* Gumperz (1968) argued that any human aggregate characterized by regular and frequent interaction by means of a shared body of verbal signs and set off from similar aggregates by significant differences in language usage constituted a speech community, a definition that gives equal importance to the structural and interactional sides of language, and does not attempt to describe either the community or the language system as separate entities. According to his approach, the community is a group of people that frequently interact with each other. But this frequency is relative, and never stable. As far as the definition of the language system shared by a speech community is concerned, Gumperz (1964: 285) claimed the following: "Regardless of the linguistic differences among them, the speech varieties employed within a speech community form a system because they are related to a shared set of social norms." In his definition, Gumperz highlighted two important components of the speech community: its members share a set of linguistics forms and a set of social norms that govern the use of those linguistic forms. In other words, there is a bidirectional interaction between linguistic forms and social norms. Social norm-development requires certain sets of linguistic forms and the use of particular sets of forms create a social frame or norm (see Kecskes 2014). This is why we can talk about Global Englishes. Let us now see how ELF relates to what we call 'language' and Global Englishes.

## 1.3 Language, Language Varieties, and ELF

In the introduction, I was very critical of the monolingual approach in linguistics. I argued that there should be a gradual shift of interest from the monolingual ideal speaker's grammar and language use to the interlocutor, whose language development and use is determined not only by individual features but also by the sociocultural environment and situations in which s/he functions. What I mean is that linguistic research should be expanded beyond studying I-language (the internal language system of an individual) to also consider E-language (the external language shared by members of a group), through the analysis of discourse and textual representation as well as the pragmatics of these levels of linguistic representation.[2] This move has been slow but certainly is happening. ELF research especially needs and also promotes this relatively new perspective.

Linguistics research has always been characterized by a unique dynamic of separatist and synergistic endeavors. This goes back to the basic question of whether language is a relatively independent cognitive faculty or an essential part of overall cognitive development. As a result, we have a number of subparadigms, each with a special focus. At the same time, however, there has always been a strong desire to cross disciplinary boundaries and pull together knowledge generated by using different perspectives of language-oriented research. Recent events point to the fact that synergetic endeavors are receiving more attention than ever before. It was a significant step when the Minimalist Program proposed that it is possible to capture knowledge of language as a function from sets of lexical items to meaning–sound pairs (see Chomsky 1995). Basically, this means that grammars are lexically rather than syntactically driven. Chomsky argued that sentences in all languages have the same phrase structure that consists of a lexical domain (VP) and a functional domain (Chomsky 1995, 2000). The lexical domain is the place of insertion of the verb and its arguments. Derivation begins with the selection of relevant lexical items that are arranged into a particular structure (or structures) using three syntactic operations: merge, agree, and move. The Lexical Learning Hypothesis (e.g., Clahsen et al. 1996; Clahsen & Muysken 1996) also claims that the development of grammar in children is largely driven by the child's gradual acquisition of lexical items. Recently in linguistics the debate has been not about the legitimacy of meaning and performance research (usage), but about the extent to which grammar research and usage research can be combined, and what role communication plays in shaping grammar. In other words, whether one can and/or needs to support the other, or whether they should not interact at all. Linguists have never denied that there is some link between structure and usage. As Chomsky (1975: 56) wrote, "surely there are significant connections between structure and function": this is not and has never been in doubt. Searle (1979) argued that "it is reasonable to suppose the needs of communication influenced [language] structure." "I agree," said Chomsky (1975: 56). Newmeyer (2003) claimed that mental grammar contributes to language use,

[2] See Chomsky (1986) about I-language and E-language.

but usage is not represented in the grammar itself. Knowledge of grammatical structure is only one of many systems that underlie usage.

Recent linguistic research (e.g., Hauser et al. 2002; Pinker & Jackendoff 2005) differentiates between aspects of language that are special to language code (Narrow Language Faculty, NLF hereafter) and the faculty of language in its entirety, including parts that are shared with other psychological abilities found elsewhere in cognition (Broad Language Faculty, BLF hereafter). The lexicon can be considered as an interface that ties NLF to the other elements of the BLF. Please look at Figure 1.1.

Kecskes' definition (2014: 23) of language makes an attempt to pull the two sides together as follows: "Language is a system of signs operated by a conceptual base that is the reflection of the socio-cultural background in which the system of signs is put to use." This definition emphasizes the unique relationship of the sociocultural background (BLF) with the system of signs (NLF) through the conceptual base. (See Figure 1.2.)

Kachru's (1985) inner, outer, and expanding circles are easy to explain on the basis of Kecskes' definition. Let us take, for instance, an outer circle country like Nigeria where English is not the native tongue, but is important for historical and economic reasons and plays a part in the nation's institutions – either as an official language or otherwise – just like in other countries with similar colonial history, such as India, Pakistan, Malaysia, Tanzania, and Kenya. What happened in Nigeria is that the English system of signs was put to use in a Nigerian sociocultural environment/background, and as a result of the long interplay of the two, the conceptual system of language users has changed and resulted in Nigerian English, which is now a variety of English. Using this approach (see

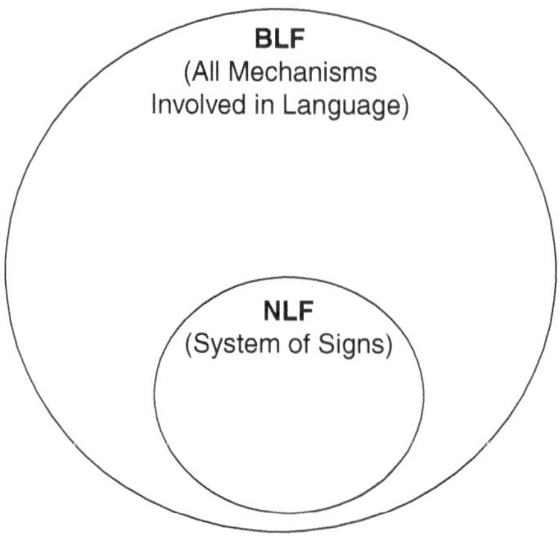


Figure 1.1 Recent linguistic theory of language

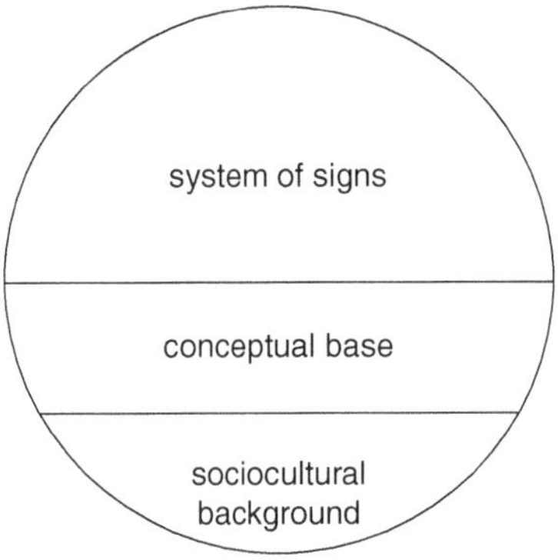


Figure 1.2 Kecskes' definition of language

Figure 1.2), we can explain the development of varieties both in the outer circle and the expanding circle, such as Chinese English, German English, Hungarian English, and so on. The main difference between the outer circle varieties and expanding circle varieties is the time, and the way the given speech communities have been using the English language, and of course the institutionalization of English in those countries. Thus, in the expanding circle countries, English language use is rarely institutionalized. Figure 1.3 illustrates the result of the interplay of the English code system with the Chinese sociocultural background, which has led to the development of a Chinese variety of English.

As you can see, this is a picture of a warning at the entrance to the Shanghai Tower. Let us take, for example, the sentence "No admittance for anyone who is drunk, insane and not properly dressed." This is a typical reflection of how the "foreign" code conveys the Chinese thought (conceptualization) that was based on the Chinese (and not English) sociocultural background.[3]

Now we should look at language and language variety from the perspective of norm-development, which always is a matter of degree. We can set up a continuum where normativization starts on the left-hand side and it reaches its highest level on the right-hand side. Of course, this is a hypothetical continuum that shows how much native-standard-driven particular language varieties are. From this respect, there are significant differences between expanding, outer, and inner circle varieties.

| | | |
|---|---|---|
| Estonian English | Indian English | American English |
| expanding circle | outer circle | inner circle |

[3] The Chinese version is: 醉酒者（drunk），精神疾病患者（insane），衣冠不整者（not properly dressed），不得入内（no admittance）。The English version is a pure literal translation.

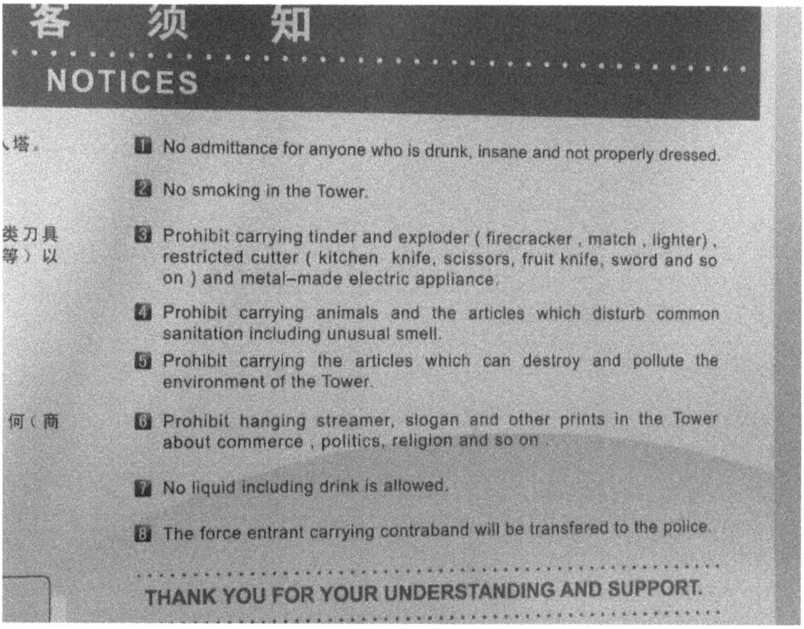


Figure 1.3 The result of the interplay of the English code system with the Chinese sociocultural background: Chinese variety of English

So, how does English as a Lingua Franca relate to all this? As I said before, ELF does not fit into the Kachruian paradigm because it is not a language, and it is not a variety of English. *Its norm-development is temporary and as a consequence, not "mature" enough to be put on the continuum above.* In order for ELF to become a variety, I believe that more normatization, standardization, and conventionalization should take place. In Figure 1.4, I demonstrate how ELF relates to the English language and Nigerian English variety.

As we can see in Figure 1.4, in ELF the English system of signs is put on a variety of different sociocultural backgrounds depending on the members of the temporary speech community. The constant entity in ELF is the English system of signs while the ever-changing entities are the sociocultural backgrounds represented by the L1s of the ELF speakers, which results in the development a unique, blended conceptual system. We may consider ELF interaction as some kind of interrupted creolization process. Cohen (2007: 370) argued that creolization is a condition in which "the formation of new identities and inherited culture evolve to become different from those they possessed in the original cultures," and then creatively merge these to create

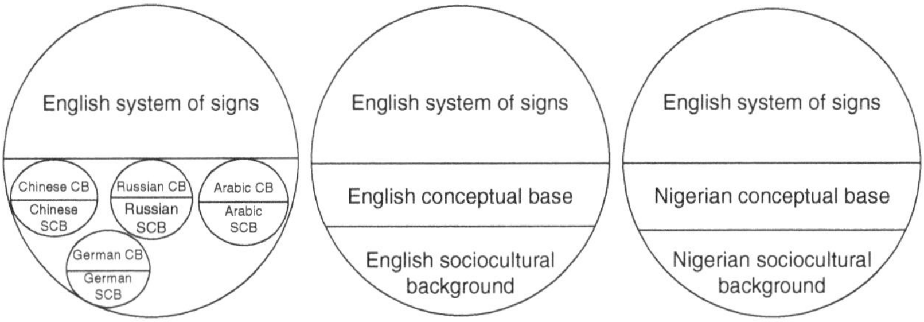


Figure 1.4 English as a Lingua Franca; native English; outer circle English[4]

new varieties that supersede the prior forms. Cohen's quoted thought in the previous sentence is completely true for ELF. However, the second part ("then creatively merge these to create new varieties that supersede the prior forms") never or very rarely happens so. This is why we can call ELF interaction *an interrupted creolization process*. In sum, we can claim that ELF is not a separate language system that can line up with varieties of English such as Indian English, Chinese English, Black English Vernacular, Hawaiian English, and German English. ELF involves the use of different varieties of English in one and the same conversation (see Matsuda & Friederich 2012). So an alternative definition of ELF can go like this: *ELF is a way to put a variety, or several varieties of English to use in interactions between speakers whose L1 is other than English.* ENL is put to action in L1 English intracultural communication while ELF is put to use in intercultural communication.

## 1.4 Intracultural Communication and Intercultural Communication

### *1.4.1 Understanding Culture*

Theoretically, human verbal communication can be considered a process with two extreme ends: intracultural communication and intercultural communication. However, communicators are practically always between, closer or further to one of the ends, creating and interpreting meaning by using their existing linguistic tools. So it would be a mistake to talk about a dichotomy. There is no such thing as pure intracultural communication or intercultural

[4] As far as the Native English system is concerned, I am fully aware of the pluricentric nature of English and the huge amount of linguistic and cultural varieties in the so-called English-speaking world as addressed in the field of variational pragmatics. But for the sake of explanation and trying to make the difference more visible between ELF, NE, and OCE, I opted for this figure.

communication. What we have is something in between, on a continuum with the two hypothetical ends. I believe that this approach can help us better understand ELF. But before we explain how the continuum works we need to define culture as understood in this book. We adopt Bates and Plog's definition according to which culture is "the system of shared beliefs, norms, values, customs, behaviors, and artifacts that the members of society use to cope with their world and with one another" (1980: 6). However, culture cannot be seen as something that is "carved" in every member of a particular society or community. It can be made, changed, manipulated, and dropped on the spot. In fact, it is not culture that can be changed, manipulated, and dropped in talk and life in general but its manifestation. Gumperz (1982) and Gumperz and Roberts (1991) talked about the fact that "culture" is not present in communication in the "old" sense of a transcendent identity that is composed of values and norms and linearly related to forms of behavior. Cultural phenomena in speech are contingent, situational, and emergent in nature. The main argument of the approach represented by Gumperz, Hymes, Blommaert, Rampton, and others is that there is no single language, culture, or communicative style. What we have is language, culture, and communicative style instantiated in several group and individual varieties. In intercultural communication, speakers have a "repertoire" of varieties of styles, and a combination of styles, which are deployed according to communicative needs in the changing context. The nationality or ethnic membership of people may suggest the possibility of ethnic or cultural marking in communicative behavior. However, the interplay of several different factors affects the emergence of "ethnically" or "culturally marked" aspects of communicative behavior that is most frequently dominated by other than cultural factors. This approach, however, should not mean that there is nothing relatively stable and unifying in culture. On this issue, there is a significant difference between the constructivist view represented by Blommaert, Gumperz, and Rampton and the socio-cognitive approach promoted by Kecskes (2010, 2013, 2014). The difference between the constructivist view and the socio-cognitive approach lies in the understanding of the nature of existing "communicative repertoires" and the ways these repertoires are deployed. According to the socio-cognitive approach, existing communicative repertoires have been developed from prior experience and communicative encounters in a language or languages including the common language of communication, that is, English in ELF (Kecskes 2013b). What the online, in situ creation of culture means is similar to what online, actual meaning construction means: the bringing about of something relatively new needed in the actual situational context by using and blending existing repertoires and newly emergent elements.

Culture, just like meaning, is characterized by both regularity and variety. It certainly is more than just an online created and co-constructed phenomenon. In communication, interlocutors can rely on two types of repository of prior experience and encounters: lexical units and communicative styles. Like lexical items, cultural patterns (often expressed in different communicative styles) code prior experience and encounters, i.e., relatively standard cultural behavior models and expectations which are activated in a given situational context. Here is, for instance, an exchange between a librarian and a student (both nonnative speakers of English)[5]:

(1) STUDENT: - I am returning these books.
LIBRARIAN: - Can I see your library card, please?
STUDENT: - Here you are . . .
LIBRARIAN: - Do you want to extend the due date of any of these books?
STUDENT: - No, thank you.
LIBRARIAN: - Here is your card. You are all set.

As we can see, in the course of the interaction these existing models (librarian–customer frame) are modified and blended with situationally emergent new elements (ad hoc generated expressions). This process of blending that relies both on existing and emerging factors constitutes the communicative encounter. *Blending means joining existing and emerging elements/factors into new intercultures.* So in the interaction, the communicative repertoires of speakers are not just deployed but are actually modified and blended with emerging elements as the process develops. The socio-cognitive approach emphasizes that this "interculture" creation means not just putting together what we have and bringing about a third phenomenon which is neither this nor that, but actually giving sense to the communicative repertoires and changing them by relating them to the actual situational context that also adds to or takes away something from what is existing. Cultural constructs and models change diachronically, while cultural representation and speech production by individuals changes synchronically. From the perspective of ELF, it is important that the participants in this conversation rely on existing ENL patterns (interaction frame between librarian and customer). They are comfortable with those in this context because they both know them quite well. So there is no problem for them to behave according to the requirements of the given cultural pattern. However, this is not always the case in ELF when the cultural frame is missing, is not recognized by the parties, or is interpreted differently by them.

[5] Conversation recorded at the University Library at SUNY, Albany.

### *1.4.2 Is There Any Difference between Intracultural or Intercultural?*

ELF communication is considered intercultural communication. So we need to discuss how ELF fits into the intra–inter relationship. The dominant view is that there is no principled difference between intracultural communication and intercultural communication (e.g., Winch 1997; Wittgenstein 2001). This is true as far as the purpose and mechanism of the communicative process is concerned. However, according to Gumperz and Cook-Gumperz (2005), monolingual people and multilingual people do not differ in *what* they do with language, but in *how* they do what they do, and this is where our focus should be. This is especially important in the case of ELF speakers. As we said earlier, we should imagine the relationship between intracultural communication and intercultural communication as a continuum and not as a dichotomy. So, as we know, a continuum has two hypothetical ends. Consequently, there is no pure intracultural or intercultural communication. Every concrete communicative event can be placed somewhere on the continuum, closer to one of the ends. However, that place keeps changing depending on several factors that affect the nature of the communicative event, such as participants, venue, language proficiency, length of event, and intersubjectivity. Therefore, the two hypothetical ends can be defined as follows: Intracultural communication occurs in interactions between members of a relatively definable L1 speech community following the conventions of language and the conventions of usage with individual choices and preferences. Intercultural communication refers to interactions between speakers who have different first languages, communicate in a common language, and, usually, represent different cultures. So the question that remains is how is this difference reflected in the language use of ELF speakers?

From a pragmatic perspective, the main difference between intracultural communication and intercultural communication is that the latter, to some extent, shifts the emphasis from the communal to the individual, as was discussed in the Introduction (see also Kecskes 2014, 2015a). I argued that standard pragmatics assumes that L1 communication depends on there being commonalities, conventions, standards, and norms between speakers and hearers. Commonalities, conventions, common beliefs, norms, shared knowledge, and the like all create a core common ground on which intention and cooperation-based pragmatics is built. (Of course, there are plenty of varieties within those commonalities.) This, however, may not be exactly so in intercultural communication. When this core common ground appears to be limited, interlocutors cannot take it for granted, rather they need to co-construct and negotiate it, at least temporarily. So, basically, there seems to be a shift in emphasis from the communal to the individual. It is not that the individual becomes more important than the societal. Rather, since there is limited common ground, it should be co-constructed in the interactional context in which interlocutors function not as users of existing schematas, cultural models or frames or as activators of existing common ground and mutual beliefs, but individuals who, based on their prior experience in different relatively stable speech communities (L1) or temporary speech communities create, negotiate, and co-construct what is missing from their actual language experience: the backing of the prefabricated language, relatively definable cultural and situational frames, and mutual understanding of norms related to the use of English. So they bring about their 'social' frame without which there is no smooth communication. This process is demonstrated in the following sequence. A man from Hong Kong and two Brazilian au pair girls are talking.[6]

(2) HKM: - Aha. But if you want to come here, what do you do? Do you have some transportation, something or do you have a car?
BF1: - We have car.
BF2: - We have our own car.
HKM: - Yeah. Who provides you with the car?
BF1: - Host family.
HKM: - Yeah. So they give you the car, yeah?
BF2: - Yeah.
HKM: - You can use the car freely, whenever you want, yeah?
BF1: - Yes and no. . . . Some of the girls have the problems with the car.
HKM: - Yeah.
BF1: - For example, they cannot go . . . more than . . . I don't know, one hundred miles for a week. Errh . . . It is up to the family . . . like people are different . . . I don't . . .
HKM: - So they can limit the mileages . . .
BF1: - Yeah.
BF2: - Most families they don't do that . . . but some of the families.

In the aforementioned example we can see that the interlocutors are talking about how the au pair girls use cars of the host families. The two Brazilian girls try to use several strategies (repetition, detailed explanation, etc.) to make the Hong Kong man understand what they are talking about, in what circumstances they are allowed to use cars by the host families. It seems that this is a scenario that they are familiar with. However, it is quite new for the HKM. But we can see that together they are co-constructing a temporary frame for the conversation with pieces of information that are mutually understandable. But, of course, it can be argued that similar exchanges happen on the intracultural end of

[6] Excerpts used in this chapter/book come from the Albany Database of Intercultural Communication (that is under development) unless otherwise noted. ADIC contains recorded conversations between native speakers and nonnative speakers of English and between non-native speakers and nonnative speakers of English.

the continuum (ENL) as well. There is no doubt about this. So let me try to explain the difference.

In the Gricean paradigm, cooperation is considered a rational behavior of human beings. It is essential that human beings are cooperative in the course of communication, subconsciously and automatically. They usually do not need specific effort for that since cooperation is part of human rationality. In ELF communication, however, this rational and usually subconscious behavior is enhanced with a conscious, often pre-planned and monitored endeavor of interlocutors to be cooperative in the common sense of the word as well, and make deliberate efforts to comprehend and be comprehended by others, and produce language that is processable and understandable by others. So it is even more emphasized that the goal of coming to an understanding is "intersubjective mutuality . . . shared knowledge, mutual trust, and accord with one another" (Habermas 1979: 3).

### *1.4.3 The Success Approach*

Based on Gumperz and Cook-Gumperz (2005), I argued that what we do in any kind of communication is similar but the ways we do them are different. Consequently, as it was mentioned in the Introduction, in analyzing ELF we should focus on the different or modified routes to success, called "the success approach" in this book. So the significant questions is: What makes ELF interlocutors successful in spite of the fact that they cannot rely on those commonalities, norms, and/or conventions that make intracultural (L1) communication relatively smooth? Some researchers' findings (e.g., House 2002, 2003; Kecskes 2007, 2015; Seidlhofer 2011) prove that intercultural communication is not necessarily the site of interactional failures, neither is it a clash of cultures. The use of semantically transparent language by nonnative speakers results in fewer misunderstandings and communication breakdowns than expected. In addition, the success approach has a profound effect on language learning and international education as well. Students using not their L1 for education but another language such as English are not considered deficient learners but learners in their own right. These learners are perfectly capable of expressing themselves through L2 and negotiate meaning by creating intercultures that can be considered as unique tools of creating meaning as, for instance, in the following sequence (3) in which a Polish woman is speaking about housing with a man from Hong Kong and a Brazilian woman (see Kecskes 2015).

(3) HKM: - How about you? . . . circumstances . . . Where do you live? You rent . . . or?
POF: - Mmm . . . I am live . . . not so far from the university.
HKM: - Hmm.
POF: - It is a college . . . you don't know . . . It is not so far. It's Albany.
HKM: - Hmm.

POF: - But I have 3 minutes . . . errh . . . to go to my work.
HKM: - Hmm.
POF: - And this house is . . . errh . . . on our own so my husband and I . . .
HKM: - Hmm.
BRF: - Doesn't have any kids?
POF: - No. don't have . . .
BRF: - No?
POF: - Yeah.
BRF: - Errh . . . Are your husband American or . . . ?
POF: - Errh . . . Actually he is . . . he is Polish. He is American but . . .
BRF: - OK.
POF: - . . . because he came into the United States when he was a child.
HKM: - Hmm.
POF: - He was something like twelve.
BRF: - All right.

As was demonstrated in this example, intercultures are co-constructed common ground elements that rely both on relatively definable cultural models and norms as well as situationally evolving features (e.g., Kecskes 2010, 2012, 2013, 2014). In this conversation the following elements can be considered intercultures (mutually co-constructed pieces of knowledge): Polish woman rents a house with her husband; they live close to work and university; husband is a Polish-American. Hence, intercultures are blends that are co-constructed by the interlocutors who rely on their existing knowledge in their L1s and L2, as well as the communicative needs triggered by the actual situational context. These intercultures can be considered *temporary norms* in ELF. They, however, are quite loose and vague in comparison to norms in traditional speech communities. But there is evidence that interlocutors co-construct some kind of norms of their own, however short a time their members spend together (e.g., Kecskes 2007, 2013, 2015; Canagarajah 2014).

## 1.5 Factors Defining Variations on the Continuum

### *1.5.1 Language Proficiency*

One of the most important factors that differs in intercultural and intracultural communication is language proficiency. Relatively high proficiency in language use allows the speaker to pay more attention to the communicative process itself rather than just to language use issues (word choice, fluency, correctness, etc.). There is usually little proficiency issue affecting intracultural (L1) communication. Consequently, one would assume that the higher the language proficiency of the ELF interlocutors, the more the communicative process resembles intracultural communication. Of course, we should recognize that there are individual differences in L1 use as well. However, those individual differences affect language use in a different way than in ELF encounters, where looking for words and building meaningful utterances may require more significant effort than in L1 communication. But we have to be careful with the language proficiency issue. Although the language gap between interlocutors may act as a barrier for intercultural communication, there can still be particular situations that suggest that the opposite can also occur. What I mean is that the success approach should also be used when we evaluate the role of proficiency in ELF encounters. There are several studies (e.g., Ting-Toomey 1999; Pearce 2005; Mancini-Cross et al. 2009) demonstrating that in specific cases, such as tourism, the language gap and intercultural inexperience of travelers can be positive rather than negative attributes in the intercultural exchange between interlocutors. The following exchange between a native speaker of American English and a Thai au pair girl records a situation when language proficiency does not work as a barrier at all. In fact, both speakers are highly motivated and interested in the topic of conversation. So as we can see below, they focus on the content rather than the "carriers" of the content, and still are able to understand each other very well.

(4) NS: Do they: um (0.5) are you teaching them any Thai? (0.2) Do they speak °Thai°?
NNS: So:metime=it difficult (to) them, sometime they (like a copy) me::? (0.5)
NS: Oh::
NNS: <When they heard> me talk on phone or something.
NS: Oh [okay.
NNS: [Some girl- (0.2) just one girl (love) to learn Thai language.
NS: ↑Oh that's so ↑cool.
NNS: Just <four years old>, she love Thai foo::d
NS: Oh↑oo
NNS: She love to speak Thai:: hh
NS: Do they- is she good?
NNS: She count one to ten in Thai.
NS: ↑Wow::, that's so [goo:d 3:30
NNS: [Yeah:: heh, she so cute, I love her.

### *1.5.2 Preferred Ways of Saying Things and Preferred Ways of Organizing Thoughts*

I argued in several papers that using a particular language and belonging to a particular speech community mean having preferred ways of saying things and preferred ways of organizing thoughts (e.g., Kecskes 2007, 2013, 2014). Also, Coulmas (1981) claimed that the more tradition-based a society is, the more its members seem to make use of situational formulas. In other words, the development of preferred ways of saying things and preferred ways of organizing thoughts in a language community is the result of conventionalization, standardization, normativization, core common ground development, historical development, and relative coherence of the speech community. However, this is not the case in ELF communication because the development of 'preferred ways' requires time, as well as a process of some kind of conventionalization. If approached from this perspective, the question of who is a 'native speaker' can also be defined. Anybody can be a 'native-like speaker' if s/he knows preferred ways in that speech community and actually uses those preferred ways. In fact, ELF speakers spending longer time together (like a one-semester seminar or group working together on a project, etc.) may result in the development of a (temporarily) emerging loose variety-like linguistic phenomenon that has its own temporary native speakers (students in the seminar, participants in the working group). The only problem is that what they have created will disappear when the group is dissolved. "Preferred ways of saying things" is expressed in a well-balanced blend of prefabricated language with ad hoc generated language. Selecting the right words and/or expressions in communication is more important than syntax. For instance, Americans *shoot a film*, *run a business*, *make love*, *do the dishes*, and *put out the fire*. The TV anchor asks you to *stick around*, and the shop assistant tells you at the end of the transaction that *you are all set*. What I am trying to say is that language socialization is directly connected with preferred ways of saying things. To a great extent, language socialization depends on the acquisition of what is expected to be said in particular situations and sociocultural frames, and what kind of language behavior is considered appropriate in the given speech community. Let's look at an example for more clarification.

(5) Husband and wife are talking.
- Are you OK, Jill?
- I am fine, Ryan.
- Do you want to talk about it?

As we can see, 'I am fine' is a formulaic expression. But Jill added 'Ryan,' the name of the husband, to the expression, which, with this action, ceased to be a formulaic expression, and in fact, conveyed the opposite meaning: 'No, I am not fine.' As his response shows the husband recognized his wife is feeling bad about something and asked if she wanted to talk about it.

Preferred ways of saying things, i.e., the use of formulaic language appears to be the heart and soul of native-like language use. In fact, formulaic language use makes language use native-like. Pawley and

Syder (2000: 164) argued that "it is knowledge of conventional expressions, more than anything that gives speakers the means to escape from the one-clause-at-a-time constraint, and that is the key to nativelike fluency." Also, Hymes (1968: 126–127) claimed that "a vast proportion of verbal behaviour consists of recurrent patterns, . . . [including] the full range of utterances that acquire conventional significance for an individual, group or whole culture." Likewise, Coulmas (1981: 1–3) argued that much of what is actually said in everyday conversation is by no means unique. Rather, a great deal of communicative activity consists of enacting routines making use of prefabricated linguistic units in a well-known and generally accepted manner. Successful coordination of social interactions heavily depends on standardized ways of organizing interpersonal encounters because conventional ways of doing things with words and expressions are familiar to everyone in the speech community so speakers can be expected to be understood according to their communicative intentions and goals. Furthermore, Wray and Namba (2003: 36) claimed "speech communities develop and retain common ways of expressing key messages." This fact also affects the development of preferred ways of organizing thoughts. Prefabricated language brings together members of the speech community; newcomers should acquire these preferred ways in order to be included in the group or community.

Several studies referred to the low rate of the use of formulaic language in intercultural communication including ELF (e.g., Kecskes 2007; Ellis et al. 2008; Prodromou 2008). Researchers argued that the main reason that interlocutors prefer semantically analyzable units is because they cannot be sure how much formulaic language their partners can process the way they do, i.e., how much their partners know preferred ways of saying things in the target language. Or they may simply do not know the formulaic expressions well. So discrepancy in formulaic language use in ELF can lead to serious misunderstandings as the following example shows:

(6) A Japanese student is talking to the department work-study student (German) in the office.
HIROKO: - I need the professor's signature on this document.
URSULA: - *Come again . . .* ?
HIROKO: - Why should I come again? I am here now.

As we can see, although the work-study student used interrogative intonation with the expression *come again*, the Korean student still misunderstood her because she did not know the formulaic function of that expression. So reliance on native-like formulas may result in communication problems. We will return this issue in the Chapter 2.

### *1.5.3 Reliance on Emergent Common Ground rather than on Core Common Ground*

Common ground refers to the "sum of all the information that people assume they share" (Clark 2009: 116) that may include world views, shared values, beliefs, and the situational context. As discussed earlier, commonalities, conventions, common beliefs, norms, shared knowledge, and the like all create a core common ground in a speech community on which members' communicative activities are based. Kecskes and Zhang (2009) argued that we need to make a distinction between core common ground and emergent common ground. Core common ground refers to the relatively static, generalized, common knowledge that belongs to a certain speech community as a result of prior interaction and experience, whereas emergent common ground refers to the relatively dynamic, actualized and particularized knowledge co-constructed in the course of communication that belongs to and is privatized by the individual(s). The former is a repertoire of knowledge that can be assumed to be shared among individuals of a speech community independent of the situational circumstances, such as when and where the conversation occurs and between whom it occurs. In contrast, the actual contextual part (emergent common ground) is knowledge that is aroused, co-constructed and/or involved as shared enterprises in the particular situational context that pertains to the interlocutors exclusively. This contingent circumstance draws attention of the interlocutors to the same entities or states and, with the formation of particular intentions therein, activates some of their prior individual experiences that join in this intention-directed action.

It is crucial to underline that this co-construction is not separated from core common ground. Co-construction, or creation of emergent common ground, builds not only on actual situational needs and context but also existing shared knowledge and information. During this process new and old are blended into a synergistic whole. This phenomenon also exists in intracultural L1 communication. However, while intracultural communication builds on existing core common ground that is the result of relatively similar prior experience of interlocutors and less on emergent common ground, ELF relies more on emergent common ground because of the limited availability of core common ground resulting from little or no mutual prior experience. So once more, what we see as difference between the two ends of the intra–inter continuum is the degree of reliance on core common ground and emergent common ground in different types of interactions. It is also important to note that emergent common ground usually builds on intercultures that are usually ad hoc creations (see example 7 below). They are created in a communicative process in which cultural norms and models brought into the interaction from prior experience of interlocutors blend with features created ad hoc in the interaction in a synergetic way. Let us look at the following excerpt in which a Korean student is talking with a Turkish student:

(7) K: - Where do you live? Near Albany?
T: - Yeah I live in Woodrick (??). do you know Woodrick?
K: - Yeah apartment right?
T: - Yes, apartment.
K: - I see.
T: - Yes I live in Woodrick with my wife. And it's beautiful.
K: - Oh . . . area
T: - Yes. I can go grocery.
K: - Mhmmm
T: - Or supermarket.
K: - Oh
T: - Or school on foot because . . .
K: - On foot?
T: - Yeah because near. It's it's .. near. It's near. But it's rainy we come here we go to school by bus. But the weather is beautiful . . . sunny . . . we like walking. Because it is healthy.
K: - I see (laughing) it's very very healthy
- My wife like . . .
- Walking?
- walking. Maybe I don't like walking. But she like so I have to walk.
- (Laughing) you are very good husband.
- Yeah. I think so.
- So usually you cook and Seda (wife) also cook
- I cook.
- Usually you cook?
- Yeah. And my wife cook. But I cook
- You like the cooking
- Yes I like cooking. I start to cooking
- Here?
- When I married.

As we can see, the Korean student and the Turkish student mutually participated in the co-construction of the following intercultures that have gained specific understanding in the exchange: living area, shopping, walking, cooking. The process of developing intercultures resulting from emerging common ground is connected with the process of shaping intersubjectivity.

### *1.5.4 Change in the Nature of Intersubjectivity*

The cognitive-oriented approach to intersubjectivity has put emphasis on the process of cooperative meaning-making (Habermas 1979) with a focus on a shared meaning as an end goal. Similarly, Rommetveit (1998: 358), who was a psychologist, viewed intersubjectivity as an end goal within social understanding. He considered it "reciprocal perspective setting and perspective taking" within a pursuit of a "state of intersubjectivity." So the term refers to the development of a shared understanding and/or focus on particular elements of the communicative process between speaker(s) and listener(s). Furthermore, in intercultural communication, including ELF, the nature of intersubjectivity seems to be changing. As discussed in Section 1.5.3, there is more reliance on language created ad hoc by individuals in the course of interaction than on prefabricated language and preexisting frames. ELF interlocutors lack full control over language skills (L2) and full knowledge of conventions, beliefs, and norms in the target language (L2) used as the medium of communication. This may lead to a more conscious approach to what is said, and how it is said. The following conversation between a female student from Japan and a female student from China appears to support my argument.

(8) CH: - And basically I don't like American food.
J: - Mhmmm.
CH: - Like there are too many . . . too much fat in it . . . . So I just . . . I cannot cook either but my roommates and friend they can cook very authentic Chinese food.
J: - Oh really?
CH: - And Chinese dish so I . . .
J: - It's good for you!
CH: -Yeah (laughing) it's good for me . . . like I just ask them to cook hometown food and then I'll be in charge for all the cleaning thing.
J: - Oh
CH: - They don't have to worry about it.
J: - It's very reasonable and fair because sometimes like cooking but they don't like cleaning
CH: - Mhmm.
J: - But you don't like cooking you like . . . .
CH: - I don't like (laughing) yeah but I have to like to be responsible for the whole dinner thing.
J: - Ahh

The example illustrates that intersubjectivity and common understanding of cooking are nicely being shaped in this exchange. The Japanese student gently makes her Chinese partner describe what her relationship to cooking is. She does not speak much but gives backchanneling support ('oh really?'; 'it's good for you'; etc.) to her partner. As we can see, both speakers have their own strategies to get the message through or get the message out of their partner. These strategies (for the Chinese person: giving much information, repetition;

and for the Japanese person: making Chinese student speak, backchanneling) help them better understand each other.

Reliance on emergent common ground, and shaping intersubjectivity through developing intercultures, all this results in a shift from the societal to the individual in the process of communication. What the individuals actually do, based on their non-target language dominated prior experience and ad hoc interpretation of the actual situational context seems to be more important than what prefabricated language and social frames and social expectations of the common language (English) can offer. So they co-create their 'social' through common individual efforts.

It is the responsibility of the participating individuals to develop their sociocultural frame for the conversation, create common ground, and find linguistic elements that are mutually processable in the actual situational context. So the basic difference between intracultural communication and intercultural communication from the perspective of intersubjectivity is that while participants in intracultural (L1) interactions can rely on existing frames that affect them top-down, in intercultural interactions participants usually must build up those frames bottom-up while negotiating meaning with their interlocutors. Diversity of individuals participating in the communicative process will result in social frames that are built on mutual understanding of different ethnicities, different individuals, different genders, etc., rather than just on the experience of one particular speech community (English).

### *1.5.5 Context-Sensitivity*

I argued that context-sensitivity works differently in intracultural and intercultural communication (Kecskes 2008, 2015a). In linguistics, context usually refers to any factor – linguistic, epistemic, physical, social, etc. – that affects the actual interpretation of signs and expressions. This is too broad a definition that does not reflect the complexity of context. Besides, this definition covers only what I call the "actual situational context." In the socio-cognitive approach, context represents two sides of world knowledge: one that is in our mind (prior context) and the other (actual situational context) that is out there in the world (see Kecskes 2014). These two sides are interwoven and inseparable. Actual situational context refers to the linguistic and extra-linguistic factors as well as the situational environment in which a given interaction takes place, while prior context encapsulates the interlocutors' previous experience with the linguistic signs used in the given situation and similar situational frame(s) that the actual situational environment resembles. So, actual situational context is viewed through prior context, and vice versa, prior context is viewed through actual situational context. Their encounter creates a third space. According to this approach, meaning is the result of the interplay of prior experience and current, actual situational experience, which are both sociocultural in nature. Prior experience that becomes declarative knowledge is tied to the meaning values of lexical units constituting utterances produced by interlocutors, while current experience is represented in the actual situational context (procedural knowledge) in which communication takes place, and which is interpreted (often differently) by interlocutors. Meaning formally expressed in the utterance is co-constructed online as a result of the interaction and mutual influence of the private contexts represented in the language of interlocutors and the actual situational context interpreted by interlocutors. This approach calls for the revision of how we understand the role of context in communication in general and in ELF communication in particular. This revision is needed because context does not exactly affect meaning production and comprehension the way it does intracultural communication. There are several reasons for this fact. One is that the actual situational context cannot play the role of catalyst in ELF, the way it does in intracultural communication, because the participants' different sociocultural background ties them to culturally different L1 communities where both prior context and actual situational context function in a variety of ways. Moreover, context-sensitiveness may also work differently because of the increasing number of "interpretation sensitive terms." Cappelen argued: "[N]atural languages contain what I'll call *interpretation sensitive terms*: terms the correct interpretation of which varies across interpreters (or, more generally, contexts of interpretation). An interpretation sensitive sentence can have one content relative to one interpreter and another content relative to another interpreter" (2008: 25). When Cappelen talks about "interpretation sensitive terms," he is not talking about nonnative speakers of a natural language. But he refers to the native speakers of a natural language. It seems to me that he is right that this notion is important in natural languages no matter whether the given language is used by a native speaker or a nonnative speaker. What these *interpretation sensitive terms* are, and how they function for nonnative speaker language users, is an important matter in ELF interaction as we will see in the examples (9) and (1)0. The content of an utterance should be understood relative to a speaker and a hearer. The same utterance can express several distinct propositions depending on the hearer. The question is what makes those "terms" interpretation sensitive in ELF interactions and how the nature of interpretation sensitive terms may depend on the culturally diverse background of interlocutors. The following excerpt is an interaction between an African French speaker and a Korean speaker. The common context is that they both live in Albany, New York, but they have different sociocultural backgrounds. The interlocutors appear to jump from one topic to another, seemingly changing their intention and interrupting the flow of communication. However, a closer look shows that they think along topic-comment lines, and co-construct a coherent narrative in which emergent intention and common ground plays an important role. The topic-comment lines are as follows: living in Albany – likes/dislikes – likes: quiet, nice neighbors – dislikes: offices and forms. Their prior context gives different understanding to terms such as school, driver station (?), and manager. The actual situational context does not help them much to specify the meanings of those key expressions (interpretation sensitive terms) so they need to negotiate their meanings in the course of interaction.

(9) K: - I like living in Albany. Because the Albany is the . . . especially I [word] almost two months . . . it's quiet . . . nice people . . . neighbor . . .
AF: - Yeah you have nice neighbors.
K: - Yeah, yeah.
AF: - The manager in the apartment is good?
K: - Yeah good.
AF: - ah . . . so you have good neighbors . . . it's quiet . . . good . . . so everybody has difficulties where they live so since you came from Korea what kind of difficulties you . . . what are the problems that you have to live in Albany?
K: - Ah I came . . . when I came here . . . the first time about . . . I applied the driver's license and you go to there
AF: - Yeah.
K: - DMV . . . yeah yeah . . . driver station
AF: - Yeah.
K: - And then they require so many documents
AF: - I see.
K: - So I had to go another office.
AF: - To apply to school.
K: - Yeah social number or . . . officer . . . anybody . . . anyway I had to go there and then . . . receive the document I gave them . . . so long time I . . . take a long time.

What I want to highlight is the context-sensitivity, which in the socio-cognitive paradigm means *actual situational context-sensitivity.* Yet it works differently in intercultural encounters and L1 encounters. There are universal contextual factors that affect language processing similarly no matter what language is actually used and how language is used. These factors are connected with general knowledge of the world such as weather, landscape, and human relations. For instance, when I say "Have a good one," it is not necessary to name whether I mean day, night, afternoon, morning: it is the actual situational context that specifies it. Or in Russian, when we say Саша и Света поженились (Shasa and Sveta got married), we do not have to refer to the fact that they got married to each other (examples from Kecskes 2014). However, most actual contextual factors are language and culture specific. Each language has interpretation-sensitive lexical items, expressions, and utterances where some or all of the knowledge necessary for processing is taken for granted in the given culture because this knowledge is part of core common ground in that speech community. So no detailed wording is needed because actual situational context does the rest. For instance, when in Russian we say "Как дела?" (How are things?), speakers know what the word "дела" (things) refers to. Basically, the closest equivalent of this expression in English is "How are you doing?" This is where the major problem of intercultural communication with context occurs. *Whose context are we talking about in an ELF communicative encounter?* Is it the prior context of the L1 or the prior context of the L2 or the actual situational co-constructed context or all three? If we go back to the definition of intercultures, then our answer should be "all three." However, we should know that the lower the proficiency of speakers is in the target language, the more likely they will be affected by the prior context of the L1 and ignore or pay little attention to the actual situational context. So context-sensitivity in these cases cannot work the way it does *in intracultural (L1) communication where salience and common ground are governed by the (relatively) same sociocultural background.* However, as already discussed, this does not mean that there is much more misunderstanding in intercultural communication than in intracultural encounters. Interlocutors negotiate and co-construct meaning, and work out their differences by relying more on semantics than the actual situational context. This is illustrated in example 10 in which a Japanese student and an American student are talking through Skype (data collected by Emiko Kamiya).[7]

(10) A: ..You know (.) I used to play tennis myself.
J: Oh really.
A: Yeah I (..) I just I used to play () the first serve? ((gesture))
J: [Mm hm?
A: [You know? then (.) you know? () a couple of () [()
J: [Ahhhhhh
A: I never () but played a little bit (here and there?)
J: Ahahaha
J: [I
A: [Hahaha
J: I can just play (0.3) SOFT tennis?
A: Sof (..) now soft tennis (.) you play with a racket and a tennis ball though right?

7 This is not an ELF encounter. It is native speaker–nonnative speaker communication that belongs to intercultural communication just like ELF communication.

J: Ah (1.2) white ball↑
(1.4)
A: White ball↓
J: Yeah (.) gom? (.) gom ball?
(1.4)
A: gom ball
J: a (.) I don't know
A: HAHAHA
J: ((laugh))
A: Are you using a (gumball?)? to play tennis? hehehe
J: Mmm (..) Yyeah (.) maybe hahaha
A: I use my () hehe=
J: =fffff

Let us briefly go over this example. The Japanese student is explaining to the American student that she also played a game similar to tennis. However, she does not know the right word in English for softball so she uses the ad hoc constructed phrase 'soft tennis' and tries to explain to the American what she really means by telling about the ball they used. However 'gom ball' (instead of 'rubber ball') does not get her through because of (1) wrong pronunciation, and (2) wrong choice of word ('gum' instead of 'rubber'). As we can see, she uses 'gom' (gum) for she has prior experience with that word rather than with 'rubber.' Actual situational context does not help the interlocutors much in this situation. What they rely on is their prior context, prior experience connected to their L1. They try to make sense of that experience together. Although there is a discrepancy between those experiences, their differences are worked out after all in the actual situational context. But it is important to note that the actual situational context does not help them much in getting their message through. Through individual efforts they create the actual situational context, the frame for their conversation.

## 1.6 Summary

Throughout this chapter, I have made an attempt to describe the nature of ELF and explain how ELF communication (intercultural) differs from ENL communication (intracultural). As a main difference it was mentioned that there is a shift from the communal/societal to the individual when moving toward the intercultural end on a continuum because conventions, common beliefs, norms, shared knowledge, and the like that constitute a core common ground in L1 are quite limited in ELF interaction so the participants should negotiate and co-construct them. This shift is a very important issue in the socio-cognitive framework, not only practically but theoretically as well (Kecskes 2008, 2010, 2014). This view is opposite to the *sociocultural view* that is based on

Vygotsky's ideas (1978) promoted by several scholars (e.g., Lantolf and Thorne 2006; van Compernolle 2014). In this summary we need to discuss the difference between the socio-cognitive and the sociocultural approaches because ELF research seems to have been influenced more by the sociocultural view (e.g., Grazzi 2014; Lim 2016). We do this comparison here in the summary because in order for me to discuss it, first I had to introduce my view on the nature of ELF.

Sociocultural theories require a shift from "the individual human mind" as the single unit of analysis in understanding human thought to the recognition of the socially and culturally constituted practices through which human thinking and behavior develop (see Scribner 1997). Informed by such a theoretical perspective, language learning in students is viewed as a process of changing participation in the sociocultural activities of students' communities, where identity development is conceptualized as socially, culturally, and historically constructed (Rogoff 2003).

There are two problems with the sociocultural view from the perspective of the socio-cognitive approach and ELF. First, the sociocultural view puts emphasis on the actual situational experience of language users but does not mention how important their prior experience is. Second, the sociocultural view has led to a plurilingual view of language proficiency that deemphasizes languages as separable and discrete entities, and instead focuses attention on the individual's ability to move between and across languages in contextually appropriate ways.[8]

Unlike the sociocultural approach, the socio-cognitive approach emphasizes that both the actual situational experience (and context) and prior experience (and context) are equally important in meaning construction and comprehension but to varying degrees. This helps us to make better sense of the differences between intracultural and intercultural communication. In ELF, we have less core common ground to rely on, less support from the actual situational context, less knowledge of conventions of English, less language proficiency so intersubjectivity needs a more careful, more conscious, more anticipatory behavior which primarily uses individual resources and secondarily relies on extralinguistic and sociocultural factors that are very much part of L1 communication. However, we should be careful here. As I emphasized earlier, we needed the continuum approach to communication with two hypothetical ends to demonstrate the dynamism of the communicative

[8] It would also be a mistake to deemphasize languages as separate and discrete entities. Vygotsky (1978) never promoted any idea like that. His followers did. Vygotsky said that when we enter school, language becomes the main regulator of thinking. So the weak version of the Whorfian principle is in place. It says that linguistic categories and usage influence thought and certain kinds of non-linguistic behavior.

process with its up and down movements on the continuum. This shift from the societal to the individual is a dynamic one, which can change even within one interaction. When we talk about this shift we mean more like a tendency full of alternations.

ELF interlocutors use a common language that is not the L1 of any of the participants. Sometimes they succeed in their language production and comprehension in ways that are different from those used in L1. How does their language use relate to linguistic creativity? This is the question that I will attempt to answer in the next chapter.

# 2 Linguistic Creativity in ELF

Jespersen (1904: 16–17) described phraseology as an 'indispensable' dimension of language competence. But with the Chomskian "revolution" in 1965, formulaic language was pushed to the periphery of linguistics, not having a place in generative syntax. Recently the landscape has been changing. There is more discussion on the essence of linguistic creativity and the role of prefabricated language in language production in general, and its relationship to linguistic creativity.

Language use in any human language is about the alternation of prefabricated lexical and grammatical units and ad hoc generated chunks and sentences that are amalgamated into simple and/or more complex utterances in speech production (see Kecskes 2016). This alternation is crucial for English as a Lingua Franca because this is where the main difference between English as a Native Language use and ELF use can be identified. Since ELF users cannot rely on the norms, standards and conventions of ENL to the extent that native speakers do, they need to co-construct or co-create those in their temporary speech communities. As a consequence, ELF users are supposed to produce more ad hoc generated language than rely on prefabricated units of the target language when creating utterances than their ENL counterparts. This is where ELF language production and interpretation mainly differ from ENL users' production and interpretation.

The two types of processing (analytic – holistic) could be viewed as forming a continuum. Speakers of any language in their actual language use move up and down on a continuum whose hypothetical ends are "prefabricated language" and "ad hoc generated language":

<————————————————————————————→

Prefabricated language                    Ad hoc generated language

In both ENL and ELF, speakers move up and down on the continuum when they use English in actual situational contexts. They are always in between the two poles. This means that they use more or less prefabricated and ad hoc generated language depending on several factors such as communicative need, intention, topic, actual situational context, and speech partners. Skehan argued that "language users are adept at shifting in and out of the analytic mode and move between the systems quite naturally" (Skehan 1998: 54).

In a study (Kecskes 2015), I have already claimed that the "idiom principle" (Sinclair 1987) is the most salient guiding mechanism not only in L1 but in any language production. However, the principle generates less formulaic language in L2 (medium of communication) than L1 because there are several factors that are not present in L1 but exist in L2, affecting the functioning of the idiom principle to a different degree. Such factors include limited core common ground, language proficiency, willingness to use certain formulas, language fluency of other participants, and others. These factors affect movement on the language use continuum and determine the combination of prefabricated units with ad hoc generated units. As a result, the actual production of formulaic expressions in the L2 will likely be lower than in L1 most of the time. This, however, does not mean that people in their L2 use are more creative linguistically than in their L1 or vice versa. The idiom principle always has priority over the open choice principle. The question is how this priority can be demonstrated and what effect it has on production. To make sense of the operation of the idiom principle that created a basic difference between ENL and ELF use, we will have to examine the nature and operation of linguistic creativity. Several studies in ELF research have emphasized that a conceptualization of creativity is particularly relevant for ELF (e.g., Langlotz 2006; Holmes 2007; Prodromou 2007; Pitzl 2012, 2018; Wang 2013).

## 2.1 Background

I have to start with what I have already mentioned in the Introduction. Human creativity is always in some sense a response to a regulating order. Consequently, creativity and variation are impossible without reference to "existing patterns." Let me quote Csikszentmihalyi again: "'new' is meaningful only in reference to the 'old.' . . . Without rules there cannot be exceptions, and without tradition there cannot be novelty" (Csikszentmihalyi 1999: 314–315). This is true no matter whether we focus on the product-oriented or process-oriented understanding of linguistic creativity. These two strands differ in goals: (a) product-oriented studies investigate diverse language forms and constructs with a potential for creative use ("vehicles of creativity" [Veale 2012: 12]); and (b) process-oriented studies aim to give a fuller understanding of the mental processes that underlie creative thought and explain the nature of creativity that affects language production mechanisms. Although the goals are different, there is some overlap between the two strands with regard to the resources of language creativity. This is quite noticeable in ELF research as it will be explained later.

Let me make it clear at this point that when discussing ELF, I will mainly be focusing on a process-oriented view of linguistic creativity, i.e., the process through which language is created in the course of interaction. So my main concern is creativity as understood in Cartesian linguistics.[1] The central doctrine of Cartesian Linguistics maintains that the general features of grammatical structure are common to all languages and reflect certain fundamental properties of the mind (Chomsky 1966). So this is not what scientists understand using the term 'creativity' which refers to creating new ideas, new theories, new approaches, and, in linguistics, new words, new expressions, poetry. Cartesian creativity is innate. Chomsky argued that the creative aspect of language use is the "central fact to which any significant linguistic theory must address itself" and thus "a theory of language that neglects this 'creative' aspect is of only marginal interest" (Chomsky 1964: 7–8). All human beings have the ability to produce and understand an infinite number of novel sentences – sentences that are new in the linguistic experience of the speaker/hearer and perhaps also new in the history of their language use. Chomsky (1964: 7) stated that "it is evident that rote recall is a factor of minute importance in ordinary use of language, that a minimum of the sentences which we utter is learnt by heart as such that most of them, on the contrary, are composed on the spur of the moment." Chomsky's approach is a clear overemphasis on the creative (combinatorial) aspect of language use based on syntax. However, real language use data show that we are much less original (at least in selection of linguistic units) in using language than we imagine because of the huge amount of prefabricated language units and chunks we use in actual language production. But this does not mean less creativity, as we will see later.

The importance of formulaic, prefabricated language was noticed in earlier linguistic research. Hymes (1962) pointed out that an immense portion of verbal behavior consists of linguistic routines. Bolinger (1976: 2) suggested that speakers do at least as much remembering as they do putting together. Fillmore (1976: 4) also found that an enormously large amount of natural language is formulaic, automatic and rehearsed, rather than propositional, creative, or freely generated. With the appearance of large corpora, understanding formulaic language has become even more complicated. Working with large corpora, Altenberg (1998) took it so far as to claim that almost 80 percent of our language production can be considered formulaic. Whatever the proportion actually is, one thing is certain: speakers in conventional speech situations tend to do more remembering than putting together. Our everyday interactions are often restricted to short routinized interchanges where we act as

[1] "Cartesian" is an adjective relating to Descartes, his mathematical methods, or his philosophy, especially with regard to its emphasis on logical analysis and its mechanistic interpretation of physical nature.

the given situational 'frame' requires. Let us look into a typical conversation between a customer and a store assistant that may make my point more clear (see Kecskes 2016):

(1) Conversation between store assistant (A) and Customer (B).
A: - What can I do for you?
B: - Thank you, I am just looking.
A: - Are you looking for something particular?
B: - No, not really.
A: - If you need help, just let me know.

As you can see, none of the expressions used by the speakers appear to be freely generated. Each of them can be considered a formulaic expression that is tied to this particular kind of frame – conversation between customer and shop assistant in a store. A great deal of language production (both oral and written) does not involve improvising phrases and sentences *ex nihilo* from a vocabulary of several thousand words or lexical items and a basic stock of internalized grammatical patterns or rules: this is what exactly what Chomsky argued for. Furthermore, Pawley and Syder (1983) claimed that although few people are able to encode, either in advance or while speaking, anything longer than a single clause of eight to ten words, they all regularly produce far longer fluent, pause-free, multi-clause utterances in spontaneous speech, mainly because they employ many prefabricated units and utterances. Thus, what we seem to do is to retain language in chunks, and this way much of our mental lexicon is stored in lexical chunks and expressions rather than just in separate words. Pawley and Syder (1983: 208) argued that "memorized clauses and clause-sequences form a high proportion of the fluent stretches of speech heard in everyday conversation. . . . Coming ready-made, [they] need little encoding work," so speakers can concentrate on "constructing a larger piece of discourse by expanding on, or combining ready-made constructions." This basically means that *genuine linguistic creativity appears to be a discourse phenomenon rather than a sentence phenomenon* as generative Cartesian linguists and syntacticians have claimed. The economizing role of memorized lexical phrases makes speakers free to match the tone and rhythm of their utterances to their conversational purpose. It equally allows addressees to pay attention to the larger structure of the discourse rather than to individual lexical items. Pawley and Syder (1983) claimed something very interesting about the size of the postulated stock of familiar usages. Whereas "the number of single morpheme lexical items known to the average mature English speaker is relatively small; a few thousand," they suggest that "the number of sentence-length expressions familiar to the ordinary mature English speaker probably amounts, at least, to several hundreds of thousands." This is where ELF speakers fall short: they may know a huge number of words in English, however, the number of sentence-length or semi-sentence-length expressions familiar to them is much smaller than in the case of ENL users.

What I have tried to succinctly address is that formulaicity is very important for both L1 and L2 development and use. The huge stock of prefabricated units in the mind of ENL speakers that are ready to be called upon when need occurs is mainly the result of normativization, conventialization, standardization, emergence of shared expectations, and core common ground development of native speakers in a particular language or speech community. As said earlier, there is evidence (e.g., Gumperz 1968; Eckert 1992; Kecskes 2015) that when people are together even only for a short time they create a speech community that starts to develop their language use norms from scratch. I have also demonstrated that English as a Lingua Franca speakers frequently coin or create their own ways of expressing themselves effectively, and the mistakes they may make will carry on in their speech, even though the correct form is there for them to imitate (Kecskes, 2015). For instance, in one of my former studies, the data reported that several participants in a spontaneous conversation adopted the phrase "native Americans" to refer to native speakers of American English (Kecskes, 2007). Although in the 'think aloud' conversation session, the correct expression 'native speaker of American English' was repeated several times by one of the researchers, the erroneous formula "native Americans" kept being used by the Lingua Franca speakers. They even joked about it and said that the use of target language formulas coined by them in their temporary speech community was like a 'joint venture' and created a special feeling of camaraderie in the group. On that account, the endeavor of creating normative use by developing formulas in a speech community is a part of human rationality. Gumperz (1968) argued that any human aggregate characterized by regular and frequent interactions and by means of a shared body of verbal signs set off from similar aggregates by significant differences in language usage. We can therefore confirm here again: the more time a group or a community of people spends together, the more we can expect them to start to give special meaning to certain strings of linguistic signs and units. As a result, *language use will increasingly bear the distinctive mark of prefabricated and formulaic expressions combined by ad hoc generated linguistic units.* According to Eckert (1992) the crucial defining characteristics of the community is a persistence over time and commitment to shared understanding.

## 2.2 Idiom Principle versus Open Choice Principle

If we want to understand the alternation and interplay of prefabricated and ad hoc generated language use, we should start with the *economy principle*. It is worth discussing how this principle has become dominant in linguistic research, and why it is relevant to ELF use. Focusing on linguistic evolution, Leopold (1930) discovered that there are two contradictory tendencies in any linguistic systems: Linguistic development follows two opposing tendencies, that is, toward distinctness on the one hand, and economy on the other. Either of these poles prevails, but both are present and alternately preponderant (Leopold 1930: 102). The tendency to distinctness originates from the fact that any speaker has, at any time, the predominant intention of being understood. The tendency to economy is "the innate tendency of man, wisely given him by nature, not to spend more energy on any effort than necessary" (Leopold 1930: 102). As a result, in concrete communicative acts, one of the two factors usually prevails on the other, generating different balances depending on the social or professional level. It is significant to highlight that Zipf (1949) came to similar conclusion when investigating speech as a natural phenomenon. He discovered that an inclination to economy is a criterion regulating any aspect of human behavior, which is governed by this Principle of Least Effort. Martinet (1955) was the first scholar to provide a coherent definition of linguistic economy as the unstable balance between *the needs of communication* that are always changing, and *natural human inertia*, two essential forces contributing to the optimization of the linguistic system. Also, Martinet claimed that any change occurring within the linguistic system which is never static is explained by means of this dichotomy. On the one hand, a single act of communication requires clearness and precision, which multiply conspicuous units, and, on the other hand, a remarkable organic inertia, which produces effort relaxation, less numerous, less specific, and more frequently occurring units, whose result is usually a hasty and careless expression. While inertia is a permanent, immutable component, people's communicative needs change constantly, so the nature of this balance is continually modified.

Moreover, in the *Relevance Theory* (Sperber and Wilson 1995), *economy* has been used with two functions: first, to explain how cognitive processes are linked to utterance interpretation (processing efforts must be balanced by cognitive effects); second, to explain how communication may be successful (inferences complete the underspecified content of the utterance to obtain its intended meaning). In other words, economy is a property of the cognitive system devoted to both utterance production and interpretation (and not just interpretation as RT theorists like to say), and is also required in order to ensure successful communication, by the computational devices, which are combined with linguistic decoding to yield the intended meaning of an utterance.

And as an additional point, the Principle of Least Effort takes us back to formulaic language use as well. There is psycholinguistic evidence that fixed expressions and formulas have an important economizing role in speech production (cf. Miller & Weinert 1998; Wray 2002). Sinclair's (1991) *idiom principle* says that the use of prefabricated chunks may "*illustrate a natural tendency to economy of effort*" (Sinclair 1991: 110). This can be interpreted thus: in communication we want to achieve more cognitive effects with less processing effort. So formulaic expressions ease the processing overload not only because they are *ready-made* and do not require of the speaker/hearer any putting together, but also because their salient meanings are easily accessible in online production and processing. Wray (2002) maintained that by favoring formulaic units speakers are able to reduce both their own processing – the larger the units, the fewer the operations needed to construct the message – and also the processing load of the hearer. On that account, she argued that there are major benefits to the speaker in ensuring that the hearer does not have to engage in too much processing. Wray also proposed that both parties are to some extent obliged to find ways of minimizing their processing, because the grammar of human language is too complex for human memory to cope with all the time (Wray 2002:15). Thus Wray converged with Sinclair's proposal (1991) that the formulaic option, which he calls the *idiom principle*, is the *default processing strategy*. Analytic processing, the *open choice principle* in Sinclair's terminology, is invoked only when the idiom principle fails. I believe that this is a crucial point for English as a Lingua Franca research. But one could ask why I am insisting on this? Because *being the default processing strategy, the formulaic option (i.e., idiom principle) is expected to be most salient in language production in general including ELF.* It means that the speaker is expected to come up primarily with utterances that contain ready-made, formulaic expression(s) if possible and plausible. If it is not, the *open choice principle* steps in. This looks like a logical mechanism in L1 production where participants can rely on the mutual understanding of formulaic expressions that are motivated by common ground, conventions, commonalities, norms, common beliefs, and mutual knowledge. Besides, the use of formulas will assure them that they will be understood since formulaic expressions are usually not polysemic. Thus, a group of nagging questions reveal themselves at this point: Is that also the case in ELF speakers when they use their L2? Does their mind, pre-wired for the *idiom principle*, continue functioning with the required conditions (partly) missing? In order for us to answer these questions, we first need to look at how the idiom principle works in L1 language production and then in L2.

Let me make clear that in L1 production there is hardly any doubt about the salience of the idiom principle. Coulmas (1981: 1–3) argued that much of what is actually said in everyday conversation is by no means unique. Rather, a great deal of communicative activity consists of enacting routines making use of prefabricated linguistic units in a well-known and generally accepted manner. He further claimed that successful coordination of social intercourse heavily depends on standardized ways of organizing interpersonal encounters. Howarth (1998) also talked about the fact that native speaker linguistic competence has a large and significant phraseological component. To unpack his argument, it seems to me that he is referring to the importance of the ability to sound idiomatic (i.e., achieving native-like selection, in the words of Pawley and Syder 1983) in language production and comprehension. This, in fact, has a profound effect on how we explain ELF interaction because both figurative and formulaic language are the result of conventionalization and standardization, which is supported by regular use of certain lexical units for particular purposes in a speech community. This is usually why ELF speakers have limited access to idiomatic and formulaic expressions in the target/common language.

To reiterate what I have been discussing, Martinet (1955) also commented about the unstable balance between the needs of communication and natural human inertia. At first glance, these two sides might look contradictory but, in fact, they are not: each conditions the other. In other words, human inertia results in search for existing combination of linguistic units with firmly established meanings. *This is what our prior experience-based salience and our least effort principle predispose us for.* However, the needs of communication require speakers to be as clear and understandable as possible. The question is: so what connects inertia and communicative need? The short answer is formulaic language. As we know, people using a particular language – who belong to a particular speech community – have preferred ways of saying things (cf. Wray 2002; Kecskes 2007) and preferred ways of organizing thoughts (Kecskes 2007, 2014). Preferred ways of saying things are generally reflected in the use of formulaic language and metaphorical/figurative language, while preferred ways of organizing thoughts can be detected through analyzing, for instance, the use of subordinate conjunctions, clauses, discourse markers, and sequential structure of discourse segments. Selecting the right words and expressions and formulating utterances in ways preferred by the native speakers of that language (native-like selection) is more important than syntax. The following example from a sign in an Austrian hotel catering to skiers (source: *Octopus*, October 1995, Champaign, IL, p.144) demonstrates this clearly. As we can see, the sentence shows off-kilter word choices but seemingly accurate syntax.

(2) Not to perambulate the corridors in the hours of repose in the boots of descension.
Correct form: Don't walk in the halls in ski boots at night.

It is clear that the author of this sign compiled this sentence by using a dictionary verbatim to convey the meaning needed for the warning sign. As you can see, the result is understandable but a native speaker would never say anything even close to this sentence. Why is that so? Native speakers usually follow the principle of preferred ways of saying things and preferred ways of organizing thoughts in the given speech community, which determines word selection and the proper match of words within a sentence. As previously mentioned, the more speech communities persist, the more their members can rely on norms and conventions of language use. Now we will examine where formulaicity comes from.

## 2.3 Psychological Saliency of Word Sequences

By 'formulaic language' we usually mean multi-word expressions which are stored and retrieved holistically rather than being generated *de novo* with each use. Collocations, fixed semantic units, frozen metaphors, phrasal verbs, speech formulas, idioms, and situation-bound utterances can all be considered as examples of formulaic language (Howarth 1998; Wray 1999, 2002, 2005; Kecskes 2000, 2007, 2015). These word strings occurring together tend to convey holistic meanings that are either more than the sum of the individual parts, or else diverge significantly from a literal, or word-for-word meaning and operate as a single semantic unit (Gairns and Redman 1986: 35). With the emergence of corpus linguistics, there has been a considerable increase in interest in multi-word sequences. Corpus linguists goes beyond the Bolingerian "remembering and putting together" (Bolinger 1976) dynamism of language use and mostly sides with Altenberg (1998), as mentioned earlier, who claimed that "80 percent of our language production can be considered formulaic." This is perfectly so if we accept Wray's (2002: 9) definition of formulaic sequences: "a formulaic sequence [is] a sequence, continuous or discontinuous, of words or other elements, which is, or appears to be, prefabricated: that is, stored and retrieved whole from memory at the time of use, rather than being subject to generation or analysis by the language grammar." Is there someone out there who can make sense of this definition? According to Wray, then, we should consider most language production prefabricated.

There is no doubt about the fact that an immense portion of verbal behavior consists of linguistic routines. But what is the nature of these linguistic routines? Why do they exist in the language? Are we to understand them as the results of the inner dynamic and functioning of the linguistic system, or perhaps the consequence of extrinsic sociocultural needs? The answer is both: Multi-word sequences clearly demonstrate the distinction between conventions of language and conventions of usage. This division has been made by several researchers including Searle (1979) and Morgan (1978). According to Searle: "It is, by now, I hope, uncontroversial that there is a distinction to be made between meaning and use, but what is less generally recognized is that there can be conventions of usage that are not meaning conventions" (1979: 49). In fact, this distinction is expressed even more concisely by Morgan:

In sum, then, I am proposing that there are at least two distinct kinds of convention involved in speech acts: conventions of language ... and conventions in a culture of usage of language in certain cases ... The former, conventions of language, are what make up the language, at least in part. The latter, conventions of usage, are a matter of culture (manners, religion, law ... ). (Morgan 1978: 269)

To demonstrate the difference between the two types of conventions, let us look at the following examples:

(3) Renting a car
CLERK: - **Can I help you**, sir.
CUSTOMER: - Yes. I have a reservation.
CLERK: - **Your name, please**.
CUSTOMER: - Ben Carlson.
CLERK: - **May I see your driver's license**, Mr. Carlson?

As we can see, none of the expressions used by the interlocutors look freely generated. Each of them can be considered a formula that is tied to this particular kind of situational frame. However, if we consider the following conversation, we may see something different.

(4) Bill and David are talking.
BILL: - <u>If we want</u> to be on time <u>we will need</u> to take a taxi.
DAVID: - OK, <u>my friend</u>.

Let's just compare the expressions in bold with the expressions underlined. What is common in them is that they are all frequent collocations consisting of words that are often used together. But the question is: are they considered formulas here? And, do they have some kind of psychological saliency as formulas for the native speakers? Well, we must be cautious with the response because frequency is only one criteria based on which we can identify formulaic expressions. The problem is that the role of frequency seems to be overemphasized in present-day linguistics, especially in corpus linguistics. Recent research analyzing written and spoken discourse has established that highly frequent, recurrent sequences of words, variously called lexical bundles, chunks, and multiword expressions, are not only salient but also functionally significant. Cognitive research demonstrated that knowledge of these ready-made expressions is crucial for fluent processing. The recurrent nature of these units is discussed in the relevant literature (McEnery & Wilson 1996; Biber et al. 1999). Simpson-Vlach and Ellis (2010) also confirmed that large stretches of language are adequately described as collocational streams where patterns flow into each other. However, we should note that Sinclair's (1991) idiom principle is not primarily based on frequency that results in long lists of recurrent word sequences (Biber et al. 1999; Biber et al. 2004), because these sequences hardly give any chance to distinguish where we have conventionalized formulas or where we have just frequently occurring word chunks that lack psychological saliency. Biber et al. (1999: 990), in their study of lexical bundles, defined formulaic language as sequences of word forms that commonly go together in natural discourse, irrespective of their structural make-up or idiomaticity, and argued that conversations have a larger amount of lexical bundle types than academic prose. However, there seems to be a clear difference from the perspective of psychological saliency between sequences such as 'to be on time' or 'take a taxi' on the one hand, and 'if we want,' 'we will need to,' and 'my friend' on the other. Although all these expressions are high on any frequency-based list, I think *we need to distinguish between groups of prefabricated expressions that have psychological saliency for speakers of a particular language community as results of conventionalization, and loosely tied, frequently occurring word-sequences (usually consisting of common words) such as "if they want," "if we need," and "tell them to.* Simpson-Vlach and Ellis (2010) argued that psycholinguistically salient sequences like "on the other hand," "suffice it to say," "welcome aboard," "you are all set" cohere much more than would be expected by chance. They are glued together, and thus measures of association, rather than raw frequency, are likely more important and relevant to these formulaic expressions.

Let us now go over the second language studies in this regard. They mostly emphasize the importance of frequency rather than psychological saliency in processing formulaic language. For instance, Ellis et al. (2008) argued that formula processing by nonnatives, despite their many years of English as a second language (ESL) instruction, was a result of the frequency of the string rather than its coherence. For learners at that stage of development, it is the number of times the string appears in the input that determines fluency. Additionally, Ellis et al. argued that tuning the system according to frequency of occurrence alone is not enough for native-like accuracy and efficiency. They further claimed that what is additionally required is tuning the system for coherence – for co-occurrence greater than chance. Likewise, Ellis et al. (2008) concurred that this indeed solves the two puzzles for linguistic theory posed by Pawley and Syder (1983): native-like selection and native-like fluency. Therefore, native speakers have extracted the underlying co-occurrence information, often implicitly from usage. On the other hand, nonnative speakers – even advanced ESL learners with more than ten years of English instruction – still have a long way to go in their sampling of language. These learners are starting to recognize and to become attuned to more frequent word sequences, but they need help to recognize distinctive formulas. So why is this issue important for ELF speakers? The fact of the matter is that the development of psychological validity/saliency of these expressions in L2 is a matter of not only frequency and exposure to language use, but also immersion in the culture and understanding the sociocultural environment. The latter is of course predicated upon the degree to which the nonnative speaker wishes to use those formulaic expressions. *Frequent encounters with these expressions for nonnative speakers help but are not enough to develop psychological saliency*, as the following encounter between a Korean student and a clerk at the Registrar's office demonstrates:

(5) Korean student (Lee) and Registrar (Clerk) encounter.[2]
LEE: - Could you sign this document for me, please?
CLERK: - *Come again* . . . ?
LEE: - Why should I come again? I am here now.

To recapitulate, we can see that in spite of the distinctive intonation used by the clerk when uttering 'come again,' the Korean student processed the expression not as a formula but as a freely generated expression with literal meaning. So what really counts is the measures of association, rather than raw frequency. What creates psychological saliency is the discursive function in a particular context of that expression. The functional aspect is what makes immersion in the target culture important for nonnative speakers, because that is where those functions come from.

## 2.4 Linguistic Creativity in ELF

Now that we have examined the role of formulaic elements in language use in general, we shall turn to the issue of linguistic creativity in ELF. A relatively small number of studies (e.g., Langlotz 2006; Holmes 2007; Prodromou 2007; Pitzl 2012, 2018; Wang 2013) have addressed this problem. As an example, Pitzl's study (2012) discussed this topic in depth. She proposed a working definition of linguistic creativity which, in her words is "the creation of new (i.e., non-codified) linguistic forms and expressions in ongoing interaction/ discourse or the use of existing forms and expressions in a non-conventional way" (Pitzl 2012: 38). This can be considered both a product-oriented and a process-oriented definition, although Pitzl's main goal is to accommodate the linguistic forms and expressions created by ELF speakers in interactions which do not represent the 'preferred ways of saying things' by ENL speakers. Furthermore, relying on Widdowson's and Pope's research, Pitzl (2012) emphasizes the importance of the idea of "potentialities already available" put forward by Pope who used that with regard to creativity in general: "'[i] nvention,' then, is hardly ever a making-up entirely from scratch. It is the 'coming-in' and in effect the 'coming-together' of potentialities already available" (Pope 2005: 64). Similarly, Widdowson talked about his concept of virtual language, which refers to a speaker "exploit[ing] linguistic resources

[2] This exchange is similar to example (6) in Chapter 1. But they are different recordings.

to produce a novel combination, not allowable by the conventional code, but nevertheless a latent possibility which is virtual in the language though not actually encoded" (Widdowson 1997: 137).

I think we must be careful with the idea of 'potentialities already available' and 'virtual language' in ELF production. The truth of the matter is that there are no concrete examples in Pitzl (2012) to illustrate what this really means in practice. In my view, 'potentialities already available' takes us back to Chomsky who speaks about a potential of speakers to create infinite number of sentences within the potentials of a coded system (conventions of language: grammar). If the potential of creating a given form or utterance or sequence derives from the system itself, we must consider that form or utterance or sequence a possible product of the system although it is not coded yet. But it may or may not be coded as the result of further/future development. Here are some examples:

(6) L1: You ain't gotta go to work today.
I don't say nothing to nobody.
L2: They started the meeting off on a bad foot.
The crualism of those people was not understandable.
You are not very rich in communication.
You are poor like the mouse in a church. (Hungarian speaker).

These are all "potentialities already available" that were created by stretching the system, creating something that is not encoded in the system yet. The problem with ELF speakers is that when they use English they rely not only on their existing limited English language system but also their L1 system. So their 'creations' can often be considered as the result of a hybrid or synergic system which is neither English nor Russian, German, or whatever the L2 of the ELF speaker is, but a blend of the two systems (see Kecskes 2010).[3] That dual language system can create utterances like (6) or utterances that follow in example (7).

(7) Japanese and Korean students
- In Japan many place has mirror in the road but in US there is no mirror
- Right I haven't seen one here
- You noticed that right?
- **Driver US is . . . they will stop line in Japan driver don't stop stop line**
- Mhmm

Let us take a look at the highlighted utterance, which is indeed unintelligible. It does not make sense although English words are used. And, there is no way to call that production the result of a creative act. Cornbleet and Carter (2001: 64)

[3] The interlanguage researchers spoke about a similar phenomenon (see, for instance, Selinker 1972).

Table 2.1 *Type-1 and Type-2 creativity*

| Type-1 Creativity | Type-2 Creativity |
|---|---|
| Brings about individual realizations of the normative system | Brings about individual realizations of the normative system |
| Realizations stay within the boundaries of the normative system | Realizations transcend the boundaries of the normative system |
| rule-generated (cf. Chomsky 1972) | rule-generating |
| combinational (cf. Boden 1999) | exploratory-transformational (cf. Boden 1999) |
| norm-following (cf. Kachru 1992) | norm-developing (cf. Kachru 1992) |
| exonormative | endonormative |
| Brings about (synchronic linguistic) **variation** | Has the potential to bring about (diachronic language) **change** |

point out "inventiveness can only communicate if it's understandable." So the two types of productions (examples 6 and 7) are both the results of the extension of the system but while examples in (6) result in meaningful units, example (7) does not make much sense.

Pitzl (2012: 36) gives a good summary of the two types of creativities that we have been discussing (see Table 2 above).

Let me now unpack what we have just emphasized. For ELF, (Type-2) creativity is of crucial importance because this type of linguistic creativity can go beyond established norms, and bypass existing rules and break current conventions. However, it is very important that this activity or production should make sense within the confines of the actual situational context, and point toward a possible further (norm) development of the existing system. The question is where to draw the dividing line between the products and creations that can still be considered the output of the existing system or a *temporary communicative extension* of the system (TCE hereafter). By TCE I mean *expressions and utterances that violate the existing norms and conventions but still make sense in a given actual situational context and can be considered a possible output of the English language system.* Here are some examples:

Let's rest the sleeping lion.
We connect with them.
Can you illuminate my cigarette?

As you can see, these expressions make sense within the system of English. But they are not preferred ways of saying things at all, and unlikely to be used by other speakers. What I am trying to call attention to here is that TCEs play a crucial role in ELF, for they are the results of what I call "deliberate creativity" (see Kecskes 2016). Before discussing deliberate creativity, it is critical to see how idiomatic/formulaic language use fits into the dichotomy that

Pitzl has already described. She argues: "In order to be able to investigate and describe variation and change within a particular language or variety, linguists commonly distinguish the levels of grammar, lexis, morphology, pronunciation and also the use of idioms, although this last level is where matters tend to get fuzzy" (Pitzl 2012: 36). In fact, linguists have never considered the use of idioms a distinguishable level of grammar. If one does so, yes, matters tend to get 'fuzzy.' So, once again, I will recapitulate that we are required to meticulously distinguish between the conventions of language (levels of grammar) and conventions of usage. The use of idiomatic/formulaic language belongs to the conventions of usage – a distinction that will be very important for us in what comes next.

## 2.5 Deliberate Creativity

In ELF, both the idiom principle and the economy principle are present, just like in L1. But in ELF the functioning of these two principles cannot produce formulaic language the way it does in L1. But because of the priority of the idiom principle in any language production there is a pressure on the hybrid, synergistic system that ELF users rely on to produce more formulaic language. But what type of formulaic language is that? To answer this question, we need to recall the Bolingerian view. Bolinger's "remembering and putting together" cannot work the way it does in L1 because for "remembering" ELF speakers would need to have access to the same psychological saliency of formulas as L1 speakers have access to, and this is hardly possible in ELF. However, this problem may be solved by what I have previously called 'deliberate creativity' (Kecskes 2016: 11–12). In my understanding, *deliberate creativity is a process that is used by ELF speakers to create and/or co-construct from scratch formulas which either resemble those of L2 (English) or L1 (speaker's L1); or are just the result of temporary communicative extension of the system (TCE).* In order for us to understand this type of ELF processing, we need to examine the nature of this deliberate creativity.

We have to start with a discussion about two factors that affect ELF production and comprehension: first, psychological saliency of formulaic expressions, and second, the process – rather than the production – side of linguistic creativity. We have already discussed the former so we will focus on the latter. How does idiomatic/formulaic language use fit into creative language processing? Our point of departure should be the hypothesis that prefabricated language does not preclude linguistic creativity. In fact, there is quite a bit of evidence for this in corpus linguistics. Skehan (1998: 54) talked about the fact that "language users are adept at shifting in and out of the analytic mode and move between the systems quite naturally." Some researchers even mentioned that the two types of processing (analytic – holistic) could be viewed as forming a continuum (cf. Skehan 1998; Wray 2002; Carter 2004). In the course of interaction, prefabricated expressions may mean islands of temporary stability demonstrating varying degrees of variation and possibilities for further development in sync with the dynamics of discourse. In this sense, "*linguistic creativity refers to the ability of combining prefabricated units with novel items (ad hoc generated items) in a syntax-and discourse-affecting way to express communicative intention and goals, and create new meaning*" (Kecskes 2016: 12). This ability is an essential part of a person's language competence that is deployed mainly subconsciously and automatically based on the existing knowledge of the speaker and his/her actual situational communicative needs. As a result, *linguistic creativity is a graded phenomenon* ranging from the more conventional and predictable to the less conventional and unpredictable. The more conventional and predictable side is operated by the idiom principle, while the less conventional and more unpredictable side of the continuum is governed by the open choice principle. Of course, these are just hypothetical ends of the continuum on which there are constant alterations in any communicative process.

CONVENTIONAL and PREDICTABLE ———UNCONVENTIONAL and UNPREDICTABLE

Let me further explain that more reliance on the right end of the continuum (open choice principle) can be called *deliberate creativity* (Kecskes 2016). It is 'deliberate' because it is mostly a conscious process in which language users prefer to generate their own utterances rather than resorting to prefabricated units or the combination of ad hoc generated units and ready-made expressions. The process exists in both L1 and ELF, however, its nature may differ significantly depending on which language the speaker (L1 or L2) uses, and also on a code-switching mode. In L1, deliberate creativity is reflected mainly in the ways in which the speaker tries to manipulate speaker meaning, while in L2 or ELF it can be demonstrated through the significant overuse of ad hoc generated utterances and less reliance on L2 (English, target language) formulaic expressions.

### *2.5.1 Deliberate Creativity in L1*

The speaker can fully control what s/he wants the audience to believe/understand but s/he cannot control what the audience will actually believe/understand. The two aspects of speaker meaning (individual and conversational) and recipient design give the chance to the speaker to manipulate speaker meaning according to his/her needs; that is, to leave meaning conversationally open for interpretation or to signal intention with cues and markers. In the abovementioned cases, the speaker aims to promote his/her own agenda by trying to manipulate the interpretation process. There are several instances of this case.

However, here we will focus only on two of them: (1) alerting addresses to what the speaker means, and (2) manipulating hearer's salience.

### *2.5.1.1 Alerting Addressees to what the Speaker Means*

(8) ROY: - Is there something wrong, Susie?
SUSIE: - I am fine, Roy.
ROY: - I would have believed you if you hadn't said "Roy."
SUSIE: - OK, OK, just stop . . . . . .

In example (8) the background is that Roy notices that there is something wrong with Susie, and he asks her about it. Susie responds with a relatively neutral expression like 'I am fine,' which is a usual routine response to that type of a question. However, she wants to call Roy's attention to the fact that everything is not fine. She is adding the conversational partner's name 'Roy' to the routine expression. This move, in fact, results in an entirely different communicative effect. Thus, 'I am fine' is a formulaic expression as long as it is a full utterance. But if something else is added to it, it loses its formulaic touch. This is what happens in many other formulaic expressions such as 'you are pulling my leg.' If you add a plural marker [s] to the word 'leg,' formulaicity is lost: 'you are pulling my legs.' Hence, in example (8), Roy understands Susie's alert, as his response demonstrates: 'I would have believed you if you hadn't said "Roy."' However, in spite of the speaker's effort alerting addressees to what s/he means can be unsuccessful because the hearer still can process the utterance as s/he wishes. This is what we will see in the following excerpt (see also example in Kecskes 2014 used for a different purpose).

(9) The excerpt from the movie *Coogan's Bluff.*
A man and a young woman are sitting in a restaurant after meal. The woman stands up abruptly and reaches for her purse.

W: - I have to be going.
M [seeing that she reaches for her purse]: - What are you doing?
W: - Dutch.
M: - You are a girl, aren't you?
W: - There have been rumors to that effect.
M: - Sit back and act like one.
W: - Oh, is that the way girls act in Arizona?

When the girl is leaving and wants to pay, the man expresses his objection by asking 'What are you doing?' The girl understands perfectly what the man is asking, so she tells him 'Dutch,' which translates into her willingness to pay for her own share of the bill. The man shows his dislike in a very indirect, but still expressive way: 'You are a girl, aren't you?' This implies that girls usually are not expected to pay when with a man, which in actual fact is a vulgar assumption. At the same time, the girl's response indicates that she knows perfectly well what the man is getting at. Then the man hints at what he expects the girl to do by uttering, 'Sit back and act like one,' implying that he does not want her to pay the bill. This inductively developed sequence is a tangible example for elaborated recipient design and creative use of language where nothing is said directly, still there is no misunderstanding for the speaker adequately alerts the hearer to what he means.

*2.5.1.2 Manipulating Hearer's Salience* There are cases when the speaker tries to manipulate what s/he thinks will be highly salient to the hearer. This assumption is usually based on collective salience. We can demonstrate this manipulation through two cases:

**A) Canceling or Degrading Highly Salient Meaning**

(10) In one of his films, *Survivors,* Robin Williams says the following:
- "I had to sleep with the dogs. Platonically, of course . . . "

The speaker thinks that the sexual connotation of 'sleep with' (collective salience) is so strong that a clarification is necessary, so he tries to cancel this effect with the adverb 'platonically.' Let me look back on Giora (2003) who claimed that both salient information and contextual knowledge run in parallel, and salient, but contextually inappropriate, information may not be discarded. This is the main reason why the speaker thought that the collective salience effect could be canceled with the adverbial 'platonically.'

**B) Practice of Explicitly Cueing Low-Salience Meanings** Givoni, Giora, and Bergerbest (2013: 30) argued that "where multiple meanings of a stimulus differ in terms of degree of salience, there seems to be a need for a procedure that will prompt the activation of senses low on salience, in case they make up part of the intended meaning."

Given that salient meanings are activated initially, cues may be required, alerting the processor to the possibility that initial outputs of the automatic process of decoding should undergo 're-coding.' This procedure can be referred to as the practice of explicitly cueing low-salience meanings. Givoni et al. (2013: 29) also gave the following example:

(11) The variety of secondhand goods available at no cost to the consumer was astonishing at the Really Really Free Market, held at Anisq'Oyo' park this past Saturday. This market was "free" in all senses of the word. (McEniry 2011)

The phrase 'in all senses of the word' draws attention to the less salient meanings of 'free.' In addition to the salient meaning 'without cost' or 'free of charge,' the less salient meanings 'liberty/freedom (to exchange)' and 'without regulation' are also activated.

Now we will need to look at how deliberate creativity works in ELF.

### *2.5.2 Deliberate Creativity in ELF*

As discussed earlier, deliberate creativity refers to a language production process when language users are driven by the open choice principle rather than by the idiom principle. Since ELF interlocutors are all nonnative speakers of English, we will need to look first at how the default idiom principle affects their L2 use at different levels of proficiency. Recent research in L2 (relevant to ELF) has demonstrated that there is a difference in formulaic language use between less and more proficient nonnative speakers. Based on longitudinal studies, both Howarth (1998) and Ortactepe (2012) came to the conclusion that less proficient learners pick up formulaic expressions and overuse them, while more advanced learners prefer to generate their own sentences rather than resorting to prefabricated units.

Wray and Perkins (2000: 23) argued that formulaic expressions provide nonnative speakers with survival phrases that achieve basic socio-interactional functions. They have automatic access to prefabricated chunks, and this eases communication, especially in the early stages of language learning (cf. Nattinger & DeCarrico 1992; Wray 2002). However, there is a problem with this practice for a couple of reasons. First, L2 or ELF users may pick up formulas easily, but this may happen without their clear knowledge of the conceptual load attached to those expressions with psychological saliency in the given speech community. It may take them quite a long time through a trial and error process to actually master appropriate use of those expressions. Second, their selection of formulas may be subjective (e.g., Kecskes 2007; Ortactepe 2012). L2 users/learners pick up expressions that they like for various reasons, and may overuse them: 'you know'; 'you bet'; 'I'll talk to you later'; 'let me tell you something'; etc. Also, according to Segalowitz and Freed (2004: 403), at later stages of language development, formulaic expressions function as a database for nonnative speakers from which learners abstract recurrent patterns, leading to the mastery of grammatical regularities. Wray (2002: 147) considers this creative tendency of advanced learners as a major problem resulting from the production of perfectly grammatical utterances that are simply not used by native speakers. This claim is in line with my finding about the language use of Lingua Franca speakers (see report in Kecskes 2007). Further, Pawley and Syder (1983) referred to this kind of 'deliberate creativity' of relatively advanced L2 learners as a process of over-generating and producing grammatical, non-idiomatic utterances due to not having accumulated the native repertoire of formulaic expressions as native-like competence and fluency demand such idiomaticity (see in Ellis 2003: 12).

The danger for Lingua Franca speakers in the use of formulaic language, is that they often pick up these expressions without comprehending the socio-cultural load attached to the expressions. This is especially true for situation-bound utterances in which it is usually the figurative meaning that is dominant rather than the literal meaning. In ELF communication, if one of the interactants does not know this figurative meaning and processes the utterance literally, misunderstanding or confusion may occur, such as in the following conversation.

(12) Conversation between a Chinese student and a Turkish student:
T: - You look worried. *Why don't you tell me what bothers you?*
CH: - I have no reason not to tell you.
T: - Ok, then go ahead.

Here the Turkish student used the expression 'why don't you tell me . . . ' in a figurative sense as a formula, but the Chinese student seems to have processed it literally. At least this is what his response shows. He assured the Turkish student that there was no reason for him not to tell his friend what bothered him. I would not call this case a complete misunderstanding, but certainly there was some kind of slight confusion between the two ELF speakers. In order to avoid cases like this, ELF speakers usually stick to literal meanings of expressions rather than figurative ones. The use of semantically transparent language resulted in fewer misunderstandings and communication breakdowns than was expected in my studies (Kecskes 2007, 2015). This finding corresponds with House's observation about the same phenomena (House 2003).

The most important and unique role of deliberate creativity in ELF is the endeavor of ELF speakers to create their own formulas, their own formulaic language and their own metaphors instead of relying on the target language: using the English language system to create their own varieties of formulas and metaphors. Deliberate creativity in ELF is a kind of compensation for not having full access to formulaicity and idiomaticity in the target language. It is a response to immediate communicative pressure and needs. This phenomenon fully confirms the general priority of the idiom principle as most salient in any language production. Speakers – monolinguals or multilinguals alike – make an effort to use formulas, no matter which language of theirs they use. In my former studies, the formulas our international interlocutors created can be split into two categories (Kecskes 2007, 2015). In the first category, we can find expressions that are used only once and demonstrate an effort to sound metaphorical. This endeavor is usually driven either by the L1 of the speaker in which there may be an equivalent expression for the given idea or by not remembering the exact words within the sequence. For instance:

(13) Formulas that demonstrate an effort to sound metaphorical.
- it is almost skips from my thoughts.
- you are not very rich in communication.
- take a school.

(14) Not remembering the exact words within the sequence
draw the limits (cf. 'draw the line'),
preserve their face (cf. 'save [sb's] face'),
turn a blank eye (cf. 'turn a blind eye')
(These examples are from the VOICE database)

The other category comprises expressions that are created on the spot during the conversations and are also picked up by the other members of the temporary speech community. One of the participants creates or coins an expression that is needed in the discussion of a given topic. It becomes a part of the interculture creation process (cf. Kecskes 2013a). This unit functions like a target language formula, the use of which may be accepted by the participants in the given temporary speech community, as demonstrated by the fact that other participants also pick it up and use it. However, this is just a temporary formula that may be entirely forgotten when the conversation is over. This is a typical example of how intercultures are created. For instance:

(15) Formulas created on the spot or ad hoc.
- we connect each other very often
- native American (in the sense of native speaker of American English, see explanation in Section 2.1)

The avoidance of genuine formulaic language, the creation of temporary formulas and preference for semantically transparent expressions can be explained by another factor. The analysis of the database and the 'think aloud' sessions in two studies (see Kecskes 2007, 2015) shed light on something that is hardly discussed in the literature. It seems that multiword chunks might not help L2 language use and ELF use in the same way they help L1 processing. Speaking about L1 communication, Wray (2002) pointed out that if processing is to be minimized, it will be advantageous to work with large lexical units where possible, storing multiword strings as a whole as if they were single words. In some cases this will make it possible for speakers to go to their mental lexicon and pull out a single entry that expresses a complete message meaning (e.g., 'are you enjoying your day?'; 'fancy meeting you here!'). However, ELF speakers usually do not know how flexible the formulas are linguistically, namely, what structural changes they allow without losing their original function and/or meaning. Linguistic form is a semantic scaffold;

if it is defective, the meaning will inevitably fall apart. This is one of the things that Lingua Franca speakers worry about, as was revealed in the 'think aloud' sessions.

The 'unnaturalness' of their language production from a native speaker perspective is caused more by imperfect phraseology than by inadequate conceptual awareness. These imperfections differ from the kind of alteration and elaboration of conventional phrases that native speakers produce. If native speakers do alter conventional expressions, they usually make any necessary changes to the grammar and syntax as a matter of course. By doing so they can usually ensure that the expression flows uninterruptedly from word to word and expression to expression, and this really helps processing. However, this does not appear to work the same way for Lingua Franca speakers who may not be able to continue the expression if they break down somewhere in the middle of its use. Let us now look at example (16):

(16) A Korean and a Turkish student are talking:
T: - I like but . . . they like but they haven't time. I see in Albany too many people like sport. And they run and fitness.
K: -Yeah.
T: - They fitness. Too many people play tennis. So I think they sport . *They, they keep yourselves healthy. . .They keep healthy yourselves . . .*
K: - Healthy.
T: - Yes.
K: - I agree with you.

As you can see, the Turkish student tried to use the formula 'keep oneself healthy.' However, he had a problem with the use of the appropriate pronoun. Instead of using 'themselves,' he inserted 'yourselves' into the formula. However, he did not realize that the problem is not with the place of the pronoun in the sequence but with the selection of the pronoun.

Formulaic language use in ELF communication points to the fact that with no native speakers participating in the language game, the Lingua Franca interlocutors can't always keep the original rules of the game. Also, I argued in my previous studies, that actual speech situations in Lingua Franca communication can mostly be considered *open social situations* which do not necessarily encourage the use of formulaic language (Kecskes, 2007). In L1 communication we have many more closed social situations than in ELF defined by the parameters and values taken for granted in them (see Clark 1996: 297). The result of these closed social situations is a highly routine procedure. To illustrate, let us look at the example below:

(17) BAR
CUSTOMER: - Two vodka tonics.
BARTENDER: - Coming up . . .

MUSEUM TICKET BOOTH
CUSTOMER: - Three adults and one child.
CLERK: - Which row?

In these examples representing L1 closed social situations, the participants know their roles. This correlates with Clark (1996) claiming that the interlocutors' rights, duties and potential joint purposes are usually quite clear. What they merely need to establish for that occasion is the joint purpose, which can be done with a routine procedure. The first interlocutor initiates the conversational routine, often with a phrasal unit, and the second interlocutor completes it by complying as in example (17). In other words, use of conversational routines and formulas requires shared background knowledge, which is indeed scarce in Lingua Franca communication. Therefore, it is quite clear why ELF communicators avoid using target language (English) formulas, and why literality and semantically transparent language play powerful roles for them.

## 2.6 Summary

Language use is a well-balanced alternation between more conventional and novel, ad hoc generated units and a blend of the two. It does not matter whether the speaker uses his/her L1 or L2, this creative blending of prefabricated units with ad hoc generated ones prevails. The only question is what can be considered dominant in a particular moment in the interaction, and this always depends on the speaker's communicative intention and needs.

What makes language a language is the presence of norms, standards and conventions, both in the linguistic system and in its practical use. Commonalities, conventions, common beliefs, shared knowledge, and the like all create a core common ground, a kind of collective salience on which L1 communication is based. This inherent endeavor of human beings to create mutual understanding in any speech community results in an everlasting process of reoccurring attempts for normativization and conventionalization in the language system through its use. Prefabricated language functions as core common ground. This endeavor is present in ELF as well. However, when this, often prefabricated-language-created, core common ground appears to be missing or limited, ELF interlocutors cannot take them for granted, rather they need to co-construct them, at least temporarily. So, there appears to be a shift in emphasis from the communal to the individual, from the more conventional to the less conventional, from the more formulaic to the less formulaic as we claimed in the introduction. So the importance of deliberate creativity increases in L2 language use in general, and ELF in particular because it is used not only for generating language ad hoc but also generating new formulas from scratch. In ELF there is more reliance on language created ad hoc by individuals in the course of their interaction than on prefabricated language and preexisting frames as is the case in L1. Furthermore, in ELF communication more conscious recipient design may be involved than in L1 communication, in which interlocutors do not have to deal with language skill issues, and may rely on more 'remembering,' more spontaneous speech and less monitoring. In the Gricean paradigm, cooperation is considered rational behavior of human beings. Thus, it is essential that human beings are cooperative in the course of communication subconsciously and automatically. In ELF, however, this rational and subconscious behavior is enhanced with a conscious, often monitored, endeavor of interlocutors to be cooperative and make deliberate efforts so as not only to comprehend others but also produce language that is processable by others. So it is even more emphasized that the goal of coming to an understanding is "intersubjective mutuality . . . shared knowledge, mutual trust, and accord with one another" (Habermas 1979: 3). This is exactly where the importance of co-constructing language comes in, and this is why deliberate creativity is a driving force in intercultural interactions including ELF. It also changes the way we need to think about interactional competence, which is the topic of the next chapter.

# 3 Interactional Competence

## 3.1 A Puzzle for ELF Research

When native speakers of a language communicate with each other, they rely on standards, norms, routines, and other aspects of the core common ground that are essential elements of their interactional competence (IC hereafter) in their common language. But what about interactional competence in languages other than L1? What kind of interactional competence is activated in Lingua Franca communication? Is that the same type of interactional competence that L2 learners rely on when using their L1? Or is that a modification of the existing L1-based interactional competence? Do Lingua Franca users have two separate competencies? That is, an L1-dominated interactional competence and an L2- or Lx-dominated interactional competence, or a blend of the two? How does interactional competence affect Lingua Franca interaction? These are the overarching questions that are going to be addressed in this chapter.

I will argue that there is just one IC that is flexible and dynamic enough to adsorb and apply new skills and information coming through *any* language channel. *Interactional competence means the ability to deploy interactional resources (turn-taking, repair, boundaries, speech acts, etc.) through available linguistic resources as needed by the speaker/hearer to express their communicative intentions in actual situational contexts.* This interactional competence is something like a continuum with two ends: basic interactional competence (BIC hereafter) and adapted interactional competence (AIC hereafter). Thus, language use is a constant move on this continuum. Using ELF, we are closer to the BIC end of the continuum, and when using an L1, L2, or Lx with native speakers of those languages, we are closer to the AIC end of the continuum for we attempt to rely on frames, routines, and patterns that are essential in the use of that particular language.

My approach to be described here is a modified version of what was published in Kecskes et al. (2017).[1] Interactional competence has a nucleus

[1] My co-authors of Kecskes et al. 2017 may not agree with the interpretation I am going to give in this chapter, so what I will be talking about does not reflect their views.

in human beings that we called "basic interactional competence" (BIC). BIC comprises knowledge of the principled ways in which utterances/actions can be discursively linked, or fitted to each other, to achieve interaction. The empirical reality of BIC was demonstrated by Bruner's (1975, 1983) and Trevarthen's (1977, 1979) findings in pre-linguistic infancy and early childhood, when children quickly develop a recognition of linkages between their own actions and the (re)actions of others. BIC develops as a part of human rationality through which any speaker of any language (let it be L1, L2, or Lx) can tacitly analyze ways in which successive utterances/actions are linked. These linkages may be of prior utterances/actions to each other, of present utterances/actions to prior ones, or present utterances/actions to wanted or unwanted future ones. These linkages are constraining of what is said next, and of the situated meaning of specific utterances/actions based on how they are fitted to what has been said, is now being said, or may yet be said.

BIC does not equal to L1 interactional competence. In other words, it is an inherent feature of human beings. This potential is gradually instantiated into concrete manifestations of communicative ability through L1 socialization. Through the socialization process a child develops what we call *adapted interactional competence* (AIC hereafter) that is L1-based interactional competence (Kecskes et al. 2017).[2] We already emphasized that as people interact in their native language and native culture, they rely on this basic knowledge of the way interactional components can be sequentially linked, and also on knowledge of routinized procedures and practices built on that basic knowledge (Kecskes et al. 2017). So when learners acquire a new language and interact in L2 in a new culture, they have to learn how to substantiate BIC in the new language, and how to adapt the routinized procedures and practices of their native culture to their counterparts in the new culture. In order to do so, they need to detect, analyze, and adjust to all the differences, and for doing so, they have and must have BIC to draw on. So in developing interactional skills in a new language, learners rely on three factors: *BIC, existing interactional knowledge (AIC tied to L1), and the emerging recognition of communicative practices and routinized procedures in the target language (modified AIC).* In fact, the interplay of the three factors is very critical in English as a Lingua Franca. So the remaining question is this: are all those three characteristics present in Lingua Franca interactions? Will Lingua Franca speakers adapt to the communicative practices and routinized procedures of the language of communication (English), or just do whatever is needed in the actual interaction, using BIC as default? In reality, there are few guidelines for ELF interactants about what patterns and routines to follow. That may, however, vary

[2] Here I use the term "adapted interactional competence" rather than "applied interactional competence."

from case to case depending on the members of the temporary speech community. This is exactly where there is a crucial difference between L2 language development and ELF use from the perspective of interactional competence. In ELF, there is a move from L1-based AIC to BIC (less reliance on language-specific practices and routines, which will be explained later), while in L2 development there is a slow (or faster) move on the interactional competence continuum from BIC to AIC. BIC serves as a skeleton, and the 'flesh' is later added as needed in the given speech community, as skills develop and are routinized in the new language. If proficiency is low in L2, communication is still possible because of BIC. Thus, language learners gradually develop the culture-specific knowledge to interact effectively in a host culture, which is referred to as adapted interactional competence. Let me highlight that it is not claimed that BIC supplants the various ways in which the interconnectedness of a succession of utterances has been analyzed, but rather that BIC is a fundamental competence that underlies them. By way of illustration, the Gricean maxims presuppose that speakers and hearers tacitly 'analyze' the connections between utterances, but Grice (1975) does not specify the basis for making such analyses. I argue that in fact this is the main reason we need BIC.

Lingua Franca communication may demonstrate some kind of AIC-neutral process for the first sight. But this is just seemingly so. As I said earlier, there is a constant move on the interactional competence continuum from AIC to BIC. So what happens when a person from Hong Kong, another from Brazil, and a third one from Poland interact? Whose specific AIC will they follow? Or will they stick to the target language's AIC (English)? I think the short answer is neither. The unique feature of the ELF communication is that there is no need to follow any of the AICs. Interlocutors may use the English language system according to their immediate needs without any specific constraints, expectations or norms of usage of a specific language. So far it makes sense but what will happen to target language expectations and norms in ELF interactions? Whose expectations and norms should interactants follow? ELF interlocutors seem to use a system of signs (the English language) without specific adaptation to its AIC to express their communicative intention while relying on BIC and the constraints and requirements of the actual situational context. So the applications of any specific routines or norms would cause more harm than good unless they are temporary norms and routines created during that particular encounter or several encounters within the same temporary speech community. There is research that supports these assumptions. In fact, some studies have demonstrated that nonnative speakers of English in intercultural interactions using the linguistic code (the English language) as their core common ground rely mainly on the literal meaning of words and expressions (e.g., House 2003; Cieslicka 2006; Kecskes 2007, 2015b). So if one of the interlocutors uses an expression that is a representative of preferred ways of saying things in the given speech community, and the other interlocutors are not familiar with that expression, that may cause trouble in understanding in the ELF interaction. This is what happens in the following encounter:

(1) Gertrud and Xiaolu are standing at the door of Human Resources.

GERTRUD: - Here is the door.
XIAOLU: - Who should go in first?
GERTRUD: - Be my guest.
XIAOLU: - We are not guests here.

As illustrated above, we can see that Xiaolu completely misunderstood the expression 'be my guest' that is often used by native speakers of American English in similar situations. The reason of misinterpretation was that Xiaolu processed the utterance literally, not as a situation-bound utterance. It seems to me that she probably had never heard the expression used in that sense. If that is so, it quite confirms what I argued above. The application of any specific routines or norms might cause more harm than good in the ELF communication. The only exception is when those temporary norms and routines are created during that particular encounter or several encounters within the same temporary ELF speech community.

After analyzing a small corpus of ELF interactions, I argued that in the course of ELF conversations ELF speakers tend to create temporary formulas and temporary norms (Kecskes 2015b). Moreover, in the previous chapter, I called them temporary communicative extensions of the system (TCE hereafter). The interactional competence that is put to use in ELF interactions is substantiated through the interplay of the use of the linguistic code and BIC (that may result in TCEs) as prompted by the immediate communicative needs of the interlocutors. Let us take a look at the following conversation where a Polish woman (PAF) is speaking about housing and English studies with a male from Hong Kong (HKM) and a female from Brazil (BIF).[3]

(2) Polish woman on housing and English studies.

HKM: How about you? . . . circumstances . . . Where do you live? You rent . . . or?
PAF: Mmm . . . I am live . . . not so far from the university.
HKM: Hmm.
PAF: It is a college . . . you don't know . . . It is not so far. It's Albany.
HKM: Hmm.
PAF: But I have 3 minutes . . . errh . . . to go to my work.
HKM: Hmm.
PAF: And this house is . . . errh . . . on our own so my husband and I . . .
HKM: Hmm.
BIF: Doesn't have any kids?

[3] Source: Albany Corpus of Intercultural Communication

PAF: No. don't havc . . .
BIF: No?
PAF: Yeah.
BIF: Errh . . . Are your husband American or . . . ?
PAF: Errh . . . Actually he is . . . he is Polish. He is American but . . .
BIF: Ok.
PAF: . . . because he came into the United States when he was a child.
HKM: Hmm.
PAF: He was something like twelve.
BIF: All right.
PAF: So . . . you know . . . but he . . . he speaks Polish, yeah.
HKM: Do you speak Polish at home?
PAF: Yes. (Giggle.) Why, that's my problem. (giggling) I don't have . . . too much connection with American so . . .
HKM: Hmm.
PAF: . . . my English is still poor. (giggling)
PAF: You know, I can understand but I have a problem with speaking. That's my . . .
HKM: Hmm.
PAF: . . . yeah . . . that's my . . . really big problem.
HKM: Hmm.
PAF: . . . even though I've been here for over five years so . . .
HKM: Hmm.
PAF: . . . sometimes I feel myself like stupid. Oh, my god, over five years, I cannot speak English perfect . . .
HKM: Do you think that you can learn English without practicing it, you know. It doesn't show anything like stupidity, you know, it is just the lack of practice.
PAF: Ah . . . I know. I try to, I try to learn because . . . you know, errh . . . I work here for not so long. That's six months, so . . .
HKM: Hmm.
PAF: . . . before dark I stay home. I stay home so I learn . . . I learn English from TV, from newspaper, and I've been taking several courses . . . from somebody . . .
HKM: Hmm.
PAF: . . . I mean ESL courses.
HKM: Hmm.
PAF: And I think that helps me a lot.
HKM: Hmm.
PAF: But it's not . . . it's not enough for me so . . . I try to take every English courses . . . you know, I try to speak at my work . . .
HKM: Hmm.
PAF: . . . more . . .
HKM: Hmm. I see.

It is clear that the Polish woman is frustrated because she thinks her English is not good enough. However, we can see that what she says makes perfect sense, and what she does (response, turn-taking, explanation, etc.) furthers the interactions smoothly. Her BIC tacitly helps her analyze the ways in which successive utterances are linked. These linkages in turn limit not only what is said next, but the situated meaning of specific utterances/actions based on how they are fitted to what has been said, is now being said, or may yet be said. Although HKM says nothing else but [hmmm] three times, the Polish woman understands that as request or an encouragement for further information. So the questions of both partners are adequately answered. At the same time there is very little in the conversation that would show that English norms, standards, or conventions have been used. The linguistic system of the English language is put to use without any, or very little, application of usage standards and norms of either English or the L1 of the participants. Thus, communicative strategies based on BIC are used according to the immediate communicative needs of participants. The approach to interactional competence presented above, however, does not match the contemporary understanding of the notion in applied linguistics and second language acquisition. In order to understand the differences we will need to clarify where the deviations are, and discuss the nature of interactional competence as presented here.

## 3.2 The Nature of Interactional Competence

In recent years, research on interactional competence has been blooming in the fields of applied linguistics and second language acquisition. The term "interactional competence" has been used by various researchers with different shades of meaning in several different areas of second language learning, use and teaching. Since I have no space here to review the relevant literature (see Young 2011, 2014 for an excellent summary), I will focus only on those aspects of research that are relevant for ELF. The crucial issue is whether we understand interactional competence as the ability of the individual to communicate with others, which is part of human rationality, or as a mutually created construct by interlocutors, as contemporary approaches claim. Young (2011) argued that interactional competence is not to be described in the knowledge and actions of an individual participant in an interaction. Instead, IC is the construction of a shared mental context through the collaboration of all interactional partners. We need to look deeper into this claim for it will help us understand the unique nature of ELF communication. Mehan (1982: 65) formulated the problem as follows: "'Competence' becomes interactional in two senses of the term. One, it is the competence necessary for effective interaction. Two, it is the competence that is available in the interaction between people." Kramsch (1986: 367) developed this idea further by claiming,

> Whether it is a face-to-face interaction between two or several speakers, or the interaction between a reader and a written text, successful interaction presupposes not only a shared knowledge of the world, the reference to a common external context of communication, but also the construction of a shared internal context or "sphere of intersubjectivity" that is built through the collaborative efforts of the interactional partners.

Also, Kramsch (1986) called this basis of successful interaction interactional competence.

So, it is Kramsch's view that forms the basis for present-day understandings of interactional competence that is created by all participants in social interaction. Young (2011) further argued that the definition of IC includes the pragmatic relationship between participants' employment of linguistic and interactional resources and the contexts in which they are employed. He underlined that the third aspect of IC is not the ability of a single individual to employ those resources in any and every social interaction. "Rather, IC is how those resources are employed mutually and reciprocally by all participants in a particular discursive practice. This means that IC is not the knowledge or the possession of an individual person, but is co-constructed by all participants in a discursive practice, and IC varies with the practice and with the participants" (Young 2011: 431).

Hence, in order for us to better grasp interactional competence, it is crucial, at this point, to return to the discussion of what role intersubjectivity plays in language production and comprehension that was started in Chapter 1. Everyone in the world has his/her own subjective viewpoint of events, actions, behaviors, contexts, etc. Intersubjectivity, as I understand it, means that we all influence and are influenced by others to some degree. We must always take into account how our actions will affect others, just as we ourselves are constantly affected by the actions and words of the people around us, which makes us both individual and universal thinkers and actors. Intersubjectivity was first inferred empirically from studies of infant development by Trevarthen (1977, 1979).[4] While studying interaction between preverbal infants and their mothers, Trevarthen noticed that around two months of age, infants produced actions of body, hands and face that were associated with the vocalizations of the mother. It was clear that, although each mother–infant pair was developing a different style of mutual activity, a general pattern of development in social behavior was common to all. Trevarthen (1977: 241) summarized this as follows:

> I believe a correct description of this behavior, to capture its full complexity, must be in terms of mutual intentionality and sharing of mental state. Either partner may initiate a 'display' or 'act of expression' and both act to sustain a sharing and exchange of

[4] The short review of preliminary works on intersubjectivity is based on Young (2011).

initiatives. Both partners express complex purposive impulses in a form that is infectious for the other.

Relying on Trevarthen's research on intersubjectivity, Wells (1979, 1981) further studied children's language development through interaction. He argued that collaborative activity provides the natural context for first language development and that children learn through exploring their surroundings with others. Wells (1981: 46–47) defines intersubjectivity as following:

> Linguistic interaction is a collaborative activity, and this applies just as much to the production and interpretation of individual utterances as it does to longer stretches of discourse. Any act of linguistic communication involves the establishment of a triangular relationship between the sender, the receiver, and the context of situation. The sender intends that, as a result of his communication, the receiver should come to attend to the same situation as himself and construe it in the same way. For the communication to be successful, therefore, it is necessary (a) that the receiver come to attend to the situation as intended by the sender; (b) that the sender knows that the receiver is so doing; and (c) that the receiver know that the sender knows that this is the case. That is to say, they need to establish *intersubjectivity* about the situation to which the communication refers. (Emphasis in original)

Furthermore, Young (2011) argued that Wells's theory has inspired much work on the development of IC, and some studies of how learners develop IC have taken intersubjectivity as evidence of IC. I believe that there is no doubt about the fact that communication is a collaborative effort. But it is important how we understand the interplay of the individual and social sides in the process. As I have repeatedly emphasized, interlocutors are both egocentric and cooperative and therefore interlocutors' linguistic behavior is shaped by the interplay of their egocentrism and cooperativeness (Kecskes 2014, 2017b). So I think Kramsch and Young and their followers take the social side of interaction too far and overlook the importance of the individual ability and contribution to interaction. What I mean by individual contribution is when production and comprehension are motivated by subconscious egocentrism of the interlocutor that is based on his/her prior experience rather than the social requirements of the actual situational context. This is especially important for ELF speakers who share very little core common ground, and, therefore, their communicative actions are dominated by their prior experience rather than commonly shared experiences as is the case in relatively stable speech communities. The following short excerpt from example (2) clearly demonstrates my point:

(3) BIF: Errh . . . Are your husband American or . . . ?
PAF: Errh . . . Actually he is . . . he is Polish. He is American but . . .
BIF: Ok.
PAF: . . . because he came into the United States when he was a child.
HKM: Hmm.
PAF: He was something like twelve.

BIF: All right.
PAF: So . . . you know . . . but he . . . he speaks Polish, yeah.

As you can see, the Brazilian woman asks the Polish woman about her husband. The Polish woman keeps talking about her husband although she does not receive any further questions. She just babbles what is on her mind, not taking account whether her partners are interested in her information. This is indeed a typical example of egocentrism overriding cooperation. It is not the actual situational context that requires or triggers that behavior. In fact, it is just what is on the Polish woman's mind for that moment, and she is ready to continue talking about it no matter what the other interlocutors think.

As said in the Introduction we human beings are just as egocentric (as individuals) as we are cooperative (as social beings). Several studies (e.g., Giora 2003; Barr and Keysar 2005; Keysar 2007) claimed that speakers and hearers commonly ignore their mutual knowledge when they produce and understand language. This behavior is called 'egocentric' because it is rooted in the speakers-hearers' own knowledge instead of their mutual knowledge. If this claim is accepted then a speaker's utterance cannot be just recipient design based on actual situational experience because it is also affected by individual prior experience. 'Egocentrism' in the socio-cognitive approach to pragmatics (Kecskes 2010b, 2014) refers to attention-bias that is the result of prior experience of an individual, meaning that interlocutors activate and bring up the most salient information to the needed attentional level in the construction (by the speaker) and comprehension (by the hearer) of the communication. This issue is especially important when interlocutors use their L2 or Lx, like in ELF. What is most salient for L2 users is usually motivated by their L1 prior experience or limited L2 experience. There is nothing negative about egocentrism if the term is used in this sense. What is significant is that this concept should not be confused with 'egotistic,' which refers to a person who is self-centered and focuses only on his/her agenda.

Individual egocentrism is important because it helps us understand how interactional competence is put to use in social encounters. According to the socio-cognitive approach, all social encounters are created by the contributions of individual participants who are constrained by social frames that have been normativized in the given speech community. However, those constraints are not compulsory; individuals may or may not follow them. *Interactional competence is an individual ability* that makes it possible for human beings to interact competently and successfully with other human beings in social encounters. In short, the individual and societal are present all the time. The key issue here is the extent to which interlocutors have access to core common ground. If societal circumstances in the speech community provide broad core common ground, speakers in that community may rely on a wide range of prefabricated language and social frames provided by presumed background information shared by participants in interactions. However, if this core common ground is not present to the extent it is in L1, L2 or ELF users must co-construct it, which is not an easy task, given the different socio-cultural background the participants represent in intercultural interactions. ELF speakers/hearers need to rely on their individual judgment rather than ready-made patterns and practices to succeed in ELF interactions. While creating temporary core common ground, interlocutors rely on BIC rather than any specified AIC because the routinized and normativized language use of either the target language (English) or any of the languages of the participant will not be much of help. Relying on something that is common such as the 'naked' language system and basic interactional competence, participants in ELF situations build up the 'flesh' on the skeleton together. This 'intersubjectivity,' however, does not mean that interactional competence is not in the knowledge and actions of individual participants in an interaction. The point is that we should not mix up the ability with the product; that is to say, the result of the ability being put to use or the process through which co-construction happens. *Collaboration, intersubjectivity, and effort to create shared mental context are all outcomes of the ability that is called "interactional competence" of human beings.* So intersubjectivity is about how a relative match can be created between different communicative needs of various interlocutors with diverse backgrounds. However, it is important to note that co-construction is not interactional competence and it is not intersubjectivity itself. It is a process that is used by people who are interactionally competent and rely on and/or develop intersubjectivity. But what does it really mean that someone is interactionally competent in a language other than L1?

## 3.3 The Relationship of BIC and L2 Interactional Competence

### *3.3.1 Understanding L2 Interactional Competence in the Literature*

The main idea of much of the work in the development of what is being referred to as "L2 interactional competence" (e.g., Hall et al. 2011; Hall & Pekarek Doehler 2011; Pallotti & Wagner 2011; Pekarek Doehler & Pochon-Berger 2015) is that learning a language is not enough for successful communication with native speakers or nonnative speakers; language learners must also be able to *interact competently* with native speakers and, in our case, with other nonnative speakers (ELF). Of course, there is no doubt about this. But much work on L2 interactional competence has some key shortcomings in common. One is that it ties interactional competence to the language being spoken (e.g., the phrase "L2 interactional competence" itself, and its being contrasted with "L1 interactional competence"). In our view, "L1 interactional competence" or

"L2 interactional competence" are adapted interactional competencies. So I think the "L2 interactional competence" view overlooks BIC, and the fact that BIC is not tied to any specific language (see Bruner 1975, 1983; Sanders 1987, 1997; Levinson 2006; Schegloff 2007). It is the far left end of the interactional competence continuum where it is still relatively language-neutral, i.e., it is not developed into concrete practices and routines of a particular language. BIC comprises knowledge of principled ways across languages in which a succession of utterances/actions by alternating speakers are substantively interconnected to form an *interaction*, and not a random collection. Furthermore, BIC underlies interactional performance but does not determine it. Language learners bring BIC with them into the language learning situation and into L2 interactions. Kecskes et al. (2017) posited that it is this basic knowledge of how interactions work that L2 learners already have that enables nonnative speakers (NNSs hereafter) to interact with other NNSs in L2 as a Lingua Franca, without shared knowledge of the interactional procedures and practices of a host (dominant) culture to guide them. It is also claimed that it is this basic knowledge of the workings of interaction that enables NNSs to recognize and learn what studies of L2 interactional competence focus on; culture- and language-specific interactional routines and practices among natives of the host culture and language NNSs are learning. Another shortcoming of the L2 interactional competence research is a tendency to focus primarily on the knowledge of the procedures and practices of a host culture (e.g., Cekaite 2007; Hall et al. 2011; Hall & Pekarek Doehler 2011; Young 2011; Pekarek Doehler & Pochon-Berger 2015). Nevertheless AIC is also influenced by language processing, social comfort and confidence, individual differences, preferences, and several other factors that Cekaite (2007: 45) enumerates thus:

> Interactional competence involves a range of skills for using language to accomplish social actions, including social aspects of language use such as knowing when, how, and with whom to engage in conversational activities. ... In this study it is defined as participants' knowledge of the interactional architecture of a specific discursive practice, including knowing how to configure a range of resources through which this practice is created. ... It entails knowledge of linguistic resources (lexis and syntactic structures) constituting particular activities ... ; pragmatic skills, such as topic introduction and maintenance ... ; turn-taking and sequential organization of talk ... ; and the communicative roles associated with the practice.

As a result of the approach described in this quote, studies of second language acquisition on interactional competence have been paying primary attention to the extent of NNSs having learned specifics of routinized procedures and practices in the host culture. Young (2011: 427) argued that L2 interactional competence is a matter of learning "recurring episodes of social interaction in context, episodes that are of social and cultural significance to a community of speakers." Moreover, Hall and Pekarek Doehler (2011: 2–3) formulated that it is a matter of learning "routinized yet context sensitive procedures with which we reason our way through the moment-to-moment unfolding of our interactions." In addition, Cekaite's (2007) study of the development of "L2 interactional competence" by a seven-year-old Kurdish girl, Fusi, in a Swedish classroom analyzes specifics of the process. She notes Fusi's progressive modulation of her disagreement as indicative of learning certain social norms in a Swedish classroom. She also regards Fusi's progress in turn-taking practices as having a (socio)linguistic basis: "her self-selection [as next speaker] is also more verbally elaborate and syntactically close to Swedish language norms" (Cekaite 2007: 57). By the same token, Pekarek Doehler and Pochon-Berger (2015: 233) posed the question of whether "interactional competence [is] simply transferred from the L1 to the L2 or is it re-elaborated in the L2?" And their response, based on their survey of research to date, is:

> [W]e start to have empirical evidence testifying to the fact that interactional competence is not simply transferred from the L1 to the L2, but is recalibrated, adapted in the course of L2 development. (235)

We can agree with this claim. But it is crucial to examine what exactly Pekarek Doehler and Pochon-Berger meant by 'recalibration.' Based on the way the concept of recalibration was described in their work, we can assume that they mean that learners have to *adapt* the interactional competence that they already have to the routines and norms of a new culture. There is no doubt that for NNSs to *perform competently* in the tasks and activities of a new language and culture, they have to adapt the routinized procedures and practices of their native culture to those of the host culture. However, Pekarek Doehler and Pochon-Berger (2015) refer to what IC learners already have as "L1 interactional competence." This terminology intelligibly indicates that they have taken a theoretical stance contrary to Kecskes et al. (2017); that *all* interactional competence is language- and culture-specific. They further describe learners as starting with "a highly limited set of techniques for accomplishing a given action (such as taking a turn, initiating repair, proffering a disagreement)." Pekarek Doehler and Pochon-Berger (2015: 262) further argue that, "Over time, these techniques become *diversified*, allowing participants to deploy more **locally adapted and interactionally accepted** conduct" [our emphasis], resulting in "*a growing ability to recipient design talk and to deploy context-sensitive conduct*" [emphasis in original]. So far, so good, but the remaining nagging problem is this: if L2 interactional competence is tied to the acquisition of the 'locally adapted and interactionally accepted conduct' of a host culture, then we can hardly account for the fact that NNSs from different cultures and different native languages can interact with each other competently in L2 as a Lingua Franca

(English as a Lingua Franca, in our case). As I have discussed, when using English as a Lingua Franca, movements on the interactional competence continuum take place in the left part of the continuum where basic knowledge of how interaction works is applied. BIC underlies whatever repertoire of "techniques for accomplishing a specific action" persons learn that are culture- and language-specific, both in their native culture and then those of any other culture(s) they move into. So what we have in ELF is not necessarily just a 'recalibration' but rather an activation of existing BIC skills in order to perform the necessary interactional moves in the actual situational contexts. These BIC skills are not specified routines or practices of any language, rather they are specified by the communicative needs of language users. Interlocutors in ELF do not wish to move into any language- and culture-specific language use. They want to succeed through applying **relatively** culture-neutral, actual situation-specific communicative skills and strategies. The main difference between AIC in English as a Native Language and AIC in English as a Lingua Franca is that in the latter speakers have more reliance on BIC than in AIC in English, where reliance is on routinized linguistic behavior and frames as required by the native speaker speech community (English). So the learning Pekarek Doehler and Pochon-Berger have described is not a matter of having to learn that turns should be taken, repair initiated as needed, or that talk should achieve recipient design and be context-sensitive. In fact, these are indeed aspects of interaction that language users must already know from infancy to have ever linked utterances/actions together into an interaction, no matter what L1 and their native culture is – what we attribute to BIC. So what has to be learned is *how to achieve* turn-taking, the initiation of repair, and so forth *in L2*, or *in the host culture,* which would only confront NNSs when it comes to learning language- and culture-specific interactional procedures and practices which result in AIC. In this sense, ELF is unique because best results in ELF interactions can be reached only if language- and culture-specific interactional procedures and practices are, at least to some extent, avoided. Here is an interaction of a man from Hong Kong with three Brazilian au pair girls.

(4) Brazilian au pair girls talking to a man from Hong Kong on living circumstances:

HKM: Ah . . . so you people are here au pair, hmm?

BNF/BSF/BIF: Yeah/Hmm.

HKM: Tell me something about . . . so you live together with the families, yeah?

BNF/BSF/BIF: Yeah.

BNF: Ah . . . I am here the nanny.
HKM: Hmm.
BNF: And we take care of the kids. They give you . . . food and they host us for home a year . . .
HKM: Do they give you some stipends? Some money?
BNF/ BSF/BIF: Yeah.
BNF: We, we, we, we are paid.
HKM: Aha.
BNF: And they pay . . . our studies. And . . .
HKM: How about living circumstances? Do you have your separate room, or . . . ?
BNF/ BSF: Yeah. Yes
HKM: Tell me something about it.
BSF: Ah . . . we have to have our own room.
HKM: Hmm.
BNF: decent room
BIF: Yeah.
HKM: Do they have huge house, probably.
BSF/BIF/BNF: Yeah.
BSF: And . . . we have to get credit to the program.
BNF/BSM: Yeah.
HKM: Hmm.
BIF: And we cannot work for forty-five hours a week.
BNF/BSF: Yeah.
HKM: Four or five hours a week?
BNM/BSM/BIM: No. Forty-five hours.
HKM: Forty-five hours.
BNF/BSF/BIF: Yeah.
HKM: Yes.
BNF: And we cannot work more than ten hours a day.
HKM: Aha. I understand. So you know, there are limitations.
BIF: Yeah. And we have two-week vacation.
BNF: Paid vacation.
HKM: Paid vacation?
BNF: Paid, paid. BIF/BSF: Yeah.
HKM: Good. So you get money for that period.
BNF/BIF/BSF: Yeah. Hmm.Yes.
HKM: So you enjoy it basically.
BNF/BIF/BSF: Yeah. Not bad.

As you can see, the sequence is about the living conditions of the three Brazilian au pair girls. All the four interlocutors speak fluent English so the conversation goes smoothly. The language they use does not reflect any language-specific practices, strategies, routines, and expressions. There are only a couple of formulaic expressions used ('take care of'; 'how about') in the whole sequence. The interlocutors rely mainly on their BIC combined with literal use of English.

### *3.3.2 How Does BIC Support the Development and Use of AIC in L2?*

Cekaite (2007) identifies knowledge of L2 and language processing as an influence on how competently NNSs interact. In her study of the seven-year-old Kurdish girl, Fusi, in a Swedish classroom, Cekaite attributes Fusi's improved ability to participate competently in part to improved mastery of Swedish, including an expanded lexicon and improved tense markings. An aspect of Fusi's growing linguistic resources that Cekaite ties directly to interaction involves turn-taking: "the timing of Fusi's self-selections may be seen to indicate her emerging competencies, in that precision timing involves the speaker's language processing skills . . . which allow her to produce a novel and relevant contribution in a split second" (Cekaite 2007: 58). These observations underscore that knowledge of the language is needed for learners to apply BIC to a tacit analysis of the ways utterances/actions in L2 are being linked, and from there to learn routinized procedures and practices in the host culture. So the 'flesh' is added to the skeleton as the proficiency in the target language is growing. Moreover, Cekaite (2007) described the symptoms of an influence on how competently Fusi interacted in L2, her lack of social confidence and comfort as a conspicuous outsider. Early on, Fusi did not participate; she avoided it and hid, followed by limited speaking that was overly aggressive, overly loud. Pekarek Doehler and Pochon-Berger (2015) attributed this to Fusi's not yet having learned more native-like ways of participating in classroom interactions. But we should not overlook an ancillary basis for the ways she initially interacted. She just may have thought that she did not know how to interact with her peers. She was frustrated because she thought what she could say in the new language sounded wrong and did not express what she wanted. She seemed to be exhibiting the emotional stresses of, and childish reaction to, being an outsider among peers, especially in the performance-oriented environment of the Swedish classroom. All these factors contributed to Fusi's interactional behavior.

Another influence on how competently people perform in interactions is individual differences. As I elaborated in some detail previously, there are differences between people psychologically and experientially, which may decrease their core common ground (Kecskes, 2014). So this has a direct bearing on the extent of troubles people may have with pragmatic and social understandings, and what they must work on to interact *with each other* more competently over time. These individual differences will be most substantial between NNSs who are native speakers of different languages and natives of different cultures when interacting in L2 as a Lingua Franca. But these differences can be expected to decrease over time with repeated interactions through the learning that reduces their differences and expands their common ground. As discussed earlier, the more time they spend together, the more routines and frames they will develop, which will significantly contribute to the specification of AIC. In addition, because there are such individual differences, we need to be cautious about overgeneralizing the result in performance in interactions to the interplay between learning L2, and adapting its use in interaction to the norms, standards, and expectations of its native speakers in the host culture. This reveals that there are important variations in individual willingness, preference, and choice to make these adaptations (e.g., Ortactepe 2012; Kecskes 2014, 2015). Ortactepe (2012) conducted a longitudinal, mixed-method study that relied on the assumption that international students as newcomers to American culture, experience bilingual development through conceptual socialization that enables them to gain competency in the target language through exposure to the target language and culture. By collecting qualitative and quantitative data three times over a year, the study examined the linguistic and social development of Turkish bilingual students as a result of their conceptual socialization in the United States. Ortactepe further provided evidence that L2 learners' conceptual socialization relies predominantly – contrary to what previous research says – on learners' investment in language rather than only on extended social networks. By examining formulaic language use, she found that in case of advanced language learners, the use of formulaic language depends not on proficiency but on acceptance, preference and willingness of use. This finding corroborates with the fact that an advanced L2 speaker cannot be expected "simply to abandon his/her own cultural world" (Barro et al. 1993: 56). Furthermore, Adamson (1988) pointed out that nonnative speakers are often reluctant to accept and share the values, beliefs and presuppositions of an L2 community even if they have been living there for a long period of time and can speak the language quite well. Besides, some recent studies have pointed out that NNSs may have some kind of resistance toward the use of NS norms and speech conventions to maintain their own identity, and so they may deliberately commit pragmatic negative transfer (e.g., Al-Issa 2003; Siegal 1996). It seems to me that this kind of behavior has a significant effect on the development of AIC in the target language. Frames, practices, and language use patterns are accepted or rejected in the target culture depending on individual preferences, motivation, and willingness of use. This is an additional explanation why in ELF interactions interlocutors seem to abandon AIC of the target language and rely more on BIC skills to make themselves understood by their partners who are similarly situated.

## 3.4 Basic Interactional Competence at Work in ELF

In a recent newsletter, Young (2014) proposed that interactional competence is "an individual's knowledge and employment of these resources [that] is contingent on what other participants do; that is, [interactional competence] is distributed across participants and varies across different interactional practices." Kecskes et al. (2017), however, argued that this approach overlooks the difference between, on the one hand, the knowledge needed to *perform* in interactions *competently* (AIC) – though we agree with Young (2014) that such knowledge does vary, and is distributed when people interact – and, on the other, the knowledge needed *to interact at all, coherently* (BIC), which does not and could not vary in those ways. Merging these two factors has been a vulnerability of the concept of 'competence' that has followed it since Chomsky (1965) first introduced it. It surfaces whenever this distinction between a theory of competence and a theory of performance is disregarded or its importance overlooked. This is arguably what happened when work on second language acquisition expanded to include a concern with learners' ability to perform competently in interactions with native speakers of L2 in a host culture, and came to refer to that as "L2 interactional competence."

Let me reiterate that BIC underlies the development of routinized procedures and practices in a learner's native culture, and the learning and adaptations of those that NNSs make to interact competently in L2 with other nonnative speakers (ELF) and native speakers in their host culture. So BIC includes the ability to make interconnection within action–reaction pairs. Such interconnections entail relevancies and constraints between utterances/actions that apply across tasks and activities, and most importantly here, in languages. When an utterance/action is interconnected with ones that precede and follow it in mutually constraining ways, it is *interactionally* meaningful, *which is not the same as culturally or linguistically meaningful.*

In ELF it happens all the time that interlocutors produce interactionally meaningful utterances that are not necessarily culturally meaningful in the target language environment (ENL) and/or contain linguistic errors (see previous conversational excerpts). Of course, even though BIC (knowledge of the way *interaction* works) is not language specific, the extent of the tacit analysis NNSs make of interconnections between utterances/actions does depend on the extent of their knowledge of L2. Interacting competently in L2 depends primarily on learning L2 well enough to be able to discern and construct interconnections between specific utterances/actions based on principles of such interconnection learners already know. The extent to which one is able to recognize such various interconnections correlates to one's knowledge of the language being uttered. As a case in point, Young and Miller (2004) reported the progress of a Vietnamese learner of English toward taking an active part in interactions with an ESL writing instructor who provided feedback to guide his revisions of an essay. In early conferences, the NNS was almost entirely passive, responding with 'okay' and 'yeah' to points that the instructor made. But after several such conferences, the NNS started to take a more active role.

Young and Miller's focus was the progress this student made in becoming more able to actively participate and perform competently in the revision work that these conferences were about. But Young and Miller's (2004) analysis focuses on the difficulties NNS was having at first, as studies of the development of L2 interactional competence typically do, and not NNS's successes from the outset. It should be noted that even the relatively passive responses the student uttered at first were nonetheless produced in turn slots where a response was called for. Moreover, those utterances/actions achieved responses in those slots even though they were not efficacious, and arguably they were the 'right' response to avoid overreaching in an activity and role he had not yet learned. In the same vein, this NNS was taking an active part in making these interactions succeed, within the limited understanding he had of that task and his role in it.

There seems to be a clear-cut distinction between NS–NNS communication and NNS–NNS (ELF) communication from the perspective of reliance on BIC. In NS–NNS communication the NNS participant(s) usually attempt to rely on AIC of the target language as much as possible – although individual preferences and motivation are in effect – given the fact that their NS partners use their L1-based (English) AIC systematically. In ELF communication, however, the need for the target language AIC is limited. But interlocutors still need to have a framework for tacitly analyzing the gradual unfolding of interactions in which they participate for the interconnections between utterances/actions that form an interaction: BIC appears to be that framework. Without that, it would only be within known (L1-based AIC) or newly learned (L2-based AIC) interactional routines that they could produce utterances/actions responsive to what came before, or anticipatory of what might follow, could initiate or make repairs, or could detect and remedy possible misunderstandings based on a bad 'fit' between an utterance/action and what preceded or followed it. Let me go over an interaction between a Chinese and a Korean student that demonstrates that interlocutors are not limited regarding such basics of interaction to a repertoire of language-specific interactional routines. In fact, they are not constrained by any specific interactional routines of the English language.

(5) CH: - I surely . . . do you think there are many activities in Albany . . . are . . . . Do you many activities are in Albany to s . . . . keep healthy ?
K: - Yeah, actually on campus you know there is a I surely . . . do you think there are many activities in Albany . . . are . . . . Do you many activities are in Albany to s . . . . keep healthy ?
CH: - Yeah, actually on campus you know there is a gym.
K: - A gym . . . ah I heard . . . I heard students can swim.
CH: - Yeah go there.
K: - Yeah.
CH: - For free.

K: - Did you visit there?
CH: - Mmm I only went to the gym and went swimming . . . . Like at the very beginning of last semester.
K: - Oh how was it?
CH: - It's good.
K: - Really?
CH: - You know it was at the beginning of the semester so basically there weren't so many students
K: - Ahhh.
CH: - Working out there.
K: - Right.
CH: - So it's good for students definitely with the high level . . . so you can go to the gym and swimming pool to keep yourself healthy. And you can always cook by yourself.
K: - Right right.
CH: - And basically I don't like American food.
K: - Mhmmm.
CH: - Like there are too many . . . too much fat in it . . . . So I just . . . I cannot cook either but my roommates and friend they can cook very authentic Chinese food.
K: - Oh really?
CH: - And Chinese dish so I . . .
K: - It's good for you!

What makes this excerpt thought provoking is the fact that the two subjects are semi-fluent in English; however, they do not rely on any language- or culture-specific practices, patterns or expressions. Still the dialogue goes on smoothly because they rely on the framework of BIC. They produce utterances responsive to what came before, or anticipatory of what might follow as in the following excerpt.

(6) CH: - Yeah, actually on campus you know there is a gym.
K: - A gym . . . ah I heard . . . I heard students can swim.
CH: - Yeah go there.
K: - Yeah.
CH: - For free.

As you might have noticed, the Chinese student mentions 'a gym' with no particular goal. But the Korean's response contains relevant information about the place, which gives the Chinese student the chance to continue and personalize this relevance. The Korean supports his turns by back-channeling. This pattern continues in the next part of the conversation. When the Korean feels that more information is needed, or detects that the flow of conversation need some 'uplift,' he uses short questions such as 'did you visit there?', 'how was it?'

(7) K: - Did you visit there?
CH: - Mmm I only went to the gym and went swimming . . . . Like at the very beginning of last semester.

K: -Oh how was it?
CH: -It's good.
K: -Really?
CH: -You know it was at the beginning of the semester so basically there weren't so many students.
K: -Ahhh.
CH: -Working out there.
K: -Right.

So, in this illustration, when the Chinese student feels that there is nothing further to say about gym and swimming because his partner has nothing to do with those he decides to change the topic and starts to talk about food.

(8) CH: - So it's good for students definitely with the high level . . . so you can go to the gym and swimming pool to keep yourself healthy. And you can always cook by yourself.
K: - Right right.
CH: - And basically I don't like American food.
K: - Mhmmm.
CH: - Like there are too many . . . too much fat in it . . . . So I just . . . I cannot cook either but my roommates and friend they can cook very authentic Chinese food.
K: - Oh really?
CH: - And Chinese dish so I . . .
K: - It's good for you!

The aforementioned ELF interactions have demonstrated that the success of NNSs in interacting with other NNSs relies on something in addition to, and more basic than, their repertoire of socioculturally appropriate practices and techniques (AIC: L1- or L2-based interactional competence). It equally depends on their having knowledge of how interactions work per se. BIC is the basis for tacitly analyzing and contributing to the coherence of current talk in situ. Also, BIC is considered the foundation for the formation of the culture-specific procedures and practices of interaction in one's native culture and those of other cultures one may move into. It is thus the basis for the development of the more specific and diverse repertoire of socioculturally appropriate procedures and practices that learners acquire (AIC), as they become more proficient in a language. But in ELF interactions, the specificity of the repertoire of socioculturally appropriate practices, procedures, and patterns may hamper rather than further the interaction, as was stated several times. So interlocutors prefer relying on BIC and use communicative strategies that are not biased by the target language or their L1s but co-constructed in the interactional process, as can be seen in examples (6), (7), and (8). At the same time, greater proficiency in English enables more subtle and complex tacit analyses of linkages among utterances/actions based on BIC, through which speakers make situational adaptations during interaction. The abovementioned examples highlight the ways ELF speakers respond to questions, self-edit word choices and utterances, or try to avoid misunderstandings and keep the conversation going. Hence, even though, analytically, BIC plays a more visible role in interactions between speakers who are less proficient in L2, and/or Lingua Franca speakers with limited core common ground, we can see the essential, though more subtle, role BIC plays in the interactions of more proficient speakers. This can be demonstrated in the conversation between an African French speaker and a Korean student.

(9) AF: - Let's talk about ... let's talk about housing. You say you live in Albany so how is the place where you live? Can you describe the place where you live?
K: - What? Sorry.
AF: - I mean the place where you live. You said you live in Albany right?
K: - Place? What place? Korea.
AF: - Place ... place ...
K: - Ah place ... describe in Albany.
AF: - Yeah is it a good place? How is it? How are the houses there? Can you walk out straight and get the first ... do you like the place where you live here in Albany?
K: - I like living in Albany. Because the Albany is the ... especially I spent almost two months ... it's quiet ... nice people ... neighbor ...
AF: - Yeah you have nice neighbors.
K: - Yeah and making friends ...
AF: - The manager in the apartment is good?
K: - Yeah good.

As the conversation illustrates, these two interlocutors are fluent in English. Still, a problem occurs during the conversation when the AF student uses the word 'place' inquiring about the dwelling of the Korean student who does not understand how the word fits into the conversation. It is not that he does not understand the word. In fact, the problem is that he cannot recognize it as a word that can refer to dwelling. Actually the word 'place' is commonly used by native speakers of English in this sense. So what we see here is that language specificity can cause trouble in ELF interactions. But the problem is easily solved by the AF student who uses several short questions and the word 'house' to make clear what he means. To conclude, BIC has helped both interlocutors. The Korean knows that the AF uses the word 'place' appropriately in referring to something that is unclear for him. So he keeps trying to make sense of it by asking short questions for clarification namely, 'What? Sorry.'; 'Place? What place? Korea.' His third reaction which is, 'Ah place ... describe in Albany,' reveals that he just comprehended it. So this tacit analysis of the 'misfit' between a succession of utterances is based on BIC. This provides ways for the ELF speaker to infer and respond to the purpose of a question through taking into account its 'fit' with prior talk. The word 'place' was a misfit for the Korean but his BIC urged him to try further to figure out if he was right or wrong. His third response shows success, the realization of how the word 'place' fits into the sequence. As far as the AF speaker is concerned, his analysis served to reveal whether such techniques as repair or understanding checks are warranted in the sequence. BIC provided a basis for reworking and improving on means of achieving understanding.

## 3.5 Summary

In this chapter, we have discussed the interactional competence (IC) that ELF users put to use in ELF interactions. It was argued that interactional competence means the ability to deploy interactional resources (turn-taking, repair, boundaries, speech acts, etc.) through available linguistic resources as needed by the speaker/hearer to express their communicative intentions in actual situational contexts. IC was presented as a continuum with two ends: basic interactional competence (BIC) and adapted interactional competence (AIC). Thus, language use is a constant move on this continuum. ELF users are closer to the BIC end of the continuum, and, when using an L1, L2, or Lx with native speakers of those languages, language users usually move closer to the AIC end of the continuum for they begin to rely on frames, routines, and patterns that are essential in the use of that particular language. BIC is knowledge of the way successive utterances/actions can be substantively interconnected into a meaningful interaction and not merely a random collection. We regard BIC as the basis on which learners infer and adopt the practices and norms of native speakers in a host culture, as well as interact competently with other learners in L2 as a Lingua Franca (ELF).

Now that we have seen what it means for ELF speakers/hearers to be interactionally competent, we should turn to the issue of how this competence develops in the sociocultural environment in which interlocutors function.

# 4 Sociocultural Background Knowledge

## 4.1 The Problem: Whose Sociocultural Background?

In Chapter 1, I provided a working definition of language as follows: "Language is a system of signs operated by a conceptual base that is the reflection of the sociocultural background in which the system of signs is put to use." This definition emphasizes the unique relationship of the sociocultural background with the system of signs (Narrow Language Faculty, NLF hereafter) through the conceptual base. In linguistic analysis, it is assumed that people who speak the same L1 share not only linguistic knowledge of the language system (NLF) but also a relatively similar sociocultural background that affects them in a distributed way when NLF is put to use. Linguistic competence and interactional competence paired with the sociocultural background knowledge (SBK hereafter) go hand in hand. That is to say, they are reflections of the phenomenon that we call 'language.' What have been analyzed for the most part in present day linguistics, pragmatics or applied linguistics research are everyday conversations or written language production where participants have similar sociocultural backgrounds (L1s). What we know as the field of linguistics is based on this kind of analysis which assumes, but hardly attempts to demonstrate, that all participants are somewhat equally familiar with and affected by the meaning-supporting sociocultural background and relevant strategies of verbal interaction or writing strategies, which is not quite true. There are many individual variations of how L1 sociocultural background affects language processing in L1. In fact, this sociocultural background is individually distributed. Durkheim (1982: 7) expressed the view that anything properly called a collective belief will be "external to individual consciousnesses." However, it is true that this relatively common sociocultural background, this collective salience, is what gives some kind of coherence (in a very broad sense of the term) to language processing in L1. SKB is some kind of relatively similar understanding of the world for people who belong to a given speech community. It serves as a basis for developing conventions, standards, norms, and common beliefs that represent what was called "core common ground" (see Kecskes and Zhang 2009). But the more diverse the speech community is, the less one can rely on a relatively common sociocultural background (see Rampton 1995).

So the question is: how does sociocultural background operate in ELF? Does sociocultural background have some relative coherence for ELF users? A crucial part of ELF studies (e.g., Hüllen 1992; Firth 2009; House 2014) have emphasized that ELF is a medium of communication which can be given substance with different national, regional, local, and individual cultural identities. This means that ELF does not carry specific identities. It is not a language in terms of which speakers define themselves (Hüllen 1992; House 2003). House (2014: 364) argued that when English is used as a Lingua Franca for communication, it is in principle *neutral* with regard to the different sociocultural backgrounds of its users. However, Baker (2015) criticized this approach by saying that ELF cannot be neutral with regard sociocultural backgrounds and I agree. In ELF, none of the sociocultural backgrounds of the participants and the target language (English) are dominant, but of course this does not mean that ELF is 'neutral': ELF interlocutors do not give up their identity and shut down the effect of their L1 sociocultural background and limited L2 sociocultural background. So ELF has great potential for international and intercultural communication because in ELF interactions there are no fixed norms, well-established conventions or standards, as was discussed in Chapter 1. It should be noted that ELF speakers get into a number of temporary speech communities where different varieties of English are deployed and represented. This forces them to constantly co-construct emergent common ground, collectively make sense of the actual situational context, rely on BIC rather than specific AICs and work out strategies that make smooth communication possible. In order to understand why the shortage of shared sociocultural background knowledge affects ELF the way we have described, we shall need to discuss the nature of this knowledge.

## 4.2 What Do We Consider Sociocultural Background Knowledge?

Interlocutors' talk can never be all-inclusive to convey every aspect of meaning. Gumperz argued that, as a consequence, some combination of 'practical reasoning' and 'unstated, taken-for-granted background knowledge' is needed to fill in what is left unsaid (Gumperz 2001: 216). So, we can ask the questions: what is this 'unstated, taken-for-granted background knowledge'? In short, we can say that *sociocultural background knowledge comprises sociocultural practices and experiences that a member of a speech community (temporary or relatively stable) is and has been exposed to and uses to make sense of the world around him/her.* All of this is reflected in core common ground and collective salience and beliefs for individuals in a given speech community, which has a profound effect on meaning production and comprehension as well as language behavior of speech community members. The more homogeneous and (relatively) stable a speech community is, the larger the effect of the core common ground and collective salience is. Conversely, the more diverse a speech community is, the more limited the reliance on core common ground and collective salience is, and the more there is need for co-construction of common ground. In other words, smooth communication is hardly possible without some, at least minimal, common ground. Thus, speech community members gain sociocultural knowledge from having been and being acculturated in their speech community. This is the basis for core common ground and collective salience that help speech community members to behave like insiders in the community. If this is lacking, or limited, interlocutors may feel like outsiders, as is the case of ELF where interlocutors do not feel and, most of the time, do not want to feel like insiders of an English L1 speaking community. The following conversation between a Korean student and a Chinese student demonstrates this very clearly.

(1) K: - And then language problem. Sometimes I obviously look like a foleign .. foreign person ... foreigner here ... so they assume I don't speak English so they sometimes ... I don't know ... they sometimes don't understand what I'm saying ... even though I'm speaking English. It hurts me a lot ... I don't know.
CH: - Could you follow them?
K: - Of course.
CH: - But they find it hard to follow you?
K: - Mhmm I don't know why. I think it's because of my ... how I look like you know . I don't know it hurts me a lot.
CH: - I don't think it matters very much because just for your physical appearance. Did you try slowing down your space?
K: - *Yes eventually they understand I can speak English but still in their mind they have strong strategy ... I mean ... I'm sorry ... stereotypes prejudice like ... you look foreign.*
CH: - Foreigner.
K: - And you probably don't speak English so they don't even bother themselves to speak to me.

As we can see, the Korean student and Chinese student clearly express their frustration about not feeling as members of the Albany speech community in which they have been living. They talk about their physical appearance, their language use and the prejudice of some members of the speech community. What frustrates them most is what the Korean student says as: 'they sometimes don't understand what I'm saying ... even though I'm speaking English.' Yes; although he uses the same code system as the native speakers do, something is still missing. This "something" is the other side of language use: the sociocultural background knowledge that would help him use the right intonation, select the preferred words in a given context, use the appropriate situation-bound utterances and understand implications and contextualization cues, including both verbal and nonverbal, etc. *Broadly speaking, everything that goes with a language minus the code system can be considered sociocultural background knowledge.* Nevertheless, the nature and functioning of this knowledge – what exactly it encompasses and how people access and activate the appropriate knowledge at a given conversational moment – are still not clear and are under investigation.

## 4.3 The Relationship of Sociocultural Background Knowledge to Linguistic Knowledge and Conceptual Knowledge

### *4.3.1 Understanding the Three Knowledges*

One of the most complicated issues of present day linguistics is the relationship of three knowledges: linguistic knowledge, conceptual knowledge, and encyclopedic knowledge. Language philosophy, theoretical linguistics, cognitive linguistics, computational linguistics, and pragmatics have been addressing this issue from different perspectives. Unfortunately, we have no room here to go into detail and summarize the different approaches. What we are interested in, however, is how the relationship between the three knowledges affects ELF, and why this relationship matters in ELF.

My definition of language (see Section 4.1 and in Chapter 1) is based on the relationship of these three knowledges. In that definition, there are three important entities, namely, system of signs, conceptual base, and sociocultural background. So it would be logical to assign linguistic knowledge to the system of signs, conceptual knowledge to the conceptual base, and encyclopedic knowledge to the sociocultural background. However, it is not that simple. Goddard is probably right when he said, "knowledge of all kinds is integrated in the mind to such an extent that it does not make any sense to partition it into two distinct realms" (1998: 15). But we still need to partition knowledge if we want to understand where the difficulties and uniqueness of ELF use are. Or at least so we can distinguish different types of knowledge in ELF for a better understanding.

Let us see what linguists say about this issue. Some works in theoretical linguistics (e.g., Gruber 1985; Kiefer 1990; Bierwisch and Schreuder 1992) talked about the need to distinguish between three types of knowledge: *linguistic knowledge*, which, roughly speaking, concerns the core (mostly literal) meaning of lexical items; *conceptual knowledge*, which has to do with the possible modifications and conceptualizations of the core meaning in various actual situational contexts; and *encyclopedic knowledge*, which comprises the rest, i.e., world knowledge that is associated with a word, but which is not immediately relevant to linguistic structure. Take for instance, the lexical item 'plate' that has its core meaning something like 'a flat dish.' The fact that this lexical item can be used also as a nonphysical entity as in the sentences: "I have too much on my *plate*" or "dinner is twenty dollars a *plate*" belongs to our conceptual knowledge. Basically, conceptual knowledge comprises the different possible senses of the lexical item. Everything beyond that, like the knowledge that *plate* is used to eat food from, that it is usually made of porcelain, metal or some artificial material and is usually oval or round belong to our encyclopedic knowledge. Another example can be the verb 'shoot.' Its core meaning is something like 'kill or wound (a person or animal) with a bullet or arrow.' Also, our conceptual knowledge comprises different other possible senses of the label 'shoot' such as 'to *shoot* questions at someone,' or fling (The volcano shot lava into the air) or to direct suddenly or swiftly (He shot a smile at his wife). At the same time, there are quite a number of things which we know about 'shoot' which do not play any role (at least most of the time) in its semantic interpretation. Beyond what we have just mentioned, we know that we need an instrument or tool to execute the action *'shoot'* like a weapon or a volcano or metaphorically a laugh. We also know that 'shoot' presupposes a swift and rapid move. It is of utmost importance to highlight that this approach to three different knowledges makes sense, but how does this relate to what we call 'sociocultural background knowledge'? Can sociocultural background knowledge be equated with encyclopedic knowledge as is done in some of the existing literature (e.g., Fillmore 1982; Croft and Cruse 2004; Evans 2006)? Basically, one can argue that sociocultural background knowledge comprises everything we know about the world. So should we distinguish conceptual knowledge from encyclopedic knowledge, or we should handle them as one entity? The answer to this question is not straightforward, but it is timely as it may allow us to pinpoint the main problems for ELF use, which are connected with how we understand conceptual knowledge and encyclopedic knowledge rather than linguistic knowledge. What we know is that linguistic knowledge is relatively easy to define: that is coded, and (relatively) standardized. Languages do not differ that much with respect to core meanings of lexical items denoting basic objects and actions in the world, but they may exhibit essential differences as to conceptual knowledge and, to some extent, encyclopedic knowledge. The core meaning of the verb 'cut' denoting 'make an opening, incision, or wound in something with a sharp-edged tool or object' exists in many languages. However, the various conceptualizations of that action are at odds in different languages. Take for instance, 'cut to the chase' which is indeed a very American way to mean 'make your point.' Likewise, there is no English translation for Hungarian 'meg*vág*tam egy kis pénzzel,' which means 'I squeezed some money out of him' in which the literal equivalent of *cut* (*vág*) is used.

### *4.3.2 Views on Separating Linguistic Knowledge from Conceptual Knowledge*

Linguistic approaches (e.g., generative linguistics and lexical semantics) usually focus on and discuss linguistic knowledge and encyclopedic knowledge. Linguistic knowledge (dictionary knowledge) is supposed to cover the idiosyncrasies of particular words, whereas encyclopedic knowledge covers everything regarding the underlying concepts. In cognitive linguistics, however, semantic representations which constitute the semantic pole of a linguistic sign are equated with "conventionalized conceptualizations" (Langacker 1988: 94). This view integrates encyclopedic knowledge into the lexicon. So there are no separate linguistic knowledge and encyclopedic knowledge. In cognitive linguistics, meaning emerging from language use is a function of the activation of conceptual knowledge structures as guided by context. Consequently, there is no principled distinction between semantics and pragmatics (e.g., Fauconnier 1997; Evans 2006). Thus, language is seen as a repository of world knowledge and a structured collection of meaningful categories which help us deal with new experiences and store information about old ones (Geeraerts 1997). It can be deduced that our linguistic knowledge is rooted in our experience with the world; this is what language in use expresses. So if language is a system for categorization of the world, one can argue that there does not seem to be any need to postulate a systemic and structural level of meaning that differs from the level where world knowledge is associated with linguistic forms. However, I beg to differ from an ELF perspective because each language categorizes the same world out there differently. What's more, Slobin (1997) argued that language is a transmitter of real-world experiences, and that these experiences are filtered through language into verbalized events. If that were not the case, ELF speakers would not face the constant problem of linguistic and conceptual differences in Chinese English, Bulgarian English, Indian English, German English, etc. The differences between languages are most significant at the conceptual level. This is where the different world views of different speech communities are conventionalized and developed into a relatively standardized code system. That is the main reason why ELF speakers consider linguistic knowledge as relatively similar in each variety of English. This is why they treat the code system as their core common ground. In a way, everybody who speaks English uses the same code system. ELF users all know, at a particular level of proficiency, the semantics of the word 'patronize' – to act as a patron of, support – as in 'they patronized the local stores.' However, what not all ELF speakers may know is the conceptual load that is attached to this word depending on its direct object. If the direct object is inanimate – take for instance the sentence above – there is no problem: the meaning is neutral or positive. But if the direct object is animate the meaning becomes negative. It refers to a condescending treatment, some kind of superiority like in the following encounter:

(2) KELLY: - I am sure you did your best. The accident was not your fault.
BILL: - Please do not *patronize* me. I will take the responsibility.
Bill does not like Kelly's patronizing tone. He is fully aware that he was wrong and is ready to take responsibility.

So, in most cases, linguistic knowledge in English is available for the ELF speakers (depending on their proficiency) while conceptual knowledge may or may not be accessible.[1] This is where the major difference lies between L1 use and ELF use. *While speakers in L1 seek and establish common ground on the conceptual level, ELF speakers do that on the linguistic level.* The separation of linguistic knowledge and conceptual knowledge is quite clear in L2 (e.g., Kecskes 2003; Baker 2015).

Furthermore, cognitive linguists have had a go at keeping linguistic knowledge separate from conceptual knowledge. Bierwisch argued that there is a clear distinction between a word's purely linguistic meaning and the interpretation that a word may have relative to conceptual knowledge (cf. Bierwisch 1981; Bierwisch and Schreuder 1992; Taylor 2000). As you may have already suspected, this two-level model distinguishes between a linguistic-semantic level of meaning and an essentially non-linguistic, conceptual level of interpretation. In fact, encyclopedic knowledge is provided only in the act of interpreting the word in its context, while the word meaning itself is underdetermined with respect to its possible interpretations in different kinds of context. This position seriously constrains polysemy in the mental lexicon and relegates it to the conceptual level. That is to say, words have a number of meanings because of their various possible conceptual interpretations. So, it could be argued that the goal of dictionary knowledge (linguistic knowledge) is only to collect all possible interpretations under a unitary semantic entry. This corroborates with what Taylor (2000:130) pointed out as "on the two-level model, interpretation of an expression emerges through the interaction of the unitary semantic representation with conceptual information, relative to a context." So the dictionary knowledge (linguistic knowledge) versus encyclopedic knowledge controversy opposes two extreme conceptions of word definitions. According to the dictionary approach, a word is described in terms of linguistic elements only,

[1] This may depend on factors such as frequency of occurrence or noticing.

without recourse to world knowledge, whereas an encyclopedic definition includes "an indication of the different species or different stages of the object or process denoted by the word, the main types of behavior of this object or process" (Mel'cuk & Zholkovsky 1984: 88). Let me highlight that the debate on the separation of the conceptual and linguistic-lexical level does not necessarily go on between generativists and cognitivists, although it concerns the basic difference between the two perspectives. Rather, it involves linguists from both sides. For instance, Bierwisch is a generativist and Wierzbicka is a cognitivist, but they are on the same side although their reasons are different. Also, several researchers who are considered cognitive linguists, have argued for keeping lexical semantics separate from conceptual semantics. Take, for instance, Haiman (1980: 355), who claimed that while theoretically untenable, the distinction between dictionaries and encyclopedias has "the happy property of working very well in practice." Similiarly, Gibbs (1996) claimed that cognitive linguists would not argue against the idea that there is a mental lexicon that might be independently accessed during sentence processing. In his view, part of the confusion about the role of cognitive structure in language use and processing results from the failure to distinguish between different levels at which cognition and language interact. Moreover, Wierzbicka (1996) strongly believes that word meaning can and has to be defined at the linguistic (lexical) level. She argued that the acquisition of another language demonstrates very well how important lexical semantics is. She said that "for anyone seriously trying to learn another language and understand another culture, the proposition that words cannot be defined can hardly be anything but bad news" (Wierzbicka 1996: 256). Also, she said that the "belief that a dictionary definition represents nothing other than a selection from a (real or imaginary) encyclopedic entry, with the choice being determined by practical considerations and having no theoretical justification, leads to stagnation in lexical semantics" (p. 336). As we can see, Wierzbicka makes the distinction between linguistic knowledge and encyclopedic knowledge, claiming linguistic knowledge is essentially shared between all speakers of a particular language, while encyclopedic (real-world) knowledge is not. She pointed out that there is linguistic evidence that the human mind itself draws a distinction between a mental dictionary and a mental encyclopedia (Wierzbicka 1996: 344). On that account, the nature of available linguistic evidence is summarized by Taylor (2000: 16) who argues that acquisition is not a process of building up a concept from its constituent parts, but rather the gradual elaboration of a knowledge network. Another important observation comes from Harnad (1990: 343–344):

Once one has the grounded set of elementary symbols provided by a taxonomy of names (and the iconic and categorical representations that give content to the names and allow them to pick out the objects they identify), the rest of the symbol strings of a natural language can be generated by symbol composition alone, and they will all inherit the intrinsic grounding of the elementary set.

This implies that higher order symbols can be interpreted without direct acquaintance with reality. We should not think, however, that these higher order symbols are not grounded in experience at all. They, together with their underlying symbolic representations, are derived from the sensory representations and thus indirectly grounded in experience. Actually, the real issue here is not whether the content of lexical units is grounded in experience or not, because in most cases they are grounded in experience either directly or indirectly. *What is important for us is that linguistic symbols can entirely be cut off from their original source and live a life of their own, independent from the conceptual system to a particular extent and from a particular perspective.* Just think about this issue from an ELF perspective: ELF speakers have access to the symbols (words) in English but they have very limited direct experience with the target language reality in which those are grounded for the native speakers. So ELF speakers may have linguistic knowledge but lack or have access to only limited conceptual knowledge as we have demonstrated in the above examples.

Based on the instances of mono- and multilingual development, it might be overstepping to claim that linguistic units (words) reflect specific, autonomous linguistic knowledge that is separate from various types of conceptual knowledge. However, *it might very well be that some linguistic knowledge that is attached to the word form is partly autonomous from the rest of our conceptual system* (see Gibbs 1996; Kecskes 2003). We can take the expression 'chicken out' as an example. The basic meaning of the expression can be defined as 'to decide not to do something because you are too frightened.' There is no actual situational context that can cancel the negative conceptual load attached to the phrase. In all actual contexts its negative connotation is present. Take for instance, the utterance 'at the last minute, Sally chickened out of the race.' No contextual support is needed for the expression to call upon the negative conceptual load. Consequently, we can say that the conceptual load is already tied to the semantics of the expression. In other words, the conceptual load becomes its word-specific semantic property. In that regard, Croft and Wood (2000: 55) argued:

it is not the case that any time we think we must conceptualize our experience the way that our language requires us to. But it is the case that any time we express our thoughts in language, we must conceptualize our experience in the way that our language requires us to. Cognition may be linguistically neutral, but language is not semantically neutral.

Slobin (1991) also made a similar point when he described "thinking for speaking" as the appropriate domain for the influence of language on thought.

The issue here is not necessarily whether language influences thought or not, but to what extent. The world is always given to us under some construal for our purposes. Thus, the remaining question is: how much of this construal is provided by the language we speak?

### *4.3.3 What Could Be the Solution?*

To answer this question, we must go back to Wierzbicka's thought reflecting a second language perspective. She argued that basically the process of second language learning is proof that the proposition that words cannot be defined is wrong. She rejects the belief that a dictionary definition represents nothing other than a selection from a (real or imaginary) encyclopedic entry, with the choice being determined by practical considerations and having no theoretical justification. Wierzbicka makes the distinction between linguistic knowledge and encyclopedic knowledge because she is convinced that linguistic knowledge is essentially shared between all speakers of a particular language, while encyclopedic (real-world) knowledge is not. So far, she is right, but she does not clarify the nature of what she calls "encyclopedic knowledge" because she equates it with what I have called sociocultural background knowledge. So the problem is not solved yet. But we are on the right track because we are using a multilingual view, the perspective of ELF. When bringing a multilingual view into the debate, we should say that the relationship between the three knowledge types is much more complex than just a simple trichotomy. The main problem is that world knowledge is available for human beings in two ways: (1) A part of world knowledge is encapsulated in the lexical items that we use in a language. That is why cognitive linguists argue that it does not make sense to separate linguistic knowledge from encyclopedic knowledge. In a way, they are right because when we use a word, that triggers both what they call linguistic knowledge (grammatical information about the word, its relations to other words, synonymy-antonym, etc.) and encyclopedic knowledge that comprises what Mel'cuk and Zholkovsky (1984) called an indication of the different species or different stages of the object or process denoted by the word, the main types of behavior of this object or process. This kind of encyclopedic knowledge sounds like something encoded in the word; what we have called 'conceptual knowledge.' But, then, where is the other part of world knowledge that is not encoded in the lexical items? (2) It looks like that 'second' type of world knowledge is not directly connected with our language system, rather, it comprises behavior practices, models, and social frames that are called upon when we use a language. We will take a closer look at these two sides of sociocultural background knowledge, namely, conceptual knowledge and encyclopedic knowledge, in the following section.

## 4.4 A Possible Model of Knowledge Distribution

### *4.4.1 The Relationship of Three Knowledges in the Model*

What I propose here is a model in which we have the linguistic knowledge on one side, and the sociocultural background knowledge (world knowledge) on the other side. There is constant interaction between the two sides. For analytic reasons, within the sociocultural background knowledge we should distinguish between conceptual knowledge and encyclopedic knowledge.

Linguistic knowledge ———— Sociocultural background knowledge
conceptual knowledge — encyclopedic knowledge

According to this model, meaning is constructed in the dynamic interplay of actual situational context and lexical items, with the context representing the actual, present, situational, ever-changing side of sociocultural background and the lexical item(s) embodying previous experiences and relations in the sociocultural background (see Kecskes 2003, 2014). This is how the three knowledges are intertwined and function together. The lexical items with their semantic properties (linguistic knowledge) represent prior reoccurring experience (conceptual knowledge), and the actual situational context triggers the other part of world knowledge that we previously called encyclopedic knowledge. The difference between the two types of sociocultural background knowledge is that the conceptual knowledge part is immediately tied to linguistic knowledge while the other type of sociocultural background knowledge (encyclopedic knowledge) is called upon as needed in the actual situational context.

It seems to me that ELF users have the least problem with linguistic knowledge that is mainly reflected in their language proficiency. Linguistic knowledge is learnable both systematically (schools, institutions) or asystematically (natural environment). It represents core knowledge that ELF interlocutors share and rely on, no matter which variety of English (Chinese English, German English, French English, Russian English, etc.) they speak. This linguistic core knowledge gives some core common ground for the interlocutors to rely on. However, conceptual knowledge is different. The problem is that conceptual knowledge that is tied to the semantics of a lexical item is quite conservative and occasionally seems to be old-fashioned or obsolete because it may be rooted in the past experience of the given speech community. Language only partly reflects the actual social world around us because of this delay in conceptual coding. It will take a while for some neologisms such as 'sharrow' (road marking), 'procott' (intentionally buy things) or 'placemaking' to be fully part of common conceptual knowledge.

Words with their semantics are needed not only to symbolize concepts but also to stabilize them, keep them tidy and make them definable. This, however, can only be done if a word or formula has some elements in its meaning that are relatively constant, i.e., part of the language system and not totally dependent on actual use and context. So I need to repeat Leibniz's argument one more time here: "*Si nihil per se concipitur, nihil omnino concipietur*": that is, "if nothing can be understood by itself nothing at all can ever be understood" (Leibniz 1903: 430). Human communication would hardly be possible if words did not have any relatively permanent elements in their meaning, and meaning formation would only be the matter of online production. If, however, these relatively constant elements of meaning really exist, the cognitive linguists' claim that word meanings may not apply at all without the supporting cognitive structures and mechanisms becomes questionable (at least to some extent).

It is conceptual knowledge where languages differ, as discussed in Section 4.3.2. The problem is that, unlike linguistic knowledge, this knowledge cannot be learned in a systematic way. It is socioculture experience that is encoded in the language. This sociocultural experience is reflected in the preferred ways of saying things and preferred ways of organizing thoughts in a speech community (see Kecskes 2014, 2015b). For instance, Americans 'run a business,' 'shoot a film,' and 'make love.' The Turkish 'estagfurullah' [I ask pardon of God] which is a very commonly used rejoiner is also a good example. Or the different uses of 'eat (chi-)' such as 'chī kǔ, 吃苦 eat hardships' → suffer from unhappy things 'chī kuī, 吃亏 eat losses' in Chinese.

As a result, coming with different L1-based sociocultural backgrounds, ELF interlocutors do not know how familiar their partners are with English L1-based conceptual knowledge. That is why English-based conceptual knowledge cannot serve as a part of their core common ground. The other part of sociocultural background knowledge that we labeled as 'encyclopedic knowledge' is some kind of general knowledge about the world. This knowledge is usually triggered by actual situational context and may be shared, at least to some extent, with other members of the temporary ELF speech community. So this knowledge, to some extent, serves as a part of core common ground for ELF users.

### *4.4.2 Words and Concepts (the Interplay of Linguistic Knowledge and Conceptual Knowledge)*

The central element of lexical pragmatics is the way we understand the relationship of word and concept, i.e., linguistic knowledge and conceptual knowledge. We need to look deeper into this relationship because we mentioned several times that this is the key to understanding difficulties in ELF use.

The conceptual system and linguistic system are related through the interdependence of concepts and words. Most of the controversy centers around the question of how concepts and words are related to one another. A natural language possesses an inventory of lexical forms, and these are mapped onto the concept network (Cruse 1992: 290). The question is: how does this mapping take place? It is true that concepts are represented by words, but this representation is rather contradictory on two points. First, there is no one-to-one relationship between the concept and the word: the overall concept usually extends beyond the sections labeled with a word. Second, the semantic domain of a word also contains specific properties that are not present in the concept. As a result, sometimes there are several different lexical routes to one and the same concept.

When we discuss the relationship between concept and word, a distinction has to be made between two approaches. Kurt Baldinger (1980: 278) described this distinction in the following way: "Semasiology . . . considers the isolated word and the way its meanings are manifested, while onomasiology looks at the designations of a particular concept, that is, at a multiplicity of expressions which form a whole." The semasiological perspective focuses on the word and explores how concepts (conceptual meanings) are associated with that word. So semasiology targets polysemy and the multiple applicability of a lexical item. In contrast, the onomasiological approach takes the concepts as its starting point and investigates what words can express a particular concept. The subject of onomasiology is synonymy, name-giving, and the selection of an expression from among a number of possible alternatives (cf. Geeraerts 1997). It is clear from this distinction that semasiology refers to processes of meaning while onomasiology involves naming. As a result of the thought–word interaction in online language production, thought usually undergoes several changes as it turns into speech. During this process, conceptual categories (concepts) are mapped on linguistic categories (words). Here is an example of how this happens when English as L2 is used.

(3) A male native speaker of English is having a conversation with a Thai female student. He wants to know whether she likes sports or not. The Thai student initially says she likes 'football' and then immediately replaces that with 'soccer.'

NNS (Thai woman) NS (American man)
NS: - . . . .So do you like sports?
NNS: - I love sports.
NS: - What sports do you love?
NNS: - I love football.. Op- in here we call soccer.
NS: - Oh okay.

As we can see, in replacing football with soccer, NNS probably wanted to provide NS with an accurate identification of the sport she liked. According to collective salience of her culture, the Thai woman used the right label 'football.' However, she realized that that label for the concept might not work in the actual situation context for the American man. In addition she likely anticipated that if NS understood her to be identifying American football, he could ask follow-up questions that she would be unable to answer. In the NNS's mind 'football' is the label that has priority based on her L1-experience. However, she realized that for the American the label has another most salient meaning. In order to avoid misunderstanding, the Thai student changed the word for 'soccer' that matched the actual situational context.

As we have mentioned, the problem is that there is no one-to-one relationship between concepts and words. There have been long debates about how much autonomy a lexical unit can have. In other words, is it just a form which reflects the conceptual system and is filled with meaning when it is actually used? Or does a lexical unit have some kind of autonomy which allows for some consistency in its semantic content and a two-way relationship of semantics with both the conceptual level and the lexical level involved (see Bierwisch in Section 4.3.2)? Can one argue that, from the perspective of the conceptual system, concepts should be considered as stable mental representations, or are they flexible, temporary, context-dependent constructions (c.f. Lamberts and Shanks 1997: 3)?

From the perspective of ELF, we can say that ELF users experience and practice differences between a word and a concept, mainly because of the two different sides of sociocultural background knowledge that we discussed. It is important to highlight that concept is a thought category. Concepts help formulate preverbal thoughts (cf. Levelt 1989). We do not know about these thoughts until they are mapped on words. What is uttered is considered the reflection of thought. But what does the following example tell us about the linguistic knowledge versus conceptual knowledge relationship?

(4) Car rental brochure, Tokyo:
WHEN PASSENGER OF FOOT HEAVE IN SIGHT, TOOTLE THE HORN. TRUMPET HIM MELODIOUSLY AT FIRST, BUT IF HE STILL OBSTACLES YOUR PASSAGE THEN TOOTLE HIM WITH VIGOUR.

In this example the word selection makes the sentence funny. We may understand what the writer wanted to say, what his thoughts were, but the concept–word mapping has been grossly unsuccessful. Based on the word selection, it is clear that preverbal thought reflects the Japanese way of thinking. The question is: what has led to this verbal formulation? The fact is that the writer did a semantic rather than a conceptual translation. He put the Japanese conceptual construal into English words. In fact, the sociocultural frame 'renting a car' in which the sentence was produced is part of encyclopedic knowledge for both Japanese and American people. So the frame exists but what language formulation that frame requires is culture specific.

### 4.4.3 *Encyclopedic Knowledge*

Now we have to examine how the uncoded part of sociocultural background knowledge affects ELF production. In our understanding, encyclopedic knowledge refers not only to extralinguistic information about the world but also to a structured system of knowledge, organized as a network. Rosch's (1977) view of category structure and its implications for reasoning (e.g., Lakoff and Johnson 1980) have had an important impact on the emergence of schema theory. Schema theory is a theoretical framework that has been developed in the cognitive sciences over the last two decades. The central concept, 'schema,' has gone by a number of other names, including 'cultural model' (Holland and Quinn 1987; D'Andrade 1992), 'frame' (Minsky 1975; Fillmore 1982), 'mental model' (Johnson-Laird 1983), 'idealized cognitive model' (Lakoff 1987), 'folk model' (D'Andrade 1987), and 'script' (Schank and Abelson 1977). Encyclopedic knowledge is mostly represented in cultural models and schemas that provide scenarios or action plans for individuals of how to interpret speech situations and behave in a particular situation, or how to interpret the behavior of others in one or another situation. Cultural schemas for social interaction are cognitive structures that contain knowledge for face-to-face interactions in a person's sociocultural environment. The following encounter between a Hungarian man and three Chinese women illustrates how these cultural models work.

(5) The four people are going into a restaurant in Albany, NY. The Hungarian stops at the receptionist desk while the three Chinese women are walking into the restaurant looking for an empty table.
H: - Where are you going?
CHI: - There is a vacant table over there.
H: - Please wait till we are seated.

According to US customs, when walking into a restaurant, you usually wait to be taken to a table. In China, there is a different model: usually (though not always) you are free to occupy whichever table is available. Not knowing the US model, the three Chinese women acted according to their own. I argued before that cultural models provide a kind of reference library for possible plans of action for oneself or possible interpretation of actions of others (see Kecskes 2014). These models are not learned directly as models, but are inferred by each of us from what we see and experience with those other people around us. But what we see and experience are never the models themselves.

What we infer from experience is pieces of information, images, features that keep a model together. What we infer depends directly on what parts of the given scenario are saliently and repetitively present in the messages we experience for us to pull out the regularities on which we will base our construction of the model behind them. Thus systematic and repeated changes in speech or cultural behavior in one generation will be learned by the next generation as part of the givens of language or culture.

The core of cultural models that people in the same speech community share changes diachronically through systematic and repeated shifts that can come from sociopolitical changes, technological changes, environmental changes and the like. For instance, currently, gender specific expressions such as 'policeman,' 'chairman,' and 'freshman' are replaced by gender neural expressions such as 'police officer,' 'chairperson,' and 'first-year student'. Of course, usually there is trouble if people try to force the linguistic system to accept something that is conceptually unfounded, for example, Justin Trudeau's[2] attempt to change 'mankind' to 'peoplekind.' These attempts are the result of a sociopolitical practice that prefers the use of gender neutral terms in language. Those sociopolitical practices may prevail if the given speech community will find them important to keep and use them repeatedly.

The application of the core of a cultural model, however, changes synchronically. Usually no situation occurs exactly the same way as we have experienced it in any previous time. See, for instance, example (6) where a librarian speaks with a student:

(6) L: - Returning?
S: - Yeah.
L: - Your ID, please.
S: - Here you are?
L: - Anything to check out?
S: - These two books, please.

This sequence works like a framework for further similar encounters. The cultural frame can be filled in with different utterances. Individuals always adapt cultural models to the situation at hand to fit their needs. Also, people use cultural models as devices to facilitate effective interaction with others in the various communities to which they belong. In this way, individuals not only shape cultural models, but also are constrained by them. Most of these cultural models come from people's past experiences, but they are constantly recreated in use. It is important to note that people are not required to follow cultural conventions (whether in the use of cultural models or in other ways). In any

[2] Canadian Prime Minister.

given time they can ignore or modify cultural models in a particular situation. Most cultural models can (and often do) show slight variations across groups to which we all belong – groups that can be formal or informal, long-lived or evanescent, imposed or voluntary, and so forth.

## 4.5 How Is Sociocultural Background Knowledge Handled in ELF?

Baker (2009) argued that linguistic and cultural forms expressed through ELF are likely to be hybrid, dynamic, and continuously adapting to local needs, global influences, and the demands of communicating across cultures. He lamented that, apart from Meierkord's (2002) study, there is little empirical evidence from ELF settings, and none from expanding circle environments; that is, specifically concerned with understanding how cultural frames of reference and communicative practices operate in such a liminal manner in intercultural communication through English. The situation has not changed much, as we can see in Baker's book (2015). What we do have on this issue in ELF is House's argument (House 2014) that was already quoted: when English is used as a Lingua Franca for communication, it is in principle neutral with regard to the different sociocultural backgrounds of its users. We discussed in Section 4.1 that House may not be quite right. However, Risager (2006) has taken this matter too far. She spoke not about neutrality but separation of language and culture. Building on the understanding of dynamism in critical theory, or as Risager views it, the complex and global flow of language and culture, she claimed that, from the perspective of users of English as a second or foreign language, languages and cultures can be separated. In order to explain what she means by this, she makes a distinction between cultures and languages in the generic sense and in the differential sense (Risager 2006: 4–5). In the generic or universal sense, language and culture are intertwined the way some theories such as linguistic relativity proposed (e.g., Whorf 1939; Gumperz and Levinson 1996). Language is always an enactment and embodiment of culture, so the two cannot be separated. However, Risager believes that when examining specific languages and cultures such as English, in the differential sense, language and culture can be separated. Her main argument is that all languages, and especially international languages such as English or Spanish, can in practice (i.e., during actual instances of use) take on new cultural meanings. She refers to those as *languacultures* (Risager 2006: 110), which depend on users and context. In this sense, "the link between language and culture is created in every new communicative event" (Risager 2006: 185). As a result, a language such as English will have as many languacultures as there are speakers of the language, and, in this sense, there is no identifiable culture to which a language is inseparably tied. She goes even further than that. She believes that at the individual psychological level, i.e., at the level of an individual's linguistic competence or resources, language and culture are again inseparable, and develop in tandem based on the individual's life experiences. She believes that this individual perspective may have led to confusion over the relationship between specific languages and cultures, and consequently claims that languages such as English are in some way directly tied to British or US culture as in strong forms of linguistic relativity (Whorf 1939). What is important for us here is that while maintaining that languages are never culturally neutral for their users, Risager's approach to the relationship between languages and cultures allows English use in ELF to be separated from the cultures of the inner circle countries. However, this is not quite so if we accept what I suggested above: a part of inner circle culture (let it be Australian English, American English, or British English) is encapsulated in the lexical items in English. So Chinese, German, Russian, Korean, etc. learners/users of English have this conceptual knowledge available to them to a certain extent depending on their proficiency level. So it is a mistake to suggest that target language culture is separated from the use of English as a Lingua Franca. The problem is that the ELF interlocutors cannot rely on that knowledge as the inner circle interlocutors can because it is unknown how much of this conceptual knowledge of inner circle English the outer and expanding circle interlocutors share. The example below demonstrates this point quite clearly.

(7) Jianwei, Mary, Andy, and Liya are sitting at a table and eating.
JIANWEI: - Can I eat that last piece of sandwich?
LIYA: - **Be my guest.**
JIANWEI: - But it's not yours.

This example displays very well why we cannot separate inner circle culture from ELF. There are three nonnative speakers and one native speaker at the table. The Chinese student asks for permission to eat the last piece of sandwich. The Russian student uses a formula to respond, which is a situation-bound utterance, encouraging or allowing someone else to take action like in the following encounter:

A: *Do you mind if I order another glass of beer?* B: *Not at all – be my guest.*

As you can see, the possessive pronoun 'my' in the set phrase 'be my guest' does not necessarily refer to possession. However, the Chinese student in example (7) processes the utterance based on its literal meaning because he may not know the functional meaning of the situation-bound utterance in this figurative use 'be my guest.' So, a slight misunderstanding occurs.

On continuing our discussion about sociocultural background knowledge, we need to point out that the issue was discussed by Kramsch from a second language acquisition perspective. Kramsch (1993: 233) viewed second language communication as operating in a 'third place' between the users' first languagc and culturc (L1/C1) and thc targct languagc and culture (L2/C2), but being part of neither. She claimed that second languages operate along a "cultural faultline" ( 205) in which communicative practices are freed from the norms of both L1/C1 and L2/C2, which opens up new perspectives on languages and cultures. Baker (2015) suggested that the notion of liminality, as proposed by Rampton (1995), shares many features with Kramsch's third places. Rampton studied communication between different ethnic groups within the United Kingdom. He identified "liminal moments" or "crossings" (Rampton 1995: 167) when language users who are not part of a given language community adopt that language for their own purposes or needs at least temporarily. This results in a code-alteration (Rampton 1995: 280) of the L2 by minority or outside users. Rampton argued that such crossings are quite common in the L2 classroom and are a part of L2 teaching and learning practice. Relying on Rampton's approach, Brumfit (2006) proposed that L2 learning and use can be considered a liminal process that leads users into new areas, in which languages and their cultural codes are unique to each individual and communicative encounter.

Baker (2015) emphasized the importance of these approaches and noted that although none of these authors had talked specifically about ELF communication, the notions of third places and liminality have much to offer in highlighting the fluid, dynamic, and novel communicative practices and language–culture connections that might be expected in such contexts. Definitely both the third space approach and liminality are relevant to our discussion about the interplay of linguistic, conceptual and encyclopedic knowledge in meaning production and comprehension in ELF. However, the question is whether ELF users do something different from what L1 users do. Seemingly, the answer is 'yes.' But this is just the tip of the iceberg. What is beneath is more complex. L1 users rely on the relative, synchronically available 'end product' of language development[3]: a relatively coherent system of signs and a relatively coherent sociocultural background knowledge that serves as a support system. This is what LaPolla (2010: 13) claims about language development:

> Language is the cumulative result of the actions of many individual humans, but their actions are not with the intention to create language; language is the unintended byproduct of their attempts to communicate effectively (constrain the addressee's inferential process effectively) on an individual level. It forms as if guided by some invisible hand, much the way economies and paths in fields develop.

But, how is that related to ELF? We should think about the following: ELF users enter into a communicative encounter with their full knowledge of L1, different levels of linguistic, conceptual, and encyclopedic knowledge of L2

[3] There is no real end product because language keeps changing.

and an individual understanding of the actual situational context. From there, they start the cumulative process which is usually very short: to put together what they have in order to create core common ground that they can rely on while communicating with each other. Although this is a short process (ELF speech communities are only temporary), people generally try to do similar things to what they do in L1 but some of those things are more articulated than in L1. So ELF users also primarily rely on prefabricated language (the idiom principle works), and if they do not have enough they produce new ones. They seek common ground, and if they do not have enough of it they create some. They try to make sense of the actual situation context, and if that does not fit in their existing repertoire they co-construct one, and so on and so forth. So, one could argue that *they create their own variety of ELF for the time they spend together.* And in this endeavor, it is linguistic knowledge that helps them most, since that is what they all share to some extent.

## 4.6 Shared Knowledge

Shared knowledge is an essential concern in any communication. In Section 4.3.1 we discussed three types of knowledge. But how much of those is shared? This is a crucial issue because shared knowledge is that to which interlocutors in an interaction can appeal before, during, and after the communicative event. The appeal to, or reliance on, shared knowledge is not always conscious, but it always affects the communicative interaction by either easing it along or interfering and even blocking it. The extent to which the participants share such knowledge will, therefore, affect the degree to which the communicative process will be smooth and effective. Speakers assume shared knowledge when they address others and plan their utterances accordingly. Listeners usually appeal to prior knowledge while interpreting the flow of speech. When writers plan their texts, they take into account what they presume their intended audience knows about the world. While processing written texts, readers appeal to their prior knowledge. When we misjudge shared knowledge or perceptions of other participants in the interaction, we potentially run the risk of creating instances of minor or even serious miscommunication. This can happen among speakers of the same language community, but it occurs much more frequently in ELF. Shared knowledge must, therefore, include both general knowledge of the world and conceptual knowledge related to the target speech community whose language is used as a medium of speech or instruction. But, how much out of each of the three knowledges that we discussed can be assumed to be shared in ELF? Let us go back to a quote from Gumperz (1979: 273) again:

> It is a generally accepted premise of modern conversational analysis that to engage in and sustain a significant range of verbal encounters, participants must have both

background information about the situation at hand and sociocultural knowledge, i.e., familiarity with the shared conventions governing the verbal categorization of the environment and the conduct of activities alluded to in the interaction.

Gumperz emphasized the importance and the effect of background information about the situation and shared knowledge that are both crucial elements of communication. When we read the relevant literature about shared knowledge or common ground, everybody thinks about knowledge that is not linguistic knowledge but something beyond linguistics as I described the notion of shared knowledge (e.g., Clark 1996, 2009; Stalnaker 2002; Kecskes and Zhang 2009). That makes sense when we talk about L1. Nobody thinks about the language system (linguistic knowledge) as common ground in L1. It is taken for granted. But is this the case for ELF as well? I do not think so. As we have discussed, ELF speakers share quite a bit of general knowledge about the world (encyclopedic knowledge) but very little of the conceptual knowledge that is crucial for smooth communication. So how can they smooth the communicative process without much shared common ground and collective salience? Latest research points toward linguistic knowledge as core common ground (e.g., Moore & Dunham 1995; Howarth 1998; Warga 2005; Cieslicka 2006; Kecskes 2007, 2015b; Ortactepe 2012). It is linguistic knowledge that ELF speakers share more than any other knowledge. They have all studied English or acquired it in naturalistic circumstances. They all know the code system at a level defined by their proficiency. What is crucial for them is *semantic analyzability*. The closer they stay to the code, the better the chance there will be no misunderstanding. Take for instance, the think-aloud sessions in which subjects talked about their own language production attached to data collection on formulaic language in my study (Kecskes 2007). ELF speakers explained that they usually avoided the use of formulaic expressions not necessarily because they do not know these phrases, but because they were worried that their interlocutors, who were also nonnative speakers, would not understand them properly. They were reluctant to use language that they knew or perceived to be figurative or semantically less transparent (see also Philip 2005). ELF speakers try to come as close as possible to the compositional meaning of expressions because they think that, if there is no figurative and/or metaphorical meaning involved, their partners will process the English words and expressions the way they meant them. Since ELF speakers come from different sociocultural backgrounds and represent different cultures, the mutual knowledge they may share is usually restricted to the knowledge of the linguistic code. Consequently, semantic analyzability seems to play a decisive role in ELF speech production and comprehension. This assumption is supported by the fact that the most frequently used formulaic expressions are the fixed semantic units (such as 'in fact,' 'generally speaking,' 'to be frank') and phrasal verbs in which there is semantic transparency to a much greater degree than in idioms, situation-bound utterances or speech formulas (e.g., Philip 2005; Cieslicka 2006; Kecskes 2007, 2015b).

Consequently, based on current research, we may say that the Gricean modular view receives more support from ELF users than from L1 users. For ELF speakers, what is said is usually what is communicated. As a result, inferencing looks much simpler than in L1 where the inferred meaning is usually the most salient meaning of the utterance (see Gibbs 1996; Giora 1997, 2003; Colston and Katz 2005). We will return to this issue in the upcoming chapters when we will discuss implicatures and the semantic–pragmatic interface.

## 4.7 Summary

In this chapter, we discussed the relationship and interplay of three knowledges: linguistic knowledge, conceptual knowledge, and encyclopedic knowledge. I have proposed a model in which we have linguistic knowledge on one side, and sociocultural background knowledge (world knowledge) on the other. There is constant interaction between the two sides. For analytic reasons, within the sociocultural background knowledge there was a distinction made between conceptual knowledge and encyclopedic knowledge. According to this model, meaning is constructed in the dynamic interplay of actual situational context and prior context encapsulated in lexical items. The context represents the actual, present, situational, ever-changing side of sociocultural background and the lexical item(s) used in the interaction encapsulate previous experiences and relations in the sociocultural background.

It was claimed that access to the three knowledges represented by the target language is a graded phenomenon for ELF users with the most accessible knowledge being the linguistics code, followed by encyclopedic knowledge. ELF interlocutors have the least access to conceptual knowledge tied to the target language. It is not just that they do not have enough experience in the target language to develop enough of that knowledge, but also the fact that when they use ELF they cannot be sure how much of that conceptual knowledge they share with their partners.

The three knowledges give ELF users the tools and the necessary background information that they need in order to formulate their communicative intention. In the next chapter we will focus on speaker intention, which is a central issue in Gricean pragmatics. The question is whether our understanding of intention should be modified in any way if we examine how it functions in ELF.

# 5 Speaker's Intention

## 5.1 The Problem

In the previous chapters we discussed interactional competence (IC) and socio-cultural background knowledge. Now we need to see what happens when interactional competence is put to use to express the communicative intention of the speaker/hearer in ELF interactions. But why is intention an issue in ELF for us? Why should we devote a whole chapter to intention when ELF literature, with some rare exceptions (see Hynninen 2016), does not even mention it. First of all, any legitimate pragmatic approach to ELF cannot but take intention as its object of study, because the latter undeniably constitutes the core of pragmatics as such. Second, it is important for us to examine this issue because ELF communication situates intention into a different dimension than is fashionable in current pragmatics theories.

Current pragmatics theories that derive from the Gricean theoretical framework are intention based and cooperation driven (see Kecskes 2014). According to these theories, communication revolves around recipient design and intention recognition. The speaker constructs a model of the hearer's knowledge relevant to the given situational context, and vice versa; based on the speaker's utterance, the hearer constructs a model of the speaker's knowledge relevant to the given situational context. This is, in fact, confirmed by Taillard (2002) who argued that communication creates an 'interface' between the speaker's intention structure and the addressee's intention structure which enables the coordinating role of intentions. It is this coordinating role and the commitment inherent to intentions that make it possible for the interface to reshape both of the participants' intentions. I have claimed that this is quite an idealistic approach to communication (see Kecskes 2010b, 2014). However, ELF interactions certainly show a contrasting picture. It should be highlighted that we cannot consider intention only as an a priori construct as is usually the case in current pragmatic theories. ELF communication calls attention to the emergent side of intention; this exists in L1 communication as well but not exactly to the extent as in ELF where the role of emergent intention is very significant. So we have interlocutors who start a conversation by revealing a particular intention. Then one of them may suddenly and unexpectedly change the topic based on an emergent intention that may have been triggered by any of the following factors: loss of interest, language difficulty, inconvenient topic, etc. (see Toyoda and Harrison 2002; Li et al. 2005). The following conversation between a Japanese (J) and Korean (K) student illustrates this point quite well (source: Albany Lingua Franca Database):

(1) J: - I play baseball with Japanese and Korean men
K: - Ah there must be a lot of competitions no?
J: - Hm?
K: - You know like . . . . You know like . . . you are going . . . . things are bad in Korea because of history. So maybe competitions?
J: - Competi . . .
K: - Ok maybe you guys feel like ok we have to win. Japan has to win . . . no no?
J: - No
K: - Ok that's good nice nice . . . do you like American food?
J: - Yes I like. I like steak I like hamburger
K: - Do you miss Japanese food though?
J: - Hm?
K: - Do you miss Japanese food?
J: - I like cooking

We can see that the Japanese student started to talk about his playing baseball with Japanese and Korean students with the intention to discuss his favorite sport with his colleague. However, the Korean student made a hint at the historically bad relations between Japanese and Koreans. He said that the Japanese probably felt the need to win. So, the Korean suddenly changed the course of the conversation when he felt that it might be inconvenient for the Japanese to continue talking about this topic by saying: 'Ok that's good nice nice . . . do you like American food?'

Based on the analysis of the nature of intention in intercultural interactions, the socio-cognitive approach proposed by Kecskes (2010, 2014) argued that the complexity of the communicative process requires that we consider intention both as an a priori and a co-constructed emergent phenomenon. This view emphasizes that there is a *dialectical* relationship between a priori intention and emergent intention, both of which are motivated by attention. What remains significant is the need to discuss how this approach differs from understanding intention in current pragmatic theories and how it functions in ELF.

## 5.2 Intention in Current Pragmatic Theories

One of the main differences between the cognitive-philosophical approach to pragmatics and the sociocultural interactional approach is that the former considers intention *a prior mental state* of speakers that underpins communication, while the latter regards intention as a *post factum* construct that is achieved jointly through the dynamic emergence of meaning in conversation in which sociocultural factors play the leading role.[1] Since the two approaches represent two different perspectives, it would not make much sense to reject either of them entirely. According to SCA, the complexity of the issue requires that we consider both the prior and the co-constructed emergent sides of intention when analyzing communicative processes. This view was supported and illustrated clearly by the ELF example (1).

The notion of Gricean prior intention has received much criticism especially from sociocultural-interactional pragmatics (e.g., Verschueren 1999; Marmaridou 2000; Mey 2001; Haugh 2009). What Grice (1989 [1957], [1969]) suggested is that the communicator must overtly provide evidence of his/her intention to induce a belief in the hearer. This perspective fails to capture cases of unintentionally communicated meanings (e.g., Sperber and Wilson 1986/1995; Bach 1994; Gibbs 1999; Carston 2002). Additionally, what Grice does not acknowledge is that hearers can compute meanings without probing the speaker's intentions (e.g., Davis 1998; Arundale 1999, 2006, 2008; Marmaridou 2000; Gauker 2001, 2003; Haugh 2008). Moreover, the speaker may intend to communicate a meaning and have it gleaned by the hearer, while necessarily keeping this intention covert, as typified by lying and other forms of deception (see Dynel 2011). When Levinson (2006) called to elevate Gricean intentions to the center of cognition in interaction, Haugh (2008: 102) referred to this suggestion as a "somewhat reactionary move." Haugh (2008) and Arundale (2008) argued that one problem facing current models of inference that privileges the speaker's intention in determining whether communication has occurred (whether in moving from speaker intentions to communicative acts or vice versa) is the failure to "address how the participants themselves could come to know whether the recipient's inference and attribution regarding that intention is to any extent consistent with it" (Arundale 2008: 241). This conveys that there is no account in current intention-based models given to how speakers and hearers determine something has indeed been communicated.

What is more, interactional pragmatics also provides evidence of the difficulty of locating intentions relative to meanings in discourse (rather than simply relative to utterances). For instance, Haugh and Jaszczolt (2012) argued that in tracing intentions in conversational interaction, it becomes apparent that intentions can also be characterized as being 'emergent,' as both the speaker

[1] The notion of prior intention was initially proposed by Searle (1983: 165–166). Searle's (1983) work on intentionality introduced a distinction between prior intention and intention-in-action, the latter referring to "the proximal cause of the physiological chain leading to overt behaviour" (Ciaramidaro et al. 2007: 3106). In our understanding "intention-in-action" also refers to some kind of prior cause.

and the hearer jointly co-construct understandings of what is meant (Haugh 2008; Kecskes 2010b: 60–61). To demonstrate this, Haugh and Jaszczolt (2012) used Kecskes' example (2010b: 60) arguing that John's initial intention to give Peter a chance to talk about his trip is not realized in the excerpt in (2).

JOHN: Want to talk about your trip?
PETER: I don't know. If you have questions . . .
JOHN: OK, but you should tell me . . .
PETER: Wait, you want to hear about Irene?
JOHN: Well, what about her?
PETER: She is fine. She has . . . well . . . put on some weight, though.

I suggested that John's original intention is sidelined by Peter's talking about Irene, perhaps because he thinks John might want to know about her (being his former girlfriend). I also argued that "it was the conversational flow that led to this point, at which there appears a kind of emergent, co-constructed intention" (Kecskes 2010b: 61). Correspondingly, Haugh & Jaszczolt (2012) pointed out that there is growing evidence that we need to make clearer distinctions between speaker (intended) meaning which pertains to the subjective processing domain and the utterance level, and 'joint meaning,' which pertains to the interpersonal domain at the discourse level (Carassa & Colombetti 2009; Kecskes 2008, 2010b). Thus, different types of intentions arguably have different roles to play relative to these different types of meaning. In Chapter 2, I argued for discourse level creativity in ELF. So we need to examine how this creativity of ELF speakers is put to use to express joint meaning in discourse segments, and what role prior intention and emergent intention play in that process.

## 5.3 The Interplay of Intention and Attention in the Socio-cognitive Approach (SCA)

In the SCA, the interplay of cooperation-directed intention and egocentrism-governed attention is the main driving force in meaning production and comprehension. Cooperation signifies that attention is paid to other speakers' intention. Successful communication requires communicators to recognize that others' perspectives may differ from their own, and that other people may not always know what they mean (cf. Keysar & Henly 2002; Kecskes 2014). SCA posits a dialectical relationship between intention and attention. As previously argued, the pragmatic view (cooperation centered) and the cognitive view (egocentrism centered) are concerned about intention and attention in an isolated way. There is no explicit explanation of the relations between intention and attention. Also, relevance theory defines relevance by effects of both attention and intention, but does not distinguish the two effects and never clarifies their relations explicitly, as revealed by their claim that "an input (a sight, a sound, an utterance, a memory) is relevant to an individual when it connects with background information he has available to yield conclusions that matter to him" (Wilson & Sperber 2004: 3).

### *5.3.1 Intention*

With regard to intention, the socio-cognitive view does two things: On the one hand, it incorporates the Searlean understanding of the term (Searle 1983), and on the other, it extends the notion to emphasize the dynamism of intention and its emergent nature. So the SCA not only considers the centrality of intention in conversation, as the cognitive-philosophical approach has done, but also takes into account the dynamic process in which the intention can be an emergent effect of the conversation. In this framework, intention is considered a dynamically changing phenomenon that is the main organizing force, together with attention, in the communicative process. Intention is not only private, individual, pre-planned and a precursor to action; it is also emergent and social. Let me make clear that I am not talking about a dichotomy here; rather, a priori intention and emergent intention are two sides of the same phenomenon that may receive different emphasis at different points in the communicative process. This is why we need to discuss this issue in regard to ELF as ELF interactions usually rely on emergent intention and much less on prior intention. When a conversation is started, the private and pre-planned nature of intention may be dominant. However, in the course of conversation, the emergent and social nature of the phenomenon may come to the fore. These two sides of intention are always present. The only question is *to what extent* they are present at any given moment of the communicative process. This view does not contradict Searle's (1983: 3) claim that intentionality is directedness; intending to do something is just one kind of intentionality among others. It is also in line with Joas's (1996: 158) claim that intentionality consists of the self-reflective control we exercise over our current behavior.

The basic property that renders intention a central element of communication is its functionality. There is always a reason and/or a goal behind a conversation; without intention, there would be no need to initiate communication, and we could hardly make any sense of this social action. In fact, Searle (1983) considered intention, along with other mental acts such as perception, desire, and belief, as prerequisites to communication. Let me highlight one more time that communication is a process in which intention is formed, expressed, and interpreted. From the speaker's perspective, intention is something that s/he bears in mind prior to the utterance; alternatively, it is generated in the course of conversation and expressed in the form of utterances. From the hearer's or analyst's perspective, intention of a speaker is something that is processed by the hearer simultaneously with the utterance, or after it has been completed. The primary intention expressed in a particular situation serves the function of guiding the conversation. Knowledge or information explicated in linguistic forms, implied connotation, along with inferable background, all get united to achieve comprehension and communication under the driving force of intention. One could possibly argue that this is just one side of intention. The emergent side of intention is co-constructed by the participants in the dynamic flow of conversation. This means that intention is not necessarily just an a priori phenomenon but, as we have said, it can also be generated and changed during the communicative process. This dynamism is reflected in emerging utterances: they may be interrupted and started again, which is an especially frequent phenomenon in ELF. It is not only the context, but also the dynamism of the conversational flow and the process of formulating an utterance that likewise affect and change the intention. Communicators change their mind within an utterance and start to speak about something else. To make my point clear, let us now look into the following excerpt in which three Brazilian au pair girls (BIF/BNF/BSF), a man from Hong Kong (HKM), a woman from Columbia (CDF), and a German female student (GMF) discuss the living circumstances of the au pair girls.

(3) BNF: . . . I can drive.
HKM: How about the others? How about you?
BIF: I have my own car, too. And . . . errh . . . I . . . I can use the car wherever I went . . .
HKM: Hmm.
BIF: . . . but I . . . just cannot go to . . . to New York or some cities that is big.
HKM: Hmm.
BIF: You know, but it is, it is normal. But it is just . . . errh . . .
HKM: Hmm.
BIF: . . . a regular thing.
HKM: So everyone is satisfied with that? They give you . . . It is quite ok, you know, you have your car, even though they limit the miles you can use the car for . . . It's still all right. So give you a kind of freedom.
BIF/BNF/BSF: Yeah. BNF: A little.
HKM: That's very important. Because in America it is impossible to be without a car.
BIF/BNF/BSF: Yeah.
HKM: Errh. I remember when I first came to this country, first thing I did . . . second day . . . errh . . . is to buy a car.
(All giggle.)
HKM: I came here on Friday. I bought a car on Saturday. (Giggle a little.) Just look around, you know . . .
CDF: But . . . how about your license, driving license?
HKM: I have the international . . .
CDF: Oh. The international license will work here.

HKM: Errh . . . of course after a time you can get a US license.
BSF: It is really easy.
HKM: It is not a big deal . . . It is very easy.
HKM: You want to say something.
BSF: I just wanted to say I don't have a car. That's kind of . . . not so nice taking the bus all the time, going shopping by bus, so whatever, so . . .
HKM: Hmm. You have to do your own shopping?
BSF: Sometimes my landlady gives me a ride . . . but a lot of the times I just take the bus so . . . I miss this because if I get my car, I can go wherever I want . . .
HKM: Hmm.
BSF: . . . and don't have to ask for a ride. Here I don't go to parties. Usually I don't go anywhere . . . like. How do I come back? I don't know. So you don't go. So, yeah . . .
HKM: Yeah. In Germany, you don't need a car, because . . .
GMF: I have my bike.
HKM: Yeah.
GMF: . . . by bike.
HKM: Here, it is . . . a must to have a car.
GMF: Hmm.
HKM: So you cannot live without it, so it's absolutely impossible . . . so . . . .

As we can see, the first part of the conversation is dominated by HKM. His intention is to make the Brazilian girls talk about their experience with driving a car in the United States. When he sees that the exchange is slowing down, he puts in a brief summary of what was said and some personal experience. Then, the Columbian woman steps in with a question about international license. The conversation flow gets a new trigger when BSF declares that she does not have a car with the intention to tell her story. When she finishes, HKM steps in and turns to the German student to ask for her input. What needs to be emphasized here is that newer and newer intentions emerge which are formulated by different participants during the course of the conversation. Hearers compute meanings without probing the speaker's original intentions; they, in fact, step in with the thought on their own mind. The whole conversation is characterized by the dynamism of expressing and triggering intention.

### *5.3.2 Attention*

Attention is closely related to intention; it refers to those cognitive resources available to interlocutors that make communication a conscious action. When intention is formed, expressed, and interpreted in the process of communication, attention contributes to the various stages of the process with different strength. As it happens, three factors will affect salience of knowledge and ease of attentional processing in all stages: (a) interlocutors' knowledge based on prior experience; (b) frequency, familiarity, or conventionality of knowledge tied to the situation; and (c) the interlocutors' mental state and/or the availability of attentional resources. Based on these three factors, the knowledge most salient to the interlocutors in a particular situation is the information that is included in their knowledge base, is pertinent to the current situation and is processed by the necessary attentional resources. No matter what mental state the interlocutors are in or at which stage of the communication they are operating, the most salient knowledge will be available as a result of the interplay of these three factors. This is demonstrated quite well in example (3) where BSF relates her prior (and present) experience about not having a car. The relevance of the issue is triggered by the topic on having a car in the United States. As you can see, what is most salient for BSF is her own experience concerning availability to a car.

All stages in the communicative process require the commitment of attention in order for successful communication to occur. Cognitive research (e.g., Giora 2003; Barr & Keysar 2005; Colston &Katz 2005) has documented the interlocutors' egocentric behavior in the process of communication. However, 'egocentrism' is not a negative term as discussed earlier. It refers to the state of mind of the interlocutor, who can hardly control this phenomenon because it is the result of the individual's prior experience and emergent present experience. *Egocentrism means that interlocutors act under the influence of the most salient information that comes to their mind in the given actual situational context both in production and comprehension.* Consequently, the speaker will use the linguistic resources (e.g., the lexical units) most salient for expressing his/her communicative intentions and/or goals; similarly, the hearer will cooperate by capturing those salient units and assigning them a proper place in the communicational process. Because of their different knowledge bases, the frequency/rituality of their knowledge in the situation, and the attendant attentional resources available to them for processing the salient items, the interlocutors' knowledge has different levels of salience. As a result, they conduct the attentional processing of communication in an egocentric manner.

There are specific ways in which attention contributes to different stages of communication as characterized by the processes of intention. When intention is formed, attention plays a crucial role. Consider the following excerpt from the conversation in example (3).

(4) HKM: You want to say something.
BSF: I just wanted to say I don't have a car. That's kind of . . . not so nice taking the bus all the time, going shopping by bus, so whatever, so . . .
HKM: Hmm. You have to do your own shopping?

This exchange reveals that HKM notices that BSF wants to say something. His intention is to give BSF a chance to talk. BSF intends to say that not everyone has a car; she does not either. As a result, when expressing intention in an utterance, the speaker also needs the necessary attention, so as to formulate the utterance in a comprehensible way.

The frequency or familiarity of the intention and especially of the linguistic expression in question determines the extent of attentional processing. For instance, greetings require less attentional resources and appear more automatic than the utterance above that changes the flow of conversation to some extent; the latter being less frequent and also harder to process. When intention is interpreted by the hearer, the amount of attentional resources needed is similarly proportional to the resources required in the formulation of intention. The person being greeted can easily comprehend the speaker's intention and respond to it in an effortless way. However, in example (4), HKM may need to undertake some effort in order to read the intention of BSF and deploy the relevant reaction. His response shows that he has done this: 'Hmm. You have to do your own shopping?' As you can see, he infers from BSF's utterance that one of her main problems is doing shopping without a car. Intention directs attention to relevant information resources so that the intention can be realized, and communication can be conducted in a coherent and comprehensible way. By selecting those resources, intention becomes central to the processing of communication.

The sociocultural background has an overall influence on the interplay of intention and attention. The interlocutors' prior knowledge directs their attention to becoming aware of different features, or different parts, of the same phenomenon. For example, a person who has a car and another one who does not, may form different views when talking about driving a car, as happened in the above example. Also as a consequence of this, different intentions may be formed, and the effect of interplay is also affected by the accessibility of the knowledge. As a result, communication is achieved with intentional action guaranteed by attentional processing; both are motivated by the common sociocultural background (environment). In this process, interlocutors are both cooperative (in terms of intention) and egocentric (in terms of attention). The part of knowledge that is relevant to intention, salient to attention and available in the sociocultural background will contribute to successful communication.

## 5.4 The Interplay of Recipient Design and Salience in Expressing and Comprehending Intention

I have argued that a speaker's utterance when formulating intention is shaped not only by recipient design but also by salience effect (Kecskes 2017). When fitting words into actual situational contexts, the speaker is driven not only by the intention that the hearer recognizes what is meant as intended by the speaker, but also by individual salience that affects production subconsciously. The interplay of these social (recipient design) and individual (salience) factors shapes speaker utterance. Recipient design is the result of being cooperative, which, according to Grice, is a part of human rationality. I, however, claimed that individual egocentrism that results in individual salience is just as much part of human rationality as cooperation (see Kecskes 2017). Nothing in fact shows this interplay better than ELF interactions where individual saliency of interlocutors cooperates to co-construct meaning. Example (5) demonstrates this matter quite well. The participants are HKM: a male from Hong Kong; CZM: a male from China; BSF, BIF, BNF: au pair girls from Brazil; TYF: a female from Thailand; and GMF: a female from Germany. They are discussing the issue of making friends in America.

(5) HKM: Do you think it's . . . it's kind of difficult for you to make friends here with Americans?
CZM: Hmm.
HKM: . . . generally, you know . . .
BSF: Yeah.
HKM: . . . or it's more directly than it is in China . . .
TYF: Yeah.
HKM: . . . in Singapore or that . . . it's more difficult . . . What do you think so? Why it's more difficult?
GMF: I am maybe, thinking, it's because . . . I don't know . . .
CZM: I would say the culture issue is the most thing. Because, you know, the background is different and errh . . . even the value is maybe different.
BIF: Yeah. But we have a lot of friends from other countries.
CZM: Aha.
BIF: and we . . . we really met with each other . . .
BNF: Yeah.
BIF: . . . we aren't from Americans, I don't know why.
CZM: Oh.
BSF: The Americans all the times, I guess would know how are you but they don't really want to know how you are.
CZM: Yeah.
BIF: Yeah. Yeah.
BSF: Oh, how are you, or whatever.
BNF/BIF: Yeah. Yeah. It's more . . . but it's not working. That's true.
BIF: And we have Germanies . . . Thai . . .
BNF: Thailand girls . . . and whatever . . .
BIF: . . . errh . . . and some African friends.
CZM: You don't have a friend from China? (giggling) No?
(giggling)
BIF/BSF/BNF: No. We are sorry.
(giggling)
BIF: But anyway . . . you know . . .
HKM: Ok.

Here the whole conversation is a collection of individual utterances that are about the same topic (making friends) but those utterances do not create a coherent sequence. Everybody says what is on his/her mind, what is salient for him/her based on prior experience without paying much attention to what has been said previously by others. And, there is little recipient design. But this is not necessarily a typical ELF conversation. It is one where individual saliency plays a more dominant role than cooperation in the traditional sense (not in the Gricean sense though!). It is not that the participants are not cooperative; they are, since they speak about the same topic (cooperative in the Gricean sense). But what they say is more about what they think, what is on their mind about the topic, rather than response to what others think or say.

Now we need to focus on some details about recipient design and salience. The term 'recipient design' derives from Conversational Analysis where it means the adaptation of communicative behavior to a particular addressee (Garfinkel 1967). This is one instance of audience/recipient design (Clark & Carlson 1982), in which utterances are constructed according to what others in the communicative exchange know and believe (Clark 1996). Audience design has been investigated in speech and actions in both naturalistic and experimental settings (Holler and Stevens 2007; Jacobs and Garnham 2007; O'Neill et al. 2005; Ozyurek 2002), but, according to Newman-Norlund et al. (2009) there is still considerable debate over when, how, and why it is used. As a matter of fact, the undecided issue is whether audience/recipient design is structurally linked to initial attempts to communicate, or whether it is used parsimoniously to repair erroneous attempts. Some researchers support a socio-centric approach, in which communicative behavior is designed by taking into account the knowledge and characteristics of the addressee that are assumed to be part of common ground (Clark 1996; Isaacs & Clark 1987; Nadig & Sedivy 2002). Others claim that the initial planning of utterances ignores common ground (egocentric approach), and that messages are adapted to addressees only when adjustments are required (Horton & Keysar 1996; Keysar et al. 1998).

As it was mentioned before, the socio-cognitive approach proposed by Kecskes (2008, 2010, 2014) attempts to blend the two views, and argues that both cooperation and egocentrism are present in the communication process all the time to varying degrees, and the interplay of conscious recipient design (result of cooperation) and subconscious salience (driving force behind egocentrism) is what shapes speaker's production and affects hearer's comprehension. As example (6) demonstrates, salience effect is important in ELF production and comprehension. So we will need to see how it works in ELF.

## 5.5 Understanding Salience in General and in ELF in Particular

### *5.5.1 What Is Salience?*

Salience, as a semiotic notion, refers to the relative importance or prominence of signs. The relative salience of a particular sign, when considered in the context of others, helps an individual to quickly rank large amounts of information by importance and thus give attention to that which is most important. We tend to overestimate the causal role of information (salience) we have available to us both perceptually and linguistically. In pragmatics, based on Giora's Graded Salience Hypothesis (GSH hereafter; Giora 1997, 2003), when we speak about salient information we usually mean information that *the hearer assumes* to be in central place in the speaker's consciousness when the speaker produces the utterance. It is the most probable out of all possible (Kecskes 2014). This is what we can call hearer's salience. The socio-cognitive approach differs from the GSH in that it argues that salience affects not only hearer's interpretation but also speaker's production (Kecskes 2014). However, this speaker's salience works differently from hearer's salience as we will see later. The socio-cognitive approach incorporates the GSH to a significant extent, but it does not accept all of its tenets. GSH basically is hearer-centered, while SCA focuses on both production and comprehension. So it is both hearer- and speaker-centered. The focus of GSH is on linguistic salience, specifically meaning salience in comprehension. GSH deals with lexical processing, whereas SCA's concern is both lexical (linguistic) salience and perceptual salience. While GSH uses 'context' in the sense of actual situational context, SCA emphasizes the difference and interplay between prior context encoded in lexical items and images and actual situational context (see discussion in Section 5.5.2).

The photo in Figure 5.1 shows how important perceptual salience is. It can be especially powerful if it is intertwined with linguistic salience.

As you may know, the acronym 'FCUK' stands for 'French Connection United Kingdom.' However, when someone looks at the photo the most salient meaning that comes to his/her mind has nothing to do with French Connection UK. The photo triggers a taboo word with a slightly different spelling. The salient effect is so strong that no actual situational context can override it.

The main claim of the GSH is that salient information is superior to less salient information (Giora 2003: 15), and often, though not always, to unstored information, such as novel information or information inferable from context (see Giora 2003, 10–11; also Peleg et al. 2001). As a consequence of this superiority, salient meanings of lexical units (e.g., conventional, frequent, familiar, or prototypical meanings) are processed automatically, irrespective of contextual information and strength of bias. Although context (actual

Figure 5.1 The perceptual salience triggered by the brand name

situational context) effects may be fast, they run in parallel with lexical processes and initially do not interact with them (Giora 2003, 24). In ELF, stored information is L1-dominated with less impact from L2. Context effect is more universal than language specific. It is based on world knowledge rather than knowledge of the world through a particular language, as has been discussed in the previous chapter.

Thus, according to the GSH in language processing, both salient information and contextual knowledge run in parallel, and salient information may not be filtered out even when it is contextually inappropriate. This is especially so in ELF where actual situational context, contrary to L1 communication, rarely serves as a socio-cognitive frame to help interlocutors make sense of utterances. This claim basically questions context dependency, which is one of the main tenets of current pragmatic theories.[2] While salience, according to the GSH, mainly concerns the storage of knowledge as a function of degree of familiarity, frequency, prototypicality, and conventionality, salience in SCA refers to the contingent effect of salient knowledge as a result of the attentional processing of communication in a particular situation, which facilitates or hampers the expression of intention and the subsequent achievement of communicative effects.

[2] This means that context may not have priority in defining actual situational meaning of lexical units. Occasionally lexical items can make their own context (see Gumperz 1982; Levinson 2003; Kecskes 2014).

Moreover, another significant difference between GSH and SCA is that the GSH emphasizes the importance of stored information, while SCA considers salience to be both a stored (inherent salience and collective salience) and an emergent entity (actual situational salience). According to GSH (Giora 2003: 15), for information to be salient – to be foremost on a person's mind – it needs to undergo consolidation, that is, to be stored or coded in the mental lexicon, which usually happens as through the process of conventionalization. Stored information is superior to unstored information, such as novel information or information inferable from the context: While salient information is highly accessible, nonsalient information requires strongly supportive contextual information to become as accessible as is salient information. At this point, Giora seems to equate salient information with consolidated/stored information and nonsalient information with unstored information. This is somewhat questionable because it considers salience as a relatively static property that changes mainly diachronically. According to Giora, in order for something to be salient, it should be stored in the memory. What is ranked as "the most salient meaning" at the present moment may die off after only a few decades. An example of such diachronical change is the word 'gentleman,' whose most salient meaning in the past century was 'nobleman, honorable man'; nowadays, this meaning would rank below that of 'a polite or formal way of referring to a man.'

Salient information can be 'disconsolidated' when its salience dies off and the information in question ends up as less salient or nonsalient. Giora's approach acknowledges diachronic change, but does not talk about synchronic change. In contrast, SCA emphasizes that salience is in a continual state of change not only diachronically but synchronically as well (emergent situational salience) as a result of the interplay of linguistic salience and perceptual salience. This is especially true in ELF but also in L1 communication. The following conversation in L1 English shows the interplay of linguistic salience and perceptual salience (Kecskes 2014).

(6) ALLEN and SHERRY (of the sitcom *Two and a Half Men*) are sitting in a restaurant. Allan's right eye is covered with a bandage so he does not see Sherry very well.

ALLEN: -You know, Sherry, I would really like to see more of you.

SHERRY: - Maybe, we should wait and see how the night goes.

ALLEN: - Oh, no. I mean I have only got one good eye. Can we change places?

SHERRY: - Sure.

The conversation demonstrates that Sherry completely misunderstood Allan's utterance 'I would really like to see more of you.' This may be due to the fact that she relied exclusively on linguistic salience and ignored perceptual salience in processing the utterance. Some studies referred to the fact that inherent linguistic salience seems to override perceptual salience in most cases. For instance, Osgood and Bock's (1977) study claimed that the effects of inherent salience consistently trumped those that would need to gain salience from speaker motivation. Correspondingly, Lupyan and Spivey (2010) reached a somewhat similar conclusion when they argued that language dynamically modulates visual processing.

Now we shall examine how salience affects production and comprehension. The focus of SCA on the interlocutor as a speaker-hearer results in a claim according to which there is a difference in salience effect between scenarios where the interlocutor acts as speaker and where s/he acts as hearer (Kecskes 2008: 401). This issue is especially important for ELF speakers, as we will see.

### *5.5.2 Inter-label Hierarchy Affects Speaker's Choice*

When a lexical unit (labeled for private context) is used by a speaker to produce an utterance, private contexts (prior experience of the speaker) attached to this lexical expression are activated top-down in a hierarchical order by salience. For the speaker, there is primarily an inter-label hierarchy (which item to select out of all possible ones), while for the hearer intra-label hierarchy (which out of all possible interpretations of the lexical item) hits first. The inter-label hierarchy operates in the first phase of production, when a speaker looks for words or expressions to express her/his communicative intention. As a first step, s/he has to select from a group of possibilities in order to express his/her intention. These words or expressions constitute a hierarchy from the best fit to those less suited to the idea s/he is trying to express. To explain how this works in ELF we will analyze an excerpt from the conversation of a woman from Poland (PAF) and a man from Hong Kong (HKM), a woman from Columbia (CDF) and a female student from Germany (GMF).

(7) PAF: My problem ... (Giggling) I think my problem is I scared of speaking English. I am not so open like ...
HKM: Hmm.
PAF: I ...
HKM: But you speak five minutes without stopping, you know. (All giggle.) What if you ... I am not ... very ... (All giggle.)
PAF: Of course, so ... so long.
HKM: Yeah. You have a very nice monologue there, basically with very rare number of mistakes. You know, so what's your problem? I don't understand ... How about you? What do you think ... ?
CDF: Actually everybody can understand what you are saying.
GMF: You speak slowly, that's good.
HKM: Hmm.
GMF: We understand ...
HKM: Hmm.
PAF: ... I have to think. (All giggle.)

HKM: . . . that's your monitors.., what you have said, you know. What comes out basically not bad, so . . . [hmm.] Of course again, another question is practice, but . . . the others said, I've said, . . . your English is not bad at all.. How about understanding, comprehensive?
PAF: I think I can understand almost everything.

In this example, the Polish woman starts with a statement: 'I think my problem is I **scared of** speaking English,' and she has several options to express that she is frightened when she must speak English: I fear speaking English, I am afraid of speaking English, I am frightened to speak English, etc. What comes to her mind first is not the best option: 'I scared of.' In fact, inter-label hierarchy is usually poorly handled by ELF speakers because of their limited options of word choice in the target language and the transfer push of L1. It is highly probable that the Polish woman used the expressions 'scare of' because she knew that intense fear can be expressed by the word 'scare,' or the choice was simply affected by her L1. She was quite emotional so that pushed away all other possible options even if she had any more.

From the perspective of inter-label hierarchy, it is also interesting to look at what the man from Hong Kong says when he asks for the Polish woman's opinion about her problem: 'I don't understand . . . *How about you? What do you think* . . . ?' He uses two different phrases to get the Polish woman's take on the situation. This is very common in ELF conversation. Speakers want to make sure that their partners understand them properly so they may use not one but two or even three different phrases (if they have that many) from their inter-label salience hierarchy to make sure that everybody understands what they want.

### *5.5.3 Intra-label Hierarchy*

Now we should look at how salience works for the interlocutor when s/he is in the role of hearer. The hearer has to cope with a different type of hierarchy than the speaker from her/his perspective. Thus, an intra-label hierarchy is in force when the hearer processes a lexical unit(s) in an utterance (or even an entire utterance). The label (word) uttered by the speaker hierarchically triggers the history of that particular label as used or experienced previously by the hearer (but not by the speaker). This may also be a reason for misunderstanding in the communicative process, both in L1 and ELF interactions. Compare the following (source: American sitcom) exchange in (9):

(8) BOB: Are you OK?
MARY: I am fine.
BOB: I know you are fine, but are you OK?

What we have here is that Bob has had several options to ask about Mary's well-being: 'Are you OK?,' 'Are you fine?,' 'Is everything all right?,' etc. His selection of 'Are you OK?' caused a slight misunderstanding between the two because they interpreted 'OK' differently, very individually. This happens in ELF interactions even more frequently than in L1 communication. I must refer back to example (3) in the previous chapter in which a native speaker of English is having a conversation with a Thai female student. He wants to know whether she likes sports. The Thai student initially says she likes 'football' and then immediately replaces that with 'soccer.'

(9) NNS (Thai woman)- NS (American woman)

NS: - . . . .So do you like sports?
NNS: - I love sports.
NS: - What sports do you love?
NNS: - I love football.. Op- in here we call soccer.
NS: - Oh okay.

In replacing 'football' with 'soccer,' NNS probably wanted to provide NS with an accurate identification of the sport she liked. In the NNS's mind 'football' is the label that has priority based on her L1-experience.

So far we have seen that salience is both an individual and a societal phenomenon. Prior and actual situational experience is privatized/subjectivized and prioritized in the mind of interlocutors. Their different prior experiences, their different evaluations of the actual situational context, their dynamically changing intentions and individual degrees of salience result in a subjectivized process of production and comprehension. As a result, there may be no single point in the recovery process at which a speaker's utterance *fully* matches a hearer's interpretation. This is because both a speaker's production and a hearer's interpretation are 'contaminated' by individualized pragmatic elements. Pragmatic enrichment processes work differently for speaker-hearers depending on which role they are in. Consequently, the match between the two sides keeps varying in the communicative process. This is why we think that, "we almost always fail. . . . Yet we almost always nearly succeed" (Rapaport 2003: 402). And this is why a pragmatic theory should be an interlocutor-centered one that takes the individual as a speaker-hearer. Speaker's production and hearer's interpretation should be analyzed on their own merits but we should not forget that human beings are speaker-hearers with one individual mind.

## 5.6 How Does Speaker's Utterance Express Speaker's Intention?

### *5.6.1 Inductive and Deductive Sequences*

Let me one more time go over the fact that, according to SCA, recipient design is when the speaker constructs a model of the hearer's knowledge relevant to the given situational context. Although this sounds idealistic, it is, in fact, not exactly what happens in an everyday communication especially not in ELF, which appears to be a mixture of consciously designed and subconsciously, automatically and ad-hoc generated utterances. It seems to me that the cognitive approach is not quite right when it claims that the initial planning of utterances ignores common ground, and that messages are adapted to addressees only when adjustments are required (Horton & Keysar 1996; Keysar et al. 1998). What really takes place is both conscious planning and formulating of intention and/or subconscious formulating. So, as was argued above, both recipient design and salience affect the process. However, the two factors affect the communicative process to varying degrees. This can be demonstrated through the following two excerpts. I want to emphasize here that the two excerpts are ideal for demonstrating my points. I deliberately selected sequences that help me make my claim: recipient design usually results in inductive sequences while salience effect leads to a deductive sequence. In everyday conversations it is very difficult to find sequences that show so clearly how inductive and deductive sequences are built up.

(10) Sacks (1992, II: 147)
1 Ann: I'm reading one of uh Harold Sherman's books.
2 Bea: Mm hm,
3 Ann: I think we read one, one time, about life after death'r
4 something.
5 Bea: Mm hm,
6 Ann: And uh, this is How Tuh Make uh ESP Work For You.
7 Bea: Mm hm,
8 Ann: And it's excellent.
9 Bea: Well, when you get through [with it
10 Ann: [And he talks about-

According to the recipient design view, in order to succeed, speakers must correctly express intended illocutionary acts by using appropriate words, and make their attempt in an adequate context. In this process, speakers relate propositional contents to the world (actual situational context; audience) with the intention of establishing a correspondence between words and things from a certain direction of fit. This is what happened in the Sacks example (10). Pomerantz and Heritage (2012: 211) explained the Sacks' sequence as follows: "Ann was sharing information with Bea about a book that she was reading. Instead of initially identifying the book by its title, she first identified it by the author (line 1), then mentioned a book by that author that they both had read (lines 3–4), and then gave the title of the book (line 6)." Sacks (1992, II: 149) commented the interaction in the following way: "That she goes through that kind of work to find a way to refer to the book is a most elegant sort of evidence that one does work at finding a description for something, and does have a preference, if one can use it, for building such a description as will permit the other to see that you know that they know what you are talking about."

I believe that the explanation of both Pomerantz and Heritage, and Sacks refers to a careful recipient design in which subconscious salience does not intrude. The description is a well-built inductive sequence by Ann. The next excerpt from a movie, however, shows an entirely different picture.

(11) From the movie *Angel Eyes*.
SITUATION: A policewoman (PW) in uniform is driving the car, and the man (M) sitting beside her is starring at her.
PW: - What?
M: - I was trying to picture you without your clothes on.
PW: - Excuse me?
M: - Oh no, I did not mean like that. I am trying to picture your without your uniform.
PW: - Okaay?
M: - I mean, on your day off, you know, in regular clothes.

Example (11) demonstrates a process different from what we saw in example (10). The latter represents a deductively built-up sequence. *Salience effect usually results in deductive sequences where the speaker has something on his/her mind, and this intention is formulated abruptly, rather carelessly, without specific planning,* as seems to be the case in example (11). This excerpt appears to support the claim of cognitive psychologists according to which the initial planning of utterances ignores common ground (egocentric approach), and messages are adapted to addressees only when adjustments are required (Horton & Keysar 1996; Keysar et al. 1998). *It looks like recipient design usually requires an inductive process that is carefully planned while salience effect generally appears in the form of a deductive process that may contain repairs and adjustments.*

We need to go into an in-depth analysis of what is going on in example (11): why were the man's attempts unsuccessful in the conversation? On the one hand, we have the speaker with an intention to tell the woman the reason he was looking at her the way he did; and on the other hand, there is subconscious salience that affected how he formulated his intention. So the utterance was not designed by the speaker's intention to fit his words into the actual situational context, taking into account his partner. It was an abrupt, subconscious action that resulted in wrong word selection. The nagging question is: why was word selection wrong? The short answer is that it was not directed by recipient design but was prompted by salience effect. As we have argued, salience, which operates subconsciously and automatically, may affect word selection and utterance formulation.

Let us look into the utterance 'I was trying to picture you without your clothes on.' Is this really what the speaker wanted to say and mean? I believe that the answer is: yes, *this is exactly what he wanted to mean but not necessarily what he wanted to say.* I agree with Bach (2005) that a speaker can always mean something distinct from the semantic content of the sentence he is uttering. But even if he speaks literally, and means precisely what his words mean, even that fact depends on his communicative intention (Bach 2005: 27). Wording – expressing intention in words – is a tricky thing. *Conceptualization is one thing, wording is another and meaning is a third.* There is no one-to-one relationship between any of the three.

Let us look at the difference between the three formulations of one and the same intention.

A) I was trying to picture you without your clothes on.
B) I am trying to picture you without your uniform.
C) I mean, on your day off, you know, in regular clothes.

As you can see, A and B are very similar because they both use the preposition 'without,' and the only difference is that B narrows down the concept of 'clothes' to 'uniform.' The impact is the same: the hearer is upset. Collective salience is, in effect, woman, without clothes. C, however, shows careful recipient design through well-selected words and utterance formulation. C is a repair to two unsuccessful attempts. Not using 'without' but rather 'in' clothes, and further specified by the expression 'on your day off' so there is no misunderstanding here. In sum, we can say that A and B appear to have been affected by salience while C is the result of careful recipient design.

So, what was wrong with A and B? Why did wording create the effect it did? It seems that subconscious, rather abrupt, automatic formulation of intention may have prompted expressions that were unwanted, uncontrolled and unfit in the actual situational context. This, of course, does not mean that salience effect always results in problematic utterances. Most of the time subconscious, automatic reactions prompt perfectly understandable utterances even in ELF.

### *5.6.2 Deductive, Salience-Affected Sequences in ELF*

Most of the time, ELF interactions are deductive sequences in which salience is dominant, and there is not too much recipient design. Emergent factor rather than prior intention drives the conversations in which individual discourse creativity, reliance on ad hoc created language and actual situational context-dictated factors, rather than formulas or well-planned utterances, abrupt word selection and plenty of repairs characterize the exchanges. Example (12) can be considered a typical ELF conversation between a man from Hong Kong and a student from Columbia in which salience effect dominates but there is recipient design as well.

(12) Hong Kong man (HKM) and Columbia student (CDM)

HKM : How long have you been here?
CDM: Ah . . . . Just three months, you know . . .
HKM: Three months. You just start it. The program. So it is the first semester, basically.
CDM: Yes.
HKM: Yes? And why do you . . . chemistry? I don't know . . . what . . .
CDM: Because I . . . like it and errh . . . my family . . .
HKM: You have come from Columbia, right?
CDM: Yeah, right.
HKM: And did you do some kind of studies there, in high school?
CDM: Yeah. They teach us chemistry, physics. Oh, everything.
HKM: You study chemistry when you were in high school? Yeah?
CDM: Yeah. In high school.
HKM: Ok.
CDM: Yeah. physics, calculus, in high school, we have to take these subjects.
HKM: ok.
CDM: It's not an option, you obviously . . .
HKM: Ok, good. And this is why you have to take chemistry, right?
CDM: Yes. Errh . . . because . . . errh . . . you know, everybody in the family, have the different field, like . . . you know, my, my aunt, is a . . . a lawyer . . . [HKM: Hmm.] . . . errh . . . my cousin is a physicist. [HKM: Hmm.] . . . and my brother is in business field.
HKM: And you didn't want to do . . .
CDM: Right. I want something different. Yeah. [HKM: Hmm.] We have a doctor, [HKM: Hmm.] already in the family . . . and . . .
HKM: You mention that . . . you came here because in New York City, basically, you . . . spoke Spanish for most of the time, yeah? [CDM: Yeah, yeah.] . . . and here the situation is different so . . . do you have the opportunity to speak Spanish . . . Who do you talk Spanish to?
CDM: Nobody.
HKM: Nobody?
CDM: No. Oh, I met a Columbia . . . Oh, her. [HKM: Yeah.] . . . she is from Columbia. And . . .
HKM: Do you m . . . meet her here or . . . ?
CDM/CFF: Yeah. CDM: We met here.
HKM: So she is from Columbia. What a remarkable kind of coincidence here.
CDM/CFF: Yeah.
HKM: You just meet her here.
CDM: Hmm.
HKM: Good. And you talk to her in Spanish, yeah?
CDM: Yes.

It is somewhat clear that HKM wants to know why CDM studies chemistry. So his questions are quite well planned (recipient design) but most of the time they depend on the response of CDM. When CDM mentions his family HKM has a side-question right away:

> CDM: Because I . . . like it and errh . . . my family . . .
> HKM: You have come from Columbia, right?

Salience effect is well demonstrated in CDM's responses. When he is asked about high school he does not restrict his answer to what was asked but starts to talk about high school in general: what subjects they studied there.

> HKM: And did you do some kind of studies there, in high school?
> CDM: Yeah. They teach us chemistry, physics. Oh, everything.
> HKM: You study chemistry when you were in high school? Yeah?
> CDM: Yeah. In high school.
> HKM: Ok.
> CDM: Yeah. physics, calculus, in high school, we have to take these subjects.

It is very interesting to note that both HKM and CDM use unfinished utterances that the other interlocutor uses as a trigger to say what is on his mind:

> CDM: It's not an option, you obviously . . .
> HKM: And you didn't want to do . . .

There is also clear recipient design in some of the utterances of both speakers. For instance, HKM changes the subject from chemistry to speaking languages. His understanding is that CDM has come to New York because he thought he could speak more English there. He wants to find out if CDM still has the chance to speak Spanish.

> HKM: You mention that . . . you came here because in New York City, basically, you . . . spoke Spanish for most of the time, yeah? [CDM: Yeah, yeah.] . . . and here the situation is different so . . . do you have the opportunity to speak Spanish . . . Who do you talk Spanish to?

What this sequence showed us is the clear interplay of recipient design and salience in ELF with a slight dominance of the latter.

### *5.6.3 Consequences of Salience Dominance*

It can be claimed that when salience dominates ELF interaction it may result in two things: unwanted ways of expressing intention and slight misunderstandings. I deliberately use the word 'slight' because misunderstandings are always worked out relatively easily in ELF interactions. The following conversation is an example of the first (unwanted way of expressing intention).

(13) Turkish student (T) and Korean student (K) are talking about where the Turk comes from:

T: - I don't know Albany exactly. But if I compare to my country Albany is better. Because I live in a big city in my country.
K: - Ah I see.
T: - So the city exactly names is Ankara.
K: - Ah.
T: - Ankara is dirty.
K: - Dirty? (laughing)
T: - Yes. Too many people. So it's too many noise. It's a problem. I think so . . . .
K: - So you like Albany . . .
T: - Yes I like Albany because there are not many people in Albany. And there are too many trees . . . for . . . forest?

As you can see, the Turkish student said 'Ankara is dirty.' The word 'dirty' may not have been the best way to express his opinion about Ankara but that was what had come to his mind (salience effect). That word was the highest on the salience inter-label hierarchy. The utterance caused a problem because the Korean understood the word in its direct sense. He laughed and questioned whether the Turk really meant what he said. Seeing that the Korean was surprised the Turk started to explain in detail what he meant.

The next excerpt demonstrates what happens when the salience-triggered word choice results in a slight misunderstanding:

(14) Japanese (J) and Chinese (C) students are talking.
J: - I start this August.
C: - August. Right. We have the same time. I'm only two months. I came here . . . right here . . . on August . . . also . . . yeah
J: - When you . . . stay . . . .
C: - Oh . . . one year. One year . . . yeah . . . at program. So you . . . what's your purpose of . . . **intention** of coming here?
J: - Intention
C: - Yah intention.
J: - Intention.
C: - For what purpose?
J: - Ah I'm exchange student.
C: - Oh exchange student.
J: - My Japanese university has exchange program.
C: - Oh yeah.

The use of the word 'intention' creates an understanding problem in the conversation. This phenomenon is the same as what I earlier covered. ELF speakers often use not one but two or even three different ways to express the same question, opinion or claim. This may cause misunderstandings like here. The Chinese student said: 'So you . . . what's your purpose of . . . intention of coming here?' – the use of 'purpose' and 'intention' in the same utterance may have confused the Japanese student. The sequence shows that he repeats the word twice. When the Chinese student uses 'purpose' in a separate utterance – 'For what purpose?' – the Japanese student understands without difficulty what his partner wants.

## 5.7 Summary

In this chapter, we discussed how prior intention and emergent intention together with attention result in different linguistic formulations and discourse sequences. It was emphasized that emergent intention dominates ELF interactions because of salience effect. Recipient design occurs mainly for repair and remedy purposes. Emergent intention and salience effect usually result in deductive rather than carefully planned inductive sequences. However, these sequences never appear in pure forms. They are always in between inductive and deductive, more like on a continuum with two hypothetical ends.

In the previous three chapters, we examined how interactional competence and sociocultural background knowledge are put to use in ELF interactions to formulate intention. These factors play a decisive role in what exactly is uttered by speakers and why exactly an utterance is interpreted the way it is. In the next chapter, we shall discuss the cumulative effect of these three factors on the interplay of semantics and pragmatics.

# 6 The Semantics–Pragmatics Interface

## 6.1 The Problem: Impoverished Pragmatics?

The semantic–pragmatic interface debate is about how much actual situational context the linguistic signs need in order for them to be meaningful in the communicative process. It was pointed out in the previous chapters that in ELF we can hardly put vague expressions or utterances out there and expect the actual situational context to specify their meaning as it usually happens in L1. Interlocutors should be quite specific as far as semantics is concerned because that is what they share with their partners. Pragmatic enrichment based on the target language and contextual mechanisms can hardly help the production and interpretation process in ELF, rather they may lead to misunderstandings. So seemingly there is something that I called "impoverished" pragmatics. But is that really so? A closer look shows that in fact pragmatics is invigorated in ELF rather than impoverished. OK, let me try to explain what is going on here.

I have pointed to the fact that relative constancy, which is the result of conventionalization and normativization, is what keeps language together, and what makes it meaningful. Of course, this relative constancy refers not only to the denotational meaning and function of linguistic signs but also to the way they are used by interlocutors. Language users frequently make critical efforts to find, create, shape, and keep up constancy within language use, even where only little of that exists like in ELF. They try to create their AIC (adapted interactional competence) even for a short time. They generate new formulas and metaphors that do not exist in the target language, and they co-construct emergent common ground. But their safest bet for relative constancy in their language use is the linguistic code itself that ELF users all share (at different proficiency levels) and use for communication. It gives them more constancy than anything else, including conceptual knowledge and/or encyclopedic knowledge. In ELF interactions, if interlocutors rely on what is encoded in the linguistic signs rather than on language-specific conceptual knowledge and/or encyclopedic knowledge, they can usually have fewer bumps in their communication since literal meanings are usually quite similar for any language users no matter what variety of English an ELF speaker represents.

Recent research has indicated that ELF and L2 users prefer compositionality and semantically analyzable language to figurative and formulaic language, thinking the probability of misunderstanding is lower if they stick to the codified meaning of lexical items (e.g., Cieslicka 2006; House 2002; Kecskes 2007, 2015b; Philip 2005). If we argue that semantics defines sentence meaning while pragmatics governs utterance meaning, can we then claim that these findings go against what we know about the semantics–pragmatics interface based on L1 research? In other words, does it mean that ELF users rely more on semantics than on pragmatics in their language use? If so, what does ELF reveal about the semantics–pragmatics interface? These and some similar questions will be in the focus of this chapter. We shall start with the review of the issues concerning the semantics–pragmatics distinction.

## 6.2 The Relationship of Semantics and Pragmatics

### *6.2.1 Semantic Underdeterminacy*

In the socio-cognitive approach, semantics is tied mainly to prior experience while pragmatics is tied to actual situational experience of interlocutors (Kecskes 2010a, 2014). Semantics and pragmatics as separate fields of inquiry are both about meaning so they have both developed sophisticated methods of analysis of meaning. As a consequence, their separation into different disciplines has caused lots of discussions and debates in linguistics, language philosophy, as well as theoretical pragmatics. But this is the first time, at least to my knowledge, that the issue is raised in relation to intercultural communication, specifically to ELF. The need for revisiting this issue is warranted by the nature of ELF communication where there seems to be a dominance of semantics rather than pragmatics. Or, in other words, could we say that semantics seems to grow into pragmatics in ELF. I shall come back to this matter shortly.

The Gricean modular view divides the interpretation process into two stages: what is said and what is implicated. It is, however, overlooked that the division between what is said and what is implicated was made for the sake of utterance interpretation, and for the sake of distinguishing the semantic meaning from the pragmatic meaning of an utterance. Traditionally, semantics has been responsible for compositionally construed sentence meaning, in which the meanings of lexical items and the structures in which they occur are combined. Pragmatics has been regarded as a study of utterance meaning, and hence meaning in context, and is therefore an enterprise with a different object of study. However, the boundary between them has never been clear, especially after the so-called semantic underdeterminacy view was introduced (see Carston 2002; Bach 2004; Recanati 2005). Semantic underdeterminacy describes the linguistic semantics of the utterance, that is, the meaning encoded in the linguistic expressions used. Semantics refers to the relatively stable meanings of lexical units in a linguistic system, meanings which are widely shared across a speech community using the particular linguistic system. These meanings are encapsulated in lexical items as a result of their reoccurring use. They underdetermine the proposition expressed (what is said). So the hearer has to undertake processes of pragmatic inference in order to work out not only what the speaker is implicating but also what proposition she is directly expressing (see Carston 2002).

Here, when starting discussing underdeterminacy of sentence meaning and speaker implication and utterance interpretation, without any detailed explanation (that will come later), we need to introduce two terms that will be important for us in this chapter. Saul (2002) made a distinction between 'utterer-implicature' and 'audience-implicature.' Utterer-implicatures are claims that the speaker attempts to conversationally implicate (intended by the speaker, but not necessarily recognized by the addressee). Audience-implicatures are claims that the audience takes to be conversationally implicated (recognized by the addressee but not necessarily intended by the speaker). This distinction will help us understand the behavior of both L1 and ELF speaker-hearers.

Without going into details, let us illustrate what underdeterminacy means through a couple of examples:

(1) A. John should know better [better than what or whom?]
B. Mary is too old [for what?]
C. The girls left early [left what? left for?]

As you can see, these are full sentential utterances whose encoded meaning does not seem to determine a fully propositional representation, that is, one which, in principle at least, could be assigned a truth value. As the bracketed questions indicate, these examples require completion by context before they can be judged as true or false of a state of affairs. This completion usually requires encyclopedic knowledge and includes pragmatic enrichment, both given by contextual effects.

Also, example (2) reveals semantic underdeterminacy when a hearer-implicature is needed to figure out the meaning of speaker-implicature:

(2) Andy to Sally:
ANDY: - Did you enjoy the party at the Browns' yesterday?
SALLY: - <u>Well, I got a bit drunk, and forgot to dance with Bill.</u>
ANDY: - Hope, you still had a good time.

Although it is not explicitly formulated, it is quite clear that Sally implied that she did not have a good time. And Andy managed to infer this from the utterance that did not directly and/or literally contain that information. Although the utterance was semantically underdetermined, still Andy seems to have managed to recover what the speaker wanted to say with uttering that sentence. So the utterer-implicature matched the hearer-implication (inference).

In ELF communication, the first type of underdeterminacy does not seem to cause any serious problem. If interlocutors know the literal meaning of the words they can pragmatically enrich the utterances just like native speakers do on the basis of encyclopedic knowledge. However, the second type of underdeterminacy, where a relative match between utterer-implicature and hearer-implicature is required, may cause some serious problems because it requires not only encyclopedic but oftentimes conceptual knowledge tied to the target language. If only encyclopedic knowledge is required to make the match that might not be an issue, as we have seen. If, however, conceptual knowledge attached to a frozen metaphor, a situation-bound utterance, or an idiom (all specific elements of the target language) is required to process the utterer implication, that may cause mismatch between utterer-implicature and hearer-implicature or misunderstanding, as is the case in example (3):

(3) Xiaolu is talking to Birgit (German student)
XIAOLU: - Birgit, can you make this scanner work?
BIRGIT: - Piece of cake.
XIAOLU: - What do you mean?

In this example, Birgit used a popular expression to say that it is no problem for her to make the scanner work. However, Xiaolu does not seem to have understood the expression. She was confused because the literal meaning does not fit into the actual situational context. This indeed reveals that underdeterminacy in this sense may be a real problem in ELF communication because the actual situational context cannot help if the interlocutor does not know the figurative meaning of the expression. So if we accept that semantic underdeterminacy exists, we are then forced to agree that this will have significant consequences for any analysis of ELF interaction. But, we have to be careful because there seems to be a contradiction here between what I said at the beginning of the chapter and what semantic underdeterminacy means. I claimed that semantic analyzability plays a central role in ELF interaction, for what interlocutors share mostly is the linguistic code, the relatively stable dictionary meaning of lexical items. However, semantic underdeterminacy means that the encoded meaning is vague, and is in need of contextual support and/or pragmatic enrichment. What is going on here? How can ELF users rely on semantically vague expressions? Are those expressions really semantically vague for ELF users the way they are for L1 users? It is precisely because of these questions that we have to deal with the issue of semantic–pragmatic interface in this chapter. We need to clarify what is going on for ELF users, but in order to do so, we must know more about the background of the semantics–pragmatics interface issue in pragmatics.

### *6.2.2 Constancy and Convention*

Let us for now quote Morris (1938: 6), who was quite straightforward about the semantics–pragmatics divide: "One may study the relations of signs to the objects to which the signs are applicable. . . . [T]he study of this dimension will be called semantics. Or the subject of study may be the relation of signs to interpreters. . . . [T]he study of this dimension will be named pragmatics." This basically means that pragmatics deals with concrete utterance tokens made by speakers in concrete discourse situations that are located in time and space, while semantics abstracts away from those concrete contextual factors and studies the decontextualized expression types that underlie those utterances (see Gutzmann 2014 for more discussion). From this perspective, the relation between semantics and pragmatics parallels the broader distinction between Chomsky's competence and performance or Saussure's langue and parole. Additionally, Carnap (1942: 9) was even more specific about the relationship of the two:

> If in an investigation explicit reference is made to the speaker, or, to put it in more general terms, to the user of a language, then we assign it to the field of pragmatics. . . . If we abstract from the user of the language and analyze only the expressions and their designata, we are in the field of semantics.

This approach clearly handles semantics as an abstraction of pragmatics because it is said to abstract away from the specific aspects of concrete discourse situations in which utterances are used. So what we have so far is that semantics deals with abstract sentences while pragmatics studies 'real utterances.' This makes sense; however, this is not what happens in linguistics/theoretical pragmatics where nobody is interested in 'real utterances' although they all say they are. Researchers rely on introspective data and data resulting from thought experiments, and create their own utterances to make their points when studying logical structures and relations instead of using 'real utterances.' So they do pragmatics with semantic units. It is also crucial to note that contexts given to those examples are hypothetical and not real. Recently, several researchers have questioned the reliability of data heavily dependent on the linguist's own linguistic intuition (e.g., Dabrowska 2010; Kertész & Rákosi 2012; Kecskes 2015a).

But ELF use is about real utterances, and ELF research focuses on real utterances in the Carnapian sense. This focus on natural, real language production is one of the most positive elements of current ELF research. So we will need to look at the semantics–pragmatics division from two perspectives: First, we need to relate the theoretical pragmatics perspective to real utterances produced in ELF interactions and try to explain, with their help, what exactly happens in those encounters. Second, we need to investigate if what we learn from the analysis of ELF production can help us add some new knowledge to the discussion about the semantics–pragmatics interface.

In order to execute our plan, we should further discuss the differences between semantics and pragmatics. As it has been overtly argued, we can all agree on the fact that semantics studies the literal meaning of an expression; however, the subject of pragmatics is what and how speakers communicate by using that expression. In other words, semantics is more tied to the conventional aspects and relative constancy of linguistic meaning as encoded in the lexicon, while pragmatics deals with the conversational aspects of speaker meaning in concrete discourse contexts. The difference between conventional and conversational meaning is demonstrated clearly in the use of the underlined expression in example (4).

(4) Sam is talking to his friend Archie.
SAM: - Archie, I took your girlfriend to the movies yesterday.
ARCHIE: - <u>Oh, what a good guy you are!</u>
SAM: - I am sorry if you think I did something wrong.

What we have here is that Archie's response can be interpreted in two different ways. First, if we take '<u>Oh, what a good guy you are!</u>' literally, it means that Archie is actually obliged to his friend that he was kind enough to take his girlfriend to the movies either because he did not have time to go or because he just wanted to get rid of her. Second, we can interpret Archie's utterance as ironic, meaning that he is actually very unhappy with Sam's action. Here the utterance means the opposite of what it says. Both interpretations are possible; however, encyclopedic knowledge – knowledge of the world – as well as Sam's response, suggests the second, nonliteral interpretation as the most probable one even without knowing what Sam's response is.

So if semantics is based on an abstraction of pragmatics, which goes without any aspect of actual situational context, then pragmatics should study those aspects of meaning that are actual situational context dependent. Semantics is restricted to what could be called (relatively) constant, that is, actual situational context-independent meaning. In example (4), the first reading seems to be independent of the actual situational context in a sense that actual situational context does not help the hearer as expected. It is the reading that comes to anybody's mind if no actual situational context is given, say, the sentence is written on a board, and we ask students to interpret it. This is the literal interpretation of the sentence based on its compositionality. The second reading can be made possible by the actual situational context. If we bring in salience, the whole thing becomes even more interesting. If we take the actual situational context-free interpretation, the most salient meaning will be the literal meaning of the expression. If we add the actual situational context, as in example (4), the most salient interpretation will be the figurative (ironic) one for both native speakers of English and nonnative speakers of English. But why will they not differ?[1] The answer lies in encyclopedic knowledge that is universal in this case. If someone takes his/her friend's girlfriend to the movies without a prior agreement with the friend, that friend might not be very happy about it. This interpretation is the result of general common sense that is not biased by any language or culture-specific factor.

Besides the two criteria, namely conventionality and constancy, which we have discussed, there is also the traditional criterion of truth conditionality which represents the core for the truth-conditional semantics in the Fregean tradition. According to this view, semantics concerns those aspects of meaning that are truth conditional, which means that they are relevant for determining the truth conditions of a sentence. Truth conditions are conditions under which a sentence is true. For example, 'Mr. Brown lives in a new house' is true precisely when there is a Mr. Brown who has a house which is new. Truth conditions of a sentence do not necessarily reflect current reality. They are merely the conditions under which the statement would be true. Gutzmann (2014) argued that conventionality, constancy and truth-conditionality go hand-in-hand. If we take them together, we can use them as a means to distinguish semantics and pragmatics.

According to this approach, semantics concerns the conventional, constant and truth-conditional content, while pragmatics deals with conversational, context-dependent, non-truth-conditional meaning; this is summarized below:

*Semantics vs. Pragmatics*

| Semantics | Pragmatics |
|---|---|
| conventional | conversational |
| constant (prior context-dependent) | actual situational context-dependent |
| truth-conditional | non-truth-conditional |

There are several other interpretations and explanations of the semantics–pragmatics distinction. However, our goal is not to review them all, but to relate to a widely accepted view of what happens in ELF interactions. Now that we

[1] I have tried it in my class with sixteen subjects (nine native speakers and seven nonnative speakers).

have a better understanding of the interface, we shall go over the production and interpretation process.

## 6.3 Pragmatic Models

### *6.3.1 The Standard Pragmatic Model*

As discussed earlier in this book, the modular view (e.g., Grice 1975; Searle 1979) posits the temporal priority of linguistic input which assumes, for the most part, that lexical processes are impenetrable and do not interact with contextual information initially. According to this standard pragmatic model, context comes into play following lexical processes, thus allowing for contextually incompatible meanings to be involved at the initial access phase. In other words, the standard pragmatic model gives temporal priority to literal meanings. The literal meaning of the utterance is accessed first; while this would be enough for literal interpretation, nonliteral language would require further processing. In case of nonliteral language, the initial, obligatory, literal stage would be supplemented by an optional stage of adjustment to contextual information. This is supposed to result in the derivation of the contextually compatible meaning.

According to the standard pragmatic model in our example (4), 'Oh, what a good guy you are!' would initially be interpreted literally. However, Sam's response shows that he went directly for the nonliteral interpretation. So no literal interpretation happened. And, no extra effort was needed although the standard pragmatic model expects that nonliteral language requires extra (and more complex) inferential processes invited by contextual misfit. So it looks like the standard view does not explain example (4) succinctly.

### *6.3.2 The Direct Access View*

The standard pragmatic model has been challenged from different perspectives by linguists, cognitive psychologists, pragmaticians, and psycholinguists, who assign a primary role in language comprehension to contextual information (e.g., Gibbs 1994, 2002; Sperber & Wilson 1995; Giora 1997, 2003). This approach, usually called 'the direct access view,' claims that contextual information interacts with lexical processes very early on. Consequently, a rich and supportive context would affect comprehension to such a significant extent that only deliberate, intended, contextually compatible meanings would be accessed directly. Contextually incompatible meanings, even if they are literal meanings, will not be considered. Thus, the direct access view gets some support from our example (4). As you can recall, Archie's 'Oh, what a good guy you are!' utterance was not interpreted literally first because of the strong contextual bias given by Sam's uttering:

'Archie, I took your girlfriend to the movies yesterday.' World knowledge attached to this utterance overrides the possible literal interpretation. In other words, it calls attention to the fact that young men are usually not supposed to take their friend's girlfriend to the movies without prior consent of the other party. However, the problem is not solved either by the modular view or the direct access view that are built on a possible hierarchical relationship between literal and nonliteral meaning. A seemingly right solution was suggested by Giora's (1997, 2003) GSH, which was reviewed in a previous chapter, but we need to continue discussing it here as well since the salient effect is crucial for ELF communication.

### *6.3.3 Salience Effect*

As discussed in Chapter 5, the GSH posits the priority of salient (coded, context-independent, prominent) meanings that are processed initially, regardless of either literality or contextual bias. That is to say, context may affect comprehension immediately, but it is ineffective in blocking (contextually incompatible) salient meanings, since it does not interact with lexical processes but runs in parallel (cf. Peleg et al. 2001). In order to be salient, meanings of words, phrases, or sentences, including the conventional interpretations of idioms, speech formulas, or proverbs, have to be coded in the mental lexicon and, in addition, enjoy prominence due to their conventionality, frequency, familiarity or prototypicality. Let us take an example from the British sitcom *Keeping Up Appearances*.

(5) Hyacinth Bucket's advertisement in the newspaper:
'Experienced hostess offers her services for special occasions.'

No matter in what contextual environment this sentence appears, it will always have a sexual connotation. No actual situational context can override the most salient meaning of the sentence.

Giora argued that salience is a matter of degree, which is determined primarily by frequency of exposure and experiential familiarity with the meaning in question. Salient meanings are assumed to be accessed immediately upon encounter of the linguistic stimulus through a direct lookup in the mental lexicon. Hence, less salient meanings will lag behind. Non-salient meanings require extra inferential processes, and, in most cases, strong contextual support. Thus, given similarly strong contexts, literal and nonliteral utterances would involve similar initial processes if they are similarly salient. They would not, if they involve salience difference. In example (6), we can see that both the literal meaning and the nonliteral one are equally salient.

(6) Bill fell into a large hole. His friend, Ben, is passing by and notices that Bill is in trouble. He looks down into the hole. Bill says:

BILL: - Give me a hand. I must get out of here.
BEN: - I do not think I can reach you. I need a rope.

What we have in this example is that both the literal and nonliteral meaning of 'give me a hand' are equally salient. Still, when I asked my native speaker students whether the literal or the nonliteral meaning is most salient for them in this case, only two out of sixteen said that the literal meaning is what they thought of as the most salient one. All the others opted for the nonliteral interpretation. This makes sense since the nonliteral meaning of this expression is more frequently used than the literal one in the L1 (American English) community.

I argued that salience is the result of prior experience (Kecskes 2006, 2010b, 2014), and this is largely why it affects individuals differently: they have different prior experiences with the world around them. This is especially true for people who do not belong to the same speech community, such as ELF speakers representing different L1s. In the socio-cognitive approach, distinction is made between prior experience (the cumulative effect of prior contexts) and actual situational experience (the context of the ad hoc speech situation). But, in fact, what Giora talks about in her GSH is connected with prior experience only, and is linguistic salience.[2] I need to underline again that, not belonging to the same speech community, ELF speakers have different prior experiences with lexical units in the target language, which results in different saliences. For ELF users, emergent situational salience can be as important as prior experience-based linguistic salience. The interplay of linguistic salience and emergent situational salience may present a serious issue in ELF. In fact, example (7) demonstrates this matter:

(7) Park, a Korean student, and Masha, a Russian student, have finished their meal in a restaurant. The waitress is putting the bill on the table.
WAITRESS: - Just take your time.
MASHA, POINTING AT THE BILL: - Shall we go Dutch?
PARK: - What do you mean?
MASHA: - Do you want to split the bill?
PARK: - Oh, yes.

In this example, although emergent situational salience (waitress putting the bill on the table and Masha pointing at the bill) is supposed to help Park to a great extent in processing Masha's intended meaning, yet Park has no idea what Masha means by 'Shall we go Dutch?' This is mainly because she relies only on linguistic salience, that is the literal meaning of the utterance, which does not match the actual situational context in this example. Therefore, Park requires some clarification. Masha's second question makes perfect sense literally, and the

[2] This is linguistically definable salience because it is encapsulated in the lexical items.

word 'bill' matches the actual situational context so Park understands it without difficulty. What is so far clear to us is that ELF interlocutors generally experience similar problems to Park's quite frequently. They process an utterance literally when its meaning does not fit into the actual situational context. Since context in these cases is not much help, further negotiation or direct support from the partner is needed, as it happens in example (7).

In the following section, we shall summarize what we have discussed so far, and then further look into the semantics–pragmatics interface based on what we have learned about ELF communication.

## 6.4 Semantics Growing into Pragmatics in ELF

### *6.4.1 Diachronic and Synchronic Pragmatics*

As we have reviewed issues concerning the semantics–pragmatics interface in the previous sections, we have made several important notes about how those issues relate to ELF. We have discussed that ELF users prefer semantic analyzability to figurative and formulaic language. Also, semantic underdeterminacy does not seem to affect their speech activities to the extent it does in L1, for they cannot count on actual situational contextual support in the same way as it works in L1. Furthermore, we have found out that constancy and conventionality that are built in the lexical items for L1 users also work for ELF users as far as literal meanings are concerned; they share the coded literal meaning with other ELF users depending on their proficiency. As far as the standard pragmatic model is concerned, it appears to work better for ELF users than for L1 users because ELF users seem to first process literal meaning, and they may stick to that sometimes even if there is a mismatch with the actual situational context. The application of the GSH to ELF encounters confirms that the most salient meaning for ELF users in interpretation is usually the literal meaning of an expression. This fact will have a profound effect on how we will understand what an implicature is in ELF as we will see in the next chapter. However, now we must summarize the differences between L1 and ELF communication from the perspective of the semantics–pragmatics divide.

- Semantic content and compositionality dominates both expressing intention and interpreting it. The standard pragmatic model works (literal meaning processed first).
- Linguistic code seems to play the role of core common ground.
- Actual contextual support for comprehension is not significant. Pragmatic enrichment is minimal: it mainly represents general world knowledge rather than language specific features.
- What is said is usually equal or close to what is communicated.

- Prior context (coded in lexical items) is more dominant than actual situational context.
- The more target language specific utterances are, the less the speaker can be sure that they will be interpreted as meant.

All the above reveals the dominance of semantics over pragmatics in ELF, at least seemingly. But is that really true? How does pragmatics work for ELF? Does semantics not, in fact, grow into pragmatics in ELF communication, taking over some functions of pragmatics? Or rather, are semantic features pragmatized in ELF?

It is essential that pragmatics for ELF speakers cannot be just something "they communicate over and above the semantic content of the sentence," as King and Stanley (2005: 117) assumed for L1. For ELF speakers, the semantic content is usually the conveyed content, or at least it is close to the conveyed content. If this is not clear from their utterance, they try to reinforce it through some pragmatic strategies such as repetition, paraphrase, or other procedures. Here is a brief exchange between a student with African French as L1 (AF) and a Korean student (K).

(8) AF: - ah . . . so you have good neighbors . . . it's quiet . . . good . . . so everybody has difficulties where they live so since you came from Korea what kind of difficulties you . . . what are the problems that you have to live in Albany?
K: - Ah I came . . . when I came here . . . the first time about . . . I applied the driver's license and you go to there.
AF: - Yeah.
K: - DMV . . . yeah, yeah . . . driver station.
AF: - Yeah.
K: - And then they require so many documents.
AF: - I see.
K: - So I had to go another office.
AF: - To apply to school.
K: - Yeah social number or . . . officer . . . anybody . . . anyway I had to go there and then . . . receive the document I gave them . . . so long time I . . . take a long time.
AF: - Yeah so the difficulty for you is to get a driver's license here in the US.

In this excerpt, which was used in Chapter 1 as well, but for another purpose, we can see that the Korean student is talking about her difficulties obtaining a driver's license in Albany. There is, in fact, no figurative or formulaic language use in the excerpt. The Korean student makes special efforts to make sure that the AF student can follow her. For instance, she pays attention to the backchanneling of her partner by saying 'DMV,' but wants to make sure that the AF student understands her properly so adds 'driver station,' which is a strange, ad hoc-created semantic unit but makes perfect sense in the given context.

For nonnative speakers – especially speakers with lower language proficiency – who participate in intercultural interactions, *pragmatics is very close to semantics.* In L1 communication, 'what is said' rarely coincides with 'what is communicated.' This is why Gricean pragmatics gives such importance to implicatures. "Speakers implicate, hearers infer" (Horn 2004: 6). In L1, it rarely happens that nothing is implied beyond semantics of the sentence. However, in intercultural communication what the speaker says is what s/he usually (but not always) means. In most cases, utterance meaning is what the corresponding sentence means literally. This fact gives a strong support to Bach's (2007: 5) claim:

> [I]t is a mistake to suppose that "pragmatic content is what the speaker communicates over and above the semantic content of the sentence" (King & Stanley 2005: 117). Pragmatics doesn't just fill the gap between semantic and conveyed content. It operates even when there is no gap. So it is misleading to speak of the border or the so-called interface between semantics and pragmatics. This mistakenly suggests that pragmatics somehow takes over when semantics leaves off. It is one thing for a sentence to have the content that it has, and another thing for a speech act of uttering the sentence to have the content it has. Even when the content of the speech act is the same as that of the sentence, that is a pragmatic fact, something that the speaker has to intend and the hearer has to figure out.

Bach's claim is true not just for L1 communication but for *any* communication including ELF as well. Pragmatics does not take over when semantics leaves off; rather, *pragmatics is always there.* In fact, pragmatics is there even when the utterance means what the sentence says. *The semantics of the sentence is pragmatized.* In other words, semantics and pragmatics are intertwined and almost inseparable, at least in ELF. A part of pragmatics is encoded in the lexical items and utterances, and another part of pragmatics requires actual situational support in the target language (English, in the case of ELF communication). The latter is often referred to as pragmatic enrichment as described by contextualists. The problem, however, is that the diachronically semantisized part of pragmatics (semantics) does not work without the other, that is, the synchronic part of pragmatics, which comes into effect in actual situational contexts. Basically, all that we call semantics is the result of pragmatic actions and processes attaching reoccurring conceptual load to lexical items and utterances. Pragmatic features – actual situational experiences being standardized, conventionalized and normativized over time – grow into semantic features. This is how word-specific semantic properties (Cruse 2002; Kecskes 2003, 2010a) of expressions such as 'chicken out,' 'pass away,' 'blackmail,' and 'kidnap. develop. This process makes language development dynamic and ever changing. In short, semantics originates from pragmatics. The former is a summary of prior reoccurring contexts, a repository of the history of use of lexical items. It is nothing other than *diachronic pragmatics as opposed to synchronic pragmatics*. However, the semantisized part of pragmatics (or diachronic pragmatics) affects synchronic pragmatics (and vice versa), and occasionally overrides actual contextual selective power. The problem of ELF users is that this diachronic pragmatics, which represents a built-in conceptual load in lexical items, is not usually part of the learning process that EFL (or sometimes ESL) learners (later ELF users) go through. They learn the pure literal meaning or core meaning of the lexical items, but not the conceptual load that is tied to them and is an essential part of actual use of those lexical items.

### *6.4.2 Prior Context and Actual Situational Context Revisited*

When discussing the semantics–pragmatics divide, we always face the same issue: the relationship and interplay of prior context and actual situational context. We have already talked about this phenomenon in Chapter 1. Now we will relate those views to the semantics–pragmatics distinction to explain the semantically biased behavior of ELF speakers. As stated earlier, prior context is tied to semantics or what I called "diachronic pragmatics." And actual situational context is tied to pragmatics, more specifically to "synchronic pragmatics." It seems to me that the traditional semantic view (literalism) and the novel pragmatic view (contextualism) may go wrong in their way of handling the role of prior context and prior experience. As a reminder, according to the traditional view, we must distinguish between the proposition literally expressed by an utterance ('what is said' by the utterance, i.e., its literal truth conditions) and the implicit meaning of the utterance ('what is communicated' by a speaker producing the utterance). The former level is the object of semantics; the latter level is the object of pragmatics. In addition, followers of the pragmatic view emphasize the importance of semantic underdetermination according to which the encoded meaning of the linguistic expressions used by a speaker underdetermines the proposition explicitly expressed by the utterance.

As for the traditional view, truth conditions may be ascribed to a sentence (of an idealized language system), independent of any contextual considerations. The opposing pragmatic view says that a sentence has complete truth conditions only in context. The semantic interpretation of utterances, in other words the propositions they express, their truth conditions, is the result of *pragmatic processes of expansion and contextual enrichment*. The followers of the semantic view may not be right when they think that any linguistic sign can be independent of any contextual considerations. No linguistic sign or expression can be independent of context because they, in fact, carry context (reoccurring prior context), they encode the history of their prior use (reoccurring prior context) in a speech community. The supporters of the pragmatic view may go wrong when they do not emphasize that expansion and contextual enrichment are the results of the individual's prior experience. Suffice it to say, both sides appear to be mistaken to some extent because they talk about *context* without making a distinction between its two sides: *prior context* and *actual situational context*. The proposition literally expressed (sentence meaning) is the result of collective prior experience of speaker-hearers of a given speech community. This is expanded and/or enriched by prior experience, current situational experience and/or the communicative need of a concrete speaker when s/he uses that utterance (speaker's meaning). The speaker privatizes the collective experience by enhancing/enriching the content with his/her private experience. Inferred meaning (hearer-implicature) is the reflection of the interplay between prior experience of the speaker and prior experience of the hearer in an actual situational context. Prior context as understood in the socio-cognitive paradigm is declarative knowledge, while actual situational context represents procedural knowledge (see Kecskes 2014). Moreover, Bezuidenhout (2004) claimed that parallels exist between the declarative–procedural divide, the semantics/pragmatics interface and the competence/performance distinction. She proposed that a clear-cut distinction must be made between procedural knowledge, which belongs to the performance system and is pragmatic, on the one hand, and the lexical conceptual knowledge, which belongs to the competence system and is semantic, on the other. This is in line with what the socio-cognitive approach claims: lexical conceptual knowledge is the basis for prior context that is encoded in the lexical items while procedural knowledge, which is pragmatic, is triggered by the actual situational context. To make our point clear, let us look at the sentences in example (9).

(9) Stan and Sally are engaged (to each other).
Some (not all) boys like baseball.
I need to change (clothes).

According to the socio-cognitive approach, all of the sentences above are complete without the parentheticals, and express a truth conditional, actual situational context-independent proposition. I want to emphasize *actual situational context-independent* proposition, because what those sentences are not independent of, is prior context. Prior context, reoccurring use – without the elements in parenthesis in example (9) – makes their meaning clear even without the actual situational context. The speaker can say Stan and Sally are engaged true or false without concern for 'to whom.' The speaker can say some boys like baseball true or false without concern for whether all do, and can say she needs to change true or false without considering in what way (clothes? diet? priorities? career?) The parentheticals add what that speaker was talking about, specifically, an added propositional element based on the actual situational context. But that is a new proposition. The one it supplants is still adequate in itself as the expression of a proposition. So I argue that *it is a mistake to claim that no sentence is complete without (actual situational) context.* It is more the case that speakers can mean more than the sentence itself means, because actual situational context may supply the rest. Nevertheless the sentence does say something completely, and sometimes it is exactly what the speaker means (see utterer-implicatures).

In the socio-cognitive approach and ELF, underdeterminacy of sentence meaning may exist only from the perspective of the hearer. The speaker's utterance is not underdetermined in any way unless the speaker deliberately wants it to be. The speaker expects that his/her utterance fits into the actual situational context, or creates an actual situational context. Let us look at this issue in L1 communication first, and then in ELF. The following conversations (10A and 10B; from Kecskes 2014) will support this point:

(10A) Sam is talking to his friend, Andy.
SAM: - Coming for a drink?
ANDY: - Sorry, I can't. *My doctor* won't let me.
SAM: - What's wrong with you?

(10B) The same situation with one change.
SAM: - Coming for a drink?
ANDY: - Sorry, I can't. *My mother-in-law* won't let me.
SAM: - What's wrong with you?

In example (10A), we can see that Andy says that he cannot go to have a drink with Sam because his doctor does not let him drink. Sam's question, 'what's wrong with you?' can definitely be interpreted as an inquiry about Andy's health. Andy's use of 'my doctor' gives prior context support to that interpretation. Traditionally doctors can prohibit people drinking for health reasons. However, in example (10B), when Andy says that his mother-in-law does not permit him to go and have a drink with his friend, we can see that the whole actual situational context is changed. Based on traditional collective saliency (prior context) no one would think that Andy listens to his mother-in-law. So the question 'what's wrong with you?' may mean something like 'are you out of your mind?' or 'are you in trouble?'

Now let us take an example and see how this works in ELF.

(11) A Japanese student (J) and a Korean student (K) are talking.
J: - OK it's been three or . . . three months so far right? Do you like living in Albany? Living in America?
K: - Yes I like.
J: - What makes you like this life? What is your . . . like .. What you like about living in Albany?

K: - I stay here only 4 month in this semester so I have no time. I go to many place . . . I went to Boston, Washington DC, of course New York City.
J: - That's a lot wow.
K: - Next month I will go to San Francisco.
J: - San Francisco wow. West coast.
K: - Grand Canyon, Niagara.
J: - Oh. So many plans are coming wow.
K: - I like traveling.
J: - I can see that.
K: - I like nature. The US has many nature.

In this example, the Japanese student wants to know if the Korean student likes Albany, and starts with a direct question, which creates the frame of the conversation. He does not get a direct answer because the Korean student begins to talk about his travel with which he changes the topic of the conversation. Here no prior context breaks the dominance of actual situational context. The same goes for the rest of the discourse segment.

So the examples from L1 and ELF discourse demonstrate that context plays both a selective (actual situational context) and a constitutive role (prior context). Actual situational context is viewed through prior context. Thus, meaning is the outcome of the interplay of prior and current experience (actual situational context). We can imagine the relationship of prior context and actual situational context during interaction as a continuum.

Prior context <————————————————→Actual situational context

What I want to emphasize here is that there is constant movement on the continuum. Depending on how speaker intention is expressed, either or neither side can be dominant (see examples 10A, 10B, and 11). Also, prior context tied to salience is as important as actual situational context connected to relevance. Our experience develops through the regular recurrence of similar situations that we tend to identify with given contexts. Additionally, the standard (prior, recurring) context can be defined as a regular situation of which we have repeated experience, about which we have expectations as to what will or will not happen (Kecskes, 2014), and on which we rely for understanding and predicting how the world around us works. Gumperz (1982: 138) claimed that utterances somehow carry with them their own context or project a context. Referring to Gumperz's work, Levinson (2003) claimed that the message versus context opposition is misleading because the message can carry with it, or forecast, the context. All of this shows that semantics (diachronical pragmatics) is as important as synchronic pragmatics in language production and comprehension. But how does this work for ELF speakers? I have argued that ELF speakers heavily rely on semantics. But semantics is about historically encoded meaning, reoccurring contexts, frequent encounters, and built-in collective salience. And I also said that ELF speakers do have only limited access to all these things in the target language. So what is going on here then? Is there, in fact, a contradiction between these two claims?

### *6.4.3 How Can ELF Speakers Rely Mainly on What They Have Limited Access To?*

This issue is not as complicated as it looks. What we call 'dictionary knowledge' and what constitutes a significant part of semantic knowledge is learnable for ELF speakers. Learnability and learning is a key concern here. ELF speakers who represent a particular variety of English (Chinese English, Russian English, German English, Korean English, etc.) have studied and/or experienced ESL, the target language system and vocabulary, at least to some extent. Their variety of English is an approximation to what is considered a nativelike variety. The process of approximation is usually characterized by learning rather than learning by using in EFL environment where the target language sociocultural background is not directly present. This changes in an ESL environment such as immigrants acquiring English in the USA where the target culture is present, and learning usually takes place through using the language in everyday situations.[3] But no matter whether the route toward English leads through classroom learning or learning by usage, what is common for everyone, no matter which variety of English they speak, is the core knowledge of the system of signs that makes them "English speakers." This core knowledge consists of a basic system of signs and semantic core (vocabulary). English language learners are exposed to these two core linguistic entities in classroom circumstances and in a target language environment as well. We can agree with Swan (2012: 388) that, in a sense, EFL leads to ELF use. However, we should add that not only EFL but ESL and any other kinds of learning of English will lead to ELF use when users of any variety of English engage in interaction with representatives of other varieties of English. In addition, Swan (2017: 513) argued that many of the world's English learners merely seek an effective working knowledge of the language, without wanting or needing a high level of accuracy. This has nothing to do with the recent growth in the Lingua Franca use of English or the implied existence of a new class of ELF users. So ELF users do not constitute a new class/group of English language users because, in fact, they use their own varieties of English without creating a new variety or developing some kind of normativity because there is little reoccurrence in ELF situations. This makes standardization and conventionalization possible

[3] Of course, I am aware of the fact that EFL and ESL is more like a continuum than a dichotomy. Concrete learning environments usually show the dominance of either EFL or ESL factors.

only to a limited extent (see discussions in previous chapters). As a consequence, ELF users' prior context background is more tied to their varieties of English than to some kind of ELF core, or norm, as some ELF researchers claim. Further, Swan (2012: 381) explained the situation of many ELF users, where they disregard the native speaker norms in terms of correctness as follows:

> However, many lingua franca English speakers are certainly unconcerned about emulating NS norms of correctness except in so far as these are likely to serve their communicative purposes, and are perfectly satisfied with approximations that are transparent and effective. For such speakers it seems quite reasonable to say that the forms they use have their own validity, and should not in principle be judged by NS norms or labeled "mistakes."

Also, Swan and Widdowson had a debate about ELF (see Swan 2012 and Widdowson 2013). We have no space here to cover that debate, which is, in fact, not quite relevant to the semantics/pragmatics divide. However, what they said about learning and using is important for us. As far as my definition goes, we can talk about ELF when different varieties of English are put to use in communicative encounters. We have argued that those varieties are usually based mainly on EFL and partly on ESL. EFL classroom learning is more about structure (usage) and semantics while ESL is more about use (practice) and pragmatics. Consequently, EFL learners need more usage practice, while ESL learners may need firmer semantics or more core knowledge of the language to clarify for themselves why people say what they say the way the say it in English as a native language. This may give them the necessary awareness and confidence in using English for communicative purposes. So ELF seems to pull together these two things. No matter the source of knowledge of English (EFL or ESL), in ELF interaction, ELF speakers put that knowledge to use, so it would be unwise to talk about a switch between EFL and ELF or ESL and ELF. Rather, what we see here is the use of different varieties that are biased either for semantics or pragmatics. The best way to put it would be just to say that both sides are present all the time among both types of speakers (EFL or ESL). The only question is to what extent this bias exists? When learned semantics (diachronic pragmatics) is put to use in intercultural encounters, it is expected to function as synchronic pragmatics. This justifies to some extent what Bach (2002: 284) said: "Semantic information is encoded in the sentence; pragmatic information is generated by, or at least made relevant by, the act of uttering the sentence." But we should not forget about another important claim of Bach (2004: 27), according to which "sentences have the properties they have independently of anybody's act of uttering them. Speakers' intentions do not endow them with new semantic properties." There are no new semantic properties added when an utterance is made but those that are encoded should continue functioning pragmatically as well. Thus, a continuum between these two hypothetical parts is justified.

Diachronic pragmatics <——————————————→Synchronic pragmatics

To make it clear, ELF speakers enter into an interaction with a significant 'load' of semantic knowledge, biased by their variety of English, and are expected to function with that in the conversation where synchronic pragmatics knowledge is also required. What they really do is develop their existing 'semantic skills' into 'pragmatic skills' by adding BIC (reminder: basic interactional competence). But with interlocutors having that particular combination of knowledge and skills, actual situation context cannot play the same selective and determinative role in ELF interactions than it does in L1 interactions.

So, if the ELF user does not know or recognize the encoded part of the utterance, the actual contextual pragmatics (synchronic pragmatics) will not be much help. Thus, encoded pragmatics (diachronic pragmatics) becomes part of conceptual knowledge, which is the basis for semantics as we covered in Chapter 4. In that chapter, it was stated that the expression 'chicken out' is used as a synonym to the word 'surrender.' However, it has a conceptual load according to which the action of surrendering is the result of cowardice. This connotation does not need any contextual support. In fact, no actual situational context can cancel this negative connotation: The word is immune to any contextual intrusion. A similar example could be the expression 'it's not my cup of tea,' whose most salient meaning is its figurative one, that is, 'it's not my business or favourite; it's not something I like/do/care for/etc.' In these and similar expressions, the pragmatic functions have been lexicalized, and so they have become a part of semantics rather than pragmatics (if we follow the traditional divide between the two). Thus, it seems to me that this is what ELF users struggle with regularly. If they are not familiar with the built-in, diachronic pragmatics, no actual situational contextual support will ever help. Here is an illustration of the problem in example (12):

(12) Japanese student (J) at the checkout in Walmart. She is paying with credit card. The transaction is over and the cashier is giving the check to the student.
CASHIER: - You are all set.
J: - Do you need anything else?
CASHIER: - No, you are done.

In this example we can see that after the cashier uses the situation-bound utterance 'you are all set,' the Japanese student looks confused and responds with a question, which shows she does not understand. In spite of the clear actual situational context and the supportive situational frame, the Japanese student does not seem to understand the utterance because she has problems with semantics rather than pragmatics. So synchronic pragmatics support does not appear to work well without understanding semantics (encoded pragmatics).

## 6.5 Summary

It was argued in this chapter that, when we examine the semantics–pragmatics division from the perspective of ELF communication, we can see a clear dominance of semantics. The linguistic code works like common ground and utterance production is governed by semantic analyzability. The standard pragmatic model seems to be working better in intercultural interactions than in L1 interaction based on which it was originally developed. In ELF production, speakers compose their utterances relying on the literal meaning of words rather than using figurative and formulaic language. Since hearers also process utterances based on compositionality and literalness first, understanding is not that big of a problem as studies on misunderstandings reported earlier (e.g., Carroll 1988; Gass & Varonis 1991; Pride 1985). As a result of this heavy dominance of semantics, we could detect what I coined as an *impoverished pragmatics* in intercultural interaction. But it was argued that this only seems to be the case. What in fact happens is that pragmatics is always there. There are two side of pragmatics: diachronic pragmatics and synchronic pragmatics. The results of diachronic pragmatics are encapsulated in lexical items and called "semantics." Synchronic pragmatics is triggered by actual situational context. Meaning, both in production and comprehension, is the result of the interplay of these two sides of pragmatics. So pragmatics is always there. The only question is which side of it is more dominant in any sequence of conversation or language use. It looks like in intercultural interactions the semantics side is usually dominant.

No matter from what perspective we look at production and comprehension, semantic competence (i.e., knowledge of what is literally expressed) is still vastly the most important factor in the productive and interpretative process. So for analytic purposes we should keep the divide. There are reasons to be pessimistic as to the prospects of any theory of linguistic interpretation that fails to give central importance to literal meaning. Cappelen and Lepore (2005: x) gave a strong argument against contextualism:

> The common thread that runs throughout our criticism of contextualism is that it fails to account for how we communicate across contexts. People with different background beliefs, goals, audiences, perceptual inputs, etc. can understand each other. They can

agree or disagree. They can say, assert, claim, state, investigate, or make fun of the very same claim. No theory of communication is adequate unless it explains how this is possible. Contextualists cannot provide such an explanation.

Cappelen and Lepore are correct, even from the perspective of ELF. The pragmatized semantics that ELF interlocutors use in interaction is the result of blending their dictionary knowledge of the linguistic code (semantics) with their basic interpersonal communicative skills and sometimes unusual, not necessarily target-language-based, pragmatic strategies that suit them very well in their attempt to achieve their communicative goals. In the upcoming chapter we will examine how ELF speakers produce utterer-implicatures and infer hearer-implicatures.

# 7 Implicatures

## 7.1 The Problem

This chapter is aimed to add to the preceding chapter in which we argued that the semantics–pragmatics distinction is about how much context the linguistic signs need so as to convey what the speaker intends. As we discussed in Chapter 6, actual situational context cannot help ELF interlocutors the way it does in L1 so they need to rely on what the linguistic signs actually say (semantics), and create a frame of their own that is, ideally, not tainted either by the target-language cultural frames or their L1 cultural frames. Now, the underlying question for this chapter is: how will this approach of the ELF interlocutors affect implicature that is a fundamental concept in Gricean pragmatics?

In order for us to answer this question we need to delve deeper into the relatively long, but quite precise, definition of the term 'implicature' by the *Stanford Encyclopedia of Philosophy*:

> Implicature denotes either (i) the act of meaning or implying one thing by saying something else, or (ii) the object of that act. Implicatures can be part of sentence meaning or dependent on conversational context, and can be conventional (in different senses) or unconventional. Figures of speech such as metaphor, irony, and understatement provide familiar examples. Implicature serves a variety of goals beyond communication: maintaining good social relations, misleading without lying, style, and verbal efficiency. Knowledge of common forms of implicature is acquired along with one's native language at an early age.

As you can see, it is argued in the definition that implicatures are acquired at early age along with one's native language in a speech community. If that is so, our ELF speakers are in trouble because they might not necessarily have access to implicatures in English *at an early age*. The development of understanding indirect figurative speech that partly serves as basis for implicatures starts to shape at a relatively early stage in L1 when children enter into the period of formal operations around ages ten to eleven (see Piaget 1977). In addition, some existing literature, with the focus on implicature processing in L2 learners and multilinguals, confirmed the claim that implicature processing depends on variables such as age and language proficiency. Also, it has been argued that implicatures are dependent on 'conversational context.' This, however, somewhat contradicts what we previously argued, namely, that actual situational context does not help ELF speakers the way it does in L1. ELF interlocutors usually co-create their own actual situational context and build common ground and situational frames in that particular context. The third problem that the definition of implicatures raises is that implicatures facilitate and are the basis for figures of speech such as metaphor, irony, sarcasm, and many times even formulaic language. They usually (not always though) imply a meaning beyond the literal sense of what is explicitly stated. In this regard, several questions pop up: How will ELF speakers tackle the aforementioned problems? Are there specific ways or strategies with which ELF speakers handle implicatures? If ELF speakers stick to semantic analyzability, will that mean that their language use will not rely on implicatures (in the Gricean sense) as much as is the case in L1?

This last question presupposes that in intercultural interactions implicatures may work not exactly as they do in L1. If so, what is the difference? Implicatures are a phenomenon that affects any speakers of any language in a similar way, which is top-down. Therefore, they are heavily influenced by prior experience-biased salience both in comprehension and production. Also, in order for us to have a better understanding of implicatures in ELF, we must emphasize that most definitions of implicatures that define them as "implying one thing by saying something else" are problematic for ELF. I claim that implicatures do not always imply one thing by saying something else. Occasionally they imply what is said. This sounds strange because 'imply' means that something is not directly said. But in ELF, modularity is not always present. As a result, sometimes there is no difference between what is said and what is communicated. But it is still legitimate to ask, 'what did the speaker imply?' and the short answer is: 's/he implied what s/he said.' This is somewhat different from the Gricean understanding of implicature, as it will be discussed later. The example below demonstrates what I have claimed so far.

(1) PETER: - *I put the guidebook on the table for you.*
JASON: - OK, thank you.

In the utterance 'I put the guidebook on the table for you,' the message is exactly what the utterance says. And, Jason comprehends it that way. If that works in L1, it is even more crucial for ELF speakers because, as has been emphasized several times, they mostly rely on semantic analyzability and compositional meaning. For them to produce and infer compositional meaning-based speaker implicature is easier than inferring a nonliteral meaning-based implicature.

I agree with Bach (2005) that a speaker can always mean something distinct from the semantic content of the sentence s/he is uttering. But even if s/he speaks literally and means precisely what his/her words mean, that also depends on his/her communicative intention (Bach 2005: 27). That is to say, it is the speaker, not the sentence that does the implicating. And the hearer still must infer properly that what the speaker said was what s/he actually meant. Bach further argued that what a speaker could, in a given situation, plausibly be taken to implicate will be constrained by the semantic content of the sentence – certainly it matters what the sentence means – but this does not make implicature a property of the sentence itself. The point of the matter is that both implicating and inferring are pragmatic acts. Therefore, we need to clarify our approach to this crucial notion in pragmatics before diving into the analysis of ELF implicatures.

## 7.2 Implicatures in Pragmatics

### *7.2.1 The Gricean Approach*

In the Gricean pragmatics, 'utterance' is the product of a verbal act, a communicative unit which may consist of single words, phrases, clauses, and clause combinations uttered in an actual situational context with/without intonation and/or gesture selected by the utterer. By saying something the speaker intends to convey some meaning that either coincides with what is said or communicates some literally unsaid information. Thus, 'implicature' usually refers to this literally unsaid information that can be conveyed by intonation and/or gesture (or other extra-linguistic factors) or by actual contextual support. But sometimes the speaker means what s/he says, as we saw in example (1). In those cases, there is basically no difference between what is said and what is implicated as far as speaker's intention is concerned. But even in those cases we should talk about 'implicatures'; the utterer implicates/implies what s/he says. In the Gricean paradigm, implicature is supposed to cover a number of ways in which literally unsaid information can be conveyed. The relationships between these ways are demonstrated in the chart below:

utterance
what is said implicature
conventional nonconventional
conversational nonconversational
generalized particularized

Let me say that, in this chapter, we have no intention to get into the everlasting debate of understanding different types of implicatures in the

Gricean paradigm. We do not need that for our discussion on implicatures in ELF. Besides, I agree with Kent Bach (1999) who denies the existence of conventional implicatures altogether. He argues that some putative conventional implicatures, like those of *but*, are really entailments, and others, like those of *luckily*, are higher-order comments on the content of a speech act. Attempting to explain how implicatures function for ELF users, our interest is in what Grice calls "conversational implicatures" and defines them as follows: Conversational implicature is triggered by "certain general features of discourse" rather than by the conventional meaning of specific words (Grice 1975). Communication (conversational exchanges) is governed by the COOPERATIVE PRINCIPLE, the content of which is detailed in the four MAXIMS of CONVERSATION and their submaxims. When one of the interlocutors seems not to follow the COOPERATIVE PRINCIPLE, his/her conversational partner(s) will nevertheless assume that, contrary to appearances, the principle is observed at some deeper level. Here is a short summary of the principle and the maxims, just as a reminder for the readers:

**The COOPERATIVE PRINCIPLE:**

To be concise, make your conversational contribution such as is required, at the stage at which it occurs, by the accepted purpose or direction of the talk exchange in which you are engaged.

**The MAXIMS of CONVERSATION**

QUALITY: Try to make your contribution one that is true.

1. Do not say what you believe to be false.
2. Do not say that for which you lack adequate evidence.

QUANTITY:

1. Make your contribution as informative as is required (for the current purposes of the exchange).
2. Do not make your contribution more informative than is required.

RELATION: Be relevant.

MANNER: Be perspicuous.

1. Avoid obscurity of expression.
2. Avoid ambiguity.
3. Be brief.
4. Be orderly.

According to the Gricean approach, implicatures are the results of failing to observe the maxims. There are five major ways of failing to observe a maxim: flouting, violating, infringing, opting out and suspending. We have neither space nor need here to review all these cases. Here is one example for flouting and another for violating.

(2) Flouting the Manner Maxim: in most cases, such flouting involves absence of clarity, brevity and transparency of communicative intentions, as the example below demonstrates:
FRANK: - Didn't you promise to take part in this project?
CARL: - Well, I was probably in a good mood.

As you can see, this is not a clear, direct answer. It means that while being in a good mood, Carl may have agreed to participate in the project. But on second thought, he might want to opt out.

(3) Violating a maxim is quite the opposite of flouting a maxim. Violating a maxim attempts to prevent or at least discourage the hearer from seeking implicatures. It encourages taking utterances at face value. The example below displays the violation of the Relation Maxim:
PETER: - Did you like my presentation?
MARY: - I think the attendance was quite impressive.

Mary's response indirectly implies that she did not like the presentation. But the utterer-implicature encourages Peter to focus on the attendance instead.

### *7.2.2 Current Theories*

Current pragmatics is basically hearer-centered rather than interlocutor-centered (see Kecskes 2010b, 2014). The term 'implicature' has often been misinterpreted by pragmaticians. The Gricean implicature is an aspect of speaker meaning, that is, what is said and what is implicated by the speaker. Although Horn (2004) and Bach (2001) called attention to the difference between implicating and inferring, not everybody has listened. Horn (2004: 6) said: "speakers implicate, hearers infer"; and Bach (2001) argued that "people sometimes confuse infer with imply . . . when we say that a speaker or sentence implies something, we mean that information is conveyed or suggested without being stated outright. . . . Inference, on the other hand, is the activity performed by a reader or interpreter in drawing conclusions that are not explicit in what is said." So the speaker puts out there an utterance implicating something, which has to be inferred by the hearer. Grice, though unintentionally, may also have contributed to some misunderstanding by bringing the 'audience' in. According to Grice, a speaker's intending to convey that P by saying that Q is not enough for the speaker to implicate that P. The audience must also need to believe that the speaker believes that P to preserve the assumption of the speaker's cooperativeness. With this claim, Grice attempted to give some degree of intersubjectivity to the notion of conversational implicature. However, speakers have authority over what they utterer-implicate, but they cannot fully control what they conversationally implicate (Saul 2002). Through example (4), we can show how this works in ELF:

(4) A Japanese student (Akiko) and a Dutch student (Ned) are talking:
AKIKO: - Are you all right, Ned?
NED: - Never better.
AKIKO: - You could be better?
NED: - Oh, no. I mean I am all right.

As you can see, Ned used a formulaic expression that confused Akiko who did not seem to have understood it properly. Ned did not do any recipient design when uttering 'never better.' The phrase was uttered subconsciously without any control. That was the most salient expression that came into Ned's mind. He, the speaker, utterer-implicated that he was very well. However, he could not control how Akiko would interpret the expression, and what she would infer from it. There was a slight misunderstanding between them because Akiko's interpretation was based on semantic analyzability, i.e., the compositional meaning of the expression.

From the speaker's perspective, what really matters is what the audience is required by the speaker to believe, not necessarily what the audience does actually believe. This is where speaker's egocentrism comes in. It is also the main reason why we argued earlier that individual egocentrism is just as much part of human rationality as cooperation is (see Kecskes 2014, 2017, and previous chapters). Further, Davis (1998: 122) argued that Grice was wrong to include audience-oriented criteria in his characterization of conversational implicature. In other words, the speaker's intentions do not depend on what anyone else presumes: "to mean or imply something is to have certain intentions" (Davis 1998: 122). As discussed in the previous chapter, Saul (2002) highlights the distinction between 'utterer-implicatures' and 'audience-implicatures.' Utterer-implicatures are claims that the speaker attempts to conversationally implicate (intended by the speaker, but not necessarily recognized by the addressee/audience). However, audience-implicatures are claims that the audience takes to be conversationally implicated (recognized by the addressee/audience but not necessarily intended by the speaker).

There have been several attempts in pragmatic theorizing to revise/correct the problems of the modular view and recognize pragmatic features of the speaker's meaning (e.g., Sperber and Wilson 1986; Carston 2002; Moeschler 2004: explicature/implicature; Burton-Roberts 2006: what-is-A-said/what-is-B-said; Bach 2001: what is said/impliciture/implicature). However, they have not gone far enough because they still were interested primarily in utterance interpretation, without paying due attention to private/individual knowledge, prior experience and the emergent, rather than the a priori only, intentions of the speaker.

The main problem with the hearer-centered views is that hearers want to or can only recover speaker meaning from a hearer perspective. They have to figure out speaker's intention by relying on linguistic signs (sentence uttered) and their own intuition biased by their understanding of the immediate situation, their prior experience and sociocultural background knowledge. As a result, what is actually 'recovered' is hearer meaning, in the sense of how the hearer interprets what the speaker said. The proposition the speaker produces will not be (cannot be) exactly the same as that which will be recovered by the hearer, because interlocutors are individuals with different cognitive predispositions, different commitments, different prior experiences and different histories of use of the same words and expressions. So there is always some slight difference between what the speaker implied and what the hearer inferred/recovered, but there is nothing wrong with that. And, we can still communicate with each other quite well. This is the case even in ELF where the gap between utterer-implicatures and audience implicatures is usually smaller than in L1 communication.

### *7.2.3 Can We Call "Utterer-Implicature" What Does Not Implicate Anything More Than What Is Said?*

Now briefly we have come back to this question again because it is crucial for ELF to answer it. "Implicate" usually means "not directly said." The dictionary meaning goes as follows: "convey (a meaning) indirectly through what one says, rather than stating it explicitly." But I claimed that implicatures in ELF do not always imply one thing by saying something else. Occasionally they imply what is said. This is mainly due to the fact that we discussed in the previous chapter. ELF users are on the semantics side of the semantics–pragmatics interface because they cannot count on contextual support as they can in L1. So if semantic analyzability prevails then there is little room for implicatures in the Gricean sense. But ELF interlocutors still implicate something that can be inferred in different ways even if they are very close to what is said.

Now before discussing implicature processing we will need to review the existing literature on implicature processing by nonnative speakers. Those studies do not focus either on oral conversation or on ELF. Their primary focus is written L2. But why do I need them then, especially since I have not been doing literature reviews in this book? I think that some of the findings shall be useful for us when we want to understand what could occur in implicature production and comprehension in ELF.

## 7.3 Former Research on Implicature Processing by Nonnative Speakers

There is almost no research on implicatures in ELF communication (at least to my knowledge) with the exception of Widdowson (2017) who related implicatures to creativity in ELF. I shall come back to this issue shortly. But first we need to review some of the findings in L2 pragmatics literature.

When we talk about implicature production and comprehension in ELF, we should underline that we cannot expect ELF users to act communicatively in accordance with the conventions of the societal culture of a native-speaking community. In spite of this, almost all of the existing literature on L2 and multilinguals implicature processing is based on the assumption *that L2 users and multilinguals should act according to the target language norms and conventions*. Thus, ELF conversations are out of the scope of that research since, as was discussed in previous chapters, ELF users, most of the time, do not follow target language norms and conventions. Besides, those L2 studies focused only on comprehension. If I want to categorize them, we can distinguish three different types of studies: one type examined implicature processing by using traditional data collection methods such as multiple choice, Discourse Completion Tests (DCT), cloze tests, or oral tests where the correct answers were usually predetermined by the researchers. In the second type, subjects were expected to interpret other people's implicature based on written or oral texts; and finally, the third type was experimental in nature.

In fact, Antoniou (forthcoming) reviewed most of the literature on L2 implicature processing including all three types I just mentioned. He argued language proficiency is an important predictor of implicature performance. As a consequence, L2 implicature processing can be described in terms of two stages. First, an early stage at which multilinguals have not yet reached an adequate level of language proficiency in the L2. This results in low level L2 implicature performance in comparison to native speakers. Second, a later stage that starts when L2 users/multilinguals have reached "a threshold level of language proficiency."[1] This developmental stage leads to "native-like implicature understanding," as Antoniou said. He also argued that at this stage, language proficiency no longer predicts implicature performance. I shall review the studies that confirm his claim in the next section.

### *7.3.1 Studies with Traditional Data Collection Methods*

The designs of these studies shared a common feature: they all offered learners predetermined interpretations in the form of multiple choice

[1] Antoniou does not define what he means by "threshold level proficiency."

selections. Multiple choice items presented learners with alternatives constructed by researchers. In these tasks the drawback was that the studies did not investigate learners' own interpretation of the alternatives in this project.

One of the pioneers of implicature studies was Bouton. In his first study (Bouton 1988), he investigated the effect of learners' cultural background on their ability to derive meaning from conversational implicatures in L2 English. With a fairly large sample size (n=436) and diverse cultural backgrounds (e.g., German, Spanish, Portuguese, Chinese, Korean, Japanese, and Taiwanese), he used a written multiple-choice task in which subjects had to choose the best implication in a conversation between two people. His findings suggested that highly proficient nonnative speakers of English with an average TOEFL score of 550 had different interpretations of implicatures compared to native speakers approximately 21 percent of the time.[2] Later, Bouton (1992) focused on the effect of target culture exposure, length of stay, and teaching intervention (1994) on implicature processing. He used various instruments (namely, structure test, cloze test, dictation, and multiple-choice tasks) to evaluate the ability to comprehend conversational implicatures in his studies. On that account, he noted that the improvement of the participants was particularly visible in items that required familiarity with the American culture. Similiarly, he argued that one impediment for the nonnative speakers in having nativelike interpretations in conversational implicatures was their lack of ability in understanding criticism. He also found that length of stay had a positive effect on implicature processing (Bouton 1994). Moreover, Bouton's (1994) study on the effect of instruction revealed that formal instruction was successful when it focused on implicatures that are formulaic in nature. He used an experimental group of fourteen nonnative speakers of English who received instruction on four different types of conversational implicatures. The instruction was six hours of class time spread over a six-week period. Participants received definitions of each type of implicature, and they also received examples of how those implicatures may work in different contexts. The control group consisted of fourteen nonnative speakers of English who did not get any instruction on implicatures. The findings showed that production of the experimental group was better than that of the control group. Later, Taguchi (2005) and Taguchi, Li and Liu (2013) continued Bouton's work, and investigated the relationship between (L2) proficiency and comprehension of implied meaning in spoken dialogues as measured by accuracy and speed of comprehension. The study had 46 native English speakers as the control group and 160 Japanese students at different levels of English proficiency. The thirty-eight-item computerized listening task was followed by multiple-choice questions that measured the

[2] TOEFL score out of 600.

participants' ability to understand different types of conversational implicatures including indirect requests, indirect refusals, negative implied meaning, and non-negative implied meaning. Their findings demonstrated that accuracy of the interpretation of conversational implicatures significantly increased with L2 proficiency. In addition, Taguchi et al. (2013) also investigated the comprehension of conventional and non-conventional implicatures in Chinese, and the research design was similar to Taguchi (2005). Their findings were also similar: There was a significant correlation between the implicature type and accuracy, but not between implicature type and comprehension speed. Participants' proficiency level affected their accuracy. More proficient learners outperformed their peers at lower levels.

### *7.3.2 Explaining Implicatures*

Shively, Menke, and Manzon-Omundson (2008) investigated irony in Spanish films by L2 learners of Spanish. Irony can be considered a type of conversational implicature. Their innovative approach compared the effect of different modalities on the comprehension of conversational implicatures. They used the same test items in both written and audio-visual format. The project had fifty-five L2 learners of Spanish as subjects. They were presented with eight contexts (six with irony and two with distractors). Twenty-seven subjects took the written and twenty-eight took the audio-visual format of the task. Following each context, the subjects were asked to write or say what they thought the implicatures meant. Again, the results were not that significant as they argue that the recognition of irony improved with the proficiency level. The different modes of presentation (written and audio-visual) did not lead to a significant difference in participants' scores either.

A recent study by Köylü (2018) aimed to test comprehension of conversational implicatures by L2 learners by asking learners to report their own interpretation of what the researcher identified as implicatures. The task he used was an audio-visual task comprised of twenty scenes from the popular TV series *Friends*. The results demonstrated that the comprehension of conversational implicatures improved with L2 proficiency. In order to find the answer to his research question, he speculated that learners first need to be able to decode linguistic and contextual cues to understand the literal meaning of an utterance. Following that, they should recognize the gap between the literal and the intended meaning. He thought that it was only after these steps had been taken that L2 learners could use cues to make inferences about speakers' implied intentions. Also, he argued that stages of acquisition of conversational implicatures grow parallel with stages of proficiency growth.

As we can see, all studies in Sections 7.3.1 and 7.3.2 tested the level of understanding conversational implicatures in L2. Their main findings were that the higher the subjects' proficiency was, the closer was their interpretation to that of L1 speakers. In fact, that is not news to us at all. Lower-level proficiency relies mainly on literal meaning recognition while non-literal interpretations require understanding language at a higher, usually figurative, level. If the utterer-implicature requires beyond-literal interpretation, that will hardly work for subjects with lower levels of proficiency because they are preoccupied with semantic decoding. This is in accordance with all kinds of implicature interpretation, especially if the utterer is an L1 speaker and the interpreter is an L2 speaker. On that account, Slabakova (2010) and Slabakova & Mayo (2013) suggested that implicature understanding is achieved using universal mechanisms of language use. Their account predicts that if learners know the semantics of the target language and have sufficient language processing capacity in the L2, then pragmatic computations should not constitute a problem for them. So the Slabakova findings confirmed what we have argued before: there is no difference as far as the computing mechanisms are concerned between L1 and nonnative speakers. Yet, the way they use those mechanisms might differ.

### 7.3.3 *Experimental Studies*

Experimental implicature studies focused mainly on multilingual children. There are no clear findings that would claim or suggest that implicature comprehension in multilingual and monolingual children differs significantly. For instance, Antoniou and Katsos (2017) compared three groups of school-aged children (six to nine years old): multilingual children (in Standard Modern Greek, Cypriot Greek, English, and, in some cases, an additional language), children who were bi-dialectal (in Standard Modern Greek and Cypriot Greek), and monolingual children (in Standard Modern Greek). Multilingual and bi-dialectal children were recruited from Cyprus and monolingual children in Greece. All multilinguals attended an English-instruction school. Approximately half of the subjects were mainly exposed to/used Cypriot Greek (Cypriot Greek-dominant) and the rest were mostly exposed to/used English (English-dominant). The majority of subjects had started being exposed to their L2 (Cypriot Greek or English) before their third year of life. The researchers tested each group in the interpretation of various implicatures (relevance, manner, scalar implicatures, and novel metaphors). Bi-dialectal and multilingual children took the test in Cypriot Greek (dialect of the community and bi-dialectals' dominant, first dialect) and monolinguals in Standard Greek. Also, language proficiency in Greek was tested for all participants as well. Based on a previous study by Siegal et al. (2007), Antoniou and Katsos expected that multilingual – and possibly bi-dialectal – children would excel in implicature comprehension relative to monolinguals. They used a picture-selection test in which subjects were presented with a statement (e.g., the figurative sentence 'George's father was a melting snowman.') and had to respond by selecting one of two pictures (e.g., a sad man or an angry man); a judgment task was used for scalar implicatures. Their findings proposed that lower expressive vocabulary in Greek for multilinguals and bi-dialectals as compared to monolinguals (with bi-dialectals having a higher vocabulary than multilinguals), but no group differences in implicature performance. They also concluded that there were no differences with monolinguals whether considering the Cypriot Greek- or the English-dominant multilingual sub-group. As a result, Antoniou and Katsos suggested that multilingual and bi-dialectal children can be expected to have similar levels of implicature comprehension to monolinguals, even when their proficiency in the language of testing may be lower.

In another study, Antoniou (forthcoming) confirmed that language proficiency predicted implicature comprehension in the monolingual and bi-dialectal groups, but only age was a significant positive predictor in multilinguals. Based on their findings, the authors came up with the result that multilingual children are comparable to monolinguals (and bi-dialectals) in their implicature understanding skills, but this is achieved, possibly, by using different resources. Besides, they suggested that the positive contribution of age in multilinguals can be attributed to a non-verbal cognitive factor that develops with age.

It is also worthwhile to highlight that there are several other studies, namely, Dupuy et al. (2018), Syrett, Austin et al. (2016), and Syrett, Lingwall et al. (2017), which also reported no significant differences between bilingual and monolingual children in scalar implicature comprehension. In fact, in a more recent study, Antoniou, Veenstra, Kissine, and Katsos (forthcoming) conducted another test of the hypothesis of superior implicature comprehension in bilingual children.[3] In this study, they used a test that assessed both accuracy and processing speed of comprehension for various implicature types. They included implicatures that had not been previously investigated in multilinguals, such as contrastive implicatures (e.g., when the phrase 'open window' implicates that there is another window in the situation) and irony. The experiment included three groups of participants (ten to twelve years old): French-Dutch bilingual, Dutch-West Flemish bi-dialectal, and Dutch monolingual children; all bilingual children were dominant in French, but attended a Dutch-instruction school from their third year, and testing took place in Dutch. Their results indicated that, with control items involving no implicature, all groups performed very well and were equally fast. Moreover, there was significant variation in implicature performance on a number of variables other than the monolingual/multilingual status. First, implicature performance positively

[3] See description in Antoniou (forthcoming).

correlated with working memory (though not with vocabulary). There was, however, little evidence that the relation between implicature understanding and working memory differed in the three groups. This suggests that all groups relied on their working memory resources similarly when interpreting implicatures. Second, novel metaphors and irony were the hardest for all children to understand, regardless of how many languages or dialects they spoke. Third, implicature responses to critical items in all sub-tests were slower than literal responses to control items. Based on these findings, the researchers suggested that implicature processing is effortful for all children. Nonetheless, what matters for us here is that more effort was needed when critical items were expected to be processed. Despite this variation, however, no differences were observed between monolinguals and the other two groups either in implicature responses or in speed of implicature processing. This finding corroborates with Antoniou and Katsos' (2017) study, despite bilinguals' and bi-dialectals' lower vocabularies in the language of testing.

Based on these results, and building on previous work by Slabakova (2010), Slabakova & Mayo (2013), and Kecskes (2015b), Antoniou et al. (forthcoming) proposed an account of bilingual pragmatic development and processing according to which bilinguals have a single pragmatic system – at least for the kind of pragmatic competence that is required for implicature interpretation – that is language-independent and that develops and operates in a similar way to monolinguals. We can agree with this statement, but not necessarily with the part that says the "single pragmatic system" is language-independent. We have, in fact, explained this in the previous chapters. What's more, Antoniou et al.'s (under review) data show that there is a point in language development at which language proficiency stops being a significant predictor of pragmatic comprehension (even though there is still variability in pragmatic performance). The authors argued that "these results suggest separation of pragmatics from language." It seems to me that they have taken it too far by suggesting "separation of pragmatics from language." It is unclear though what they mean by "language" here. As a matter of fact, they probably opted for the separation of pragmatics from semantics. If so, this is contrary to what we said in the previous chapter: diachronic pragmatics (semantics) and synchronic pragmatics are intertwined both in production and comprehension.

The cross-linguistic evidence we have reviewed (see also Grice, 1989; Katsos et al. 2016) indicates that implicature comprehension and pragmatic maxims of conversation are universal properties of language use. This suggests that maxims of conversation are represented as a single pragmatic system and that, across their languages, multilinguals have experience equal to monolinguals with pragmatic aspects of language. Finally, Antoniou et al. (forthcoming) found that pragmatic comprehension draws on working memory, but there was little evidence that bilinguals or bi-dialectals used these resources differently from monolinguals when interpreting implicatures. The last two considerations indicate that pragmatic comprehension possibly develops and operates similarly in multilinguals and monolinguals. Siegal and colleagues' (2007) research suggested that bilingual children exhibit precocious pragmatic development. Their findings highlighted that bilingual children of preschool age are better than monolinguals in detecting utterances that violate Gricean maxims and in understanding scalar implicatures. However, research by Antoniou and colleagues (2017, under review), Dupuy et al. (2018), Johnson (1991), and Syrett and collaborators (2016, 2017) found no differences between multilingual and monolingual children in pragmatic comprehension. This has been shown for a wide range of implicatures (relevance, scalar, manner, contrastive implicatures, metaphors, and irony), with different methodologies (picture-selection, judgment tasks), for both comprehension accuracy and speed of processing, for different age groups (three to twelve years old), for different language and cultural groups, and regardless of whether multilingual children were tested in their L1 or L2. These studies also had little evidence that multilingual children rely more or use differently their executive control resources than their monolingual counterparts in the process of understanding implicatures. So we can ultimately determine that the bulk of the evidence suggests that implicature understanding develops and operates similarly in multilingual and monolingual children. Now we shall relate the findings presented above to the discussion about how implicatures are processed by nonnative speakers, including ELF interlocutors.

## 7.4 Processing Implicatures

### *7.4.1 A Possible Processing Model*

One might ask: how do we understand implicatures? And, what makes us capable of correctly processing something that is not said directly in the Gricean sense? In order for us to answer these questions, we should go back to Chapter 4 where I proposed a model that explains the relationship between three factors: linguistic knowledge, conceptual knowledge, and encyclopedic knowledge. In this model, we have linguistic knowledge on one side of a continuum and sociocultural background knowledge (world knowledge) on the other side. As I previously argued, there is constant interaction between the two sides. For analytic reasons, which will become important now, within the sociocultural background knowledge I suggested that we distinguish between conceptual knowledge and encyclopedic knowledge.

Linguistic knowledge —————————— Sociocultural background knowledge
conceptual knowledge — encyclopedic knowledge

In this model, meaning is constructed in the dynamic interplay of actual situational context and semantic content of lexical items, with the context representing the actual, present, situational, ever-changing side of sociocultural background and the lexical item(s) encapsulating previous experiences and relations in the sociocultural background. The lexical items with their semantic properties (linguistic knowledge) represent prior reoccurring experience (conceptual knowledge) and the actual situational context triggers the other part of world knowledge that we have called encyclopedic knowledge. *So the difference between the two types of sociocultural background knowledge (world knowledge) is that the conceptual knowledge part is immediately tied to linguistic knowledge (semantics) while the other type of sociocultural background knowledge (encyclopedic knowledge) is called upon as needed in the actual situational context*. But, how does that work for implicatures? There are two cases when speaker-hearers have no problem, or only a slight problem with implicatures: A) If what is said is what is meant, compositional meaning prevails. The only problem in this case can be proficiency in case of ELF speakers. This is what some of the aforementioned studies referred to; that the hearer does not understand a word or expression. Here are examples for both instances:

(5) L1 speakers
JIM: - You look exhausted.
ANDY: - Tell me about it. *I have been on the road for 22 hours.*
JIM: - You better take a rest.

The compositional meaning of the utterance makes it easy to connect exhaustion with traveling. There is a match between utterer-implicature and hearer-implicature. Not like in the next example:

(6) ELF speakers: a Hungarian student (Sandor) and a German student (Manfred) are talking.
SANDOR: - I think Sue's argument was incorrect.
MANFRED: - *You may have missed the boat there*. I guess she was right.
SANDOR: - It was not about a boat.
MANFRED: - Sorry, you may not have understood her point.

As you can see, the Hungarian student, Sandor did not seem to have understood the idiomatic expression 'missed the boat' used by Manfred, the German student. This is not an implicature problem. It appears to be primarily a language problem, but is it? Later we will return to this issue. Now we should look at the other case.

B) No problem is expected to occur if the implicature can be processed on the basis of general encyclopedic knowledge that most people are familiar with, no matter what their L1 or previous language experience is, as is the case in example (7).

(7) MARY: People usually listen to me.
ANNE: *You're lucky because you're pretty.*
MARY: -What does prettiness have to do with attention?
ANNE: - A lot.

As you can see, the utterer-implicature is that pretty people are usually listened to. This is supposed to be quite a well-known stereotypical way of thinking no matter what language someone speaks (knowledge of the world). It is understood thus by Mary but, as her reaction shows, she does not agree with it.

### *7.4.2 Processing Problems*

The real problem in producing implicatures (utterer-implicatures) and processing implicatures (audience implicatures) occurs when speaker-hearers, especially ELF ones will/must rely on conceptual knowledge that is culture-specific or linguistic knowledge where diachronic pragmatics prevails and some culture-specific conceptual property is encoded in a lexical item or expression such as 'chicken out,' 'patronize,' 'cake walk,' and 'kick the bucket.' Let us see examples for both cases:

(8) A Turkish student (TS) is talking to a Korean student (KS).
KS: - Do you know where Arnold is?
TS: - *There is a Humvee outside.*
KS: - What do you mean?
TS: - *His girlfriend is in the military.*
KS: - Okay..?
TS: - That Humvee is used by military personal.

As you might have guessed, there are two problems here: First, the Turkish student used an utterer-implicature that did not take into account the possible limitations of the hearer's background knowledge. There was no recipient design at all. The utterer-implicature included two requirements for the Korean student. He should know what 'Humvee' is. [High Mobility Multipurpose Wheeled Vehicle (HMMWV; colloquial: Humvee) is a family of light, four-wheel drive, military trucks and utility vehicles produced by AM General.] This is the short name for that type of vehicle in American culture, which is culture-specific knowledge. Besides, the Korean student was expected to know that Arnold's girlfriend is in the military. This information could not be inferred without knowing what Humvee is. As the Korean's interpretation shows neither of the utterer-implicatures went through, and the Turkish student had to give an explanation. Now let's look at example (9).

(9) A Chinese student (CS) is helping a Russian student (RS) use the ATM.
CS: - Olga, put your card in the reader there, and then type in your PIN number when it prompts.
RS: - *Don't patronize me.* I know how to use an ATM.
CS: - You don't want me to help? Sorry . . . ..

In this example, although the Chinese student gave a detailed explanation of how to use the ATM the Russian student took offense. She thought that what was said, communicated not only the process of how to use the ATM but also some condescending message. This, however, was not the intention of the Chinese student. He meant what he said without any 'beyond literal' meaning. This is the danger of utterer-implicatures: when they are inferred by the hearer, s/he may feel that something is implied by the speaker even if this is not the case. This is the strongest justification for us to use the term "utterer-implicature" even when there is nothing implied by the speaker beyond what is said. In this exchange there was also some confusion on the Chinese side because of the verb 'patronize.' He did not seem to have clearly understood what the Russian girl's offended tone implied.

One of the most typical examples of the crucial role of conceptual knowledge in processing implicature is the so-called Pope Q implicature. This is a type of relevance-based implicature which Bouton labelled pope' questions, (Pope-Q) after the prototypical example "Is the Pope Catholic?" (see Bouton 1988, 1994). This is a seemingly unrelated response that is applied to indicate (usually in a good-natured way) that a question has been asked to which the answer is very obvious, as in (10).

(10) KATE: - Do you think it will rain tomorrow?
BOB: - *Is the Pope catholic?*

The interesting thing is that we can lexicalize this pragmatic function in different ways such as 'do bears fly?'; 'does the sun come up in the east?'; etc. All these expressions refer to the same thing: 'isn't something obvious?' However, there is an important issue here for ELF users. Most of the lexicalizations of this pragmatic function are language- and culture-specific. The more culture-specific they are, the more difficulty ELF users face in inferring the right meaning. In one of my previous studies (Kecskes 2001: 258), I used the following example:

(11) AMY: - Don't you think Jim drinks a bit too much?
BILLY: - *Is the Pope catholic?*

While analyzing the data, I noticed that some of the nonnative speaker subjects gave very odd interpretations. Let us look at some of their responses:

Russian student (2 years in the USA, female, age 23): "Catholics drink too much."

Spanish student (6 months in the USA, female, age 27): "Billy thinks that catholic people drink too much."
Spanish student (8 months in the USA, male, age 22): "Billy confused catholic with alcoholic."

As you can see, all interpretations were incorrect and showed that the utterer-implicature did not match the audience-implicatures. The main reason of this discrepancy was that the compositional meaning of the utterance did not make sense in the given situation. So the interpretation was based on guessing rather than inferring the right meaning. There are, of course, cases when L2 speakers infer the right meaning, but they just do not seem to like what the utterer-implicature implies, even if it perfectly matches the hearer-implicature, as in (12).

(12) Ulrike is a German student and Joe is an American one.
ULRIKE: - Don't you think that the dean was quite rude to me?
JOE: - *Is the Pope catholic?*
ULRIKE: - I think so. But why do you ask?
JOE: - What?

In this example, I do not think that Ulrike 'missed the boat.' She was perfectly aware of the conveyed meaning of the question. But she pretended to have interpreted it literally, which seemed to have confused Joe a bit.

Thus, we should be careful when analyzing this type of implicatures because some of the lexicalizations of the pragmatics function (something is obvious) are widely used like 'is the Pope catholic?' or 'do bears fly?' while others are created in the course of conversation, as in example (13). It seems that what they have in common is only their communicative function: express something that is obvious.

(13) Example from Bouton (1988: 191).
Two roommates are talking about what they are going to do during the summer.
FRAN: My mother wants me to stay home and entertain the relatives when they come to visit us at the beach.
JOAN: Do you have a lot of relatives?
FRAN: *Does a dog have fleas?*

In this brief exchange, the expression Fran used is not very common or may have been generated in the course of conversation.[4] Now this discussion has led us to examine how salience affects implicature use in general and in ELF in particular.

[4] Of course, I am aware of the fact that Bouton made up that example. But it still illustrates my point quite well.

## 7.5 Salience and Implicatures

We argued several times that language production and comprehension are motivated not only by cooperation but also egocentrism, both of which are parts of human rationality (see, for instance, Kecskes 2014, 2017, and previous chapters). In producing and processing implicatures, figurativity and formulaicity play a decisive role, and create a major difference between L1 and non-L1 users. Both figurativity and formulaicity are connected with salience. Peleg et al. (2001) argued that context may affect comprehension immediately, but it is ineffective in blocking (contextually incompatible) salient meanings, since it does not interact with lexical processes but runs in parallel. But, how does this concern ELF? Well, very significantly, because salience effect cancels the decisive role of the literal-figurative dichotomy in production and comprehension and makes salient meaning the center of attention. As a consequence, the most salient meaning of a word, expression or utterance prevails both in production and comprehension, and that most salient meaning can be either figurative or literal or both. So in top-down processing (comprehension) and online production, what matters is the most salient meaning that is based on prior experience, familiarity, frequency, prominence, etc., and that, as a cumulative effect, will override any contextual effect. If we agree on this, then we can say that both utterer-implicature and audience-implicature may work differently for an L1 speaker-hearer than for an ELF speaker-hearer. More processing effort is needed on the ELF side. This is basically what the experimental studies that I reviewed above have demonstrated. In example (6) we already highlighted this problem and promised to come back to it with more explanation. So here are two more examples to illustrate this point:

(14) L1 speakers
TOM: - Are you coming to the Quincy Jones' concert?
SALLY: - *It's not my cup of tea.*
TOM: - OK, I understand. Not everyone likes his music.

(15) ELF speakers (Russian and Chinese)
SASHA: - Are you coming to the Quincy Jones' concert?
XIAO: - *It's not my cup of tea.*
SASHA: - What does tea have to do with the concert?
XIAO: - OK, I just do not like Quincy's music.

In both cases the utterance 'It's not my cup of tea' means the same thing indirectly: I do not like QJ and/or his music so I won't go to the concert. What is implicated is almost like what is said for the L1 speakers. No special processing effort is needed. Based on their L1 prior experience, a particular familiarity develops with this kind of figurative and formulaic expressions as a result of language socialization. As Tannen and Öztek (1981: 54) argued, "cultures that have set formulas afford their members the tranquility of knowing that what they say will be interpreted by the addressee in the same way that it is intended, and that, after all, is the ultimate purpose of communication." Therefore, formulaic expressions and figurative language usually do not complicate L1 production and use, rather they simplify them. Utterer-implicature more often than not matches audience-implicature. This is the second point where we can see the importance of understanding implicatures as more than expressions that convey something above literal and/or compositional meaning, as in the Gricean paradigm.[5] In fact utterer-implicatures can mean exactly what the utterance says: nothing more, nothing less. What really counts is what message that *wording* usually conveys to the speakers of that language community. It is important to note that formulaic and idiomatic expressions are usually not polysemic. They mean and (usually) imply the same thing for the members of the speech community. In other words, they function like frozen implicatures. But, how is this possible? And, what is 'frozen' in them? How does this happen? A particular communicative act and/or repeated speech event gets worded in a particular, usually metaphoric way (but not always) that may convey some meaning above compositional/literal meanings of words in the expression such as 'it's not my cup of tea' (not my favorite), 'help yourself' (take whatever you want), 'stick around' (don't go away), 'be my guest' (allowing, permitting). But it can also happen that the compositional meaning of an expression gets similar privileged status, such as 'what can I do for you?,' 'this way, please,' 'I have nothing to wear.' Because of repeated use and recurrence, the expression may become privileged to denote that particular communicative act or speech event, no matter that the wording may be not the literal way to describe that act or event. So what counts is the functional meaning of the expression, i.e., the communicative function that the expression conveys. The functional meaning of the expression can override the compositional meaning of the words that makes up the expression. This is how the functional meaning becomes the most salient meaning of the expression in the given speech community (like in the expressions just mentioned). If these expressions are used in the given speech community, there is no modular effect. No literal meaning is processed first. The most salient meaning prevails, no matter whether it is the literal/compositional meaning or the figurative meaning of the expression. The implication in the expression, the metaphorism, is not dead. These are not dead implicatures or metaphors but they are 'frozen' in the sense that they stopped denoting anything but the functional meaning attached to

[5] The first point was explained with example (8).

them. So L1 speakers produce these formulaic expressions quite often, as Tannen and Öztek (1981: 54) have said. What can be better for smooth communication than a perfect match between an utterer-implicature and an audience implicature? What is implicated in the utterer-implicature is fully recovered in the audience-implicature, as in example (16):

(16) JACK: - *You are beating around the bush.* Tell me what really happened.
JENNY: - Nothing really happened between me and Bill. I already told you.
Jenny's response shows that she was fully aware of the meaning of the idiomatic expression 'You are beating around the bush' ('not speaking directly about the issue').

It is true that in L1 no literal meaning is processed first: the most salient meaning gets processed first, be it either literal or figurative. Interlocutors jump to the best interpretation (the most salient one) that fits the context. But still, Widdowson may be wrong when he says that those formulaic expressions are not implicatures for L1 speakers. No special inference is needed for the hearer to process them. Here is what Widdowson (2017: 277–278) said talking about the Gricean maxims and implicature:

But it must be stressed that these maxims relate to presuppositions of familiarity. So for example if in conversation with a fellow native speaker of English I were to say that somebody had been barking up the wrong tree, or had shot himself in the foot, since these are familiar idiomatic phrases they would not be noticed as maxim violations and there would be no implicature. If, however, I wanted to give a more incisive edge to my meaning, I could play on words, as the phrase goes, and creatively adjust the wording of these idiomatic expressions. I might say 'he is not just barking up the wrong tree but up the wrong wood' or 'he has just shot his whole family in the foot.' Such rewordings *do* give rise to implicatures in that they depart from the customary patterns of use in order to achieve a special effect.

It is clear that for Widdowson, 'implicature' means something that departs from the familiar and 'customary patterns of use.' He further argued that there is no implicature without bilateral condition of mutual norm recognition. He said the following: "If the condition of mutual norm familiarity is not met, there is no implicature" (Widdowson 2017: 278). So the criteria for implicature are twofold for him: maxim violation ["When a maxim is violated, the effect is what Grice refers to as an 'implicature'"], and bilateral condition of mutual norm recognition. Let us see how this works for formulaic language in L1 and for ELF in general.

Can we argue that there is no implicature in L1 when we use a well-known formulaic expression like in examples (6), (14), and (16)? I think in all these examples the two criteria Widdowson talks about are met. There is a violation of a maxim, and there is bilateral norm recognition. So there is utterer-implicature that should be inferred by the hearer, i.e. that matches audience-implicature. 'You are beating around the bush' means/implies 'you are not telling what exactly happened,' 'It's not my cup of tea' means/implies 'it is not what I like.' This is clearly saying something and meaning something else. So there is a clear maxim violation. But that violation is 'frozen'; it is not a one-time occurrence, and as such is valid for most of the situations in which the given expression is used. So as this 'violation' is always there, it does not count as such any more. There is no need for any special cognitive effort to figure out what the speaker implies. This way the use of these expressions meets language-use norms, which is mutually recognized. As I said before, there is a perfect match between utterer-implicature and audience-implicature. Why is this possible? It seems to me that it is the common sociocultural background in L1 that results in conceptual knowledge, which leads to mutual understanding of those frequently occurring linguistic expressions.

Now we need to examine how this phenomenon is different for ELF users. Widdowson connected implicature use in ELF with creativity. He considers ELF creativity as acts of intended non-conformity, deliberate departures from an expected norm (Widdowson 2017: 277). He claimed that in the pragmatic case these departures are intended to have a particular perlocutionary effect – to make an utterance emphatic, ironic, amusing and so on. Also, he emphasized that to be a non-conformist in this way is to act against what Grice (1975) called the cooperative principle. According to Widdowson, the maxim that is of particular relevance to creativity is the so-called 'maxim of manner,' which calls for perspicuity of expression. Thus, when people communicate, they would normally be expected to conform to this clarity condition, avoid obscurity and ambiguity and make their meanings as transparent as possible. Thus, creative uses of language go against this maxim since they are of their nature non-conformist and unexpected, and so they quite naturally give rise to implicatures. So far so good! But then Widdowson (2017: 278–279) said the following:

> But this bilateral condition of mutual norm recognition typically does not apply in contexts of interaction between ELF users. If one or more than one of them is a non-native speaker, as is frequently the case, they exploit whatever linguistic resources they have at their disposal to get their meaning across and whatever non-conformities they produce are not usually intended to be noticed as such, and even if they are, the recipient may well not be able to ratify the intention. If the condition of mutual norm familiarity is not met, there is no implicature. In what sense, then, can ELF usage be considered creative?

I do not agree with Widdowson's argument that implicature occurs only if the condition of mutual familiarity is met. If that were true, there would be almost no implicature in ELF communication. Furthermore, Widdowson (2017: 279) continues arguing like this:

> According to the co-operative principle, an implicaturc comcs about when a departure from the default norm is intended and recognized as such. The usual assumption is that this norm is preconceived a schematic construct already known by the participants as a basis for their co-operation. But when ELF users co-operate in their communication – since they come from different linguacultural backgrounds – they cannot rely on such shared preconceptions. How do ELF users from Lecce and Leicester, for example, or from Bangkok and Barcelona manage to communicate? The answer, I suggest, is that they negotiate pro-tem norms online in the adaptive, emergent process of their very interaction. The co-operative principle still applies, as it must apply to all communication, but it is acted upon in ways that do not require conformity to conventional native speaker ways in which the principle is put into practice.

I argue that Widdowson is right that ELF users lack core common ground that would enable them to use and process implicatures the way L1 users do: Since they come from different linguacultural backgrounds, they cannot rely on shared preconceptions. But that does not mean that they do not use implicatures. The cognitive mechanisms for implicatures are the same no matter what language someone uses. However, linguistic knowledge, conceptual knowledge and encyclopedic knowledge that all are needed for implicatures vary significantly in ELF users, especially conceptual knowledge that is the key for implicatures as we saw in the previous examples. So ELF users cannot act and cannot be expected to act in accordance with the conventions of the societal culture of a native-speaking community. They must create their own temporary norms and conventions with implicatures in them.

## 7.6 Summary

All of our arguments, examples and reviewed studies on implicature comprehension in L2 and multilingual subjects demonstrated that there is no fundamental difference between L1, L2, and ELF users as far as mechanism used for implicature processing is concerned. Although all studies that were reviewed focused on comprehension, and were conducted in unlifelike situations, two of their findings confirmed what I said about implicature use in ELF. First, there is a significant dependency on proficiency. The more proficient interlocutors are in the target language, the better their implicature performance is expected to be. Thus, understanding the code is a precondition of any comprehension and also production. Also, Antoniou et al.'s (forthcoming) research showed that there is a point in language development at which language proficiency stops being a significant predictor of pragmatic comprehension. The authors even suggested separation of pragmatics from language. It seems to me that by 'language' they probably understood the code system with codified meanings of lexical items. Beyond the threshold they talk about, what really counts is encyclopedic knowledge and conceptual knowledge that is language and culture-specific.

A second point that was made in several studies on L2 implicatures is about what types of implicatures were most difficult for the subjects to process. Findings revealed that implicatures that relied on formulaic and figurative language – namely, novel metaphors, irony, and idiomatic expressions – where specific conceptual knowledge was required for correct processing were especially hard for subjects to comprehend.

Since ELF users have only limited access to core common ground and collective salience of the target language, and the bilateral condition of mutual norm recognition does not support their implicature production and inferencing, they rely more on ad hoc generated implicatures than frozen ones or conventionalized ones. But examples demonstrated that ELF users produce and comprehend implicatures just as frequently as their L1 counterparts. And at this point, I argued that Widdowson is right when he connects implicature use in ELF with linguistic creativity. Instead of depending on mutual conceptual knowledge that drives implicature use in L1, ELF users rely on co-constructed and temporarily shared knowledge bases to behave as "normally" and naturally as L1 speakers do when they use and comprehend implicatures.

What was said about implicatures matches our discussion about the semantics–pragmatics interface. Preference for semantic analyzability creates "utterer-implicatures" that usually do not implicate anything beyond what is said in ELF. But still we have kept calling them implicatures and not "implicitures" or "explicatures" as they are called in the Gricean literature because they are the results of the same mechanism as is the case in L1. What we can observe in ELF interactions is a kind of pragmaticization of semantics which is a synchronic, one-off phenomenon in which coded meaning, sometimes without any specific pragmatic enrichment based on the target language, obtains temporary pragmatic status. ELF speakers need this online pragmaticalization process because they cannot rely on pragmatic effects as happens in L1. Target-language norms and frames do not work well in ELF so interlocutors usually need to build up their own frames in the course of interaction. Actual situation context does not help much because it may be understood differently by interlocutors. So ELF users will produce and interpret a pragmatic act including implicatures mainly based on its semantic content that is pragmaticized not by the actual contextual effect or core common ground but by prior context and knowledge and co-constructed emergent common ground. So there is no impoverished pragmatics here. What we have is pragmatics with some different emphasis than we experience in L1. Pragmatics in ELF relies not necessarily on existing norms, standards and conventions but rather on emergent intention, innovation, emergent common ground, online frame building and one-off strategies. This ELF-type of pragmatics leads us to our next topic which is modality. It will also reveal some unique features of the linguistic behavior of ELF speakers, as we will see in the next chapter.

# 8 Modality

## 8.1 The Problem

Modality is as much part of the heart and soul of language as formulaicity and figurativity. In fact, these three elements all help us to adhere to one of our main principles in communication; that is, we do not say what we think, and do not always think what we say. For this, we need a language system that reflects this double-sidedness of our communication and interaction with others. Modality is about giving an opinion on reality. Or, more precisely, it is concerned with this opinion itself, a quality that separates it from the categories of tense and aspect. On that account, Palmer (2001: 1) expanded on the definition by adding that modality is concerned with the status of the proposition that describes the event. So the point of the matter is that modality does not refer to reality itself but to its interpretation and description by a speaker. In other words, the use of modal expressions reflects the speaker's way of thinking about reality. This is the main reason that it is very important for us to examine this category in ELF. Let me start by stating that ELF users do not create new modal expressions; they rely on the rich repertoire that the English language offers to them. It also needs to be highlighted that those English modal expressions do not necessarily reflect the mindset of ELF users with different L1s: Those modals reflect the mindset of native speakers of English. Thus, the following underlying questions will be relatively covered in this chapter: what do ELF users do with the rich English language repertoire of modals? Which modals do they mostly rely on, and why? And, how do they modify the senses of modals in their ELF use?

Modality is a crucial part of our everyday language use. Just like formulaic units and figurative phrases, modal expressions are determined by diachronic pragmatics; that is, they are reflections of standardization, conventionalization, and normativization in a language. We can consider modal expressions as semantic units that give ample varieties for L1 speakers (or any other speakers of English) to express their relationship to the world through synchronic pragmatics referring to different categories of modality including possibility, probability, necessity, ability, permission, etc.

However, this is not a smooth process, and it creates two problems from the perspective of ELF. First, the only available approach of accessing modality in ELF is through the modal carriers of English used by native speakers. As I have said, ELF users will hardly create new modal expressions. It is not like creating new formulas or implicatures. They will only use the modals that are accessible for them. Nonetheless, we know that those modal carriers will work differently in ELF interactions, which takes us to the second problem as previously formulated by Hinkel (1995: 337), who argued that "the usage of the root modals must, have to, should, ought to, and need to in NS and NNS writing appears to be culture and context dependent." Context dependency is something objective that works in L1 although not the way as it does in ELF (see more in-depth discussions in previous chapters). But culture dependency is a different issue. As it happens, our culture may motivate us in how we express modal categories (e.g., possibility, probability, necessity, permission, ability), and certainly ELF speakers are far from representing any even relatively homogenous culture. So it is a significant issue for us to examine how modality works in ELF, whether there is any kind of pattern-like use there. In other words, will ELF users stick to the root semantics of modal expressions, or will they completely reconceptualize them according to their immediate needs in the process of communication? Also, will modality be as central a category in ELF as it is in L1, or will ELF speakers rely on modality much less than in L1? It goes without saying that nonnative proficiency and their different language and cultural backgrounds are expected to bring new dynamics to modality use in English as a Lingua Franca. But before we talk about modality use we need to cover knowledge about modality that has immediate relevance to ELF.

## 8.2 What Is Modality?

### *8.2.1 Definitions*

Let us start with a quote from Van der Auwera and Plungian (1998: 80) that sets our theoretical lens: "Modality and its types can be defined and named in various ways. There is no one correct way. The only requirement is that one makes clear how one uses one's terms." We can agree with this statement. In fact, this is the main principle that will drive what follows.

Summarizing research on modality, Hoye (1997) argued that there seems to be a human tendency of evaluating experiences and opinions in terms of modal categories. He maintained that "[the] capacity to envisage things other than they actually are or were ('things being otherwise'), to hold competing and incompatible world views, is fundamental to our everyday thinking" (1997: 40). Modality thus offers the possibility to describe situations not only the way in which they actually occur, but also in the ways they can be, could have been, should be, would be, must be and so on; how they are 'otherwise.'

We can certainly contrast unmodalized utterances with modalized utterances: Unmodalized utterances are used by the speaker to describe reality in its actual circumstance; they denote that the speaker perceives a situation as true (*realis*). In contract, modalized utterances describe scenarios that are theoretically possible but not known by the speaker for sure to be the actual case (*irrealis*). To make this point clear, let us look at examples (1) and (2):

(1) Peter *mailed* the letter yesterday.
(2) Peter *may have mailed* the letter yesterday.

As you can see, when the speaker produced the unmodalized utterance of 'Peter mailed the letter yesterday,' he made a factual assertion about a state of affairs that he considered to be the case. The utterer-implicature is that the letter was definitely mailed according to the knowledge of the speaker. By contrast, when the speaker said 'Peter may have mailed the letter yesterday,' he expressed a state of affairs which was possibly real even if it was not in fact the case. The utterer-implicature, here, is that the mailing may or may not have happened.

Additionally, linguists (e.g., Palmer 1990, 2001, 2003; van de Auwera & Plungian 1998; Downing & Locke 2002; Hoye 1997) consider modality a semantic category that covers such notions as possibility, probability, necessity, volition, obligation and permission and ability. Historically, as a semantic category, modality has gone through a myriad of developments, and is in constant change in English as well as in any other language. Moreover, Leech (2003, 2013) discussed several changes including declines and increases in modality use. Investigating recent changes in the spoken English language, Bowie, Wallis and Aarts (2013) demonstrated that there is not only decline in the use of core modals (for instance, should, may, could, shall, ought to) but also in some cases, there is increase (such as need to, want to, supposed to). These diachronic changes are the results of several variables including sociocultural developments, demographics, economic changes, and the inner development of language. So there is no doubt that ELF may bring in changes as related to the relatively standard modality use in the English language. However, the real question for us is whether these changes induced by ELF are fleeting, or if they will leave some traits in the global use of English. We shall cover all these issues shortly.

### *8.2.2 Epistemic and Root Modality*

Our goal here is to select/create an approach that gives us the best possible way to highlight those questions that are especially important for ELF. So, we are not going to cover all various subcategorizations of modals in existing linguistic literature. Therefore, we should start with making a difference between *speaker-oriented modals* (or epistemic modals) and *agent-oriented modals* (also known as root modals) with two further subcategories: deontic and dynamic modals.

We consider epistemic modals as speaker-oriented while deontic and dynamic modals as agent-oriented (see, for instance, Bybee & Fleischman 1995). Speaker-oriented (or epistemic) modals are said to communicate the degree of speaker commitment to the truth of the proposition that forms the complement of the modal. They present the speaker's subjective take on reality. Agent-oriented (or deontic and dynamic) modals are concerned with the necessity or possibility of acts performed by morally responsible agents, such as obligation and permission (e.g., Lyons 1977; Palmer 1986, 1990; Sweetser 1990; Bybee & Fleischman 1995). These modals express the way the speaker wishes or desires to see reality. The following utterances are expected to demonstrate these differences: examples (3) and (4) stand for epistemic modality while examples (5) and (6) represent deontic modality:

(3) This must be the house we are looking for.
(4) Taking a course in pragmatics should be useful for you.
(5) The dog should be operated on.
(6) You may leave the room if you have signed this document.

Besides the epistemic/deontic distinction, there is a third area of modal meaning that is often recognized by linguists, that is the *dynamic* modality, which includes the notional categories of real-world ability, possibility, and intention/willingness (see von Wright 1951; Palmer 1990). Also, dynamic modality refers to the ability or the requirement of the agent to do something. It is nonsubjective in contrast to the similar deontic modality, and is usually expressed with [can] or [will]. The following examples make this distinction clearer.

(7) Your friend can play the piano very well.
(8) Peter will be a teacher in an elementary school.

Sometimes the same utterance can be interpreted as expressing both epistemic and deontic modality like in example (9):

(9) You must be very tolerant to other people's views.

This utterance can be interpreted in two different ways and paraphrased as either "I definitely infer/conclude that you are very tolerant to other people's views" or as "You are required to be very tolerant to other people's views." The first meaning is epistemic whereas the second is deontic.

Table 8.1 is a simplified summary of modal categories.

Deontic and dynamic modality represent two sides of root modality. Thus, we shall talk about two types of modal meanings:

Table 8.1 *Modal categories*

| Epistemic | Deontic | Dynamic |
|---|---|---|
| necessity | obligation | ability |
| probability | permission | volition |
| possibility | | |

**Modal Meanings**

A) Epistemic modality: meanings that are to do with the speaker's judgment about things and events.

You may be mad at me.
Jim is probably right.
They must be home by now.

B) Root (deontic-dynamic) modality: meanings that are to do with an ability to control things or with the necessity or possibility of acts performed by morally responsible agents, such as obligation and permission. Meanings of root modality can also express the speaker's desire for the world to be in a particular way or state.

Sally can develop computer programs.
The kids should return home by ten.

### *8.2.3 Linguistic Means of Expressing Modality*

We are not aiming to provide a full picture of the many ways modality can be expressed in English in this book. However, a basic summary is needed so that we can go back to them when examining their use in ELF.

Modal auxiliaries proper: can, could, may, might, must, ought to, shall, should, will, would

Marginal modal auxiliaries: need, dare, have to, used to

Other expressions of modality:

- modal adverbs, e.g., maybe, probably, surely, certainly
- modal auxiliary equivalents, i.e., paraphrases of modal meanings (e.g., be possible, be willing to, be necessary that ...)

**Root Meanings of Modal Auxiliaries**

**ability** (can/could): Can you swim?

**permission** (can/could, may/might): Can/May I leave the table?

**obligation** (must, ought to, shall/should): No, you must/ought to/should stay.

**volition** (will/would): I will leave the room anyway. I would leave the room if I were you.

**possibility** (may/might): The guests may arrive late.
**prediction** (will/shall): I'm afraid, I won't/shan't be able to come.
**habitual activity** (will/would): In the evening, father would stand by the window and watch the cars go by.

There are two main issues when we analyze modal use in ELF. The first one is connected with the scale of modal strength, and the second is about category boundaries between root modals and epistemic modals. Let us look at the first issue:

(10) You should tell me the truth.
(11) You must tell me the truth.

As you see, both of these examples represent deontic modality and refer to some kind of obligation that is agent oriented. But they express the speaker's desire or force about the obligation in different strength. In (11), the speaker is committing the addressee to the act of telling the truth in a more definite and forceful manner than in (10). This type of scaling is a significant issue in ELF, as was illustrated in a study by Kecskes and Kirner-Ludwig (2017). In their study, they analyzed Asian English Language Learners' (AELs hereafter) preferred use of 'should' and 'must' in their written datasets produced by Chinese, Japanese, and Korean EFLs in the International Corpus Network of Asian Learners of English (ICNALE hereafter).[1] They compared the results to English Native Speaker (ENS hereafter) production based on English Web Treebank corpus (EWTC hereafter).[2] Their findings showed that AELs use 'must' and 'should' significantly differently than ENS due to their alleged culturally intrinsic sense of togetherness and joint responsibility for their society. The assumption that Western societies tend to be more individualistic than Asian ones, which appear to demonstrate a more collective conception of societal responsibility, has been widely established in the literature (e.g., Triandis 1993; Nelson & Fuvish 2004; Desai 2007). By showing that AELs tend to position themselves systematically as 'I' and 'we' when it comes to deontic demands or suggestions in regard to their community's welfare and harmony, the authors were able to pin this assumption down to concrete numbers. While ENS samples confirmed coherence in expressing more individualistic stances throughout, the AEL data is considerably consistent in emphasizing each individual's collective responsibility toward one's family's and community's well-being and happiness. At the same time,

[1] All in all, ICNALE contains 1.8 million words of controlled L2 English speeches and essays by over 3,500 college undergraduate and graduate students in ten countries and areas in Asia as well as L1 productions by 350 English native speakers.
[2] English Web Treebank corpus (EWTC) contains 16,624 sentences (254,830 tokens) of web text.

respect, manners, politeness and consideration for each other are regularly referred to in collocation with 'I/we must/should' patterns.

Additionally, the other issue that we shall address here is category boundaries between root modals and epistemic modals. These categories (namely, the epistemic sub-categories, the deontic and dynamic ones) are not fixed entities. In other words, one can argue that they are user and context sensitive. In fact, Küronya's (2013) thesis corroborates with our argument; she argued that it looks like the notions of possibility, permission and ability blur in ELF. There seems to be not only one modal force at work in the case of some instances but sometimes two or even three modal notions are denoted at the same time. As a matter of fact, this makes it difficult for an analyst to distinguish between the three modal sub-categories for all of them correspond to possibility (epistemic possibility, permission = what is possible in a deontic sense; ability = what is possible in a dynamic sense).

What needs to be highlighted here is that there is no formal criterion for the classification of modal meaning, as Nuyts et al. (2010: 20) aptly put it: "there are no systematic(ally occurring) and reliable structural (syntactic or morphological) or other 'behavioral' characteristics distinguishing between the different meanings." However, one exception was in Kecskes and Kirner-Ludwig's (2017) study in which they attempted to generate a formal syntactic-semantic criteria to classify modal meanings of the modal verbs 'must' and 'should' into either deontic or epistemic. They also found that the use of a continuum between epistemic modality and root modality would work better that a dichotomy to allow for interpretations ranging from epistemic suggestions to deontic (self-)obligation and command. In addition, Dutra (1998) pointed to the fuzziness and high degree of synonymy inhabiting the notions obligation and necessity, requiring placement of any modal usage on a continuum between necessity, i.e., something that is essential in a certain situation has to be done, and obligation, i.e., something that has to be done due to one's duty or one's moral or legal responsibility. Also, Zalaltdinova (forthcoming), in her thesis, uses a continuum approach (epistemic–deontic). She aims to identify characteristic features of modality use demonstrated by intermediate and advanced ELLs to examine the change, if any, in the characteristic set of modality use featured by advanced as compared to intermediate ELLs. Although her focus is limited to evaluation and advice-giving in written peer feedback, it is still important for ELF that she also proposed using a continuum rather than a dichotomy to lay out the interrelations between evaluation and suggestion on the one hand, and their relation to epistemic and deontic modality in the specific context of feedback on the other. Figure 8.1 represents epistemic modality on the one side of the continuum, and deontic modality on the other side. The distinction between epistemic and deontic modality is crucial for Zalaltdinova's study, because

Figure 8.1 The continuum representing epistemic modality on the one side of the continuum, and deontic modality on the other side.

she thinks it enables her to capture whether the use of modality by ELLs contains traits of their L2 sociocultural value system.[3]

Justifying the modal continuum, Zalaltdinova argued that the continuum approach treats modality as the expression of a degree of commitment to the proposition expressed, an approach aligned to the engagement theory (Aijmer 2016: 502). Focusing on her analysis perspective, Zalaltdinova claims that evaluations and suggestions are related to modality in the following way: epistemic is closer to evaluation and deontic is aligned with suggestion. Since it would be highly unconventional to encounter an evaluation to be expressed through the notion of obligation, permission or desirability, evaluation is more closely associated with epistemic modality. Zalaltdinova argues that the less 'modalized' a proposition is, the more it will move toward the center of the continuum where "naked assertions" are placed, which, according to Coates (1987: 116), "imply total commitment to the truth of the proposition expressed." In Zalaltdinova's datasets, suggestions in the evaluative feedback of participants can shift toward either end of the continuum, depending on a writer's commitment to the proposition expressed. She says that deontic modality in suggestions will give a very strong, almost assertive effect to a proposition. The degree of the writer's commitment is so high that the speaker does not simply give an opinion, but a call for action. Very often suggestions will occupy the position closer to the middle of the continuum, for instance, when the combination of deontic and epistemic modality occurs. It is unlikely for suggestions to be expressed in unmodalized propositions. We will return to Zalaltdinova's results later, but first we will need to discuss briefly the research that is available on modality in ELF and L2.

## 8.3 Frequency and Message Content Analysis

There seems to be a dearth of scholarly research on modality in ELF, and the little research that is available is mainly based on written data with few exceptions that analyze oral production. So, research on modality in ELF seems to be going in two directions: First, there are studies that focus mainly

[3] Such traits include using primarily epistemic modality to convey politeness or uncertainty, and to mitigate negative judgment and criticism in peer feedback.

on frequency of use of modals in ELF – this type of studies constitutes the majority – and they compare the results to that of native speakers. Second, however, there are a few studies that looked further and investigated if there is anything unique in the use of modals in ELF.

### *8.3.1 Frequency Studies*

Let me first go over two studies that focus on modality use in two different approaches. We should start with Laitinen's (2016) study, which investigated how the ongoing changes in the system of modality in English are reflected in Lingua Franca use. In his paper, he disclosed that ELF uses polarize the diffusion of changes. This makes perfect sense for us if we think about ELF as a language-use mode rather than an emerging language system. The second study, on the other hand, represents another interesting approach. Zalaltdinova (2018) explored how ELLs of different backgrounds (namely, Chinese, German, and Brazilian) use their knowledge of modality for advice/suggestion-giving in English, and observed their usage patterns. Her primary goal was to look at L2 users with different sociocultural backgrounds as a group of ELF users rather than each representing a different language. One of the most significant findings was that ELLs as L2 users demonstrate some kind of common patterns of modality use regardless of their sociocultural background. This is a very important suggestion that warrants further discussion and research.

Now we need to have a closer look at the two studies. Using a diachronic perspective Laitinen (2016) examined the use of modal expressions in ELF. He was interested in how the ongoing changes in the system of modality are reflected in Lingua Franca use. His results suggest that in cases of substantial recent changes in the core varieties of English, Lingua Franca uses, as we already said, polarize the diffusion of change. ELF evidence shows that ELF falls between American English and British English in terms of diachronic changes of core and emergent modal frequencies. The quantitative patterns of ELF use contribute to ongoing variability in ways that accelerate diffusion of grammatical change. This verifies that many of the items that have undergone substantial recent increases exhibit substantially larger quantitative shifts in nonnative use, such as 'should' and 'might.' Similarly decreasing developments are further polarized as seen with many outgoing core modal items. Low frequency modals such as 'ought to' and 'shall' have almost disappeared from nonnative use. Thus, Laitinen's conclusions (2016: 175) suggest that a diachronically informed angle to Lingua Franca use offers a new vantage point not only to ELF but also to ongoing grammatical variability. It is clear to us that Laitinen's focus is on quantitative patterns based on frequency in

Table 8.2 *Modal devices*

| N | Modality device | Examples |
|---|---|---|
| 1. | Imperative mood | *Finally,* ***buy*** *only things you need.* |
| 2. | Deontic modal verb *should* | *Second, you* ***should*** *set small steps to overcome your phobia.* |
| 3. | Deontic modal verb *must* | *Second, you* ***must*** *try to think positively and practice the relaxation exercises every day.* |
| 4. | Epistemic modal verb *could* | *Cooking at home and then lunching at work* ***could*** *save a lot of money and keep saving time.* |
| 5. | Epistemic modal verb *would* | *And meditation training for deep and slow breathing techniques, muscle relaxation* ***would*** *be also helpful.* |
| 6. | Epistemic adverbs | *I saw some advice that will* ***probably*** *help you.* |
| 7. | Parenthetical clauses *I think/I believe* | *Because* ***I think*** *the foundation competence is most important in our work.* |

datasets. Hence, the findings are quite compelling, even though ELF does not constitute a focused variety that has been coded in grammars as American English and British English have. In ELF, several extending-circle varieties are represented that do not have any particular coherence because of their temporary occurrences. So it is important to note that this comparison is not quite valid since it is used with reference to two things that are fundamentally different and therefore not suited to comparison.

In her study, Zalaltdinova (2018) analyzed 270 advice-giving ELLs' essays from the EF-Cambridge Open Language Database for the use of modal devices by learners at elementary, intermediate and advanced proficiency levels from China, Germany, and Brazil. She used MANOVA, VanValen's test and Discriminant Function Analysis as main statistical tools. The author was interested in identifying common patterns in modality use in a group of nonnative speakers who represented three different L1s. Table 8.2 shows the modal devices that the research focused on.

An essential aspect of the project was to group ENLs according to their sociocultural backgrounds to see whether a pattern of modality existed and, if yes, whether it was reliant on the subjects' sociocultural background. Zalaltdinova made sure that L1s of the participants stood far apart from one another in their language family relationships: i.e., German (Indo-European, Western Germanic), Chinese (Sino-Tibetan, Sinitic), and Portuguese (Indo-European, Neo-Latin). Her idea was to find out how radically different sociocultural backgrounds of the participants affect their modality use, and how that use relates to ENLs' modality use patterns. With this approach, Zalaltdinova attempted to deemphasize the binary view of native/nonnative comparisons, and focus rather on the "fine-grained, comprehensive understanding of . . . pragmatic ability and its development" (Gablasova et al. 2015: 21; also Wortham 2008) by ELLs, using native preferences as a springboard rather than an ideal usage to adhere to. This reasoning speaks to the fact of not incorporating any control group of English native speakers.

The results of the study show that the development of pragmatic knowledge of modality use – with regard to the use of modal devices with epistemic or deontic meanings for advice/suggestion giving in this case – is not linear a process. In other words, modification of ELLs' pragmatic competence does not follow a predictable course of moving from the least-aligned-with-ENS preferences of pragmatic choices to the most aligned ones. Thus, advanced ELLs show more flexibility in the use of modal devices by, for example, incorporating more complex epistemic modals as well as deontic modality in their use. This flexibility and variety was previously confirmed with Laitinen (2016) as well. So modality use is a complex process, with factors regulating the process extending beyond the level of language proficiency.

Although Zalaltdinova's results are quite surprising, there is no evidence that ELLs demonstrate patterns of modality use depending on their own sociocultural group. Zalaltdinova argues that while some ELLs groups are organized by their sociocultural background, at the advanced or intermediate proficiency levels they could be distinct in terms of relative frequencies of modal device use. The applied methods of analysis did not capture any statistically significant variation or well-identifiable patterns of modality use among groups of ELLs organized by their sociocultural backgrounds. She concluded that it is possible that ELLs demonstrate some common patterns of modality use no matter what sociocultural group they are part of. She found that while elementary ELLs demonstrate dispersed use of both epistemic and deontic modal devices, intermediate ELLs align to a high degree in their preferences for epistemic modals. As far as advanced ELLs are concerned, they deemphasize the use of some epistemic modal devices and are more flexible in incorporating the use of diverse modal devices, including deontic ones. Zalaltdinova speculates that this could be an indication of ELLs development of some common strategies to cope with the difficulties of English language use. That is to say, the reason for advanced ELLs being more flexible than intermediate ELLs in their choices of modal devices could be explained by the fact that the advanced ELL's pragmatic competence starts to reveal the outcomes of the modification of existing pragmatic competence. Under the influence of emergent L2 information, pragmatic competence of advanced ELLs has been gradually modified, and as a result, reflects a unique bidirectional "symbiosis of pragmatic rules and expectations of both languages" (Kecskes 2014: 80). In other words, the sociocultural background knowledge of their L1 and L2 is blended, which led to the emergence of the "synergism of information and knowledge" guiding learners' language use (Kecskes 2010c: 96).

### *8.3.2 Message Content and Cultural Values*

Zalaltdinova's paper emphasized that pragmatic and sociocultural assumptions represent fundamental points of reference that seem rarely questioned by members of a language community in which values and common background beliefs appear to be mutually shared. To some extent, Hinkel's study (1995) contradicts Zalaltdinova's findings mainly in regard to the influence of L1 sociocultural background on the use of modals. As discussed in Chapter 4, sociocultural background knowledge and beliefs also include views on what is required, expected, necessary, and appropriate. All these are connected with the use of modals in languages. Several studies (e.g., Schachter 1983; Strevens 1987; Schmidt 1993) have found that assumptions, world views, values, beliefs and points of reference are almost always transferred from LI to L2 language use. In fact, Hinkel referred to a number of papers in which researchers also established that there may be little connection between, on the one hand, linguistic proficiency and exposure to L2 social and conceptual constructs, and, on the other hand, the willingness or ability to assume L2 sociocultural beliefs and norms (Schmidt 1983; Adamson 1988; Adamson & Regan 1991). Also, Adamson (1988) claimed that nonnative speakers do not necessarily come to share the values and beliefs of an L2 community, despite having lived there for periods of time up to ten years. Moerman (1988: 4) corroborated that even those nonnative speakers who have developed a relatively high L2 proficiency may interpret L2 social frameworks according to L1 notional paradigms and "principles of interpretation." I need to highlight that all of the above are very significant for ELF from a modality-use perspective.

We need to call attention to the fact that Hinkel's subjects were all Asians who had a relatively extensive exposure to L2 social constructs and cultural norms, and had a certain degree of familiarity with L2 sociocultural frameworks. In her study, out of the total 450 nonnative participants, 195 students were speakers of Chinese, 87 of Japanese, 72 of Korean, 63 of Indonesian, and 33 of Vietnamese. According to Hinkel (1995), each of these language groups represents a culture heavily influenced by Confucian, Taoist and/or Buddhist philosophy, tradition and cultural values (see also Cushman & Kincaid 1987). We also need to point out the fact that all NNSs had achieved relatively high English language proficiency with a mean TOEFL score of 583. In Hinkel's study, the usage of modal verbs of obligation and necessity in the NNS texts was compared to that of essays written by NS of American English. The topics of NS essays were selected to match those of NNS texts. Both NS and NNS essays were written in response to assigned topics, including academics, politics, family, friendships, traditions, patriotism, and racism. Due to the fact that there were more essays of NNSs than NSs, and the NS essays were 62 percent longer than those of NNSs, Hinkel, in order to allow for comparisons of NS and NNS data pools, randomly selected a statistically representative sample of thirty essays per topic from NS and NNS sets. To analyze the data, the number of words in each essay was counted, followed by a count of the occurrences of 'must,' 'have to,' 'should,' 'ought to,' and 'need to' per essay and examined accordingly with root meanings; however, modal verbs with epistemic meanings were excluded. The findings indicated that in essays on academics, NNS usage of root modals 'must' and 'should' differed significantly from that of NSs, with NNSs using more of these modal verbs in their essays. On the other hand, in the essays written on politics, NSs used 'must' and 'need to' at higher rates than NNSs did; 'must' was not encountered in NNS on this topic. The NS and NNS usage of the modals of obligation and necessity – namely, 'must,' 'have to,' 'should,' and 'ought to' – exhibited significant differences in essays on family roles and relationships. Moreover, the topics dealing with friendships showed a similar trend, with the NNS rate of root modal use in both topics exceeding that of NSs. In the essays discussing traditions, NSs rarely employed root modals, while NNSs employed them at a relatively high rate. On the topic of patriotism, NSs used the modal verbs 'should' and 'need to' but did not use 'must' and 'have to.' NNSs utilized a wider variety of modal verbs when addressing this topic, and used them, with the exception of 'need to,' in greater ranges. In essays written about racism, NNSs did not use the modals 'must' and 'have to,' but as is apparent from range values, NSs employed a comparatively high number of them, as well as 'should' and 'need to.' In general, Hinkel concluded that NNS writing did not contain many root modals when discussing racism. Overall, the differences in NS and NNS use of modals of obligation and necessity were significant for 'must,' 'have to,' and 'should.' There were fewer significant differences found in the use of 'ought to' and 'need to.'

The comparisons of NS and NNS values showed that the use of root modals is largely topic dependent, and the greatest ranges in the use of 'must,' 'have to,' and 'should' were found in NNS essays describing family roles, family responsibilities and traditions. Hinkel pointed out that family and family obligations represent one of the fundamental values in many Confucian and Taoist societies, where loyalty to kin and tradition, as well as the responsibility for maintaining these values, are essential social presuppositions whose quality and importance find few parallels in Anglo-American societies. The gradience of root modality is reflected in the NNSs' use of 'have to' in essays discussing family, friendships and patriotism.

Hinkel argued that numerous usages of 'must' and 'should' in NNS texts are likely to appear different from those that NSs would employ and seem to be culture specific and culture bound. The results of her study indicate that the usage of root modals 'must,' 'have to,' 'should,' 'ought to,' and 'need to' in NS and NNS writing appears to be culture and context dependent. The fundamental social values and presuppositions that are associated with the notions of harmony maintenance, family and group responsibility, and extrinsically imposed obligation and necessity are often expressed through root modality in NNS writing.

Inspired by Hinkel's study, Kecskes and Kirner-Ludwig (2017) chose a cross-cultural approach with a focus on differences in native and nonnative speakers' deontic and epistemic uses of those two auxiliary modals that have been classified by, for example, Biber et al. (1999), as the two that mainly express obligation and necessity: namely, 'must' and 'should.' Although the study was corpus based, where frequency indicators played an important role, the authors' primary goal was to identify culture-specific motivations in the use of the two modal verbs by Asian Learners of English and to demonstrate how those relate to the use of the two items in language produced by L1 speakers of English. Thus, the authors proposed a combination of syntactic and semantic annotation criteria, arguing that Hinkel's criterion of topical frame as well as sole corpus-linguistic and quantitative analyses will not be sufficient when approaching highly complex, polysemous and multifunctional linguistic devices such as modal auxiliaries. They demonstrated that no single method or measurement is enough to produce expressive and meaningful results. The key lies in a symbiotic combination of quantitative and qualitative tools and specifically corpus-pragmatic tools. Their semantic criteria, for instance, did apply to a good majority of samples, but the authors argued that language will just not be tamed in any such way. The application of their criteria showed that their semantic sub-categories, for instance, formed much more of a continuum than individual functional sectors (also cf. Zalaltdinova forthcoming). As displayed in Figure 8.2, some items, particularly D4, i.e., the expression of one's personal values and moral beliefs, and E1, i.e., the more or less imposing and binding sharing of a suggestion or advice, seem to overlap frequently.

The authors found that, whereas ENSs and AELs alike did demonstrate a preference in the less face-threatening modal *should* over the more direct *must* in deontic uses, as Hinkel (1995) suggested, both *must* and *should* tend to be used more deliberately and more aimfully by AELs than by ENSs, who seem to apply them much more vaguely and polysemously. One could certainly argue that this is per se not a surprising result, considering that a language learner would, in general, be expected to consistently cling to what they have learned about the use of certain modal verbs in the target language. At the same time, a native speaker will – often unconsciously – tend to use modals more creatively or vaguely, while often not even being aware of any additional semantic layers a modal might bring to an utterance (e.g., Perkins 1983).

Figure 8.2 Merging semantic criteria

This seems to contradict those findings, or more like speculations (cf. Carrió-Pastor 2014; Laitinen 2016), that ELF users apply modality more 'creatively' in their language use than English native speakers. Hinkel's study also confirmed what Kecskes and Kirner-Ludwig (2017) said about the effect of classroom learning on the use of modals. Of course, spontaneous ELF speech situations significantly differ from writing where there is not much for the writer to co-construct or negotiate with the readers.

Kecskes and Kirner-Ludwig's data showed that AELs' use of *must* and *should* reflects cultural values different from the ones expressed in native English speech. AELs in the datasets used *must* and *should* significantly differently than ENSs due to their alleged culturally intrinsic sense of togetherness and joint responsibility for their society. The assumption that Western societies tend to be more individualistic than Asian ones that demonstrate a more collective conception of societal responsibility was basically confirmed by the modality use of AELs. By showing that AELs tend to position themselves systematically as *I* and *we* when it comes to deontic demands or suggestions in regard to their community's welfare and harmony, the authors were able to pin this assumption down to concrete numbers. While ENS samples demonstrated coherence in expressing more individualistic stances throughout, the AEL data is significantly consistent in emphasizing each individual's collective responsibility toward one's family's and community's well-being and happiness. At the same time, respect, manners, politeness, and consideration for each other were frequently referred to in collocation with *I/we must/should* patterns.

### *8.3.3 Similar Patterns Studies*

In this section, we will be looking into two studies that are mainly focused on L2 writing rather than on ELF. However, they are of significant importance to us, because they demonstrate that if language users have a similar genre or topic, the differences in modality use between native speakers and nonnative speakers are not that significant.

In the first study, Carrió-Pastor (2014) presents a traditional comparative study based on academic writing samples. The findings do not give us much more than was expected, that is, there are differences between native speakers and nonnative speakers in the use of modality even if those differences are not significant because of the common genre of the samples. The author aimed to determine whether language variation may be identified in cross-cultural communication when modal verbs of ability and possibility are used by speakers with different linguistic backgrounds. Another goal of the study was to find out whether English writers tend to be more explicit than Spanish writers when both groups use English to communicate. The author used two corpora that consisted of a set of fifty academic papers written in English by Spanish scholars, and a set of fifty academic papers written in English by native English-speaking researchers. Both corpora were analyzed to identify synchronic language variations. The results demonstrated that there are disparities in the use of possibility and ability modal verbs. I think that this kind of finding is expected in any type of study like this.

In the second study, Mur-Dueñas (2016) studied the use of modal hedging verbs in ELF business communication. She analyzed the occurrences of 'may,' 'might,' 'could,' 'can,' and 'would' in two small corpora. The English as a Lingua Franca Business Management (ELFBM hereafter) sub-corpus comprises twenty-four RAs published in three journals (namely, *British Management Journal*, *Journal of Management Studies*, and *Research Policy*), in which a great percentage of publications are authored by nonnative English scholars representing different similects. The English Business Management (ENGBM hereafter) sub-corpus comprises twenty-four RAs published in three different journals (namely, *Academy of Management Journal*, *Journal of Management*, and *Strategic Management Journal*), in which a very high percentage of publications are authored by ENL scholars affiliated to Anglophone institutions. Although the two datasets are very limited, they contain research articles in business management. Mur-Dueñas was interested in the epistemic meanings of the modal verbs 'may,' 'might,' 'could,' 'can,' and 'would.' Whereas the epistemic value of 'may,' 'might,' and 'could' is unquestionable, there is more controversy regarding the extent to which 'can' expresses epistemic modality. But we do not need to go into details at this point. The hedging modal verbs were searched for in the two sub-corpora using Wordsmith Tools 4.0. The author emphasized that all concordances obtained were carefully analyzed and those tokens which did not contribute to expressing the authors' lack of full commitment were dismissed. This is very important because it shows that Mur-Dueñas tried to go beyond frequency analysis. What she found was that the overall frequency of use of these modals showed that the authors' stance is similar in both sub-corpora. However, when the particular use of each hedging modal verb is examined in detail, similarities and differences arise between both sub-corpora in the type of constructions in which they are used and in the combinations or clusters they form. This contrastive analysis demonstrates preferred lexico-grammatical realizations of the expression of tentativeness entailing the use of particular hedging modal verbs in one or the other sub-corpus. Mur-Dueñas argued that some such realizations which are only used, or used to a greater extent, in the ELFBM sub-corpus may be considered ELF innovations, creative expressions (Seidlhofer 2011) or emerging patterns (Jenkins et al. 2011). She pointed out that tokens of "we may" followed by a main discourse verb (e.g., "we may also postulate," "we may argue," "we may also infer," and "we may say that") are only found in the ELFBM sub-corpus. Similarly, 'may' used as part of the anticipatory it-pattern containing a discourse verb seems to be characteristic of the ELFBM corpus. Below, you can see the two examples from this study:

(12) However, it may be argued that by increasing his/her stake in the firm, the manager may overwhelm other minority shareholders. (ELFBM2)

(13) As a result, it may be suggested that more controlling modes of HRM will be more effective when an organization is characterized by low quality EOR. (ELFBM14)

It is important to note that in the ENGBM sub-corpus 'may,' 'would,' 'could,' and 'might' have been found to be used when suggesting possible avenues for further research. However, in the ELFBM sub-corpus only 'may' and 'could,' which seem to be distinctively preferred over the rest, have been found. Although the paper is very restricted in focus, and the so-called ELF database is more like an L2 corpus authored by nonnative speakers of English, there is one reason why I find the study important for ELF. I believe that it reveals that there is no anarchy in modality use in ELF. Writers – and also speakers in other studies – tend to try to follow ENL standards that they consider as guidelines or reference points. *If the genre is the same (like in this study: research article) L2 language users and native speakers do not show striking differences.* In fact, L2 users follow the same patterns that are dictated by ENLs. The results of another studies – Piqué, Posteguillo, and Andreu-Besó (2001) – reveal almost identical results in which they looked at the use of modal verbs in three corpora representing different genres. Moreover, Mur-Dueñas argued in her study that the results show a similar frequency of use of hedging modal verbs in the two sub-corpora, which may point to some degree of homogenization of published written outcomes, at least within the same discipline. Even though the texts in the ELFBM sub-corpus are authored by scholars from varied linguacultural backgrounds, the frequency of use of these particular interpersonal features in their research papers is rather similar to that in ENL research papers.

### *8.3.4 Quantitative and Qualitative Analysis*

The only available resource in which ELF modality has been the direct focus of the study, both quantitatively and qualitatively, is Küronya's thesis (2013). Thus, in the following section, I will be reviewing some parts of it for it has relevant implications in this book. I need to emphasize that there are some limitations in the study's design, data collection and some claims in the thesis, but here, for the sake of furthering research in ELF modality, we shall focus on the positive sides only. Küronya aimed to describe how modal expressions are employed in ELF discourse, and particularly what kind of modal meaning they denote. The data was retrieved from the Vienna-Oxford International Corpus of English (VOICE), and in her work, she devised a mixed-method analysis. In the quantitative analysis, she selected only those modal expressions used most frequently, at least 300 times in the VOICE. The qualitative analysis focused on this part of her data. She examined these occurrences in terms of the following questions:

- Are they used in a deontic, epistemic or dynamic sense?
- Which modal-subcategory can they be assigned to?
- Do they co-occur with other modal carriers?
- Are there any strategies that speakers use in order to ensure mutual understanding?

The author further narrowed down the number of analyzed modal units. She argued that since instances of the selected modal carriers in VOICE are too abundant to be analyzed qualitatively within the framework of her thesis, only thirty occurrences of each modal expression were examined. And, equal shares of random occurrences were selected from each domain. The frequency analysis showed that modal auxiliaries were used in 68.7 percent, lexical items with modal meaning such as 'possible,' 'able,' 'perhaps,' 'maybe,' 'probably,' 'need,' 'think' in 21.1 percent, and 'verbs of intermediate status' such as 'dare' and 'ought to' in 10.2 percent. The frequencies of modal carriers revealed that the set of modal auxiliaries – with the exception of *shall* – are central when it comes to uttering modal meaning in ELF communication. Other types of modal carriers (namely, marginal modals, modal idioms, or lexical items) however, were not used frequently. When considering the semantics of the most frequently used modal carriers, they could be assigned to four clusters of modal meanings. The first one is deontic obligation that was expressed by the auxiliary *must* as well as by *have (got) to* and *need.* Comparing the frequencies of 'have to' to those of 'must' and 'need,' 'have to' plays a considerable role when it comes to denoting the idea of obligation (in 74.3 percent). The second field of modal meaning is the one of epistemic possibility, deontic permission and dynamic ability. Küronya argued that although they are distinct notions of modality – e.g., modals 'can,' 'could,' 'may,' as well as adjectives 'able' and 'possible' – they are closely interrelated in ELF use. She also concluded that notions of possibility, permission and ability blur.

As we mentioned in Section 8.2.3, according to Küronya it is not one modal force that is at work in some instances but sometimes two or even three modal notions are denoted at the same time. In the end, to identify the three modal subcategories should be difficult since all of them correspond to possibility (epistemic possibility, permission = what is possible in a deontic sense; ability = what is possible in a dynamic sense).

The third field of modal meaning was the one of different shades of epistemic modality: the speaker's commitment: epistemic possibility, probability and certainty. The modal carriers for this category are 'must' and the past tense form of 'think' for epistemic necessity; 'probably' and 'think' for epistemic probability; 'might,' 'perhaps,' and 'maybe' for signaling epistemic possibility. The fourth cluster was volition. The auxiliary 'will' was assigned to this category although it denotes this modal notion only to a very restricted extent. Most instances of 'will' have predominantly predictive function. Finally, Küronya mentioned that it was impossible to assign the auxiliaries 'would' and 'should' to any of the four clusters since their mechanisms of denoting meaning were quite complex. In their core semantic meaning, they seem to denote epistemic modality, whereas if considered on a discourse level, they were used to fulfill another function. They were found to denote weak obligation (should) and epistemic probability (would).

In conclusion, Küronya claimed that considering the frequencies of certain modal expressions in connection to the meaning they denote, it became obvious that speakers of ELF are very vague and tentative concerning their utterances. This is to say, epistemic modality used for hedging seems to play a considerable role. Deontic modals with lower modal strength are preferred over those with greater force. This is mainly true for hedging *realis* statements. Modal expressions frequently co-occur with epistemic hedging devices. Expressions of deontic obligation and epistemic necessity are often toned down a little, by means of epistemic modality. It is important to note that modal expressions used for hedging purposes are usually mono-semantic, thus they only express epistemic modality: ‘perhaps,’ ‘probably,’ ‘maybe,’ ‘might,’ as well as parenthetical constructions with ‘I think.’

As far as deontic obligation is concerned, Küronya found that speakers select rather weak forms for signaling this type of meaning. Whereas ‘need’ has been shown to be the one denoting the weakest deontic obligation, ‘have (got) to’ as well as ‘should’ were found to be a little stronger. Still, however, they are rather weak compared to ‘must,’ which seems to be of very strong deontic force. Interestingly, ‘must’ is hardly used for denoting obligation whereas in particular the vague ‘have (got) to’ is very frequent. The same was found to be true in cases where speakers obliged their communication partners to future actions. Whereas ‘must’ is not used at all for directives in ELF discourse, the remaining three expressions (‘need,’ ‘should,’ ‘have to’) seem to be central. The author found that directives also occur in the form of indirect speech acts using modality. Most frequent are the constructions ‘Can I,’ ‘Could I,’ and ‘May I’; in other words, those of the cluster of possibility, ability and permission. These constructions appear to be rather vague since their deontic force is expressed in an indirect manner. At the same time, Küronya also found that speakers of ELF appear to use strategies to ensure mutual understanding. They repeat a modal expression as well as paraphrase the signaled modal notion. These are two ways of achieving clarity and, in consequence, mutual intelligibility.

## 8.4 Summary

At the beginning of this chapter, I asked the question of whether changes in the use of modals induced by ELF are temporary only, or whether they will leave some traits in the global use of English. Based on the available studies, I am quite skeptical about the global effect of ELF modality use at this point: Studies based on the analysis of datasets do not point in that direction. But further research is definitely needed to answer this and other pertinent questions. Looking at the reviewed literature and combining it with the claims and suggestions presented in the previous chapters, we shall emphasize three important points about ELF modality use.

### *8.4.1 Learning Experience*

Most of the ELF users have been language learners in an instructional environment. Of course, they constitute only a portion of ELF users, but a significant portion, so we must pay attention to them. They have been exposed to English in school environments rather than in spontaneous speech situations. The instructional environment probably presented them with modality in a structured way in which modal verbs were learned as semantic units with a core meaning(s). To this core meaning, language learners related their communicative need (usually consciously), and their sociocultural background (usually subconsciously). It is definitely true that their use of modals does not have any kind of "boxed-in" characteristics. They feel free to select from the available modal units (proficiency) what they think is appropriate (sociocultural background) or best carries their approach and commitment (immediate communicative need).

### *8.4.2 L1 Effect and Cultural Influence*

ELF speakers are nonnative speakers of English, and they speak different L1s that also express modality recognized as a universal category by linguists. However, it might not be a good idea to extract the semantic categories of modality of one language (in our case English) and then transfer any definition of modality to another language, since the other language might expose different semantic categories. For instance, Li (2003) demonstrated that the modal systems in English and Chinese are very different things in their hypernyms, distinctive properties and syntactic behavior in the assertive, the nonassertive and the passive. Based on L1 influence, and also taking into account different sociocultural backgrounds, we can expect significant reconceptualization of modals in ELF use. But the questions is, is it. in fact, really the case? The studies that we reviewed do not necessarily point us in that direction. There is reconceptualization, and there is also L1-based cultural influence, but not to a significant degree. What we see is the dominance of the immediate communicative need that shall be discussed in Section 8.4.3.

### *8.4.3 Immediate Communicative Need*

It seems to me that one of the most significant findings in the reviewed papers is that the use of modality in ELF demonstrates some kind of vagueness. Deontic modals with lower modal strength are preferred over those with greater force, and epistemic modality is widely used for hedging. Sometimes it is difficult to say what modal role is assigned to an expression or utterance. In some instances there is not only one modal force at work but occasionally two or even three modal notions are denoted at the same time. I believe that ELF speakers tend to leave the doors open. That is, they put out some message there, and then negotiate and co-construct the rest. In that process they rely on target-language use as reference points. They try to stick to the original rules of the game by keeping the semantic features of the modals rather than modifying those too much. This basically confirms what we have been arguing in this book. Semantic analyzability prevails no matter what ELF uscrs do. That is their main reference point and all other features of the co-construction process, including pragmatics strategies and frame development, are built around that reference point. In the next chapter, we shall look at the results of the process of co-construction and analyze the structures ELF users produce.

# 9 Dialogic Sequences and Odd Structures

## 9.1 The Problem

Pragmatics is mainly an utterance-based inquiry. It is about utterance interpretation which has resulted in a hearer rather than a speaker-hearer approach in this discipline. That creates a problem when we examine ELF production exclusively from a pragmatic standpoint. But, why is that so? Analysis of intercultural interactions shows that utterances of ELF speakers are occasionally not well-formulated, may even sound unintelligible and difficult to understand. As we discussed in Chapter 2 of this book, research in intercultural pragmatics (e.g., Kecskes 2007, 2013; Kecskes & Assimakopoulos 2017; Decock & Spiessens 2017; Giora & Haugh 2017) has demonstrated that in intercultural interactions participants are creative on a discourse level rather than on an utterance level. The two foremost underlying reasons why this is so are limited language proficiency and communicative pressure. These two may result, among other difficulties, in ill-formed but still processable utterances. However, one can argue that well-structuredness has never been a criterion for comprehensible language production. Interlocutors produce clumsy utterances in their L1 as well, and they are still comprehended. Nonetheless, at this point, there is a basic difference between L1 and ELF production and comprehension. While L1 speakers can rely on conventions, norms, and common cultural frames to make sense of clumsily structured utterances, this additional support is absent in ELF since interlocutors need to create their own temporary context and frame in the course of interaction. So analyzing not only utterances but larger segments of interactional sequences may give us the chance to look into the mechanisms of co-construction processes, and find explanations for the unconventional structure of an utterance, as well as a way to examine the real purpose of the speaker.

In this chapter, I will focus on two important issues. First, I will discuss why it would make sense to extend the pragmatic perspective, and examine utterance as part of a dialogic sequence, which may fit ELF analysis better than just an utterance-based approach. Second, by building on the dialogic approach, we will analyze utterance structures formally and contextually, focusing mainly on the speaker's intention rather than just on the hearer's interpretation. We will use the *Humpty Dumpty* approach to language use (see Carroll 1871: *Through the Looking-Glass*) which is demonstrated through the conversation between Humpty Dumpty and Alice below:

> "When I use a word," Humpty Dumpty said in rather a scornful tone, "it means just what I choose it to mean – neither more nor less."
> "The question is," said Alice, "whether you can make words mean different things – that's all."
> "The question is," said Humpty Dumpty, "which is to be master – that's all."

In explanations about what Humpty Dumpty understood by word meaning in this exchange, and elsewhere in Lewis Carroll's book, it is often said that Alice was quite skeptical about Humpty's ability to pick the proper meaning of words. What exactly did Humpty want to say with the utterance: "When I use a word it means just what I choose it to mean – neither more nor less"?

It seems to me that he was trying to address that, as a speaker, he is the one who decides what his words mean. Thus, he made a strong point about speaker's intention. It is his decision of what words he picks express his intention. Based on his choice, the hearer then will have to figure out his message. Of course, there are constraints on Humpty's selection of words besides communicative intention (namely, salience, proficiency of ELF users, actual situational contexts, topic, partners, etc.). But still, he is the *boss*. Given his resources he selects the best solution for him. So this speaker-centered approach will be our guiding mechanism in looking at utterance structures in ELF. But first we should discuss how the dialogic view can help us better understand what the ELF speaker does.

## 9.2 The Dialogic Approach

The leading concern of pragmatics, namely the utterance analysis, has continuously been a challenge for researchers for good reasons. First, it is an arduous task to come up with a clear-cut definition for an utterance because, in oral production, we often do not know where an utterance begins and ends; and this, indeed is true for ELF. Second, the meaning of an utterance resides both in the building elements of an utterance (lexical units), and in the subsequent utterances produced in response. Consequently, pragmatics, which is also defined as a theory of meaning in context, has been looking for meaning 'constituents' both inside and outside the utterance. As a result, there has developed an approach that I called *pragma-dialogue* (see Kecskes 2012). This approach calls attention to the dialogic nature of communication by emphasizing that interlocutors are actors who act and react (e.g., Cooren 2010; Weigand 2010a; Kecskes 2012; Weigand & Kecskes 2018). This means that the speaker-hearer not only interprets but also reacts to the other interlocutor's utterance.

Throughout this chapter, we shall use two terms – *dialogue* and *discourse* – repeatedly, so a working definition of these two terms is called for. Discourse is a broad term that is used to refer to spoken and written language used in different social contexts. And, dialogue is a written or spoken conversational exchange between two or more interlocutors. As we are mainly interested in the nature of mechanisms that unfold in an oral interaction, we will focus more on the dialogic rather than the discourse features of ELF exchanges.

According to the basic dialogic principle, human beings are dialogic individuals (social individuals) who communicate in dialogic interaction not only by producing and understanding utterances but also by acting and reacting (e.g., Buber 1955; Weigand 2010a, 2010b). The dialogic principle defines dialogue as a sequence of actions and reactions. A sequence of speech acts can be considered as a dialogue, a highly structured activity involving (at least) two agents. The structure of real dialogues has been extensively studied by ethnomethodologists (see Garfinkel 1972; Turner 1974; Schenkein 1978; Psathas 1979), who have advocated the necessity of non-quantitative, ethnic methods in the analysis of social interactions.

Let me just highlight one more time that a dialogue is a sequence of utterances, and it is a reciprocal conversation between two or more entities. Buber (1955) argued that genuine dialogue can be obtained between two people "no matter whether spoken or silent." He further claimed that, "each of the participants really [must have] in mind the other or others in their present and particular being and turn to them with the intention of establishing a living mutual relation between himself and them" (Buber 1955: 22). More simply, genuine dialogue can be understood as a momentary experience in which participants are consciously mindful of the other/s. Preserving the original Buberian idea of dialogue being a reciprocal conversation in which interlocutors are consciously aware of the partners, current researchers of dialogue studies (e.g., Cooren 2010; Tracy & Craig 2010; Weigand 2010a, 2010b; Weigand & Kecskes 2018) go one step further and emphasize that dialogue is constituted by the interactive purpose of coming to an understanding, which is based on the sequence of actions and reactions. The following conversation demonstrates that point:

| | | |
|---|---|---|
| (1) | Action-directive | Jim: - I need a ticket to Cleveland. |
| | Info-request | Clerk: - Return? |
| | Signal-non-understanding | Jim: - Say that again. |
| | Info-request | Sara: - Do you want a return ticket? |
| | Agreement | Jim: - Yes, I do. Thanks. |

What's more, Weigand (2010b) argued that action and reaction are not two actions of the same type that are arbitrarily connected and only formally distinguished by their position in the sequence. Action and reaction are functionally unalike types of actions, that is to say, action is initiative while reaction is responsive. In utterance-based pragmatics, this distinction is usually not made. According to Weigand, orthodox speech act theory that is exclusively based on illocution should be adjusted. On that account, she claimed that Searle's theory of conversation as based on single illocutionary acts put together by what Searle (1995: 26) calls "collective intentionality" ignores the interdependence between action and reaction. In order to interpret an utterance properly, the interlocutor has to arrive at an understanding not only of the communicative function of the utterance but also of the communicative agenda of his/her dialogue partner, i.e., what s/he really wants to achieve in the dialogue. As a result, the underlying interests of the dialogue partners become evident through dialogic sequences. This is in line with the socio-cognitive approach that we should go beyond single utterance to fathom the communicative agenda of interlocutors (Kecskes 2010b, 2014). ELF communication serves several examples that support this point. Let us look at the following short excerpt to clarify our point:[1] The participants are a man from Hong Kong (HKM hereafter) and a woman from Poland (PAF hereafter).

(2) HKM: - How about you? ... circumstances ... Where do you live? You rent ... or?
PAF: - Mmm ... I am live ... not so far from the university.
HKM: - Hmm.
PAF: - It is a college ... you don't know ... It is not so far. It's Albany.
HKM: - Hmm.
PAF: - But I have 3 minutes ... errh ... to go to my work.
HKM: - Hmm.
PAF: And this house is ... errh ... on our own so my husband and I ...
HKM: - Hmm.

In this dialogue, the Polish speaker has a communicative agenda to explain where she lives in Albany to her partner from Hong Kong. The curious thing is that the HKM does not say much. But as Buber said, silence or one-word backchanneling also counts as a communicative act. Whenever the PAF says something, HKM responses with a 'hmm,' which is interpreted by the PAF that more information is needed. So this results in building on information about her living circumstances. Those bits and pieces are in fact informative, but can hardly be considered full utterances with the exception of the last two

[1] The excerpt is from the Albany Database of Intercultural Communication that contains recorded conversations between nonnative speakers and nonnative speakers and native speakers and nonnative speakers.

comprehensible utterances. The dialogic sequence is quite atypical because the HKM does not appear to be cooperative enough. So the Polish woman does not always recognize if her statement has been understood or not. She goes on talking about the subject, but the sequence can still be considered a dialogue where action and reaction shadow each other. As a result, the interdependence between dialogic partners is undeniable. One needs comprehensive information, the other provides it, and the responses of the HKM (whatever form they appear) lead to further actions. Now we will need to have a closer look at this type of interactions.

## 9.3 Odd Structure (OS) in ELF Dialogue

It would be too arduous a task for us to analyze the structural and contentual characteristics of ELF production in general.[2] So we have decided to give an insight into unfolding ELF interaction by focusing only on one essential feature of ELF production, namely odd structures (see Kecskes & Kirner-Ludwig 2019). We will use a dialogic lens emphasizing the collaborative and emergent nature of ELF talk. As it was already stated, dialogue drives discourse in the sense of a contingent evolution of ideas. Also, odd structures (OS hereafter) are essential parts of this dialogue-building process that leads to discourse segments that reflect how mutual understanding is achieved in ELF.

Now we need to define what we consider an OS. We consider a structure as 'odd,' if it either (a) violates the structural dimension, i.e., saliently and conventionally expected sequences, (b) breaks the topical or situational frame of a conversation or (c) fulfills both of these criteria at the same time (for details, see Section 9.5). While we do not deny that the perception of a structure as 'odd' – and its labelling as such – may be inherently subjective, and will be influenced by a number of extra-linguistic factors that cannot be defined in any default manner, we propose the classification of a structure as 'odd,' and have decided to analyze odd structures for two main reasons. First, we propose that we need a combination of top-down and bottom-up analysis of dialogic segments to systematically dismantle discourse-internal dynamics and principles underlying intercultural interaction. Second, by relying on the original Gricean speaker-centered approach, we will try to better understand speaker's behavior that results in the production of an OS. We aim to identify pattern-like consistencies in these structures, and with regard to how they are dealt with by the speakers: which OS-types do actually cause a breakdown in conversation and which ones do not. In this chapter, we are merely going to introduce this

[2] From now on, the chapter heavily relies on the samples that were analyzed in the paper Kecskes & Kirner-Ludwig, "Odd Structures in ELF Discourse" that is in press in the *Journal of Pragmatics*.

approach as a tool to better understand what ELF interlocutors do from a structural and contentual perspective.

We claim that the analysis of an OS should not only focus on the structure itself, but also examine the dialogic sequence in which it is identified. An OS will potentially put the smoothness of a conversation at risk. But this does not mean that it will definitely trigger a problem. There are two possibilities: (a) either the linearity of the conversation will not be affected due to the interlocutors not acknowledging or reacting to the OS at all or (b) the recipient will launch strategies to establish common ground with the utterer of the OS and seek to bridge the gap caused by it in order to continue the dialogue intact.

While it has been claimed before that a meaningful and reliable analysis of intercultural communication discourse scenarios must take into conjoint consideration that dialogue is both a process as well as an entity (cf. Kecskes 2012, 2014), there is a noticeable dearth of approaches that would extensively pick this idea up, and propose facilitating methods for such a holistic analysis. Various studies have highlighted that single utterances are reflections of individual human cognition, while a span of utterances within a discourse segment reflects sociocultural factors (cf. e.g., Grosz & Sidner 1986; Mann & Thompson 1988; Moore & Paris 1993; Passonneau & Litman 1997; Taboada & Habel 2013). We argue that an approach comprising both a bottom-up as well as a top-down analysis is needed so as to systematically dismantle discourse-internal dynamics and principles underlying any kind of interaction. So OSs within ELF are used as linguistic springboards in order to demonstrate the added value of a systematic bidirectional (or double) analytic approach to interlocutors' coping (problem-solving) strategies.

## 9.4 Why Look at Odd Structures? – To Better Understand What the Speaker Does

The Gricean idea of implicature is inherently linked to speaker meaning – i.e., to what is said and what is implicated by the speaker as opposed to what the recipient makes of it – whereas pragmatic theories, as discussed earlier, have remained hearer-centered with focus on utterance interpretation (see more in Kecskes 2013b). So far, it seems to me that the speaker's position is somewhat overlooked, and the pragmatic features of speaker's meaning are somewhat neglected in the literature.

In fact, this overall tendency to focus on the recipient rather than on the speaker is not that surprising, if we consider that Grice himself seems not to have been overly preoccupied with a speaker's reasons for communicating implicatures. Concluding his discussion of conversational implicature, he merely states that "there may be various possible specific explanations, a list of which may be open," for why conversational implicature comes into being, continuing, "the conversational implicature in such cases will be disjunction of such specific explanations" (Grice 1989 [1975]: 40). Grice therefore seems to take for granted that implicatures may be variously motivated, whether arising from tropes, or other forms of language use. For instance, the speaker may intend to create a rhetorical effect (e.g., emphasize the evaluation in irony), to be polite or impolite, to invite a humorous reaction or to come across as being creative or witty, all of which may underlie the use of tropes.[3]

As discussed in Chapter 7, Grice assigns the key role to the hearer by arguing that it is not enough for the speaker to implicate something. The audience must also believe that the speaker believes what s/he intends to convey. However, we wish to claim, and demonstrate, that from the speaker's perspective what really matters is what the audience is required by the speaker to believe, not what the audience does believe. That is why Saul's (2002) distinction (utterer-implicatures as opposed to audience-implicatures) has been used consistently in this book to refer to the speaker's attempt(s) to conversationally implicate his/her intention, either recognized by the addressee or not.

OSs are appropriate for making our point about utterer-implicatures, as they only *potentially* put mutual understanding and successful communication between the interlocutors at risk. Presumably more often than not, they do actually not affect or hinder a conversation. But our primary goal is not to figure whether they do or do not, and we are not really interested in analyzing misunderstandings per se. In spite of this, when detecting OSs, we still need to seek the signs of misunderstandings because, as Kaur (2011) claimed, they come to light when the speaker is seen to make a move to correct the understanding arrived at by the recipient. It is the repairs, therefore, that "anchor the analysis as misunderstandings and … show what the participants treat as sources of the misunderstanding as well" (Schegloff 1987: 204).

It is of importance to note that we do not consider OSs as mistakes on the speaker's part; although, in particular, our first criterion of violating the structural factors may suggest so. In fact, we deem OSs as the best option a speaker is able to retrieve at the moment of speech in his/her sincere attempt to get his/her message across as fully as possible. Therefore, we are simply interested in the speaker's cognitive efforts of working around any self-perceived grammatical, lexical or idiomatic pitfalls. Suffice it to say, the speaker is not considered at fault when producing an OS. When we say that 'the best option a speaker is able to retrieve at the moment of speech' we mean that the utterance is either a result of recipient design (planning) or of salience effect (ad hoc, subconscious attempts). However, 'best option' on the speaker's part does not mean that it

[3] However, Grice did not aspire to explain why irony (or any of the other three figures) should be used. He merely sketchily depicted them by placing them among other communicative phenomena in his framework of communication.

will necessarily work best for the audience. When the speaker's best option does not work, repair attempts will follow, as we will see in the upcoming examples.

To recap, we claimed that the speaker's perspective is generally easier, and more transparent to grasp in intercultural discourse than in L1 communication because in intercultural discourse, including ELF, what is said is mostly and closely what is meant. In other words, semantic analyzability prevails (e.g., House 2002; Philip 2005; Cieslicka 2006; Kecskes 2007). We argue that while an OS has the potential to cause trouble in communication that may not necessarily be the consequence of an OS. There might be other reasons like pronunciation, misleading contextual effect and the like. But we are not interested in those. What we focus on is the nature and characteristics of OSs themselves and the speaker's strategies in (re-)establishing – to the best of their abilities – common ground so that the conversation can be picked up and continued beyond the OS. We do not investigate whether or in what way the recipient may misunderstand or seek clarification on an OS. Our approach is an etic one as we are seeking to draw inferences regarding generalizable patterns and strategies on the speakers' part in dealing with OSs that are already uttered within the frame of ELF. Now we will need to define what OSs are.

## 9.5 What Is an Odd Structure?

According to our definition, an OS is an utterance that puts forth contradictory or frame-breaking information, by fulfilling either a sub-criterion to C1 or C2 or both a sub-criterion of C1 and C2 at the same time (cf. Table 9.1).[4]

We find it indispensable, for analytic purposes, to separate the individual and social factors that govern a speaker's actions by relying on the socio-cognitive approach (Kecskes 2010, 2014). We argue that C1 is a reflection of the speaker's struggle with best-possibly expressing his/her intention. The OS presents a break-away grammatical sequence or referential vagueness, which may be followed by a back-and-forth, drop-and-pick, try-again approach on the speaker's part in reformulating his/her utterance. But we have to be careful here. We do not want to suggest that, in order to express intention successfully, adherence to standard norms of English use is required: not at all. ELF communication is quite successful with ungrammatical and unfinished utterances. But definitely, repeated attempts to put intention into L2 words and utterances may result in poorly organized sequences.

Additionally, C2 represents a reflection of social factors, i.e., the speaker's endeavor to match his/her intended thought with the actual situational context and the conversational partner(s). While trying to do that, the speaker puts

[4] Source: Kecskes and Kirner-Ludwig (2019)

Table 9.1 *Criteria for odd structures*

| | |
|---|---|
| C1 | posing a violation of the structural dimension, i.e., linguistic characteristics of formal patterns that break up traditional expected sequences: |
| a. | ⇨ structural incohesiveness |
| b. | ⇨ failing to disambiguate referential vagueness |
| C2 | |
| a. | ⇨ putting forth contradictory information, i.e., posing a violation of lexical cohesion |
| b. | ⇨ breaking the topical or situational frame of the conversation, thus creating immediate incoherence. |

forward contradictory information and/or breaks the situational and/or topical frame, which may result in incoherence, which, again, may result in confusion or misunderstanding on the recipient's part. The following samples will be presented for different types of OSs (here and henceforth, OSs are underlined in all upcoming samples):

(3) A Japanese student (J) and an African-French student (AF) are talking.
J: Do you like the place where you live here in Albany?
AF: I like living in Albany. <u>Because the Albany is the … especially I live almost two months … it's quiet … nice people … neighbor …</u>
J: Yeah you have nice neighbors.
AF: Yeah and making [incomprehensible]

In Sample (3), C1a is fulfilled by the structural dimension being violated at several points in the utterance, including the incomplete syntax in 'Because the Albany is the …, ' 'especially I live almost two months' and the two incohesively juxtaposed noun phrases 'nice people' and 'neighbor,' with the latter not even being specified by a determiner or indicated as generic by a plural {-s}. In addition to C1a, the incohesive 'neighbor' may be argued to fulfill criterion C1b, i.e., failing to disambiguate referential vagueness. However, since AF's response, including the OS is still to a considerable extent relevant and in line with Grice's maxims, it does not, in fact, seem to impede the flow of the ongoing conversation, as J's turn 'Yeah you have nice neighbors' shows.

Sample (4) is a case fulfilling both C1a (in transitioning from 'It is so nice' to the prepositional phrase 'Befar.. taking') and C2b (in seemingly deviating from the topic 'going out with friends' to 'taking one's children to bed'). The OS, however, does not seem to surprise B (who does not even have children):

(4) A Korean (K) and a Burmese (B) person are talking.
K: Sometimes you go to the restaurant with your family?
B: Oh … Usually I go with my friends.
K: Oh with your friends. It is so nice. <u>Befar.. taking your children to the bedroom?</u>

B: I don't have any children.
K: Oh you don't have any children. So you live here by yourself?
B: I live with my parents.

Particularly interesting are such cases that present contradictory information, thus fulfilling C2a and at least one more criterion as in Sample (5).

(5) A Pakistani (Pak), a Columbian (Col) and a Chinese (Ch) person are talking:
PAK: You said you live with your son. So your wife is not here.
CH: Yes, I am alone. I am with my son.
COL: Will your wife come to visit?
CH: Yes, she came yesterday.
PAK: Did she come from China?
CH: Yes, she arrived from Nanjing.

In Sample (5) the Chinese person gives contradictory information by presenting lexically incoherent information (*alone* [+all by oneself] [-company] *with my son*), although he was using the adjective *alone* as the antonym to 'with my spouse.' Still there is mutual understanding, and the conversation is unimpeded after the Chinese person's first utterance in the sample. The OS does not cause any problem because the Columbian student understood the Chinese person's use of 'alone' in this context as referring specifically to 'a person being without the spouse or life partner.'

In Sample (6) a male from Hong Kong (HKM) and a female from Poland (PAF) are talking. The Polish female produces an OS, fulfilling C1a ('he is … he is,' 'He is American but') and C2a ('he is Polish. He is American').

(6) HKM: - Errh … Are your husband American or … ?
PAF: - Errh … Actually he is … he is Polish. He is American but …
HKM: - OK.
PAF: - … because he came into the United States when he was a child.
HKM: - Hmm.
PAF: - He was something like twelve.
HKM: - All right.

When an OS results in confusion, we can identify that from either a hearer-focused or a speaker-focused perspective. In the case of a hearer-focused approach we may, on the one hand, rely on markers of confusion as indicators for preceding OSs (e.g., HKM's 'OK' in [6], or 'oh' in [4]). In some cases, hearers may even make an attempt to repair the OS so as to establish common ground, overcome the 'oddness' and carry on (e.g., [3]). On the speaker's end, they often do not simply utter the OS, but – if aware of their utterance being odd – will seek to ensure that the recipient actually understands it despite the oddness of how the utterance was worded. Strategies may include a meta-comment implicitly or explicitly double-checking whether, or to what extent, common ground has been established. Another set of strategies covers various

Table 9.2 *Possible hearer- and speaker-strategies in reaction to OSs*

| | |
|---|---|
| **1. Hearer-focused: MARKERS OF CONFUSION as INDICATORS for OSs** | |
| **$HI_1$** | Markers of confusion (*What? Excuse me? Pardon? I don't understand. What do you mean?* etc.) |
| **$HI_2$** | Other's (attempted) repair |
| **$HI_3$** | Check for common ground (*right? correct?* etc.) |
| **2. Speaker-focused: (REPEATED) SELF-REPAIR as an INDICATOR for OSs** | |
| **$SI_1$** | (Attempted) structural self-repair |
| **$SI_2$** | (Attempted) self-repair through repetition |
| **$SI_3$** | Referring to assumed common ground (*as you know; we know that … ; obviously; I mean; in other words,* etc.) |

forms of self-repair. Table 9.2 sums up the strategical domains we are focusing on.[5]

## 9.6 Methods of Data Collection

I need to reiterate that we do not assume that an OS will necessarily cause misunderstanding or non-understanding. In order to identify OSs in corpora, we rely on the hypothesis that OSs may cause, and indicate, confusion – not necessarily misunderstanding – on the recipient's part in a conspicuous manner. Our specific search for such markers corroborates with that of Kaur's observation, in which ELF speakers employ various interactional practices (e.g., repetition, confirmation, and clarification requests), so as to ensure the intactness and smoothness of a conversation (see Kaur 2009, 2010, 2011).

For purely logistical reasons, our data collection approach draws upon the hearer. We focus on the hearer's action so as to understand the utterer who has produced an OS. In the first step, we identified a set of potential OSs in discourse by focusing on hearers' stereotypical reactions in terms of markers of confusion and clarification-markers (e.g., 'right?,' 'correct?') in already existing corpora of ELF, and through manual search in raw data that we have been compiling for the Albany Corpus of Intercultural Communication (ACIC). In doing so, we have been able to identify a few non-representative strategies for $HI_2$, and $HI_3$ (see Table 9.2). In the next step, our actual analysis focuses on the speaker solely (i.e., with regard to the OSs they produce), and any patterns in their strategies to overcome the potential effect of OS. For the latter, we rely, on the one hand, on those instances of OSs that we retrieved

[5] Source: Kecskes and Kirner-Ludwig (2019).

with our hearer-focused data-compiling approach. On the other hand, we were able to retrieve a set of OSs based on seeking out any overcoming or repairing strategies on the speakers' part. I have to emphasize that this compilation of patterns and strategies had to rely on purely manual searches rather than on systematic corpus or data browsing. At this point in our study any strategies would be far too heterogeneous to be identified through pattern searches.

### *9.6.1 Corpus-Based Data Search*

We browsed for explicit markers of confusion in the hearer's reaction that would point to such structures as ELF speakers may perceive as 'odd.' We used the Vienna-Oxford International Corpus of English (VOICE, 2013), which comprises one million words of ELF interactions between around 1,250 ELF speakers with approximately 50 different first languages. Table 9.3 displays the markers of confusion (MCs hereafter) as well as the lack-of-clarity markers we selected for a piloting round of retrieving relevant instances of OSs. The formulae for the former category include 'Pardon?,' 'What do you mean?,' 'I don't understand,' and 'Excuse me?' and those contained in the second category are 'Right, but' and 'Okay but.'[6]

The search in the VOICE corpus revealed fairly manageable numbers with only 151 hits for the MCs 'Pardon?,' 'I don't understand,' 'What do you mean?,' and 'Excuse me?.' We do not wish to claim that the small number of MCs found in the corpus suggests that the level of confusion, in general, seems to be rather low in ELF. Still we still need to point out that the MCs we chose do occur in significantly small numbers in relation to the size of VOICE. This seems to confirm the findings by House (1999), Mauranen (2006), and Kecskes (2014), who have claimed before that misunderstandings appear to be much less of an issue in ELF discourse than one would assume. It should be mentioned that in addition to the twenty OSs we retrieved through systematic browsing, we manually identified another twenty-one OSs in VOICE which had not responded to our search for patterns.

In all following examples, the OS is underlined, while the hearer's verbal reaction to the OS is printed in bold. Sample (7) includes an OS according to our definition, with 'Did you correct?' fulfilling all of our C1-subcriteria at once. This utterance poses a violation of the structural dimension (C1a), i.e., cohesion, in that it uses the transitive verb 'correct' intransitively. The utterance also violates lexical cohesion in that 'correct the rent' is unidiomatic (C2a). Finally, S1 does not disambiguate the referential vagueness (C1b), which goes in lockstep with C1a, i.e., the dropping of the object, in this case 'it' (or more explicitly, 'the rent').

[6] A browse for *what[?]* turned out to yield too many instances in VOICE to deal with for this study, i.e., 6,075. The same is true for variants of *huh?, haeh?*, etc., which, therefore, were not taken into consideration.

Table 9.3 *Selected MCs and lack-of-clarity markers in VOICE*

| Markers | Raw instances total | Odd (OS) | Non-Odd | Type |
|---|---|---|---|---|
| *Pardon?* | 35 | **6** | 29 | Markers of confusion (MCs) |
| *I don't understand.* | 22 | **1** | 21 | |
| *What do you mean?* | 27 | **5** | 22 | |
| *Excuse me?* | 67 | **2** | 65 | |
| *Right, but* | 31 | **0** | 31 | Lack-of-clarity markers |
| *Okay, but* | 129 | **6** | 123 | |
| **Total** | **311** | **20** | **291** | |

(7)

(6) S2: Okay you don't have to pay anything for September. You're right. (.)
I'm sorry for this mistake
S1: Did you correct?
S2: **Par<1>don? </1>**
S1: <1> Did you </1> correct? (1) e:r <2> with the </2> rent?
S2: <2> e:m </2> (.)
**What do you mean? =**

In Sample (8), the OS is being built up gradually over two turns by S14 until S3 interrupts S14's unintelligible speech in turn 4 and explicitly states that s/he does not understand what S14 means. In turn 2, S14 presents the OS, which fulfills C1a in posing structural violations: 'are going there just to: coffee shop' – one would expect a verb in the infinitive here, or a determiner before coffee shop; 'you know that th- they have.' This OS also shows C1b in leaving unspecific and vague who *they* and what *there* in 'when they </6> are going there' refer to. S14 does not manage to dissolve the oddness, but continues to speak of *they* and *there* in turn 4 (still C1b) and again fulfills C1a by not completing the syntax after the subordinate clause 'when they're (.) they're on the streets.'

(8)

S3: No <soft. E:r </soft> I I'm: I feel really safe (.) in my country i I
S14: i mean <6> when they </6> are going there just to: coffee shop or something like that <un> xx </un> you know that th- they have (.)
S3: <6> (we have) </6>
S14: They'll go to go there to buy some e:r joint or something and when they're (.) they're on the streets (.) <7> <un> x </un> </7>
S3: **<7> what d- </7> what do y- (.) what do you mean i er don't <8> understand </8>**
S14: <8> I mean </8> when y- they are outside you know <1> and </1>
S3: <1> who are </1> outside? (.)

What we are labelling 'lack-of-clarity' markers at this point were much more heterogeneous and thus posed less smooth processing for us, as the dialogic excerpts as well as their contextual discourse were not necessarily conspicuous or transparent with regard to whether our criteria were fulfilled or not.

Sample (9) provides a range of lack-of clarity markers and MCs ('but er,' 'okay but,' 'pardon?') and at least two OSs: In S6's first turn, the whole utterance seems to build up to an OS, both on the structural and cohesion/ coherence level – S5 ignores that, though, and opens up a whole new frame (C2) with 'any: problems regarding the slivers.' This OS is full-blown odd as it also fulfills criteria C1a (ellipsis of 'are there' or 'have you found,' etc.) and C2a, as *slivers* does not seem to mean anything to S6. This becomes evident some turns later when S6 tries to overcome or rather brush over that gap of shared knowledge in responding with a referentially vague structure themselves ('it's around two per cent'), after having expressed their lack-of-understanding: 'yes yes but e:r' (line 9) may even represent an OS itself (cf. C1a, C1b).

(9)

S6: norm- normally we we have a kind of scratch in the end of the the the the coils? hh it's a: common (.) e:r (.) defect of the <un> xx </un> (mill) (.) hh and some MARKS something like that. But hh e:r (.) you can say that <un> xx </un> today you have a good quality (.) for (.) <un> xxx </un>
S5: any: problems regarding the slivers (.)
S6: yes yes (.) <1> but e:r </1> (.)
S5: <1><soft><un> xxx </un><soft></1>
S6 it's around two per cent
S5: <soft> only two per cent </soft><2> at </2> at the: annealing <un> xx </un> stage (.)
S6: <2> yes </2>
S6: <3> yes </3>
S5: <3> hm </3> okay (.) but er are the slivers i mean e:r any specific (observations) regarding of the (.) <un> xxx</un> from caster or from heating furnace or something like that?
S6: er in these cases only for the: hot steel mill (responsible)
S5: **for slivers also. (1) I'm talking about slivers now specifically**
S6: pardon?
S5: **SLIvers slivers (.) <4> slivers </4>**
S6: <4> slivers </4> yes (.)
S5: <un> xxx xx </un> (very from hot) <un> xx </un>
S6: yes (1) two per cent are out
S5: From ere r any specific <un> xxx </un> I mean the heating furnace temperatures or something like that going wrong? (1) <un> xx </un> heating of slabs is it e:r (.) any analysis or something in that field? (2)

S5 appears to find S6's responses vague from the beginning – which is why s/he adds more information, i.e., 'only two per cent at the annealing stage' – and apparently uninformative, which is why s/he repeats the question in a more specific and explanatory manner in line 15, initiating this turn and OS by the MC/lack-of-clarity marker '(hm) okay but er': 'are the slivers I mean e:r any specific observations regarding of the […].' This utterance violates the structural dimension regarding subcriteria C1a and C1b.

Sample (9) contains further odd features that are not indicated through any markers on the hearer's part. S6's utterance 'and some MARKS something like that. But hh e:r that [...] today you have a good quality for' fulfills criteria C1a (incomplete syntax: 'a good quality for [?]'), C1b in presenting referential vagueness in several instances ('something like that,' 'good quality for [what?]') and even C2, considering that the topic up till that point has been 'mistakes and deficiencies' that S5 had asked and S6 was reporting about. This becomes evident also in that S5 redirects the conversation to 'problems' (line 8) rather than reacting to S6's deviation to 'good quality' (line 7).

### *9.6.2 Data Retrieved through Manual Searches*

The second step we took in order to find odd structures in ELF discourse was to manually process such data that we have been collecting for our own database, the Albany Corpus of Intercultural Communication (ACIC). This corpus is not yet publicly available, but has been collected since 2016. The data compiled in this database combines written, oral and audio-visual language datasets produced by bilinguals, including both native speakers of English and bilingual speakers with advanced English proficiency, whose L1s are mostly – but not exclusively – Asian languages.

Our search for certain responses to OSs in the VOICE corpus had been rather systematic. However, the retrieval of potential OSs in our own raw ACIC dataset was much less straightforward. It had to be based on our introspection and any contextual markers of 'oddness' in regard to either of our criteria and subcriteria (cf. Table 9.1). Overall, however, in addition to those twenty browsed samples from VOICE, we have been able to manually identify nine instances of OSs in ACIC as well as nine more cases in VOICE excerpts, which we came across during our analyses. We picked some demonstrative examples of manually retrieved samples from ACIC:

(10) A Chinese student (Ch) and a Korean student (K) are talking.

Ch: But do you think that is live style including the food style something different from that in Korea?
K: From American or Chinese?
Ch: Korea the American live style
K: **Different from America, Korean style is different from America right?**
Ch: Mmmm..
K: Just as you mention
Ch: Yes of course
K: Girls enjoy gathering together eating and chatting.

With 'Korea the American live style,' the Chinese student in Sample (10) puts forth an OS that fulfills C1a (incomplete and incohesive structure) and C1b in that, by dropping the preposition *from* (cf. turn 1), the reference is vague. The Chinese utterance structure (turn 1) features sentence constituents in the wrong order and in turn 3 the two noun phrases are simply put next to each other with anything else elliptical. One could furthermore argue that 'live style' (as opposed to *life style*) is lexically challenging or rather goes against collective saliency. In addition, 'something' may have been mixed up with 'somehow' or 'somewhat' as 'something' itself is redundant. So, as we can see, referential vagueness is found in the Chinese utterance. The Chinese speaker neither specifies what lifestyles he would like the Korean's opinion about (Korea versus which?) nor provides even a preposition that would disambiguate the reference. The Korean interlocutor therefore rephrases what s/he believes the Chinese student meant, i.e., that the 'Korean style is different from [the] America[n],' and checks for the Chinese's confirmation ('right?').

Sample (10) is a typical example for how OS is produced and what may happen after it has been uttered. The OS 'Korea the American live style' was the result of salience effect. The Chinese student produced it without any planning. The OS is ungrammatical but it did not matter. The Korean response 'Different from America, Korean style is different from America, right?' does not show misunderstanding or confusion. It is a reinforcement that the Korean wants to hear from the Chinese student: Yes, the Korean life style is different from the American one. So grammar or correctness is not necessarily an issue here. Neither is it in Sample (11).

(11)

| | |
|---|---|
| HKM: | How about you?...circumstances...Where do you live? You rent...or? |
| PAF: | Mmm...I am live...not so far from the university. |
| HKM: | Hmm. |
| PAF: | It is a college...you don't know...It is not so far. It's Albany. |
| HKM: | **Hmm.** |
| PAF: | But I have 3 minutes...errh...to go to my work. |

In Sample (11), the Pakistanis student (PAF hereafter) presents two structures that we classify as OSs: one in turn 4 and another one in turn 8. Both put forth contradictory information, thereby fulfilling C2a: 'It is a college ... you don't know' seems to clash with what the student from Hong Kong (HKM hereafter) question actually aimed for, namely where PAF lives. HKM acknowledges the incoherent response with 'Hmm' in turn 5 and again in turn 7, when, in turn 6, PAF does still not resolve the confusion on HKM's part reference. Finally, in turn 9, when PAF actually does clarify that she lives in a house, but embeds this detail in a second OS: 'And this house is ... errh ... on our own so my husband and I ... .' The latter fulfills criteria C1a and C2a.

## 9.7 Analyzing Speakers' Strategies in Overcoming Oddness

Now that we have established a sound and systematic pattern of defining OSs, and determining some ways to identify them in ELF discourse, we will take a

Table 9.4 *Speaker strategies in our dataset*

| Speaker strategy to overcome an OS | Sum | % |
|---|---|---|
| 9.7.1 (Attempted) structural self-repair | 9 | 20% |
| 9.7.2 (Attempted) self-repair through repetition/paraphrasing | 18 | 40% |
| 9.7.3 (Attempted) self-repair through added information | 13 | 28.9% |
| 9.7.4 Referring to assumed common ground | 5 | 11.1% |
| | 45 instances<br>in 32 OSs<br>in 20 excerpts | 100% |
| 9.7.5 More than one repair strategies within two subsequent turns | 19 instances | 42.2% |

closer look at pattern-like consistencies that speaker strategies have in common with regard to overcoming the oddness created by OSs. Understanding such patterns will provide implications to better understand what speakers choose to do. Above we proposed an etic rather than an emic approach when analyzing samples featuring an odd structure. Those patterns we focus on include speakers' (attempted) repair of OSs through structural self-repair, repetition, adding clarifying information and referring to presupposed common ground so as to double-check if mutual understanding has been accomplished. Finally we examine samples that contain more than one strategy being applied.

All samples in the upcoming subsections come from both the corpus and the manual searches we conducted, which brought forth all in all thirty-eight OSs in thirty-five text excerpts. We selectively use these samples disregarding the hearer and solely focusing on the speaker. The overall distribution of the four strategies we found on the speakers' side count sixty-one tokens all in all and is displayed in Table 9.4:

Note that we will henceforth not indicate the hearers' responses anymore, but will continue to indicate OSs by underscore and *speakers' self-repair strategies in bold italics.*

### *9.7.1 (Attempted) Structural Self-repair*

Attempted structural self-repair – references to common ground aside – is one of the two rarest strategies used in our data set. Sample (12) includes four OSs:[7] two of them uttered by S1, who attempts to repair the first one ('but it is a

[7] S2 poses a violation of the structure, in that s/he breaks the clause structure twice: "which one" is repeated and neither "which one do you" nor "the yes or the no" are syntactically cohesive (C1a). Whereas "which one" may still be understood as referring to any option of topic (cf. S1's first turn), "the yes or the no" additionally can be argued to break the topical frame in that it does not

subject it's a maltese which one do you d- do you d- did it learn to know erm?') by paraphrasing it, thereby producing another OS, i.e., '*If there is a some topic you would rather speak in erm English for example OR in maltese*.' The makeup of the latter utterance is structurally adjusted in that S1 inserts a defining relative clause ('[*some topic*] *you would rather speak in*') so as to specify the reference, while they retain the framing conditional clause structure so to lighten S2's cognitive processing load. While S2's OS ('<7> in maltese so which one </7> (.) which one do you (1) the (.) the yes or the no') remains unrepaired, since S1 does not actually ask for clarification, but rather pursues their original agenda, thereby producing yet another OS ('Is there something? (1) according to you'). When S2 finally asks for clarification, S1 starts another attempt at repairing their original OS both on the structural level, falling back on 'subject' (rather than 'topic'), but combining with a clarification about languages. This repair turns out to be structurally and referentially successful.

Sample (12) represents a similarly complicated dialogic sequence.

(12)

S1: If there is any subject you would like to talk about in maltese or in english (.) i <6> mean </6> but it is a subject it's a maltese which one do you d- do you d- did it learn to know erm?
S2: <6> yes </6>
S1: *If there is a some topic you would rather speak in (.) erm English <7> for example (.) OR in maltese </7>*
S2: <7> in maltese so which one </7> (.) which one do you (1) the (.) the yes or the no
S1: Is there something? (1) according to you
S2: Pardon?
S1: ***About e:r er some subject about which you would rather speak in maltese (.) than in english***

Sample (12) includes four OSs, three of them uttered by S1 and the fourth by S2. The latter responds to S1's first OS ('If there is a some topic you would rather speak in (.) erm English <7> for example (.) OR in maltese') by indicating their confusion ('in maltese so which one </7> (.) which one do you'), which itself turns out to be an OS. However, probably due to their own confusion, S2 does not take the opportunity to repair their OS. What's more, S1 is interrupting them with another one of their own ('Is there something? (1) according to you'). Rather than asking for clarification in regard to S2's OS, S1 seems to process and follow up only on S2's MC ('Pardon?'), and does so by repairing their OS as follows: S1 picks up what they had already asked in their turn preceding S2's OS, i.e., 'a

transparently refer to anything in the preceding turns at all (C2a). Partly due to the fact that S1 and S2 interrupt or at least overlap with each other, they seem to be talking past each other, too. Thus, when S1 puts forth his referentially vague question "Is there something?" (C1b), followed by the seemingly incomplete structure "according to you" (C1a), S2's "Pardon?" merely expresses their confusion about what is expected from them at this turn.

some topic you would rather speak in erm English,' by rephrasing topic as 'subject' and repairing the structure by inserting the originally missing bridge into the originally intended but not managed relative clause ('*about which you would rather speak*'). Finally, instead of the implicit choice between *English or Maltese* in the original structure, S1 chooses a much more explicit wording, i.e., '*rather [...] in maltese (.) than in english.*'

Seven out of the nine instances we identified for structural self-repair turn out to occur with adding information such as in (6), and with repetition such as in (10). In Sample (13) we even find three strategies applied at once: structural repair, repetition and added information.

(13)

| | |
|---|---|
| S2: | But you needed also FRIENDS in turkey would send you <2> material </2> |
| SS: | <2> @@@@ </2><3> @@ </3> |
| S1: | <3> haeh excuse me </3> |
| S2: | ***= you need a lot of FRIENDS in turkey or your Family collecting materials =*** |
| S1: | = I'M Turkish it doesn't MATTER (.) so |

Even though, in Sample (13), it seems that S1 utterance 'haeh excuse me' is not even an MC, but rather a double-check for what S2 had said, and they had not heard due to the group's laughter. S2 still grasps the opportunity to not only repeat the most essential components of their structure (i.e., 'FRIENDS in turkey,' 'material'), but also decides to structurally repair some of the flaws they apparently realized they had made: the past tense form 'needed' now is 'need,' 'material' is transformed into the plural, and the syntactical structure incohesively merging the two clauses 'you needed also FRIENDS in turkey' and 'would send you material' is reworded into 'a lot of FRIENDS in turkey or your Family collecting materials.' So S2 definitely makes quite an effort to repair their OS for S1, but seemingly more so out of self-motivation.

### *9.7.2 (Attempted) Self-repair through Repetition and Paraphrasing*

Repetition and paraphrasing has turned out to be the most frequent strategy in our dataset (40 percent). We argue that in Sample (14), S10's first turn ('so you have <2> to decide </2> which part is true or which part </1> is <soft> not <soft>') is in fact an OS – not due to any structural incohesiveness, but with regard to breaking the topical frame. While it could have been possible that S13's 'excuse me?' refers to not having heard S10's first turn (soft enunciation and overlapping speech, indicated by <2> and </2>), the fact that S10's structure does neither tie in with S13's 'they might do it' nor even with S13's preceding utterance ('but anyway,' etc.), leads us to argue in favor of S10's utterance being an OS. S10 interprets S13's 'excuse me?' as the plea to repeat what they just said and so they do – without an effort to repair, though.

(14)
S13: But anyway it was good because (2) they're saying it so you get it and you know what it is and you it can help you if you need it for your country and tha- er that that was the most positive thing if they were saying something and they're not doing it? But a- at least they're saying it (.) <6> so </6>
SX-5: <6><soft> @ </soft> </6>
SS: @<7>@@ </7> @ <1> @@@@@@ </1>
S13: <7> they might do it </7>
S10: <1> so you have <2> to decide </2> which part is true or which part </1> is <soft> not <soft>
S13: <2> who knows <2>
S13: Excuse me?
S10: ***you have to decide whi- which half it's is true or which is not***
S13: Well I was more with the er Nordic which (.) they seem like they're speaking the- they are more like (2) know what <3> they are talking about </3>
(VOICE)

In Sample (15), the OS 'we have a but do you have a booklet?' is structurally repaired in that the speakers actually correct themselves while speaking, first intending to repeat their original structure ('do you … '), then though deviating into 'which booklet did you use.'

(15)
S1: = up north =
S2: = because <5> the </5>
S3: <5> @ </5> @@ <6> @@@@ </6> @ =
S1: <6> to spain down south </6>
S2: = and (1) er (1)
S1: to the central of europe =
S2: = this is a <7> <un> xx </un><7>
S1: <7> @@ </7> (2)
S2: what's? (9) {mobile phone rings (9)} my son is (1) i hope (25) {S2 starts talking on the phone in romanian; S1 and S4 talk in spanish}
S1: we have a but do you have a booklet? (1) [S3]
S3: pardon?
S1: **do you wh- which booklet did you use?** (1)
S3: just (1) can you can you (.) give me (1) with the lithuanian flag (6) {S1 looks for booklet (6)}
S4: Mhm (1) o<1>kay </1>

### *9.7.3 (Attempted) Self-repair through Added Information*

The strategy of adding information for repair occurs relatively frequently in our dataset, i.e., in 28.9 percent of all cases – and often in connection with structural repair or repetition.

In Sample (7), discussed earlier, the OS 'Did you correct?' fulfills C1 in all its sub-features. When S2 reacts with the MC 'Pardon?,' S1 not only repeats the structure in its entirety, but also adds the obligatory direct object – seemingly when realizing that 'Did you correct' is not sufficient in conveying the message to S2. S1 even marks this moment of self-reflection by a filler 'e:r.' Note that S2 reacts with another MC ('e:m') directly overlapping with S1's self-repair attempt ('with the rent'), which is probably the reason for S2 not even processing the added information and thus asking again for clarification ('What do you mean?').

**(Sample 7 repeat)**

We continue with Sample (16) in which we have two OSs, the first one by S2: 'so I just come and improvise on the occasion good.' The latter is reacted upon by S4 with an MC ('okay but'), but since S4 continues talking at that point, S2 did not pick up any opportunity to self-repair. S4 then finishes their turn with the OS 'you had tha- s- that series about the evasion reports do you have something er similar to this day,' which triggers confusion in S2 ('the what'). S4, however, launches an attempt to repair by paraphrasing the vague preceding 'something similar' by 'the evaluation reports on er on various disciplines,' which is fairly concrete and gradually dissolves S2's confusion ('yes [so what?]?'; 'sure').

(16)

S2: well I look forward to that then so I just come (.) and (2) improvise on the occasion good (.)

S4: {eats while talking} okay but er (.) in fact {someone pours water} (.) <soft> erm </soft> (.) <un> xxx </un> be that (.) (yes are we in) Denmark (1) i would like to (.) ask you (1) {S4 stops eating} about some recent erm er developments concerning the higher education evaluations (1) do you have any (.) (of) er written material er ab- about recent evaluations or something like that be-when i was here (.) three years ago (.) you had tha- s- that series (.) about the evasion reports (.) do you have something er similar to this: day

S2: the what (.) (we are) =

S4: ***= the (.) evaluation reports on er on various disciplines***

S2: yes? (.)

S4: ***do you have er recent reports***

S2: sure (.)

S4: ca- can i <6> take </6>

S2: <un><6> x</6>xx </un>

S4: one or <@> two </@> (.)

### 9.7.4 *Referring to Assumed Common Ground*

Our dataset features a number of samples that show the speaker referring to assumed, or presupposed common ground like in the former Samples (4) and (8). We will be discussing Samples (17) and (18) in this subsection.

(17)

HKM: Do you speak more English here?

CDM: You are right.

HKM: But why you speak more English here?

CDM: Because, you know, I don't know, I don't see any…errh…Spanish people

HLM: Here?

CDM: No. like in New York City. ***You see, you know, every…in every corner, you see, I don't know, everybody, somebody who speak Spanish.***

HKM: Yeah.

CDM: And you went to a store, and they speak to you in Spanish.

HKM: Ok.

In Sample (17), CDM seems to utter two OSs: first 'Because, you know, I don't know, I don't see any … errh … Spanish people,' and then 'You see, you know, every … in every corner, you see, I don't know, everybody, somebody who speak Spanish.' Within the latter, CDM inserts several common ground check marks, i.e., 'you see' – 'you know' – 'you see,' thereby composing a second OS.

In Sample (18), S1 produces two OSs as well, i.e., 'but the question is should we talk about because if we (start of the) money then i don't know how to make it because' and 'WHENEVER they are going to deliver all points which are in the menu? i don't mind how what they spend.' In order to repair at least the latter, they insert the marker 'okay?' so to check for existing common ground with S3, although S1 does not await S3's confirmation.

(18)

| | |
|---|---|
| S1: | you get a monthly report <1> of them and </1> yes <2> and and @@@ </2> |
| S3: | <1> yeah of course </1> |
| S3: | <2> yes of course they they they promised to </2> yah: (.) <3> sure </3> (1) |
| S1: | <3> @ </3> |
| S3: | but the so (.) okay. (1) but the question is (.) should we talk about because if we (start of the) money (1) <soft> then i don't know how to make it <9> because </9></soft> (1) |
| S1: | <9> yeah </9> |
| S3: | WHENEVER (.) they are going to deliver (.) all points (.) which are in the menu? (1) i don't mind how <@> what they spend. </@> (.) ***okay?*** But I think <4> that </4> at the <5> end of the day they </5> will come (.) |
| S1: | <4> yeah </4> |
| S1: | <5> i understand yeah </5> |
| S3: | With the: (.) with the money to me. (.) that they do not have money for the execution. (.) yeah? |
| S1: | <soft> okay </soft> = |

### 9.7.5 *More than One Strategy within a Two-Turn Range*

In nineteen cases, we found more than one repair strategy applied to one OS on the speakers' part. These instances make up for more than 42 percent of the samples in the dataset, so they are fairly frequent overall. We will discuss two particularly clear examples in this subsection.

Sample (7) is an obvious case of not only repeating the OS word-by-word, but then also adding more information, i.e., 'with the rent.'

(Sample 7 repeat)

Sample (19) is similarly straightforward in that S1 seeks to repair their OS ('we have a but do you have a booklet?'), first by beginning to ask the same question again ('do you'), but then repairing their structure by switching for 'which booklet' – which implicitly specifies that they are referring to the selection of booklets available and asking for one in particular. In addition, S1 chooses to turn the present tense in their OS into a past form, which seems much more coherent with the context of their question.

(19)

S1: = up north =
S2: = because <5> the </5>
S3: <5> @ </5> @@ <6> @@@@ </6> @ =
S1: <6> to spain down south </6>
S2: = and (1) er (1)
S1: to the central of europe =
S2: = this is a <7> <un> xx </un><7>
S1: <7> @@ </7> (2)
S2: what's? (9) {mobile phone rings (9)} my son is (1) i hope (25) {S2 starts talking on the phone in romanian; S1 and S4 talk in spanish}
S1: we have a but do you have a booklet? (1) [S3]
S3: pardon?
S1: **do you wh- which booklet did you use?** (1)
S3: just (1) can you can you (.) give me (1) with the lithuanian flag (6) {S1 looks for booklet (6)}
S4: Mhm (1) o<1>kay </1>

## 9.8 Discussion on Speaker Meaning

In the first part of this chapter, we emphasized that we consider OSs as the best option a speaker is able to retrieve at the moment of speech in their sincere attempt to get their message across as fully as possible. Our focus has been on utterer-implicatures rather than hearer-implicatures (cf. 2002). The samples have demonstrated that speaker's utterance is characterized not only by recipient design but also by individual salience. This claim is not exactly in line with current pragmatic theories according to which 'speaker meaning' can be understood in two ways. First, it is considered an emergent and negotiated construct that is not necessarily a matter of the speakers' actual cognitions (see Schegloff 1988; Arundale 2005; Haugh 2008). Second, speaker meaning may refer just to what particular, individual speakers *mean*; what they have in mind to be talking about, and perhaps doing, in producing an utterance without much concern for the hearer's understanding (e.g., Keysar et al. 1998; Giora 2003; Keysar 2007).

Our findings give support to the socio-cognitive approach (cf. Kecskes 2010b, 2014, 2017) which is an attempt to combine the pragmatic view with the cognitive view into a coherent blend by arguing that speaker's utterance is shaped by the interplay of recipient design and salience as discussed in Chapter 5. Samples presented here demonstrate that the interplay of these social (recipient design), and individual (salience) factors shape speaker utterance. Recipient design is the result of being cooperative, while salience is the outcome of individual egocentrism that builds on prior experience.

Odd structures produced by interlocutors in intercultural interactions including ELF demonstrate this interplay of recipient design and salience very clearly: either one or the other comes to the fore, or a blend of the two. Speakers appear to be off the track, as in Samples (4) and (7), where the OS seems to deviate from the topic, or put confusing structures together as in Samples (9) and (13) and/or use vague references as in Sample (10). These are all signs of individual salience where speakers utter what is on their mind first without particular attention to their partners. There are, of course, counter examples where seemingly conscious attempts are made to give concrete, clear, well-designed information to the partner. However, these attempts may also result in odd structures mainly because of proficiency issues, and/or uncertainty in common ground as in Samples (11) and (6).

Further analysis of our samples demonstrates that initial planning of utterances in intercultural encounters appears to be mainly dominated by salience effect; self-repair, search for common ground and co-construction of meaning kick in when either the utterer anticipates mismatch or a problem before that occurs and uses self-repair (Samples [6] and [11]), or they make adjustments when an OS results in confusion (such as Samples [6], [13], and [16]). Based on the analysis, we are inclined to argue that real recipient design in ELF usually happens when speakers notice that there is something wrong with their utterance. For the ELF interlocutor to notice that something is wrong, it is not necessary to see any confusion in the communicative behavior and utterance production of his/her partner. It is enough if the speaker anticipates trouble, or makes a judgment about possible confusion even without a concrete sign from the other interlocutor. If there is any concrete sign, repair usually occurs right away in several different ways.

Samples demonstrate some difference between L1 and ELF concerning the interplay of recipient design and salience effect that leads to the production of odd structures. When producing an utterance in L1, the interlocutor can rely on a wider inter-label hierarchy when selecting words than in ELF where, because of language proficiency issues, this inter-label hierarchy offers fewer options. So the best option of the speaker at the moment of speech is the one that is selected (recipient design) or triggered (salience effect) from the limited repertoire.

## 9.9 Summary

This chapter has made an attempt to take a closer look at speaker production in ELF by introducing a dialogic approach to the analysis of a newly established category that I called odd structures. OSs put forth contradictory or frame-breaking information. In violating particular patterns, they potentially put mutual understanding and successful communication between interlocutors at risk. However, the important thing is that OSs do not necessarily lead to non-understanding or misunderstandings between ELF interlocutors. They can be unnoticed, unreacted to, or reacted to as if no oddness has occurred. It was argued and demonstrated that a dialogic turn-by-turn, action–reaction approach to discourse segments will give us a better understanding of how these structures are created and deployed.

The analysis of OSs shows that oddness may be triggered, and also be the result of the speaker's effort to formulate what is on his/her mind to the best of his/her knowledge. However, contrary to what happens in L1, in ELF the interplay of recipient design and salience is strongly affected by deficient proficiency and uncertainty about assumed common ground. So the primary goal of the speaker is to formulate his/her intention not necessarily as required by the context and the audience but as s/he is able to under communicative pressure. As a result, this somewhat limited ability is reflected in most of the odd structures. So the characteristics features of oddness given in Table 9.1, and their demonstrations by numerous examples, are basically the reflections of speaker's effort in shaping his/her utterance. In spite of the oddness of those structures we, do not consider them mistakes because conversationally OSs usually make sense and do not necessarily lead to misunderstanding. Thus, the characteristics of oddness we proposed are reflections of a speaker's effort in shaping his/her utterance. This being said, it is striking that, in most of our examples, the contradictory information put forth (cf. C2a) seems to be the primary trigger for repair attempts, while lexical ambiguity is only a secondary one. This means, overall, that OSs more often than not pose issues on a content-level, and not so much with regard to a speaker's selection of words.

Also, one of the goals of the presented analysis was to identify speakers' strategies that are used in overcoming oddness. These categories, as we said several times, are the results of an etic rather than an emic approach. But through our data collection methods we have tried to 'legitimize' them as existing ones that the speakers actually rely on. As part of this legitimization process, we have identified instances of repair strategies used by the speakers in 73.3 percent of cases within the forty-one OSs samples we investigated. This high percentage suggests that speakers are, in fact, significantly active and determined in seeking to create common ground and to communicate effectively. Only in 26.7 percent of all cases did speakers choose the non-repair of their OSs. But it has to be kept in mind that in most of these instances, they might have chosen to launch a repair, but were not able to do that due to being interrupted by their interlocutors, or simply due to not realizing themselves that they just had produced an OS.

Our approach had to step out of the strict confines of utterance- and intention-based pragmatics diving into the field of dialogue and discourse analysis. As Horn and Kecskes (2013) pointed out, this is an essential route for socio-cultural-interactional pragmatics and intercultural pragmatics that have both been making equal attempts to broaden the scope of pragmatics. Thus, our analysis of OSs has been pointed in the same direction analogous to the rest of this book.

We have come a long way in these nine chapters. We have not only discussed the most important issues in ELF from a pragmatic perspective but also used some methods to analyze ELF production to get information about the main characteristics and nature of this language-use mode. This book is just one attempt out of many to shed light on what exactly happens in ELF communication. Many more will come …

# Epilogue

I think I need to pick up where I finished in Chapter 9. One of the main goals of this book was to broaden the scope of pragmatics through examining English as a Lingua Franca from several different perspectives. During my investigation and discussions in the different chapters, I have tried not to leave the Gricean paradigm. What I have intended to do is to add something to the Gricean way of thinking that originates in intercultural communication. My previous book, *Intercultural Pragmatics* (OUP 2014), was the first step on this path. This book represents the second step. I hope some more will come.

It was not easy to write this book. On the one hand, there is a huge amount of literature on ELF out there and it is growing by the day. ELF is a hot topic: scholars research it, debate it, and write about it. In spite of this there are still uncharted territories in the field that need to be addressed. This is what I have tried to do in this book. Topics like the role of sociocultural background knowledge, intention, implicature, semantics–pragmatics interface, modality, etc. have not been addressed much within ELF research. I have not ignored the existing literature but it was hard to find what would be relevant to those topics from the available literature. Still, I think I have managed to include much existing literature and make it relevant to my discussion points. Of course, not all the views presented in this book are new. I have "recycled" some of my previously presented ideas or related them to ELF. I think this is natural. But many of the ideas I have put forward are expected to be quite innovative. They were born of my thinking about ELF while writing papers and this book. I am sure some of them will be picked up by researchers and be analyzed, discussed, approved, or rejected.

All in all, I think ELF helps us, as pragmaticians, better understand how language works when the logic of the language may take occasional turns different than in L1, and the pillars that the structure of that language sits on may stand less firmly than in L1 but the 'building' still stands. I will explain this briefly.

## E.1 Hybridity and Synergism

I hope the discussions and examples have proven that although ELF is not a language in its own right, it is still used in a somewhat systematic way that characterizes any language use mode. It was demonstrated that this language use mode involves the use of several varieties of English. The use of ELF shows hybridity on the one hand and synergism on the other. Hybridity because when, for instance, a Russian speaker, a French speaker, and a Chinese speaker use English for communication, the process represents three different varieties of English: Russian English, French English, and Chinese English. But ELF use also shows synergism because the three varieties in this example rely on a core linguistic code that is put to use in order to develop a frame for their actual situational context or modify an existing target language frame according to the speakers' immediate needs. The usage varieties that the three Englishes represent contribute to the co-construction of a discourse sequence that facilitates the process of understanding between the participants. So the three varieties serve one purpose and work with the core linguistic code to create an amicable environment for communication.

What ELF users do and the way they do it is governed by human rationality that shows the interplay of social cooperation and individual egocentrism. Their language behavior does not differ much from what they do in their L1. Basic human language behavior is very similar no matter what language is used. The three main components of meaning production and comprehension are always there: code system, sociocultural context and interlocutors with their communicative needs. As we discussed, the mechanisms of language behavior are the same but they work differently in ELF environment. ELF speakers try to organize their own frames, develop their own temporary vocabulary, establish rapport with each other, and attempt to set up temporary norms, etc. In this process they do not dismantle language, rather they recreate it temporarily according to their needs. And this 'language building' still relies on how the logic and mechanism of language work in general. So if there is little in terms of pragmatics that can be used from the target language, no problem, the participants will build up temporary frames and create temporary formulas and norms to make the communicative process smooth. But, of course, there is still something that makes Elf communication distinguishable from L1 communication.

## E.2 Differences of Native Varieties of English and ELF

I see the main differences between the use of native varieties of English (American, Australian, British, New Zealand) and the use of ELF mainly in two things:

### E.2.1 The Extent to which Interlocutors Can Rely on Ready-Made, Relatively Preexisting Frames and Prefabricated Language, and How Much They Must Co-construct Those

We argued that any language use is an alternation between prefabricated and ad hoc generated sentences that gain communicative meaning in the actual situational context. As a consequence, linguistic creativity is considered a discourse level rather than a sentence level creativity, which includes combining ready-made language with ad hoc generated language in a creative way that satisfies communicative needs. The only question is that how much interlocutors need to/should/could/wish to rely on prefabricated elements and frames rather than on ad hoc language generation. We can easily answer this question if we consider this alternation a continuum with two hypothetical ends such as prefabricated —— ad hoc generated language. Each interaction in any language use means an up-and-down movement on the continuum. It was argued that in L1 we are usually closer to the prefabricated end of the continuum while in ELF we are closer to the ad hoc generated end, where more co-construction is usually needed.

Of course, I do not want to say that there is no co-construction in L1. Yes, there is, and a lot of it. However, in L1 that co-construction is usually a question of choice, while in ELF it is more likely a question of necessity. L1 speakers can decide whether they wish to use available frames and prefabricated language in social encounters: they are all given to them. But ELF speakers hardly have this choice because they have limited common ground and shared knowledge about how much their partners are familiar with target language norms, formulaicity and figurativity. So to stay on the safe side, they would rather stick to semantic analyzability, ad hoc language generation (see Chapter 9) and reliance on the linguistic system as core common ground, which leads us to the second issue.

### E.2.2 The Semantic–Pragmatic Interface

The semantic–pragmatic interface debate is about how much actual situational context the linguistic signs need in order to be meaningful in the communicative process. The analysis of ELF has given something new to this debate. It was argued that target language-based pragmatic mechanisms and contextual effects do not work the way they do in L1. So, seemingly, there is something that I called "impoverished" pragmatics in ELF. However, a closer look showed that in fact pragmatics is invigorated rather than impoverished. There is a kind of pragmaticalization of semantics – a synchronic, one-off phenomenon in which coded semantic meaning, sometimes without any specific pragmatic enrichment based on the target language, obtains temporary pragmatic status.

So ELF interlocutors appear to create their own pragmatics. This phenomenon has made us rethink how implicatures work in ELF.

In L1, there is a lot of implication and inferencing. It is a great way in L1 to subtly communicate to your partners what your opinion is on a topic, event, person or anything else without actually coming out and saying it. Suggestive language is an essential part of the language game. In fact, with some exaggeration we could say that we usually do not say what we think directly. Indirectness is an indispensable language phenomenon. How much of that do we have in ELF? Not much. Suggestive language is largely missing in ELF. To use suggestive language in ELF means taking a serious risk. The ELF speaker can be easily misunderstood or non-understood at all. Semantically analyzable language is preferred by ELF interlocutors. Why? Because suggestive language requires strong actual contextual support. The selective role of actual situational context in an encounter is strong and decisive if the understanding of that context is similar for each interlocutor. This, again, requires core common ground and shared sociocultural background knowledge (see Chapter 4). Since this is quite limited in ELF, interlocutors usually avoid the use of indirectness and suggestive language. As a consequence, implicatures in the Gricean sense are rare to find in ELF interactions. That is why I suggested that we should revise what we understand by "implicature."

ELF will not disappear. In fact, it will grow and change constantly. As it stands now, we have a strong argument for calling it a language use mode rather than a language. But there is something that we should not forget about. We have emphasized in several chapters that there are two very important characteristic features of any language use: economy and normativity. People need prefabricated language to satisfy their subconscious desire to be as economical as possible in language use. Also, the more people spend time together and have relatively common communicative goals to express, the more the results of their endeavor for normativity are visible in the form of frames and formulas. This is how economy and normativity are intertwined in language use. And this is how a new variety of language, or even a new language altogether, may start to develop . . .

# References


Adamson, H. D. (1988). *Variation theory and second language acquisition*. Washington, DC: Georgetown University Press.

Adamson, H. D., & Regan, V. (1991). The acquisition of community speech norms by Asian immigrants learning English as a second language: A preliminary study. *Studies in Second Language Acquisition*, *13*, 1–22.

Aijmer, K. (2016). Modality and mood in functional linguistic approaches. In J. Nuyts & J. Van der Auwera (Eds.), *The Oxford handbook of modality and mood* (pp.495–513). Oxford: Oxford University Press.

Al-Issa, A. (2003). Sociocultural transfer in L2 speech behaviors: Evidence and motivating factors. *International Journal of Intercultural Relations*, *27*, 581–601.

Altenberg, B. (1998). On the phraseology of spoken English: The evidence of recurrent word-combinations. In A. P. Cowie (Ed.), *Phraseology: Theory, analysis, and applications* (pp.101–122). Oxford: Clarendon Press.

Antoniou, K. (2019). Multilingual pragmatics: Implicature comprehension in adult L2 learners and multilingual children. In N. Taguchi (Ed.), *The Routledge handbook of pragmatics and second language acquisition*.

Antoniou, K., & Katsos, N. (2017). The effect of childhood multilingualism and bilectalism on implicature understanding. *Applied Psycholinguistics*, *38* (4), 787–833.

Antoniou, K., Veenstra, A., Kissine, M., Katsos, N. (in press). The Impact of Childhood Bilingualism and Bi-dialectalism on Pragmatic Interpretation and Processing. In *Proceedings of the 42nd Annual Boston University Conference on Language Development*.

Antoniou, K., Veenstra, A., Kissine, M. & Katsos, N. (2019). How does childhood bilingualism and bi-dialectalism affect the interpretation and processing of implicature? *Bilingualism: Language and Cognition,* 1–18.

Arbib, M. A., Oztop, E., & Zukow-Goldring, P. (2005). Language and the mirror system: A perception/action based approach to communicative development. *Cognition, Brain, Behavior*, *3*, 239–272.

Archibald, A., Cogo, A., & Jenkins, J. (2011). *Latest trends in ELF research*. Newcastle: Cambridge Scholars Publishing.

Ariel, M. (2008). *Pragmatics and grammar*. Cambridge: Cambridge University Press.

Arundale, R. B. (1999). An alternative model and ideology of communication for an alternative to politeness theory. *Pragmatics*, *9*, 119–154.

Arundale, R. B. (2005). Pragmatics, conversational implicature and conversation. In K. L. Fitch & R. E. Sanders (Eds.), *Handbook of language and social interaction* (pp.41–63). Mahwah, NJ: Lawrence Erlbaum.

Arundale, R. B. (2006). Face as relational and interactional: a communication framework for research on face, facework, and politeness. *Journal of Politeness Research*, *2*(2), 193–216.

Arundale, R. B. (2008). Against (Gricean) intentions at the heart of human interaction. *Intercultural Pragmatics*, *5*, 229–258.

Bach, K. (1994). Conversational implicature. *Mind & Language*, *9*(2), 124–162.

Bach, K. (1999). The myth of conventional implicature. *Linguistics and Philosophy*, *22* (4), 327–366.

Bach, K. (2001). Grice, H. Paul. In R. Wilson & F. Keil (Eds.), *The MIT encyclopedia of the cognitive sciences* (pp.59–60). Cambridge, MA: MIT Press.

Bach, K. (2002). Giorgione was so-called because of his name. *Noûs*, *36*, 73–103.

Bach, K. (2004). Minding the gap. In C. Bianchi (Ed.), *The semantics/pragmatics distinction* (pp.27–43). Stanford: CSLI Publications.

Bach, K. (2005). Context ex machina. In S. Zoltán (Ed.), *Semantics vs. pragmatics* (pp.15–45), Oxford: Oxford University Press.

Bach, K. (2007). Regressions in pragmatics (and semantics). In N. Burton-Roberts (Ed.), *Pragmatics* (pp.24–44). Basingstoke: Palgrave Macmillan.

Baker, P. (2017). *American and British English: Divided by a common language?* Cambridge: Cambridge University Press.

Baker, W. (2009). The cultures of English as a Lingua Franca. *TESOL Quarterly*, *43*(4), 567–592.

Baker, W. (2015). *Culture and identity through English as a lingua franca*. Boston/ Berlin: DeGruyter Mouton.

Baldinger, K. (1980). *Semantic theory: Towards a modern semantics*. Oxford: Blackwell.

Barr, D. J., & Keysar, B. (2005). Making sense of how we make sense: The paradox of egocentrism in language use. In H. L. Colston & A. N. Katz. (Eds.), *Figurative language comprehension* (pp.21–43). Mahwah, NJ: Lawrence Erlbaum.

Barro, A., Byram, M., Grimm, H., Morgan, C., & Roberts, C. (1993). Cultural studies for advanced language learners. In D. Graddol, L. Thompson & M. Byram (Eds.), *Language and culture* (pp.55–70). Clevedon: Multilingual Matters.

Bates, D. G., & Plog, F. (1980). *Cultural anthropology* (2nd ed.). New York: Alfred A. Knopf.

Bezuidenhout, A. (2004). Procedural meaning and the semantics/pragmatics interface. In C. Bianchi (Ed.), *The semantics/pragmatics distinction* (pp.101–131). Stanford: CSLI Publications.

Biber, D., Conrad, S., & Cortes, V. (2004). If you look at . . . : Lexical bundles in university teaching and textbooks. *Applied Linguistics*, *25*, 371–405.

Biber, D., Johansson, S., Leech, G., Conrad, S., & Finegan, E. (1999). *Longman grammar of spoken and written English*. London: Pearson Education.

Bierwisch, M. (1981). Basic issues in the development of word meaning. In W. Deutch (Ed.), *The child's construction of language* (pp.341–387). London: Academic Press.

Bierwisch, M., & Schreuder, R. (1992). From concepts to lexical items. *Cognition*, *42*, 23–60.

Björkman, B. (2010). Spoken lingua franca English at a Swedish technical university. Unpublished doctoral dissertation, University of Stockholm, Sweden.

Björkman, B. (2011a). Pragmatic strategies in English as an academic lingua franca: Ways of achieving communicative effectiveness? *Journal of Pragmatics*, *43*(4), 950–964.

Björkman, B. (2011b). The pragmatics of English as a lingua franca in the international university. *Journal of Pragmatics*, *43*(4), 923–925.

Björkman, B. (2013). *English as an academic lingua franca: An investigation of form and communicative effectiveness*. Boston/Berlin: De Gruyter Mouton.

Boden, M. A. (1999). Computer models of creativity. In R. Sternberg (Ed.), *Handbook of creativity* (pp.351–372). Cambridge: Cambridge University Press.

Bolinger, D. (1976). Meaning and memory. *Forum Linguisticum*, *1*, 1–14.

Bouton, L. F. (1988). A cross-cultural study of ability to interpret implicatures in English. *World Englishes*, *7*(2), 183–196.

Bouton, L. F. (1992). The interpretation of implicature in English by NNS: Does it come automatically–Without being explicitly taught? *Pragmatics and Language Learning*, *3*, 53–65.

Bouton, L. F. (1994). Conversational implicature in the second language: Learned slowly when not deliberately taught. *Journal of Pragmatics*, *22*, 157–67.

Bowie, J., Wallis, S.A. & Aarts, B. (2013). Contemporary change in modal usage in spoken British English: Mapping the impact of "genre". In J. I. Marín-Arrese, M. Carretero, J. A. Hita & J. van der Auwera (Eds.), *English modality: Core, periphery and evidentiality*, Topics in English Linguistics [TiEL], Band 81 (pp.57–94). Boston/ Berlin: De Gruyter Mouton.

Bowles, H., & Cogo, A. (Eds). (2015). *International perspectives on English as a lingua franca: Pedagogical insights*. London: Palgrave.

Brumfit, C. (2006). A European perspective on language as liminality. In C. Mar-Molinero & P. Stevenson (Eds.), *Language ideologies, policies and practices* (pp.28–43). London: Palgrave Macmillan.

Bruner, J. (1975). From communication to language: A psychological perspective. *Cognition*, *3*, 255–287.

Bruner, J. (1983). *Child's talk: Learning to use language*. Granada: W.W. Norton.

Buber, M. (1955). Dialogue. In *Between man and man* (R. G. Smith, Trans., pp.1–39). Boston, MA: Beacon Press.

Burton-Roberts, N. (2006). *Cancellation and Intention*. Paper given at the Workshop on Explicit communication, University of Granada, Spain.

Bybee, J., & Fleischmann, S. (1995). Modality in grammar and discourse: An introductory essay. In J. Bybee & S. Fleischmann (Eds.), *Modality in grammar and discourse* (pp.1–14). Amsterdam: John Benjamins Publishing.

Canagarajah, A. (2007). Lingua franca English, multilingual communities and language acquisition. *The Modern Language Journal*, *91*, 923–939.

Canagarajah, A. (2014). In search of a new paradigm for teaching English as an international language. *TESOL Journal*, *5*(4), 767–785.

Cappelen, H. (2008). Content relativism and semantic blindness. In M. García-Carpintero & K. Max (Eds.), *Relative truth* (pp.265–286). Oxford: Clarendon Press.

Cappelen, H., & Lepore, E. (2005). *Insensitive semantics*. Blackwell Press.

Carassa, A., & Colombetti, M. (2009). Joint meaning. *Journal of Pragmatics*, *41*(9), 1837–1854.

Carnap, R. (1942). *Introduction to semantics*. Cambridge: Harvard University Press.

Carrió-Pastor, M. L. C. (2014). Cross-cultural variation in the use of modal verbs in academic English. *Sky Journal of Linguistics*, *27*(1), 153–166. Linguistic Association of Finland.

Carroll, L. (1871). *Through the looking glass*. London: Macmillan.

Carroll, R. (1988). *Cultural misunderstanding: The French-American experience*. Chicago: University of Chicago Press.

Carston, R. (2002). *Thoughts and utterances: The pragmatics of explicit communication*. Oxford: Blackwell.

Carter, R. (2004). *Language and creativity: The art of common talk*. New York: Routledge.

Cekaite, A. (2007). A child's development of interactional competence in a Swedish L2 classroom. *Modern Language Journal*, *91*, 145–162.

Chomsky, C. (1972). Stages in language development and reading exposure. *Harvard Educational Review*, *42*(1), 1–33.

Chomsky, N. (1964). *Current issues in linguistic theory*. The Hague: Mouton.

Chomsky, N. (1965). *Aspects of the theory of syntax*. Cambridge, MA: MIT Press.

Chomsky, N. (1966). *Cartesian linguistics: A chapter in the history of rationalist thought*. New York: Harper & Row.

Chomsky, N. (1975). *The logical structure of linguistic theory*. New York: Plenum press.

Chomsky, N. (1986). *Knowledge of language: Its nature, origin and use*. New York: Praeger.

Chomsky, N. (1995). *The minimalist program*. Cambridge, MA: MIT Press.

Chomsky, N. (2000). Minimalist inquiries: The framework. In R. Martin, D. Michaels & J. Uriagereka (Eds.), *Step by step: Essays on minimalist syntax in honor of Howard Lasnik* (pp.89–155). Cambridge, MA: MIT Press.

Ciaramidaro, A., Adenzato, M., Enrici, I., Erk, S., Pia, L., Bara, B. G. & Walter, H. (2007). The intentional network: How the brain reads varieties of intentions. *Neuropsychologia*, *45*(13), 3105–3113.

Cieślicka, A. (2006). Literal salience in on-line processing of idiomatic expressions by second language learners. *Second Language Research*, *22*(2), 115–144.

Clahsen, H., & Muysken, P. (1996). How adult second language learning differs from child first language development. *Behavioral and Brain Science*, *19*, 721–723.

Clahsen, H., Eisenbeiss, S., & Penke, M. (1996). Lexical learning in early syntactic development. In H. Clahsen (Ed.), *Generative perspectives on language acquisition* (pp.129–159). Amsterdam: Benjamins.

Clark, H. H. (1996). *Using language*. Cambridge: Cambridge University Press.

Clark, H. H. (2009). Context and common ground. In J. L. Mey (Ed.), *Concise Encyclopedia of Pragmatics* (pp.116–119). Oxford: Elsevier.

Clark, H. H., & Carlson, T. B. (1982). Hearers and speech acts. *Language*, *58*, 332–373.

Clyne, M. (1994). *Intercultural communication at work: Cultural values in discourse*. Cambridge/New York: Cambridge University Press.

Coates, J. (1987). Epistemic modality and spoken discourse. *Transactions of the philological society*, *85*(1), 110–131.

Cogo, A., & Dewey, M. (2012). *Analysing English as a lingua franca: A corpus-driven investigation*. Bloomsbury Publishing.

Cohen, R. (2007). Creolization and cultural globalization: The soft sounds of fugitive power. *Globalizations*, *4*(3), 369–384.

Colston, H. L., & Katz, A. (Eds.). (2005). *Figurative language comprehension: Social and cultural influences*. Hillsdale, NJ: Lawrence Erlbaum.

Cooren, F. (2010). *Action and agency in dialogue: Passion, incarnation, and ventriloquism*. Amsterdam/Philadelphia: John Benjamins.

Cornbleet, S., & Carter, R. (2001). *The language of speech and writing*. London: Routledge.

Corson, D. (1995). *Using English words*. Dordrecht, Netherlands: Kluwer Academic Publishers.

Coulmas, F. (Ed.). (1981). *Conversational routine: Explorations in standardized communication situations and prepatterned speech*. The Hague: Mouton.

Croft, W., & Cruse, D. A.(2004). *Cognitive Linguistics*. Cambridge University Press.

Croft, W., & Wood, E. J. (2000). Construal operations in linguistics and artificial intelligence. In L. Albertazzi (Ed.), *Meaning and cognition: a multidisciplinary approach* (pp.51–78). Amsterdam: John Benjamins.

Cruse, D. A. (1992). Antonymy revisited: Some thoughts on the relationship between words and concepts. In *Frames, fields, and contrasts* (pp.289–306). Hillsdale, NJ: Lawrence Erlbaum.

Cruse, D. A. (2002). Language, meaning and sense: semantics. In N. E. Collingen (Ed.), *An encyclopedia of language* (pp.87–104). Oxfordshire: Routledge.

Csikszentmihalyi, M. (1999). Implications of a systems perspective for the study of creativity. In R. Sternberg (Ed.), *Handbook of creativity* (pp.313–335). Cambridge: Cambridge University Press.

Cushman, D., & Kincaid, L. (1987). Asian perspectives on communication theory. In L. Kincaid (Ed.), *Communication theory: Eastern and western perspectives* (pp.11–20). San Diego, CA: Academic Press.

D'Andrade, R. (1987). A folk model of the mind. In D. Holland & N. Quinn (Eds.), *Cultural models in language and thought* (pp.113–147). Cambridge: Cambridge University Press.

D'Andrade, R. (1992). Schemas and motivation. In R. D'Andrade & C. Strauss (Eds.), *Human motives and cultural models* (pp.23–44). New York: Cambridge University Press.

Dąbrowska, E. (2010). Naive vs. expert intuitions: An empirical study of acceptability judgments. *The Linguistic Review*, *27*, 1–23.

Davis, W. (1998). *Implicature, intention, convention, and principle in the failure of Gricean theory*. Cambridge: Cambridge University Press.

Decock, S., & Spiessens, A. (2017). Customer complaints and disagreements in a multilingual business environment. A discursive-pragmatic analysis. *Intercultural Pragmatics*, *14*(1), 77–114.

Desai, J. (2007). Intergenerational conflict within Asian American families: The role of acculturation, ethnic identity, individualism, and collectivism. *Dissertation Abstracts International*, *67*, 7369.

Deterding, D. (2013). *Misunderstandings in English as a lingua franca: An analysis of ELF interactions in south-east Asia* (Vol. 1). Walter de Gruyter.

Downing, A., & Locke, P. (2002). *A university course in English grammar*. London: Routledge.

Du-Babcock, B. (2009). English as a business lingua franca: A framework of integrative approach to future research. In L. Louhiala-Salminen & A. Kankaanranta (Eds.), *International business communication: The ascent of international business communication* (B-109, pp. 45–66). Helsinki: HSE Print.

Dupuy, L., Stateva, P., Andreetta, S., Cheylus, A., Déprez, V., & Henst, J. B. V. D. (2018). Pragmatic abilities in bilinguals: The case of scalar implicatures. *Linguistic Approaches to Bilingualism*. doi:10.1075/lab.17017.dup.

Durkheim, E. (1982). *The rules of sociological method*. (W. D. Halls, Trans.). New York: The Free Press. (Original work published in 1895).

Dutra, D.P. (1998). *The acquisition of English root modality by non-native speakers*. Unpublished doctoral dissertation, University of Florida.

Dynel, M. (2011). A web of deceit: A neo-Gricean view on types of verbal deception. *International Review of Pragmatics*, *3*, 137–165.

Eckert, P. (1992). Communities of practice: Where language, gender and power all live. In K. Hall, M. Bucholtz & B. Moonwomon (Eds.), *Proceedings of the 1992 Berkeley Women and Language Conference: Locating power* (pp.89–99). Berkeley: Berkeley Women and Language Group.

Ehrenreich, Susanne. (2016). English as a lingua franca (ELF) in international business contexts: key issues and future perspectives. In K. Murata (Ed.), *Exploring ELF in Japanese academic and business contexts* (pp.135–155). London and New York: Routledge Taylor & Francis Group.

Ellis, N. C. (2003). Constructions, chunking, and connectionism: The emergence of second language structure. In C. J. Doughty & M. H. Long (Eds.), *The Handbook of second language acquisition* (pp.63–103). Malden, MA: Blackwell.

Ellis, N. C., Simpson-Vlach, R., & Carson, M. (2008). Formulaic language in native and second language speakers: Psycholinguistics, corpus linguistics, and TESOL. *TESOL Journal*, *42*, 375–396.

Evans, V. (2006). Lexical concepts, cognitive models and meaning construction. *Cognitive Linguistics*, *17*(4), 491–534.

Fauconnier, G. (1997). *Mappings in thought and language*. Cambridge: Cambridge University Press.

Fillmore, C. J. (1976). The need for a frame semantics within linguistics. *Statistical Methods in Linguistics*, *12*, 5–29.

Fillmore, C. J. (1982). Frame semantics. In Linguistic Society of Korea (Ed.), *Linguistics in the morning calm* (pp.111–137). Seoul: Hanshin Publishing Co.

Firth, A. (1996). The discursive accomplishment of normality: On 'lingua franca' English and conversation analysis. *Journal of Pragmatics*, *26*(2), 237–259.

Firth, A. (2009). The lingua franca factor. *Intercultural Pragmatics*, *6*(2), 147–170.

Firth, A., & Wagner, J. (1997). On discourse, communication and (some) fundamental concepts in SLA research. *The Modern Language Journal*, *81*, 285–300.

Gablasova, D., Brezina, V., McEnery, T., & Boyd, E. (2015). Epistemic stance in spoken L2 English: the effect of task and speaker style. *Applied Linguistics*, *38* (5), 613–637.

Gairns, R., & Redman, S. (1986). *Working with words: A guide to teaching and learning vocabulary*. Cambridge: Cambridge University Press.

Garfinkel, H. (1967), *Studies in ethnomethodology*. Upper Saddle River, NJ: Prentice Hall.

Garfinkel, H. (1972). Remarks on ethnomethodology. In J. J. Gumperz & D. H. Hymes (Eds.), *Directions in sociolinguistics pages* (pp. 301–324). New York: Holt, Rinehart & Winston.
Gass, S. M., & Varonis, E.M. (1985). Miscommunication in native/nonnative conversation. *Language in Society*, *14*(3), 327–343.
Gass, S. M., & Varonis, E.M. (1991). Miscommunication in nonnative speaker discourse. In N. Couplan, H. Giles & J. M. Wiemann (Eds.), *"Miscommunication" and problematic talk* (pp. 121–145). Thousand Oaks, CA: Sage Publications.
Gauker, C. (2001). Situated inference versus conversational implicature. *Nous*, *35*, 163–189.
Gauker, C. (2003). *Words without meaning*. Cambridge, MA: MIT Press.
Geeraerts, D. (1997). *Diachronic prototype semantics*. Oxford: Clarendon Press.
Gibbs, R. (1994). *The poetics of mind*. Cambridge: Cambridge University Press.
Gibbs, R. (1996). Why many concepts are metaphorical. *Cognition*, *61*, 309–319.
Gibbs, R. (1999). *Intentions in the experience of meaning*. Cambridge: Cambridge University Press.
Gibbs, R. (2002). A new look at literal meaning in understanding what is said and implicated. *Journal of Pragmatics*, *34*(4), 457–486.
Giora, R. (1997). Understanding figurative and literal language: The graded salience hypothesis. *Cognitive Linguistics*, *8*(3), 183–206.
Giora, R. (2003). *On our mind: Salience context and figurative language*. New York: Oxford University Press.
Giora, R., & Haugh, M. (Eds.). (2017). *Doing pragmatics interculturally: Cognitive, philosophical, and sociopragmatic perspectives* (Vol. 312). Berlin: Walter de Gruyter.
Givoni, S., Giora, R., & Bergerbest, D. (2013), How speakers alert addressees to multiple meanings. *Journal of Pragmatics*, *48*(1), 29–40.
Goddard, C. (1998). *Semantic analysis: A practical introduction*. Oxford: Oxford University Press.
Graddol, D. (1997). *The future of English?* London: The British Council.
Graddol, D. (2006). *English next*. London: The British Council.
Gramkow Anderson, K. (1993). *Lingua franca discourse: An investigation of the use of English in an international business context*. Unpublished master's thesis, Aalborg University, Aalborg, Denmark.
Grazzi, E. (2014). The sociocultural dimension of ELF in the English classroom: A case study on web-mediated activities. *Textus*, *27*(1), 155–172.
Grice, H. P. (1975). Logic and conversation. In P. Cole & J. L. Morgan (Eds.), *Syntax and semantics* (Vol. 3, pp.41–58). New York: Academic Press.
Grice, H. P. (1989). Meaning. In *Studies in the way of words* (pp.213–233). Cambridge, MA: Harvard University Press. [Grice, H. P. (1957). Meaning. *The Philosophical Review* *66*(3), 377–388.] [Grice, H. P. (1969). Utterer's meaning and intentions. *The Philosophical Review, 78*(2), 147–177.]
Grosz, B. J., & Sidner, C. L. (1986). Attention, intentions, and the structure of discourse. *Computational Linguistics*, *12*(3), 175–204.
Gruber, J. S. (1985). Lexical, conceptual, and encyclopedic meaning. *Quaderni de Semanlica*, *2*, 254–267.
Gudykunst, W. B., & Kim, Y.Y. (1992). *Communicating with strangers: An approach to intercultural communication*. New York: McGraw-Hill.

Gumperz, J. J. (1964). Linguistic and social interaction in two communities. In B. Blount (Ed.), *Language, culture and society* (pp.283–299). Cambridge, MA: Winthrop.

Gumperz, J. J. (1968). The speech community. In A. Duranti (Ed.), *Linguistic anthropology: A reader* (pp.66–73). Wiley-Blackwell.

Gumperz, J. J. (1979). The retrieval of socio-cultural knowledge in conversation. *Poetics Today*, *1*(1/2), 273–286.

Gumperz, J. J. (1982). *Discourse strategies*. Cambridge: Cambridge University Press.

Gumperz, J. J. (2001). Contextualization and ideology in intercultural communication. In A.D. Luzio, S. Gunthner & F. Orletti (Eds.), *Culture in communication: Analysis of intercultural situations* (pp.35–54). Amsterdam: John Benjamins Publishing Company.

Gumperz, J. J., & Cook-Gumperz, J. (2005). Making space for bilingual communicative practice. *Intercultural Pragmatics*, *2*(1), 1–23.

Gumperz, J. J., & Levinson, S. (Eds.). (1996). *Rethinking linguistic relativity.* Cambridge: Cambridge University Press.

Gumperz, J. J., & Roberts, C. (1991). Understanding in intercultural encounters. In B. Jan & J. Verschueren (Eds.), *The pragmatics of intercultural and international communication* (pp. 51–90). Amsterdam: John Benjamins.

Gumperz, J. J., & Tannen, D. (1979). Individual and social differences in language use. In F. Charles J., K. Daniel & W. S.-Y. Wang (Eds.), *Individual differences in language ability and language behavior* (pp.305–325). New York: Academic Press.

Gutzmann, D. (2014). Semantics vs. pragmatics. Accessed www.danielgutzmann.com /work/semantics-vs-pragmatics. Forthcoming in L. Matthewson, C. Meier, H. Rullmann & T. E. Zimmermann (Eds.), *The companion to semantics*. Oxford: Wiley.

Habermas, J. (1979). *Communication and the evolution of society.* Toronto: Beacon Press.

Haiman, J. (1980). Dictionaries and encyclopedias. *Lingua*, *50*, 329–357

Hall, J. K., & Pekarek Doehler, S. (2011). L2 interactional competence and development (Chapter 1). In *L2 Interactional Competence and Development* (Vol. 1, pp.1–15). Bristol, UK: Multilingual Matters.

Hall, J. K., Hellerman, J., & Pekarek Doehler, S. (Eds.). (2011). *L2 interactional competence and development*. Bristol, UK: Multilingual Matters.

Harnad, S. (1990). The symbol grounding problem. *Physica D*, *42*, 335–346.

Haugen, E. (1972). The ecology of language. In A. S. Dil (Ed), *The ecology of language: Essays by Einar Haugen*. (pp. 344–366). Stanford: Stanford University Press.

Haugh, M. (2008). Intention in pragmatics [Special issue]. *Intercultural Pragmatics*, *5* (2), 99–110. Berlin: Mouton de Gruyter.

Haugh, M. (2009). *Face, communication and social interaction*. Sheffield, UK: Equinox Pub.

Haugh, M., & Jaszczolt, K. (2012). Speaker intentions and intentionality. In K. Allan & K. Jaszczolt (Eds.), *Cambridge handbook of pragmatics* (pp.87–112). Cambridge: Cambridge University Press.

Hauser, M.D., Chomsky, N., & Fitch, W.T. (2002). The faculty of language: What is it, who has it, and how did it evolve? *Science*, *298*, 1569–1579.

Hinkel, E. (1995). The use of modal verbs as a reflection of cultural values. *TESOL Journal*, *29*(2), 325–343.

Holland, D., & Quinn, N. (Eds.). (1987). *Cultural models in language and thought*. Cambridge: Cambridge University Press.

Holler, J., & Stevens, R. (2007). The effect of common ground on how speakers use gesture and speech to represent size information. *Journal of Language and Social Psychology*, *26*, 4–27.

Holmes, J. (2007). Making humour work: Creativity on the job. *Applied Linguistics*, *28* (4), 518–537.

Holmes, P., & Dervin, F. (Eds.) (2016). *The cultural and intercultural dimensions of English as a lingua franca*. Bristol, UK: Multilingual Matters.

Horn, L. R. (2004). Implicature. In L. R. Horn & G. Ward (Eds.), *The handbook of pragmatics* (pp.3–28). Oxford, Blackwell.

Horn, L., & Kecskes, I. (2013). Pragmatics, discourse and cognition. In *The language-cognition interface* (pp.353–375). Geneva-Paris: Librairie Droz.

Horton, W. S., & Keysar, B. (1996). When do speakers take into account common ground? *Cognition*, *59*, 91–117.

Howarth, P. (1998). Phraseology and second language proficiency. *Applied Linguistics*, *19*, 24–44.

House, J. (1999). Misunderstanding in intercultural communication: Interactions in English as lingua franca and the myth of mutual intelligibility. In C. Gnutzmann (Ed.), *Teaching and learning English as a global language* (pp.73–89). Tübingen: Stauffenburg.

House, J. (2002). Developing pragmatic competence in English as a lingua franca. In K. Knapp & C. Meierkord (Eds.), *Lingua Franca Communication* (pp.245–267). Frankfurt am Main: Peter Lang.

House, J. (2003). Misunderstanding in intercultural university encounters. In J. House, G. Kasper & S. Ross (Eds.), *Misunderstanding in social Life: Discourse approaches to problematic talk* (pp.22–56). London: Longman.

House, J. (2009a). Introduction: The pragmatics of English as a lingua franca [Special issue]. *Intercultural Pragmatics*, *6*(2), 141–145.

House, J. (2009b). Subjectivity in English as Lingua Franca discourse: The case of you know [Special issue]. *Intercultural pragmatics*, *6*(2), 171–193.

House, J. (2014). *Managing academic institutional discourse in English as a lingua franca*. Amsterdam/Philadelphia: Benjamins.

Hoye, L. F. (1997). *Adverbs and Modality in English*. London/ New York: Longman.

Hüllen, W. (1992). Identifikationssprachen und Kommunikationssprachen. Über Probleme der Mehrsprachigkeit/Languages of identification and languages of communication. On problems of multilingualism. *Zeitschrift für germanistische Linguistik*, *20*(3), 298–317.

Hymes, D. H. (1962). The ethnography of speaking. In T. Gladwin & W. C. Sturtevant (Eds.), *Anthropology and human behavior* (pp.13–53). Washington: The Anthropology Society of Washington.

Hymes, D. H. (1968). The ethnography of speaking. In J. A. Fishman (Ed.), *Readings in the sociology of language* (pp.99–138). The Hague, Paris: Mouton de Gruyter.

Hynninen, N. (2016). *Language regulation in English as a lingua franca: Focus on academic spoken discourse*. Berlin/Boston: De Gruyter Mouton.

Isaacs, E. A., & Clark, H. H. (1987). References in conversation between experts and novices. *Journal of Experimental Psychology: General*, *116*, 26–37.
Jackson, H. (2013). *Words and their meanings*. London: Routledge.
Jacobs, N., & Garnham, A. (2007), The role of conversational hand gestures in a narrative task. *Journal of Memory and Language*, *56*, 291–303.
Jenkins, J. (1996). Native speaker, non-native speaker and English as a foreign language: Time for a change. *IATEFL Newsletter*, *131*, 10–11.
Jenkins, J. (2000). *The phonology of English as an international language*. Oxford: Oxford University Press.
Jenkins, J. (2006a). Current perspectives on teaching world Englishes and English as a lingua franca. *TESOL Journal*, *40*, 157–181.
Jenkins, J. (2006b). Global intelligibility and local diversity: Possibility or paradox? In R. Rubdy & M. Saraceni (Eds.), *English in the world: Global rules, global roles* (pp.32–39). London: Continuum.
Jenkins, J. (2007). *English as a lingua franca: Attitude and identity*. Oxford: Oxford University Press.
Jenkins, J., Cogo, A., & Dewey, M. (2011). Review of developments in research into English as a lingua franca. *Language Teaching*, *44* (3), 281–315.
Jespersen, O. (1904). *How to teach a foreign language?* London: S. Sonnenschein & Co.
Joas, H. (1996). *The creativity of action*. Chicago: University of Chicago Press.
Johnson, J. (1991). Developmental versus language-based factors in metaphor interpretation. *Journal of Educational Psychology*, *83*(4), 470.
Johnson-Laird, P. N. (1983). *Mental models*. Cambridge: Harvard University Press.
Kachru, B. B. (1985). Standards, codification and sociolinguistic realism: the English language in the outer circle. In R. Quirk & H. G. Widdowson (Eds.), *English in the world: Teaching and learning the language and literatures* (pp.11–30). Cambridge: Cambridge University Press.
Kachru, B. B. (1992). *The other tongue: English across cultures*. Champaign: University of Illinois Press.
Kankaanranta, A., & Planken, B. (2010). BELF competence as business knowledge of internationally operating business professionals. *Journal of Business Communication, Special Issue on Language Matters, Part 2*. 47, 380–407.
Katsos, N., Cummins, C., Ezeizabarrena, M. J., Gavarró, A., Kraljević, J. K., & Hrzica, G. (2016). Cross-linguistic patterns in the acquisition of quantifiers. *Proceedings of the National Academy of Sciences*, *113*, 9244–9249.
Kaur, J. (2009). Pre-empting problems of understanding in English as a lingua franca. In A. Mauranen & E. Ranta (Eds.), *English as a lingua franca: Studies and findings* (pp.107–123). Newcastle upon Tyne: Cambridge Scholars Publishing.
Kaur, J. (2010). Achieving mutual understanding in world Englishes. *World Englishes*, *29*(2), 192–208.
Kaur, J. (2011). Intercultural communication in English as a lingua franca: Some sources of misunderstanding. *Intercultural Pragmatics*, *8*(1), 93–116. https://doi.org/10.1515/IPRG.2011.004.
Kecskes, I. (2001). The graded salience hypothesis in second language acquisition. In M. Putz, S. Niemeier & R. Dirven (Eds.), *Applied cognitive linguistics* (Vol. 1, pp.249–271). Berlin/New York: Mouton de Gruyter.

Kecskes, I. (2000). A cognitive-pragmatic approach to situation-bound utterances. *Journal of Pragmatics*, *32*(6), 605–625.

Kecskes, I. (2003). *Situation-bound utterances in L1 and L2*. Berlin/New York: Mouton de Gruyter.

Kecskes, I. (2006). On my mind: thoughts about salience, context and figurative language from a second language perspective. *Second Language Research*, *22*(2), 219–237.

Kecskes, I. (2007). Formulaic language in English lingua franca. In I. Kecskes & L. R. Horn (Eds.), *Explorations in pragmatics: Linguistic, cognitive and intercultural aspects* (pp.191–219), Berlin/New York: Mouton de Gruyter.

Kecskes, I. (2008). Dueling contexts: A dynamic model of meaning. *Journal of Pragmatic*, *40*(3), 385–406.

Kecskes, I. (2010a). Situation-Bound Utterances as pragmatic acts. *Journal of Pragmatics*, *42*(11), 2889–2897.

Kecskes, I. (2010b). The paradox of communication: A socio-cognitive approach. *Pragmatics and Society*, *1*(1), 50–73.

Kecskes, I. (2010c). Dual and multilanguage systems. *International Journal of Multilingualism* *7*(2), 91–109.

Kecskes, I. (2012). Is there anyone out there who really is interested in the speaker? *Language and Dialogue*, *2*, 283–297.

Kecskes, I. (2013a). Why do we say what we say the way we say it? *Journal of Pragmatics*, *48*(1), 71–84.

Kecskes, I. (2013b). Focus on the speaker: An introduction. Special issue. *Journal of Pragmatics*, *48*(1), 1–4.

Kecskes, I. (2014). *Intercultural pragmatics*. Oxford, UK: Oxford University Press.

Kecskes, I. (2015a). Intracultural communication and intercultural communication: Are they different? *International Review of Pragmatics*, *7*, 171–194.

Kecskes, I. (2015b). Is the idiom principle blocked in bilingual L2 production? In R. Heredia & A. Cieslicka (Eds.), *Bilingual figurative language processing* (pp.28–53). Cambridge: Cambridge University Press.

Kecskes, I. (2016). Deliberate creativity and formulaic language use. In K. Allan, A. Capone & I. Kecskes (Eds.), *Pragmemes and theories of language use (Perspectives in pragmatics, philosophy & psychology)*, *9*, 3–20.

Kecskes, I. (2017a). From pragmatics to dialogue. In E. Weigand (Ed.), *The Routledge handbook of language and dialogue* (pp.77–92). New York: Routledge.

Kecskes, I. (2017b). The effect of salience on shaping speaker's utterance. *Reti, saperi, linguaggi, 1/2017 a.* *6*(11), 5–34. doi:10.12832/87352

Kecskes, I., & Assimakopoulos, S. (Eds). (2017). *Current issues in intercultural pragmatics*. Amsterdam/Philadelphia: John Benjamins.

Kecskes, I., & Kirner-Ludwig, M. (2017). "It would never happen in my country I must say": A corpus-pragmatic study on Asian English learners' preferred uses of "must" and "should". *Corpus Pragmatics, 1*(2), 91–134.

Kecskes, I., & Kirner-Ludwig, M. (forthcoming). (2019) Odd structures in intercultural discourse segments. *Journal of Pragmatics*. DOI: 10.1016/j.pragma.2019.04.007.

Kecskes, I., & Zhang, F. (2009). Activating, seeking and creating common ground: A socio-cognitive approach. *Pragmatics and Cognition*, *17*(2), 331–355.

Kecskes, I., Sanders, R. E., & Pomerantz, A. (2017). The basic interactional competence of language learners. *Journal of Pragmatics*, *124*, 88–105.

Kertész, A. & Rákosi, C. (2012). *Data and evidence in linguistics: A plausible argumentation model.* Cambridge: Cambridge University Press.

Keysar, B. (2007). Communication and miscommunication: The role of egocentric processes. *Intercultural Pragmatics*, *4*(1), 71–84.

Keysar, B., & Henly, A. S. (2002). Speakers' overestimation of their effectiveness. *Psychological Science*, *13*(3), 207–212.

Keysar, B., Barr, D. J., & Horton, W. S. (1998). The egocentric basis of language use: Insights from a processing approach. *Current Directions in Psychological Science*, *7*, 46–50.

Kidwell, M. (2000). Common ground in cross cultural communication: Sequential and institutional contexts in front desk service encounters. *Issues in Applied Linguistics*, *11*(1), 17–37.

Kiefer, F. (1990). Linguistic, conceptual and encyclopedic knowledge: some implications for lexicography. In T. Magay & J. Zigány (Eds.), BudaLEX '88 proceedings: *Papers from the 3rd International EURALEX Congress. Budapest.*

King, J. C., & Stanley, J. (2005). Semantics, pragmatics, and the role of semantic content. In S. Z. Gendler (Ed.), *Semantics versus pragmatics* (pp.111–164). Oxford: Oxford University Press.

Kirkpatrick, A. (2010). Researching English as a lingua franca in Asia: The Asian Corpus of English (ACE) project. *Asian Englishes*, *31*(1), 4–18.

Kirkpatrick, A. (2011). *English as a lingua franca in ASEAN: A multilingual model.* Hong Kong: Hong Kong University Press.

Koole, T., & ten Thije, J. D. (2001). The reconstruction of intercultural discourse: Methodological considerations. *Journal of Pragmatics*, *33*(4), 571–587.

Korta, K., & Perry, J. (2015). Pragmatics. *The Stanford Encyclopedia of Philosophy.* https://plato.stanford.edu/entries/pragmatics/

Köylü, Y. (2018). Comprehension of conversational implicatures in L2 English. *Intercultural Pragmatics*,*15*(3).

Kramsch, C. (1986). From language proficiency to interactional competence. *The Modern Language Journal*, *70*(4), 366–372.

Kramsch, C. (1993). *Context and culture in language teaching.* Oxford: Oxford University Press.

Küronya, K. (2013). Modality in English as a lingua franca communication (Dissertation). University of Vienna.

Laitinen, M. (2016). Ongoing changes in English modals: On the developments in ELF. In O. Timofeeva, A. Gardner, A. Honkapohja, S. Chevalier, M. Hundt, & G. Schneider (Eds.), *New approaches to English linguistics: Building bridges* (pp.175–196). Amsterdam, Netherlands: John Benjamins.

Lakoff, G. (1987). *Women, fire and dangerous things: What categories reveal about the mind.* Chicago: University of Chicago Press.

Lakoff, G., & Johnson, M. (1980). *Metaphors we live by.* Chicago: University of Chicago Press.

Lamberts, K., & Shanks, D. (1997). *Knowledge, concepts and categories.* Cambridge, MA: MIT Press.

Langacker, R. W. (1988). An overview of cognitive grammar. *Topics in Cognitive Linguistics*, *3*.

Langlotz, A. (2006). *Idiomatic creativity: A cognitive-linguistic model of idiom-representation and idiom-variation in English*. Amsterdam: Benjamins.

Lantolf, J. P., & Thorne, S. (2006). *Sociocultural theory and the genesis of second language development*. Oxford: Oxford University Press.

LaPolla, R. J. (2010). *Arguments against 'subject' and 'direct object' as viable concepts in Chinese*. Frankfurt: Universitätsbibliothek Johann Christian Senckenberg.

Leech, G. (2003). Modality on the move: the English modal auxiliaries 1961–1992. *Topics in English Linguistics*, *44*, 223–240.

Leech, T. K. (2013). Finding space for non-dominant languages in education: Language policy and medium of instruction in Timor-Leste 2000–2012. *Current Issues in Language Planning*, *14*(1), 109–126.

Leibniz, G. W. (1903). *Opuscules et fragments inédits de Leibniz: Extraits des manuscrits de la Bibliothèque royale de Hanovre par Louis Couturat*. Paris: F. Alcan.

Leibniz, G. W. (1976[1679]). *Philosophical Papers and Letters* (2nd ed.). L. E. Loemker (Ed. & Trans.). Dordrecht, Holland/Boston: D. Reidel.

Leopold, W. (1930), Polarity in language. *Curme volume of linguistics studies*, *6*(4), 102–109. doi:10.2307/521989

Levelt, W. J. M. (1989). *Speaking: From intention to articulation*. Cambridge, MA: MIT Press.

Levinson, S. C. (1983). *Pragmatics: Cambridge textbooks in linguistics*. Cambridge University Press.

Levinson, S. C. (2003). Language and mind: Let's get the issues straight! In G. Dedre & S. Goldin-Meadow (Eds.), *Language in mind: Advances in the study of language and cognition* (pp.25–46). Cambridge: MIT Press.

Levinson, S. C. (2006). On the human "interactional engine". In N. J. Enfield & S. C. Levinson (Eds.), *Roots of human sociality: Culture, cognition, and interaction* (pp. 39–69). Berg/ Oxford University Press.

Leyland, S. (2011). *The language of exile*. Liverpool: Erbacce-Press.

Li, H. Z., Yum, Y. O., Yates, R., Aguilera, L., Mao, Y., & Zheng, Y. (2005). Interruption and involvement in discourse: Can intercultural interlocutors be trained. *Journal of Intercultural Communication Research, 34*(4), 233–254.

Li, R. (2003). Modality in English and Chinese: A typological perspective. Doctoral dissertation, University of Antwerp.

Lim, S. (2016). Learning to teach intelligible pronunciation for ASEAN English as a ingua franca: A sociocultural investigation of Cambodian pre-service teacher cognition and practice. *RELC Journal*, *47*(3). https://doi.org/10.1177/0033688216631176.

Liu, P., & Liu, H. (2017). Creating common ground: The role of metapragmatic expressions in BELF meeting interactions. *Journal of Pragmatics*, *107*, 1–15.

Lupyan, G., & Spivey, M. J. (2010). Redundant spoken labels facilitate perception of multiple items. *Attention, Perception and Psychophysics*, *72*(8), 2236–2253.

Lyons, J. (1977). *Semantics* (Vols. 1–2). Cambridge: Cambridge University Press.

MacKenzie, I. (2013). *English as a lingua franca: Theorizing and teaching English*. London: Routledge.

Mackenzie, N. M. (2014). Teaching early writers: Teachers' responses to a young child's writing sample. *The Australian Journal of Language and Literacy*, *37*(3), 182.

Mancini-Cross, C., Backman, K. F., & Baldwin, E. D. (2009). The effect of the language barrier on intercultural communication: A case study of educational travel in Italy, *Journal of Teaching in Travel & Tourism*, *9*(1–2), 104–123.

Mann, W. C., & Thompson, S. A. (1988). Rhetorical structure theory: Toward a functional theory of text organization. *Text*, *8*(3), 243–281.

Marmaridou, S. (2000). *Pragmatic meaning and cognition*. Amsterdam: John Benjamins.

Martinet, A. (1955). *Economie des changements phonetiques: Traite de phonologie diachronique*. Bern: Francke.

Matsuda, A., & Friedrich, P. (2012). Selecting an instructional variety for an EIL curriculum. In Aya Matsuda (Ed.), *Principles and Practices of Teaching English as an International Language* (pp.17–27). Channel View Publications.

Mauranen, A. (2003). The corpus of English as a lingua franca in academic settings. *TESOL Journal*, *37*(3), 513–527.

Mauranen, A. (2006). Signaling and preventing misunderstanding in English as lingua franca communication. *International Journal of the Sociology of Language*, *177*, 123–150.

Mauranen, A. (2012). *Exploring ELF: Academic English shaped by non-native speakers*. Cambridge: Cambridge University Press.

McEnery, T., & Wilson, A. (1996). *Corpus linguistics*. Edinburgh: Edinburgh University Press.

McEniry, S. (2011). Free in all senses of the word. *The Bottom Line*. Accessed https://thebottomline.as.ucsb.edu/2011/04/free-in-all-senses-of-the-word.

Mehan, H. (1982). The structure of classroom events and their consequences for student performance. In P. Gilmore & A. Glatthorn (Eds.), *Children in and out of education: Ethnography and education* (pp.59–87). Washington, DC: Center for Applied Linguistics.

Meierkord, C. (2002). "Language stripped bare" or "linguistic masala"? Culture in lingua franca communication. In K. Knapp & C. Meierkord (Eds.), *Lingua franca communication* (pp.109–134). Frankfurt: Peter Lang.

Mel'cuk, I., & Zholkovsky, A. (1984). *Explanatory combinatorial dictionary of modern Russian*. Vienna: Wiener Slawistischer Almanach.

Mey, J. (2001). *Pragmatics*. London: Blackwell.

Mey, J. (2013). A brief sketch of the historic development of pragmatics. In Keith Allan (Ed.), *The Oxford Handbook of the History of Linguistics* (pp. 587–611). Oxford: Oxford University Press.

Miller, J., & Weinert, R. (1998). *Spontaneous spoken language: Syntax and discourse*. Oxford: Clarendon Press.

Minsky, M. (1975). A framework for representing knowledge. In P. H. Winston (Ed.), *The psychology of computer vision* (pp.211–277). New York: McGraw-Hill.

Moerman, M. (1988). *Talking culture: Ethnography and conversation analysis*. Philadelphia: University of Pennsylvania Press.

Moeschler, J. (2004). Intercultural pragmatics: a cognitive approach. *Intercultural Pragmatics*, *1*(1). https://doi.org/10.1515/iprg.2004.007.

Mollin, S. (2006). *Euro-English: Assessing variety status*. Tübingen: Gunter Narr Verlag.

Moore, C., & Dunham, P. J. (Eds.). (1995). *Joint attention: Its origins and role in development*. Hillsdale, NJ: Lawrence Erlbaum.

Moore, J. D., & Paris, C. L. (1993). Planning text for advisory dialogues: Capturing intentional and rhetorical information. *Computational Linguistics*, *19*(4), 651–694.

Morgan, J. L. (1978). Two types of convention in indirect speech acts. In P. Cole (Ed.), *Syntax and Semantics* (Vol. 9, pp.261–280). New York: Academic Press.

Morris, C. W. (1938). Foundations of the theory of signs. *In International encyclopedia of unified science* (pp.1–59). Chicago: Chicago University Press.

Mur-Dueñas, P. (2016). Modal hedging verbs in English as a lingua franca (ELF) business management research articles. *Kalbotyra: Romanu Ir Germanu Studijos*, *69*, 153–178. doi:10.15388/Klbt.2016.10371.

Murray, N. (2012). English as a lingua franca and the development of pragmatic competence. *ELT Journal*, *66*(3), 318–326.

Nadig, A., & Sedivy, J. (2002). Evidence of perspective-taking constraints in children's on-line reference resolution. *Psychological Science*, *13*(4), 329–336.

Nattinger, J. R., & DeCarrico, J. S. (1992). *Lexical phrases and language teaching*. New York: Oxford University Press.

Nelson, K., & Fivush, R. (2004). The emergence of autobiographical memory: A social cultural developmental theory. *Psychological review*, *111*, 486–511.

Neuliep, J. W. (2006). Editorial welcome. *Journal of Intercultural Communication Research*, *35*(1), 1–2.

Newman-Norlund, S. E., Matthijs, L. N., Newman-Norlund, R. D., Volman, I. A. C., De Ruiter, J. P., Hagoort, P., & Toni, I. (2009). Recipient design in tacit communication. *Cognition*, *111*, 46–54.

Newmeyer, F. J. (2003). Grammar is grammar and usage is usage. *Language*, *79*, 682–707.

Nicoll, J. (1990). The King's English. *Newsgroup: rec.arts.sf-lovers*.

Nuyts, J., Byloo, P., & Diepeveen, J. (2010). On deontic modality, directivity, and mood: The case of Dutch mogen and moeten. *Journal of Pragmatics*, *42*(1), 16–34.

O'Neill, M., Bard, K. A., Linnell, M., & Fluck, F. (2005). Maternal gesture with 20-month-old infants in two contexts. *Developmental Science*, *8*(4), 352–359.

Ortaçtepe, D. (2012). *The development of conceptual socialization in international students: A language socialization perspective on conceptual fluency and social identity*. Cambridge: Cambridge Scholars Publishing.

Osgood, C. E., & Bock, K. J. (1977). Salience and sentencing: Some production principles. In S. Rosenberg (Ed.), *Sentence production: Developments in research and theory* (pp.89–140). New York: Lawrence Erlbaum.

Ostler, N. (2005). *Empires of the world: A language history of the world*. New York: Harper Collins.

Ozyurek, A. (2002). Do speakers design their co-speech gesture for their addressees? The effects of addressee location on representational gestures. *Journal of Memory and Language*, *46*(4), 688–704.

Pallotti, G., & Wagner, J. (Eds.). (2011). *L2 learning as social practice: Conversation analytic perspectives*. National Foreign Language Resource Center.

Palmer, F. R. (1986). *Mood and modality*. Cambridge: Cambridge University Press.

Palmer, F. R. (1990). *Modality and the English modals* (2nd ed.). London/ New York: Longman.

Palmer, F. R. (2001). *Mood and Modality* (2nd ed.). Cambridge: Cambridge University Press.

Palmer, F. R. (2003). Modality in English: Theoretical, descriptive and typological issues. In R. Facchinetti, M. Krug & F. Palmer (Eds.), *Modality in contemporary English* (pp.1–17). Berlin/ New York: Mouton de Gruyter.

Passonneau, R. J., &. Litman, D. J. (1997). Discourse segmentation by human and automated means. *Journal of Computational Linguistics*, *23*(1), 103–139.

Pawley, A., & Syder, F. H. (1983). Two puzzles for linguistic theory: Nativelike selection and nativelike fluency. *Language and Communication*, *5*, 191–226.

Pawley, A., & Syder, F. H. (2000). The one-clause-at-a-time hypothesis. In H. Riggenbach (Ed.), *Perspectives on fluency* (pp.163–199). Ann Arbor: University of Michigan Press.

Pearce, P. L. (2005). *Tourist behavior: Themes and conceptual schemes*. Clevedon, UK: Channel View Publications

Pekarek Doehler, S., & Pochon-Berger, E. (2015). The development of L2 interactional competence: Evidence from turntaking organization, sequence organization, repair organization and preference organization. In T. Cadierno & S. W. Eskildsen (Eds.), *Usage based perspectives on second language learning* (pp.233–268). Berlin: De Gruyter Mouton.

Peleg, O., Giora, R., & Ofer, F. (2001). Salience and context effects: Two are better than one. *Metaphor and Symbol*, *16*(3–4), 173–192.

Perkins, M. R. (1983). *Modal Expressions in English*. London: Frances Pinter Publishers.

Philip, G. (2005). Figurative language and the advanced learner. *Research News: The Newsletter of the IATEFL Research SIG*, *16*, 16–20.

Phillipson, R. (1998). Globalizing English: Are linguistic human rights and alternative to linguistic imperialism? *Language Science*, *20*(1), 111–121.

Piaget, J. (1977). *The development of thought: Equilibration and cognitive structures*. New York: The Viking Press.

Pinker, S., & Jackendoff, R. (2005). The faculty of language: What's so special about it? *Cognition*, *95*, 201–236.

Piqué, J., Posteguillo, S., & Andreu-Besó, J. V. (2001). A pragmatic analysis framework for the description of modality usage in academic English contexts. *ELIA: Estudios de Lingüística Inglesa Aplicada*, *2*, 213–224.

Pitzl, M-L. (2012). Creativity meets convention: Idiom variation and remetaphorization in ELF. *Journal of English as a Lingua Franca*, *1*(1). https://doi.org/10.1515/jelf–2012–0003.

Pitzl, M-L. (2018). *Creativity in English as a lingua franca: Idiom and metaphor*. Berlin: De Gruyter Mouton.

Pitzl, M-L., Breiteneder, A., & Klimpfinger, T. (2008). A world of words: Processes of lexical innovation in VOICE. *Vienna English Working Papers*, *17* (2), 21–46.

Pomerantz, A., & Heritage, J. (2012). Preference. In J. Sidnell & T. Stivers (Eds.), *The handbook of conversational analysis* (pp.201–228). Oxford: Blackwell.

Pope, R. (2005). *Creativity: Theory, history, practice*. New York: Routledge.

Pride, J. B. (1985). *Cross-cultural encounters: Communication and miscommunication*. Melbourne: River Seine Publications.

Prodromou, L. (2007). Bumping into creative idiomaticity. *English Today, 23*(1), 14–25.
Prodromou, L. (2008). *English as a lingua franca: A corpus-based analysis*. London: Continuum.
Psathas, O. (Ed.). (1979). *Everyday language: Studies in ethnomethodology*. New York: Irvington.
Rampton, B. (1995). *Crossing: Language and ethnicity among adolescents*. London: Longman.
Rapaport, W. J. (2003). What did you mean by that? Misunderstanding, negotiation, and syntactic semantics. *Minds and Machines 13*(3), 397–427.
Recanati, F. (2004). *Literal meaning*. Cambridge: Cambridge University Press.
Recanati, F. (2005). Literalism and contextualism: Some varieties. In G. Preyer & G. Peter (Eds.), *Contextualism in philosophy: Knowledge, meaning, and truth* (pp.171–196). Oxford: Clarendon Press.
Recanati, F. (2012). Pragmatic enrichment. In G. Russell & D. G. Fara (Eds.), *Routledge companion to the philosophy of language* (pp.67–78). London, Routledge.
Risager, K. (2006). *Language and culture: Global flows and local complexity*. Clevedon: Multilingual Matters.
Rizzolatti, G., & Craighero, L. (2004). The mirror-neuron system. *Annual Review of Neuroscience, 27*, 169–192.
Rogoff, B. (2003). *The cultural nature of human development*. New York: Oxford University Press.
Rommetveit, R. (1998). Intersubjective attunement and linguistically mediated meaning in discourse. In S. Bråten (Ed.), *Intersubjective communication and emotion in early ontogeny* (pp. 354–371). Cambridge: Cambridge University Press.
Rosch, E. (1977). Human categorization. In N. Warren (Ed.), *Advances in cross-cultural psychology* (pp. 1–72). London: Academic Press.
Sacks, H. (1992). *Lectures on conversation*. Schegloff, Oxford: Blackwell.
Sanders, R. E. (1987). *Cognitive foundations of calculated speech: Controlling understandings in conversation and persuasion*. New York: State University of New York Press.
Sanders, R. E. (1997). The production of symbolic objects as components of larger wholes. In J. O. Greene (Ed.), *Message production: Advances in communication theory* (pp.245–277). Mahwah, NJ: Lawrence Erlbaum.
Saul, J. M. (2002). Speaker meaning, what is said, and what is implicated. *Nous 36*(2), 228–248.
Schachter, J. (1983). A new account of language transfer. In S. Gass & L. Selinker (Eds.), *Language transfer in language learning* (pp.98–111). Rowley, MA: Newbury House.
Schank, R. C., & Abelson, R. P. (1977). *Scripts, plans, goals, and understanding: An enquiry into human knowledge structures*. Hillsdale, NJ: Lawrence Erlbaum.
Schegloff, E. A. (1987). Analyzing single episodes of interaction: An exercise in conversation analysis. *Social Psychology Quarterly, 50*(2), 101–114.
Schegloff, E. A. (1988). Presequences and indirection: Applying speech act theory to ordinary conversation. *Journal of Pragmatics, 12*, 55–62.
Schegloff, E. A. (2007). *Sequence organization in interaction: A primer for conversation analysis I*. Cambridge: Cambridge University Press.
Schenkein, J. (Ed.). (1978). *Studies in the organization of conversational interaction*. New

Schmidt, R. (1983). Interaction, acculturation, and the acquisition of communicative competence: A case study of an adult. In N. Wolfson & E. Judd (Eds.), *Sociolinguistics and language acquisition* (pp.137–174). Cambridge, MA: Newbury House.

Schmidt, R. (1993). Consciousness, learning and interlanguage pragmatics. In G. Kasper & S. Blum-Kulka (Eds.), *Interlanguage pragmatics* (pp.21–42). Oxford: Oxford University Press.

Scribner, S. (1997). A sociocultural approach to the study of mind. In E. Tobach, R. J. Falmagne, M. B. Parlee, L. M. W. Martin & A. S. Kapelman (Eds.), *Mind and social practice: Selected writings of Sylvia Scribner* (pp.266–280). Cambridge: Cambridge University Press.

Searle, J. R. (1979). *Expression and meaning: Studies in the theory of speech acts.* Cambridge: Cambridge University Press.

Searle, J. R. (1983). *Intentionality: An essay in the philosophy of mind.* Cambridge: Cambridge University Press.

Searle, J. R. (1995). *The construction of Social Reality.* New York: Simon & Schuster.

Segalowitz, N., & Freed, B. F. (2004). Context, contact, and cognition in oral fluency acquisition: Learning Spanish in at home and study abroad contexts. *Studies in Second Language Acquisition*, *26*, 173–199.

Seidlhofer, B. (2001). Closing a conceptual gap: The case for a description of English as a Lingua Franca. *International Journal of Applied Linguistics*, *11*(2), 133–158.

Seidlhofer, B. (2004). Research perspectives on teaching English as a Lingua Franca. *Annual Review of Applied Linguistics*, *24*, 209–239.

Seidlhofer, B. (2009a). Accommodation and the idiom principle in English as a Lingua Franca. *Intercultural Pragmatics*, *6*(2), 195–215.

Seidlhofer, B. (2009b). Common ground and different realities: World Englishes and English as a lingua franca. *World Englishes*, *28*(2), 236–245.

Seidlhofer, B. (2011). *Understanding English as a lingua franca*. Oxford: Oxford University Press.

Selinker, L. (1972). Interlanguage. *International Review of Applied Linguistics in Language Teaching*, *10*(1–4), 3–34, 209–232. https://doi.org/10.1515/iral.1972.10.1-4.209.

Shively, R. L., Menke, M. R., & Manzon-Omundson, S. M. (2008). Perception of irony by L2 learners of Spanish. *Issues in Applied Linguistics*, *16*, 101–132.

Siegal, M. (1996). The role of learner subjectivity in second language sociolinguistic competency: Western women. *Applied Linguistics*, *17*, 356–382.

Siegal, M., Matsuo, A., Pond, C., & Otsu, Y. (2007). Bilingualism and cognitive development: Evidence from scalar implicatures. In *Proceedings of the Eighth Tokyo Conference on Psycholinguistics* (pp.265–280). Tokyo: Hituzi Syobo.

Simpson-Vlach, R., & Ellis, N. C. (2010). An academic formulas list: New methods in phraseology research. *Applied Linguistics*, *31*, 487–512.

Sinclair, J. (1987). Collocation: A progress report. In R. Steele & T. Treadgold (Eds.), *Language topics: Essays in honour of Michael Halliday* (pp.319–331). Amsterdam: John Benjamins.

Sinclair, J. (1991). *Corpus, concordance, collocation*. Oxford: Oxford University Press.

Skehan, P. (1998). *A cognitive approach to language learning*. Oxford: Oxford University Press.

Slabakova, R. (2010). What is easy and what is hard to acquire in a second language? *Proceedings of the 10th Generative Approaches to Second Language Acquisition Conference (GASLA 2009), Cascadilla Proceedings Project, 20*, 280–294.

Slabakova, R., & Mayo, M. D. P. G. (2013). Whether to teach and how to teach complex linguistic structures in a second language. In M. Whong, G. Kook-Hee & H. Marsden (Eds.), *Universal grammar and the second language classroom* (pp.187–205). Amsterdam: Springer.

Slobin, D. (1991). Learning to think for speaking: Native language, cognition, and rhetorical style. *Pragmatics*, *1*(1), 7–25.

Slobin, D. I. (1997). Mind, code, and text. In J. Halman, J. Bybee & S. Thompson (Eds.), *Essays on language function and language type: Dedicated to T. Givón* (pp.437–467). Amsterdam: John Benjamins Publishing.

Sperber, D., & Wilson, D. (1986). *Relevance: Communication and cognition*. Oxford: Basil Blackwell.

Sperber, D., & Wilson, D. (1995). *Relevance: Communication and cognition* (2nd ed.). Oxford: Blackwell.

Stalnaker, R. C. (2002). Common ground. *Linguistics and Philosophy*, *25*, 701–721.

Strevens, P. (1987). Cultural barriers to language learning. In L. Smith (Ed.), *Discourse across cultures* (pp.169–178). New York: Prentice Hall.

Swan, M. (2012). ELF and EFL: Are they really different? *Journal of English as a Lingua Franca*, *1*(2), 379–389.

Swan, M. (2017). EFL, ELF, and the question of accuracy. *ELT Journal*, *71*(4), 511–515.

Sweetser, E. (1990). *From etymology to pragmatics*. Cambridge: Cambridge University Press.

Syrett, K., Austin, J., Sánchez, L., Germak, C., & Lingwall, A. (2016). The influence of conversational context and the developing lexicon on the calculation of scalar implicatures. *Linguistic Approaches to Bilingualism*, *7*(2), 230–264.

Syrett, K., Lingwall, A., Perez-Cortes, S., Austin, J., & Sánchez, L. (2017). Differences between Spanish monolingual and Spanish-English bilingual children in their calculation of entailment-based scalar implicatures. *Glossa: A Journal of General Linguistics*, *2*(1), 31.

Taboada, M., & Habel, C. (2013). Rhetorical relations in multimodal documents. *Discourse Studies*, *15*(1), 59–85.

Taguchi, N. (2005). Comprehending implied meaning in English as a second language. *Modern Language Journal*, *89*, 543–562.

Taguchi, N., Li, S., & Liu, Y. (2013). Comprehension of conversational implicature in L2 Chinese. *Pragmatics & Cognition*, *21*, 139–157.

Taillard, M. O. (2002). Beyond communicative intention. *UCL Working Papers in Linguistics*, *14*, 189–207.

Tannen, D., & Öztek, P. C. (1981). Health to our mouths: Formulaic expressions in Turkish and Greek. In F. Coulmas (Ed.), *Conversational routine* (pp.37–54, 516–534). The Hague: Mouton.

Taylor, J. (2000). The network model and the two-level model in comparison. In B. Peeters (Ed.), *The lexicon-encyclopedia interface* (pp.115–143). Amsterdam: Elsevier.

Ten Thije, J. D. (2003). The transition from misunderstanding to understanding in intercultural communication. In I. Komlósi László., P. Houtlosser & M. Leezenberg (Eds.), *Communication and culture: Argumentative, cognitive and linguistic perspectives* (pp.197–214). Amsterdam: Sic Sac.

Ting-Toomey, S. (1999). *Communicating across cultures*. New York: Guilford Press.

Toyoda, E., & Harrison, R. (2002). Categorization of text chat communication between learners and native speakers of Japanese. *Language Learning & Technology*, *6*(1), 82–99.

Tracy, K., & Craig, R. T. (2010). Studying interaction in order to cultivate practice: Action-implicative discourse analysis. In J. Streeck (Ed.), *New adventures in language and interaction* (pp.145–166). Amsterdam: John Benjamins Publishing.

Trevarthen, C. (1977). Descriptive analyses of infant communicative behaviour. In H. R. Schaffer (Ed.), *Proceedings of the Loch Lomond symposium, Ross Priory, University of Strathclyde, September, 1975: Studies in mother-infant interaction* (pp.227–270). London and New York: Academic Press.

Trevarthen, C. (1979). Communication and cooperation in early infancy: A description of primary intersubjectivity. In M. Bullowa (Ed.), *Before speech* (pp.321–347). Cambridge: Cambridge University Press.

Triandis, H. C. (1993). Collectivism and individualism as cultural syndromes. *Cross-Cultural Research: The Journal of Comparative Social Science*, *27*, 155–180.

Turner, R. (Ed.). (1974). *Ethnomethodology: Selected readings*. Harmondsworth: Penguin.

Van Compernolle, R. A. (2014). *Sociocultural theory and L2 instructional pragmatics*. Clevedon: Multilingual Matters.

Van der Auwera, J., & Plungian, V. (1998). Modality's semantic map. *Linguistic Typology*, *2*(1), 79–124. https://doi.org/10.1515/lity.1998.2.1.79.

Veale, T. (2012). *Exploding the creativity myth: The computational foundations of linguistic creativity*. London: Bloomsbury.

Verschueren, J. (1999). *Understanding Pragmatics*. London: Edward Arnold.

Vettorel, P. (Ed.). (2015). *New frontiers in teaching and learning English*. Newcastle: Cambridge Scholars Publishing

VOICE. (2013). *The Vienna-Oxford International Corpus of English*. Accessed http://voice.univie.ac.at/

*Von Wright, G. H. (1951). An essay in modal logic*. Amsterdam: North Holland.

Vygotsky, L. S. (1978). *Mind in society*. Cambridge: Harvard University press.

Wang, Y. (2013). Non-conformity to ENL norms: a perspective from Chinese English users. *Journal of English Lingua Franca*, *2*(2), 255–282.

Warga, M. (2005). 'Je serais très merciable': Formulaic vs. creatively produced speech in learners' request closings. *Canadian Journal of Applied Linguistics*, *8*, 67–94.

Weigand, E. (2010a). *Dialogue: the mixed game*. Amsterdam/Philadelphia: Benjamins.

Weigand, E. (2010b). Language as dialogue. *Intercultural Pragmatics*, *7*(3), 505–515.

Weigand, E., & Kecskes, I. (Eds). (2018). *From Pragmatics to Dialogue*. Amsterdam and Philadelphia: John Benjamins.

Wells, G. (1979). Describing children's linguistic development at home and at school. *British Educational Research Journal*, *5*(1). https://doi.org/10.1080/0141192790050109.

Wells, G. (1981). *Language as interaction*. Cambridge University Press.

Whorf, B. L. (1939). The relation of habitual thought and behavior to language. In J. Carroll (Ed.), *Language, thought and reality: Selected writings of Benjamin Lee Whorf.* Cambridge, MA: MIT Press.

Widdowson, H. G. (1997). EIL, ESL, EFL: Global issues and local interests. *World Englishes*, *16*(1), 146–153.

Widdowson, H. G. (2012). ELF and the inconvenience of established concepts. *Journal of English as a Lingua Franca*, *1*(1), 5–26.

Widdowson, H. G. (2013). ELF and EFL: What's the difference? Comments on Michael Swan. *Journal of English as a Lingua Franca*, *2*(1), 187–193. Vienna: De Gruyter.

Widdowson, H. G. (2017). The cultural and creative use of English as a Lingua Franca. *Lingue e Linguaggi*, *21*, 275–281.

Wierzbicka, A. (1996). *Semantics: Primes and universals.* Oxford: Oxford University Press.

Wilson, D., & Sperber, D. (2004). Relevance theory. In L. Horn & G. Ward (Eds.), *The handbook of pragmatics* (pp.607–632). Oxford: Blackwell.

Winch, P. (1997). Can we understand ourselves? *Philosophical Investigations*, *20*(3), 193–204.

Wittgenstein, L. (2001). *Philosophical investigations* (3rd ed.). Oxford/Malden: Blackwell.

Wortham, S. (2008). Linguistic anthropology of education. *Annual Review of Anthropology*, *37*, 37–51.

Wray, A. (1999). Formulaic language in learners and native speakers. *Language Teaching*, *32*, 213–231.

Wray, A. (2002). *Formulaic language and the lexicon.* Cambridge: Cambridge University Press.

Wray, A. (2005). Idiomaticity in an L2: Linguistic processing as a predictor of success. In B. Briony (Ed.), *IATEFL 2005: Cardiff conference selections* (pp.53–60). Canterbury: IATEFL.

Wray, A., & Namba, K. (2003). Formulaic language in a Japanese-English bilingual child: A practical approach to data analysis. *Japanese Journal for Multilingualism and Multiculturalism*, *9*(1), 24–51.

Wray, A., & Perkins, M. R. (2000). The functions of formulaic language: An integrated model. *Language and Communication*, *20*, 1–28.

Young, R. F. (2011). Interactional competence in language learning, teaching, and testing. In E. Hinkel (Ed.), *Handbook of research in second language teaching and learning* (Vol. 2, pp.426–443). Routledge.

Young, R. F. (2014). AL Forum of the Applied Linguists Interest Section of TESOL International Association: *What is interactional competence?* Accessed http://newsmanager.commpartners.com/tesolalis/textonly/printall.php?id=tesolalis20140827.

Young, R. F., & Miller, E. R. (2004). Learning as changing participation: Discourse roles in ESL writing conferences. *Modern Language Journal*, *88*(4), 519–535.

Zalaltdinova, L. (2018). "Stop doing this at once!": The preferred use of modality for advice-giving by English language learners. *Intercultural Pragmatics*, *15*(3), 349–373.

Zalaltdinova, L. (forthcoming). Modality as a reflection of pragmatic competence (PhD thesis).

Zhu, H. (2015). Negotiation as the way of engagement in intercultural and lingua franca communication: Frames of reference and Interculturality. *Journal of English as a Lingua Franca*, *4*(1), 63–90.

Zipf, G. K. (1949). *Human behavior and the principle of least effort*. Cambridge, MA: Addison-Wesley Press.

# Index

actual situational context, 13, 26, 27, 31, 38, 40, 42, 43, 45, 58, 71, 76, 77, 92, 99, 101, 102, 104, 110, 112, 120, 124, 125, 129, 130, 131, 132, 137, 140, 142, 143, 145, 146, 147, 148, 150, 151, 152, 153, 156, 157, 159, 160, 161, 173, 213, 233, 234, 235
ad hoc generated language, 33, 45, 234
Anglo-Saxon, 16
applied linguistics, 5, 9, 17, 74, 91
Asian Corpus of English (ACE), 4, 16
attention, 5, 9, 11, 13, 17, 19, 21, 31, 35, 41, 43, 48, 58, 61, 63, 77, 79, 113, 114, 116, 117, 119, 120, 121, 123, 124, 136, 145, 148, 163, 164, 174, 177, 195, 203, 207, 229

bi-directional interaction, 20
bilateral, 179, 180, 182
bilingual pragmatic development, 171
blending, 26, 27, 67, 158

Cartesian linguistics, 47
closed social situations, 66, 67
co-constructed common ground, 31
co-construction, 7, 35, 36, 78, 93, 205, 206, 229, 233, 234
code system, vi, 2, 23, 24, 93, 96, 111, 181, 233
collective conception, 189, 198
collective salience, 6, 62, 67, 91, 93, 104, 111, 126, 154, 182
combinational, 58
common ground, i, 5, 6, 8, 11, 17, 28, 33, 35, 36, 38, 40, 41, 42, 43, 46, 49, 51, 67, 69, 71, 76, 77, 83, 89, 92, 96, 97, 101, 102, 110, 111, 123, 130, 131, 137, 147, 157, 160, 181, 182, 211, 213, 215, 216, 222, 226, 227, 229, 230, 234, 235
commonalities, 6, 14, 28, 30, 35, 51
communicative repertoires, 26, 27
compositionality, 138, 143, 147, 157
conceptual knowledge, 94, 96, 97, 99, 100, 101, 102, 104, 108, 110, 112, 137, 140, 151, 156, 172, 173, 174, 175, 180, 181, 182
conceptual load, 63, 97, 99, 149, 156
conceptual system, 22, 24, 99, 103, 104
connotation, 62, 99, 118, 145, 156
constructivist view, 26
contact language, 17
context dependent, 142, 143, 185, 197
context sensitive, 80
context-sensitivity, 38, 40
contextual enrichment, 150
contextualism, 150, 157
contextualization cues, 94
continuum, i, vi, 23, 24, 26, 28, 30, 31, 35, 42, 43, 45, 46, 60, 69, 71, 79, 81, 90, 136, 153, 154, 156, 172, 190, 191, 197, 234
convention, 54, 141
conventionality, 119, 125, 143, 145, 147
conventionalization, 24, 33, 52, 55, 67, 126, 137, 154, 184
conversational analysis, 110
cooperation, 5, 6, 13, 28, 30, 68, 77, 113, 116, 122, 123, 164, 177, 233
core knowledge, 101, 154, 155
core meaning, 94, 150, 204
corpus-pragmatic, 197
creativity, i, viii, 7, 12, 44, 45, 46, 47, 48, 56, 58, 59, 60, 63, 64, 67, 116, 132, 166, 180, 182, 234
cross-cultural approach, 197
cultural model, 105, 106
culture-specific conceptual property, 174
culture-specific knowledge, 71, 174

declarative, 39, 151
declarative knowledge, 39, 151
decontextualized, 141
default processing strategy, 51
deliberate creativity, 58, 59, 60, 68
deontic modality, vi, 187, 189, 190, 191, 194
diachronic language, 58
diachronic pragmatics, 149, 150, 155, 156, 157, 171, 174, 184
dialogic sequence, 206, 210, 211, 223

dichotomy, 25, 28, 50, 58, 117, 154, 177, 190
discourse, 8, 11, 17, 19, 21, 48, 52, 54, 56, 60, 76, 115, 116, 132, 136, 141, 142, 153, 162, 200, 201, 202, 203, 206, 208, 210, 211, 213, 216, 217, 219, 220, 221, 230, 233, 234, 249
discourse analysis, 17, 230
discourse level, 116, 202, 206, 234

egocentrism, 13, 76, 77, 116, 120, 122, 123, 164, 177, 228, 233
ELF interlocutors, 2, 12, 30, 31, 37, 44, 63, 67, 71, 92, 101, 102, 108, 112, 147, 158, 159, 160, 165, 172, 211, 229, 235
emergent common ground, 35, 38, 182, 183
emergent intention, 13, 40, 113, 114, 116, 117, 136, 183
encyclopedic knowledge, 94, 96, 97, 100, 101, 102, 105, 109, 111, 112, 137, 139, 140, 142, 143, 172, 173, 181, 182
endonormative, 58
English as a Lingua Franca in Academic Settings (ELFA), 16
English as a Native Language, 2, 17, 45, 81
epistemic modality, vi, 187, 190, 191, 200, 202, 204
exonormative, 58
explicature, 5, 164
exploratory-transformational, 58
extension of the system, i, 58, 59
extralinguistic, 43, 105

figurative language, 52, 178, 182
formulaic expression, 33, 48, 51, 61, 164, 179
formulaic language, viii, 7, 8, 33, 34, 45, 46, 47, 50, 52, 53, 55, 58, 59, 63, 64, 65, 66, 84, 111, 138, 147, 148, 157, 160, 179, 256
formulaic sequence, 53
frame, 13, 20, 27, 29, 38, 42, 48, 54, 104, 105, 106, 125, 153, 156, 159, 183, 197, 205, 206, 210, 213, 214, 219, 222, 224, 229, 233
functional domain, 21
functional meaning, 108, 178

generative syntax, 45
Germanic languages, 15
Gricean paradigm, i, 1, 5, 30, 68, 161, 162, 178, 232
Gricean pragmatics, i, 1, 8, 112, 149, 159, 161

Haugenian approach, 9
heterolytic, 5
human rationality, 20, 30, 49, 70, 74, 85, 122, 128, 164, 177, 233

idiom, 46, 50, 51, 54, 59, 60, 63, 64, 110, 140
Idiom principle, 49
implicature, 1, 5, 9, 139, 140, 147, 151, 159, 160, 161, 162, 163, 164, 165, 166, 167, 168, 169, 170, 171, 173, 174, 175, 176, 177, 178, 179, 180, 181, 182, 186, 211, 232, 235
impoverished pragmatics, 157, 182
individual factors, 5, 122, 228
individual saliency, 122, 123
inference, 115, 139, 140, 179
intentionality, 75, 115, 117, 209, 243
interactional competence, i, 1, 68, 69, 70, 71, 72, 74, 75, 77, 78, 79, 80, 84, 86, 88, 90, 91, 113, 136, 137, 156
intercultural communication, 11, 25, 28, 30, 32, 34, 37, 38, 41, 43, 92, 107, 138, 149, 211, 232
intercultural interactions, 6, 11, 38, 68, 71, 78, 114, 149, 157, 160, 206, 228
intercultural pragmatics, 206, 230
interculture, 27, 65
Interlanguage, 19
interlanguage pragmatics, 17
interpretation sensitive terms, 39
interrupted creolization process, 24
intersubjectivity, 7, 14, 28, 36, 37, 38, 43, 75, 78, 163
intracultural communication, 25, 28, 31, 35, 38, 39

language proficiency, 8, 28, 31, 43, 46, 101, 149, 160, 166, 169, 170, 171, 181, 194, 195, 206, 229
language socialization, 33, 178
lexical conceptual knowledge, 151
lexical domain, 21
Lexical Learning Hypothesis, 21
linguistic code, 71, 72, 111, 137, 140, 157, 158, 233
linguistic creativity, 12, 45, 46, 56, 58, 59
linguistic knowledge, 91, 94, 96, 97, 99, 100, 101, 102, 104, 110, 111, 112, 172, 173, 174, 181
linguistic routines, 47, 53
linguistic salience, 124, 126, 146
literal, 8, 23, 53, 56, 64, 71, 82, 94, 108, 138, 140, 142, 143, 144, 145, 146, 147, 150, 157, 160, 168, 169, 171, 175, 177, 178, 179
literalism, 150

maxim, 9, 162, 163, 179, 180
meaning construction, 26, 43
mental grammar, 21
mental lexicon, 48, 65, 97, 126, 145
merging, 224

metaphor, 2, 140, 159
metaphorism, 16, 178
modality, i, 1, 183, 184, 185, 186, 187, 188, 190, 191, 192, 193, 194, 195, 196, 197, 198, 199, 200, 201, 202, 203, 204, 232
monolingual approach, 20
monolithic, 5, 9
multifunctional linguistic devices, 197
multilingual competence, 6
multilinguals, 6, 64, 160, 166, 169, 170, 171

natural human inertia, 50, 52
needs of communication, 21, 50, 52
nonliteral meaning, 145, 146, 160
nonnative speakers, 8, 11, 19, 27, 29, 39, 55, 56, 63, 71, 78, 84, 85, 111, 143, 165, 166, 167, 169, 172, 193, 195, 199, 204
norm, 3, 19, 20, 23, 24, 58, 155, 179, 180, 182
normative system, 58
normativization, 23, 33, 49, 67, 137, 184
norm-developing, 4, 58
norm-following, 58

odd structures, 210, 220, 229, 230
open choice principle, 46, 49, 51, 60, 63
open social situations, 66

perceptual salience, vi, 124, 125, 126
pidginization, 19
politeness, 5, 190, 191, 198
potentialities already available, 56, 57
pragmatic competence, 171, 194
pragmatic creativity, 12
pragmatic development, 172
pragmatic enrichment, 8, 139, 140, 149, 182, 234
pragmatic perspective, 1, 28, 206, 231
pragmatic strategies, 10, 148, 158
pragmaticalization process, 182
preconstituted forms, 10
prefabricated language, 7, 10, 33, 37, 45, 47, 59, 67, 78, 110, 234, 235
preferred ways of saying things, 32, 34, 52, 56, 58, 72, 102
presupposition, 5
Principle of Least Effort, 50
prior context, 38, 41, 42, 112, 124, 143, 148, 150, 151, 152, 153, 155, 182
prior experience, 7, 13, 26, 29, 35, 38, 39, 42, 43, 52, 76, 77, 119, 120, 123, 127, 138, 146, 150, 151, 160, 164, 165, 177, 228
procedural knowledge, 39, 151
process-oriented, 46, 47, 56
product-oriented, 46, 56
proficiency, 10, 12, 19, 31, 41, 63, 71, 83, 84, 88, 96, 97, 108, 111, 137, 147, 166, 167, 168, 169, 170, 173, 181, 185, 193, 194, 195, 204, 207, 220, 229, 230
proposition, 98, 100, 139, 150, 151, 165, 184, 187, 191
prototypicality, 125, 145
psychological saliency, 54, 55, 56, 59, 63

recipient design, 7, 60, 62, 68, 77, 80, 113, 121, 123, 129, 130, 131, 132, 133, 134, 164, 174, 212, 228, 229, 230
reference, 12, 17, 46, 75, 105, 107, 141, 193, 195, 200, 204, 220, 221, 223
relevance, 5, 87, 116, 120, 153, 169, 172, 175, 180, 185
Relevance Theory, 50, 116
rule-generated, 58
rule-generating, 58

salience, 5, 41, 51, 52, 61, 62, 93, 119, 120, 121, 123, 124, 125, 126, 127, 128, 129, 130, 131, 132, 134, 135, 136, 143, 145, 146, 153, 160, 176, 177, 207, 212, 221, 228, 229, 230
scalar, 169, 170, 172
schema, 105
second language acquisition, 1, 5, 9, 17, 74, 79, 85, 108
semantic analyzability, 7, 8, 10, 111, 140, 147, 157, 160, 164, 165, 182, 213, 234
semantic content, 8, 11, 104, 132, 148, 149, 161, 173, 182
semantics–pragmatics interface, i, viii, 1, 7, 8, 137, 138, 141, 142, 147, 165, 182, 232
shared knowledge, 6, 8, 28, 30, 35, 42, 67, 75, 79, 110, 182, 219, 234
situational formulas, 33
Situation-Bound Utterances, 53, 64, 94, 112
sociocultural background, viii, 2, 22, 39, 78, 91, 92, 94, 95, 100, 101, 102, 104, 105, 107, 108, 109, 112, 113, 121, 136, 154, 165, 172, 173, 180, 235
sociocultural frames, 33
sociocultural frameworks, 195
sociocultural-interactional pragmatics, 230
speech acts, 5, 54, 69, 90, 203, 208
speech community, 2, 10, 19, 24, 28, 32, 34, 35, 38, 41, 49, 52, 53, 63, 65, 67, 71, 72, 77, 81, 91, 92, 93, 101, 102, 106, 110, 139, 146, 151, 159, 178
success approach, 11, 30, 32

synchronic linguistic, 58
synchronic pragmatics, 147, 150, 153, 155, 156, 157, 171, 184

target culture, 56, 84, 154, 167
target language, 7, 9, 12, 34, 37, 38, 41, 45, 49, 60, 65, 67, 70, 71, 78, 83, 84, 85, 86, 88, 92, 99, 108, 109, 112, 128, 137, 140, 146, 148, 149, 154, 158, 159, 166, 169, 181, 182, 197, 204, 233, 234
temporary norms, 31, 71, 72, 181, 233
temporary speech communities, 19, 29, 45, 92
temporary speech community, 49, 65
third space, 38, 109

underdeterminacy, 138, 139, 140, 147, 152

varieties of English, 2, 19, 25, 92, 154, 155, 192, 233
Vienna-Oxford International Corpus of English (VOICE), 4, 16, 201
virtual language, 56, 57

Lightning Source UK Ltd.
Milton Keynes UK
UKHW021620030622
403870UK00019B/559

9 781107 503373